Four Tools to Enhance Your Students' Learning!

1 Integrated Campaigns in Action
These actual advertising and promotional programs are described by the people and advertising agencies involved in creating them.

2 Interviews with Advertising Professionals
In various points throughout the text, interviews and quotes from advertising professionals have been integrated into the chapters.

PART 1 The IMC Foundation

1 Integrated Marketing Communications

TWITTER

Social Networking and the Future of Marketing Communications

Do you "tweet"? Less than a decade ago, no one would have understood this question. Now, the language of Twitter is part of the cultural lingo. Tweets are reported on the national news, via traditional media, and on various Web sites. Celebrities, sports figures, businesspeople, and politicians use this new social networking forum.

Two questions have emerged about Twitter. First, is it only a flash in the pan? Second, can the company generate profits?

In terms of the first question, many wonder if Twitter's sudden popularity may diminish just as quickly. MySpace and other social networking sites have experienced declining interest. *Fortune*'s Jessie Hempel suggests a risk she labels the "hype cycle," in which "People realize that this is lame and they leave. They don't come back until it is a useful technology."

To combat concerns that Twitter will only be viewed as the latest fad, the company's cofounder Biz Stone states that, "We are building a company to last." To do so, the company's leaders have tried to ". . . focus on value before we optimize profits." Value can be delivered to two important segments: individual users and businesses. Stone notes that the company's goal is to deliver value at what he terms, "both ends of the spectrum," which means for both small and large businesses. The common link is that small and large firms can both use Twitter to create a better customer experience.

In the summer of 200 offered examples of how s nesses create positive experiences through Twi local bakery sends out when its cookies are fr warm out of the oven. Loc the bakery quickly descen up the inventory. Anothe tweets the "pie of the da enthusiasts.

Source: Getty Images–Thinkstock.

3 Increased Emphasis on Social Media
As one of the most rapidly evolving aspects of advertising and promotion, coverage of social media has been added wherever it has impacted marketing communications.

PERSONAL SELLING

Personal selling offers a face-to-face opportunity to build relationships with consumers. It takes place in both consumer and business-to-business transactions. Personal selling may result in the acquisition of new customers in addition to influencing current customers to increase levels of purchases. It is also used to service and maintain existing relationships. The goal of personal selling should not be limited to simply making sales. An additional objective should be to develop longer-term relationships with customers. In **relationship selling**, the goal is to create a customer for life, not for a single transaction.

Figure 11.11 identifies the standard steps in the selling process. A quality data warehouse accompanied by effective database technologies provides key tools that assist in personal selling.

Generating Leads

The first task in personal selling, especially for business-to-business relationships, is producing quality leads. Figure 11.12 identifies some of the most common methods. Making personal sales calls is costly, which makes generating quality leads crucial.

Referrals are ideal leads, because most recommendations are made by satisfied individuals. Referrals give the salesperson a head start. Making contact with purchasing agents or buyers in business organizations is often difficult. Using the name of the person who gave the referral can help the salesperson get past any gatekeepers. Also, if someone has given a referral, then the potential lead becomes more receptive to the sales call and has a more positive attitude toward the salesperson. The best referrals are from current customers.

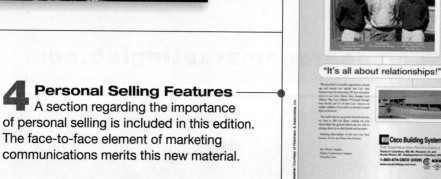

▼ Building relationships with customers is an important component of personal selling.

"It's all about relationships!"

Ceco Building Systems
THE CONSTRUCTION PROFESSIONALS
1-800-474-CECO (2326)

Source: Courtesy of Robinson & Associates, Inc.

4 Personal Selling Features
A section regarding the importance of personal selling is included in this edition. The face-to-face element of marketing communications merits this new material.

INTEGRATED
ADVERTISING, PROMOTION, AND MARKETING COMMUNICATIONS

FIFTH EDITION

KENNETH E. CLOW

University of Louisiana at Monroe

DONALD BAACK

Pittsburg State University

Prentice Hall

Boston   Columbus   Indianapolis   New York   San Francisco   Upper Saddle River
Amsterdam   Cape Town   Dubai   London   Madrid   Milan   Munich   Paris
Montreal   Toronto   Delhi   Mexico City   Sao Paulo   Sydney   Hong Kong
Seoul   Singapore   Taipei   Tokyo

Editorial Director: Sally Yagan
Editor-in-Chief: Eric Svendsen
Executive Editor: Melissa Sabella
Director of Editorial Services: Ashley Santora
Editorial Project Manager: Meeta Pendharkar
Editorial Assistant: Elisabeth Scarpa
Director of Marketing: Patrice Lumumba Jones
Senior Marketing Manager: Anne Fahlgren
Marketing Assistant: Melinda Jensen
Senior Managing Editor: Judy Leale
Production Project Manager: Kelly Warsak
Senior Operations Supervisor: Arnold Vila
Operations Specialist: Cathleen Petersen

Creative Director: Christy Mahon
Senior Art Director: Kenny Beck
Text Designer: LCI Design
Cover Designer: LCI Design
Manager, Rights and Permissions: Hessa Albader
Media Project Manager: Lisa Rinaldi
Media Assistant Editor: Denise Vaughn
Full-Service Project Management: Jennifer Welsch/ BookMasters, Inc.
Composition: Integra Software Services
Printer/Binder: R.R. Donnelley/Willard
Cover Printer: Lehigh-Phoenix Color/Hagerstown
Text Font: 10.5/12, Times New Roman

Credits and acknowledgments borrowed from other sources and reproduced, with permission, in this textbook appear on appropriate page within text.

Microsoft® and Windows® are registered trademarks of the Microsoft Corporation in the U.S.A. and other countries. Screen shots and icons reprinted with permission from the Microsoft Corporation. This book is not sponsored or endorsed by or affiliated with the Microsoft Corporation.

Many of the designations by manufacturers and seller to distinguish their products are claimed as trademarks. Where those designations appear in this book, and the publisher was aware of a trademark claim, the designations have been printed in initial caps or all caps.

Library of Congress Cataloging-in-Publication Data

Clow, Kenneth E.
    Integrated advertising, promotion, and marketing communications / Kenneth E. Clow, Donald Baack.—5th ed.
        p. cm.
    Includes bibliographical references and index.
    ISBN-13: 978-0-13-253896-1 (pbk. : alk. paper)
    ISBN-10: 0-13-253896-2
    1. Communication in marketing.   2. Advertising.   I. Baack, Donald.   II. Title.
HF5415.123.C58 2012
659.1—dc22

2010044390

10 9 8 7 6 5 4 3 2 1

Prentice Hall
is an imprint of

www.pearsonhighered.com

ISBN 13: 978-0-13-253896-1
ISBN 10:   0-13-253896-2

To my sons Dallas, Wes, Tim, and Roy, who provided encouragement, and especially to my wife, Susan, whose sacrifice and love made this textbook possible.

—Kenneth E. Clow

I would like to dedicate my efforts and contributions to the book to my wife Pam; children Jessica, Daniel, and David; and grandchildren Danielle, Rile, Andy, Emilee, Jason, Damon, Tatum, and Joe.

—Donald Baack

Brief Contents

Contents

**PART 4
IMC Promotional Tools 282**

PART 5

IMC Ethics, Regulation, and Evaluation   366

14   Regulations and Ethical Concerns   366

15   Evaluating an Integrated Marketing Program   392

Preface

Advertising, promotions, and marketing communications are integral components of marketing. If your students are marketing majors, understanding how companies can effectively communicate with customers and potential customers creates the foundation they need to develop effective marketing skills. This will help them succeed in their marketing careers.

If they are not marketing majors, consider all of the marketing communications around them. Any company or organization they work for will be involved in marketing its products or services. Understanding how marketing communications are developed and why will be valuable knowledge. It will help them comprehend the methods used by the people in the marketing departments where they will work and will provide them with better information to function as a consumer.

We created *Integrated Advertising, Promotion, and Marketing Communications,* in part, to help students understand the importance of integrating all marketing communications (IMC) and how they are produced and transmitted. When our first edition was written, almost all marketing communication textbooks focused exclusively on advertising. As your students know from their everyday experiences and the courses they have taken in college, marketing communications includes much more than that. It includes promotions, such as coupons, price discounts, and contests. Marketing has expanded to blogs on the Internet, customer reviews of products, messages delivered to cell phones, and newer programs, such as buzz marketing. These venues are vital ingredients in effectively reaching consumers. These must also be carefully integrated into one clear message and voice for customers to hear.

We prepared this textbook and all of the additional materials in a way that will best help your students to understand integrated marketing communications. Students need opportunities to apply concepts to real-life situations. This helps them clearly understand and retain the ideas. As a result, we have prepared a variety of end-of-chapter materials that are designed to help them practice using the concepts. These materials include integrated campaigns in action, integrated learning exercises, discussion and critical-thinking exercises, creative exercises, and cases.

WHAT'S NEW IN THE FIFTH EDITION?

The fifth edition of *Integrated Advertising, Promotion, and Marketing Communications* offers some exciting new features. The most dynamic is the addition of the Integrated Campaigns in Action series, which concludes nearly every chapter. These actual advertising and promotional programs are described by the people and advertising agencies involved in creating them. As part of the professor's ancillary package, additional materials for in-class presentations should lead to a more dynamic and well-rounded learning experience. Other new features in this edition include:

- **Interviews with advertising professionals.** At various points throughout the text, interviews and quotes from advertising professionals have been integrated into the chapters. Some are as lengthy as a full description of the development of the Motel 6 advertising program by Stan Richards, founder of The Richards Groups, whereas others are short as one-sentence commentaries on various marketing and promotions topics, but they all will give your students an important perspective on real-world applications.

- **Increased emphasis on social media.** One of the most rapidly evolving aspects of advertising and promotion has been the demand for increased usage of social media. This edition presents a great deal of new material on these important changes, including the book's opening vignette about Twitter. Coverage of social media has been added wherever it has impacted marketing communications.

- **New opening vignettes and cases.** Many of the chapter opening vignettes are brand new to this edition, and each chapter includes one new case. These materials keep the book fresh and current.

- **Inclusion of personal selling.** Based on responses from reviewers of the previous edition, a section regarding the importance of personal selling has been added to Chapter 11. The face-to-face element of marketing communications merits this new material.

- **New advertisements.** Throughout the text, many new advertisements have been added. Many of these resulted from interactions with advertising agencies. Oscar Meyer, Interstate Batteries, and Bridgestone advertisements are included, all helping to keep the content as fresh and current as possible.

- **Updated examples.** New examples of marketing communications principles have been incorporated to provide up-to-date information about companies students can relate to. New discussion and critical-thinking exercises have been created to help students understand and apply the materials presented in each chapter.

INTEGRATED LEARNING PACKAGE

We have created several devices that are designed to help students learn the materials in this text. Advertising and marketing communications are interesting and enjoyable subjects, and these materials have been developed to make learning interactive and fun!

- **Integrated Campaigns in Action.** The most exciting and unique new feature in this textbook is a series of presentations about actual marketing programs, as created and designed by professional agencies. Bill Breedlove from the Pink Jacket Creative advertising agency will relay a great story about an event marketing program set up for 200 people attending a trade show. He will also tell you about his firm's successful guerilla marketing program for Engobi. Lee McGuire will discuss an integrated marketing campaign for selling Skyjacker lift kits. Kraft and the mcgarrybowen advertising agency share information on the newest Philadelphia Cream Cheese campaign. Each of these short stories is accompanied by additional materials that you can use to provide additional information about the advertisements and marketing campaigns. These features appear and the end of each chapter and in the instructor's PowerPoint materials.

- **Lead-in vignettes.** Each chapter begins with a vignette related to the presented topic. The majority of the vignettes revolve around success stories in companies most students will recognize, such as PetSmart. In this edition, new vignettes have been introduced, including stories about Twitter, Platinum Motorcars, GoDaddy.com, and even one about Barbie. The vignettes introduce your students to the concepts presented throughout the chapter.

- **International marketing discussions.** Some of you have traveled to other countries. Most of you interact with students from around the globe. Global, international business is all around. This makes understanding international marketing issues important. This book features international concerns that match the presented materials. Also, a section called "International Implications" is found at the end of every chapter.

- **Critical-thinking exercises and discussion questions.** The end-of-chapter materials include a variety of exercises designed to help your students comprehend and apply the chapter concepts. These exercises are designed to challenge students' thinking and encourage them to dig deeper. The best way to know that your students have truly learned a concept or theory is when they can apply it to a different situation. These critical-thinking and discussion exercises require them to apply knowledge to a wide array of marketing situations.

- **Integrated learning exercises.** At the end of each chapter, a set of questions guides students to the Internet to access information that ties into the subject matter covered. These exercises provide students an opportunity to look up various companies and organizations to see how they utilize the concepts presented in the chapter.

- **Creative Corner exercises.** A new feature has been added to this edition. Most students enjoy the opportunity to use their creative abilities. As a result, we feature a new exercise called the "Creative Corner," which asks students to design advertisements and other marketing-related materials. The exercises are designed to help students realize that they are more creative than they might think. Ken Clow has taught students who said they had zero creative ability. Yet these same students were able to produce ads that won ADDY awards in student competitions sponsored by the American Advertising Federation (AAF). If you don't know anything about the AAF student competition, go the organization's Web site at **www.aaf.org**. Entering the annual competition is exciting, and participating looks great on a student's resume.

- **Cases.** Two cases are provided at the conclusion of each chapter. They were written to help students learn by providing plausible scenarios that require thought and review of chapter materials. The short cases should help students conceptually understand chapter components and the larger, more general marketing issues.

PEARSON MYMARKETINGLAB

Pearson's mymarketinglab (**www.mypearsonmarketinglab. com**) gives students the opportunity to test themselves on key concepts and skills, track their progress through the course, and use the personalized study plan activities—all to help them achieve success in the classroom.

The mymarketinglab that accompanies *Integrated Advertising, Promotion, and Marketing Communications* includes:

- **Ad exercises.** Give your students the opportunity to view a variety of advertisements and test their understanding of how they apply IMC concepts.

- **Personalized study plans.** Pre- and posttests are directed to help students understand and apply the concepts where they need the most help.

- **Critical Thinking Challenge Questions.** These questions measure core critical-thinking skills through the context of marketing applications. To answer these questions, students will need to recognize assumptions, evaluate arguments, identify relevant issues, draw inferences, spot logical flaws, and recognize similarities between arguments. Knowledge of marketing content picked up through the text and the class will help students zero in on the correct issues, but they will still need to exercise critical judgment in order to get the correct answer.

- **Audio PowerPoints.** Pearson's MyMarketingLab also offers the instructor PowerPoints in an audio format for students taking classes online or as a supplemental teaching aid to the classroom lectures.

Find out more at **www.mypearsonmarketinglab.com**.

INSTRUCTOR'S RESOURCE CENTER

Media-Rich PowerPoint Presentation. This PowerPoint presentation features print advertisements, slides that build concepts over several steps, discussion questions, Web links, and video snippets. The PowerPoint presentation not only includes ads from the text but also additional ads. The slides, Web site links, video clips, and questions form a coherent presentation for the class. The print advertisements are accompanied by questions or captions relating them to the concepts within the chapter. Integrated learning experiences take the class to Web sites referenced in the text. These files are available as a download from the Instructor's Resource Center.

PowerPoint BASIC. This simple presentation includes only basic outlines and key points from each chapter. No animation or forms of rich media are integrated, which makes the total file size manageable and easier to share online or via e-mail. BASIC was also designed for instructors who prefer to customize PowerPoint and want to be spared from having to strip out animation, embedded files, or other media-rich features. These files are available as a download from the Instructor's Resource Center.

Instructor's Manual. This resource provides support and suggestions for instructors. A complete outline is provided for each chapter, including key words and their definitions, important themes, references to text figures, and the material's implications for marketing professionals. Review questions, discussion questions, and application questions are all answered thoroughly by the authors, and the chapter-opening vignettes are also explained. Suggestions for classroom projects and presentations are also included. These files are available as a download from the Instructor's Resource Center.

Test Item File. The test file has been expanded to include approximately 3,500 true-false, multiple-choice, and short-answer questions. It includes page references and difficulty level so that instructors can provide greater feedback to students. These files are available as a download from the Instructor's Resource Center.

TestGen-EQ. The TestGen-EQ test-generation software is a computerized package that allows instructors to custom design, save, and generate classroom tests. The test program permits instructors to edit, add, and delete questions from the test bank; analyze test results; and organize a database of tests and student results. The new software allows for greater flexibility and ease of use. It provides many options for organizing and displaying tests, along with a search and sort feature. These files are available as a download from the Instructor's Resource Center.

IMC Video Library. A video library is available for use in the classroom. Using today's popular newsmagazine format, students are taken on location and behind closed doors. Each news story profiles a well-known or up-and-coming company leading the way in its industry. Teaching materials to accompany the video library are available in the Instructor's Manual.

ACKNOWLEDGMENTS

We would like to thank the following individuals who assisted in the development of the first five editions through their careful and thoughtful reviews:

We are grateful to these reviewers for the fifth edition:

Joni Jackson, Robert Morris University

Rick Morris, University of North Texas

Charles Larson, Northern Illinois University

Charlie Schwepker, University of Central Missouri

John Bennett, University of Missouri

Prema Nakra, Marist College

Linden Dalecki, Pittsburgh State University

Kathleen Havey, University of Maryland

Bryan Johnson, Pennsylvania State University

Debbie Campbell, Temple University

We are grateful to these reviewers for portions of the fourth edition:

John Bennett, University of Missouri–Columbia

MaryEllen Campbell, University of Montana, Missoula

Donna Falgiatore, St. Joseph's University

Deanna Mulholland, Iowa Western Community College

Jim Munz, Illinois State University

Prema Nakra, Marist College

Allen Smith, Florida Atlantic University

Amanda Walton, Indiana Business College

We are grateful to these reviewers for the third edition:

Jeffrey C. Bauer, University of Cincinnati–Clermont

MaryElllen Campbell, University of Montana, Missoula

Sherry Cook, Missouri State University

Catherine Curran, University of Massachusetts–Dartmouth

Michael A. Dickerson, George Mason University

Donna Falgiatore, St. Joseph's University

Charles S. Gulas, Wright State University

Diana Haytko, Missouri State University

Al Mattison, University of California–Berkeley

Deanna Mulholland, Iowa Western Community College

Jim Munz, Illinois State University

Charlie Schwepker, University of Central Missouri

Eugene Secunda, New York University

Allen E. Smith, Florida Atlantic University

Bonni Stachowiak, Vanguard University

Rod Warnick, University of Massachusetts–Amherst

Patti Williams, Wharton Business School

We are grateful to these reviewers for the second edition:

Robert W. Armstrong, University of North Alabama

Jerome Christa, Coastal Carolina University

Stefanie Garcia, University of Central Florida

Robert J. Gulovsen, Washington University–Saint Louis

Sreedhar Kavil, St. John's University

Franklin Krohn, SUNY–Buffalo

Tom Laughon, Florida State University

William C. Lesch, University of North Dakota

James M. Maskulka, Lehigh University

Darrel D. Muehling, Washington State University

Esther S. Page-Wood, Western Michigan University

Venkatesh Shankar, University of Maryland

Albert J. Taylor, Austin Peay State University

Jerald Weaver, SUNY—Brockport

We are grateful to these reviewers of the first edition:

Craig Andrews, Marquette University

Ronald Bauerly, Western Illinois University

Mary Ellen Campbell, University of Montana

Les Carlson, Clemson University

Newell Chiesl, Indiana State University

John Cragin, Oklahoma Baptist College

J. Charlene Davis, Trinity University

Steven Edwards, Michigan State University

P. Everett Fergenson, Iona College

James Finch, University of Wisconsin–La Crosse

Thomas Jensen, University of Arkansas

Russell W. Jones, University of Central Oklahoma

Dave Kurtz, University of Arkansas

Monle Lee, Indiana University–South Bend

Ron Lennon, Barry University

Charles L. Martin, Wichita State University

Robert D. Montgomery, University of Evansville

S. Scott Nadler, University of Alabama

Ben Oumlil, University of Dayton

Melodie R. Phillips, Middle Tennessee State University

Don Roy, Middle Tennessee State University

Elise Sautter, New Mexico State University

Janice E. Taylor, Miami University

Robert L. Underwood, Bradley University

Robert Welch, California State University–Long Beach

Although there were many individuals who helped us with advertising programs, we want to thank a few who were especially helpful. We appreciate the owners and employees of advertising agencies Pink Jacket Creative, The Richards Group, mcgarrybowen, and Gremillion & Pou for providing us with a large number of advertisements. We want to thank Benny Black for his time explaining his highly successful company, Platinum Motorcars. Stan Richards, Mary Price, Dave Snell, Elena Petukhova, and Carrie Dyer (The Richards Group) were very generous with their time, as were Bill Breedlove and Elena Baca (Pink Jacket), Shama Kabini (Marketing Zen), Brian and Sarah Warren (Emogen Marketing Group), Lee McGuire (Skyjacker), Paula Ramirez (1400 Words), Tim Clow and Jane Hilk (Oscar Mayer), Howard Friedman (Kraft), Tori Emery, Brittany Bowman, and Rick Thornhill (mcgarrybowen), Shauna McLean Tompkins (Boxcar Creative), Bo Bothe (Brand Extract) and Anne Gremillion (Gremillion & Pou).

On a personal note, we would like to thank Leah Johnson, who signed us for the first edition of the book. Thank you to Melissa Sabella, James Heine, Meeta Pendharkar, Ashley Santora, and Sally Yagan for helping with this edition as it moved forward and to Kelly Warsak and Jen Welsch (BookMasters) for guiding the production process. We would also like to thank the entire Prentice Hall production group.

Kenneth Clow would like to thank the University of Louisiana at Monroe for providing a supportive environment to work on this text. He is thankful to his sons Dallas, Wes, Tim, and Roy, who always provided encouragement and support.

Donald Baack would like to thank Mimi Morrison and Paula Palmer for their continued assistance in all his work at Pittsburg State University. Eric Harris has been a great help in his role as department chairperson. He helped make the workload manageable during the preparation of the manuscript.

We would like to especially thank our wives, Susan Clow and Pam Baack, for being patient and supportive during those times when we were swamped by the work involved in completing this edition. They have been enthusiastic and understanding throughout this entire journey.

1 Integrated Marketing Communications

TWITTER

Social Networking and the Future of Marketing Communications

Do you "tweet"? Less than a decade ago, no one would have understood this question. Now, the language of Twitter is part of the cultural lingo. Tweets are reported on the national news, via traditional media, and on various Web sites. Celebrities, sports figures, businesspeople, and politicians use this new social networking forum.

Two questions have emerged about Twitter. First, is it only a flash in the pan? Second, can the company generate profits?

In terms of the first question, many wonder if Twitter's sudden popularity may diminish just as quickly. MySpace and other social networking sites have experienced declining interest. *Fortune*'s Jessie Hempel suggests a risk she labels the "hype cycle," in which "People realize that this is lame and they leave. They don't come back until it is a useful technology."

To combat concerns that Twitter will only be viewed as the latest fad, the company's cofounder Biz Stone states that, "We are building a company to last." To do so, the company's leaders have tried to " . . . focus on value before we optimize profits." Value can be delivered to two important segments: individual users and businesses. Stone notes that the company's goal is to deliver value at what he terms, "both ends of the spectrum," which means for both small and large businesses. The common link is that small and large firms can both use Twitter to create a better customer experience.

In the summer of 2009, Stone offered examples of how small businesses create positive customer experiences through Twitter. One local bakery sends out a tweet when its cookies are fresh and warm out of the oven. Local fans of the bakery quickly descend to buy up the inventory. Another bakery tweets the "pie of the day" to its enthusiasts.

CHAPTER 1

CHAPTER OBJECTIVES

After reading this chapter, you should be able to answer the following questions:

1 How does communication take place?

2 What is an integrated marketing communications program?

3 Are there any new trends affecting marketing communications?

4 How does an integrated marketing communications program create value?

5 What are the components of an integrated marketing communications program?

6 What does the term *GIMC* mean?

At the other extreme, Best Buy has created what it terms the Twelpforce, which consists of 700 employees who are available to answer customer questions and inquiries using Twitter, to make almost instant connections while shopping. Stone believes the model allows Best Buy to effectively engage with current and potential customers. Twitter also assists Dell in selling computers over the system.

The employees at Twitter have developed Twitter 101, or a "Suite of Education," according to Stone, designed to show companies how to effectively use the system.

In essence, to survive in the long term, Twitter's management team seems to be intent on moving past just being viewed as "babbling spam" to create meaningful information in the most relevant way. A series of new features has been released that are designed to make certain the company continues to grow.

The second question remains, can the company generate profits? Some analysts speculate that Twitter may well be worth over $1 billion, but the actual cash flow and profit figures have not yet been realized. Biz Stone and cofounder Evan Williams are working on methods to generate those profits, but argue that building the base of the company remains more important. By late 2009, the company still did not use "traditional advertising"

methods; however, in the late spring of 2010 Twitter began selling advertising space on the site.

As with any new and growing company, obstacles have appeared. Hackers were able to access some of Twitter's planning documents and then posted them online. Security concerns remain for many users.

At the same time, optimism abounds among the company's 55 employees, who are located in a single building in San Francisco. "We have a lot of growing still to do," Stone notes, adding, "We are thinking big."

Social networking sites and other forms of instant communication are changing the face of business. At the forefront will be marketing communications. Although traditional advertising methods remain the cornerstone of many promotional programs, these new methods of interaction and communications with customers simply cannot be ignored as the world becomes increasingly interconnected. There is, as Biz Stone has noted, value to be gained by enhancing the customer's experience through these unique new communication channels.[1]

OVERVIEW

The global marketplace consists of a complex set of competitors battling for customers in a rapidly changing environment. New companies are formed on a daily basis. Small businesses, Internet-based operations, and global conglomerates are all part of the worldwide marketing environment.

A wide variety of media are available to the leaders of these companies. Advertising and marketing methods range from simple stand-alone billboard advertisements to complex, multilingual global Web sites. The number of ways to reach potential customers continually increases while alternative methods expand and become increasingly popular.

In the face of these sophisticated and cluttered market conditions, firms try to be heard. Marketing experts know that a company's communications must speak with a clear voice. Customers must understand the essence of a business and the benefits of its goods and services. The vast variety of advertising and promotional venues combined with a multitude of companies bombarding potential customers with messages makes the task challenging.

This first chapter explains the nature of an integrated advertising and marketing communications program. First, communication processes are described. Understanding how communication works builds the foundation for an integrated marketing program. Next, an integrated marketing communications program is described. Finally, the integrated marketing communications process is applied to global or international operations, creating a *globally integrated marketing communications (GIMC)* program.

THE NATURE OF COMMUNICATION

1 How does communication take place?

Communication is transmitting, receiving, and processing information. When a person, group, or organization attempts to transfer an idea or message, communication occurs when the receiver (another person or group) comprehends the information. The model of communication shown in Figure 1.1 displays the pathway a message takes from one person to another.[2]

Communication plays a key role in any advertising or marketing program. Consider a person planning to dine at a quick-service chicken restaurant. In the communications model (Figure 1.1), suppose the **senders** are chicken fast-food companies. Restaurants such as KFC, Chick-fil-A, Popeye's, Church's Chicken, Bojangles, and Raising Cain's Chicken Fingers try to capture the customer's attention. Most of these firms hire advertising agencies. Some utilize in-house marketing groups.

Encoding is forming verbal and nonverbal cues. In marketing, the person in charge of designing an advertisement takes an idea and transforms it into an attention-getting message. The commercial consists of cues being placed in various media, including television, magazines, and billboards. The message may also be encoded on the firm's Web site, a social media page, or a Twitter account.

Messages travel to audiences through various **transmission devices.** Marketing communications move through various channels or media. The channel may be a television station carrying an advertisement, a Sunday paper with a coupon placed in it, the Internet, or a billboard placed along the interstate.

Decoding occurs when the message reaches one or more of the receiver's senses. Consumers both hear and see television ads. Others consumers handle (touch) and read (see) a coupon offer. It is even possible to "smell" a message. A well-placed perfume sample might entice a buyer to purchase both the magazine containing the sample and the perfume being advertised. People who are hungry tend to pay closer attention to advertisements and other information about food.

Quality marketing communication occurs when customers (the **receivers**) decode or understand the message as it was intended by the sender. In the case of Chick-fil-A, effective marketing communications depend on receivers getting the right message and responding in the desired fashion, such as by making a trip to the local Chick-fil-A restaurant or becoming loyal fans on the company's social media page.

FIGURE 1.1 ▶
The Communication Process

// = Noise

Chick-fil-A's approach to social media provides an excellent example of a successful communication strategy that integrates the Web site with both online and off-line advertising to build a loyal customer base.[3] Before launching a social media site, Chick-fil-A's third-party digital agency discovered that Chick-fil-A was mentioned in more than 500 profiles on Facebook and that one particular fan page had 25,000 "fans." The customer who started the fan page continues to help administer the official Chick-fil-A fan page. The goal of this social media program was to engage consumers. According to John Keehler, director of interactive strategy at ClickHere, "One of the mistakes we'd seen is brands would gather a lot of friends but wouldn't get people to interact with them."

▲ Effective marketing communication is important in the highly competitive chicken fast food industry.

The Facebook page allows fans to interact with Chick-fil-A. Traditionally, "Cow Appreciation Day" is held each July, and young customers are encouraged to dress like a cow and post their photos on the Facebook fan page. To build the base of members, in the past coupons have been offered as part of a "Chicken Wave" during the kickoff of the college football season. Other promotions through Twitter and Facebook have resulted in a Facebook community with more than 1 million members. Currently, any new Chick-fil-A store opening is first announced on Facebook. Customers are encouraged to visit the new restaurant and participate in grand-opening festivities.

▼ Each July, Chick-fil-A encourages young customers to dress like a cow.

The key to the social media utilization is a compatible off-line program. Successfully integrated communications use multiple channels that provide the same message. Many Chick-fil-A commercials invite people to "Eat Mor Chikin.'" All advertising and promotional venues present the same tagline and theme. This increases the chances that consumers will perceive the same message and further build the company's strong brand presence.

In the communication process, **feedback** reflects how the receiver responds to the sender. In marketing communications, this includes purchases, inquiries, complaints, questions, store visits, blogs, and Web site hits.

Noise is anything that distorts or disrupts a message, including marketing communications. It can occur at any stage in the communication process, as shown in Figure 1.1. The most common form of noise affecting marketing communications is **clutter.** Examples of noise that can affect the advertising messages are provided in Figure 1.2.

The marketing professionals involved in the communication process pay attention to each aspect of the communications model to ensure that all audiences receive a consistent message. They try to be sure the message cuts through noise and clutter. In the case of chicken quick-service restaurants, increases in market share, sales, and brand loyalty are common objectives the marketing team attempts to achieve.

Communicating with consumers and other businesses requires more than simply creating attractive advertisements. In the next section, the nature of integrated marketing communications is described. An effective integrated marketing communications program integrates all marketing activities into a complete package designed to effectively reach the target market or audience.

FIGURE 1.2 ►
Examples of Communication Noise

- Talking on the phone during a commercial on television
- Driving while listening to the radio
- Looking at a sexy model in a magazine ad and ignoring the message and brand
- Scanning a newspaper for articles to read
- Talking to a passenger as the car passes billboards
- Scrolling past Internet ads without looking at them
- Becoming annoyed by ads appearing on a social media site
- Ignoring tweets on Twitter because they are not relevant
- Being offended by the message on a flyer for a local business

INTEGRATED MARKETING COMMUNICATIONS

② What is an integrated marketing communications program?

An integrated marketing communications program can be built on the foundation provided by the communications model. **Integrated marketing communications (IMC)** may be defined as the coordination and integration of all marketing communication tools, avenues, and sources in a company into a seamless program designed to maximize the impact on customers and other stakeholders. The program should cover all of a firm's business-to-business, market channel, customer-focused, and internally directed communications.[4]

Before further examining an IMC program, consider the traditional framework of marketing promotions. The **marketing mix** is the starting point. As shown in Figure 1.3, promotion is one of the four components of the mix. For years, the traditional view was that promotional activities included advertising, sales promotions, and personal selling activities. This view has been expanded to incorporate online and alternative methods of communication. It also includes activities such as database marketing, direct response marketing, sponsorships, online marketing, social media, guerrilla marketing, alternative marketing, and public relations programs.

Consequently, a complete IMC plan reaches every element of the marketing mix: products, prices, distribution methods, and promotions. While this textbook primarily deals with the promotions component, it should be noted that, in order to present a unified message, the other elements of the marketing mix will be blended into the program.

AN INTEGRATED MARKETING COMMUNICATIONS PLAN

The strategic marketing plan forms the basis for integrated marketing communications. The plan should coordinate every component of the marketing mix in order to achieve harmony in the messages and promotions relayed to customers and others.

FIGURE 1.3 ►
The Components of Promotion

- Current situational analysis
- SWOT analysis
- Marketing objectives
- Target market
- Marketing strategies
- Marketing tactics
- Implementation
- Evaluation of performance

Figure 1.4 lists the steps required to complete a marketing plan. The first, a *current situational analysis*, is the process of examining the firm's ongoing market situation. Next, a *SWOT analysis* is conducted to examine factors present in the organization's internal and external environments. It should identify internal company strengths and weaknesses along with the marketing opportunities and threats that are present in the external environment.

The next step, defining primary *marketing objectives*, establishes targets such as higher sales, an increase in market share, a new competitive position, or desired customer actions, such as visiting the store and making purchases. Marketing objectives are identified along with key *target markets*. A comprehensive understanding of these markets helps the marketing team prepare effective integrated marketing communications.

Based on the marketing objectives and target market, *marketing strategies* are produced. Marketing strategies apply to all the ingredients of the marketing mix, plus any positioning, differentiation, or branding strategies. From these strategies, *marketing tactics* guide the day-by-day activities necessary to support marketing strategies. The final two steps in the marketing plan are stating how to *implement* the plan and then specifying methods to *evaluate performance*.

The steps of the strategic marketing plan help pull all company activities together into one consistent effort. This provides guidance to company leaders and marketing experts as they coordinate the firm's total communications package.

EMERGING TRENDS IN MARKETING COMMUNICATIONS

Many forces have impacted the field of marketing communications. Economic pressures have caused the company leaders who hire advertising agencies to recognize that they cannot pay out unlimited dollars for marketing programs. Emerging social trends have affected marketing messages and means of communication. The introduction of new technologies has also influenced the field. As a result, three new trends have emerged (see Figure 1.5).

❸ Are there any new trends affecting marketing communications?

Emphasis on Accountability and Measurable Results

First, an emphasis on accountability and measurable results has arisen. Advertising agencies are expected to produce tangible outcomes. Promotional dollars must be spent carefully. Any coupon promotion, contest, rebate program, or advertising campaign must yield observable gains in sales, market share, brand awareness, customer loyalty, or other observable results to be considered successful.

This drive for accountability and measurability is being led by chief executive officers (CEOs), chief financial officers (CFOs), and chief marketing officers (CMOs). According to Martyn Straw, chief strategy officer of the advertising agency BBDO Worldwide, corporate executives and business owners are tired of "funneling cash into TV commercials and glossy ads" that keep increasing in cost while appearing to do less and less.

- Emphasis on Accountability and Measurable Results
- Changes in tasks performed by key players
- Explosion in the use of alternative media

As a result, many companies have become less inclined to rely on 30-second television spots. Instead, alternative communication venues and methods are combined with special events where names, profiles, and addresses of prospective customers can be collected and tracked. Straw suggests that marketing is not viewed as a cost, but rather as an investment in which promotional dollars should generate sales and profits.[5]

Changes in Tasks Performed

The second new trend is changes in the tasks performed by the players in advertising programs. The first person facing new job responsibilities is the *account executive* who is employed by an advertising agency (see Figure 1.6). This person sells, directs, and oversees advertising and promotional programs for client companies. Growing demand for accountability means the account manager carefully examines each marketing campaign and looks to provide evidence of success to show prospective clients. The account manager develops overall strategic communication plans for client companies while, at the same time, overseeing individual promotional activities.

The *brand* or *product manager* oversees a specific brand or line of products for the client company. When sales of a brand slow, the brand manager looks for ways to boost them. The brand manager works diligently with the advertising agency, specialists in trade and consumer promotions, and other individuals and agencies involved in conveying brand image to customers. The brand manager organizes the activities of multiple individuals and agencies while integrating each marketing campaign. The goal is to ensure customers encounter the same consistent voice.

Two other groups face new responsibilities. *Creatives* are the people who develop the actual advertisements and promotional materials. Most creatives are employed by advertising agencies. Some work for individual companies; others are freelancers. An *account planner* is the voice of the consumer within the agency. It is his or her job to represent the consumer's viewpoint to the agency's creative staff and to be involved in the development of an advertising campaign. In this new era where attracting attention to a company, good, or service is difficult, creatives and account planners are being asked to contribute ideas about the strategic marketing direction of the firm and the types of communication that are the best for reaching each target audience.

The result is that a new partnership among account executives, brand managers, account planners, and creatives has emerged. Most advertising and marketing agencies do more than create ads. They assist the client company in developing the entire integrated communications program.

Emergence of Alternative Media

The third new trend is the emergence of alternative media. Internet marketing communications have evolved from simple Web-based advertisements to interactive Web sites, blogs, and social networks. Handheld technologies such as smartphones and text-messaging systems have created a new landscape and, in some cases, nearly a new language. Alternative interactive marketing techniques are designed to create experiences with a brand and not just simple purchases.

Many companies have cut expenditures on traditional media commercials and have moved to nontraditional or alternative media. Procter & Gamble, AT&T, Johnson & Johnson, Kraft Foods, Verizon, and Toyota are spending less on television advertising and have shifted funds to digital media. As a General Motors executive noted, "Some 70 percent of consumers who shop for a new car or truck do Web research."[6] The same holds true for countless other products.

FIGURE 1.6 ▶
Key Individuals in an Advertising Program

- Account executive
- Brand or product manager
- Creatives
- Account planners

Currently, younger consumers with considerable amounts of purchasing power are less inclined to watch television. Instead, they engage in technology-based interactions with friends around the world through various social media sites. The marketing challenge becomes finding ways to reach these consumers, who are increasingly sophisticated at blocking out traditional advertising messages. Merely capturing their attention is not enough. Marketing communication now includes finding ways to engage and interact with consumers in ways that create positive, long-term experiences.

THE VALUE OF IMC

Advances in technology and communications have dramatically changed marketing. Consumers may be reached in a variety of ways.[7] Engaging consumers requires an entirely new, carefully integrated approach. Figure 1.7 lists reasons for this shift to greater integration of advertising and marketing communications programs.

▲ Handheld technologies such as smartphones and text-messaging devices have changed the landscape of advertising and marketing.

Source: Getty Images–Thinkstock.

Advances in Information Technology

Technology enables instant communications among business executives, employees, channel members, and customers around the world. It creates both opportunities and threats for marketing communications. Consumers have access to a wealth of information about companies, products, and brands. They can communicate with each other, sending both favorable and unfavorable ratings and information. Messages travel almost instantaneously across social media sites and as mobile texts. Marketers are adapting methods to communicate and vend products effectively in this new communication-rich age. They also monitor what consumers are saying in blogs and online forums.

4 How does an integrated marketing communications program create value?

Advances in information technology allowed self-styled makeup maven Lauren Luke to sell cosmetics around the world. She started by offering them on eBay and then moved to posting videos that she recorded in her bedroom on YouTube. The videos have been viewed 50 million times. Her YouTube channel now has over 250,000 subscribers.

It is not just entrepreneurs such as Lauren Luke who have taken advantage of the opportunities present in today's information and technology-rich environment. In just 6 months. Dell generated $1 million in sales from individuals who contacted the firm using Twitter.[8]

Changes in Channel Power

A marketing channel consists of a producer or manufacturer vending goods to wholesalers or middlemen, who, in turn, sell items to retailers, where the same items are finally sold to consumers. Numerous technological developments have changed the levels of power held by members of the channel.

Retailers often maintain channel power by controlling shelf space and purchase data. Retailers determine what products and brands are placed on store shelves and made

● Advances in information technology	● Increase in brand parity
● Changes in channel power	● Emphasis on customer engagement
● Increase in global competition	● Increase in micro-marketing

◄ **FIGURE 1.7**
Reasons for Integrating Advertising and Marketing Communications

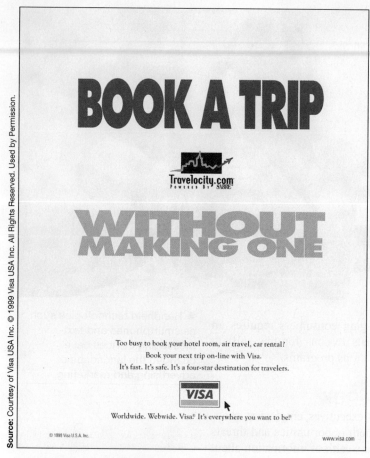

▲ This VISA advertisement encourages consumers to book vacations online.

available to consumers. Through checkout scanners, retailers know what products and brands are selling. Many retailers share the data with suppliers and require them to ensure that store shelves remain well stocked. The size and power of mega-retailers means manufacturers and suppliers have no choice but to follow the dictates of these "mega" stores.

At the same time, the growth of the Internet and other methods of communication have shifted some channel power to consumers.[9] Consumers can obtain information about goods and services and purchase them using the Internet and other resources. The Visa advertisement in this section encourages consumers to book hotel rooms, air travel, and car rentals online. Internet-driven sales have grown at a tremendous rate. Online retail sales grew from $31 billion in 2001 to $156 billion in 2009 (see Figure 1.8). Online purchases made up 5 percent of retail sales in 2008. This figure is projected to rise to 8 percent by 2012.[10]

To illustrate the effects of technology on channel power, consider an individual in the market for a mobile phone provider. First, she completes an Internet search. She identifies several possible brands and narrows them down to three. Next, she travels to a local mall to investigate the carriers. Asking questions of the salespeople helps her gather additional information. After returning home, she logs onto the Web sites of the three brands to learn about warranties, the types of phones being offered, and about company policies, such as how easy it is to change calling plans, plus other details about rollover minutes and other services. She then goes to various forums and blogs to read what other consumers have to say about the three brands.

After gathering sufficient information to make a decision, she can use Internet sources, the telephone, or a personal visit to the carrier's store to finalize the purchase. She may even play one carrier off against another to negotiate a better price. Soon, she has a new phone, along with the paperwork used to complete the transaction. The buyer was in charge of the entire process. Although individuals still purchase the majority of

FIGURE 1.8 ▶
Online Retail Spending, 2001–2009

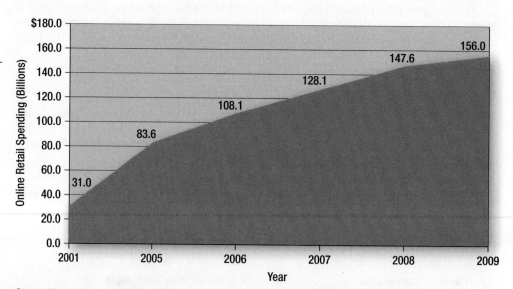

Source: Adapted from Cate T. Corcoran, "Delivering the Goods: E-Tailing Sales to Rise But Gains Seen Slowing," *Women's Wear Daily,* 197, no. 94 (May 5, 2009), p. 1; "Online Retail Spending, 2001–2007, and Projections, 2008," *The 2009 Statistical Anstract: Online Retail Sales* (*www.census.gov/com_a/statab/wholesale_retail_trade/online_retail_sales*, accessed November 23, 2009).

products in brick-and-mortar stores, many are shifting to these more technology-driven methods of gathering information.

The same principles apply to business-to-business purchasing activities. Buyers who shop on behalf of organizations and other company members seeking business-to-business products also tap into these resources (i.e., Web sites, databases). Consequently, the same kind of shift in channel power may be taking place in the business-to-business sector.

Increases in Global Competition

Information technology and communication advances have dramatically changed the marketplace in other ways. Competition no longer comes from the company just down the street—it may be from a firm 10,000 miles away. Consumers want quality, but they also want low prices. The company that delivers both quality and price makes the sale, regardless of location. Advancements in delivery systems make it possible for purchases to arrive in a matter of days.

In this environment, integrating advertising and other marketing communications becomes extremely important. Advertising alone cannot maintain sales. The situation is further complicated for manufacturers when retailers hold stronger channel power and control the flow of merchandise to consumers. In that circumstance, manufacturers invest in trade promotions (dealer incentives and discounts) to keep products in various retail outlets. Encouraging retailers to promote a manufacturer's brand or prominently display it for consumer viewing requires an even greater expenditure of promotional dollars. Manufacturers also invest in consumer promotions (coupons, contests, sweepstakes, bonus packs, and price-off deals) to retain customers. The goal is to keep a brand attractive to the retailer.

The global mobile phone market provides a model of this new global marketplace. Figure 1.9 displays market shares for the top brands in the industry. Nokia is the market leader, Samsung is number two, and the number three brand is LG.[11] The primary way Samsung, LG, Motorola, Sony Ericsson, and other companies gain market share is by taking it away from other brands.[12] As the market leader, Nokia often becomes the main target of such efforts.

As manufacturers battle for market share, a retailer, equipped with scanner data, controls product placement and shelf-space allocation. To gain prominence for a particular brand at the retail level, the manufacturer's marketing team coordinates all advertising, trade promotions, and consumer promotions in an effort to maximize marketing dollars by gaining maximum exposure to consumers and retailers. Retailers, in turn, focus attention of programs that help maintain customer loyalty to the store. They also try to maintain positive relationships with manufacturers. A successful partnership between the retailer and manufacturer helps to build a stronger customer base over time.

◀ **FIGURE 1.9**
Market Share of Top Brands in the Global Mobile Phone Market

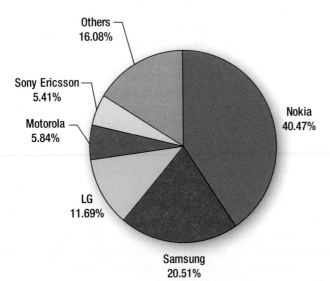

Source: "Wireless/Mobile Statistics," *www.mobileisgood.com/statistics.php*, accessed November 23, 2009.

▲ To minimize brand parity effects, companies such as Asics use advertising to create a strong brand name in the mind of consumers.

Increase in Brand Parity

Many of the products that are currently available offer nearly identical benefits. When consumers believe that most brands provide the same set of attributes, **brand parity** results. From the consumer's perspective, this means that shoppers select from a *group* of brands rather than one specific brand.[13] Brand parity means quality becomes less of a concern, because consumers believe that only minor quality differences exist between brands. When this happens, purchase decisions are based on other criteria, such as price, availability, or a specific promotional deal. The net effect may be a steady decline in brand loyalty.[14] Brand loyalty has also been reduced by the growing acceptance of private brands.

A recent survey revealed that consumers are willing to switch brands in most product categories and do not have one specific brand they must buy or believe is significantly superior.[15] In response to this trend, marketing teams tried to create messages that suggest a company's products were different. Although these messages were designed to convince consumers that the company's brand was superior and not the same as the competition, they often did not move consumers from the perception of brand parity. As a result, some companies have moved to different marketing tactics.

Emphasis on Customer Engagement

The expanding number of available brands that are perceived as being roughly equivalent has led to another response. Many new marketing efforts have been made to engage customers with the brand at every contact point as methods of building loyalty. A **contact point** is any place where customers interact with or acquire additional information about a firm. Customer engagement programs often utilize digital media; however, they should also become part of a more integrated marketing approach.

Effective engagement provides an avenue for two-way communication. It can be built by offering incentives and reasons for the consumer to communicate with the company. For customers to take advantage of these initiatives, however, they must develop emotional commitments to the brand and have feelings of confidence, integrity, pride, and passion for the brand.[16] The brand, in turn, must deliver on its promises and provide reasons for consumers to continue to engage with the company.

Increase in Micro-Marketing

Marketing involves identifying the firm or product's target market and identifying the appropriate media to reach members of each particular market segment. With the burst into the information age and the expanding number of communication technologies, the influence of mass-media television advertising has declined dramatically. VCRs, DVR systems, and using the remote to channel surf all allow consumers to watch programs without commercials. Many television advertisements are not seen, even by those people watching a particular program. The same scenario takes place in other forms of mass advertising.

Consequently, many marketing professionals have shifted efforts to micro-marketing techniques. These programs focus more on individuals and micro-segments rather than the mass population. According to Rex Briggs, founder of Marketing Evolution, " . . . going into the future you're going to see more fragmentation of the media mix and more digital."[17]

Advertising agencies often assist in these marketing efforts. Until 1970, almost all advertising agencies focused solely on the advertising part of the marketing plan. Now, however, many agencies spend substantial amounts of time assisting clients in developing and refining of IMC programs.[18] In addition to advertisements, agencies design Web content, create special events, and look for opportunities to build two-way communication systems with customers.

IMC COMPONENTS AND THE DESIGN OF THIS BOOK

Figure 1.10 presents an overview of the IMC approach used in this textbook. As shown, the foundation of an IMC program consists of a careful review of the company's image, the buyers to be served, and the markets in which the buyers are located. Advertising programs are built on this foundation, as are the other elements of the promotional mix. The integration tools located at the peak of the pyramid help the company's marketing team make certain all of the elements of the plan are consistent and effective.

5 What are the components of an integrated marketing communications program?

The IMC Foundation

The first section of this text builds the foundation for an IMC program. Chapter 2 describes the corporate image and brand management elements. Strengthening the firm's image and brands answers the question, "Who are we and what message are we trying to send?" Branding includes the development of quality packages and labels that speak with the same voice as other marketing messages.

Chapter 3 describes buyer behaviors. The steps of the consumer purchasing process explain how individuals make choices. Marketers identify the motives leading to purchases and factors affecting those decisions. Then, the IMC program can be designed to influence consumer thinking. Business-to-business buyer behaviors are also examined. Knowing how to reach purchasing managers and other decision makers within target businesses is another critical element in an integrated communications plan. Discovering viable business-to-business marketing opportunities plays a vital role in overall company success.

Chapter 4 explains the IMC planning program. This includes identifying all target markets. Consumer market segments are identified using demographics and psychographic variables as well as benefits sought and usage information. Business markets are segmented by understanding the demographics of the company's buying team, noting who the end users will be, and by determining the benefits other businesses expect to receive from the goods and services to be purchased. The plan is complete when communications budgets have been developed and all appropriate media have been identified.

Advertising Tools

The second section of this text is devoted to advertising issues. Advertising management, as described in Chapter 5, addresses the major functions of advertising, the general direction the company takes, and the selection of an advertising agency. The functions performed by various advertising agency personnel are also noted.

◀ **FIGURE 1.10**
Overview of Integrated Marketing Communications

Several advertising theories, which are explored in Chapter 6, are available to help creatives design advertisements. The various advertising appeals that can be used, including those oriented toward fear, humor, sex, music, and logic, are explained in the chapter.

Chapter 7 reveals the ingredients involved in creating effective message strategies. The messages are delivered via various executional frameworks, which are various ways to construct the actual commercial or advertisement. Creatives and other advertising professionals know that effective advertising includes the use of effective sources or spokespersons and following well-established principles of success.

IMC Media Tools

The third section of this book contains information regarding both traditional and new cutting-edge methods of reaching potential customers. First, the traditional media channels, including television, radio, outdoor, magazines, and newspapers, are described in Chapter 8, along with the advantages and disadvantages of each medium. The roles provided by media planners and media buyers are also explained.

Chapter 9 is devoted to issues associated with the Internet, with the term *e-active marketing* used to summarize the various activities involved. E-active marketing integrates e-commerce programs with more recent trends in online interactive marketing. These include social networks, blogs, and customer reviews. In these forums, consumers play active roles in receiving and sending messages. Consequently, the channel deserves special attention from the marketing department.

Many communication channels are available beyond both the traditional networks and the Internet. These methods are described in Chapter 10, titled "Alternative Marketing," and include buzz marketing, guerrilla marketing, product placements and branded entertainment, and lifestyle marketing. Brand communities are also examined.

▼ This advertisement for Security Finance offers quick approval for back-to-school loans.

Promotional Tools

The next level of the IMC pyramid adds database and direct response marketing programs, personal selling, trade promotions, consumer promotions, public relations efforts, and sponsorship programs. When marketing managers carefully design all of the steps taken up to this point, the firm is in a better position to integrate these activities. Messages presented in the advertising campaign can be reinforced with a variety of communication promotions.

Database and direct response marketing programs are outlined in Chapter 11. The chapter first describes effective data collection and analysis. Then, the information gained can be used to develop data-driven marketing programs, including permission marketing, frequency programs, and customer relationship management systems. It is also employed to enhance effective personal selling activities.

Consumer and trade promotions are described in Chapter 12, which has the general title of "Sales Promotions." Trade promotions include trade incentives, cooperative advertising, slotting fees, and other promotions and discounts that help the manufacturer or channel member to push the product through the distribution channel. Consumer promotions are

Source: Courtesy of Joplin Globe.

directed at end users and include coupons, contests, premiums, refunds, rebates, free samples, and price-off offers.

Chapter 13 focuses on public relations programs that connect with consumers in positive ways. This involves emphasizing positive events and dealing with negative publicity. In many cases, the marketing team utilizes public relations efforts to help a sponsorship program achieve the greatest impact.

Integration Tools

The top level of the IMC program adds the integration tools needed to make sure all customers are effectively served. Chapter 14 begins with an examination of the many legal and regulatory issues that are part of the advertising and promotions environment. Ethical issues in marketing communications are also discussed. Ethical systems should go beyond simply meeting the letter of the law.

The final chapter of this textbook, Chapter 15, explains the evaluation of integrated marketing communications programs. Evaluations can begin prior to any promotional campaign and continue during the campaign to postcampaign evaluations. These evaluations generate valuable information to alter campaigns before they are commercially introduced. They also provide input to modify programs that have already run. A promotions evaluation process holds everything together and drives the entire IMC process. Fully integrated marketing requires a careful linkage between planning and evaluation processes.

INTERNATIONAL IMPLICATIONS

The same trends that exist among advertising agencies in the United States occur in the international arena. Instead of IMC, international marketing is called *GIMC*, or a *globally integrated marketing communications program*.[19] The goal is still the same—to coordinate marketing efforts across all platforms. The challenges are greater due to larger national and cultural differences in target markets.

Marketers can employ two different strategies for global companies. The first approach is **standardization,** in which the idea is to feature a uniform product and message across countries. The goal of this approach is to generate economies of scale in production while creating a global product using a more universal promotional theme. The language may be different, but the basic marketing message will be the same.

The second approach to global marketing is **adaptation.** Products and marketing messages are designed for and adapted to individual countries. Thus, the manner by which a product is marketed in Mexico will be different from how it is marketed in Italy, India, or Australia.

The GIMC approach is easier to apply when a company relies on the standardization method; however, GIMC can and should be used with either adaptation or standardization.[20] To reduce costs, careful coordination of marketing efforts should occur across countries. Even when a firm uses the adaptation strategy, marketers from various countries can learn from each other. Members of the marketing department should not feel like they have to reinvent the wheel. Synergy can occur between countries and regions. More important, learning can occur. As telecommunications continue to expand, contacts between peoples of different countries are much more frequent.

International marketing experts recognize that a commercial targeted for customers in France may also be viewed by people in Spain using satellite technologies. Therefore, a company should try to transmit a consistent theme, even when there are differences in local messages. In terms of marketing, the philosophy many companies use is "market globally, but act locally." When marketers design or encode messages, they need to have the freedom to tailor or alter the message so that it fits the local culture and the target market. The final message conveyed in each country often varies. Development of a GIMC is the final extension to an IMC plan. With its completion, companies are able to compete more effectively both at home and abroad.

6 What does the term *GIMC* mean?

In many of the upcoming chapters, this section will present some basic information about various integrated advertising and marketing campaigns. The insights resulted from personal interviews with members of the advertising agencies and client companies. Some of the brands include:

- Argent Financial (Emogen Marketing Group)
- Oscar Mayer (Oscar Mayer and mcgarrybowen advertising agency)
- Skyjacker (Skyjacker)
- Wayport Austintatious (Pink Jacket Creative)
- Just Curb It (Gremillion & Pou)

In addition, your professor will have access to Power-Point presentations that include insights and background materials from the agencies and companies involved. These features bring to life the exciting process of building integrated advertising and marketing campaigns.

Your instructor has additional information about the ads, visuals, and displays used in the campaigns featured in upcoming chapters.

Source: Author Supplied Image.

▲ The Richards Group provides a full range of integrated marketing communications services.

 # SUMMARY

Communication is transmitting, receiving, and processing information. It is a two-way street in which a sender must establish a clear connection with a receiver. Effective communication forms the basis for a solid and successful marketing program.

The components of the communication process include the sender, an encoding process, the transmission device, the decoding process, and the receiver. Noise is anything that distorts or disrupts the flow of information from the sender to the receiver.

In the marketing arena, senders are companies seeking to transmit ideas to consumers, employees, other companies, retail outlets, and others. Encoding devices are the means of transmitting information and include advertisements, public relations efforts, press releases, sales activities, promotions, and a wide variety of additional verbal and nonverbal cues sent to receivers. Transmission devices are the media and spokespersons that carry the message. Decoding occurs when the receivers (customers or retailers) encounter the message. Noise takes many forms in marketing, most notably the clutter of an overabundance of messages in every available channel.

Integrated marketing communications (IMC) takes advantage of the effective management of the communications channel. Within the marketing mix of products, prices, distribution systems, and promotions, firms that speak with one clear voice are able to coordinate and integrate all marketing tools. The goal is to have a strong and positive impact on consumers, businesses, and other end users.

A new era is unfolding in the fields of advertising, promotions, and marketing communications. Marketing departments

and advertising agencies, as well as individual account managers, brand managers, and creatives, encounter strong pressures. They are being held accountable for expenditures of marketing communications dollars. Company leaders expect tangible results from promotional campaigns and other marketing programs. As a result, new partnerships are forming among account executives, creatives, and the companies that hire them. The duties of the account manager have expanded in the direction of a more strategically oriented approach to advertising and marketing communications. Those preparing to become advertising or promotions professionals must be aware of both accountability issues and the new aspects of these jobs, including accounting for all of the new forms of alternative media.

IMC plans are vital to achieving success. The reasons for their importance begin with the explosion of information technologies. Channel power has shifted from manufacturers to retailers and is now shifting to consumers. Company leaders must adjust in order to maintain a strong market standing, and IMC programs can assist in this effort. New levels of competition drive marketers to better understand their customers and be certain that those end users are hearing a clear and consistent message from the firm. As consumers develop a stronger sense of brand parity, whereby no real differences in product or service quality are perceived, marketers must re-create a situation in which their brand holds a distinct advantage over others. This may be difficult, because consumers collect and integrate information about products from a wide variety of sources, including technological outlets (Web sites) and interpersonal (sales reps) sources. Quality IMC programs help maintain the strong voice a company needs to ensure that its message is heard. An additional challenge is the decline in effectiveness of mass-media advertising. IMC helps company leaders find new ways to contact consumers with a unified message and to engage them in long-term relationships.

When a firm conducts business internationally, a GIMC, or globally integrated marketing communications system, can be of great value. By developing one strong theme and then adapting that theme to individual countries, the firm conveys a message that integrates international operations into a more coherent package.

This text explains the issues involved in establishing an effective IMC program. The importance of business-to-business marketing efforts is noted, because many firms market items as much to other companies as they do to consumers. Successful development of an IMC program should help firms remain profitable and vibrant, even when the complexities of the marketplace make these goals more difficult to reach.

KEY TERMS

communication Transmitting, receiving, and processing information.

senders The person(s) attempting to deliver a message or idea.

encoding The verbal (words, sounds) and nonverbal (gestures, facial expressions, posture) cues that the sender utilizes in dispatching a message.

transmission devices All of the items that carry a message from the sender to the receiver.

decoding When the receiver employs any of his or her senses (hearing, seeing, feeling) in an attempt to capture a message.

receivers The intended audience for a message.

feedback Information the sender obtains from the receiver regarding the receiver's perception or interpretation of a message.

noise Anything that distorts or disrupts a message.

clutter Exists when consumers are exposed to hundreds of marketing messages per day, and most are tuned out.

integrated marketing communications (IMC) The coordination and integration of all marketing communication tools, avenues, and sources in a company into a seamless program designed to maximize the impact on customers and other stakeholders.

marketing mix Consists of products, prices, places (the distribution system), and promotions.

brand parity Occurs when there is the perception that most goods and services are essentially the same.

contact points The places where customers interact with or acquire additional information about a firm.

standardization When a firm features uniform products and market offerings across countries with the goal of generating economies of scale in production while using the same promotional theme.

adaptation Occurs when products and marketing messages are designed for and adapted to individual countries.

REVIEW QUESTIONS

1. Define communication. How does it play a crucial role in marketing and business?
2. What are the parts of an individual communications model?
3. Who are the typical senders in marketing communications? Who are the receivers?
4. Name the transmission devices, both human and nonhuman, that carry marketing messages.
5. Define clutter. Name some of the forms of clutter in marketing communications.
6. Define integrated marketing communications (IMC).
7. What are the four parts of the marketing mix?
8. What steps are required to write a marketing plan?
9. How has the job of an advertising account executive changed? How has the job of a brand manager changed? How has the job of a creative changed? How has the job of account planner changed? How do the four jobs interact in the new marketing environment?
10. What reasons were given to explain the growth in importance of IMC plans in this chapter?
11. How has the growth of information technology made IMC programs vital to marketing efforts?
12. What is channel power? How has it changed in the past few decades?
13. What is brand parity? How is it related to successful marketing efforts?
14. What is a contact point? How are contact points linked to customer engagement?
15. What is micro-marketing?
16. What are the components of an integrated marketing communications program, as outlined in this textbook?
17. What is a GIMC? Why is it important for multinational firms?
18. What is the difference between standardization and adaptation in GIMC programs?

CRITICAL THINKING EXERCISES

Discussion Questions

1. Do you use Twitter? If so, how do you use it? Ask 10 people who are not taking this course if they use Twitter and how they use it. Can you identify any local businesses that use Twitter? How does the company use it? What about a national company? Based on this information, write a paragraph about how Twitter is being used and how it can be used by businesses.

2. The marketing director for a furniture manufacturer is assigned the task of emphasizing the furniture's natural look in the company's integrated marketing communications program. Discuss the problems the director might encounter while developing this message and in ensuring that consumers understand the message correctly. Refer to the communication process in Figure 1.1 for ideas. Explain how noise or clutter interferes with the communication process.

3. What do you typically do during commercials on television? What percentage of the time do you watch commercials?

What makes you watch? Ask these same questions of 10 other people. What type of activities do people engage in during commercials?

4. For years, Nike's advertising tagline was "Just do it." What meaning is conveyed by the tagline? Do you think this conveys a clear message about the company's operations?

5. Brand parity has become a major issue for companies. Identify three product categories where the brand you purchase is not very important. Why is the brand not important? Identify three product categories where the brand is important. What brand or brands do you typically purchase in each category?

6. The marketing director for a manufacturer of automobile tires has been asked to integrate the company's marketing program internationally. Should the director use a standardization or adaptation approach? How could the company be certain that its marketing program will effectively be integrated among the different countries in which it sells tires?

INTEGRATED LEARNING EXERCISES

1. Access the Web site of Chick-fil-A at **www.chickfila.com**. Access the Web sites of Chick-fil-A's competitors: KFC (**www.kfc.com**), Popeye's (**www.popeyes.com**), Church's Chicken (**www.churchschiken.com**), and Bojangles (**www.bojangles.com**). Which sites have a link to Facebook, Twitter, or other social media site? Compare and contrast the information available and the design of each company's Web site. Which Web site did you like the best? Why? Which one did you like the least? Why?

2. Ron Jon Surf Shop is probably the best known retail store brand for ocean gear in Florida. In Hawaii, the dominant name is Hilo Hattie. Go to the Hilo Hattie Web site at **www.hilohattie.com**. Compare it to the Ron Jon site at **www.ronjons.com**. Do the two sites have relatively common themes? Which is the more attractive site? Why?

3. Find each of the following companies on the Internet. For each company, discuss how effective its Web site is in communicating an overall message. Also, discuss how well the

marketing team integrates the material on the Web site. How well does the Web site integrate the company's advertising with other marketing communications?

   a. Revlon (**www.revlon.com**)

   b. J.B. Hunt (**www.jbhunt.com**)

   c. United Airlines (**www.united.com**)

   d. Steamboat Resorts (**www.steamboatresorts.com**)

4. Information is one key to developing a successful integrated marketing communications program. Access each of the following Web sites and examine the information and news available on each site. How would this information help in developing an integrated marketing campaign?

   a. *Brandweek* (**www.brandweek.com**)

   b. *Adweek* (**www.adweek.com**)

   c. *Mediaweek* (**www.mediaweek.com**)

   d. *Branding Asia* (**www.brandingasia.com**)

STUDENT PROJECT

Creative Corner

One of Procter & Gamble's fastest growing products is Febreze. The product targets individuals who do not like washing laundry and has been positioned by P&G as an alternative method of completing this chore. An ideal target market would seem to be the 18 million college students in the United States. With busy class schedules, work, and social events, they may believe they do not have enough time to do laundry. For jeans and other clothes that are not quite dirty yet, Febreze offers the chance to "refresh" the clothes and kill any possible odors. John Paquin, Executive

Vice-President at the advertising agency WPP Grey Worldwide, which handles the Febreze product, states that "washing is not a convenient part of the lifestyle at college." He also recognizes that "mainstream media buys [such as television] are not effective for the 18- to 22-year-olds."[21] For more information about Febreze, access the Febreze Web site at **www.febreze.com**.

1. Identify alternative media you would use to reach 18- to 22-year-old college students.

2. Design an advertisement for Febreze aimed at the college demographic. Where would you place your ad? Why?

SHOULD ZAPPOS.COM GO TO EUROPE?

One of the major success stories in online retailing has been the emergence and growth of Zappos.com. Founded in 1999 by Nick Swinmurn, the company's initial focus was on selling shoes (the name *Zappos* is derived from the Spanish word for "shoes") to people looking for a large inventory with exactly the right model in stock. The company's warehouse and order-fulfillment zone contains over 3 million pairs.

Zappos.com now offers additional items, including clothing, bags, housewares and beauty products. A visitor to the company's Web site can expect a purchase to be shipped within a few days. If the item does not fit or the customer decides it isn't right, she can return the item for full credit, with free return shipping, for up to 1 year. Phone orders are taken by friendly, upbeat, sales representatives referred to as the Customer Loyalty Team.

One of the primary features of Zappos.com is management's emphasis on great customer service. New employees are required to enroll in a 4-week training program designed to teach them how to work in the call center, even if they will eventually be placed elsewhere. During the course of the training, CEO Tony Hsieh offers to "buy them out," with a cash payment of $2,000, should the individual decide to leave within the first 90 days of his or her job. Those who remain have a high dedication to serving customers. This includes directing customers to competitors when Zappos does not have a particular item in stock.

The Zappos culture features 10 core values that employees are happy to recite. These include thoughts such as "Deliver WOW Through Service," "Pursue Growth and Learning," "Create Fun and a Little Weirdness," and "Be Passionate and Determined." Members of the Zappos team are encouraged to be spontaneous, have fun, and stay excited. The workplace features free food and a pleasant, friendly environment.

By 2010, Zappos.com had expanded into other product lines, including clothing, bags, and accessories. At the same time, more than once the question was posed, "Should we move into the European market?"

One concern might be with the main product line, clothing and footwear. When Zappos executive Aaron Magness was asked specifically about differences in fashion in European countries, he responded, "We don't really think that fashion is the concern. The real challenge is from logistics and vendor relationships. Most vendors have specific distribution relationships by country, so we wouldn't be able to sell everything everywhere."

With regard to purchasing habits and methods of payment, Magness noted, "While they may be slightly different, we accept multiple types of payment options which allow for the international customer to be able to shop. Europeans seem to be accelerating their online shopping habits, so the customer base is there and ready to buy."

When asked to discuss customer service, Magness stated, "Customer service may mean different things to different people. Next day delivery is very important and a big deal in the US. Is it the same in Europe? In Germany, many retailers offer same day delivery. In London, shipping is very expensive. In France, there are a lot of delays and strikes. We would need to find out what service levels people are looking for."

Finally, the issue of marketing communications arose. Magness noted that, "We'd have to find what is important to the customer and stand behind that."

▲ **Zappos.com has achieved success by providing excellent customer service.**

Source: Thinkstock Royalty Free.

1. Would the image or theme that Zappos.com portrays to its customers in the United States translate to the European market? Explain.

2. Do you think Zappos.com should utilize a standardization or adaptation approach to both the products offered and the marketing messages to be sent?

3. Examine Figure 1.11. Explain how each feature would be the same or different for Zappos.com, if the company entered the European market.

- Company logo
- Product brand name and company name
- Business cards
- Letterhead
- Carry home bags (paper or plastic)
- Wrapping paper
- Coupons
- Promotional giveaways (coffee mugs, pens, pencils, calendars)
- Design of booth for trade shows
- Advertisements (billboards, space used on cars and busses, television, radio, magazines, and newspapers)
- Toll-free 800 or 888 number
- Company database

- Cooperative advertising with other businesses
- Personal selling pitches
- Characteristics of target market buyers
- Characteristics of business buyers
- Sales incentives provided to salesforce (contests, prizes, bonuses, and commissions)
- Internal messages
- Company magazines and newspapers
- Statements to shareholders
- Speeches by company leaders
- Public relations releases
- Sponsorship programs
- Web site

CASE 2   A NEW SALSA SENSATION

Hector Fernandez created a salsa that became legendary within just a few years. Hector operated a successful restaurant, El Casa Grande, in Taos, New Mexico, for many years. A new chapter in his life opened when he was approached by two of his best customers, who offered to help him produce and market his salsa throughout the state, with the goal of reaching regional distribution in 5 years.

As a first step, Hector located the home office of a major advertising agency in Albuquerque. The agency positioned itself as being a "full-service" organization. Hector wondered exactly what that meant. He was introduced to Matt Barnes, who was to serve as his marketing and promotions consultant.

Matt's first questions were about Hector's salsa: "What makes your salsa better?" and "Is there a way we can convince people of the difference?" Hector responded that his customers

▲ Hector had a great salsa, but no brand name and no marketing communication plan.

Source: Thinkstock Royalty Free.

often commented about both the taste and the texture of the salsa. He had a secret formula that had a few unusual seasonings that made his salsa burst with flavor. Hector also believed that it was less "runny" than others.

The next item the two discussed was potential customers. Hector noted that Tex-Mex was a popular form of dining in New Mexico as well as across the country. He believed that his salsa would appeal to a wide variety of people who enjoy Tex-Mex cuisine.

Matt's next question was simple: "Who do you think are your major competitors?"

Hector responded, "That's easy, Pace and Old El Paso."

Matt then asked what Hector thought of the two companies and their products. He suggested an investigation on both a personal and competitive basis. For example, Matt asked, "What do you think of when you hear the name Pace? How about Old El Paso?" He noted that both brands were solid and that Hector's company would need a compelling brand in order to compete.

The next step was a visit to the Web site of each company (**www.pacefoods.com** and **www.oldelpaso.com**). They noticed that the two companies offered some products that were the same and others that were not.

Matt asked Hector what he thought about the advertising and promotions for each company and its products. Hector replied, "Well, to tell you the truth, I only remember one television ad. It said something about one of the two companies was located in New York City instead of near Mexico, but I can't remember which was which." They concluded that it was possible that these companies do not engage in a great deal of traditional media advertising or that Hector was simply too busy with his own company to notice. Hector noted that he used a DVR to watch television and that he listened to satellite radio in both his restaurant and his car.

Matt suggested that Hector should look in Sunday papers for the past several weeks to see if either company was offering price-off coupons or other promotions, such as a contest or sweepstakes. He told Hector it would be a good idea to attend events where salsa was being sampled or sold, such as at county fairs, Mexican heritage events, and at ballparks and other sports stadiums where nachos were on the menu.

The two then discussed a crucial issue: How could Hector's new company convince grocers and others to designate some shelf space for his salsa, thereby taking space away from some other product?

Finally, Matt handed Hector a package of materials (see Figure 1.11). He asked Hector to consider how to reach every possible type of customer for his product, including grocery stores, other restaurants, and individual consumers shopping for salsa. He suggested that Hector would need to think about what type of sales tactics to use, which promotional programs were most important, and how the company should look—from its logo, to its letterhead, to the business cards handed out by sales representatives. Remember, Matt stated, "Everything communicates."

1. Can you think of a brand name that could be used not only for salsa, but for any other product related to salsa that Hector's company might sell?

2. How can Hector's company compete with Pace and Old El Paso? Is there a market niche the company can locate?

3. What kinds of advertising and promotions tactics should the company use? Will the tactics be the same in 5 years?

2 Corporate Image and Brand Management

BARBIE

Brand Rejuvenation in a New Era

What should a company do when a long-standing, powerful brand begins to age and lose its luster? General manager and senior vice president for the Barbie brand, Richard Dickson, confronted the problem facing the leading product line at Mattel. The Barbie collection experienced a dramatic decline in sales. In essence, the buzz shifted to newer, seemingly more twenty-first century doll lines, especially the Bratz line from outside Mattel and the American Girl brand from within the company. The Bratz line was viewed as being "edgier" and more ethnically diverse. The American Girl line appealed to older girls.

For many years, Barbie dolls and accessories enjoyed a rich tradition of popularity and status as a cultural icon. The first edition, produced in 1959, quickly became a national commodity. The companion Ken doll was launched in 1961. Christie, an African American doll, emerged in 1968. In 2000, the Barbie line held an astonishing 80 percent market share. The Barbie line's peak year of sales, 2002, was the financial pinnacle.

In the years that followed, Barbie's market share dropped dramatically and reached bottom in 2009, when it fell to less than 50 percent. When Richard Dickson was assigned the task of rejuvenating the line, he created a team of in-house brand managers and sent them to the mod-baroque, Kelly Wearstler–designed Viceroy hotel in Santa Monica, California. "I wanted people to see what it was like to be surrounded by a signature style," Dickson reported.

Dickson's team responded with a new model, the "Generation of Dreams" Barbie line. They also mandated that all Barbie products be consistent with the brand's identity. For several years, powerful retailers such as Wal-Mart had influenced the doll's specs, creating what Dickson called "brand goulash." Further, the number of licensees of Barbie products was greatly reduced.

Changes were made to the marketing program. Dickson insisted that a real-life Barbie dream home be designed and built in Malibu, California. Fashion giant Diane von

CHAPTER 2

CHAPTER OBJECTIVES

After reading this chapter, you should be able to answer the following questions:

1 How does a corporate image affect consumers, other businesses, and the company itself?

2 What elements are involved in identifying, creating, rejuvenating, or changing a corporation's image?

3 What are the different types of corporate names?

4 What are the characteristics of effective logos?

5 What different kinds of brands can firms offer?

6 How are brands developed, built, and sustained in order to build brand equity and fend off perceptions of brand parity?

7 What current trends affect private labels?

8 How are packages and labels used to support an IMC program, both domestically and in foreign settings?

Furstenberg created life-size Barbie apparel for *Fashion Week* magazine. To pay for the programs, the number of traditional 30-second television advertising spots was reduced. The Barbie Web site was expanded to include contests, games, videos, and a virtual world.

Initial results of these efforts were promising. In 2009, sales rose by 18 percent in one quarter, the largest increase in 3 years. The new line created additional publicity and buzz, which also generated greater interest.

Mattel directly confronted Bratz with a copyright infringement lawsuit, which it won. The essence of the lawsuit was that Mattel is the legal owner of the Bratz dolls, which are manufactured by archrival MGA Entertainment. The ruling by a federal judge was reached, in part, because Bratz's creator Carter Bryant was working at Mattel under an exclusive contract when he came up with the idea for the doll.

The jury's $100 million judgment did not include punitive damages. Both sides claimed victory based on the jury's decision.

The future of the doll industry remains clouded. One trend, known as *age compression*, dramatically affects all traditional toy manufacturers and retailers. Children simply abandon certain toys, including dolls, at much younger ages. Both the Barbie and Bratz lines continue to adapt, with more mature clothing options for dolls combined with more mature marketing presentations.

Further complications emerge from the fad-driven nature of the toy industry, with Tickle Me Elmo and Cabbage Patch Kids serving as prime examples. Although the Mattel brand remains strong, the company continues to face challenges as the world of children and toys continues to evolve.[1]

OVERVIEW

Managing an organization's image remains one of the most critical ingredients in the successful development of an integrated marketing communications plan. A **corporate image** reflects the feelings consumers and businesses have about the overall organization and its individual brands. Advertising, consumer promotions, trade promotions, personal selling, the company's Web site, and other marketing activities all affect these consumer perceptions. A strong brand creates a major advantage for any product or service. When the image of an organization or one of its brands becomes tarnished, sales revenues and profits can plummet, and then rebuilding or revitalizing the image becomes a difficult task.

Brand managers are responsible for developing and maintaining a quality image, which has a "bottom line" that can even be assigned a value on accounting statements. Advertising managers and other marketing experts try to create messages that (1) sell products in the short term and (2) build a firm's image over time. Advertising agencies consider both goals when designing advertisements and promotional campaigns.

The marketing team seeks to understand the firm's image and the strengths of individual brands in order to make solid connections with consumers and business-to-business customers. A strong IMC foundation combines an analysis of the firm's image and brands with assessments of consumer and business buyer behaviors. The marketing team then prepares consistent messages designed to reach every individual who might purchase a company's products.

The first part of this chapter examines the activities involved in managing a corporation's image, including its name and logo. The second part addresses ways to develop and promote the various forms of brand names. Brand equity and brand parity are described. Finally, packages and labels, which should be part of a marketing communications program, are assessed. Ethical and international considerations also are noted.

❶ How does a corporate image affect consumers, other businesses, and the company itself?

CORPORATE IMAGE

A corporate image summarizes what the company stands for as well as how it is known in the marketplace. Whether it is the "good hands" of Allstate Insurance or the "good neighbors" at State Farm Insurance, creating a specific impression in the minds of clients and customers should be the goal of image management. Insurance companies often accomplish this by stressing helpfulness, safety, and security as elements of a strong image.

Consumer beliefs about a firm are far more important than how company officials perceive the image. Corporate names such as Dell, Toyota, Kraft Foods, and ExxonMobil create impressions in the minds of clients and customers. Although the specific version of the image varies from consumer to consumer or business-to-business buyer, the overall image of a firm is determined by the combined views of all publics. These can be positive or negative.

Components of a Corporate Image

Consumers encounter many elements as they interact with a company. Consumer perceptions of the goods and services being offered create a primary component of a corporate image. A recent study suggested that the quality of a company's goods and services ranks as the most important component of corporate image. The willingness of a firm to stand behind its goods and services when something went wrong was second. Third on the list were perceptions of how the firm dealt with customers, such as by being pleasant, helpful, or professional.[2]

Each firm's image consists of a unique set of features. The corporate image of an automobile manufacturer such as Porsche, Mazda, Toyota, or General Motors might be based on the following: (1) evaluations of vehicles, (2) whether the company is foreign or domestic, (3) customer views of each company's advertisements, and (4) reactions to the local dealership. A corporation's image often includes consumer assessments of company employees. In fact, the mechanic trying to repair a vehicle at a local Mr. Goodwrench garage might become the dominant factor that shapes a customer's image of General Motors.

▼ A State Farm advertisement stressing driver safety.

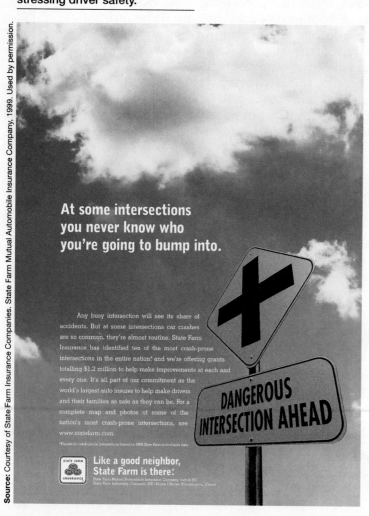

At some intersections you never know who you're going to bump into.

Any busy intersection will see its share of accidents. But at some intersections car crashes are so common, they're almost routine. State Farm Insurance has identified ten of the most crash-prone intersections in the entire nation,* and we're offering grants totalling $1.2 million to help make improvements at each and every one. It's all part of our commitment as the world's largest auto insurer to help make drivers and their families as safe as they can be. For a complete map and photos of some of the nation's most crash-prone intersections, see www.statefarm.com.

*Figures for crash-prone intersections based on 1998 State Farm auto claims data.

Like a good neighbor, State Farm is there.®
State Farm Mutual Automobile Insurance Company (not in NJ)
State Farm Indemnity Company (NJ)—Home Offices: Bloomington, Illinois

DANGEROUS INTERSECTION AHEAD

Tangible Elements	Intangible Elements
1. Goods and services sold	1. Corporate, personnel, and environmental policies
2. Retail outlets where the product is sold	2. Ideals and beliefs of corporate personnel
3. Factories where the product is produced	3. Culture of country and location of company
4. Advertising, promotions, and other forms of communications	4. Media reports
5. Corporate name and logo	
6. Packages and labels	
7. Employees	

Recently, Subaru and Mazda created programs designed to emphasize the importance of the dealership as an influence on consumer assessments of the company's image. Both firms launched aggressive remodeling plans for local dealerships, with the goal of providing a more pleasant shopping environment. These new-look dealerships helped boost the images of both Subaru and Mazda, resulting in higher sales. Subaru dealers that remodeled using the new retail format sold 54 percent more vehicles in the following year. Mazda dealers that adopted the new retail design sold 30 percent more vehicles.[3] Toyota, recognizing that many women purchase automobiles, and that an even greater number have a significant influence on the purchase decision, launched "Image USA II." The program recommended that every Toyota dealer provide a children's play area in the showroom, a coffee bar in the service area, and nicely decorated restrooms to make the showroom more inviting to women.[4]

A corporate image contains invisible and intangible elements (see Figure 2.1). When consumers learn that a pharmaceutical or cosmetic company has a policy that prohibits product testing on animals, this information will be integrated into their attitudes about the firm. Personnel policies and practices impact the firm's image. Strikes and labor disputes often have a negative impact on a firm's image. Executive pay and whether a company accepted bailout money from the federal government during the recent recession impact how consumers view various businesses. The beliefs and attitudes consumers have about Japan might influence their views of companies such as Sony and Toyota.

Negative publicity has the potential to stain or damage consumer perceptions of a corporation's image. Examples include the damaged reputations of financial institutions, General Motors, and Chrysler immediately after the companies received bailout money from the federal government.

The Role of a Corporate Image—Consumer Perspective

From a consumer's perspective (or business customer perspective), a corporate image serves several useful functions. These include the items displayed in Figure 2.2.

A well-known corporate image offers customers *positive assurance* about what to expect. A can of Coke or Pepsi purchased in Anchorage, Alaska, features a taste that is comparable to one purchased in Liverpool, England, or Kuala Lumpur, Malaysia. KFC serves the same or similar meals in San Francisco as the ones sold in Minneapolis or Paris. Products ordered online from Bed, Bath and Beyond are the same as those purchased in the retail store.

- Provides confidence regarding purchase decisions
- Gives assurance about the purchase when the buyer has little or no previous experience
- Reduces search time in the purchase decision
- Provides psychological reinforcement and social acceptance of the purchase

Pity you have nothing left to wish for.

It's all come true. The endless horizon. The precise handling. And the way the sounds and sensations of the night resonate throughout the open cockpit. The 911 Turbo Cabriolet delivers the road in its most potent form. Perhaps it's time you followed your dreams. Porsche. There is no substitute.

The new 911 Turbo Cabriolet

PORSCHE

▲ Porsche maintains a strong and positive corporate image that influences consumer purchase decisions.

Positive assurance generates greater value when customers purchase goods or services with which they have *little experience*. Consider families on vacation. Many travelers look for names or logos of companies from their native areas. Purchasing from a familiar corporation seems "safer" strategy than buying something from an unknown company. Taking a room at a hotel the consumer has never heard of feels riskier than utilizing a familiar one. Thus, a family visiting Brazil might normally not stay at the Holiday Inn, but the recognizable name makes it a lower-risk option.

Another significant role corporate image plays for customers will be *reduced search time*. Purchasing from a familiar firm saves time and effort. An individual or company loyal to Ford spends fewer hours searching for a new car than does someone without such loyalty. The same holds true when purchasing low-cost items such as groceries or office products. Search time is saved when a consumer purchases items from the same organization, such as Campbell's, Nabisco, Kraft, or 3M.

For many individuals, purchasing from a highly recognized company provides psychological reinforcement and social acceptance. *Psychological reinforcement* comes from feeling that a wise choice was made and the belief that the good or service will perform well. *Social acceptance* may be derived from knowing that other individuals have purchased from the same firm. Family members and friends are likely to accept the choice. The Porsche advertisement in this section illustrates the power of psychological and social forces on the purchase of an expensive item, an automobile.

Recently, Interbrand produced a list of the top 100 corporate brands. Companies that offer portfolios of products and brands, such as Procter & Gamble, were not included. In addition, companies that are privately held, such as VISA, or companies that operate under different names in different countries, such as Wal-Mart, were not included. The list only notes corporations that provide products under one name. Using these criteria, Interbrand ranked Coca-Cola as the top global corporate brand. IBM was second. Table 2.1 provides a complete listing.

TABLE 2.1 Top 10 Corporate Global Brands

Rank	Company	Brand Value (billions)	Country of Ownership
1	Coca-Cola	$68.7	United States
2	IBM	$60.2	United States
3	Microsoft	$56.6	United States
4	General Electric	$47.7	United States
5	Nokia	$34.8	Finland
6	McDonald's	$32.2	United States
7	Google	$31.9	United States
8	Toyota	$31.1	Japan
9	Intel	$30.6	United States
10	Disney	$28.4	United States

Source: Based on "The 100 Top Brands," *BusinessWeek* (August 6, 2007), pp. 59–64.

- Extension of positive customer feelings to new products
- Ability to charge a higher price or fee
- Consumer loyalty leading to more frequent purchases
- Positive word-of-mouth endorsements
- Higher level of channel power
- Ability to attract quality employees
- More favorable ratings by financial observers and analysts

◀ **FIGURE 2.3**
Corporate Image: Benefits to Companies

The Role of a Corporate Image—Company Perspective

From the viewpoint of the firm itself, a highly reputable image generates many benefits, which are noted in Figure 2.3. First, a quality corporate image provides the basis for the development of *new goods and services*. When potential customers are familiar with the corporate name and image, the introduction of a new product becomes much easier. Long-term customers are willing to give something new a try and transfer trust in and beliefs about the corporation to new products.

A strong corporate image allows a company to *charge more for goods and services*. Most customers believe they "get what they pay for." Better quality is often associated with a higher price. This can lead to improved markup margins and profits for the firm.

Further, firms with well-developed images have more loyal customers. Customer loyalty results in patrons *purchasing products more frequently*. Loyal customers also are less likely to make substitute purchases when other companies offer discounts, sales, and similar enticements.

Heightened levels of customer loyalty are associated with *positive word-of-mouth* endorsements. Favorable comments help generate additional sales and attract new customers. Consumers and business buyers have more faith in personal references than other forms of advertising or promotion.

Positive customer attitudes create corporate equity, which provides *greater channel power*. Retailers offer brands that are viewed positively by customers. Retailers want brands that pull customers into stores. A company with a high positive image retains control and channel power.

Attracting quality employees can be another advantage of a dominant corporate image. Just as consumers are drawn to strong firms, potential workers apply for jobs at companies with solid reputations, which reduces recruiting and selection costs. Employee turnover may also be reduced.

A strong corporate reputation often results in *more favorable ratings* by Wall Street analysts and other financial institutions. This helps when a company raises capital. Further, legislators and governmental agencies tend to act in a more supportive manner toward companies with strong and positive reputations. Lawmakers are less inclined to pursue actions that might hurt the business. Members of regulatory agencies are less likely to believe rumors of wrongdoing.

Building a strong corporate image provides tangible and intangible benefits. Both customers and organizations benefit from a well-known firm with an established reputation. Organizational leaders devote considerable amounts of time and energy to building and maintaining a positive organizational image. Client companies expect advertising account managers and creatives to help design marketing programs that take advantage of the benefits of a strong corporate image.

IDENTIFYING THE DESIRED IMAGE

2 What elements are involved in identifying, creating, rejuvenating, or changing a corporation's image?

The corporation's image can be a major part of its success. To promote the desired image, the marketing team first evaluates the nature of the company's current image. Future communications can be tailored to promote the proper image. These communications

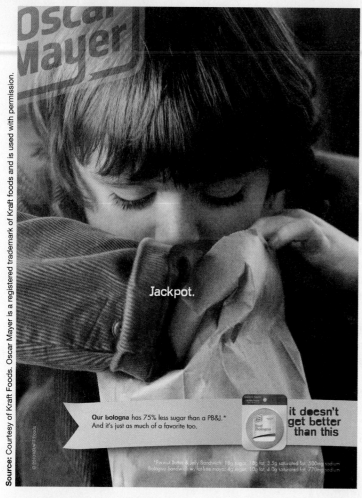

Jackpot.

Our bologna has 75% less sugar than a PB&J.* And it's just as much of a favorite too.

it doesn't get better than this

*Peanut Butter & Jelly Sandwich: 18g sugar, 18g fat, 3.5g saturated fat, 500mg sodium
Bologna Sandwich w/fat-free mayo: 4g sugar, 10g fat, 4.0g saturated fat, 770mg sodium

▲ The strong Oscar Mayer brand makes the introduction of new products easier.

should reach every constituency, including customers, suppliers, and employees.

Company leaders study the firm's image to identify the firm's strengths and weaknesses. A strong image can be combined with an opportunity present in the external environment to create a strategic advantage.

As the advertising team examines a company's image, other consumers, especially noncustomers of the firm, should be approached to discover their views. Once the marketing team understands how others see the company, decisions can be made regarding how to correct any misperceptions and/or build on the image that customers currently hold.

CREATING THE RIGHT IMAGE

In each industry, the right image sends a clear message about the unique nature of an organization and its products. A strong image accurately portrays what the firm sells. This is even true for large corporations, such as Kraft Foods, that offer multiple brands. Recently, top management at Kraft Foods developed the phrase "Make today delicious" in an effort to unify the corporation and its various brands by focusing its 100,000 employees in a unified direction. To support the effort, Kraft's leadership team established seven core values to reinforce the Kraft Foods image across all brands.[5]

In a business-to-business operation, creating the right image may be challenging. Calumet faced that situation, because most consumers and businesses only knew the firm as a petroleum company. The goal for the company's advertising agency, Gremillion & Pou, was to establish a different corporate image for Calumet. Recognizing that people knew little about the company, the creative staff at Gremillion & Pou created an advertising campaign called "All things Calumet" with the tagline, "Products you use every day." The Calumet advertisement in this section attempts to change the organization's image from a petroleum company to one that produces important ingredients used in everyday products, such as lipstick, candles, gum, and crayons.[6]

REJUVENATING AN IMAGE

Rejuvenating an image helps a firm sell new products and can attract new customers. At the same time, reinforcing previous aspects of an image helps the company retain

ALL THINGS CALUMET
PRODUCTS YOU USE EVERY DAY

CALUMET

▲ An advertisement conveying the message that Calumet ingredients are in products used every day by consumers.

loyal patrons and those who are comfortable with the original image. The key to successful image reengineering is to remain consistent with a previous image while at the same time incorporating new elements to expand the firm's target audience.

Rejuvenating a firm's image can be difficult. It takes time and effort and more than just advertising. To combat declining sales, Ruby Tuesday began with a new advertising campaign. Advertising was only part of the process. The company also changed the décor in over 900 restaurants, replacing interiors with a clean, uncluttered modern look. Menus were changed. Employees were retrained and provided with new uniforms. The goal was to create a new in-restaurant experience. To achieve success, the marketing team that embarks on image rejuvenation programs should be patient and address every aspect of the company's marketing approach.[7]

Holiday Inn encountered a similar situation. Consumers viewed the hotel chain as being outdated with old décor. To rejuvenate this image, over $1 billion was spent on interior and exterior renovations and updates and 150 properties that did not meet the new standards were sold. The proceeds were invested in the remaining hotels. Helen Travers, a corporate travel planner, stated, "It's about time. My clients haven't stayed in Holiday Inns in years [because] the chain hasn't kept up." Holiday Inn's marketing team also created a new logo. The goal was to rejuvenate the brand and regain lost business travelers.[8]

CHANGING AN IMAGE

It is difficult to completely change the image people hold regarding a company. Changing an image becomes necessary when target markets have begun to shrink or disappear or the firm's image no longer matches industry trends and consumer expectations. At that point, company leaders carefully consider what they wish to change, why they wish to make a change, and how they intend to accomplish it.

The marketing professionals at AT&T recognized the need to change its image, believing that many consumers associated the company with the old-fashioned landline phones and the huge yellow telephone directories. Consumers did not view AT&T as a leader among high-speed digital networks and mobile phones. With the purchase of Cingular, AT&T entered into the mobile phone service and networking industries. At the time of the purchase, company executives decided to keep the AT&T name and convince consumers that the company was now new and could meet everyone's communication needs. Still, the image change had not occurred as hoped.

To further modify consumer perceptions of AT&T, company officials incorporated Cingular's orange color into its brand, monthly billing statements, interiors of retail stores, and to the company's Web site. To coincide with the addition of the color, AT&T launched a national advertising campaign featuring mobile professionals and young people from all over the world using AT&T wireless products. The company also partnered with Apple to launch the iPhone.[9] These rebranding efforts successfully refurbished AT&T's image to something more modern for younger customers, but that remained familiar to older AT&T customers.

Changing an image requires more than one well-made commercial or press release or adding color to a logo and retail store signage. It begins with internal company personnel and products and then moves outward to suppliers, other businesses, and especially to consumers.[10]

Sometimes changing an image requires trying to change the view of the industry or service itself. Consider the advertisement in this section created by Newcomer, Morris and Young for St. Patrick's Behavioral Hospital. The purpose of the ad campaign was to inform individuals that mental health care was available and that it was socially acceptable to use the services of St. Patrick's. It did not brand your loved one as "crazy." The hospital's services could restore life to a loved one.

▼ This advertisement was created for St. Patrick's Behavioral Health Hospital to help change the public's perception of mental health care.

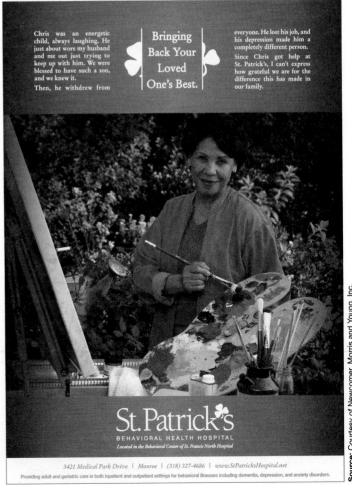

Chris was an energetic child, always laughing. He just about wore my husband and me out just trying to keep up with him. We were blessed to have such a son, and we knew it. Then, he withdrew from everyone. He lost his job, and his depression made him a completely different person. Since Chris got help at St. Patrick's, I can't express how grateful we are for the difference this has made in our family.

Bringing Back Your Loved One's Best.

St. Patrick's
BEHAVIORAL HEALTH HOSPITAL
Located in the Behavioral Center of St. Francis North Hospital

3421 Medical Park Drive | Monroe | (318) 327-4686 | www.StPatricksHospital.net
Providing adult and geriatric care in both inpatient and outpatient settings for behavioral illnesses including dementia, depression, and anxiety disorders.

▲ The Snoring Center is an overt name.

3 What are the different types of corporate names?

CORPORATE NAME

A corporate name is the overall banner for operations. According to David Placek, president and founder of Lexicon, Inc., "The corporate name is really the cornerstone of a company's relationship with its customers. It sets an attitude and tone and is the first step toward a personality."[11]

Corporate names can be divided into the following four categories based on their actual, implied, or visionary meaning (see Figure 2.4).[12]

Overt names include American Airlines, Kraft Foods and BMW Motorcycles USA. *Implied names* include FedEx and IBM (International Business Machines). *Conceptual names*, such as Google, Twitter and Krispy Kreme, take a different approach. The name "Google" evokes a vision of a place where an endless number of items can be found, and "Krispy Kreme" suggests confectionaries filled with tasty crème. Monster.com, Nabisco, and Calumet are examples of *iconoclastic names*.

The first two categories (overt and implied) are easier to market, because they will be recalled by consumers. The other two categories (conceptual and iconoclastic) require greater marketing efforts to ensure that consumers connect the corporate name with the goods and services.

FIGURE 2.4 ▶
Categories of Corporate Names

- Overt names. Reveal what a company does.
- Implied names. Contain recognizable words or word parts that convey what a company does.
- Conceptual names. Capture the essence of what a company offers.
- Iconoclastic names. Represent something unique, different, and memorable.

4 What are the characteristics of effective logos?

CORPORATE LOGOS

A logo adds an additional aspect to a corporation's image. A **corporate logo** is the symbol used to identify a company and its brands. Each logo should be designed to be compatible with the corporation's name. Many organizations have spent millions of dollars selecting and promoting corporate names and logos. A strong corporate name featuring a well-designed logo helps consumers remember specific brands and company advertisements. Search time is reduced when consumers look for specific product names that are identified by effective logos. Quality logos and corporate names should meet the four tests shown in Figure 2.5.[13]

Logos are especially important for in-store shopping. The mind processes visuals faster than it does words. A corporate logo may be more quickly recognized by shoppers. Logo *recognition* can occur at two levels. First, a consumer might remember seeing the logo in the past. It is stored in memory, and when it is seen at the store that memory is jogged. Second, a *familiar* logo may remind the consumer of the brand or corporate name. This reminder can elicit *positive* (or *negative*) *feelings* regarding either the corporation or branded item.

Successful logos *elicit shared meanings across consumers*, a process known as **stimulus codability**. Logos with high stimulus codability evoke consensual meanings within a culture or subculture (such as the Prudential Rock). Logos with a high degree of codability are readily recognized, such as Apple, McDonald's, and Pepsi. Companies

FIGURE 2.5 ▶
Four Tests of Quality Logos and Corporate Names

- Recognizable
- Familiar
- Elicits a consensual meaning among those in the firm's target market
- Evokes positive feelings

using logos with a low degree of codability spend more money on advertising. At first, Nike spent a considerable amount of funds to make the "swoosh" more recognizable, because early on the swoosh, by itself, did not conjure any specific image.

Sometimes a company's marketing team may wish to update or modify a logo, as was the case with Pepsi. According to Pepsi Vice President Frank Cooper, a change was needed as the company moved "out of traditional mass marketing and mass distribution." A logo was needed that was "more dynamic and more alive" to engage consumers. The new logo took 5 months to create and cost over $1 million. Additional costs were incurred when the company placed the new logo on delivery trucks, vending machines, stadium signage, and point-of-purchase materials.[14]

▲ Sartor Associates designed five different logos for Achievers, Inc.

BRANDING

Many of the benefits of a strong corporate image also apply to brands. The primary difference between the two is that of scope. **Brands** are names assigned to individual goods or services or to a group of complementary products. A corporation may own multiple brands. For instance, Hormel Foods carries several brands, including Dinty Moore, Jennie-O Turkey Store products, Chi-Chi's Mexican products, Valley Fresh, Farmer John, and SPAM.

An effective brand name allows a company to charge more for products. Strong brands provide customers with assurances of quality and reduce search times in the purchasing process. Transference might occur to other brands sold by the same company. For the first time in 119 years, Hormel Foods ran a television and print ad campaign spotlighting the entire portfolio of Hormel brands. The campaign tagline "Life Better Served" was aimed at consumers who purchased one or two of Hormel's brands, but were not aware of Hormel's other products. According to the ad agency BBDO, it involved "pulling the blanket off of the brand" so consumers could see what other quality brands and products were available through Hormel.[15]

5 What different kinds of brands can firms offer?

TYPES OF BRANDS

Brands develop histories. They have personalities. They include strengths, weaknesses, and flaws. Figure 2.6 identifies several types of brands.

Family Brands

Many brands produce family trees. A **family brand** means a company offers a series or group of products under one brand name. The Campbell's brand is assigned to various lines of soups and other vegetable products. Consumers seeing the Campbell's brand

◀ **FIGURE 2.6**
Types of Brands

- **Family brands.** A group of related products sold under one name.
- **Brand extension.** The use of an established brand name on products or services not related to the core brand.
- **Flanker brand.** The development of a new brand sold in the same category as another product.
- **Co-branding.** The offering of two or more brands in a single marketing offer.
- **Ingredient branding.** The placement of one brand within another brand.
- **Cooperative branding.** The joint venture of two or more brands into a new product or service.
- **Complementary branding.** The marketing of two brands together for co-consumption.
- **Private brands.** Proprietary brands marketed by an organization and sold within the organization's outlets.

expect a certain level of quality in existing products and any product line addition or modification, such as Healthy Choice soups. These transfer associations occur as long as the new product remains within the same product category. When the additional products added that are not related to the brand's core merchandise, the transfer of loyalty does not occur as easily.

Brand Extensions

A common approach used by firms to enter new markets or to expand current market is the development of additional brands. **Brand extension** is the use of an established brand name on new goods or services. The extension may not be related to the core brand. For example, Nike has been successful in extending its brand name to a line of clothing. Black & Decker has been successful in extending its brand name to new types of power tools. The company was not as successful in extending the line to small kitchen appliances.

Flanker Brands

Flanker brands provide an alternative to brand extensions. A **flanker brand** is the development of a new brand by a company in a good or service category in which it currently has a brand offering. Procter & Gamble's primary laundry detergents are Cheer and Tide. Over the years, P&G has introduced a number of additional brands, such as Ivory, Dreft, and Gain. In total, P&G offers eight different brands of detergents in North America (see Table 2.2). The company's marketing team introduces flanker brands to appeal to target markets a brand is not reaching. This helps the company to offer a more complete line of products and reach a higher percentage of customers. It also creates barriers to entry for competing firms.

A flanker brand may be introduced when company leaders believe that offering the product under the current brand name might adversely affect the overall marketing program. Hallmark created the flanker brand Shoebox Greetings to sell cards in discount

TABLE 2.2 Brands Sold by Procter & Gamble

• Cosmetics	• Downy
• CoverGirl	• Dreft
• Max Factor	• Era
• Dish washing	• Febreze Air Freshners
• Cascade	• Gain
• Dawn	• Ivory
• Ivory	• Tide
• Joy	• Body wash and soap
• Hair care	• Camay
• Aussie	• Ivory
• Head & Shoulders	• Olay
• Herbal Essences	• Old Spice
• Infusion 23	• Safeguard
• Pantene	• Zest
• Laundry & fabric care	
• Bounce	
• Cheer	

stores as well as Hallmark outlets. At first, the Hallmark brand was only sold in retail stores carrying the Hallmark name. The marketing team discovered that although Shoebox Greeting cards are lower priced, they allowed Hallmark to attract a larger percentage of the market, even in its own stores. Firms operating in high-end markets may use flanker brands to compete in low-end markets. They are also is used in international expansion. Procter & Gamble sells Ariel laundry detergent in Latin America, Europe, the Middle East, Asia, and Africa, but not in the United States. Offering different brands for specific markets helps a firm to operate in international markets.

Co-Branding

Co-branding, the combination of two brands, takes three forms: ingredient branding, cooperative branding, and complementary branding (see Figure 2.7). **Ingredient branding** is the placement of one brand within another brand, such as Intel microprocessors in HP computers. **Cooperative branding** is the joint venture of two or more brands into a new good or service. The advertisement in this section features a cooperating branding venture by Citibank that combines American Airlines and MasterCard. **Complementary branding** is the marketing of two brands together to encourage co-consumption or co-purchases, such as Seagram's 7 encouraging 7-Up as a compatible mixer or Oreo milkshakes sold in Dairy Queen stores.

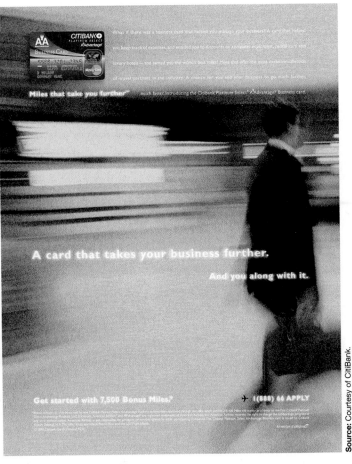

Source: Courtesy of CitiBank.

▲ An example of cooperative branding.

Co-branding succeeds when it builds brand equity in both brands. When Monsanto created NutraSweet, consumer trust was built by placing the NutraSweet logo on venerable and trusted brands, including Diet Coke, Wrigley's Chewing Gum (Wrigley's Extra), and Crystal Light. The strategy worked. NutraSweet is now the standard of quality in the sweetener industry.[16]

Co-branding creates some risk. If the relationship fails to do well in the marketplace, normally both brands suffer. To reduce the risk of failure, co-branding is often undertaken only with well-known brands. Co-branding of goods and services that are highly compatible generally will be less risky. Ingredient and cooperative branding tend to be less risky than complementary branding because both companies have more at stake and devote greater resources to ensure success.

For small companies and brands that are not as well known, co-branding will be an excellent strategy. Finding a well-known brand willing to co-brand with a lesser-known product may be difficult. When such an alliance is made, the co-brand relationship often builds brand equity for the lesser-known brand, as was the case for NutraSweet. Co-branding also provides access to distribution channels that may be otherwise hard to obtain.

◀ **FIGURE 2.7**
Forms of Co-Branding

DEVELOPING STRONG BRANDS

Developing a strong brand begins with discovering why consumers buy a brand and why they rebuy the brand. In assessing a brand, the professionals at the Brand Extract agency ask the following questions:

- Where does your brand stand now?
- What are your objectives?
- What are you doing in terms of building your brand and business?
- What are your brand's strengths? Weaknesses?
- Which opportunities should be pursued first? Where are the pitfalls?[17]

The answers to these questions assist the company's marketing team or its agency in developing a plan that cultivates a stronger brand position.

A primary feature that keeps a brand strong occurs when it contains something that is **salient** to customers. Salience comes from several sources. A product or brand that has benefits consumers consider important and of higher quality than other brands enjoys salience. The view that the brand represents a good value also creates this advantage. The belief that the brand is superior to other brands because of its image leads to customer loyalty based on these salient properties.[18]

BUILDING BRAND PRESTIGE

Two important processes help establish stronger brand prestige. First, the brand name should be prominently promoted through repetitious ads. The overwhelming numbers of brands and advertisements consumers see make repetition essential to capturing the buyer's attention. Repetition increases the odds that a brand and its accompanying message will be stored in long-term memory and recalled.

Second, the brand name should be associated with the product's most prominent characteristic. Many consumers associate Crest with "cavity prevention." Coca-Cola seeks to associate its name with a product that is "refreshing." For BMW, it is "performance driving." For 3M it is "innovation."

Setting a product apart from the competition should be the goal of brand development. Market researchers identify the "one thing" the brand stands for, that consumers recognize, and that is salient to them. When these are present, more powerful brand recognition occurs. In the marketplace for automotive suspension systems, the Skyjacker brand is well-known to many consumers, distributors, and automobile manufacturers.

▼ In the athletic shoe market, Reebok has built a strong brand name.

Source: Courtesy of Reebok International.

SUSTAINING BRAND SUCCESS

After brand recognition has been achieved, the next step will be to prolong its success. A long brand life results from finding one unique selling point and staying with it. Tide has been viewed as a powerful laundry detergent for decades. To sustain that success, the marketing team at Tide continues to pay attention to its image. Recent advertisements note how well Tide cleans clothes, using themes such as "Tide knows fabrics best," "Dirt can't hide from Tide," "If it's got to be clean, it's got to be Tide," and "Style is an option. Clean is not." To make sure the message will be seen and heard, Tide employs traditional mass media advertising, alternative media including YouTube and Facebook, signs known as *wild postings* in urban locations, and sponsorship of events in South Beach, Florida, and other resort areas.[19]

Some brands eventually experience decline. If a company waits too long to respond, the result might be the eventual death of the brand. If caught in time, a brand can be revived and given new life. The marketing team pays careful attention perceptions of each brand and well how it performs over time.[20]

BRAND EQUITY

One major problem many established companies encounter is *brand parity*, which occurs when there are few tangible distinctions between competing brands in mature markets. Customers see only minor product differences, and, in many product categories, even minor variations are hard to identify.

Brand equity is a set of characteristics that are unique to a brand. It helps to fight the brand parity problem. In essence, brand equity is the perception that a good or service with a given brand name is different and better.

As shown in Figure 2.8, brand equity creates several benefits. First, it allows the company to charge a higher price. The company retains a greater market share than would otherwise be expected for an undifferentiated product. Brand equity provides channel power as the company deals with retailers. This power leads to improved position in terms of shelf space and displays. Brand equity also influences wholesalers by affecting what they stock and which brands they encourage customers to purchase. Wholesalers normally stock several brands but place greater emphasis on high-equity brands.

1. Allows manufacturers to charge more for products
2. Creates higher gross margins
3. Provides power with retailers and wholesalers
4. Captures additional retail shelf space
5. Serves as a weapon against consumers switching due to sales promotions
6. Prevents erosion of market share

◀ **FIGURE 2.8**
Benefits of Brand Equity

In business-to-business markets, brand equity often allows a company to charge a higher price. Equity influences selections in the buying decision-making process. Products with strong brand equity are often selected over products with low brand equity or brands that firms know less about. The same scenario occurs in international markets. Brand equity opens doors to foreign firms, brokers, and retailers and provides privileges that products with low brand equity cannot obtain.

Brand equity often dissuades consumers from looking for cheaper products, special deals, other or incentives. It prevents erosion of a product's market share, even when a proliferation of brands is coupled to promotional maneuvers by those competitors.

Steps to Building Brand Equity

Brand-name recognition and recall can be built through repetitive advertising. Building brand equity, however, requires the company to achieve more than brand recognition. Recognition is only the first phase of the marketing program. The other steps are shown in Figure 2.9.

The first step to building brand equity, *researching and analyzing what makes a brand distinctive*, includes identifying the unique selling point to be promoted. Many

1. Research and analyze what it would take to make the brand distinctive.
2. Engage in continuous innovation.
3. Move fast.
4. Integrate new and old media.
5. Focus on domination.

◀ **FIGURE 2.9**
Steps in Building Brand Equity

products compete in mature markets, which means that companies that do not *continuously innovate* and move forward fall behind. It may be tempting for Procter & Gamble not to tinker with Tide. Doing so, however, might lead to a steady erosion of market share to brands offering new features. Instead, Procter & Gamble's management team expanded the Tide family of detergents to include Tide Coldwater and Tide Kick. Tide Kick is a combination measuring cup and stain penetrator. The result of this continuous innovation was a 2.6 percent gain in sales during a time in which industry sales increased less than 1 percent.[21]

Today's customers want innovations and new products. They also want them *fast*. Handbag designer Coach used to introduce new products quarterly. Now new items are released monthly. Coach CEO Lew Frankfort states that "For brands to stay relevant, they have to stay on their toes. Complacency has no place in this market." In any given month, new products account for up to 30 percent of U.S. retail store sales.[22]

Another ingredient in building brand equity is to *integrate new and old media*. Consumers are bombarded with advertising messages from a multitude of sources. Therefore, the marketing team integrates all messages while looking for new, nontraditional and online communication methods. Although television, radio and magazines remain key media, newer alternative advertising methods can help strengthen a brand name. Recently, Mountain Dew reduced its television, radio, and print media budgets from $57 million to $21.6 million. Funds were shifted to branding subcultures, such as action sports partnerships and sponsorships, indie music with Green Label Sound, and video game partnerships. The shift of expenditures was to incorporate the media being used by younger consumers. Mountain Dew's name was shortened to Mtn Dew, to better match a younger market.[23]

Pepperidge Farm took similar steps. The advertising campaign theme, "Connecting through cookies" was developed. A social media site targeted at women, **www.artofthecookie.com**, was a primary component of the company's online efforts. A quote on the site stated "Our friendship with our girlfriends makes our lives much richer." The site allowed women to connect with each other and also displayed video clips of Sally Horchow's cross-country trip from Las Vegas to Nantucket. During the trip, Horchow spoke to women about making and maintaining friendships. Horchow, the author of *The Art of Friendship: 70 Simple Rules for Making Meaningful Connections,* also served as one of the site's hosts.[24]

The Pepperidge Farm Web site was supported by print ads and a public relations initiative involving a survey of American women on the topic of friendship. The ads ran in *Country Living, Good Housekeeping,* and *Redbook.* The headline for each was "Friendship. Is yours an art form or a lost art?" The goal of the social media site and the print ads was to forge emotional connections with customers that are difficult to create with broadcast advertising alone.

A growing number of companies, including Blockbuster, Chick-fil-A, Coca-Cola, Sony, and Microsoft, advertise on social network Web sites such as Bebo, Buzznet, Facebook, and MySpace. According to eMarketer, over $2 billion per year is spent on advertising on these types of Web sites.[25]

Brand equity involves *domination*, the strongly held view that the brand is number one in its product category. Domination can take place in a geographic region or in a smaller product category or market niche. To dominate, the brand must be viewed as number one in some way. Intel processors hold this status. Domination means delivering on the promise. Customers must believe that the Intel processor is the best.

▼ Skyjacker has built a high level of brand equity through domination in the vehicle suspension market.

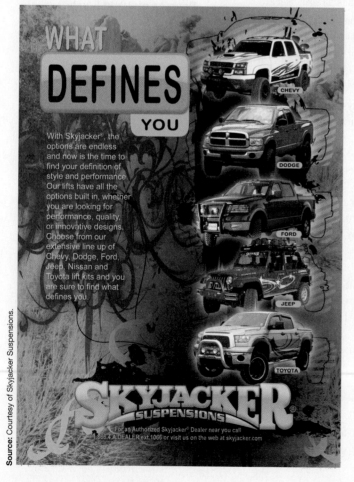

▶ FIGURE 2.10
Top 10 Most Powerful Brands

Brand	Trust Rate (%)	Distrust Rate (%)	BPI
Sony	9.2%	1.8%	75.1
Johnson & Johnson	5.7	0.5	55.3
Kraft	5.2	0.6	48.7
Procter & Gamble	5.8	1.1	48.2
Campbell's	3.5	0.4	32.9
Toyota	4.1	1.2	28.0
Tylenol	3.2	0.6	27.2
Dell	5.1	2.1	27.0
General Mills	2.7	0.2	25.9
HP	4.0	1.5	23.5

Source: Based on Fred Crawford, "Branding Isn't Like High School," *Retail Merchandiser* 47, no. 6 (July–August 2007), pp. S4–S9.

Measuring Brand Equity

Trying to determine whether brand equity exists is difficult. Marketing experts use **brand metrics** to measure returns on branding investments. Attitudinal methods are used to track brand awareness, recall, and recognition. To increase their power, these factors can be tied with other variables (e.g., brand awareness coupled with intent to buy). Brand awareness can also be connected to use of either the product class (mustard) or the brand (Kraft, Grey Poupon). When measuring awareness, recall, and recognition, a brand can be recalled for negative as well as positive reasons.[26]

Recognizing that popular brands are not always powerful brands, AlixPartners developed a method for measuring a brand's strength based on its popularity, its level of trust, and its level of distrust. Figure 2.10 identifies the top 10 most powerful brands, according to AlixPartners.[27] According to this firm, the best brands in the future will be those that have a high level of awareness, are trusted by consumers, and have low levels of distrust, resulting in higher brand power index (BPI) scores.

DSN Retailing used a different method for measuring brand equity, asking consumers to identify their most preferred brand in a particular product category.[28] Figure 2.11 displays the list that emerged.

▶ FIGURE 2.11
Most Preferred Brands

Women's Apparel
1. Hanes (39%)
2. Levi's (10%)
3. Victoria's Secret (6%)
4. Liz Claiborne (4%)
5. Nike (4%)
6. Fruit of the Loom (4%)

Snacks
1. Frito Lay/Lays (19%)
2. Doritos (10%)
3. Hershey's (6%)
4. Pringles (6%)
5. Oreos (5%)

Beverages
1. Coke (26%)
2. Pepsi (22%)
3. Dr. Pepper (6%)
4. Mountain Dew (5%)

Consumer Electronics
1. Sony (27%)
2. RCA (6%)
3. Panasonic (6%)
4. Dell (5%)
5. Duracell (4%)

Source: Based on Debbie Howell, "Top Brands," *DSN Retailing Today 44*, no. 20 (October 24, 2005), pp. 38–42.

Although these methods of measuring brand equity can provide valid information, CEOs and other corporate leaders often want real, hard numbers. One such method for generating hard numbers is known as the *revenue premium* approach. The method compares a branded product to the same product without a brand name. To calculate a brand's revenue premium, the revenue generated by a particular brand will be compared to a private-label brand. The difference is the revenue premium, or value, of that brand and would equate to the brand equity that has accrued.[29]

7 What current trends affect private labels?

PRIVATE BRANDS

Private brands (also known as *private labels* and *store brands*) are proprietary brands marketed by an organization and normally distributed exclusively within the organization's outlets. Private brands have experienced a roller-coaster ride in terms of popularity and sales. To some individuals, private brands carry the connotation of a lower price and inferior quality. Historically, the primary audiences for private labels were price-sensitive individuals and low-income families. This is no longer true. Retailers invest significant dollars to develop private brands, which now account for approximately 22 percent of all unit sales in the United States.[30]

Many consumers report that they cannot tell the difference in quality between national brands and private brands. In a Nielsen survey of 54,000 consumers, 72 percent said private brands are equivalent to national brands.[31] Even high-income individuals have reported purchasing more private brands, especially during difficult economic times. These changes, as well as others that have occurred in the private-brand arena, are summarized in Figure 2.12.[32]

Advantages to Retailers

Although private labels still tend to be priced between 5 and 20 percent lower than national brands, they also generate higher gross margins than national brands, because there are no middlemen. Higher margins enable retailers to earn higher profits on private brands or, alternatively, to reduce the prices of the private brands to make them more attractive to price-sensitive consumers. Retailers that maintain the higher markup on private labels have the opportunity to use some of the margin for advertising and promotions of the brands.

An emerging trend in retailing is that loyalty toward retail stores has been growing while loyalty toward individual brands has been on the decline. Rather than going to outlets selling specific brands, many shoppers visit specific stores and are willing to buy from the brands offered by those stores. The increase in loyalty to retailers has caused several department and specialty stores to expand the number of private-brand products offered. This requires the retailer to develop private brands that are congruent with consumer images of the company.[33]

Savvy retailers recognize the value of private labels and how they can be used to differentiate the store from competing retailers and from national brands. These stores promote these labels as distinctive brands aimed toward specific market segments. The emphasis is on meeting needs of consumers with a quality product rather than simply on price.

JCPenney has been successful utilizing private branding in apparel lines. JCPenney offers more than 30 private labels, accounting for more than 40 percent of sales.[34] Liz Sweeney of JCPenney stated, "We are dedicated to creating and managing winning private

FIGURE 2.12 ▶
Changes in Private Brands

- Improved quality
- Perceived as a value purchase
- Higher loyalty toward retail outlets and lower loyalty toward specific brands
- Used to differentiate retail outlets
- Increased advertising of private brands
- Increased quality of in-store displays and packaging of private brands

brands that develop customer loyalty. This means managing and marketing our key private brands as true brands versus labels."[35] For instance, the trendier fashion lines were promoted with a TV ad on the Academy Awards and with magazine ads in *Cosmopolitan* and *People*. The company's Web site featured runway shows of the private lines along with fashion tips from the lines' designers. The uniqueness of the ad campaign was that the ads focused exclusively on JCPenney's fashion-forward clothes and none of the store's national brands.[36]

New trends in the use of private labels are emerging. Currently, retailers spend marketing dollars on improving the actual label, on designing noticeable in-store displays, and on packaging. Retailers without large national ad budgets rely more on displays and attractive packaging. A drab, cheap package does not convey the message that a private brand is the equivalent of or is better than a national brand. For many consumers, the distinction between private labels and national brands is blurred. Unless a customer is familiar with the store's private brand labels, the individual might think she is purchasing a national brand.[37]

▲ Private labels are often displayed in retail store windows and made to look as attractive as manufacturers' brands.

Some retailers go one step further by designing the advertising of private brands apart from the store's regular advertising program. Recently, Sears launched a series of advertisements featuring its Kenmore and Craftsman brands. Sears was only mentioned in the context of being the place to purchase Kenmore and Craftsman products. A similar approach was used for other Sears brands, such as Lands' End, and Kmart's private labels, which include Martha Stewart, Jaclyn Smith, Route 66, Structure, and Joe Boxer. The purpose of promoting these private brands separately is to help establish the name as a bona fide brand competing head-to-head with national brands and to distance the brand from its retail parent.

Responses from Manufacturers

Manufacturers are responding to the inroads made by private labels in various ways. Figure 2.13 lists some of the most common tactics.[38] A manufacturer can *focus on a few core brands* rather than split advertising dollars among a large number of brands. The core brands are *advertised heavily*. This helps the manufacturer maintain its brand name and reinforces the message that consumers are making the right decision when they purchase the manufacturer's national brand. The goal is to create bonds with consumers both before and after purchases.

Manufacturers may attempt to reduce the impact of private labels on sales by *expanding product offerings*. By aggressively introducing new products and new versions of current products, a manufacturer can maintain the loyalty of its current customers and be seen as an innovator. Hanesbrands, Inc. owns a number of well-known brands, such as Bali, Playtex, Champion, L'eggs, Barely There, Outerbanks, Duofold, and Hanes. The company expanded into the active wear market with the Hanes Sport casual collection.

- Focus on core brands.
- Increase advertising.
- Introduce new products.
- Focus on in-store selling and packaging.
- Use alternative methods of marketing.

◀ **FIGURE 2.13**

Tactics Used by Manufacturers to Combat Gains Made by Private Labels

Source: Based on Vanessa L. Facenda, "A Swift Kick to the Privates," *Brandweek* 48, no. 31 (September 3, 2007), pp. 24–28.

▲ Hanes Sports has introduced new products into the active lifestyle wear market.

The surge in popularity of active lifestyle clothing created an increase in sales of other related products, such as the sports underwear featured in the Hanes ad in this section. Hanes Sport now manufactures products for women, men, and children.

To further combat the impact of private brands, manufacturers can *focus on in-store selling* to emphasize core brands. Also, *alternative methods of marketing*, such as brand communities and social networks, can increase loyalty to a brand rather than a private label.

Impact of Economic Conditions

Private brands tend to fare better in recessions and slow economic times, when consumers try to save money. Sales for national brands often decline during slow economic cycles. Consequently, many companies cut advertising dollars to reduce costs. A study conducted by the University of North Carolina over a 20-year period revealed that companies that cut advertising budgets during recessions tended to lose more market share to private labels during the bust cycle. Further, these companies seldom recovered the full market share when a boom cycle followed. In contrast, companies that maintained ad expenditures tended to maintain market share and had stock prices that were 1.3 percent higher.[39]

The success of private brands has influenced both manufacturers and retailers. Each pays careful attention to where this trend leads in the next decade. One response manufacturers can use would be moving beyond traditional advertising methods to maintain sales rather than losing them to private labels.

PACKAGING

In many large retail stores, most employees are either stockers or cashiers. Few know anything about the products on the shelves. Therefore, the product's package represents the final opportunity to make an impression on a consumer. Marketing surveys have revealed that only 31 percent of purchases are planned prior to reaching a retail outlet. This means 69 percent of purchase decisions are made in the store. Other research indicates that when consumers walk within 10 to 15 feet of a product, the item has 3 seconds to catch the consumer's attention.[40]

An effective package design stand outs. It tells consumers what is inside and offers additional appeals. Traditionally, the primary purposes of packaging were those shown in Figure 2.14. Now, however, packages and labels are increasingly viewed as a key part of a company's integrated marketing communications program. It makes little sense to spend millions of dollars on advertising only to lose the sale in the store because of a lackluster, dull package design that is not attractive to potential customers.[41]

Most retail purchase decisions are made based on familiarity with a brand or product at a retail store. Consequently, a unique and attractive package that captures the

8 How are packages and labels used to support an IMC program, both domestically and in foreign settings?

FIGURE 2.14 ▶
Primary Purposes of Packaging

- Protect the product inside.
- Provide for ease of shipping, moving, and handling.
- Provide for easy placement on store shelves.
- Prevent or reduce the possibility of theft.
- Prevent tampering (drugs and foods).

buyer's attention increases the chances the product will be purchased, sometimes as an impulse buy. For many years, winemakers strongly resisted the use of marketing tactics for fear of being perceived as having questionable quality. Products such as Blue Nun, Ripple, and Boone's Farm were major marketing successes, but they did not enjoy reputations for high quality. Recently, however, some wineries have begun to accept the value of a quality package. Many Australian wineries captured market share based on the knowledge that men (who are more likely to make wine purchases) look at a wine's country of origin, followed by grape variety, and finally aesthetics. Australian wine is perceived as new, different, and of sufficient quality, especially in the Shiraz lines. As a result, attractive bottles featuring names such as Vale, Valley Hill, and Cloudy Bay with images of mountain peaks and vineyards receding in the distance have been designed. Bottle color is crucial; buyers prefer dark, warm, and intense colors (red and blue). These changes and the successes of the Australians have caused French and German winemakers to change packages and labels to compete.[42]

New Trends in Packaging

Some of the new trends in packaging are based on changes in the ways in which consumers use products (see Figure 2.15). In the foods market, foods that are fast, convenient, portable, and fresh are preferred by customers. A quality package accommodates these needs. Recent research by DuPont revealed that half of consumers surveyed said that taste and freshness were more important than price, convenience, and brand name. Packaging determines if a food item maintains its freshness. A consumer who experienced inferior packaging was more likely to switch to another brand on the next purchase.[43]

▲ Smaller households have led to the creation of smaller packages.

The marketing team at Alcoa Rigid Packaging watched consumers as they purchased groceries and stocked refrigerators. The team noticed that the standard 3-by-4-can (12-pack) beverage box was too large for the refrigerator, and consumers would only take out a few cans at a time to cool. It seemed logical that if more cans were cold, consumers might drink more. This observation led to the design of a box that was easier and more convenient to use, the 6-by-2-can box, which is longer and slimmer. The newly designed 12-pack fits into the refrigerator door or on a shelf. It is also self-dispensing. As a can is taken out, a new one automatically slides down to the front of the box. This innovation improved sales for both Alcoa and soft-drink manufacturers, who embraced the new package.[44]

Another recent trend in packaging is the use of recycled and biodegradable materials. Although regulations are a factor, large retailers such as Wal-Mart and Tesco and environmentally conscious consumers are also driving the change to greener packaging. Creating packaging that meets all of the other marketing needs that is also made of recycled or biodegradable materials can be challenging.[45]

The trends in packaging in international markets are much the same as in the United States. Ease of use is a key feature. When shipping products overseas, however, one key issue is that the buyer must feel reassured the package will not break or become contaminated.

- Meets consumer needs for speed, convenience, and portability
- Must be contemporary and striking
- Must be designed for ease of use

◀ **FIGURE 2.15**
New Trends in Packaging

LABELS

Labels on packages serve several functions. First, they must meet legal requirements. This includes identifying the product contained in the package and any other specific information about content, such as nutritional information on foods. The Food and Drug Administration (FDA) regulates food labels in the United States. Also, many times warranties and guarantees are printed on the label.

The label represents another marketing opportunity. Many times the label will be the only distinguishing feature of an item, such as a 12-ounce bottle of beer or a 1-gallon container of milk. A typical label contains the company's logo and the brand name. Labels may reveal special offers and other tie-ins, such as a box of cereal with a toy contained inside.

Labels often carry terms designed to build consumer interest and confidence in making the purchase. Word such as "gourmet," "natural," "premium," "adult formula," and "industrial strength" help make the product appear to be a better buy. A company's image, brand, logo, and theme extend to the design of the package and label, which allows the marketing team the opportunity to make the sale when the consumer is in the store making a purchasing decision.

ETHICAL ISSUES IN BRAND MANAGEMENT

A variety of ethical issues are associated with brand management. For years, the most common problem was *brand infringement*, which occurs when a company creates a brand name that closely resembles a popular or successful brand, such as Korrs beer. In that case, the courts deemed the brand an intentional infringement on the Coors brand, and the name was abandoned. Another brand-infringing company that was forced by the courts to give up its name was Victor's Secret.

Brand infringement is more complex when a brand becomes so well-established that it may be considered a generic term, such as a Kleenex tissue or a Xerox copy. Band-Aid encountered the problem in the 1970s, forcing the marketing team to make sure the product was identified as "Band-Aid Brand Strips" rather than simply "band aids," to keep the competition from being able to use the name. The most vulnerable new brand names might be Google and Twitter, because the names have entered everyday conversation, as in "I Googled myself" or "I tweeted you."

Another form of unethical behavior, according to many sources, is *cyber squatting,* or *domain squatting*. This is the controversial practice of buying domain names (e.g., *barnesandnoble.com, kohls.com, labronjames.com,* etc.) that are valuable to specific people or businesses in the hopes of making a profit by reselling the name. At the extreme, **www.whitehouse.com** was a pornographic Web site. Any new company trying to build a presence in the online marketplace might find itself stifled by domain squatters. Names matter, and cyber squatters are willing to take advantage of that to make profits at someone else's expense.

INTERNATIONAL IMPLICATIONS

In international markets, product development, branding, and maintaining an image are more complex. As noted previously, firms use either an *adaptation* strategy or a *standardization* strategy in promotional programs. These two approaches can be applied to the products themselves as well as to brand names. With standardization, the same brand name and product are sold in all countries. With adaptation, the brand and/or the actual product may be different in each country or region. This can mean a product may be viewed as a local brand. Mr. Clean uses the adaptation brand approach for the same products. Items are sold under the names of Mr. Proper and Maestro Limpio, as well as other names in various countries.

Using a standardized global brand reduces costs. Instead of advertising each local brand with a separate communication strategy, one standardized message can be sent. Standardized global brands also allow for the transference of best practices from one country to another. Further, purchasing a standardized global brand can be viewed as a better choice than buying a local brand. The global brand might have a higher perceived quality. The consumer's self-concept of being cosmopolitan, sophisticated, and modern can be enhanced when buying a global brand.[46] As the world continues to shrink through advances in telecommunications, consumers are becoming increasingly similar, displaying comparable consumer characteristics and purchase behaviors. This may lead to greater use of standardized global brands.

Despite all of the advantages of global brands, some efforts to standardize brand names have met with resistance. A number of global brands that were introduced were not received with enthusiasm. Although consumer behavior might have converged somewhat throughout the world, local idiosyncrasies still exist. Global brands enjoy the most success in high-profile, high-involvement products. Local brands have performed the best in low-involvement everyday products. Automobiles and computers have done well as global brands. Food, candy, and some soft drinks have done better using a local-brand approach.[47]

A common GIMC strategy is to "think globally, but act locally." This approach applies to branding. Developing global brands might be the ultimate goal; however, the marketing team will still consider each local market's unique features and be sensitive to supporting and developing local brands. According to Eileen Campbell, CEO of Millward Brown Group, the success of global brand is largely dependent on the brand's ability to adapt to local needs and tastes: "Cultural relevance is important." For example, the "Real Beauty" campaign developed by Ogilvy and Mather for Unilever's Dove featured images of women in underwear in Western countries, but was modified to reveal a face behind a woman's veil for the Middle East.[48]

As in the United States, the importance of brand name may have diminished somewhat in other countries. Figure 2.16 identifies the percentages of consumers who indicated that they consider the brand name when purchasing food products. In almost all countries, taste, quality, and price are the dominant factors influencing food purchases. In China, health benefits are ranked number one. This decline in the importance of the brand name in the international market can be contributed to the rise of high-quality private labels and the ability of consumers to use online sources and networking to gain knowledge about the contents of various brands.[49]

Packaging and labeling issues are complex for global firms. The label must meet the legal requirements of the country where the product is sold. An attractive label is an attention-getting device that can draw the consumer to the product and is vitally important in the United States as well as Asian countries where purchases, in part, are driven by the appeal of the label.[50] At the same time, some culturally sensitive items, such as lingerie and other personal products, carry labels that basically disguise or hide the contents. Packages must also be able to withstand the rigors of being shipped longer distances, meet any legal restrictions, and be as cost-effective as possible.

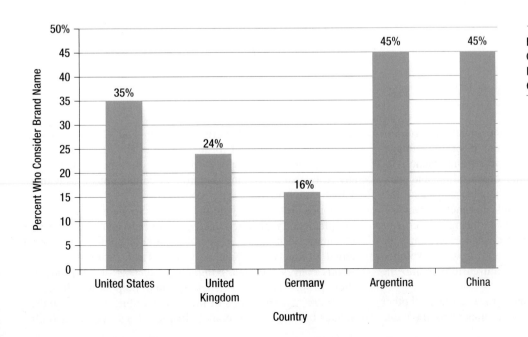

◀ **FIGURE 2.16**
Percentage of Consumers Who Consider the Brand Name When Purchasing Food Products, by Country

Home Federal Bank

Home Federal Savings and Loan opened its doors in 1924. A strong, responsible institution, it weathered the Great Depression, World War II, and the savings and loan crisis of the 1980s. In 2009, Home Federal celebrated its 85th anniversary; hired a new president and CEO, James R. Barlow; and received a charter to become Home Federal Bank (HFB).[51]

Gremillion & Pou had been Home Federal's advertising agency since 1988. When the institution moved from being a savings and loan to a bank, Gremillion & Pou was asked to:

- Refresh the brand and create a new logo that was progressive, without losing the equity of the 85-year-old logo
- Introduce and reinforce a new brand promise
- Introduce Home Federal as a bank
- Create market awareness of the new HFB brand
- Work closely with HFB and its partners to ensure that the brand promise is consistently communicated across all customer touch points

Your instructor has additional information about the ads, visuals, and displays used in this campaign.

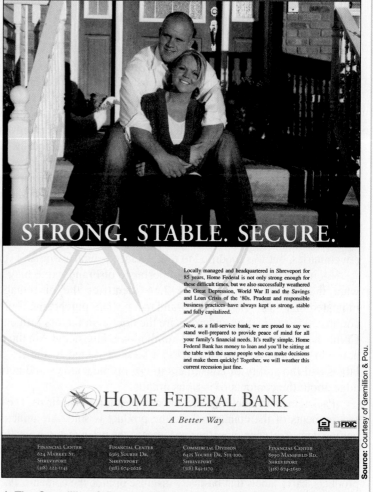

Source: Courtesy of Gremillion & Pou.

▲ The Gremillion & Pou advertising agency faced the challenge of creating a new brand for a company that was already well-known and respected.

SUMMARY

An effective integrated marketing communications program emphasizes a strong and positive company or corporate image. An image consists of the feelings consumers and business-to-business customers have toward the organization and each individual brand. An image has both tangible and intangible components. Tangible elements include products, advertisements, names, logos, and services provided. Intangible elements consist of policies and practices that change or enhance the company's image in the consumer's mind. A well-developed and well-established image benefits both customers and the company in many ways.

A corporate name is the overall banner under which all other operations occur. The corporate logo accompanying the name

is the symbol used to identify a company and its brands, helping to convey the overall corporate image. The firm's name and image are important not only to general customers, but also to any firms that might purchase from or conduct business with a manufacturer or service provider.

Brands are names given to goods or services or groups of complementary products. Effective brands give the firm an advantage, especially in mature markets containing fewer actual products or where service differences exist. Strong brands convey the most compelling benefits of the product, elicit proper consumer emotions, and help create loyalty. There are many versions of brands, including family brands, flanker brands, and co-brands. In each, brand equity is built by domination or the recognition that the brand has one key advantage or characteristic.

Creating an effective image is a difficult task. It is important to know how all publics view the firm before seeking to build or enhance an image. Rejuvenating the image involves reminding customers of their previous conceptions of the company while at the same time expanding into a closely related area of concern. Once an image is strongly pressed into the minds of customers, it becomes difficult, if not impossible, to change.

Private brands, or private labels, have become important components in the success of both producers and retailers. Consumers now view private brands as having quality equal to or close to that of more famous manufacturer brand names.

At the same time, customers expect price advantages in private label products. Consequently, effective management of brands and products includes creating a mix of offerings that both end users and retailers recognize as a beneficial range of choices.

Company leaders remain aware of legal and ethical brand challenges. Brand infringement is both a domestic and international problem. The generic problem may also influence a new generation of products and services.

International marketers utilize both standardization and adaptation tactics with regard to brands and products. Packages and labels must meet the legal and cultural needs of individual countries.

KEY TERMS

corporate image Overall consumer perceptions or end-user feelings toward a company along with its goods and services.

corporate logo The symbol used to identify a company and its brands, helping to convey the overall corporate image.

stimulus codability Items that easily evoke consensually held meanings within a culture or subculture.

brands Names generally assigned to a good or service or a group of complementary products.

family brand When a company offers a series or group of products under one brand name.

brand extension The use of an established brand name on goods or services not related to the core brand.

flanker brand The development of a new brand by a company in a good or service category in which it currently has a brand offering.

co-branding Offering two or more brands in a single marketing effort.

ingredient branding A form of co-branding in which the name of one brand is placed within another brand.

cooperative branding A form of co-branding in which two firms create a joint venture of two or more brands into a new good or service.

complementary branding A form of co-branding in which the marketing of two brands together encourages co-consumption or co-purchases.

salient When consumers are aware of the brand, have it in their consideration sets (things they consider when making purchases), regard the product and brand as a good value, buy it or use it on a regular basis, and recommend it to others.

brand equity A set of brand assets that add to the value assigned to a product.

brand metrics Measures of returns on brand investments.

private brands (also known as *private labels*) Proprietary brands marketed by an organization and normally distributed exclusively within the organization's outlets.

REVIEW QUESTIONS

1. What is meant by the term corporate image? What are the tangible aspects of a corporate image?

2. How does a corporation's image help customers? How does it help the specific company?

3. How will company leaders know when they have created the "right" image for their firm?

4. What is a corporate logo? What are the characteristics of an effective corporate logo?

5. What is meant by the term stimulus codability?

6. What is a brand? How is a brand part of a corporation's overall image?

7. Describe the use of brand extension and flanker-brand strategies.

8. Identify and describe three types of co-brands.

9. How has private branding, or private labeling, changed in the past decade?

10. What are the characteristics of a strong and effective brand name?

11. What is the difference between brand equity and brand parity?

12. Why is brand equity important? How is it measured?

13. What role does a product's package play in the marketing program?

14. How can a label support an IMC program or advertising campaign?

15. What ethical issues are associated with brand management?

16. How do the concepts of standardization and adaptation apply to products, brand names, and marketing strategies?

CRITICAL THINKING EXERCISES

Discussion Questions

1. Dalton Office Supply Company has been in operation for over 50 years and has been the predominant office supply company in its region during that time. Approximately 85 percent of Dalton's business is based on providing materials to other businesses. Only 15 percent comes from walk-in customers. Recently, low-cost providers such as Office Depot have cut into Dalton's market share. Surveys of consumers indicate that Dalton has an image of being outdated and pricey. Consumers did report that Dalton's customer service was above average. What image should Dalton project to regain its market share? Outline a plan to rejuvenate the company's image.

2. Henry and Becky Thompson plan to open a new floral and gift shop in Orlando, Florida. They want to project an image of being trendy, upscale, and fashionable. They are trying to decide on a name and a logo. What should be the name of the company? What kind of logo should be developed?

3. Brand and corporate image are important in purchase decisions. What brands or corporations do you consider to have a positive image? Why? Which brands or corporations should attempt to change images? Why? Explain how to accomplish this task. Name brands that require need rejuvenation. How can it be accomplished for each brand?

4. Figure 2.11 lists the most preferred brands in four categories. Survey 10 individuals who are not in your class and ask them to identify the most preferred brand in the categories of women's apparel, snacks, beverages, and consumer electronics. Tally your results and compare them to Figure 2.11. What similarities and differences do you see? From the survey of the 10 individuals, what do you think makes a brand the "most preferred"?

5. Go to a local retail store. Choose five packages that are effective. Describe why they are effective. Choose five labels that are effective at capturing attention. What are the attention-getting aspects of each label?

6. The management team at Terminix Pest Control has decided to expand through co-branding. To gather more information about Terminix, access its Web site at **www.terminix.net**. What kind of co-branding would you suggest? Which companies should Terminix contact?

INTEGRATED LEARNING EXERCISES

1. Web sites are an important element of a company's image. Access the Web sites of the following companies to get a feel for the image each company tries to project. Is the image projected on the Web site consistent with the image portrayed in the company's advertisements?

   a. Bluenotes (**www.bluenotesjeans.com**)

   b. Portillo's Restaurants (**www.portillos.com**)

   c. BMW Motorcycles (**www.bmwmotorcycles.com**)

   d. McDonald's (**www.mcdonalds.com**)

   e. HP (**www.hp.com**)

2. A major consulting firm that has been a leader in extending marketing knowledge and in the area of brand development is the Boston Consulting Group. Other companies that have actively been involved in brand development include Lexicon Branding and Corporate Branding. Access each firm's Web site. What kinds of services does each provide?

   a. Boston Consulting Group (**www.bcg.com**)

   b. Lexicon Branding, Inc. (**www.lexicon-branding.com**)

   c. Corporate Branding (**www.corebrand.com**)

3. Brand extension and flanker branding are common strategies for large corporations. Access the following Web sites. Identify the various brand extension strategies and flanker brands used by each company.

   a. Marriott Hotels (**www.marriott.com**)

   b. Procter & Gamble (**www.pg.com**)

   c. Sara Lee Corporation (**www.saralee.com**)

   d. VF Corporation (**www.vfc.com**)

4. Private labels are an important source of revenue for many retail stores and manufacturers. The Private Label Manufacturers' Association promotes manufacturers that produce private labels. Visit the organization's Web site at **www.plma.com** and identify the press updates, store brands, and upcoming events that illustrate the importance of private labels for both retailers and manufactures.

5. Look up one of the following companies on the Internet. Discuss the image conveyed by each company's Web site. What positioning strategy does it use? What changes or improvements could these companies make?

   a. Scubaworld (**www.scubaworld.com**)

   b. Union Pacific Railroad (**www.uprr.com**)

   c. Bicycle Museum of America (**www.bicyclemuseum.com**)

   d. Metropolitan Transportation Commission (**www.mtc.ca.gov**)

   e. Canyon Beachwear (**www.canyonbeachwear.com**)

STUDENT PROJECT

Creative Corner

The brand name, package, and label are three critical elements a marketing manager considers when introducing a new product. Pick one of the products from the following list. Assume that you are the new product manager and that your company has introduced a new brand within the product category. Your first task is to choose a brand name. Using the Internet, identify three key competitors and make a case for how the brand name you select will help the item stand out in the marketplace. If needed, what type of package will be used? What elements will be placed on the label?

Products

1. A new brand of skis for recreational boating
2. A new line of eyeglasses
3. A new chocolate candy bar
4. A new line of jeans
5. A new energy drink
6. A new perfume or cologne

CASE 1   NIKE'S DILEMMA

The sport of golf has a long, storied tradition. Originating in Scotland, the game requires concentration, hand–eye coordination, stamina, and often at least a small level of wealth. The average golfing enthusiast tends to have an income higher than the average in a geographic area.

The first decade of the new millennium indicated conflicting opinions about the sport. On the one hand, the number of new golf courses grew by nearly 500 per year for much of the decade. Television ratings for some golf tournaments rose. Most analysts would agree that the emergence of Tiger Woods onto the national stage affected both of these trends.

At the same time, contradictory viewpoints about the popularity of golf could be found. Jim Kass, the research director of the National Golf Foundation, an industry group, said that a gradual but prolonged slump in golf defies the adage, "Once a golfer, always a golfer."

Kass noted that about 3 million golfers quit playing each year. A lower number takes up the sport. Kass commented, "The man in the street will tell you that golf is booming because he sees Tiger Woods on TV." Mr. Kass said, "But we track the reality. The reality is, while we haven't exactly tanked, the numbers have been disappointing for some time."

The major competitors in the golf ball manufacturing market are:

- Bridgestone
- Callaway
- TaylorMade
- Top-Flite
- Maxfli
- Titleist
- Nike

Titleist remains the dominant force in golf ball manufacturing, for years holding a greater than 30 percent market. The Titleist Pro V1 and Pro V1x balls were viewed by many golfers as the best in the industry.

Source: Thinkstock Royalty Free.

▲ What impact do Tiger Woods and other golfers have on the products they endorse?

Nike had begun to make some in-roads when Woods began using its golf balls full time in 2000. The company only held a 1 percent share in 1999, but that amount had increased to 12 percent by late 2001. The steady growth of the brand faced substantial challenges by the end of the decade.

First, a major recession decreased the number of people willing to spend substantial amounts of money to play. In general, monies spent on leisure time activities were reduced, as households watched budgets more carefully.

Then, in late 2009, the Tiger Woods scandals began. Woods, who had carefully crafted an image as a family man and true professional, suddenly became tabloid fodder, as a series of women came forward claiming that they had extramarital affairs with the golfing legend.

Many companies quickly dropped Woods as an endorser or spokesperson. It was feared that the damage to his image would spread and taint the names and reputations of various companies. Nike was by far the most threatened by this turn of events. Woods was closely associated with the company, wearing the Nike swoosh on his golf cap in every tournament.

Some analysts believed that following his return to the sport after a leave of absence golf would attract a wide audience of viewers enticed by the scandal. The situation became more complex when Nike released the "Have You Learned Anything?" commercial in which the voice of Wood's father questioned some of his actions. Some viewed the ads as "compelling"; others just called it "creepy." Analysts believed that some fans, especially females, would turn away in wide numbers. Without question, the marketing team at Nike had major challenges to overcome as the new decade was to unfold.

1. Assess the impact of the Tiger Woods scandal on Nike's image and the Nike brand.

2. At the time of the scandal, should Titleist have attempted to take advantage of Nike's misfortune? If so, how? If not, why not? What about the other competitors in the marketplace?

3. Should Nike try to develop new brands to accompany the Crush, ONE, Power Distance, Hole in One, and Juice Plus 312 balls? If so, what kinds of brands should be introduced?

4. Was the "Have You Learned Anything?" commercial an effective approach by Nike? Why or why not?

5. Assess the popularity of golf in general. Is the sport declining? If so, why? Is the image of golfers partly to blame? If the sport is growing, what has led to the growth? Compare the popularity of golf to baseball, basketball, football, and soccer. How does image play a role in each?

Source: Jim Buzinski, "Golf Loses Popularity," *Outsports.com* (http://outsports.com/jocktalkblog/2008/2/22/golf-loses-popularity/, accessed January 6, 2010).

CASE 2

A HEALTHY IMAGE

Mary Wilson was both nervous and excited as she opened her first staff meeting in the marketing department of St. Margaret's General Hospital. Mary's new role was Director of Marketing and Communications. Her primary task was to increase the visibility of St. Margaret's Hospital in order to raise the image of the institution in the eyes of the many publics served. The long-term goal was to attract the best possible physicians while increasing use of the hospital's facilities and attracting more patients.

The world of health care has changed dramatically in the past decade. Government regulations and support, concerns about lawsuits, evolving and expensive technologies, and changes in health insurance provisions affect hospitals of all sizes. In addition, St. Margaret's faces strong competition. The hospital's primary location is in a major metropolitan area in Minnesota. Two other large hospitals also offer comparable services in the same city. Each seeks to sign physicians to exclusive contracts in which they will only provide care with one organization.

The other significant challenge to St. Margaret's is its proximity to the Mayo Clinic. Clearly, Mayo holds the highest level of prestige in the state, and even in the region. Most physicians are inclined to think of Mayo first when making referrals for patients with difficult medical problems. Mayo would be viewed by most publics as the "best" care possible.

The key issues in the image of any health organization are developing trust and a feeling of confidence in the quality of care that will be received. Beyond technological advantages, other, more subtle elements of an image could have an influence. Mary noted that to most patients the nurse plays a primary role in determining how the hospital is viewed. An uncaring and inattentive nurse is likely to drive away both the patient who encountered the nurse and all of the patient's family and friends. Negative word-of-mouth, Mary said, must be held to an absolute minimum.

Mary believed St. Margaret's needed to overcome two problems. First, the name "Margaret" is not commonly used anymore. Some publics may view it as an "old-fashioned" name. Second, there was nothing distinctive about the hospital's image. The overlap in services provided (heart care, cancer treatment) made it difficult to differentiate St. Margaret's from other providers.

If there was any advantage, Mary believed it was that St. Margaret's was affiliated with the Catholic Church. It was the only nonprofit hospital of the three major competitors. This attracted both Catholic patients and some Catholic physicians. Also, the hospital was able to utilize the services of a wide variety of volunteers.

Source: Thinkstock Royalty Free.

▲ How important is image for a medical institution?

As the marketing meeting opened, the agenda was to discuss all of the ways St. Margaret's could build its client base. The task would not be easy, but everyone in the room believed the hospital offered high-quality services in a caring atmosphere.

1. What are the image issues in this case?

2. What are the brand-name issues? Should the brand name be changed? If so, to what?

3. What types of advertisements should Mary develop for St. Margaret's General Hospital?

4. What other types of activities could St. Margaret's pursue to build a strong and positive corporate image?

3 Buyer Behaviors

CHIPOTLE MEXICAN GRILL
A New Dimension in Dining

One simple buying decision made every day by a large number of consumers is the choice of where and what to eat for breakfast, lunch, or dinner. Those who crave Mexican food review a variety of options, including fast-food operations, such as Taco Bell and Del Taco; locally owned establishments; and dine-in chains, such as El Chico and On the Border. In this complex and competitive marketplace, a new option emerged.

A chipotle is a ripened, dry, smoked jalapeno. It features a smoky, hot flavor and is often added to Mexican and Southwestern dishes. In 1993, Steve Ells based a new business as well as the original company name on this single ingredient, and the Chipotle Mexican Grill was born. He notes, "I had a very simple idea: Offer a simple menu of great food prepared fresh each day, using many of the same cooking techniques as gourmet restaurants. Then serve the food quickly, in a cool atmosphere. It was food that I wanted, and thought others would like too. We've never strayed from that original idea. The critics raved and customers began lining up at my tiny burrito joint," which was in Denver, Colorado.

Chipotle Mexican Grill food items may be purchased in a variety of ways, including dine-in, call-in, or online. The menu is relatively simple, with a series of options for each menu item. The choices include burritos, fajitas, and tacos featuring pork, shredded beef, chicken, steak, and vegetarian fillings along with side dishes such as a salad, chips, and pinto or vegetarian black beans. Drinks include margaritas, beers, and soft drinks. Ordering is quick and easy. As one marketing expert noted, "The menu is kind of like a Subway— only for Mexican food."

Early rave reviews about the generous portions and the quality of the meals helped the original restaurant grow to a second location within 3 years. Seeing the potential for growth, McDonald's purchased a minority interest in Chipotle, which made it possible for the company to quickly expand the number of units. By 2003, 300 new restaurants were open. Later in the decade, the company began

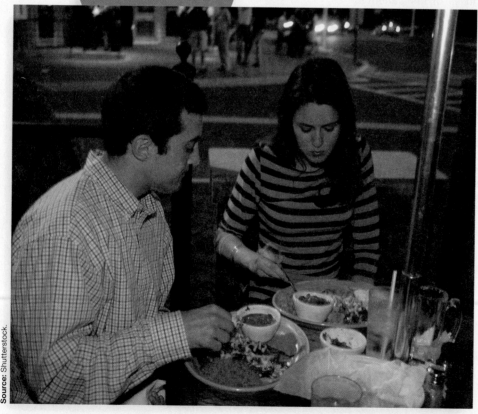

CHAPTER OBJECTIVES

After reading this chapter, you should be able to answer the following questions:

1 What elements are involved in internal and external information searches by consumers, as part of the purchasing process?

2 What three models explain how individuals evaluate purchasing alternatives?

3 What trends are affecting the consumer buying environment?

4 How do the roles played by various members of the buying center and the factors that influence them impact business purchases?

5 What types of business-to-business sales are made?

6 What are the steps of the business-to-business buying process?

7 How does dual channel marketing expand a company's customer base and its sales?

8 How can a company overcome international differences when adapting to buying processes?

to add nearly 100 new locations per year, topping 800 units by mid-2009.

Chipotle restaurants feature artistic, classy interiors. Each is brightly lit and clean. The stores have an open-kitchen design. Customers interact directly with the staff and watch as their orders are processed.

Another unique feature includes the methods used by the chain's corporate governance to select ingredients. In an effort to upgrade its foods, the company switched from yellow corn, which could contain genetically modified corn, to organic white corn, which does not. Chipotle purchases organic beans whenever possible. By mid-2004 Chipotle was offering naturally raised, antibiotic-free chicken from Bell & Evans in 50 restaurants in Washington, D.C., New York, and Ohio, and 8 restaurants in Chicago and New York use naturally raised beef. In 2009, ABC News "Nightline" featured a free-range pig farm from which Chipotle acquires some of its pork. Ells reported, "You have to be concerned where your food comes from and how the animals were raised. I call it 'Food with Integrity.'"

By the late 1990s, McDonald's acquired majority ownership of the company, although Steve Ells remained the operational manager. The link to McDonald's increased Chipotle's buying power, leading, for example, to a better supply of avocados as well as to more rapid expansion of locations.

Chipotle maintains a relatively limited advertising budget. Most of its advertisements feature humor. An online presence and word-of-mouth have supported the company's growth and success for over a decade.

Which factor leads a customer to purchase food at Chipotle? Is it the organic ingredients, the quick-and-simple ordering methods, the quality interiors of the restaurants, the large portions, or some other element? Regardless of the decision variable, the success and growth of the chain suggests a well-designed integrated marketing communications program.[1]

OVERVIEW

Enticing people to buy goods and services should be a primary goal of integrated marketing communications. Understanding how buyers make purchase decisions helps the marketing team reach this goal. Two types of buyer behaviors—consumer buyer behaviors and business-to-business buyer behaviors—receive attention in this chapter. Understanding the steps consumers use to make purchase decisions helps the marketing team create quality communications.

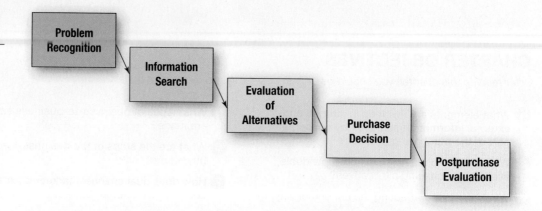

Consumer purchasing processes are examined in the first half of this chapter. Two stages in the process are the key to marketing communications. The first is the *information search* stage, in which the customer reviews previous memories and experiences looking for acceptable ways to meet a need by buying a product. The second stage is the *evaluation of alternatives* process, where the individual compares various purchasing possibilities. An effective IMC program targets potential buyers involved in these processes. A review of the traditional factors affecting consumers, along with discussion of some of the newer trends present in the consumer buying environment, is also provided.

❶ What elements are involved in internal and external information searches by consumers, as part of the purchasing process?

Business-to-business buyer behaviors are the focus of the second part of this chapter. First, the five major roles played in the buying center are reviewed. Next, the types of purchases companies make are noted, along with the steps involved in the purchasing process. Finally, dual channel marketing, which involves selling the same product to both consumers and business buyers, is discussed. Effective IMC programs identify potential customers from both markets. This leads to increased sales and helps a company maintain a strong presence in the marketplace.

▼ This advertisement for Skyjacker might trigger a search for additional information about truck suspensions and lift kits.

CONSUMER PURCHASING PROCESS

Finding ways to influence the consumer purchasing process is a vital activity. Figure 3.1 models the consumer buying decision-making process. Each step of the decision-making process is important; however, two of the components are the most directly related to developing quality integrated marketing communications: (1) information search and (2) the evaluation of alternatives. Discovering how customers seek out product information and then evaluate that information are keys to creating effective marketing messages.

The first step of the buying decision-making process occurs when the consumer notices a need or want. A problem or gap exists between an individual's current state and desired state. The need can be physical, such as hunger or thirst. It can be social, such as when a consumer visits a friend's apartment and sees his new HDTV and wants one in order to "keep up." Needs may be psychological in nature, including feelings for love, self-efficacy, or protection from fear.

A need can be triggered by a marketing communication. The advertisement for Skyjacker suspensions in this section may act as a catalyst for an individual to contact the company or a dealer that sells Skyjacker products. Many marketing communications stimulate needs or wants within consumers. Once this occurs, consumers enter the next phase of the process.

INFORMATION SEARCH

Once a problem has been recognized, the consumer begins an internal search, mentally recalling products that might satisfy the need. Often, the individual remembers how the need was met in the past. If a particular brand was chosen and the experience was positive, the consumer repeats the purchase decision, and the information search ends. When a previous purchase did not work out or the consumer wishes to try something else, a more complete internal search may result.

Internal Search

During an internal search, the consumer thinks about the brands she is willing to consider. This group may not contain every brand the consumer has experienced, because she removes brands that resulted in negative experiences. Brands she knows little about are eliminated. Consequently, the consumer quickly reduces the number of brands during an information search.

Making sure a company's brand becomes part of the consumer's set of potential purchase alternatives in an internal search is one objective of marketing communications, because it increases the chance that the brand will be purchased. A product with a high level of brand awareness or brand equity will likely to be included in the consumer's set of alternatives. The Neutrogena advertisement shown in this section uses "#1" four times to persuade consumers that Neutrogena is the number-one anti-wrinkle cream and should be considered. The purpose of the ad is to cause consumers who want an anti-wrinkle cream to consider Neutrogena as the first and best choice.

External Search

Following an internal search, the consumer makes a mental decision regarding an external search. When the customer has sufficient internal information, she moves to the next step of the decision-making process: evaluating the alternatives. A consumer who remains uncertain about the right brand to purchase undertakes an external search.

External information can be gathered from a variety of sources, including friends, relatives, experts, books, magazines, newspapers, advertisements, in-store displays, salespeople, and the Internet. The amount of time a consumer spends on an external search depends on three factors: (1) ability, (2) motivation, and (3) costs versus benefits (see Figure 3.2).[2]

Ability to Search

The ability to search partially determines the extent of an information search. Ability consists of a person's educational level combined with the specific knowledge he has about a product and the brands in that product's category. Educated individuals are

▲ A Neutrogena advertisement designed to convince consumers that the product should be the first choice when selecting an anti-wrinkle cream.

◀ **FIGURE 3.2**
Factors that affect the amount of time a consumer will spend conducting an external search

more likely to spend time searching for information. They are also more inclined to visit stores or search online prior to making decisions. Consumers possessing extensive knowledge about individual brands and product categories are better able to conduct a more involved external search. Thus, someone who knows a great deal about digital cameras has a more sophisticated ability to examine information than does someone who knows little about the technology. In addition, a person with more comprehensive knowledge of a product area often collects additional information, even when she is not in the market for the product.[3]

In terms of the amount of time an individual devotes to the external search process, an unusual phenomenon occurs. Although extensive product category knowledge means an individual has greater ability to search for external information, the consumer normally spends less time on the external search process because of the extensive knowledge she already possesses. Consumers at the other end of the spectrum also spend less time in the external search process, but for the opposite reason. They do not have knowledge about the product category and do not know what type of information to ask for or what type of information is needed, which means they lack the ability to search for information. Individuals in the middle, who have some knowledge of a product category but feel additional information is needed to make intelligent decisions, typically spend the most time searching for external information.

Level of Motivation

The degree to which an external search takes place also depends on the customer's level of motivation. The greater the motivation, the more time spent on an external search. Motivation is determined by the consumer's:

- Level of involvement
- Need for cognition
- Level of shopping enthusiasm

Individuals experience greater motivation to search for information when involvement levels are high. **Involvement** reflects the extent to which a stimulus or task is relevant to a consumer's existing needs, wants, or values. When a consumer deems a product to be important, it becomes more likely she will engage in an external search. The amount of involvement is based on factors such as the *cost* of the product and its *importance*. The higher the price, the more time an individual will spend searching for information.

The same holds true for importance. Choosing clothes might not be an important decision to some young males, which suggests their clothing purchases typically have low involvement. Picking a tuxedo for the high school prom, however, may spur greater involvement and a higher level of information search due to the social ramifications of dressing poorly at such an important event. The higher level of involvement emerges from the addition of a new element—a major occasion in the person's life.

The **need for cognition** personality characteristic identifies individuals who engage in and enjoy mental activities. Mental exercises have a positive impact on the information search process. People with high needs for cognition gather more information and search more thoroughly.

The search also depends on a person's **enthusiasm for shopping**. Customers who enjoy shopping undertake a more in-depth search for goods and services. The three factors—involvement, need for cognition,

▼ Enthusiasm for shopping has an impact on the amount of time spent on an external search.

and enthusiasm for shopping—combine to determine the individual's motivation to search for additional information.[4]

Cost Versus Benefits

The final factors that influence an information search are the *perceived costs* versus the *perceived benefits* of the search. Higher perceived benefits increase the tendency to search.

The ability to reduce purchase risk becomes a benefit that many consumers seek while examining external information. Additional information lowers the chances of making a mistake in the purchase selection. The cost of the search consists of several items:

- The actual cost of the good or service
- The subjective costs associated with the search, including time spent and anxiety experienced while making a decision
- The opportunity cost of foregoing other activities to search for information (e.g., going shopping instead of playing golf or watching a movie)

Higher perceived subjective costs associated with collecting external information search lessen the likelihood that the consumer will conduct a search.[5]

The three factors that make up an external search (ability, motivation, costs versus benefits) are normally considered simultaneously. When the perceived cost of a search is low and the perceived benefit is high, a consumer has a higher motivation to search for information. A consumer with a minimal amount of product knowledge and a low level of education is less likely to undertake an external search, because the consumer lacks the ability to identify the right information.

From a marketing communications perspective, the search process represents an important time to reach the consumer. The consumer's objective in making the effort to perform an external search is to acquire information leading to a better, more informed decision. The marketing team provides information that leads consumers to the company's products. One ideal time to attempt to influence the decision-making process occurs when the consumer has not yet made up his mind. Marketing experts utilize three models of the information search process: (1) attitudes, (2) values, and (3) cognitive mapping.

Consumer Attitudes

Consumer attitudes can be influenced by effective marketing communications. An **attitude** is a mental position taken toward a topic, a person, or an event that influences the holder's feelings, perceptions, learning processes, and subsequent behaviors.[6] Attitudes can drive purchase decisions. A consumer holding a positive attitude toward a brand becomes more likely to buy it. Someone who enjoys an advertisement also will be more likely to purchase the product.

Attitudes consist of three components: (1) affective, (2) cognitive, and (3) conative.[7] The *affective* component consists of the feelings or emotions a person has about the object, topic, or idea. The *cognitive* component refers to a person's mental images, understanding, and interpretations of the person, object, or issue. The *conative* component contains an individual's intentions, actions, or behavior. One common sequence of events that takes place in attitude formation is:

$$\text{Cognitive} \rightarrow \text{Affective} \rightarrow \text{Conative}$$

Most of the time, a person first develops an understanding about an idea or object. In the case of marketing, these ideas center on the benefits of the good or service. Thoughts about the product emerge from watching or reading advertisements. Other thoughts may result from exposures to information from other sources, such as the Internet or a friend's referral. Eventually, these ideas become beliefs the consumer holds about a particular product.

▼ This advertisement for St. Francis North Hospital is designed to influence a person's beliefs about the facility and its brain-imaging technology.

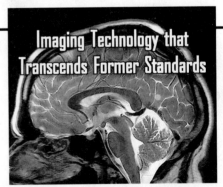

Providing brain imaging with uncompromised image quality, even with patient motion due to young age or uncontrollable tremors.

St. Francis North Hospital is pleased to announce that we now offer a state-of-the-art high definition magnetic resonance (HDMR) system, the Signa® EXCITE 1.5T. Similar to high definition television, HDMR provides physicians with highly detailed pictures to help them evaluate a wide range of patient conditions, including stroke, musculoskeletal, abdominal, breast and vascular disease. This system provides outstanding image quality for a confident diagnosis, and less likelihood of patient rescans, even in the most challenging circumstances.

Once again, St. Francis leads the way in our region with its continual effort to make the most advanced diagnostic equipment available to your doctor, and provide the best healthcare for you.

ST. FRANCIS NORTH HOSPITAL
An Affiliate of St. Francis Medical Center

3421 Medical Park Dr. • Monroe, LA • (318) 388-1946 • www.stfran.com

First in Technology.
Foremost in Care.

For instance, a consumer seeing the St. Francis North Hospital advertisement on the previous page might develop the impression that St. Francis offers high-quality imaging technology to help detect brain disorders.

The affective part of the attitude carries the general feeling or emotion a person attaches to the idea. In the case of goods and services, the product, its name, and other features can all generate emotions. Consider your emotional reactions to the following goods and services:

- Cough medicine
- Diaper wipes
- Motorcycles
- Children's toys made in China
- *Sports Illustrated*'s annual swimsuit issue
- Condoms

What emotions and thoughts did you associate with diaper wipes? The Pampers diaper wipe advertisement shown in this section attempts to influence emotions. When considering the items listed here, note that some emotions or attitudes about them seem relatively benign. Others are more strongly held. Cough medicine does not typically evoke an emotional response; however, the swimsuit issue or condoms may generate stronger reactions.

Decision and action tendencies are the conative parts of attitudes. Therefore, when a person feels strongly enough about the swimsuit issue, she might cancel a subscription to *Sports Illustrated*. Most attitudes are not held that strongly. Some people might feel favorably about a topic, such as green marketing, but this does not necessarily change their purchasing behaviors.

Attitudes develop in other ways. An alternative process is:

Affective → Conative → Cognitive

Advertisements and other marketing communications can first appeal to the emotions or feelings held by consumers in order to move them to "like" a product and make the purchase (the conative component). Cognitive understanding of the product comes after the purchase. For example, a woman may see the ad for Platinum Motorcars on the next page and be drawn to the idea of being "pampered" in a luxury car, along with her significant other. Emotionally, she has a desire to rent the car and takes action. Cognitive reasoning about renting the luxury car follows the emotional experience.

Some attitudes result from a third combination of the components, as follows:

Conative → Cognitive → Affective

Purchases that require little thought, that have a low price, or do not demand a great deal of emotional involvement might follow this path. For instance, while shopping for groceries a customer may notice a new brand of cookies on sale. The person may have never seen the brand or flavor before, but, because it is on sale, decides to give it a try. As the consumer eats the cookies, he develops a greater understanding of the product's taste, texture, and other qualities. Finally, the consumer reads the package to learn more about contents, including how many calories were devoured in each bite. He finally develops feelings toward the cookies that might affect future cookie purchases.

No matter which path is taken to develop attitudes, each component will be present, to some extent. Some attitudes are relatively trivial (e.g., "I like ping pong, even though I hardly ever get

▼ What emotions does this advertisement for Pampers Wipes elicit?

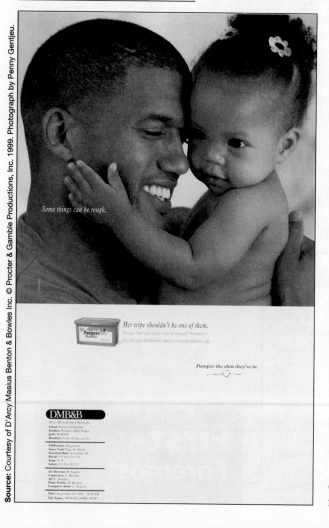

Some things can be rough.

Her wipe shouldn't be one of them.

Pamper the skin they're in.

to play"). Others are staunchly held, such as "I hate cigarette smoke!" Both are associated with feelings toward things, including products in the marketplace that may eventually result in purchases.

Consumer Values

Attitudes reflect an individual's personal values. **Values** are strongly held beliefs about various topics or concepts. Values frame attitudes and lead to the judgments that guide personal actions. Values tend to endure. They normally form during childhood, although they can change as a person ages and experiences life.

Figure 3.3 identifies some of the more common personal values. Individuals hold them to differing degrees. Factors that affect a person's values include the individual's personality, temperament, environment, and culture. By appealing to basic values, marketers try to convince prospective customers that the company's products align with their values.

In terms of consumer decision-making processes, both attitudes and values are influential. A good or service tied to a relatively universal value, such as patriotism, helps the firm take advantage of the linkage and present the product in a positive image. Levi Strauss attempted to do this with its recent "Go forth" campaign that was replete with American imagery. The campaign was based on research by Levi Strauss that found teenagers and individuals in their 20s were more patriotic and optimistic about the United States. The goal was to transfer positive feelings of patriotism to Levi's products.[8]

Attitudes are also featured in marketing communications. Most people consider being "put on hold" to be a nuisance. An advertising creative can tap into that attitude and use it to present a good or service in a more favorable light. Making the time pass pleasantly while on hold turns a negative attitude into a more positive experience.

Cognitive Mapping

The manner in which individuals store information further affects decisions, because it impacts what is recalled. Knowing how people store, retrieve, and evaluate information assists the company's marketing team in developing advertisements and marketing communications. The first step is to understand how various thought processes and memories work.

Cognitive maps are simulations of the knowledge structures and memories embedded in an individual's brain.[9] These structures contain a person's assumptions, beliefs, interpretation of facts, feelings, and attitudes about the larger world. These thought processes interpret new information and determine a response to fresh information or a

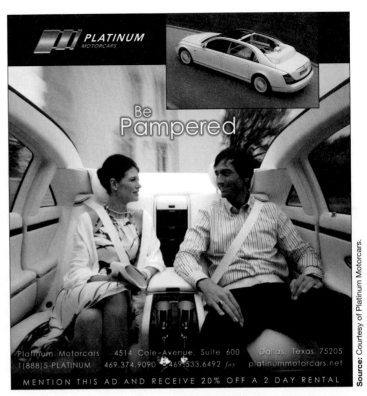

Source: Courtesy of Platinum Motorcars.

▲ This advertisement for Platinum Motorcars focuses on the affective component of an attitude.

Personal Values	
● Comfortable life	● Pleasure
● Equality	● Salvation
● Excitement	● Security
● Freedom	● Self-fulfillment
● Fun, exciting life	● Self-respect
● Happiness	● Sense of belonging
● Inner peace	● Social acceptance
● Mature love	● Wisdom
● Personal accomplishment	

◀ **FIGURE 3.3**
Personal Values

FIGURE 3.4 ▶
A Cognitive Map for Ruby Tuesday

novel situation. Figure 3.4 depicts a simplified hypothetical cognitive map of an individual thinking about a Ruby Tuesday restaurant.

Based on the cognitive structures illustrated in Figure 3.4, when this customer thinks about Ruby Tuesday, she connects images of it to other restaurants offering fast food and others providing dine-in services. The individual recognizes Ruby Tuesday as a dine-in establishment. The consumer believes that Ruby Tuesday offers excellent service, but that the service is slow. Next, when the person thinks of slow service, her thoughts turn to Mel's Diner. When she thinks of excellent service, she recalls Applebee's.

Cognitive Linkages

Cognitive structures contain many linkages and exist on several levels. For instance, one level of cognition may be the map shown in Figure 3.4. At another level, the cognitive map is more spatial and conjures images of the actual physical location of Ruby Tuesday and the surrounding businesses. A third cognitive level related to Ruby Tuesday is the person's recall of the interior of the restaurant along with other linkages that occur at that level. The consumer may have thoughts about Ruby Tuesday that focus on employees, including a relationship she had with a server who was a friend. Therefore, cognitive processing occurs on several levels using highly complex mechanisms.

Processing New Information

In terms of cognitive mapping, when a consumer receives information or sees an advertisement, it is processed in one of three ways. New information that is consistent with current information tends to strengthen an existing linkage. For example, when a consumer views a Ruby Tuesday advertisement promoting great service, the result might be that the ad will strengthen an existing belief, because the consumer already reached that conclusion.

A different response occurs when a message has no current linkages. A consumer who sees an advertisement featuring Ruby Tuesday's seafood selection and does not know that Ruby Tuesday offers seafood experiences a different reaction. In order for this information to remain in the consumer's mind and to become linked to Ruby Tuesday, the customer must create a new linkage between previous Ruby Tuesday images and other images of seafood.

▼ Cognitive mapping models the process consumers use to assess and evaluate information.

Source: Thinkstock Royalty Free.

Retaining Information

Hearing something once is usually not enough to cause it to be retained in a person's long-term memory, due to differences between short-term recall and long-term memories. The cognitive-mapping process explains the knowledge structures embedded in a person's long-term memory. Ordinarily, information will be retained in short-term memory for only a few seconds. As stimuli reach an individual's senses, short-term memory processes them. Short-term memory retains only five to nine pieces of information, meaning new messages are either soon forgotten or added to long-term memory. A repeated message may cause an individual to become more likely to remember it, because the message will be processed into long-term memory and placed into previously developed cognitive maps.

▲ This Sunkist advertisement is designed to establish a new linkage between Sunkist lemon juice and a salt substitute.

As a result, when a company attempts to introduce consumers to a new brand, advertisements and other marketing messages should repeat the name of the brand several times during the presentation. This repetition improves the chances of recall at a later time. To illustrate how this works, consider what happens when a person gives a phone number to a friend. To help remember it, the individual repeats the number several times.

New Concepts

Another way a consumer can process information is to link the message to a new concept. For example, if a consumer sees an advertisement from Ruby Tuesday emphasizing that it has great food but has never thought about the restaurant in terms of quality food, that linkage is not currently present. If the advertisement persuades the consumer, she might construct a linkage between Ruby Tuesday and good food without even traveling to the restaurant. If she does not believe the message, she will ignore or forget the information, and no new linkage results. A third possibility is that the consumer recalls the advertisement at a later time and decides to try Ruby Tuesday. If the food is great, then the link is established at that point. If it is not, the consumer continues thinking that Ruby Tuesday does not offer good food.

Marketing Messages

From a marketing perspective, it is easier to strengthen linkages that already exist. Adding new linkages or modifying linkages will be more difficult (see Figure 3.5). Regardless of how information is presented, repetition remains important due to the limitations of short-term memory. Consumers are exposed to hundreds of marketing messages daily. Only a few are processed into long-term memory.

Cognitive mapping and persuasion techniques designed to change attitudes or tap into strongly held values are two key ingredients of any IMC program. When the marketing team understands the needs and attitudes of the target market, messages can be structured to meet those needs. The message should capture the consumer's attention by exposing him to messages that travel effectively through a core mental processing channel or peripheral channels, either through logic or alluring emotional appeals.

Creatives attempt to design ads that reach the linkages consumers have already made between a product and other key ideas. For example, for a long time a linkage

Strengthen current linkage

Marketing Message

Modify current linkage

Create new linkage

◀ **FIGURE 3.5**
The Roles of Marketing Messages in Cognitive Mapping

FIGURE 3.6 ▶
Methods of Evaluating
Alternatives

existed between Cadillac and quality, as witnessed by the advertising and promotional phrase "This product is the *Cadillac*...[of all products in the market]." Common linkages exist between products and ideas such as quality, value, low cost, expense, fun, sex, danger, practicality, exoticness, and others. Carefully planned marketing campaigns identify linkages that entice the consumer to buy a brand and to believe in or be loyal to that brand in the future. This advantage remains as the consumer considers various purchasing alternatives.

② What three models explain
how individuals evaluate
purchasing alternatives?

EVALUATION OF ALTERNATIVES

The third step in the consumer buying decision-making process, expanded in Figure 3.6, is the evaluation of alternatives. Three models portray the nature of the evaluation process: (1) the evoked set approach, (2) the multiattribute approach, and (3) affect referral. Understanding how consumers evaluate choices helps the firm's marketing team develop materials that lead consumers to favor a given brand.

The Evoked Set Method

A person's **evoked set** consists of the brands the individual considers in a purchasing situation. An evoked set might be reviewed during both the information search and evaluation

▼ One goal of this advertisement
for BT Steakhouse is to move
the brand from a consumer's
inert set to the evoked set to be
considered the next time the
person dines out.

stages of the buying decision-making process. Two additional brand sets become part of the evaluation of purchase alternatives: the inept set and the inert set. The **inept set** consists of the brands that are part of a person's memory that are *not considered* because they elicit negative feelings. These negative sentiments are normally caused by a bad experience with a vendor or particular brand. They can also originate from negative comments made by a friend or by seeing an advertisement that the potential customer did not like.

The **inert set** holds the brands that the consumer is aware of but the individual has neither negative nor positive feelings about them. Using the terms from cognitive mapping, these brands have not been entered into any map, or they only have weak linkages to other ideas. The lack of knowledge about these brands usually eliminates them as alternatives. In other words, in most purchase situations the only brands considered are those in the evoked set.

Placing a brand name in the evoked sets of consumers may be the primary goal of a marketing message. Doing so requires promoting the brand name and that brand's primary benefit extensively and consistently using multiple media and other venues. The consumer should see the brand name frequently in as many locations as possible. Then, to make sure the name becomes part of an evoked set, the concepts described related to cognitive mapping can be employed. By tying the brand with its primary benefit, the intent is to embed the brand's name into the consumer's long-term memory. The message should be designed to establish or reinforce linkages between benefit and the brand name. When a

TABLE 3.1 The Multiattribute Model

Product	Characteristics				
Computer	Price	Style	Service contract	Software	Memory storage
Telephone	Price	Style	Speed dial	Caller ID	Cordless feature
Car	Price	Style	Safety	Room	Other features
T-bone steak	Price	Age	Fat content	Degree cooked	Seasonings
Sunglasses	Price	Style	UV protection	Durability	Prescription lenses
Sofa	Price	Style	Foldout bed	Stain resistance	Color
Credit card	Interest rate	Fees	Billing cycle	Access to ATM	Credit limit

Consider each item. Which characteristic is most important to you personally? Least important?

consumer evaluates alternatives using his evoked set and the company's brand becomes the part of the set being considered, the advertisement has been successful.

The Multiattribute Approach

Another model of consumer evaluations of purchasing alternatives is the multiattribute approach. It may be most useful for understanding high-involvement types of purchases. Consumers often examine sets of product attributes across an array of brands. The multiattribute model suggests that a consumer's attitude toward a brand is determined by:[10]

- The brand's performance on product or brand attributes
- The importance of each attribute to the consumer

The higher a brand rates on attributes that are important to the consumer, the more likely it becomes that the brand will be purchased. Table 3.1 notes various products, along with some of the characteristics that affect their selection. Each has potentially a lesser or greater value to individual consumers. Case 1 at the end of this chapter demonstrates the multiattribute model.

From an integrated communication standpoint, providing consumers with information about a brand's performance on criteria that are likely to be used is the key. This can be achieved on a brand's Web site, where consumers often gather information about high-involvement decisions. Brochures and print ads can also be prepared; however, getting them into the hands of consumers just as they desire information presents the greatest challenge.

In advertising, creatives often feature a product with multiple benefits by designing a series of messages. Advertisements highlight price, style, service contract, software, memory, storage, or other product features. Only one or two of these benefits should be presented in each message. Otherwise, the advertisement becomes overloaded with information. Consumers who see commercials featuring one or two benefits are able to learn about a brand's characteristics. Over time, consumers obtain sufficient information to evaluate the product.

▼ The multiattribute model is used in the purchase of high-involvement products, such as automobiles.

Affect Referral

A third model of consumer evaluations of purchase alternatives, **affect referral**, suggests that consumers choose brands they like the best or the ones with which they have emotional connections. The individual does not evaluate brands or think about product attributes. Instead, he buys the brand he likes the best or the one that incites positive feelings. Toothpaste, ketchup, soft drinks, and candy are

Frank Fletcher Nissan Imports
#1 Nissan Dealer in Missouri
NISSAN
SHIFT the way you move   www.fletchernissan.net   2327 South Range Line Rd. – Joplin   1-800-243-8554 or 417-781-1177

Source: Courtesy of Joplin Globe.

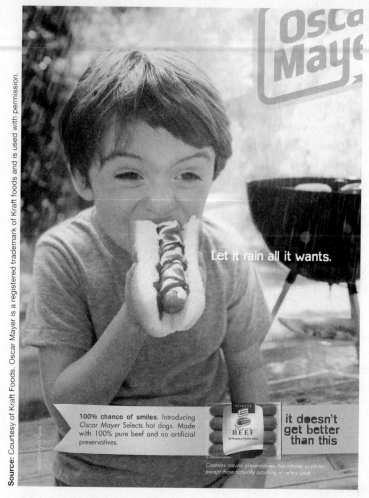

Let it rain all it wants.

100% chance of smiles. Introducing Oscar Mayer Selects hot dogs. Made with 100% pure beef and no artificial preservatives.

Contains natural preservatives. No nitrates or nitrites except those naturally occurring in celery juice.

it doesn't get better than this

▲ For some consumers, Oscar Mayer represents the best brand of hot dogs and will be purchased using the affect referral approach.

some of the products consumers normally select in this way. These purchases typically have low levels of involvement. They also tend to be frequently purchased products.

The affect referral model also explains purchases of higher priced and "socially visible" products. The emotional bond that has been established between the consumer and the brand leads to a purchase under those circumstances.

The affect referral model explains three things. First, using this approach to product evaluation saves mental energy. A quick choice is easier than going through the process of evaluating every alternative. Some purchases do not deserve much effort. The affect referral model explains those situations.

Second, a multiattribute model approach might have been used previously when making a purchase. The person has already spent a great deal of time considering various product attributes, deciding which are most critical, and reaching a decision. Going through the process again would be "reinventing the wheel." For example, a teenager buying jeans may have already spent considerable time evaluating styles, prices, colors, durability levels, and "fit" of various brands. After making the purchase, the teen continues to purchase the same brand as long as the experience remains positive. The affect referral model explains this buying behavior. Making a repurchase becomes simple and convenient.

Third, consumers often develop emotional bonds with brands. In terms of the purchase decision, an emotional bond with a product can be the strongest and most salient factor in the decision.[11] It is more important than any attribute or benefit the product can offer. Successful brands establish emotional bonds with consumers. A bond generates brand loyalty, enhances brand equity, and reduces brand parity. Consequently, consumers do not evaluate alternatives because of the bond with the brand. Harley-Davidson has developed such a bond with many of its customers. For these individuals, their feelings toward Harley-Davidson are so strong that they do not even think about other alternatives. The affect referral model explains this outcome.

TRENDS IN THE CONSUMER BUYING ENVIRONMENT

❸ What trends are affecting the consumer buying environment?

Studying the steps consumers take while making purchasing decisions helps create effective marketing communications. The environment in which purchases are made continually changes and evolves. Several trends in the consumer buying environment affect purchasing patterns. Some are listed in Figure 3.7.[12]

Age Complexity

Technology has changed the way children grow up. Children are bombarded with advertisements, video games, television shows, movies, and a myriad of other images from an early age. Most know a great deal about sex by the age of 12. Female teenagers, and even preteens, wear skimpy, revealing fashions. Many believe children are "growing up" at a much earlier age.

At the other end of the spectrum, some adults refuse to "grow old." They wear fashions that resemble those worn by college students. They still drive sports cars or convertibles. Many middle-aged adults apparently do not want to grow old, acting like younger people

- Age complexity
- Gender complexity
- Individualism
- Active, busy lifestyles

- Cocooning
- Pleasure pursuits
- Health emphasis

and buying products normally purchased by them. This trend challenges marketers to create messages that reflect these behaviors but do not offend or confuse more traditional middle-aged persons.

Gender Complexity

Gender complexity means that the traditional roles, lifestyles, and interests of men and women have become blurred. Many women attend college, delay marriage, and wait to start families. Some do not marry nor have children, choosing instead to focus on moving up the corporate ladder.

Men, meanwhile, are more likely to play an active role in parenting, help with household chores, and do more of the shopping. Since 1985, a shift in the number of men who are the primary household shopper has occurred. Almost one-third of men are now the principal shopper. Males spend 38 percent of all grocery dollars.[13] Companies such as General Foods that would normally advertise groceries to women now consider men in terms of what they buy and how they shop. In the past, an automaker such as Ford would target ads to men. Such an approach is no longer useful. Women either purchase the vehicle or have a major influence on the one that is chosen.

▼ Understanding the issues created by age and gender complexities, Guess created these two advertisements.

Individualism

Individualism has become more pronounced, especially in goods and services. Customers want companies to develop products just for them. To meet this trend, Nike now allows consumers to design their own shoes using the company's Web site. Levi Strauss allows for personalized jeans, made to fit the exact measurements given to them by the consumer, again over the Internet. Recognizing this trend, food manufacturers have increased the varieties, sizes, and flavors of foods. In the beverage industry, a total of 450 new products were introduced within a single year. Many of these new beverages were health-related items, touting that they were vitamin fortified, organic, all natural, or low calorie.[14]

Active, Busy Lifestyles

Active lifestyles have had a dramatic impact on consumer behaviors. In one survey, 47 percent of respondents stated that they would prefer additional free time over more money. The recent recession caused many individuals to work longer hours in order to protect their jobs. Many people focus less on material possessions and more on experiences with friends and family.[15]

Time pressures account for increases in sales of convenience items, such as microwave ovens, drive-through dry-cleaning establishments, and one-stop shopping outlets, most notably big box superstores. People on the go use mobile phones, Blackberries, and answering machines to make sure they stay in touch with others and do not miss any messages during busy days. The demand for convenience continues to increase.

Cocooning

Another side-effect of a busy and hectic lifestyle is cocooning. The stress of long hours at work and additional hours spent fighting commuter traffic has led many individuals to retreat and cocoon in their homes, which includes making the home environment as soothing as possible. Until recently, cocooning was demonstrated by major expenditures on elaborate homes, expensive sound systems, satellite systems with big-screen televisions, swimming pools, saunas, hot tubs, gourmet kitchens with large dining rooms, decks and porches, and moving to the country or to a gated community.

The recent recession led to changes in many marketing messages, emphasizing a positive home environment at a low cost. Others focused on being frugal to rebound from financial loses. Some ads featured the utility of shopping from home to avoid the hustle and bustle of malls and traffic.

Changes in Family Units

Divorce and remarriage have altered many family units. Remarried divorcees represent about 10 percent of the population. Divorcees tend to develop a new outlook on life. They often desire to cocoon, which changes their purchasing patterns. This group, called *second chancers,* is usually between the ages of 40 and 59 and has a higher household income. Second chancers are more content with life than are average adults. They tend to be happy with their new families but also have a different life focus. Second chancers spend less time trying to please others and more time seeking fuller, more enriching lives for themselves and their children or spouse. Although the home and cocooning continue to be a major emphasis, entertainment and vacation services also appeal to this group.[16]

Pleasure Pursuits

Some people handle the stress caused by a hectic, busy lifestyle through occasional indulgences or pleasure binges such as expensive dinners out and smaller luxury purchases. Pleasure pursuits also include "getaway" weekends in resorts and on short cruises. These self-rewarding activities make the consumer feel that all the work and effort is "worth it."

Many people respond to stress through exciting adventures. From theme parks to virtual reality playrooms, consumers enjoy the mental relaxation of experiencing things that seem almost unreal. Many gambling establishments cater to these more exotic types of vacations. IMAX theaters generate a much more exciting experience than do normal movie theaters. As the technology of fantasy continues to develop, more firms enter the marketplace to profit from consumer desires to "get away from it all."

Health Emphasis

The U.S. population continues to age, leading to two trends: (1) a blossoming interest in health and (2) maintaining youthful appearance. Many consumers try to develop a balanced lifestyle with an emphasis on nutrition, exercise, and staying active.[17]

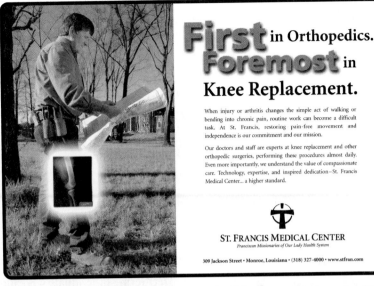

▲ With the emphasis on health and remaining active, St. Francis Medical Center promotes knee replacement following an injury or arthritis.

Developing better eating habits has changed many families. Kraft, which faced this new landscape, combated rising concerns about obesity by shifting its approach. The company began to produce more healthy, diet-oriented foods. In addition, Kraft reduced the fat content in over 200 products. The marketing message was changed to promote Kraft foods as part of a proper diet.[18]

Although consumers desire healthier foods, they also want convenience. Busy lifestyles mean consumers are less willing to cook from scratch. They prefer prepared foods that can be assembled easily and cooked quickly. Products that combine health attributes with convenience are likely to sell well.[19]

In sum, these new trends in the consumer buying environment create several challenges for marketing experts, as shown in Figure 3.8. The activity will be to monitor changes so that the company is not surprised by them. Second, companies create goods and services that are compatible with changing values. Third, marketing messages can be designed to reflect and build on the values people express. Incorporating new trends into the marketing program may be undertaken while at the same time being careful not to alienate any current customers who might not like the trends.

BUSINESS-TO-BUSINESS BUYER BEHAVIOR

❹ How do the roles played by various members of the buying center and the factors that influence them impact business purchases?

In business-to-business purchases, *people* still make the decisions. At the same time, when selling to a business organization, the marketing team knows that normally several individuals are involved. Further, corporate policies create restrictions and decision rules that affect purchasing activities. Factors such as costs, quality, and profit considerations also influence the final choice.

The **buying center** consists of the group of individuals making a purchase decision on behalf of a business. This complicates buying decisions. The buying center contains five different purchase roles, as shown in Figure 3.9. The five roles are:

- **Users**—Members of the organization who actually use the good or service
- **Buyers**—Individuals given the formal responsibility of making the purchase

- Monitor consumer environment for changes.
- Create goods and services that are compatible with the changes.
- Design marketing messages that reflect the changes.

◀ **FIGURE 3.8**
Marketing Responses to Changing Trends in the Consumer Buying Environment

FIGURE 3.9 ▶
The Buying Center

- **Influencers**—People who shape purchasing decisions by providing the information or criteria utilized in evaluating alternatives, such as engineers
- **Deciders**—Individuals who authorize the purchase decisions
- **Gatekeepers**—Individuals who control the flow of information to members of the buying center

These five roles often overlap. Also, several individuals can occupy the same role in a buying center, especially for large or critical purchases. It is not unusual for a variety of members of the organization to serve as influencers, because these roles usually are not fixed and formal.

The purchasing process will be unique in each organization. It also varies within an organization from one purchase decision to the next. Salespeople calling on a business must be able to locate members of the buying center and understand their roles in the process. When these roles change from one purchase situation to another, the marketing and selling task becomes more complex.[20]

FACTORS AFFECTING BUSINESS BUYING CENTERS

The behaviors of members in the buying center are influenced by a series of organizational and individual factors.[21] These influences change the manner in which decisions are made and often affect the eventual outcome or alternative chosen.

Organizational Influences

Several organizational factors affect the ways employees make purchasing decisions for a company. The factors include the company's goals and its operating environment (recession, growth period, lawsuits pending, etc.). Decisions are further constrained by the organization's finances, capital assets, market position, the quality of its human resources, and the country in which the firm operates.

Studies of organizational decision-making indicate that employees tend to adopt *heuristics,* which are decision rules designed to reduce the number of viable options to a smaller, manageable set. Company goals, rules, budgets, and other organizational factors create heuristics. One decision rule often employed is *satisficing,* which means that when an acceptable alternative has been identified it is taken and the search ends. Rather than spending a great deal of time looking for an optimal solution, decision makers tend to favor expedience.[22]

Individual Factors

At least seven factors affect each member of the business buying center (see Figure 3.10).[23] Each impacts how the individual interacts with other members of the center.

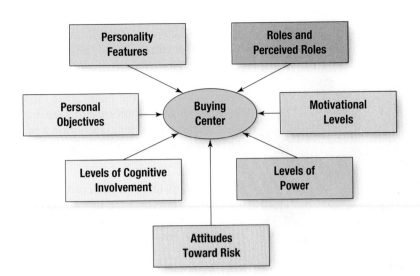

Personality

Many facets of personality exist. A decisive person makes purchase decisions in a manner different from someone who vacillates. Confidence, extroversion, shyness, and other personality traits affect both the person performing the decision-making role and others in the process. An aggressive "know-it-all" type affects the other members of a decision-making team. Such a personality feature does not always benefit the organization. An extrovert tends to become more involved in the buying process than a more introverted individual. The extrovert spends more time talking, and the introvert spends more time listening to sellers. The introvert might be too timid with salespeople, and consequently might not ask important questions.

Roles

The roles people play are influenced by an individual's age, heredity, ethnicity, gender, cultural memberships, and patterns of social interaction. Roles are socially constructed, which means people define how they intend to play roles as part of a negotiation process with others. A person's perception of how the role fits into the buying center process and the overall organization affects how the individual becomes involved in the purchase.

A buying center member who views his role as merely giving approval to decisions made by the boss (the decider) does not actively participate. Members who believe their inputs are valued and are being solicited become more active. One person might believe that his role is to provide information. Another might perceive her role as being the person who synthesizes information provided by vendors and then relating the information to the buying center to save time. Roles and perceptions of roles are major factors determining how members of the buying center engage in the decision.

Motivation

A person's degree of motivation depends on the match of the individual's goals to the organization's. A factory foreman with a personal goal of becoming the vice president of operations will be more likely to become involved in the purchasing decisions that affect his performance and that of his department. A purchasing agent who has been charged by the CEO to reduce expenses will take a more active role to ensure that cost-cutting selections are made. Many individuals are motivated by the need for recognition. Then the goal of making successful purchasing decisions becomes to ensure that others recognize the effort, because the person believes a link exists between recognition and promotions or pay raises.

Level of Power

A person's derives her level of power in the buying process from the role in the buying center, official position in the organization, and the impact of the purchase decision on a

▲ An advertisement for Sub-Zero directed toward business buyers for refrigeration units, containing the message: "Fresh is everything."

specific job. When a particular purchase decision directly affects an employee, she may try to gain more power through the buying process. For instance, a factory foreman has greater power within the buying center in the purchase of raw materials, whereas the maintenance foreman has more power in the purchase of maintenance supplies. In these situations, each strives to influence the decision that affects his or her area.

Risk

Many vendors are chosen because buyers believe the choice represents the lowest risk. Risk avoidance leads buyers to stay with current vendors rather than switching. In marketing to businesses, reducing risk is a priority, especially when signing large contracts or when a purchase might affect company profits. People tend to believe that taking risks, especially when a failure follows, affects performance appraisals, promotions, and other outcomes.

Levels of Involvement

Both consumer buyer behaviors and business buying behaviors are influenced by levels of cognitive involvement. Individuals with higher levels of cognitive capacity seek more information prior to making decisions. They also ask more questions when interacting with a salesperson. They spend more time deliberating prior to making decisions. Clearly-stated message arguments help persuade both consumers and business buyers with higher cognitive levels.

Personal Objectives

Motives, personality types, perceptions of risk, and the other individual factors influence personal objectives. These objectives can lead buyers to make purchases that help them politically in the organization, even when they are not the best choice. For example, if someone knows his boss is friends with a particular vendor, the buyer might choose that vendor even when others offer higher quality, lower prices, or both. Personal objectives in buying decisions can be tied to getting promotions, making rivals look bad, "brown-nosing" a boss, or the genuine desire to help the organization succeed.

In sum, a buying center consists of a complex set of relationships. Members can serve different roles and may play more than one role. Understanding these dynamics helps when marketing to businesses. The marketing team identifies who will make the decision, how the decision will be made, and any forces or factors that might affect the decision-making process. Examining the organizational and individual influences makes it possible to design a communications program that reaches the key people at the right time.

⑤ What types of business-to-business sales are made?

TYPES OF BUSINESS-TO-BUSINESS SALES

Business buyers make different types of purchasing decisions. The marketing team adapts to the type of decision being made. Three categories of buying activities are: (1) straight rebuy, (2) modified rebuy, and (3) new task.[24]

A **straight rebuy** occurs when the firm has previously chosen a vendor and places a reorder. This routine process involves only one or a few members of the buying center. Often the purchasing agent (buyer) and the users of the product are the only persons aware of a rebuy order. The user's role in this purchase situation is to ask the buyer to replenish the supply. The buyer then contacts the supplier and places the order. Little or no evaluation of alternatives or information takes place. These purchases often take place electronically.

When making a **modified rebuy**, the buying team considers and evaluates alternatives. As identified in Figure 3.11, a modified rebuy purchase can be made for four different reasons. First, when a company's buyers are *dissatisfied with the current vendor*, they look for new options. A greater the level of dissatisfaction creates a strong enticement to examine new possibilities. Second, if a new company offers what is perceived by a member of the buying center to be a *better buy*, the purchase decision may be revisited.

A third type of modified rebuy occurs at the *end of a contractual agreement*. Many organizations, as dictated by corporate policy, must ask for bids each time a contract is written. This situation often occurs when governmental and nonprofit organizations make purchases. The final reason for a modified rebuy is that the people in the company assigned to make the purchase might have only *limited or infrequent experience with the good or service*. When a company purchases delivery trucks, the typical time between decisions may be 5 to 7 years. This creates a modified rebuy situation, because many factors change over that amount of time. Prices, product features, and vendors (truck dealerships) change rapidly. Also, in most cases the composition of the buying group will be different. Some may have never been part of the decision to purchase delivery vehicles.

In **new task** purchasing situations, the company considers a good or service for the first time or it has been a long time since the last purchase. Further, the product involved is one with which organizational members have no or extremely little experience. This type of purchase normally requires input from a number of buying center members. A considerable amount of time is spent gathering information and evaluating vendors. In many cases, vendors are asked to assist in identifying the required specifications.

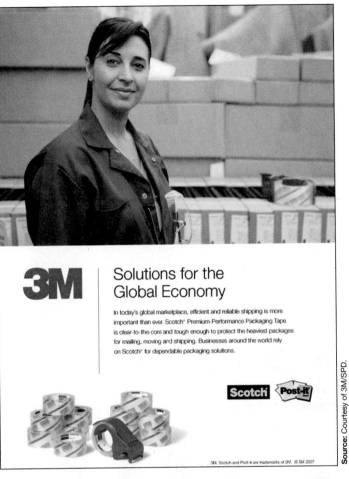

▲ A 3M advertisement directed to businesses for Premium-Performance Packaging Tape.

THE BUSINESS-TO-BUSINESS BUYING PROCESS

The steps involved in the business-to-business buying process are similar to those made by individual consumers. In new task purchasing situations, members of the buying center tend to go through each of the seven steps as part of the buying decision-making process. In modified rebuy or straight rebuy situations, one or more of the steps may be eliminated.[25] Figure 3.12 compares the consumer buying process to the business-to-business buying process.

6 What are the steps of the business-to-business buying process?

- Dissatisfaction with current vendor.
- A different vendor makes an attractive offer.
- End of contractual arrangement with current vendor.
- Individuals involved in decision process have no or little experience with the product.

◄ **FIGURE 3.11**
Reasons to Make a Modified Rebuy

FIGURE 3.12 ▶

A Comparison of the Business-to-Business Buying Process to the Consumer Buying Process

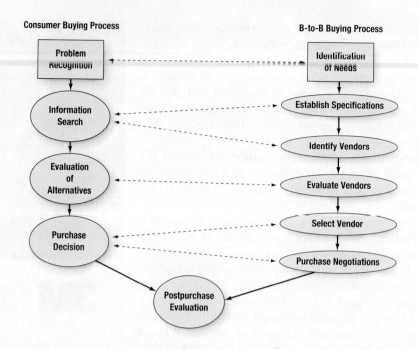

Consumer Buying Process

- Problem Recognition
- Information Search
- Evaluation of Alternatives
- Purchase Decision
- Postpurchase Evaluation

B-to-B Buying Process

- Identification of Needs
- Establish Specifications
- Identify Vendors
- Evaluate Vendors
- Select Vendor
- Purchase Negotiations

▼ Sales of rental equipment offered by Scott is based on consumer demand for the products and services.

WITH SCOTT POWERLINE,

THE JOB IS IN THE BAG.

Whatever you want, Scott's got. Plus, 24/7 service anywhere on the globe!

From bucket trucks to Mantis cranes (we're the No. 1 dealer in the world), we carry the selection and inventory to get you what you need when you need it. Plus, 24/7 service to keep you running and on the job – anywhere. See all our lines online!

Rentals • Leasing • Service • Sales

SCOTT
POWERLINE & UTILITY EQUIPMENT

One-Stop Scott

scottpowerline.com • Monroe, LA – 877-388-9269 • Lake City, GA – 877-396-1500

Identification of Needs

Just as consumers identify needs (hunger, protection, social interaction), businesses also make purchases because of needs ranging from raw materials to professional services. The manner in which business needs are determined is often different.

Many business needs are created by derived demand. **Derived demand** is based on, linked to, or generated by the production and sale of some other good or service.[26] The demand for steel used in automobiles is largely based on the number of cars and trucks sold each year. When the demand for vehicles goes down during a recession or downturn, the demand for steel also declines. Steel manufacturers find it difficult to stimulate demand because of the nature of derived demand. Derived demand results from purchases of raw materials used in the production of goods and services, such as steel, aluminum, concrete, plastic, petroleum products (e.g., jet fuel for airlines), construction materials, and others. Derived demand also exists for services. Most of the demand for mortgages depends on housing sales.

Once a need has been recognized, the order will be placed with the current vendor, if a straight rebuy is being made. When the purchase is a modified rebuy or new task, members of the buying center move to the next step.

Establishment of Specifications

In a new task purchase, the most complete specifications are spelled out. Many times, various vendors assist the buyer in developing clear specifications. In modified rebuy situations, specifications are examined to ensure that they are current and that they still meet the company's needs. Occasionally, specifications are changed, but normally these are only minor alterations.

Identification of Vendors

Once specifications have been identified, potential vendors are located and they are asked to submit bids. In most business situations, written, formal bids are required. A vendor's ability to write a clear proposal often determines whether the company will present a successful bid. Effective proposals spell out prices, quality levels, payment terms, support services, and any other condition requested by the company.

Vendor Evaluation

Evaluations of vendors normally occur at two levels. The first level, an *initial screening* of proposals, narrows the field of vendors down to three to five competitors. The number of people from the buying center involved in the initial screening depends on the dollar value of the bid and whether the product is critical to the firm's operation. As dollar values increase and the product becomes more critical, the number of individuals from the buying center involved also rises. Minor choices are often delegated to a single individual.

The second level of evaluation occurs as the firm undertakes a *vendor audit.* An audit is especially important when members of the company seek to develop a longer-term relationship with a supplier. Vendors that are the primary sources for critical components or raw materials recognize that long-term bonds benefit both the vendor and the purchasing firm. Members of the audit team often include an engineer, someone from operations, a quality-control specialist, and members of the purchasing department. The goal of the audit is to evaluate potential suppliers and each company's ability to meet demand, provide the level of quality needed, and deliver the product on time.

Vendors are people, just as members of the buying center are people. Attitudes, values, opinions, and first impressions influence evaluations made about vendors. All messages, including bids and proposals, should be carefully designed to create favorable impressions.

Vendor Selection

Once company officials have carefully studied all of the vendors and the bids have been considered, it is time to make a final choice. In the decision-making process, members of the buying center experience the individual and organizational pressures presented earlier. The selection criteria used include quality, delivery, performance history, warranties, facilities and capacity, geographic location, technical capability, and per-dollar value.[27] It is unlikely that a single vendor will be deemed superior across all selection criteria. Consequently, the marketing team for each seller emphasizes the company's specific strengths as part of its presentation. In reality, however, politics and other similar forces impact the final decision.

Negotiation of Terms

In most purchasing situations, negotiation of terms will be a formality, because most of the conditions have already been worked out. Occasionally, however, changes are made at this point in a contract or purchase. These tend to be minor and are normally negotiated by the purchasing agent. When the final agreement is set, goods are shipped or services provided. Assuming no further complications, the buying process is complete until the next cycle begins.

Postpurchase Evaluation

In the business-to-business arena, the postpurchase phase represents a marketing opportunity. Vendors that provide high-quality products, make follow-up calls, and offer additional services often move into a straight rebuy situation. They avoid going through the process again, because they are the chosen vendor unless something changes. Even for products that are purchased occasionally, the firm that gives attention to the postpurchase component of the selling process gains an edge the next time a purchase is made.

7 How does dual channel
marketing expand a
company's customer base
and its sales?

DUAL CHANNEL MARKETING

Firms sell virtually the same goods or services to both consumers and businesses in **dual channel marketing**.[28] The approach fits several situations. Perhaps the most common scenario occurs when a product sold in business markets is then adapted to consumer markets. New products often have high start-up costs, including R&D expenditures, market research, and other tasks. Businesses tend to be less price sensitive than retail consumers, which makes it logical to approach them first.

As sales grow, economies of scale emerge. Larger purchases of raw materials combined with more standardized methods of production make it possible to enter consumer markets. The benefits of economies of scale entice manufacturers to sell products previously supplied to the business sector in the retail markets. Products including digital cameras, calculators, computers, fax machines, and mobile phones were first sold to businesses and then later to consumers.

To make the move to the retail arena possible, prices must come down and products need to be user-friendly. For example, consumers can now have their photos put on a CD rather than obtain prints. The imaging technology developed by Kodak and Intel was first sold to various businesses and now is offered to retail customers. By forming an alliance with Intel, Kodak brought the cost down and developed the economies of scale necessary for consumer markets.

Spin-Off Sales

Another type of dual channel marketing—spin-off sales—occurs when individuals who buy a particular brand at work have positive experiences and, as a result, purchase the same brand for personal use. This situation often takes place with computers and computer software. Favorable feelings about more expensive items can also result in spin-off sales. A salesperson who drives a company-owned Buick for work might like it so well that one is purchased for personal use. Holiday Inn's marketing team discovered that many of its private stays come from business-related spin-offs. Approximately 30 percent of Holiday Inn's business customers also stay with the chain on private vacations.[29]

▼ 3M Post-It Sortable Cards are
sold to retail customers and in
business-to-business markets.

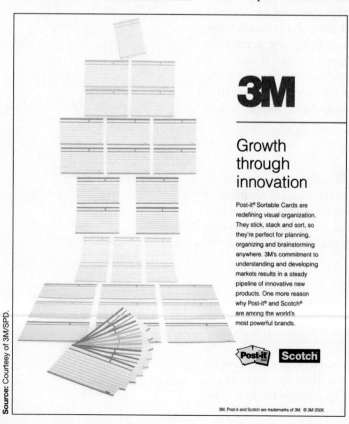

3M

Growth
through
innovation

Post-it® Sortable Cards are
redefining visual organization.
They stick, stack and sort, so
they're perfect for planning,
organizing and brainstorming
anywhere. 3M's commitment to
understanding and developing
markets results in a steady
pipeline of innovative new
products. One more reason
why Post-it® and Scotch®
are among the world's
most powerful brands.

Post-it   **Scotch**

3M, Post-it and Scotch are trademarks of 3M. © 3M 2006

Marketing Decisions

In dual channel marketing, a primary decision will be made about how to represent the product in each channel. The firm can either emphasize similarities between the two markets or focus on differences. Consumers and businesses looking for the same benefits and product features receive marketing messages that are quite similar. When consumers and business buyers value different product attributes or desire different benefits, the marketing strategy team customizes messages for the separate markets. When there are substantial differences between the two channels, the typical tactics are to:

- Use different communication messages
- Create different brands
- Use multiple channels or different channels

In some instances, the product attributes are the same, but the value or benefit of each attribute differs. Messages then focus on the benefits each segment derives from the product. Mobile phones marketed to businesses stress area coverage and service options. For consumers, mobile phone marketing messages may center on the fashionable design of the product, ease of use, or price.

To avoid confusing individuals who might see both messages from the same producer, companies may utilize dual branding. For instance, when Black & Decker launched a professional line of power tools, the DeWalt brand name was chosen. This avoided confusion with the Black & Decker name.

In most cases, business customers and consumers seek the same basic benefits from products. In these situations, a single approach for both markets will be used. Tactics include:

- Integrating communications messages
- Selling the same brand in both markets
- Scanning both markets for dual marketing opportunities

In addition to creating economies of scale, integrating consumer markets has another advantage: the potential to create synergies. Synergies arise from increased brand identity and equity. An image developed in the consumer market can then be used to enter a business market, or vice versa. Using one brand makes it easier to develop brand awareness and brand loyalty. A business customer who uses a company-owned American Express Card may obtain a card from the company for personal use.

Scanning both types of customers for new opportunities is part of dual channel marketing. For example, the firm Intuit, which sells Quicken software, discovered that individuals who use Quicken at home were willing to use a similar version for their small businesses. Capitalizing on this advantage, Quicken added features including payroll and inventory control to its business software package while maintaining the easy-to-use format. By identifying business use for a consumer product, Quicken adapted the product and captured 70 percent of the small-business accounting software market.[30]

Dual channel marketing can create a major competitive advantage as products are sold in both markets. A complete IMC planning process includes the evaluation of potential business market segments as well as consumer market segments. Firms that integrate messages across these markets take major steps toward reaching every potential customer.

INTERNATIONAL IMPLICATIONS

8 How can a company overcome international differences when adapting to buying processes?

Selling to consumers and businesses requires the marketing team to understand cultural differences related to products, messages, and selling techniques. A *cultural assimilator* will be a valuable member of the marketing team in international projects. Individual buyers and members of companies from other countries exhibit cultural differences as they consider purchasing alternatives.

It is helpful to understand the nuances of the purchasing process for transactions that take place in foreign countries. For example, at domestic U.S. trade shows it is unlikely that an actual purchase will be finalized. Instead, information is collected and transferred between the buyer and the seller. At international trade shows, however, sales are often completed. Higher-ranking members of the purchasing company attend the shows and want to complete transactions. Knowing these kinds of differences helps a company succeed in international trade.

Building a powerful brand is important in any IMC program. A strong brand means the product becomes part of the consumer's initial set of brands to consider when making a purchase. A powerful brand crosses national boundaries and becomes part of an effective GMIC program. Successful global brands are built over time. It takes a combination of high-quality products and effective marketing communications to reach that point.

In business-to-business marketing, a visible global brand presence is equally crucial. The existence of multiple vendors, increasing perceptions of brand parity, and growing use of the Internet make it impossible for a company to succeed using only price differentiation. To combat such situations, a strong brand is a necessity in the global environment. A strong brand increases the chances of being selected. As Robert Duboff writes, "It is no longer sufficient to be a great company; *you must be a great brand.*"[31]

! INTEGRATED CAMPAIGNS IN ACTION

● Argent Financial

Argent Financial Group provides comprehensive financial services and products to individuals, families, and friends. Argent is fast growing into a large corporation, but it still operated as a smaller organization. As a result, its marketing efforts were reactive rather than strategic and planned. Little coordination across subsidiaries and between offices took place.

The objective for the marketing agency, Emogen Marketing Group, was to define and promote a single brand that would increase Argent's brand recognition and value. After brainstorming with the client, Emogen suggested the following brand identity statement: "Argent is a wealth management firm comprised of highly qualified professionals helping clients manage, grow and protect assets."

Based on the brand identity statement, Emogen suggested that the new campaign stress: (1) high values, trust, and expertise; (2) relationships, not performance; and (3) that client satisfaction grows when using a single advisor. From these ideas came the new campaign tagline "Be informed, not sold."[32]

▲ The value proposition for the new Argent Campaign was "Be informed, not sold."

Your instructor has additional information about the ads, visuals, and displays used in this campaign.

 # SUMMARY

Buyer behaviors are part of the purchasing process in both consumer markets and business-to-business transactions. An effective IMC program accounts for the ways in which goods and services are purchased in both markets. The goal is to tailor marketing messages to target audiences in the appropriate media.

The consumer buying decision-making process consists of five steps. Marketing experts are aware of each step and prepare effective communications that lead most directly to the decision to buy. For the purposes of creating effective marketing communications, two of the most important are the information search stage and the evaluation of alternatives stage.

After recognizing a want or need, a consumer searches for information both internally and externally. Marketing messages attempt to place the product or service in the consumer's evoked set of viable prospects. The more involved the customer is in the search, the more likely the product will have a longer-lasting impact once purchased. Those with greater needs for cognition are attracted to the process of thinking through a decision. Those with a greater degree of enthusiasm for shopping spend more time analyzing the available alternatives. Customers consider the benefits and costs of searches and make decisions regarding how extensively they will seek information.

Evoked sets, attitudes and values, and cognitive maps explain how an individual evaluates various purchasing choices. Evoked sets reveal which products receive consideration. Attitudes and values predispose consumers toward some products and companies and away from others. Cognitive maps help the customer link thoughts about a company with other experiences. Marketing experts try to identify consumer attitudes and values that affect purchase decisions and make sure they do not offend prospects with messages. Stronger ties can be built with customers when the good or service is favorably attached to strongly held attitudes and values.

Marketers face an evolving buying decision-making environment. New cultural values and attitudes, time pressures, and busy lifestyles influence what people buy, how they buy, and the manner in which they can be enticed to buy. Many families try to isolate themselves from everyday pressures by cocooning. They also try to escape through indulgences and pleasure binges, by finding excitement or fantasy, and by planning to meet social needs. An aging baby boom population is more focused on lasting values and on health issues. Marketing experts can address these needs and lead customers to purchases based on them.

By understanding business buyer behaviors, the marketing team constructs a more complete and integrated marketing communications program. Business purchases are driven by members of the buying center. These members include users, buyers, influencers, deciders, and gatekeepers. Each role is important, even when a single person plays more than one role. Members of the buying center are human beings. This means they are influenced by both organizational and individual factors that affect various marketing decisions.

Business-to-business sales take three forms. A straight rebuy occurs when the firm has previously chosen a vendor and intends to place a reorder. A modified rebuy occurs when the purchasing group is willing to consider and evaluate new alternatives. This decision is usually based on dissatisfaction with a current vendor. A new task purchase is one in which the company buys a good or service for the first time and the product involved is one with which organizational members have no experience.

The business-to-business buying process is similar to the consumer purchase decision-making process. A more formal purchasing process includes formal specifications, bids from potential vendors, and a contract finalizing the purchasing agreement.

Dual channel marketing means that the firm sells virtually the same goods or services to both consumers and businesses. Dual channel marketing creates both economies of scale and synergies for the vendor company. It also enhances the chances that a product will be sold to every available customer. The challenge to the marketing team is to create strong and consistent marketing messages to every potential buyer, accounting for how buyer behaviors are present in purchasing processes.

KEY TERMS

involvement   The extent to which a stimulus or task is relevant to a consumer's existing needs, wants, or values.

need for cognition   A personality characteristic an individual displays when he or she engages in and enjoys mental activities.

enthusiasm for shopping   Customers who like to shop will undertake a more in-depth search for details about goods and services.

attitude   A mental position taken toward a topic, person, or event that influences the holder's feelings, perceptions, learning processes, and subsequent behaviors.

values   Strongly held beliefs about various topics or concepts.

cognitive maps   Simulations of the knowledge structures embedded in an individual's brain.

evoked set   Consists of the set of brands a consumer considers during the information search and evaluation processes.

inept set   Part of a memory set that consists of the brands that are held in a person's memory but that are *not considered,* because they elicit negative feelings.

inert set   Part of a memory set of brands that hold the brands that the consumer has awareness of but has neither negative nor positive feelings about.

affect referral   A purchasing decision model in which the consumer chooses the brand for which he or she has the strongest liking or feelings.

buying center   The group of individuals who make a purchase decision on behalf of a business.

straight rebuy   Occurs when the firm has previously chosen a vendor and intends to place a reorder.

modified rebuy   The company buying team considers and evaluates new purchasing alternatives.

new task   The company buys a good or service for the first time, and the product involved is one with which organizational members have no experience.

derived demand   Demand based on, linked to, or generated by the production and sale of some other good or service.

dual channel marketing   Selling virtually the same goods or services to both consumers and businesses.

compensatory heuristics   A purchasing decision model that assumes that no one single brand will score high on every desirable attribute and that individual attributes vary in terms of their importance to the consumer.

conjunctive heuristics   A purchasing decision model that establishes a minimum or threshold rating that brands must meet in order to be considered.

phased heuristics   A purchasing decision model that is a combination of the compensatory and conjunctive heuristics models.

REVIEW QUESTIONS

1. What are the five steps of the consumer buying decision-making process? Which two steps are the most important with regard to developing quality integrated marketing communications?

2. What is the difference between an internal search and an external search in a purchasing decision?

3. Define attitude. What are the three main components of attitude, and how are they related to purchasing decisions?

4. How do values differ from attitudes? Name some personal values related to purchasing decisions.

5. Explain what a cognitive map models.

6. What is an evoked set? Why are evoked sets, inept sets, and inert sets important to the marketing department?

7. What are the key features of the multiattribute approach to evaluating purchasing alternatives?

8. What is meant by affect referral? When is a person likely to rely on such a cognitive approach to evaluating purchasing alternatives?

9. What new trends in the consumer buying environment affect consumer purchasing decisions?

10. Name and describe the five roles played in a buying center.

11. What organizational and individual factors affect members of the business buying center?

12. Describe the three main forms of business-to-business sales.

13. Name the steps in the business-to-business buying process.

14. Describe dual channel marketing and explain why it is important to a company's well-being.

CRITICAL THINKING EXERCISES

Discussion Questions

1. For college students and other individuals with compulsive buying behaviors, a primary influence is the family. Often one or both parents are compulsive shoppers. Families that display other forms of dysfunctional behaviors, such as alcoholism, bulimia, extreme nervousness, or depression, tend to produce children who are more inclined to exhibit compulsive shopping behaviors. Why do dysfunctional behaviors among parents produce compulsive shopping behavior among children? Another component of compulsive buying behaviors is self-esteem. Again, self-esteem is partly inherited, but it also develops in the home environment. How would self-esteem be related to compulsive shopping behaviors? What influences other than family might contribute to compulsive shopping behaviors? If an individual has a tendency to be a compulsive shopper, what can (or should) be done?

2. Think about the way you purchase products and consider a recent purchase that involved an external search. Discuss your ability to search, the need for cognition, your personal level of shopping enthusiasm, and the perceived costs versus the perceived benefit of the search. How much time did you spend in the external search, and what was the outcome?

3. Study the list of personal values presented in Figure 3.3. Identify the five most important to you. Rank them from first to last. Beside each value, identify at least two products you have purchased to satisfy those values. Then,

gather into small groups of three to five students. Using the information from your list of values, discuss differences among members of the group. Identify a way to send a marketing message that will appeal to the top value from each person's list.

4. Cultural values and norms are constantly changing. Talk to your parents, grandparents, and friends and identify cultural values and norms that you believe have changed in the last 10 years. Are the values and norms you hold different from those held by your parents and grandparents? If so, why? What caused these changes to occur?

5. Review the three methods of evaluating alternatives. For each method, discuss a recent purchase you made using that method. Which method did you tend to use the most? Why?

6. A member of the buying center for a large shoe manufacturer tries to purchase soles for shoes from an outside vendor (or vendors). Study the individual and organizational factors that affect buying center members. Discuss the effect of each factor on the roles of members in the shoe company's buying center. How does the factory foreman's role differ from that of the purchasing agent? How do these roles differ from the company president's role?

7. A purchasing agent for a clothing manufacturer is in the process of selecting a vendor (or vendors) to supply the materials to produce about 30 percent of its clothes. The clothing manufacturer employs about 300 people. As the audit nears completion, what factors are most important to the purchasing agent?

INTEGRATED LEARNING EXERCISES

1. Consumers and businesses conduct external searches when they lack sufficient internal knowledge to make a wise decision. Assume you have $50,000 to $70,000 to spend on a sailboat. Locate four Web sites that sell sailboats. Select one in your price range. Why did you select that particular brand? What features are attractive to you? Would you want any additional information before making a final purchase decision?

2. Almost everyone has an opinion about tattoos. Some attitudes are positive, whereas others are negative. Few are neutral. Go to www.tattoos.com and examine the material that is on the Web site. Did this information modify your

attitude toward tattoos? What factors on the Web site influenced your attitude? Find at least one additional Web site of a company that offers tattoos. Discuss the components of the Web site in terms of which components of attitude it is trying to influence: cognitive, affective, or conative.

3. United Raw Material Solutions, Inc. is a business-to-business marketplace that brings together buyers and sellers of textiles, petrochemicals, plastics, and electronics. Access the Web site at www.urms.com. Which members of the buying center would be most interested in this site? What services and benefits do you see for buyers? For suppliers?

4. Examine the following Web sites. What kind of information is provided? Which component of attitude is the site designed to affect: cognitive, affective, or conative?

   a. Kenneth Cole (**www.kennethcole.com**)

   b. Starbucks (**www.starbucks.com**)

   c. Cadillac (**www.cadillac.com**)

   d. IKEA (**www.ikea.com**)

   e. Baby Gap (**www.babygap.com**)

5. A member of the buying center has been asked to gather information about possible shipping companies for international shipments. Visit the following Web sites. What companies have the most appealing Web sites? Beyond online materials, what additional information do they need to supply to the buying center in order to win the contract?

   a. ABC India Limited (**www.abcindia.com**)

   b. SR International Logistics, Inc. (**www.srinternational.com**)

   c. Falcon Transportation & Forwarding Corp. (**www.falcontrans.com**)

   d. Global Freight Systems (**www.globalfreightsystems.com**)

STUDENT PROJECT

Creative Corner

A local travel agency has decided to advertise in the student newspaper on your campus to promote spring break packages. They have hired you to perform the creative work. They are not sure which type of advertising approach to use. The agency knows that attitude consists of three parts: cognitive, affective, and conative. They also know that an advertisement can appeal to any one of the attitude components. The agency's management team is not sure which component to use. Consequently, they have asked you to design three advertisements, with one designed to appeal to the cognitive component of attitude, the second to the affective component, and the third to the conative component. After you have finished designing the ads, discuss the pros and cons of each and make a recommendation to the travel agency about which one to use. The ads should be for a 5-day spring break vacation on the beach in Fort Lauderdale, Florida.

CASE 1 CHOOSING A PHONE COMPANY: OPTIONS AND ALTERNATIVES

The past two decades have witnessed a dramatic shift in the ways people can talk on the phone. Landline phones, while still in common use, are being challenged by new and different technologies. AT&T, a major landline provider, has expanded to compete in areas such as mobile phones, texting, and Internet access using handheld devices.

Also, a new type of telephone technology has emerged, Voice over Internet Protocol (VoIP). This new technology allows a customer to make voice calls using a broadband Internet connection instead of a regular (analog) phone line.

Some VoIP services allow users to make calls to people who use the same service. Others allow users to call anyone who has a telephone number, including local, long-distance, mobile phone, and international numbers. Some VoIP services only work over a computer or a special VoIP phone. Others can be used with a traditional phone connected to a VoIP adapter. In addition, wireless "hot spots" in locations such as airports, parks, and cafes allow callers to connect to the Internet and use VoIP service wirelessly.

A customer owning a special VoIP phone or a regular telephone connected to a VoIP adapter will have a phone that rings like a traditional telephone. If the person's VoIP service requires him to make calls using a computer, the software supplied by the service provider alerts the user when he has an incoming call.

VoIP services do have some disadvantages. First, some VoIP services do not work during power outages unless the service provider offers backup power. Second, not all VoIP services connect directly to emergency services through 911. Third, VoIP providers may not offer directory assistance or white page listings.

The two major VoIP providers are Skype and Vonage. Skype allows customers to make calls to other Skype members free of charge. The service includes free text messaging and video calls as well. Skype offers low rates for calls of other

types. A customer can use Skype on a computer or on a mobile device. Skype works on a wide range of mobile phones, as well as on devices such as PlayStation Portable. Instant messages can be directed at individuals or group chat rooms. Skype users can also make conference calls. Skype offers customers pay-as-you-go or monthly payment options. No special equipment purchase is required in order to use Skype.

Vonage emphasizes that it provides lower-cost options when compared to AT&T. The company features international calling at greatly reduced rate. Vonage does require users to install special hardware. After signing up for an account, Vonage ships an adapter or other equipment to the customer, who must then install it and set it up. Complete instructions are provided, and setup is relatively simple. Vonage service can be purchased at Best Buy, Wal-Mart, and Target. The systems offer unlimited local and long-distance calling, call waiting, call forwarding, automatic redial, and voice mail for a single monthly fee.

Kelli is evaluating the two VoIP services and two mobile phone services. Table 3.2 provides the multiattribute evaluation approach she has developed. She is considering the attributes of sound quality, special services available, access to mobile devices, and difficulty in set up. Each attribute receives a score on a scale of 1 to 10 in terms of importance to Kelli, with 10 being the most important and 1 the least important. The four companies are then evaluated with a 10-point scale for each attribute, with 10 indicating the highest performance.

Using a **compensatory heuristics** method, Kelli assumes that no one single brand scores high on every attribute and that individual attributes vary in importance. With this model, Kelli will purchase the brand with the highest compensatory score, which is calculated by multiplying each attribute score by its importance, and then summing the total, as shown at the bottom of Table 3.2.

Using the **conjunctive heuristics** method, a threshold or minimum rating is established. A brand is eliminated if an important attribute is rated lower than a certain number. For example, Kelli has rated "sound quality" as very important (rating of 10). She may decide any service with a rating lower than 8 will be eliminated. In her situation, Skype would be eliminated because it scored only a 5. This process is followed until one brand is left.

The **phased heuristic** approach combines the two methods. Any brand with a low score on any criterion is eliminated first. Then, if a tie exists, the conjunctive heuristics method is used to decide between the two remaining contenders.

Consumers make purchase decisions using one of these methods, or some other approach. Each competitor seeks to highlight the advantages of its approach in order to maintain current customers and attract new ones.

1. Use Table 3.2 to explain the purchase decision Kelli will make using the following methods: (a) conjunctive heuristics, (2) compensatory heuristics, and (3) phased heuristics. Elaborate on which brand is chosen and which brands are not and explain why.

2. Create a similar table for two of the following products that you have recently purchased. Explain which method of evaluation could be used for each purchase decision.

   a. An automobile
   b. A dinner at a high-end restaurant
   c. A life insurance policy
   d. A new pair of jeans

Source: Thinkstock Royalty Free.

▲ VoIP services can work with just a computer, or with traditional phones.

TABLE 3.2 Example of a Multiattribute Evaluation Approach for a Phone Service

Attribute	Importance	AT&T	Vonage	Skype	Verizon
Sound quality	10	10	8	5	8
Special services	9	6	9	8	9
Mobile device access	8	8	8	5	6
Setup difficulty	6	7	5	2	8
Phone style	5	8	4	9	4
Compensatory score		300	275	219	277

3. How would the multiattribute model be expanded to include paging services?

4. If a customer bases a purchase on affect referral rather than a multiattribute method for mobile phone service, which of the companies may have an advantage? Why?

Sources: HowStuffWorks, "Skype vs. Vonage" (**http://electronics. howstuffworks.com/skype-vonage2.htm**, accessed November 24, 2009); Skype (**www.skype.com/intl/en/getconnected/**, accessed November 24, 2009); FCC, "Voice-Over-Internet Protocol" (**www.fcc. gov/voip/**, accessed November 24, 2009); Vonage (**www.vonage. com/how_ vonage_works/?refer_id=WEBHO0706010001W&lid=main_nav_how_ works**, accessed November 24, 2009).

CASE 2

CLEARING THE AIR

Most people want to live in a clean environment. Marketing cleaning products involves tactics ranging from rationality and logic to emotions and instincts. Some companies use the simplest possible terms, as basic as calling bacteria "germs." Advertisers use cartoons and simple diagrams to show how the product kills bad germs and makes things "sparkle." At the other extreme are the more complex and scientific explanations regarding a product's cleaning ability.

In this context, the market for air purifiers has grown and developed in the past decade. Smaller items, such as air freshener sprays and plug-ins made by brands such as Glade, have been available for many years. Now, newer technologies, such as HEPA hypo-allergenic filtration, are available.

The Sharper Image has been a leader in the marketing of new air cleaning technologies. The company's basic product and brand, the Ionic Breeze, has been sold through retail stores and Web sites and via infomercials and inbound telemarketing for many years.

One primary feature of all the Ionic Breeze products is silent operation. The Silent Electronic Propulsion technology made the original product the number-one air-cleaner brand in America. Through this silent air circulation technology, the company promises effective removal of airborne contaminants, reduction of common household odors, no filters to replace, low energy costs, an attractive design, ease of operation, and low maintenance.

Variations on the base model now include advancements such as the Germicidal version; the QUADRA; a smaller, plug-in bathroom version; and the new MIDI, which is smaller than earlier products. Other features associated with the Ionic Breeze are its OzoneGuard with PremAir catalyst, developed by BASF Catalysts LLC, which converts the byproduct ozone to oxygen.

Not surprisingly, competition has emerged. One of the new major players is Oreck, a company that gained fame and brand strength through its line of vacuums, which are lightweight, but powerful, carpet cleaners. A logical brand extension would be into air filtration.

Oreck promotes products that kill viruses, bacteria, mold, and fungi. One major difference is that the Oreck model moves the air. In advertisements and promotional materials, the air clearers are demonstrated as being superior because of this feature. Product materials strongly emphasize the health benefits of cleaner air. Oreck air cleaners are also featured in infomercials, on Web sites, and through standard television advertising.

Both Oreck and Sharper Image note that the air inside a house often is much more polluted than the air outside. Consumers are warned that asthma, allergies, and respiratory illnesses are on the rise. Air cleaners are offered to help.

Now, many lower-priced air cleaners are also available through retailers such as Wal-Mart and Target. Consequently, consumers have a vast array of potential prices, product features, and promotional claims to consider when choosing an air cleaning product. The future of the air cleaning business appears to be either bright or cloudy, depending on one's perspective, and consumers will undoubtedly see the number of options for methods to clear the air continue to rise.

1. How would a consumer's level of involvement, need for cognition, and level of shopping enthusiasm affect the purchase of an air filtration product?

2. Explain how cognitive mapping could be used to demonstrate a consumer's reaction to either the Ionic Breeze or the Oreck Air Cleaner.

3. Which model best explains the evaluation of alternatives when it comes to air filtration products: the evoked set model, the multiattribute approach, or affect referral?

4. Should air cleaner companies focus on fear, health, or other emotions to sell products? Explain.

Sources: Case based on information available at **www.oreck.com** and **www.sharperimage.com**.

4 The IMC Planning Process

PETSMART

It's a Dog's Life (Which Ain't Half Bad)

Not so many years ago, pets kept in homes and on farms were there to serve a purpose, which typically was either to provide companionship or to serve as protective watchdogs. It wasn't unusual for a dog to sleep outdoors (no matter what the weather), to dine on the scraps that fell from the table at night, and to endure the aches and pains that accompany the aging process in silence, or with the occasional moan.

Today, the world of pet ownership consists of an entirely new form of "parent." No longer is a dog, cat, fish, potbellied pig, or snake just a diversion—the critter is considered part of the family. The pet industry has grown from simple dog and cat food, plus a few toys along the way, to a $41 billion industry. Companies vending products to pet owners have shifted with the times.

PetSmart serves as a classic example of a company prospering in this new environment of animal indulgence. In 1986, founders Jim and Janice Dougherty secured a venture capital loan from the Phillips Van Heusen Corporation and incorporated as Pacific Coast Distributing, Inc. The primary company business, a pet owner superstore, was vending food and other basic pet supplies. As time passed, the scope of company operations grew dramatically.

By 1988, PetSmart sold pet sweaters and emphasized cutting down on pet overpopulation. Soon after, fish and birds were added to the original line of pets for sale and the company launched a new doggie salon. The era of extravagance had begun. It wasn't long until the company's original tagline, "Where high prices have been housebroken," was outdated. The most dramatic change introduced, a new corporate vision statement, appeared in 2000. PetSmart now operates, "To provide Total Lifetime Care for every pet, every parent, every time—which means that we offer solutions, superior products, unmatched services and superb customer service."

Why the change? The market continues to evolve along with the types of pet owners in the marketplace.

CHAPTER OBJECTIVES

After reading this chapter, you should be able to answer the following questions:

1 How can the three Cs of the IMC planning context form the basis for an effective advertising program?

2 What categories are used to identify consumer target markets or market segments?

3 What categories are used to identify business-to-business market segments?

4 How do the various approaches to positioning influence the selection of target markets?

5 How do the marketing communications objectives interact with the other elements of an IMC planning process?

6 What are the relationships between communications expenditures and company sales?

7 What types of marketing communications budgets may be used when developing the IMC planning program?

8 In addition to advertising, what other IMC components are selected as part of the IMC planning process?

Pets now enjoy a new type of status, often with different types of owners, including empty nesters, single professionals, and couples who have decided to delay starting a family consisting of actual children. Many of these new, more passionate pet lovers have a great deal of income to spend on their "babies." American families spend more annually on buying, feeding, and caring for pets than they do on movies, video games, and recorded music in any form.

The range of pet-related goods and services continues to expand. The list of items available in store and online includes indoor potties, pet perfumes, trench coats for dogs, and even a patented testicular implant for dogs that have been neutered, so as to not hurt the animal's self-esteem following the surgery.

Pet psychology opens up an entirely new realm. Many find relief from the troubles and woes of a dog's life through psychotherapy and animal anti-depressants. More shallow pets can rely on cosmetic procedures to keep up their self-image. Harley-Davidson branded products are available for bikers who want their pets to live on the edge.

PetSmart's competitors take animal pampering to the extreme. Doggie spas offer pedicures, professional dog walkers provide exercise, and massage therapy is available for those aching doggie muscles. Generic dog food is no longer the norm. The market is filled with specialty foods that clearly show the vegetables and other healthy nutrients in the product. At the other end of the spectrum, entire companies have formed to take care of end-products, including service agencies named Doody Duty, Scoopy-Poo, and Pooper Trooper.

In the more traditional vein, PetSmart offers vet clinics for ailing animals and adoption centers to find homes for pets (over 200,000 are placed each year). The company also sponsors charities associated with animal well-being. Today's owner wants an animal to have an excellent quality of life, from beginning to end. The net result is services oriented to ailing and dying pets along with their grieving parents.

PetSmart continues to adjust to changing conditions. The company features a strong emphasis on brand recognition and has adjusted selling techniques to meet the needs of various product lines. New signage was created in 2004. The company also opened distribution centers to make product delivery to each store more efficient.

In 2005, PetSmart began opening a series of pet hotels. Fifty hotels have been built, with an eventual goal of 435 hotels across the United States. Now a traveling pet owner has new options available, which means less guilt about leaving a pet behind.

In general, there has been a major shift in the marketplace. Pets are treated not in pet terms, but rather in human terms. This means that the number of marketing opportunities continues to increase and the nature of the competition continues to grow as the animal kingdom becomes more human-like each year. PetSmart vows to identify each new trend and respond accordingly, keeping pace in the dog-eat-dog world of animal comfort.[1]

OVERVIEW

The integrated marketing communications planning process requires careful and diligent analysis by the company's marketing personnel and any agencies the firm employs. Decisions are made with regard to matching products to marketing messages and communications tactics. Successful marketing efforts occur when the company's marketing team identifies every opportunity to make quality contacts with customers or potential customers.

This chapter describes the nature of the IMC planning process. As illustrated in Figure 4.1, it begins with an analysis of the company's context, including a review of customers, competitors, and communications. This allows the marketing team to identify potential target markets and positioning strategies that match those markets. Next, communications objectives are specified. Finally, a budget designed to achieve the communication objectives is matched with the IMC components to be employed. In addition, any international considerations are taken into account.

THE IMC PLANNING CONTEXT

1 How can the three Cs of the IMC planning context form the basis for an effective advertising program?

Developing an integrated marketing communications plan requires the analysis of the three Cs: customers, competitors, and communications. Understanding the firm's current situation and context within the industry makes it possible to specify target markets and positioning strategies. The other steps of the planning process can then be completed.

Customers

Every product or service meets the needs of a set of customers. When conducting an analysis of customers for the purposes of IMC planning, the marketing department examines:

- Current customers
- Former customers
- Potential new customers
- Competitors' customers

Current Customers

The easiest group to study will be current customers; however, the other three groups are equally, if not more, important. Members of the other groups may think in other ways or make decisions differently from a firm's current customers. They might also use other standards to evaluate products and advertisements.

FIGURE 4.1 ▶
The IMC Planning Process

An analysis of current customers helps identify the type of message that will effectively reach this group. Discovering how current customers think constitutes the first step. This includes an assessment of what they buy, why, when, where, and how they evaluate products, both while making purchases and upon completion of those purchases. In essence, the marketing team finds out what works for this group. The consumer and business buying behavior processes presented in the previous chapter may serve as a guide.

▲ For MTA, it is important to determine the most viable potential customers for STI Mud Trax tires.

Former Customers

Marketers also seek out customers who no longer purchase the company's products. Understanding why they defected may reveal important information, including whether a competitor's product enticed them away or if it was marketing tactics such as advertising, consumer promotions, or personal selling that made the difference. Then, the marketing team can identify methods to reconnect with former customers.

Potential New Customers

When seeking out potential new customers, the marketing team determines which customers the firm should seek to win. They may form a new target market or target markets. Not everyone is a viable prospect. The advertisement for STI Mud Trax Tires by MTA shown in this section was based on the observation that the individuals who are most likely to purchase the company's products consist of those who enjoy riding all-terrain vehicles (ATVs). The advertising department creates messages and utilizes media that matches this group's interests and preferences.

Competitor's Customers

The final group to study will be the competition's customers. An analysis of the processes that lead members of this group to choose the competition's offering assists the marketing team in modifying the company's approach and/or its products to better meet their needs. Alternatively, the company may conclude that members of this group cannot be persuaded to switch or are not attractive because of purchase patterns or other factors. To convince them to switch may be too costly, especially when they are brand-loyal customers.

Competitors

The second phase of an analysis of the company's context is examining competitors. The company's marketing professionals study the methods and strategies competitors employ to interact with consumers. Consumers integrate information from many sources. It helps to know what potential customers see, hear, and read about the competition.

Every domestic and foreign competitor should be identified. After listing the competing firms, an analysis can be conducted using *primary research*. In retailing, this includes visiting competing stores to study merchandise displays and observing the store's employees as they interact with customers. Members of the marketing department also talk to vendors and suppliers that have relationships with the competition, as well as wholesalers, distributors, and agents. For businesses other than retail, marketers can contact salespeople in the field to obtain additional information about the competition.

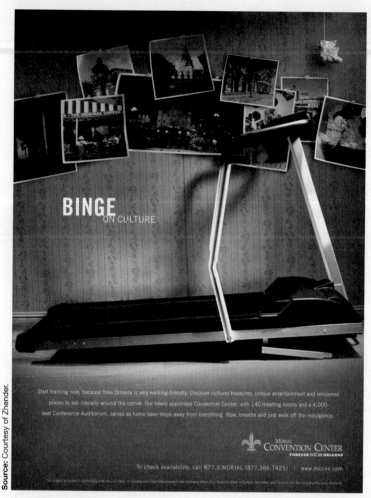

BINGE
ON CULTURE

Start training now, because New Orleans is very walking-friendly. Discover cultural treasures, unique entertainment and renowned places to eat—literally around the corner. Our newly appointed Convention Center, with 140 meeting rooms and a 4,000 seat Conference Auditorium, serves as home-base steps away from everything. Now, breathe and just walk off the indulgence.

MORIAL
CONVENTION CENTER
FOREVER NEW ORLEANS

To check availability, call 877.3.MORIAL (877.366.7425) | www.mccno.com

▲ Intense competition for convention and meeting sites makes a competitive analysis important for the Morial Convention Center of New Orleans.

▼ This advertisement for Ouachita Independent Bank was developed after an analysis of customers, competition, and communications revealed that trust is an important element in choosing a financial institution.

It's nice to trust my bank.

OIB
OUACHITA INDEPENDENT BANK

OIBank.com

Can you trust yours?

Balance. Timing. When you're on your path, you have to trust your instincts.
It's also nice to have a bank you can trust. A partner that guides you to sound financial decisions that help you in the long run... Local People, Local Trust.

FDIC

Next, the competitive analysis includes gathering *secondary data* about those companies. The first items to look at are statements competitors make about themselves. These can be found in:

- Advertisements
- Promotional materials
- Annual reports
- Web sites

By collecting as much information as possible about competitors, including messages to customers, the marketing team can respond more effectively.

The third task is to study what *other people* say about the competition. Marketers often read trade journals. The library might yield additional news articles and press releases about competitor activities. The marketing team also tries to discern how competing companies view the organizations. This provides a sense of how the company is viewed in comparison with its competition.

An analysis of the competition assists the marketing manager in understanding the company and product's situation relative to the competition. When the situation appears to be viable, the company can build on this strength. When the company is incorrectly perceived or is at a disadvantage, marketing efforts are made to reposition the product or brand.

Communications

The third component of an analysis of the company's context is an examination of communications. This includes the firm's current communications, at all levels and in all channels. Messages to current and potential customers, employees, and channel members are studied in order to find out what is working and what is not.

A further examination will be made focusing on the communications used in the industry and by competing firms. This provides an important backdrop when making decisions about the IMC components.

A communications analysis provides information that assists marketing personnel and advertising creatives in developing marketing messages and selecting the best IMC components. Marketing communications materials, including advertisements, Web blogs, sponsorships, and others are designed to integrate what is known about the firm's customers, target markets, competitors, and the product's position. Each IMC component should send a consistent message.

TARGET MARKETS

When an analysis of the company's context has been completed, the marketing group moves on to delineate the target markets to be served as well as the company's approach to product positioning. As shown in Figure 4.1, these two activities take place concurrently. In this chapter, target markets and market segmentation approaches are described first, followed by product-positioning issues.

Target markets exist in two areas: consumer markets and business-to-business markets, which may be termed market segments. A **market segment** is a set of businesses or group of individual consumers with distinct characteristics. For a market segment to be considered viable, it should pass the following tests:

- The individuals or businesses within the market segment should be similar in nature, having the same needs, attitudes, interests, and opinions. This means that persons or businesses within the segment are *homogenous.*
- The market segment differs from the population as a whole. Segments are distinct from other segments and from the general population.
- The market segment must be large enough to be financially viable to target with a separate marketing campaign.
- The market segment must be reachable through some type of media or marketing communications method.

Market researchers spend considerable resources and time working to discover viable market segments. This process, known as **market segmentation**, consists of identifying specific groups based on their needs, attitudes, and interests. The following sections describe market segmentation approaches for consumers and other businesses.

② What categories are used to identify consumer target markets or market segments?

MARKET SEGMENTATION BY CONSUMER GROUPS

Consumers, or end users, are often the primary target market for a firm's offerings. Effective IMC programs identify sets of consumers who are potential buyers. The most common consumer market segmentation approaches are listed in Figure 4.2.

Segments Based on Demographics

One primary method of segmentation employs **demographics**, or population characteristics. Typical demographic variables include gender, age, education, income, and ethnicity. Companies create goods and services to meet the needs of individual demographic segments.

Gender

Men and women purchase different products, buy similar products with different features (e.g., deodorants), desire products for dissimilar reasons (stereos, televisions), and buy the same products after being influenced by different kinds of appeals through different media. A recent study suggested that women control 66 percent, or $12 trillion, of the world's annual consumer spending. Women now influence or make purchases in product categories that were traditionally controlled by men.[2] For instance, in the United States:

- 96 percent of women are involved in purchasing high-priced electronics.
- 90 percent of women deal with financial advisors.
- 80 percent of women buy and sell stocks to make money.
- 70 percent of women are their household's primary "accountant."

Figure 4.3 offers suggestions for marketing to women. Some companies that have done well include Olay, Paige Premium, and OfficeMax. Olay advertises skin care products for all women and tells women that the company wants to help them enjoy beautiful

- Demographics
- Psychographics
- Generations
- Geographic
- Geodemographics
- Benefits
- Usage

◄ **FIGURE 4.2**
Methods of Segmenting Consumer Markets

FIGURE 4.3 ▶

Tips for Marketing to Women

- Be helpful. Focus messages on how the brand can improve a woman's life.
- Engage them. Women are excellent brand ambassadors, so involve them with the brand.
- Focus on practical, not trivial.
- Tell a story that will resonate with females.
- Provide details.
- Be positive. Don't focus on female insecurities, focus on how the brand will help women.

Source: Adapted from Nancy Pekala, "Marketing to Today's Women: Focus on Life Stages, Not Ages," *Marketing Matters Newsletter*, American Marketing Association, November 11, 2009.

skin. Paige Premium encourages women to love their bodies and places a card in each pair of denim jeans that reads "I want you to love your body. Feel comfortable in your skin. Feel comfortable in your jeans. Thanks for believing in our product." OfficeMax has created a fashion brand of office products targeted specifically at women.[3]

Women constitute a major market for unique getaways. Some travel agencies market specific travel opportunities for women. A recent survey by AAA revealed that nearly one-fourth of women in the United States have taken a getaway trip with one or more other women in the past 3 years. Further, 39 percent plan on going on a girls-only getaway in the future.[4] Some of the unique female getaway packages being offered by travel agencies include:

- A 3-day art safari at Carmel-by-the-Sea in California
- A girls-only weeklong cruise to the Galapagos Islands featuring sightseeing for giant tortoises, kayaking, scuba diving, and nature tours
- A 4-day dog-sledding adventure in the north woods of Minnesota
- A 2-day surf 'n' turf excursion at Pismo Beach in California
- A 3-day cowgirl boot camp in California's wine country that includes riding, roping, and line dancing

▼ An advertisement for Bijan targeted to females.

Other marketing programs target men. Often male market segments are identified using both gender and age. The product Just for Men targets gray-haired, mature males. Many beer commercials focus on younger men. In contrast, hunting equipment is often marketed to a more general set of males.

Gender presents the opportunity to match a product with a large category of individuals. Careful thought should be given as to whether it should be aimed at only one sex, because gender roles have shifted over the past half-century.

Age

Marketing programs often target persons of a certain age, such as children, young adults, middle-age adults, and senior citizens. Age is often combined with another demographic, such as gender. Consequently, older women may be primary targets for specific types of vitamins and medical products, such as those that combat osteoporosis. Young working women with children are more likely to notice advertisements for conveniences, including ready-made foods and snacks and even quick oil and lube change facilities. Sexual dysfunction products and other medicines target middle-aged and older men.

A particularly attractive age group is children younger than 12, because they spend $30 billion annually in the United States and influence more than $500 billion in purchases.[5] Despite criticisms from parental and other watchdog groups, advertising to children remains big business and is important to many companies. Research indicates that by the age of 3 some children recognize brand logos. Soon thereafter, they start becoming brand conscious. If brand loyalty can be obtained at a young age, the company may have a customer for an entire lifetime.

Another age-based demographic group that appeals to many firms is *seniors,* defined as individuals older than age 55. Most marketers have abandoned treating seniors as a singular market and have stopped stereotyping them in commercials. Seniors are no longer viewed as being feeble, avid gardeners, or as only being able to enjoy a blissful retirement by walking on the beach holding hands. They are not a homogeneous group. The seniors segment consists of sets of smaller groups of individuals, each with different lifestyles, interests, and opinions.[6] The companies that have been successful with seniors understand and relate to them by highlighting the value these individuals place on friendships, communities, involvements with family, and new life interests.

▲ A BMW Motorcycle advertisement targeted toward men as the primary purchasers and women as the decision-making influencers.

▼ Children are an attractive segment of consumers because they influence more than $500 billion in purchases.

Education

A person's education affects many aspects of life, including how the individual shops and the goods and services that are purchased. For example, products associated with golf and tennis are often targeted at individuals who have attended college. Marketers often combine educational level with another demographic when identifying target markets, such as college-educated males.

Income

Closely related to educational attainment is an individual's or family's income. Lower-income homes focus primarily on *necessities,* such as food, clothing, and housing needs; however, members of these households also purchase cell phones, automobiles, and other, more costly products. As income increases, household members can purchase from a greater selection of expensive items. The products, which are also known as *sundry* items, include vacations, more expensive automobiles, more fashionable clothes, and meals at high-end restaurants. They are purchased occasionally by those who can afford them, but not on a routine basis. At the extreme, *luxury* items such as yachts and private planes target the wealthy.

The furniture industry uses income segmentation to create products and advertisements. One demographic group that has received attention recently is the "exhausted affluent." Individuals in this group generate household incomes from $100,000 to $150,000. They are affluent, but identify more with the working class. They bridge the gap between, "the haves and the have nots." In furniture, they desire style and quality, but not something overly fancy. Members of this segment want furniture to be right for them; that lets them stand out, but not so much that it says "I've been too extravagant and spent

▲ This Thomasville furniture advertisement appeals to the "exhausted affluent" and the desire for style and quality.

money foolishly."[7] In contrast, many furniture sellers focus on price, appealing to those of lower income, while a select group offers high end furniture to the wealthy.

Ethnic Groups

The United States is becoming increasingly diverse. Figure 4.4 reports the buying power of the various ethnic groups in the United States compared to the Caucasian population. The increase in the number of minorities and their buying power represents both an opportunity and a threat: an opportunity for companies able to adapt their messages to other cultures and heritages. It threatens those that do not. Successful ethnic marketing requires understanding various ethnic groups and writing marketing communications that speak to specific cultures and values.

In addition to the primary U.S. ethnic groups, a large number of immigrants are arriving from India and Pakistan. Other groups are coming from the Middle East and Eastern European countries. Each ethnic group contains multiple subgroups. For example, the Asian community includes individuals of Korean, Japanese, Filipino, Vietnamese, and Chinese descent. The Hispanic community consists of persons from Latin America, Mexico, Cuba, and Puerto Rico.

Although different in many ways, several common threads exist among ethnic groups. They tend to be more brand loyal than their Caucasian counterparts. They value quality and are willing to pay a higher price for it. They value relationships with companies and are loyal to those that make the effort to establish a connection with them.

To market effectively to ethnic groups, marketing experts look for creative approaches that respect America's ethnic differences while also highlighting its similarities. Achieving this requires advertising and marketing agencies that understand the subtleties of multiculturalism. Many firms have become involved in sponsorships of minority and ethnic events to help establish ties with specific ethnic groups.

Ethnic marketing is similar to global marketing. A company may present one overall message that is also tailored to fit the needs and values of various groups. Successfully achieving this integration of the overall message with characteristics of individual

FIGURE 4.4 ▶
U.S. Buying Power by Ethnicity, 2011

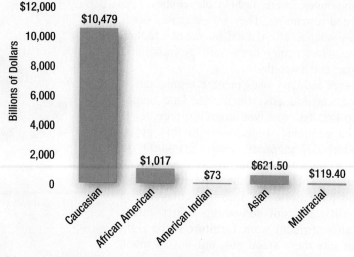

Source: Adapted from "U.S. Buying Power," *2007 Marketing Fact Book,* July 15, 2007, p. 30.

cultures should result in valuable gains in loyalty to a company and its brands and diversify the markets the company can effectively serve.

Psychographics

Demographics are relatively easy to identify. They do not, however, fully explain why people buy particular products or specific brands or the type of appeal that can be used to reach them. To assist in the marketing effort while building on demographic information, psychographic profiles have been developed. **Psychographics** emerge from patterns of responses that reveal a person's activities, interests, and opinions (AIO). AIO measures can be combined with demographic information to provide marketers with a more complete understanding of the market to be targeted.[8]

Strategic Business Insights provides a popular classification of lifestyles using psychographic segmentation. The VALS2 typology categorizes respondents into eight different groups based on resources and on the extent to which they are action-oriented.[9] The VALS2 typology includes the following segments:

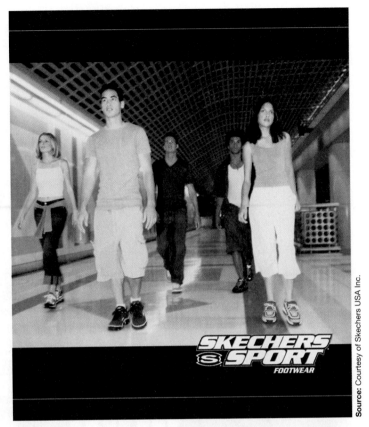

▲ This Skechers advertisement features a multiethnic approach.

- **Innovators**—Successful, sophisticated, and receptive to new technologies. Their purchases reflect cultivated tastes for upscale products.
- **Thinkers**—Educated, conservative, practical consumers who value knowledge and responsibility. They look for durability, functionality, and value.
- **Achievers**—Goal-oriented, conservative consumers committed to career and family. They favor established prestige products that demonstrate success to peers.
- **Experiencers**—Young, enthusiastic, and impulsive consumers who seek variety and excitement and spend substantially on fashion, entertainment, and socializing.
- **Believers**—Conservative, conventional consumers who focus on tradition, family, religion, and community. They prefer established brands and favor American-made products.
- **Strivers**—Trendy, fun-loving consumers who are concerned about others' opinions and approval. They demonstrate to peers their ability to buy.
- **Makers**—Self-sufficient consumers who have the skill and energy to carry out projects, respect authority, and are unimpressed by material possessions.
- **Survivors**—Concerned with safety and security, focus on meeting needs rather than fulfilling desires. They are brand loyal and purchase discounted products.

This type of information helps marketers design more effective communications. For instance, reaching Strivers requires advertisements that convey fun and trendy products. Ads for Believers should focus more on traditional and patriotic values.

A recent research project identified 11 key teenage markets based on demographic and psychographic characteristics. The largest male teen group, "Young Metrosexuals," focus on outward appearance and comprise 25 percent of all teenage men. Other male groups include "Big Man on Campus," "Technosapians," "Red-blooded Boys," "Tuned Inward," and "Under Construction." The largest female group is "Jockettes," which make up 25 percent of female teens. The Jockettes have active lifestyles and enjoy participating in sports. Other groups included "In-style Socialites," "Most Likely to Succeed," "Style Meets Thrift," and "Traditionalists." By adding psychographic information to the demographic data, a much richer understanding of the various teen groups emerges.[10]

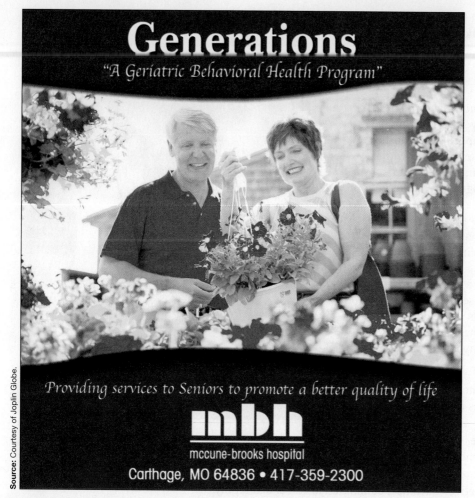

▲ An advertisement directed to seniors for the Geriatric Behavioral Health Program offered by McCune-Brooks Hospital.

Segments Based on Generations

Many marketing efforts target generational cohorts, because the approach does not require the use of psychographic information, but does possess some of the richness of psychographics. Marketing to generational cohorts relies on the common experiences and events that create bonds between people who are about the same age.

Generational segmentation proponents suggest that people experience significant events during late adolescence or early adulthood. These events create an impact on social values, attitudes, and preferences, based on shared experiences. This may lead to common preferences for music, foods, and other products. A cohort group may respond favorably to the same type of marketing appeal. Six generational cohorts are noted in Table 4.1, along with some basic characteristics.

Segmentation by Geographic Area

Marketing appeals can be made to people in a geographic area or region. Retailers often seek to limit marketing communications programs to specific areas. This helps a company conduct a campaign in a target region. The primary disadvantage of this approach may be that everyone in a geographic area receives the marketing communication, regardless of interest in the product or service. Geographic segmentation does not allow a firm to focus on a more specific target market containing only those most likely to make purchases.

TABLE 4.1 Characteristics of Generation Segments

Name of Segment	Year of Birth	Characteristics
Generation Y	1978–2002	Spend money on clothes, automobiles, college, televisions, and stereos. Ninety percent live at home or in a dorm or rent an apartment.
Generation X	1965–1977	Focus on family and children. Spend on food, housing, transportation, and personal services.
Younger boomers	1954–1964	Focus on home and family. Spend on home mortgage, pets, toys, playground equipment, and large recreational items.
Older boomers	1952–1953	Spend on upgrading homes, ensuring education and independence of their children, and luxury items, such as boats.
Seniors	Up to 1951	Most have fixed incomes. Spend heavily on health care and related medical items.

Source: Based on Dana-Nicoleta Lascu and Kenneth E. Clow, *Essentials of Marketing* (Cincinnati, OH: Atomic Dog Publishing, 2007).

Geodemographic Segmentation

A hybrid form of geographic segmentation allows companies to enrich geographic approaches to segmentation. This form of segmentation, called *geodemographics*, identifies potential customers using demographic information, geographic information, and psychographic information.

Geodemographic segmentation may be beneficial for national firms conducting direct-mail campaigns or using sampling promotions. Mailing a sample to every household in a geographic area can be expensive and unwise. Through geodemographics, samples are only sent to households matching the profile of the target market. For instance, colleges and universities use geodemographics to locate ZIP codes of communities that match particular student profiles.

One firm, PRIZM (Potential Rating Index by Zip Marketing) specializes in geodemographics. PRIZM has identified 62 different market segments in the United States. The company has categorized every U.S. ZIP code. The concept behind PRIZM is that ZIP codes represent neighborhoods containing people with relatively uniform characteristics. Consumers tend to be attracted to neighborhoods consisting of people similar to them. Recognizing that more than one market segment might live within a ZIP code, PRIZM identifies the top market segments within each ZIP code.[11]

A PRIZM-coded map of downtown Jackson, Mississippi, identifies two primary clusters. The more predominant is the "Southside City" residents. This cluster contains mainly young and elderly African Americans employed in low-paying blue-collar jobs. They tend to have lower levels of formal education, rent apartments, and read sports and fashion magazines. The second cluster within downtown Jackson holds the "Towns and Gowns" neighborhoods. Towns and Gowns inhabitants also rent apartments, but members tend to be college graduates with better-paying white-collar jobs. This group likes to ski, reads beauty and fitness magazines, and frequently uses ATM cards.[12]

Geodemographic marketing has been expanded to the Internet. The Adfinity program designed by Intelligent Interactions allows an advertiser to direct specific ads to Web users based on user-defined demographics. When users visit Web sites, they often provide their names and addresses along with other demographic information. While the user is surfing a site, Adfinity's software can access the user's file in order to place a targeted ad on the page. To extend its power and effectiveness, Adfinity formed a strategic alliance with PRIZM. When a user accesses a Web site, the user is matched with data from the 62 PRIZM clusters. Based on the lifestyle and interests of that cluster, messages are sent that match the user. A person from the cluster "Executive Suites" will see advertisements about jazz or business books, because people in this cluster tend to enjoy those items.

Benefit Segmentation

Benefit segmentation focuses on the advantages consumers receive from a product rather than the characteristics of consumers themselves. Demographic and psychographic information can be combined with benefit information to identify segments. Then, the marketing team can seek to further analyze each segment's consumers.

Benefit segmentation appears in the fitness market. Regular exercisers belong in one of three benefit segments. The first group, "Winners," do whatever it takes to stay physically fit. This segment tends to be younger, upwardly mobile, and career-oriented. The second group, "Dieters," exercise to maintain their weight and enhance physical appearance. This group tends to be females over the age of 35. They are primarily interested in reliable wellness programs offered by hospitals and weight-control nutritionists. The third group, "Self-Improvers," exercise to feel better and to control medical costs.[13] The understanding that individuals exercise for different reasons provides excellent material for designing marketing programs.

▼ The fitness industry is often segment based on the benefit each segment seeks from exercise.

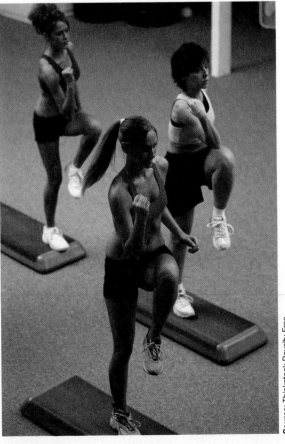

Source: Thinkstock Royalty Free.

Usage Segmentation

The final type of consumer segmentation examines groups based on usage or purchases, including the company's best customers, average users, and casual or light customers. The objective becomes to provide the highest level of service to the best customers while promoting the company to the other two groups in the attempt to maximize sales to all user groups.

Marketing teams can identify heavy users with internal databases. Bar-code scanners, point-of-sale systems, and data from credit, debit, and in-house transaction cards provide marketers a wealth of information about customers. Many companies experience a situation in which 10 to 30 percent of a company's customers generate 70 to 90 percent of total sales. Instead of using firms such as PRIZM to create customer clusters, firms develop customer clusters from in-house databases. Customers are then placed in clusters based on common attitudes, lifestyles, and past purchase behaviors. This technique offers a business the following advantages:[14]

1. A meaningful classification scheme to cluster customers based on a firm's actual customers.
2. The ability to reduce large volumes of customer data down to a few concise, usable clusters.
3. The ability to assign a cluster code number to each customer in the database. Each number is based on the customer's actual purchases and other characteristics (e.g., address, amount spent, demographics, etc.).
4. The capacity to measure the growth and migration of customers over time and from one cluster to another, which allows for the evaluation of marketing programs.
5. The ability to use a database to develop multiple clusters based on different benefits or usages.

Some businesses do not have such extensive databases. For these firms, other companies sell and provide consumer databases. These consumer databases can be linked to a customer's records through a name, address, or Social Security number. Typical information found in commercial databases includes household income, the ages of household members, the length and type of residence, information about car ownership, and telephone numbers.

3 What categories are used to identify business-to-business market segments?

BUSINESS-TO-BUSINESS MARKET SEGMENTATION

Another set of target markets may be found by identifying business-to-business market segments (see Figure 4.5). The primary goals of business segmentation efforts are to group similar organizations into meaningful clusters in order to provide better service.

Segmentation by Industry

When segmenting by industry, many marketers use the NAICS (North American Industry Classification System) coding system. NAICS allows the marketing team to examine specific industries, such as construction (23) or wholesale trade (42). There are also segments within specific categories. For example, NAICS codes health care and social assistance services as 62. A manufacturer of health-related products may find four segments, based on these subsections:

621	Ambulatory Health Care Services
622	Hospitals
623	Nursing and Residential Care Facilities
624	Social Assistance

- Industry (NAICS code)
- Size of business
- Geographic location
- Product usage
- Customer value

◀ **FIGURE 4.5**
Methods of Segmenting
Business-to-Business Markets

The segments can be broken down into smaller subcomponents. For example, Ambulatory Health Care Services includes physicians, dentists, chiropractors, and optometrists.

The NAICS system divides the economy into 20 broad sectors using a six-digit code. The six-digit code allows for stratification of industries and provides flexibility in creating classifications. The federal government records corporate information and data using the NAICS, making it a useful system for identifying market segments.

Segmentation by Size

Market segments can be identified based on a company's sales volume or number of employees. Large firms with 100,000 employees have needs that are different from smaller companies with 100 or fewer employees. Typically, for a large firm the marketing effort often focuses on the company's purchasing department. For smaller firms, the owner or general manager often makes the purchase decisions and becomes the target of marketing messages.

Segmentation by Geographic Location

Identifying market segments by geographic location can be a successful tactic. This approach benefits businesses with customers that are concentrated in geographic pockets, such as the Silicon Valley area of California. It works for other firms as well.

When the Applied Microbiology firm developed a new antimicrobial agent, the goal was to market the product to dairy farmers. The traditional agricultural marketing and distribution channel required for a national launch was estimated to be $3 million. Such a traditional marketing plan involved national advertising in agriculture magazines plus recruiting sales agents and brokers to introduce the product. Instead, Applied Microbiology used geodemographics. The marketing team identified areas with dairy herds consisting of 1,000 or more cows per ranch. These farmers were contacted for two reasons. First, large dairy farmers who adopted the product would purchase greater quantities. Second, the company's leaders believed that the larger farmers were the opinion leaders who could influence smaller farmers, thereby causing them to adopt the product as well.

Several separate direct-response pieces offering discounts for and samples of Applied Microbiology's new product were sent to larger farms. After sales started rising, farmers were asked for testimonials. The testimonials were extremely powerful, and they were then incorporated into new direct-marketing pieces. One brochure contained three testimonials and validation of the product by Cornell University. After a dairy farmer adopted the product, direct-marketing pieces were sent to farmers in the surrounding area. This method yielded excellent sales figures and reduced marketing costs to one-third of the traditional approach. Using geodemographics, marketing costs were $1 million rather than the proposed $3 million.[15]

▼ Service Metrics can use the NAICS codes to target this advertisement to specific industries.

Is your Web site moving **fast** enough

to **survive** the competition?

Find out before you're dead in the water. Service Metrics℠ measures your Web site from an end-user perspective, using detailed levels of performance metrics found nowhere else in the industry. Our reports show you how the speed of your servers, site design, vendors, and routing networks compare to your competitors'. This data helps you make improvements to keep your site at peak performance. We don't just help you compete, we give you an unfair advantage.

SERVICE METRICS
an Exodus Communications Company

The Best Measure of Performance™

Source: Courtesy of Service Metrics.

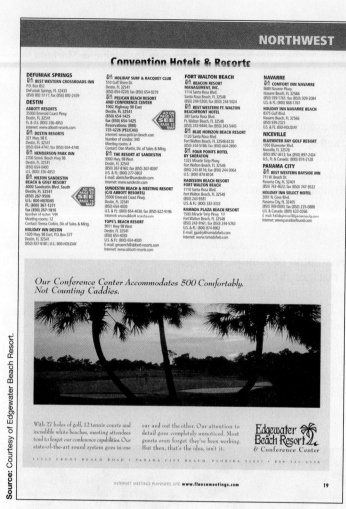

▲ An advertisement targeted to the large business conference segment.

Segmentation by Product Usage

Business markets can be segmented based on the manner in which the good or service is used. Many services (financial, transportation, shipping, etc.) have a variety of uses for distinct customers. For example, in the hotel industry a major source of revenue is booking business events and conferences. A hotel or resort can identify business market segments based on various types of events. Single-day seminars require only a meeting room and refreshments. A full conference may involve renting rooms for lodging, preparing banquets, furnishing meeting rooms, and planning sightseeing excursions. By segmenting the market based on the use of the hotel's facilities and staff, a manager can prepare marketing materials that address the needs of each specific type of conference. The advertisement for Edgewater Beach Resort shown in this section provides an example of this type of approach.

Segmentation by Customer Value

The final method of business segmentation is based on customer value. It is much easier for business-to-business firms to utilize this approach than for consumer-oriented businesses, due to the availability of in-depth data about each business customer. A more precise value can be assigned to each individual business through sales records and other sources of data and information, placing them into low-, medium-, and high-value groups.

In summary, consumer and business-to-business market segments can be identified many ways. In choosing market segments to approach, a marketer looks for groups that best match the company's goods and services, as well as the overall marketing message. Then the message can be structured to meet the needs of the various market segments and will be aligned with the company's positioning strategy.

4 How do the various approaches to positioning influence the selection of target markets?

PRODUCT POSITIONING

Each target market or market segment will be selected, in part, because the company, product, or brand position matches the segment. **Product positioning** is the perception in the consumer's mind of the nature of a company and its products relative to competitors. Positioning features variables such as the quality of products, the price, methods of distribution, packaging, image, and other factors. Typically, however, two elements stand out: (1) how the product is perceived by customers and (2) the product's standing relative to the competition.

Consumers ultimately determine the position a product holds. Marketing programs attempt to help position the product or brand effectively. Marketing communications either reinforce what consumers already believe about a product and the brand or try to shift consumer views about them. The first outcome is easier to accomplish. It also facilitates selection of target markets. When the attempt is made to reposition a product, consideration must be given as to whether the new position will continue to match existing market segments.

Positioning enables companies such as Procter & Gamble, VF Corporation, Sara Lee Corporation, and Campbell's Soups to prevent cannibalism among various brands within a product category. For instance, Campbell's produces five different types of V8 juice. Each one targets a slightly different market segment. Celestial Seasonings offers several types of tea. The advertisement shown in this section is for tea for health-conscious consumers.

Approaches to Positioning

Effective positioning can be achieved in seven different ways (see Figure 4.6). Although companies might try two or three approaches, such efforts generally only manage to confuse customers. The best method is to use one approach consistently.

Product Attributes

Any product trait or characteristic that sets it apart from other products may be considered an attribute. The Sony ad in this section is aimed at business customers. The advertisement promotes the attribute of quality, because the projector provides stronger light. The message also suggests that the featured attribute outperforms the competition.

Competitors

Using competitors to establish position can be accomplished by contrasting the company's product against others. For years, Avis ran advertisements comparing itself to Hertz. Avis admitted it was not number one, but turned that position into an advantage, because Avis was willing to "try harder" for business.

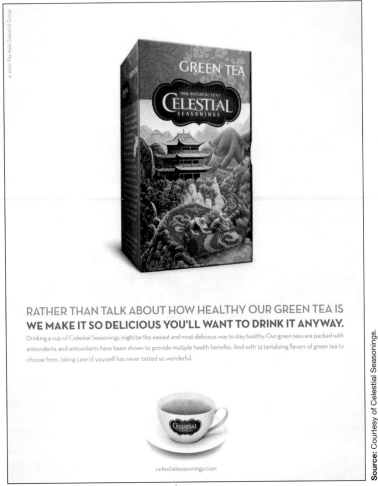

RATHER THAN TALK ABOUT HOW HEALTHY OUR GREEN TEA IS **WE MAKE IT SO DELICIOUS YOU'LL WANT TO DRINK IT ANYWAY.**

Drinking a cup of Celestial Seasonings might be the easiest and most delicious way to stay healthy. Our green teas are packed with antioxidants and antioxidants have been shown to provide multiple health benefits. And with 14 tantalizing flavors of green tea to choose from, taking care of yourself has never tasted so wonderful.

celestialseasonings.com

▲ To prevent cannibalism of its other teas, Celestial Seasonings positions each version for a different target market.

Use or Application

Positioning that involves creating a memorable set of uses for a product emphasizes the use or application approach. Arm & Hammer has long taken this approach by convincing consumers to use baking soda in other ways, such as a deodorizer in the refrigerator. Arm & Hammer is a co-brand in toothpaste, creating another use for the product and enhancing its position.

Price–Quality Relationship

Businesses that offer products at the extremes of the price range may position by price–quality relationships. At the high end, the emphasis will be on quality. At the low end, price is emphasized. Hallmark cards cost more but are for those who "only want to send the very best." Other firms seek to be a "low-price leader," with no corresponding statement about quality. Instead of focusing on low prices, Wal-Mart's tagline "Save Money, Live Better" highlights the importance of price and how it can improve the customer's quality of life.

- Attributes
- Competitors
- Use or application
- Price–quality relationship
- Product user
- Product class
- Cultural symbol

◀ **FIGURE 4.6**
Product Positioning Approaches

▲ A business-to-business advertisement positioned based on the projector's attributes.

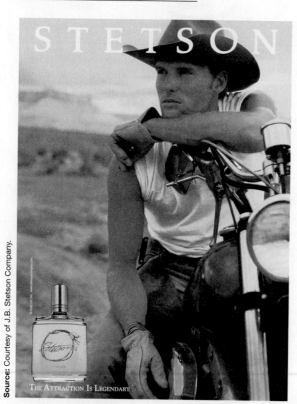

▲ An advertisement for Stetson using the cultural symbolism of cowboys as the positioning strategy.

Product User

Another positioning strategy distinguishes a brand or product by specifying who might use it. Apple Computers was originally positioned as the computer for educational institutions. The approach helped the company grow rapidly. Later, however, it was difficult to convince businesses to use Apple computers. Apple's marketing team effectively created the original position, which made it harder to change perceptions of the company.

Product Class

Position can be based on product class. In the beverage category, soft drinks compete with energy drinks and others, such as breakfast drinks. Red Bull has successfully moved into U.S. markets by uniquely positioning the product as different from soft drinks and other products. Competitors, including Full Throttle, are now trying to capture a larger portion of this market.

Cultural Symbol

Positioning a product as a cultural symbol is not easy. When the position is successfully achieved, the company holds a strong competitive advantage. For many years, Chevrolet enjoyed such a position. Chevrolet was advertised as being as American as baseball and apple pie. Later, ads portraying all of the songs written about driving a Chevrolet were designed to reinforce the message. In its advertisement shown in this section, Stetson cologne is tied to the American cowboy and the spirit of the West. The ad copy reads that "The attraction is legendary." The purpose of placing this ad in *Glamour* magazine was to entice women to purchase the product for the men in their lives.

Other Elements of Positioning

A brand's position is never completely fixed. It can be changed. In the previous decade, the Gillette brand that was traditionally firmly entrenched with men required repositioning. The company launched a massive advertising campaign aimed at women. New products, including the Sensor Excel razor and Satin Care Shave Gel, were offered by mail to consumer homes. Free samples were placed in homeroom bags for 14- and 15-year-old girls at school. Gillette's advertisements encouraged women to view the products as a key part of being physically and psychologically ready for anything. The ad copy asked "Are you ready?" and answered "Yes, I am!" This positioning matched Gillette's products for men, which were marketed using the "Best a man can get" tag line.[16]

Brand positioning applies to business-to-business marketing efforts. InterContinental Hotels Group, which owns InterContinental, Crowne Plaza, Holiday Inn, Holiday Inn Express, Staybridge Suites, and Candlewood Suites, understands the needs of business travelers and offers unique services that add value to the businessperson's stay. High-speed Internet access is available at all of the properties. At Crowne Plaza, wireless connections are available at any location on the property. Knowing that time and convenience are important to business travelers, InterContinental Hotels offers an online wireless reservation system that allows business guests to review, cancel, or modify reservations online. To ensure that business guests get a good night's sleep, Crowne Plaza offers a guaranteed wake-up call, quiet floors, sleep amenities, sleep CDs, and relaxation tips.[17] These features all emphasize the attribute and product user–based positions associated with offering all of the conveniences and services a businessperson desires.

International Positioning

In the international arena, effective positioning remains vitally important. Plans are made to establish an effective position when a firm expands into new countries. Often the positioning strategy present in one country will not work in another. Marketing experts carefully analyze the competition as well as the consumers or businesses that are potential customers. After this analysis, the marketing team chooses a positioning approach. Although the positioning strategy might need to be modified for each country, the company's overall theme and the brand image should remain as consistent as is possible.

Image and Brand

Positioning is a critical part of image and brand-name management. Consumers have an extensive set of purchasing options and can try products with specific advantages or attributes. Effective positioning, by whatever method chosen, should increase sales and strengthen the long-term position of an individual product and the total organization.

MARKETING COMMUNICATIONS OBJECTIVES

5 How do the various marketing communications objectives interact with the other elements of an IMC planning process?

An effective IMC planning process requires quality communication objectives. These objectives tie the organization's context, target markets, and positioning approaches to the ultimate selection of budget figures and IMC components, as depicted in Figure 4.1. Further, communications objectives guide account executives and advertising creatives in designing the actual advertising messages.

The process of defining and establishing communication objectives fine-tunes the IMC planning process. Communication objectives are derived from overall marketing objectives. Marketing objectives tend to be general because they are for the entire company. Some examples of marketing objectives include:

- Sales volume
- Market share
- Profits
- Return on investment

In contrast, a communications plan may emphasize a specific communications objective. Figure 4.7 lists some of the more common objectives present for profit-seeking organizations. A large firm may establish different objectives for each brand within a product portfolio. Oftentimes, a communications plan for an individual brand will emphasize a single objective.

Some programs can accomplish more than one communication objective at a time. This occurs when logical combinations of communication objectives are identified. For example, the same advertisement can develop brand awareness and enhance a brand's image. Increasing sales can be accomplished through price changes, contests, or coupons. The key is to match the objective to the medium and the message.

● Develop brand awareness	● Build customer traffic
● Increase category demand	● Enhance firm image
● Change customer beliefs or attitudes	● Increase market share
● Enhance purchase actions	● Increase sales
● Encourage repeat purchases	● Reinforce purchase decisions

◄ FIGURE 4.7
Communication Objectives

3M

Growth through reliability

Post-it® Flags make it easy to mark, flag and find important information for a wide range of applications. And thanks to our unique repositionable adhesive, Post-it® Flags stick securely and remove cleanly. 3M's reliable quality products deliver results that help drive the office supply industry. One more reason why Post-it® and Scotch® are among the world's most recognized brands.

Post-it   Scotch

3M, Post-it and Scotch are trademarks of 3M. © 3M 2006

Source: Courtesy of 3M/SPD.

▲ Before launching an advertising campaign, 3M will develop benchmark measures that can be compared to end-of-campaign results.

6 What are the relationships between communications expenditures and company sales?

Many marketing professionals believe that benchmarks are helpful tools. A **benchmark measure** represents the starting point that has been established in relation to the degree of change following a promotional campaign. In other words, the benchmark is the baseline from which future outcomes can be assessed.

When market research revealed that a dry cleaning company's name was only known by 20 percent of the community's population and that the company held a 3 percent share of the city's total market, a benchmark was present. In response, the primary communications objective for the next advertising cycle became to increase awareness and market share to 30 percent awareness and a 5 percent share. Then a campaign featuring advertisements, coupons, and discounts for certain days of the week (Tuesday specials) and to senior citizens was designed by establishing a budget that matched these IMC components. If the company achieved the desired target, this would indicate a level of success based on the previously specified benchmarks.

ESTABLISHING A COMMUNICATIONS BUDGET

The final two steps in the IMC planning process include preparing a communications budget and selecting the IMC components to be utilized (Figure 4.1). Once again, these two activities occur concurrently. In this section, budgets are described first, followed by the IMC components.

Budgets are based on communication objectives as well as marketing objectives. Communications budgets and IMC components will be different in consumer markets as compared to business-to-business markets. Normally, a much larger percentage of the budget allocations for business-to-business markets will be allocated to trade journals and telemarketing. Consumer markets are more likely to feature use of traditional media, such as television, magazines, and radio.

Many times, unrealistic assumptions are made about a communications budget. This occurs, for example, when a manager assumes there is a direct relationship between expenditures on advertising communications and subsequent sales revenues, which is highly unlikely. A more realistic relationship is shown in Figure 4.8. Several factors influence the relationship between expenditures on promotions and sales, including:

- The goal of the promotion
- Threshold effects
- Diminishing Returns
- Carryover effects
- Wear-out effects
- Decay effects
- Random events

Communication goals differ depending on the stage in the buying process that is being addressed. The hierarchy of effects model suggests that prior to making a purchase a consumer goes through the stages of awareness, knowledge, liking, preference, and conviction. The objective and stage in the hierarchy of effects model influences the objectives, budget, IMC components, and advertising message that will be sent. For example, an early advertising campaign for the Sun Life Financial company highlighted the fact that people had not heard of the organization, but would. Several humorous commercials

An unrealistic assumption about
the relationship between promotional
expenditures and sales

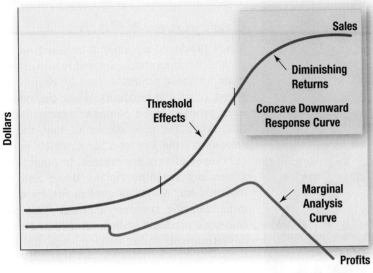

Sales-Response Function Curve

developed awareness of the brand. Over time, other aspects of the company's services and comparative advantages were featured. The entire campaign started at one place (awareness) and ended at another (encouraging action). It would not be logical to expect that early promotional expenditures would create a dollar-for-dollar relationship with sales as the campaign moved to new communication goals.

Threshold Effects

As shown in Figure 4.8, the early effects of advertising are minimal. The same holds true for all communication expenditures. At first, few behavioral responses occur, especially when only advertisements are used. Over time, a consumer who is exposed repeatedly to a company's marketing message recalls the company or brand and eventually becomes willing to make an inquiry or purchase.[18] Coupons, free samples, and other marketing tactics can help a good or service reach the threshold point sooner. **Threshold effects** are present at the point where the advertising program begins to affect consumer responses.

Threshold effects may be relatively easy to reach in some circumstances. For instance, a new good or service may be so innovative that consumers become quickly aware of its advantages and are willing to buy the item immediately. Also, when new products are introduced carrying an established, strong brand name, the threshold point will be reached more quickly.

Diminishing Returns

A point exists at which a promotional campaign has saturated the market. At that point, further expenditures have a minimal impact. The S-shaped curve displayed in Figure 4.8,

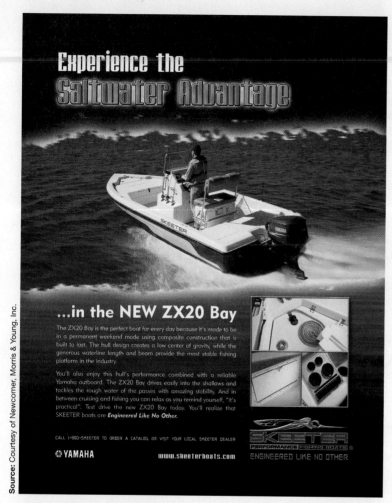

▲ For products such as boats, it is important for advertising to create carryover effects.

which represents a **sales-response function curve**, indicates diminishing returns.

Diminishing returns are part of the **concave downward function**. This means that incremental increases in expenditures in advertising result in smaller and smaller increases in sales. A **marginal analysis** reveals that further advertising and promotional expenditures will adversely affect profits, because sales increase less than what is being spent on marketing.

Carryover Effects

Many products are only purchased when needed, such as washing machines and refrigerators. Promotions for these products must be designed to create brand recall. This occurs when the consumer has been exposed to the company's message for so long that, when the time comes to buy, the individual remembers the key company, which indicates that **carryover effects** are present. In other words, when a washing machine breaks down and requires a replacement, Maytag's goal is for the consumer to remember the company's brand. This means that Maytag's products will be considered and that the advertisements have carried over until the right time.

Wear-out Effects

An additional complication to the advertising budgeting process may emerge. At a certain point, an advertisement or particular promotional campaign simply becomes "old" or "boring." Consumers tend to ignore the advertisement or just tune it out.[19] Some consumers may develop negative attitudes toward the brand if they become annoyed at the marketing communication and believe the advertisement should be discontinued. This indicates **wear-out effects**. The challenge for marketers is to continue an advertising campaign beyond the threshold effects and long enough to capture carryover effects, but not so long that wear-out effects begin to take place.

Decay Effects

When a company stops advertising, consumers begin to forget the message, indicating that **decay effects** are present. In some instances, the degree of decay is dramatic. In others, the carryover effects are strong enough that some time can lapse before the brand drops out of the consumer's consciousness. The promotional budget must be structured to avoid the problems of decay effects, which are illustrated in Figure 4.9.

FIGURE 4.9 ▶
A Decay Effects Model

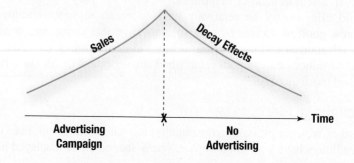

Random Events

Finally, random events affect promotions. A natural disaster or some other event can reduce the impact on any given campaign. Such events normally cannot be predicted.

TYPES OF BUDGETS

A communications budget can be prepared in a number of different ways. Figure 4.10 provides a list of the various methods that are used.[20]

❼ What types of marketing communications budgets may be used when developing the IMC planning program?

Percentage of Sales

With the **percentage-of-sales budget,** the budget is derived from either: (1) sales from the previous year or (2) anticipated sales for the next year. The major reason for using this method is simplicity. A percentage-of-sales budget is relatively easy to prepare.

The approach also has problems. First, it tends to change in the opposite direction of what is typically needed; that is, when sales go up, so does the communications budget. When sales decline, the communications budget also declines. In most cases, when sales are declining the communications budget should be increased to help reverse the trend. Further, during growth periods the communications budget may not need to be increased. The second major disadvantage of this method is that it does not allocate money for special needs or to combat competitive pressures. Therefore, many marketing experts believe the disadvantages of the percentage of sales method tend to outweigh its advantages.

Meet the Competition

The **meet-the-competition budget** seeks to prevent loss of market share. Expenditures are raised or lowered to match those of the competition. This method may be found in highly competitive markets where intense rivalries exist between competitors.

The potential drawback to meet-the-competition budgeting is that marketing dollars might not be spent efficiently. Matching the competition's spending does not guarantee success. Market share can still be lost. It is not *how much* is spent, but rather *how well* money is allocated and how effectively the marketing campaign works at retaining customers and market share.

"What We Can Afford"

The **"what we can afford" budget** sets the marketing budget after all of the company's other budgets have been determined or while determining the other budgets. Money is allocated based on what the company's leaders feel they can spend. Use of this method suggests that management may not fully recognize the benefits of marketing. Instead, company leaders view marketing expenditures as non-revenue-generating activities. Newer and smaller companies with limited finances often use the "what we can afford" approach.

Objective and Task

To prepare an **objective-and-task budget**, management lists all of the communication objectives to pursue during the year and then calculates the cost of accomplishing each objective. The communications budget represents the cumulative sum of the estimated costs for all objectives.

• Percentage of sales	• Objective and task
• Meet the competition	• Payout planning
• "What we can afford"	• Quantitative models

◀ **FIGURE 4.10**
Methods of Determining a Marketing Communications Budget

Great for growing chicks.

Want strong bones? Your bones grow until about age 35 and the calcium in milk helps. After that, it helps keep them strong. Chicks rule.

got milk?

▲ The objective-and-task method of budgeting is effective because it matches specific advertising dollars to specific advertising objectives.

Many marketing experts believe that the objective-and-task method represents the best budgeting approach because it relates dollar costs to achieving specific objectives. Unfortunately, a large company, such as Procter & Gamble, may find it difficult to use. With hundreds of products on the market, producing a budget based on objectives for each brand and product category is time consuming. Despite the challenge, some form of the objective-and-task method of setting marketing budgets is used by about 50 percent of the firms.[21]

Payout Planning

With a **payout-planning budget**, management establishes a ratio of advertising to sales or market share. This method normally allocates greater amounts in early years to yield payouts in later years.[22] By allocating larger amounts at the beginning of a new product introduction, brand awareness and brand equity are built. Then, as the brand becomes accepted and sales build, a lower percentage of advertising dollars will be needed to maintain a target growth.

The payout-planning approach is based on threshold effects and diminishing returns. A company that has reached the maximum threshold point should not continue pouring money into advertising that only results in diminishing returns. Instead, a company can maintain awareness and brand equity by more effective expenditures of marketing dollars. Future promotions and advertisement will target specific market segments and consumer groups rather than simply increasing the volume of marketing dollars spent.

Quantitative Models

In some instances, computer simulations can be developed to model the relationship between advertising or promotional expenditures with sales and profits. These models are far from perfect. They do have the advantage of accounting for the type of industry and product as the model is created. In most cases, quantitative models are limited to larger organizations with strong computer and statistics departments.

Therefore, as the marketing team constructs a budget, the assumptions that drive the process should be considered. The newness of the product, the economy, and other complicating factors must be considered during the process of tying budgeting expenditures to marketing and communication objectives. A budget is finalized when the company marketing team specifies how funds will be spent on each of the major communications tools.

8 In addition to advertising, what other IMC components are selected as part of the IMC planning process?

IMC COMPONENTS

As has been noted, marketing communications consists of much more than traditional advertising. In fact, advertising expenditures may not make up the major portion of a marketing communications budget. In terms of dollars spent, media advertising normally accounts for about 41 percent of a marketing communications budget. Trade promotions receive about 28 percent and consumer promotions average about 28 percent of overall marketing expenditures (see Figure 4.11).[23] These percentages vary considerably from industry to industry. Consumer product manufacturers spend more on trade promotions directed toward retailers. Service companies tend to spend more on media advertising.

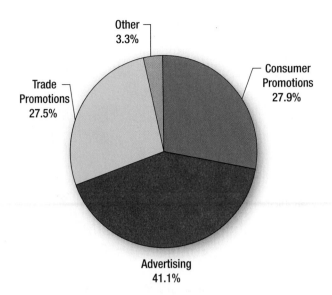

◄ **FIGURE 4.11**
Breakdown of Marketing
Communication Expenditures

Budgets also vary by product type. For example, for dolls and stuffed toys the average expenditure on media advertising as a percentage of sales is 11.2 percent, whereas for men's clothing expenditures on media advertising represent only 3.3 percent of sales.[24]

Selecting IMC components and media takes place in conjunction with preparation of the budget. Figure 4.12 highlights the ways advertising dollars are allocated among the various media. Television ranks first, primarily because of the high cost of advertising time. Internet expenditures rank fourth, but make up the fastest growing component.[25]

The clutter among the major advertising media has caused many marketing professionals to shift communication dollars to alternative methods. Figure 4.13 shows the breakdown of alternative media spending in the United States. Online and mobile advertising is the largest category. This category includes lead generation, online display and video ads, online yellow pages, and mobile phone advertising. Branded entertainment includes paid product placement along with event sponsorships. The entertainment/digital category consists of local pay TV, video-on-demand, DVR advertising, and video games. Almost $12 billion was spent in interactive marketing, which involves direct marketing by e-mail and word-of-mouth marketing. The smallest category, but one of the fastest growing, is social media advertising.[26] It includes social media pages such as Facebook, MySpace, Twitter, and numerous smaller, targeted social sites.

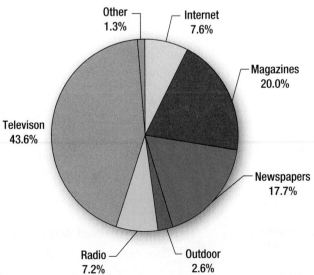

◄ **FIGURE 4.12**
U.S. Ad Spending by Media

Source: Adapted from "U.S. Ad Expenditures," *2008 Marketing Fact Book, Marketing News,* July 15, 2008, p. 22.

FIGURE 4.13 ▶
U.S. Alternative Media Spending

Source: Adapted from "U.S. Alternative Media Spending," *2008 Marketing Fact Book, Marketing News,* July 15, 2008, p. 18, 22.

Decisions regarding business-to-business IMC components are different than for consumer products. Figure 4.14 indicates how business-to-business marketing monies are allocated. Although consumers my detest telemarketing, it remains an important component of business-to-business marketing. Direct mail is used extensively along with noncatalog direct mail. Television advertising is a much smaller amount than for consumer products, while Internet marketing expenditures are much larger, and even higher than those for television. The IMC components used in business-to-business markets vary from those chosen for consumer markets.

Choosing the best IMC components remains the challenge. IMC components are selected to reach the target audience and achieve the objectives that are set while operating within the constraints imposed by budgetary concerns. Marketing personnel with a company and its various external agencies analyze the firm's context, including customers, competition, and communication within the industry (the 3Cs) to provide the background for choosing IMC components.

FIGURE 4.14 ▶
U.S. Business-to-Business
Direct Marketing Spending

Source: Adapted from "U.S. Alternative Media Spending," *2008 Marketing Fact Book, Marketing News,* July 15, 2008, p. 24.

INTERNATIONAL IMPLICATIONS

Globally integrated marketing communications (GIMC) programs are vital for international firms. Each message should fit a country's language and culture. Brand names, marketing ideas, and advertising campaigns designed for one country do not always translate correctly to another. Consequently, understanding the international market is essential. Figure 4.15 highlights the ingredients of successful GIMC plans.

Marketing campaigns do not necessarily require a unique program for each country and each cultural group within a country. It is important to make sure the company's products and marketing messages will be *understood in the region*. When needed, the message is tailored to an individual area. The goal is to *create a borderless marketing plan* that uses the same basic marketing approach for all of a company's markets. This allows each subsidiary the freedom to determine how to implement that marketing plan, in essence, to *think globally but act locally*. It also presents the opportunity to maintain a theme while targeting the message to a given region.

Another key to a successful GIMC is developing *local partnerships*. Local partners can be marketing research firms or advertising firms that are familiar with the local language and culture. These partnerships sometimes are formed by hiring a **cultural assimilator**. This individual will have an understanding of the market and speak both the language of the parent company and the local region.

Communication segmentation means creating a communications package that effectively reaches all possible target markets in another country. Many times both consumer and business-to-business segments are present.

A well-designed *market communications analysis* begins with the marketing team identifying strengths and weaknesses of local competitors and places in which opportunities exist. They must also develop an understanding of how the firm is perceived in the international marketplace.

Finally, *solid communication objectives* should be established. Linguistics is a major hurdle. Translating an English advertisement into another language requires expertise, because exact word translations often do not exist. For example, the slogan of Ruth's Steak House, "We sell sizzle as well as steaks," could not be translated into Spanish, because there is no equivalent word for "sizzle." Therefore, the translator found a Spanish idiom conveying a similar meaning in order to solve the problem.

The IMC planning process becomes more complicated in international settings; however, it is crucial in creating an effective GIMC. Language, culture, norms, beliefs, and laws all must be taken into consideration. Literal translation of a commercial's tagline might not be acceptable within a given culture. Laws concerning advertising and promotions vary by country. Cultures view ideas and objects differently. These differences should be considered when designing a communications program.

- Understand the international market
- Create a borderless marketing plan
- Think globally but act locally
- Local partnerships

- Communication segmentation strategies
- Market communications analysis
- Solid communication objectives

◀ **FIGURE 4.15**
Successful Globally Integrated
Marketing Tactics

Skyjacker

Skyjacker was established in 1974 in West Monroe, Louisiana. Skyjacker manufactures suspension lift kits and shocks for four-wheel-drive trucks, SUVs, and Jeeps. The kits and shocks are sold to warehouse distributors and distributed internationally. Skyjacker provides retailers and jobbers with point-of-purchase displays and a strong integrated marketing campaign to pull the products through the various channels.

Skyjacker engages in both consumer and trade advertising. Skyjacker uses television and print advertising to sell the products to the consumer. The company sponsors drivers and various off-road events. To support the retailers who sell the products, Skyjacker also budgets money for trade advertising and trade support.

Your instructor has additional information about the ads, visuals, and displays used in this campaign.

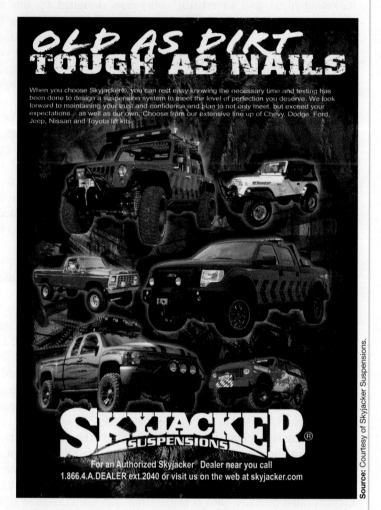

Source: Courtesy of Skyjacker Suspensions.

▲ Skyjacker uses an integrated marketing approach to reach both consumers and channel members.

SUMMARY

A marketing communication planning program begins with the analysis of the organization's context, including customers, competitors, and communications. When the analysis is complete, target markets may be selected in conjunction with product-positioning tactics.

Market segmentation identifies sets of business or consumer groups with distinct characteristics. Segments must be clearly different, large enough to support a marketing campaign, and reachable through some type of media. Consumer groups that can be segmented include those identified by demographics, including gender, age, income, and ethnicity. Markets can also be identified using psychographic, generational, and geographic delineations. Geodemographic segmentation combines demographic, psychographic, and geographic information together. Other ways to categorize consumers are by the benefits they receive from goods or services and by the ways they use products.

Business-to-business segmentation can be accomplished by targeting business customers by industry, business type, the size of the company, geographic location, usage, and customer-value calculations. Marketing managers should carefully specify the company's consumer and business market segments. All other promotions opportunity analysis processes are tied to the identification of key customers.

Product positioning represents the perceptions in consumer minds of the nature of a company and its products relative to the competition. Positioning may be based on product attributes, competitors, product uses or applications, the price–quality relationship, product class, or through the association with a cultural symbol.

Marketing objectives lead to the development of communications objectives that are matched to the product, target market, and product positioning. These objectives form the basis for developing communications budgets and selecting IMC components for actual marketing campaigns.

Globally integrated marketing communications efforts are guided by the IMC planning process. National differences, cultural concerns, language issues, and other challenges must be viewed in light of the target markets an individual company intends to serve.

KEY TERMS

market segment A set of businesses or group of individual customers with distinct characteristics.

market segmentation Identifying specific groups (target markets) based on their needs, attitudes, and interests.

demographics Population characteristics such as gender, age, educational levels, income, and ethnicity.

psychographics Patterns of responses that reveal a person's activities, interests, and opinions (AIO).

product positioning The perception in the consumer's mind of the nature of a company and its products relative to the competition.

benchmark measures Starting points that are studied in relation to the degree of change following a promotional campaign.

threshold effects The point at which an advertising or promotional program has begun to affect customer responses.

sales-response function curve An S-shaped curve that indicates when threshold effects are present and when diminishing returns are present.

concave downward function A model of the diminishing returns of advertising expenditures on sales.

marginal analysis A model that shows when additional expenditures on advertising and promotions have an adverse affect on profits.

carryover effects The point at which a consumer has been exposed to the company's message for so long that, when the time comes to buy, the individual remembers the company.

wear-out effects Declines in advertising effectiveness that occur when an ad or marketing communication becomes "old" or "boring."

decay effects Declines in advertising effectiveness that occur when advertising stops and consumers begin to forget about the company.

percentage-of-sales budget A form of communications budgeting in which budgeting is based on sales from the previous year or anticipated sales for the next year.

meet-the-competition budget A communications budget in which expenditures are raised or lowered to match the competition.

"what we can afford" budget A communications budget that is set after all of the company's other budgets have been determined or while the other budges are being set and communications money is allocated based on what company leaders feels they can afford to spend.

objective-and-task budget A communications budget in which management first lists all of the communications objectives to pursue during the year and then calculates the cost of accomplishing those objectives.

payout-planning budget A budgeting method that establishes a ratio of advertising to sales or market share.

cultural assimilator A person who is familiar with the local language and culture of a given country who is employed to help marketing efforts in that particular region.

REVIEW QUESTIONS

1. What are the three components of analysis of the IMC planning context?
2. What four categories of customers are examined when analyzing the IMC planning context?
3. What three types of research are used when analyzing the competition?
4. Define market segment and market segmentation.
5. Define demographics. How are they used to segment consumer markets?
6. How can firms take advantage of target markets by gender?
7. What generational cohorts have marketing experts identified?
8. What problems are associated with markets segmented according to geographic areas?
9. What are geodemographics? How can they be successfully used to define market segments?
10. Describe usage segmentation and benefit segmentation.
11. What are the common business-to-business market segments?
12. Describe the NAICS approach to business market segmentation.

13. Describe a usage segmentation approach in a business-to-business setting.

14. Describe a segmentation approach based on company size.

15. Define product positioning and identify the types of positioning approaches that can be used in the IMC planning process.

16. What is a benchmark measure?

17. What common marketing communications objectives do firms establish?

18. Describe the natures of threshold effects, carryover effects, wear-out effects, decay effects, and random event with regard to communications budgets.

19. Describe the methods that can be used to establish a communications budget.

20. Which IMC components are more likely to be used in business-to-business marketing communications programs, as compared to consumer markets?

21. What is a cultural assimilator?

CRITICAL THINKING EXERCISES

Discussion Questions

1. Pick a product that you have recently purchased and that you have considerable knowledge about. Conduct a context analysis. Examine the customers, competition, and communications of the product and brand.

2. An analysis of movie theaters revealed the primary moviegoers tend to be between 18 and 24 years of age. Twenty years ago, 44 percent of the individuals in this age bracket went to movies frequently. Today, less than 34 percent are frequent moviegoers.[27] Conduct a customer analysis by interviewing five individuals between the ages of 18 and 24. Based on their responses, what suggestions would you make to movie theaters to reverse this declining trend?

3. Pick one of the following industries. Discuss the types of marketing communications used in the industry by various firms or brands. What are the similarities and differences in the communication approaches being used?

   a. Tanning salons

   b. Local night clubs

   c. Local dine-in restaurants around your university or in a specific area of town

   d. Soft drinks

   e. Bottled water

4. Make a list of five consumer goods or services segmented on the basis of gender but sold to both genders. Are there any differences in the product or service attributes? Are there differences in how they are marketed? What are those differences? Do you think using a different marketing approach has worked?

5. Examine the list of demographic segmentation variables. For each demographic listed in the text, identify two products that are marketed to a specific demographic segment. Identify the specific demographic segment and explain why the product is aimed at that particular market segment. Identify one brand that has been especially successful at reaching a specific demographic segment.

6. For each of the following goods or services, identify the various benefits that consumers may derive from the good or service. Can you think of an advertisement or marketing communication that has featured the benefit as the central part of the appeal?

   a. Seafood restaurants

   b. Auto insurance

   c. Optometrist or eye-care clinics

   d. Soft drinks

   e. Aspirin or other pain relievers

7. For each of the product-positioning strategies discussed in this chapter, identify two brands that feature the strategy and explain how the strategy is used to successfully market the brand.

8. Locate five ads in a magazine. Either tear out the ads or scan them. For each ad, identify the target market of the ad, the communications objective, and the product-positioning strategy that you think is being used.

INTEGRATED LEARNING EXERCISES

1. Use a search engine to locate five companies on the Internet that sell swimwear. For each company, discuss the types of products sold, the types of promotional appeals that are used, and the types of special offers used to entice buyers. From looking at each Web site, describe the type of customer you think the company is trying to reach. Of the five companies, which one do you think does the best job of marketing itself? Why?

2. A brand's product-positioning strategy should be an integral part of the company's advertising and marketing strategy, including its Web site. Examine the following Web sites and identify the product-positioning strategy that you think is being used. Explain your choice.

   a. Polaris (**www.polarisindustries.com**)

   b. Edgewater Beach & Golf Resort (**www.edgewaterbeach resort.com**)

   c. Celestial Seasonings (**www.celestialseasonings.com**)

   d. Sony (**www.sony.com**)

   e. Stetson cologne (**www.stetsoncologne.com**)

3. For consumer markets, a leading geodemographic firm is Nielsen Claritas. Go to the Web site at **http://en-us.nielsen.com/tab/product_families/nielsen_claritas** and explore the various methods of segmentation. What information does Nielsen Claritas provide? How would it help a company develop an integrated marketing communication plan?

4. VALS psychographic segmentation can be a valuable tool for marketers as they prepare their marketing materials. Access VALS through the Strategic Business Insights (SBI) Web site at **www.strategicbusinessinsights.com/vals** and examine the characteristics of each of the groups. Then take the test to determine which group you belong to. How can VALS help marketers develop advertising messages?

5. A current trend for many companies is the development of marketing messages for specific demographic, ethnic, or lifestyle groups. This allows for a more targeted message than is possible for the mass audience. Go to the following Web sites. What types of marketing messages are on each site? How could the information on these Web sites be used to develop integrated marketing communication plans?

   a. Women (**www.ivillage.com**)

   b. Hispanics (**www.hispaniconline.com**)

   c. African Americans (**www.targetmarketnews.com**)

   d. Gays and lesbians (**www.planetout.com**)

6. Choose two of the following companies. Examine the company's Web site to determine what segmentation strategy the firm uses. Describe the intended target market for the Web site. What communication objective(s) do you think the company is trying to accomplish? What product positioning strategy is being used? Explain your responses.

   a. Sports Spectrum Greeting Cards (**www.sportsgreetingcards.com**)

   b. Ty Beanie Babies (**www.ty.com**)

   c. Sara Lee (**www.saralee.com**)

   d. Skeeter boats (**www.skeeterboats.com**)

   e. Gold Bond (**www.goldbond.com**)

STUDENT PROJECT

Creative Corner

The VALS typology has been used by a number of companies and advertising agencies to create marketing materials. Your task is to design two advertisements for DIRECTV. Pick one of the following pairs of VALS segments and design an advertisement promoting DIRECTV for each segment. When you are finished, write a paragraph explaining how the ads you created will appeal to their respective VALS segment and how the two ads are different. Before you begin work on the ads, go to the Strategic Business Insights (SBI) Web site at **www.strategicbusinessinsights.com/vals** to obtain more information about the two segments you will be targeting with your ads.

   Pair 1: Innovators and Survivors

   Pair 2: Thinkers and Makers

   Pair 3: Believers and Achievers

   Pair 4: Strivers and Experiencers

CASE 1   BOSE: HIGH-END SOUND REPRODUCTION

A case can be made that sound reproduction has become one of the areas in which technological innovations have made the most profound leaps forward. Leading the way are major competitors such as Sony, Philips, Tivoli Audio, and Bose. Many forms of sound delivery exist, some featuring earphones and headphones, and others through stand-alone speakers.

The Bose Corporation began operations in 1964. Amar G. Bose, a professor of electrical engineering at the Massachusetts Institute of Technology, became frustrated during his attempt to purchase a high-quality stereo system. He believed that the speakers that were available had impressive technical specifications but failed to reproduce the realism of a live performance.

Four years later, the first Bose product reached the market. In a very short time, Bose has delivered a series of innovations in sound.

Currently, the Bose Wave products are at the forefront of quality sound, including the Wave radio, Wave music system, and Acoustic Wave music system. Each is designed to deliver the most realistic sound through a compact, attractive device that will fit in any room in the home or office. The product can be linked with a dock that both plays and recharges an iPod. Another product allows the user to wirelessly play and store music from an Internet radio station. Other Bose products include headphones, home theater systems, speakers, and sound systems for various locations, including boats and businesses.

Bose systems are on the high end in terms of price. For example, the most widely purchased Wave music system had a list price of $499.95 in November 2009. To entice buyers, product discounts are routinely offered, including a $100.00 price reduction when the Wave is purchased with the accompanying multi-CD changer. Also, Bose offers 1-year, interest-free financing.

The Bose marketing program includes use of traditional media, most notably television, newspaper, and magazine advertising. The company's Web site allows buyers to find and purchase all items online. The company employs a limited number of retail stores that feature the Bose line. The primary marketing emphasis remains focused on quality. For example, *Fortune* rated the Bose QuietComfort headset, which cancels outside noise, as the best-quality option for headphones.

Although a company's reputation for quality may help to drive sales, outside factors can interfere. The recession which began in 2008 and continued into 2009 led many shoppers to cut back purchases, especially for more expensive luxury items. Bose was not immune to this trend. The company was forced to lay off nearly 1,000 workers, or 10 percent of its labor force, during the decline.

At the same time, Bose forged ahead, seeking to develop new technologies in areas other than sound. As the economy continues to recover, business analysts expect Bose to build on its core products while moving into new areas, furthering the growth of this innovative, energetic organization.

1. Explain how the IMC planning process would apply to future marketing efforts for Bose Wave products.

2. Identify the market segments that the Bose Wave products should continue to maintain.

3. Should Bose continue to compete based on high-price/high-quality positioning, or should it develop programs to reduce prices and entice a wider variety of shoppers?

4. What should be the primary marketing communications objectives for Bose?

5. What type of budget should be used for the Bose promotional program?

6. Which IMC components best match the target market, position, objectives, and budget for Bose products?

Sources: "Bose Confirms Layoffs," *Boston.com* (www.boston.com/business/ticker/2009/01/bose_confirms_l.html, accessed November 10, 2009), January 20, 2009; Peter Lewis, "Sounds of Silence Noise-Canceling Headphones Make Air Travel Quiet," *Fortune* (http://money.cnn.com/magazines/fortune/fortune_archive/2002/05/13/322899/index.htm, accessed November 10, 2009), May 13, 2002.

CASE 2   BURGER WARS

The world of fast food, especially the world of hamburgers and fries, continues to evolve. The dominant force for nearly 40 years has been McDonald's. The company is an icon in the United States and has expanded to nearly a worldwide reach. Recently, the McDonald's empire has come under attack from a variety of sources.

Socially, films such as *Supersize Me* criticized the basic McDonald's menu, noting high levels of calories and fat in the foods offered, complaining about the suggestive selling tactics used, and arguing that advertising to children utilizing Ronald McDonald as a spokesperson has created an unhealthy, obese, malnourished new generation. McDonald's responded with products such as salads and fruit plates, while agreeing to halt the use of trans fats in French fries and other deep-fried products. Company leaders did not agree, however, that Ronald McDonald should retire. McDonald's continues to offer birthday parties, outdoor toys, and the Happy Meal to entice kids into its stores.

The number two competitor in the world of burgers is Burger King. The company is dwarfed by McDonald's in terms of locations, revenues, and dollars spent on advertising and marketing as well as in brand recognition and recall by children and teens. In 2007, Burger King began a bold new program featuring two new spokespersons. The first is the computer-animated Burger King, placed into a variety of sports events and other unusual places. The Burger King never speaks but clearly stands out. The appeal is to a slightly older generation of burger buyers than children. The second spokesperson is Homer Simpson from the television cartoon *The Simpsons*. Homer has always been a big burger-eater. He is highly recognizable to a generation of television viewers going back for

20 years. *The Simpsons Movie*, which was released as the Burger King tie-in began, created a great deal of buzz. The film was a major success in terms of tickets sold and practically ensured that the *The Simpsons* would continue on television, and possibly in movie sequels, for the next several years. The marketing genius of signing Homer Simpson is that the television show has an audience ranging from younger children to adults. Many 20-somethings grew up with *The Simpsons* as a weekly nighttime habit.

Neither Burger King nor McDonald's can ignore other burger chains. Wendy's and Hardees have been successful in some markets. Sonic also has a following among some customers. Each utilizes a unique marketing pitch oriented to individual target audiences.

At the same time, chains offering food items other than hamburgers have also made inroads. Among the most powerful new competitors is Subway, with its "Eat Fresh" campaign, spokesperson Jared, and advertising claims regarding the lower-calorie, low-fat options available. Pizza offers further competition, led by major players Pizza Hut, Papa John's, and Dominos. Taco Bell, KFC, and Long John Silver's are additional fast-food options. Under the direction of Yum, the three are often found in the same location along the Interstate, giving a weary traveler a variety of choices under the same roof.

Both Burger King and McDonald's seek to maintain a competitive advantage through differentiation. McDonald's features include its powerful brand, accessibility across the country and around the world, and the "pull" factor, whereby children entice parents to continue to visit a unit even when other options are available. For years, Burger King relied on the advertising claim that broiled burgers taste better than fried and that in taste tests people prefer the Whopper to the Big Mac.

In the next decade, the victor in the burger wars may or may not be based on what happens on the children's front. Combinations of products, prices, delivery systems, and promotions programs might make the difference. Clearly, no company can sit still and wait to see what happens with the others.

▲ The fast-food restaurant industry is highly competitive, as major chains and independents compete for dining-out dollars.

1. Conduct an IMC context analysis for one of the following: McDonald's, Burger King, Wendy's, Hardees, or Sonic.

2. Besides children, identify the target markets that are best suited to each of the following: McDonald's, Burger King, Wendy's, Hardees, Sonic.

3. What type of product-positioning strategy does each company use? Discuss the merits of the positioning strategy. Should it be changed? Why or why not?

4. What type of promotional budget should each major competitor use?

5. Based on the information in this chapter, how would a company like Hardees or Carl's Jr. (which owns Hardees) compete effectively against McDonald's? What types of IMC communication components would work best?

5 Advertising Management

THE RICHARDS GROUP

"Some companies push products. Some sell ads. We sell the truth." This guiding principle may be found on the Web site for The Richards Group, America's largest independent advertising agency, based in Dallas, Texas; an agency so distinguished that it has been listed as one of the six most influential agencies in the United States by *Graphic Design USA*.

The firm, which at one point consisted of fewer than 60 employees, all located on one floor of an office building, has expanded to a major office building on the North Central Expressway. The company has received many awards, including *Adweek* magazine's "Agency of the Year" numerous times.

The Richards Group generates billings exceeding $1 billion annually. The organization employs more than 650 marketing professionals. Its list of current and former clients includes a variety of well-known companies, Orkin, Fruit of the Loom, T.G.I. Friday's, Zales, Red Lobster, Farmer's Insurance, and others.

Beyond these simple statistics rests a story that owner-founder Stan Richards once described as "a rocket ride," which has taken him to being named as one of *The Wall Street Journal*'s "Giants of Our Time." Many of the tactics employed by The Richards Group have been emulated by other agencies. Richards notes that his company did them first and does them best.

Stan Richards

Richards prefers hiring new employees straight out of college, because, he says with a smile, "We don't want them picking up bad habits in other agencies, before they join us." These individuals quickly discover that the offices are all completely open, with no doors or walls. More significant, Richards notes, "What we do is commingle all the disciplines, so that in every cluster of spaces we will have an art director who sits next to a brand manager, who, for example, sits next to a print production manager, so that, in those interdisciplinary villages that everyone here occupies, nobody's next door neighbor does the same thing that he or she does. What you don't get

CHAPTER OBJECTIVES

After reading this chapter, you should be able to answer the following questions:

1 What are the essential ingredients in advertising campaign management, including the role of advertising?

2 When should a company employ an external advertising agency rather than completing the work in-house?

3 How do companies choose advertising agencies?

4 What roles are played within advertising agencies and client companies?

5 What steps are completed as part of advertising campaign management?

6 What are the primary goals of advertising?

7 What are the key elements of an advertising budget?

8 What are the issues in the media-selection process?

9 How does a creative brief facilitate effective advertising?

CHAPTER 5

Source: Author Supplied Image.

▲ **Employees of The Richards Group**

is all the creative people sitting on this floor, then all the account management people on the next floor, and the media people on the floor above that."

"The reason I did that in the first place," Richards continues, "was that when we were 50 or 60 people, there was an extraordinary level of energy and electricity that just flowed through the place. You could just walk in and feel it. A lot of it was created by the casual contact people had with each other. When you have 50 or 60 people packed into a tight space, you see everybody every day.

"What agencies have always done, is when they reach that 120- to 130-person size, they then have to move to multiple floors. And the minute they do, they take a tight-knit bunch of people who really liked each other and understood each other, because they saw each other every day, and divide them up into tribes. These tribes don't always get along.

"There are lots of occasions where a creative will butt heads with a planner, because they have a different point of view. When you are packed into a tight space, and when you have a great deal of casual contact going on all day, every day, you get over that stuff, because they are your friends. When you're on a different floor, you seldom see them, and you decide, 'That's a different tribe up there, and they drive me crazy.'"

Richard's approach clearly works. "When we are hired by a client," Richards notes, "it's not just to make ads. We do so many things that are extremely important. That ad is what the consumer ultimately sees, but in order to get there, you have to have a dead-on strategy, if you're going to be successful. You go through the strategic process, you get to the right answer, and then you can execute against that answer."

Some of the success stories created by The Richards Group are relayed in various places in this textbook, including the long-standing Chick-fil-A cow campaign, the fascinating "ride" with Motel 6 described in this chapter, the company's 2010 Super Bowl commercials, and its relationships with Firestone and The Home Depot.

In the meantime, the next time you view a commercial for Corona Beer, featuring a laid-back setting on a beach in the Caribbean somewhere, and you leave the cares of the world behind you, Richards suggests, you are viewing another company success story. Corona has become the number one imported beer in the United States, passing Heineken, due, in part, to a successful advertising management program assisted by The Richards Group.[1]

OVERVIEW

1 What are the essential ingredients in advertising campaign management, including the role of advertising?

The average person encounters more than 600 advertisements per day, delivered by an expanding variety of media. Television and radio have long been the advertising staples, along with newspaper and magazine ads, billboards, signs, direct-mail campaigns, and other traditional channels. Recently, advertisements presented on the Internet, social networks, and cell phones have generated new ways to contact and interact with customers.

Today's marketers face a challenge. A company simply cannot afford to prepare advertisements for every medium. Further, the message should be designed to create an advantage in a highly cluttered world in which people are becoming increasingly adept at simply tuning ads out.

To be effective, an advertisement first must be noticed. Next, it must be remembered. Then, the message of the advertisement should incite some kind of action, such as a purchase, a shift in brand loyalty, or, at the very least, find a place in the buyer's long-term memory.

Part 2 of this textbook describes the role advertising plays in an integrated marketing communications program. Figure 5.1 portrays the overall IMC approach. The three chapters in this section focus on developing an effective IMC advertising program.

FIGURE 5.1 ▶
Overview of Integrated Marketing Communications

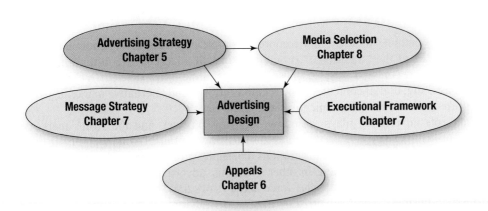

Three ingredients create effective advertisements: (1) development of a logical advertising management scheme for the company, (2) thoughtful design of advertisements, and (3) careful selection of media. Media tools and media-selection processes will be described in the next section of this textbook (Part 3); however, media selection and advertising design go hand in hand: One cannot be performed without the other. Thus, although they are presented separately in this textbook, they occur at the same time.

This chapter focuses on advertising management, which lays the groundwork for the total advertising program. One element is developing the **message theme**, which is an outline of the key idea(s) the advertising campaign conveys.

Chapters 6 and 7 describe advertising design processes. The primary issues include deciding on the leverage point to use, the major appeal in the advertising campaign, and the type of executional framework to use. A **leverage point** is the key element in the advertisement that taps into, or activates, a consumer's personal value system (a value, idea, or concept). The **appeal** is the approach used to design the advertisement that attracts attention or presents information to consumers through the use of humor, fear, sex, logic, or emotions. The **executional framework** explains how the message will be delivered. Methods include the slice-of-life approach, fantasies, dramatizations, and ads featuring animation. Figure 5.2 displays the advertising design elements.

▼ Creating eye-catching ads plays a vital role in advertising management.

OVERVIEW OF ADVERTISING MANAGEMENT

An **advertising management program** is the process of preparing and integrating a company's advertising efforts with the overall IMC message. The program consists of four activities:

1. Review the role of advertising in the IMC effort.
2. Select an in-house or external advertising agency.
3. Develop an advertising campaign management strategy.
4. Complete a creative brief.

Consistency will be the guiding principle of these four efforts. The company's goods or services and methods of doing business should match the advertising agency chosen, the strategy of the campaign, and the work of the advertising creatives. The result should be a coherent message stating the theme of the entire IMC program.

"Hey, there's a blue one."

Drivers wanted.

ADVERTISING AND THE IMC PROCESS

Advertising continues to be a major component of integrated marketing communications. It remains part of the "traditional" promotions mix of advertising, consumer and trade promotions, and personal selling. These functions, along with other activities, such as direct marketing, digital content, public relations efforts, and alternative marketing strategies, form the basis for communicating with customers.

The role advertising plays varies by company, product, and the firm's marketing goals. For some products and companies, advertising continues to be the central focus, and the other components (trade promotions, consumer promotions, and personal selling) support the advertising program. In other situations, advertising plays a secondary role, such as supporting the national sales force and a firm's trade promotion program. In the business-to-business sector, advertising often assists other promotional activities, including trade shows and personal sales calls. In the consumer sector, the reverse is often true. Advertising will be the primary communication vehicle, and other promotional tools (contests, coupons, sampling) reinforce the campaign.

Recently, Oscar Mayer launched an integrated campaign entitled "It Doesn't Get Better Than This," which featured new advertisements for all Oscar Mayer products (Deli Fresh, Bologna, Deli Creations, Hot Dogs, and Bacon). The campaign emphasized an altruistic effort called "Good Mood Mission." Consumers were encouraged to share their good moods. For each good mood shared, Oscar Mayer donated 1 pound of food to families in need. The goal was to donate 2 million pounds of food. Advertising launched the campaign through TV spots on the *Golden Globe Awards* as well as sponsorship of the show. The message was strengthened using print ads, video ads, package redesigns, public relations efforts with Kristin Chenoweth, digital and consumer-generated content on the Internet, and local event marketing featuring the Wienermobile (see Figure 5.3). The Oscar Mayer campaign illustrates the key role advertising continues to play in communications.

IN-HOUSE VERSUS EXTERNAL ADVERTISING AGENCIES

2 When should a company employ an external advertising agency rather than completing the work in-house?

When beginning an advertising program, the first issue is whether to use an in-house advertising group or an external advertising agency. Figure 5.4 compares the advantages of an in-house facility to an outside agency.

Approximately 40 percent of companies use some type of in-house facility, due to its potential advantages. Managers believe this approach *lowers costs* and gives the company better control of the message, which can be *aligned* with the brand and other company communications.[2] The *CEO can work closely* with the marketing team to make sure this

FIGURE 5.3 ▶
Oscar Mayer's "Mission to Spread Good Mood Food" Campaign

Source: Adapted from Tom Lopez, Senior Director of Marketing, Oscar Mayer, Good Morning Headquarters, January 16, 2010.

◀ **FIGURE 5.4**
Advantages of In-House versus Outside Agencies

Advantages of In-House	Advantages of Outside Agency
● Lower costs	● Reduce costs
● Consistent brand message	● Greater expertise
● Better understanding of product and mission	● Outsider's perspective
● Faster ad production	● Access to top talent
● Works closer with CEO	
● Lower turnover rate in the creative team	

Source: Adapted from Rupal Parekh, "Thinking of Pulling a CareerBuilder? Pros and Cons of Bringing an Account In-House," *Advertising Age*, **http://adage.com/print?article_id136701,** May 18, 2009.

occurs. Consequently, members of the marketing department may conclude they have a *better understanding of the firm's products and mission.* They may also think they can more *quickly produce* advertisements. Finally, an in-house program will be more consistent because of a *lower turnover rate in the creative team.*

As a result, some firms, such as CareerBuilder and Skyjacker, perform all advertising functions in-house. Others hire marketing and advertising experts to assist in the effort. Some contract specific functions, such as writing, filming, recording, and editing advertisements. Most utilize media companies to plan and purchase media time (on television and radio) and space (in magazines, in newspapers, and on billboards).

At times, an outside agency *reduces costs* when compared to less efficient in-house facilities. This occurs when in-house employees spend more time on campaigns and ad designs than an agency would. The agency offers *greater expertise* and may have *access to top talent* in the industry. Advertising agencies offer an *outside perspective* not influenced by internal corporate politics and personal biases. Agency professionals often have a better understanding of consumers and trends, because they work with a number of clients over an array of products. Often knowledge gained from one product can be transferred to other, even unrelated products.

Cost Considerations

Another factor affecting the choice of an in-house team versus an external advertising agency is the size of the account. A small account may not be attractive to an advertising agency. Smaller accounts generate lower revenues. If the agency charges a higher fee to compensate, it becomes too costly for the small firm.

Smaller accounts create other challenges for agencies. Less money is available to spend on purchasing media time and space, because the majority of the advertising budget will be spent on production of the advertisement.

One rule of thumb used by agencies is the *75–15–10* breakdown, where 75 percent of the money spent on advertising should be used to purchase media time or space, 15 percent to the agency for the creative work, and 10 percent for the actual production of the ad. In contrast, for smaller accounts, the breakdown may be 25–40–35. This means that only 25 percent of expenditures are for media purchases. The other 75 percent of the funds goes to the creative and production work.

Unless the majority of the company's advertising budget can be spent on media purchases, it may be wise either to perform the work in-house or to develop contracts with smaller specialty firms to prepare various aspects of an advertising campaign.

Crowdsourcing

A new alternative has recently emerged. **Crowdsourcing** is the process of outsourcing the creative aspect of an advertisement to the public. Unilever used this approach for its meat snack brand Peperami. Company leaders announced a creative competition on the brand's Web site. More than 1,100 entries were

▼ Skyjacker is one of a number of firms that performs all advertising functions in-house.

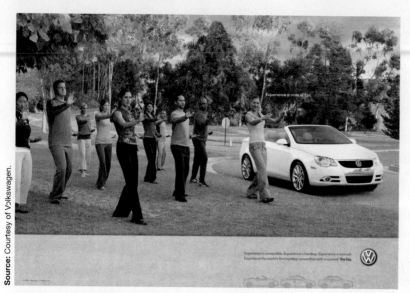

Source: Courtesy of Volkswagen.

▲ Creatives at advertising agencies tend to have greater expertise and objectivity in creating ads, such as this one designed by Crispin, Porter & Bogusky for Volkswagen.

submitted. Peperami marketing manager Noam Buchalter stated, "We were so overwhelmed with the level of entries and range of high-quality creative ideas pitched for brief that we found it impossible to pick one." Two ideas were chosen: one by Kevin Baldwin, a copywriter from London, and the other by Rowland Davies, an ex-creative director from Germany. The two ideas cost about $15,000 in prize money. They were combined into print and television campaigns produced by Smartworks, a marketing production company from South Africa.[3]

Doritos used a similar approach when creating Super Bowl ads in 2009 and 2010. Fans were invited to submit ideas for ads. An MSNBC.com poll reported that the Doritos ads were voted as the best of the Super Bowl in both years. The winning ad for 2010 triumphed over 4,000 other submissions.[4]

It may seem that crowdsourcing would be a cheaper way to create a Super Bowl commercial. In reality, the total cost was about the same as it would have been to hire a professional agency. The costs of running the contest, paying the prize money, creating the microsite to host the contest, and producing the commercial and the time spent by Doritos and the agency in choosing from the 4,000 entries were about equal to what would have been spent on an agency. The primary advantage of the crowdsourcing approach was getting fans involved and the subsequent buzz that surrounded the contest for the consumer-generated advertisement.[5]

❸ How do companies choose advertising agencies?

EXTERNAL ADVERTISING AGENCIES

Most companies hire advertising agencies to perform some or all of the advertising functions. When the decision is made to retain an external advertising agency, the company commits substantial resources to the goal of expanding its audience.

Many options are available when choosing an advertising agency. All sizes and types of agencies exist. At one end of the spectrum are the highly specialized, boutique-type agencies offering only one specific service (e.g., making television ads) or serving only one type of client. G+G Advertising of Albuquerque, New Mexico, specializes in advertising to Native Americans, a market of an estimated 10 million people.[6]

At the other end of the spectrum are the full-service agencies, including The Richards Group, that provide every type of advertising and promotional activity. These companies offer advice and assistance in working with the other components of the IMC program, including consumer and trade promotions, direct-marketing programs, digital programs, and alternative media. Figure 5.5 lists the services that full-service advertising agencies typically provide.

In addition to advertising agencies are other closely associated types of firms. *Media service companies* negotiate and purchase media packages (called *media buys*) for companies. *Direct-marketing agencies* handle every aspect of a direct-marketing campaign, either through telephone orders (800 numbers), Internet programs, or by direct mail. Some companies focus on either *consumer promotions, trade promotions,* or both. These

FIGURE 5.5 ▶
Services Provided by
Full-Service Agencies

- Advice about how to develop target markets
- Specialized services for business markets
- Suggestions about how to project a strong company image and theme
- Assistance in selecting company logos and slogans
- Preparation of advertisements
- Planning and purchasing media time and space

companies assist in developing promotions such as coupons, premiums, contests, and sweepstakes. A new group of agencies specialize in developing *online and digital services.* Boxcar Creative designs *interactive Web sites* and widgets that can be used on multiple sites. Other companies offer *social media services* to reach consumers and businesses through a wide array of Internet techniques. *Public relations* firms provide experts to help companies and individuals develop positive public images and for damage control when negative publicity arises.

One approach to advertising management, developed by the Young & Rubicam Advertising Agency, is the *whole-egg theory.* The program moves from only selling a client's products to instead helping the client attain total success in the marketplace. It requires a more fully integrated marketing approach that includes a wider array of services. As client companies began to move to more integrated marketing approaches, agencies such as Young & Rubicam and The Richards Group captured more accounts.[7]

CHOOSING AN AGENCY

The next advertising management function is choosing an agency. The process includes developing effective selection criteria for the process of hiring an advertising agency. Figure 5.6 lists the steps involved in this process.

Goal Setting

Before making any contact with an advertising agency, company leaders identify and prioritize corporate goals. Goals provide a sense of direction designed to prevent personal biases from affecting decisions. Without clearly understood goals, it becomes more difficult to know which agency to choose, because company leaders do not have a clear idea of what they want to accomplish. It also makes it difficult for agencies to react when companies submit requests for proposals. They will not be certain about what the company wants from an advertising campaign.

Selection Criteria

Stating the selection criteria constitutes the second step. Even firms with experience set criteria in advance in order to reduce any biases that might affect the decision. Emotions and other feelings can lead to poor decisions. Figure 5.7 identifies some of the major issues to be considered as part of the process. The list can be especially useful during the initial screening, when the field narrows to the top five (or fewer) agencies.

Agency Size
The size of the agency should be considered, especially as it compares to the size of the company hiring the agency. If a large firm hires a small agency, the small agency may be overwhelmed. A small firm hiring a large agency may find that the company's account could be lost or could be treated as being insignificant. A good rule of thumb to follow regarding the size of the agency is that the account should be large enough for the agency so that it is important to the agency but small enough that, if lost, the agency would not be badly affected.

Relevant Experience
When an agency has experience in a given industry, the agency's employees are better able to understand the client firm, its customers, and the structure of the marketing channel. At the same time, the client company will make sure the agency does not have any *conflicts of interest.* An advertising firm that has been hired by one manufacturer of

• Set goals.	• Request client references.
• Select process and criteria.	• Reduce list to two or three viable agencies.
• Screen initial list of applicants.	• Request creative pitch.

◀ **FIGURE 5.6**

Steps in Selecting an Advertising Agency

- Size of the agency
- Relevant experience of the agency
- Conflicts of interest
- Creative reputation and capabilities
- Production capabilities

- Media purchasing capabilities
- Other services available
- Client retention rates
- Personal chemistry

automobile tires would experience a conflict of interest if another tire manufacturer attempted to hire the agency.

An advertising agency can have relevant experience without representing a competitor. Such experience can be gained when an agency works for a similar company operating in a different industry. For example, when an agency has a manufacturer of automobile batteries as a client, the experience is relevant to selling automobile tires.

The agency should also have experience with the business-to-business side of the market, so that retailers, wholesalers, and any other channel party are considered in the marketing and advertising of the product. All of the milk advertisements in this textbook were created by Bozell Worldwide, which has become Lowe Worldwide. In addition to the milk advertisements, Lowe Worldwide's clients include Rexona, Saab, Axe, Johnson & Johnson, and Electolux. Note that the list does not include competing firms within the same industry.

Creative Reputation and Capabilities

One method of assessing an agency's creativity would include asking for a list of awards the company has received. Although awards do not always translate into creating effective advertisements, in most cases there is a positive relationship between winning awards and writing effective ads. Most creative awards are given by peers. As a result, they are good indicators of what others think of the agency's creative efforts.

Production and Media Purchasing Capabilities

These capabilities should be examined if these services are needed. A firm that needs an agency to produce a television commercial and also buy media time should check on these activities as part of the initial screening process. Many agencies either employ subsidiary companies to perform the media work or subcontract it to a media firm. The advertising agency does not necessarily need to make media buys, but it should have the capacity to make sure they are made and fit with the ads being designed.

The type of information involved in selecting an advertising agency can be difficult to obtain. The company hiring the agency should engage in thorough research. It helps to access each agency's Web page and annual report and to search for news articles about the agency. Most advertising agencies provide prospectus sheets describing company capabilities.

Other Criteria

The final three selection criteria—*other services available, client retention rates*, and *personal chemistry*—are revealed as the final steps of selection take place. These criteria help make the final determination in the selection process.

▼ The milk industry is just one of the accounts being handled by Lowe Worldwide.

In addition to the backstroke and the butterfly, I can perform a world-class chug-a-lug. With milk. It has protein for my muscles, plus essential vitamins and minerals like calcium and potassium. All of which help me get the one mineral every Olympian craves. Gold.

MILK

Where's *your* mustache?"

Reference Requests

After completion of the initial screening, the company requests references from the agencies still in the running. Most agencies post major clients on company Web sites and provide additional client information when requested. A company can obtain references of firms with similar needs. Also, when possible, the company can contact former clients of the agency. Finding out why they switched often provides valuable information, even when changes were made for legitimate reasons.

Discovering an agency's *client retention rate* reveals how effective the firm has been working with various clients, although poor service is not the only reason a firm changes agencies. Sometimes the move was made because an agency became too small to handle an account that has increased in size due to a merger or purchase of another company.

Background checks start with finding firms that have dealt with each agency. Also, talking to media agents who sell media time provides insights as to how an agency buys time and deals with customers. Companies that have formed contracts with individual agencies for production facilities or other services are excellent sources of information. Background checks help the client company make sure the agency can provide quality professional services.

Creative Pitch

When the list has been reduced to two or three finalists, the company's selection team asks each for a creative pitch. The advertising agencies chosen to compete provide a formal presentation that addresses a specific problem, situation, or set of questions, a process which is also called a *shootout*. The presentations reveal how each agency would deal with specific issues that might arise during preparation of a campaign. This helps a client company choose the agency that best understands the issues at stake and offers a comprehensive approach to solving the problem or issue.

Preparing a pitch takes time and is costly for advertising agencies; therefore, agencies only want to prepare pitches that have a decent chance of being accepted. Spending time preparing a pitch only to find out later the company had no desire to switch agencies, but were told by upper management to solicit pitches, is frustrating.[8] A company seeking to retain an advertising agency should provide sufficient time for the competing finalists to prepare the pitch. Pink Jacket Creative's Bill Breedlove reports, "I would prefer at least 30 days to prepare a pitch. Even 45 to 60 days would be wonderful sometimes, and for some companies."

Recently, Oscar Mayer, a brand under the Kraft umbrella, was looking for ways to unify its portfolio of products and contemporize its image with consumers. The mcgarrybowen agency demonstrated how Oscar Mayer could contemporize the brand and build emotional ties with customers. The agency's ideas were fresh, contemporary, and had the emotional spark the organization desired.[9]

When Kraft launched its Oscar Mayer Deli Creations sandwiches, the initial print ad developed by the brand's previous agency depicted a woman in a suit, standing with her arm bent eating one of the Deli Creation sandwiches. Karen Adams, senior director of advertising at Kraft Foods, stated, "People don't eat sandwiches that way." Instead, new ads were created showing real people in real-life situations eating sandwiches.[10] The Oscar Mayer ad in this section depicts a construction worker ready to enjoy a Deli Creation sandwich with the tagline "Oh goody, it's Monday."

▼ During the creative pitch for the Oscar Mayer account, mcgarrybowen demonstrated an ability to transform the brand to bring the emotional spark sought by the client.

Oh goody, it's Monday.

A hot, melted sandwich that tastes so fresh, it's the perfect way to kick off your week.

it doesn't get better than this

FIGURE 5.8 ▶
Pitching Do's and Don'ts

- Do listen. Allow the client to talk.
- Do your preparation. Know the client and its business.
- Do make a good first impression. Dress up, not down.
- Do a convincing job of presenting. Believe in what you are presenting.
- Don't assume all clients are the same. Each has a unique need.

- Don't try to solve the entire problem in the pitch.
- Don't be critical of the product or the competition.
- Don't overpromise. It will come back to haunt you.
- Don't spend a lot of time pitching credentials and references.

Source: Based on Heather Jacobs, "How to Make Sure Your Pitch Is Heard," *B&T Weekly* 57, no. 2597 (February 2, 2007), pp. 14–16.

Successful creative pitches result from hard work and thorough planning. Figure 5.8 highlights some of the do's and don'ts for advertising agencies in making pitches.

Agency Selection

During the presentation phase, the opportunity exists to meet with creatives, media buyers, account executives, and other people who will work on the account. *Chemistry* between employees of the two different firms becomes critical. The client company's leaders should be convinced that they will work well together. Chemistry can break or make the final decision.[11]

After completing the selection process the agency and the company work together to prepare the advertising campaign. The account executive, account planner, and advertising creative all plays key roles in the process.

ROLES OF ADVERTISING PERSONNEL

④ What roles are played within advertising agencies and client companies?

Personnel within advertising agencies perform a wide variety of roles. In small agencies, an individual may perform multiple roles. In a large agency, multiple individuals will be employed in the various departments and perform similar functions. The primary roles within the agency consist of the account executives, creatives, traffic managers, and account planners.

Account Executives

The account executive will be the key go-between for both the advertising agency and the client company. This individual stays actively involved in soliciting the account, finalizing details of the contract, and working with personnel within the agency to make sure the advertising campaign is produced according to the client's specifications. An account executive often helps the company define the theme of the overall IMC program and provides other support, as needed.

Creatives

The persons who develop and design advertisements are called creatives. They are either members of advertising agencies or freelancers. Some smaller companies provide only creative advertising services without becoming involved in other marketing programs and activities. Creatives may appear to hold the "glamour" jobs in advertising, because they get to actually create ads and marketing materials. At the same time, creatives work long hours and face enormous pressures to design effective advertisements that produce tangible results.

Traffic Managers

The traffic manager works closely with the advertising agency's account executive, creatives, and production staff. The manager's responsibilities include scheduling the various aspects of the agency's work to make sure it is completed on time. During production, the traffic manager will be responsible for making sure props, actors, and whatever else is needed has been ordered and is in place at the time of the filming or recording.

Account Planners

The account planner becomes the voice or advocate for the consumer in the advertising agency. The planner makes sure the creative team understands the consumer (or business). Account planners interact with the account executive and the client to understand the target audience of the ad campaign. The planner then works to make sure creative messages reach the right customers.

The account planner assists the client in developing long-term communication strategies and provides direction for individual advertising campaigns. In small agencies, the role may be performed by the account executive. Larger firms employ separate individuals and or departments to conduct the account planning role.

The Role of Quality Communication

Quality communication will be a vital part of the relationship between a client company and an advertising agency. A recent survey of 250 senior executives of marketing and advertising agencies revealed that these managers believed that at least 30 percent of their staff's time was wasted or used ineffectively because of poor communications from clients. Issues such as poor competitive information and lack of clarity about the company or brand's position in the marketplace were common. More disturbing was that 75 percent of the ad agencies indicated that clients go through at least five significant changes in directions given to agencies and about what they want the agencies to do. The agencies reported that, on average, they dealt with five different individuals from the client company, each with a different agenda and different directions for the agency.[12]

The company's marketing department manager works closely with the advertising agency's account manager to overcome these obstacles. The manager remains aware that missteps and changes to an advertising program are costly in terms of additional advertising agency fees as well as the less effective campaign that might result.

Clients want to know if they are getting a good value. Many clients worry that they do not understand the relationship between an agency's cost and the actual value it renders. Ron Cox, a vice president at Wrigley Jr. Company, suggests that agencies update clients regularly on the work they are doing and the results obtained. *Stewardship reports* help clients review the process and the outcome. Updating clients will be critical, especially when large amounts of money are being spent on advertising.[13]

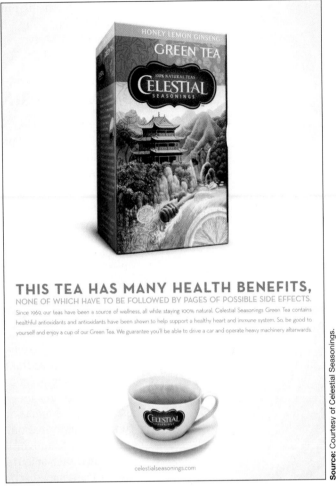

THIS TEA HAS MANY HEALTH BENEFITS,
NONE OF WHICH HAVE TO BE FOLLOWED BY PAGES OF POSSIBLE SIDE EFFECTS.
Since 1969, our teas have been a source of wellness, all while staying 100% natural. Celestial Seasonings Green Tea contains healthful antioxidants and antioxidants have been shown to help support a healthy heart and immune system. So, be good to yourself and enjoy a cup of our Green Tea. We guarantee you'll be able to drive a car and operate heavy machinery afterwards.

celestialseasonings.com

▲ The account planner represents the consumer's viewpoint so that creatives can design effective advertisements, such as this one by Celestial Seasonings for Green Tea.

ADVERTISING CAMPAIGN MANAGEMENT

Advertising campaign management is the process of preparing and integrating a specific advertising program. Whether the work is done in-house or with an external agency, the marketing manager oversees the development of the advertising campaign. An effective campaign consists of following five steps:

5 What steps are completed as part of advertising campaign management?

1. Conduct and review the advertising research.
2. Establish advertising objectives consistent with the overall IMC program.
3. Review the advertising budget.
4. Select the appropriate media based on the viewing habits of the target market.
5. Prepare a creative brief.

The advertising program should be consistent with every part of the IMC program as well as the company's mission to make sure the firm presents a clear message to key target markets. Advertising efforts are refined to gain the maximum benefit from promotional dollars.

ADVERTISING RESEARCH

When an advertising agency is hired, the team immediately seeks to understand the client's company and products. Clients try to provide accurate and timely information that assist the agency in the preparation of the campaign. To create an effective advertising program, the advertising agency's creative personnel requires information about customers, why they purchase the product, and what exactly they seek to purchase.

Products are not typically purchased solely for attributes. Customers also consider the benefits they provide. Individuals purchasing makeup, cologne, perfume, and other beauty products may not care about the ingredients and attributes, but care very much about how these items will make them look or smell. Advertising research goes beyond identifying demographic profiles or target markets. It also identifies the brand's competitors and the communications used in the industry.

To best understand a company's customers, their purchasing habits, and the other key ideas about them, various forms of advertising research are available. Key insights about how products are used, when they are used, and why can emerge from effective research. Two primary approaches exist.

Product-specific research involves identifying key product characteristics that become selling points. For example, the marketing team might try to discover the most desirable features are "apps" for a cell phone. The team may find that certain apps are used when customers are bored and are just passing time, whereas others provide specific functional information, such as the location of a restaurant while the customer drives to dinner. One feature or the other may become the focal point of a commercial.

Consumer-oriented research will be used to understand the context of a product's use. A team may discover that a pizza restaurant's clientele tends to stay longer, because the establishment offers quality family time. This more *anthropological* approach involves direct observation of consumers using the good or service. Other customer-oriented research may feature a *sociological* analysis of social class issues, trends, and family life cycle changes. Ralph Lauren may match with upper class, richer families. Another product may appeal most to empty-nest couples looking to enrich their lives in some way. A third customer-oriented approach analyzes *psychological* motives for product purchases, such as feeling sexy, powerful, or intelligent.

▼ Consumer-oriented research provides valuable information, such as why some individuals enjoy riding motorcycles.

Sometimes a company's marketing team becomes so close to products and customers that they do not see these issues. Consequently, agencies often seek out more information than is provided by clients. One common approach used by agencies to understand a client's customers is a **focus group**, which consists of consumers who are retained to talk about a particular topic, product, or brand.

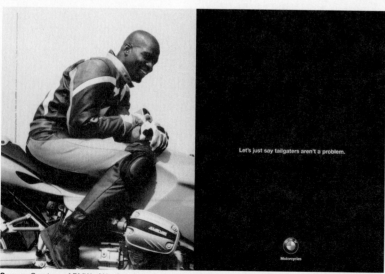

Let's just say tailgaters aren't a problem.

BMW
Motorcycles

Motel 6 and The Richards Group

During the interview with Stan Richards that was conducted for the opening vignette in this chapter, he talked about a "perfect example" of understanding a client's customers using focus groups. "We've worked with Motel 6 for 24 years," he said, "and the beginning of that relationship was a remarkable insight."

"The insight came out of our research, which was primarily qualitative. We sat behind a glass window in a focus room setting. Our account planner sat at the head of the table, moderating the session. We've got a dozen people in the room whom we recruited by phone. They don't know why they're in the room. We know that they all use Motel 6. The moderator asks, 'Where do you stay when you're on the road?' They go around the table and nobody says, 'Motel 6.'

"The moderator pushes further and says, 'Well, where else do you stay?' They go around the table again, and nobody says, 'Motel 6.' Now, why is that? They didn't know who the other people in the room were, and they didn't want to be perceived as being poor or cheap.

"Now, finally, you get somebody, by going around the table again, to say, 'You know, if it's late at night, I'll stop at a Motel 6, and I can save enough money to buy a tank of gas.' And then, somebody else across the table would say, 'I do the same thing, and I save enough money to bring a gift home to the grandkids.' And all of a sudden, the character of the room changed, because everybody had a story like that. What happened was a move from embarrassment to pride in the benefits of frugality.

"That's what the insight was all about. I am a frugal person, and if my eyes are closed, all hotel rooms look alike. I don't see any reason to overspend for lodging, when I can find a perfectly good place like Motel 6."

From this insight, The Richards Group developed the theme, tagline, and advertising approach for Motel 6 that are still used today. Richards noted that the phrase, "A clean, comfortable room, at the lowest price of any national chain," appears in every spot.[14]

Richards argues that this approach highlights the difference between simply creating an advertisement through a technique such as crowdsourcing and conducting the type of quality research that leads to a better outcome. "Let's suppose that Motel 6 has cast a wide net, that 1,000 people are working on creative, and then we're going to run the one they like best. Just run a contest. It is so unlikely that they would have gotten to the insight that really propelled their business. The insight was a really simple one, but it wouldn't have come out if people were simply just trying to sell Motel 6."

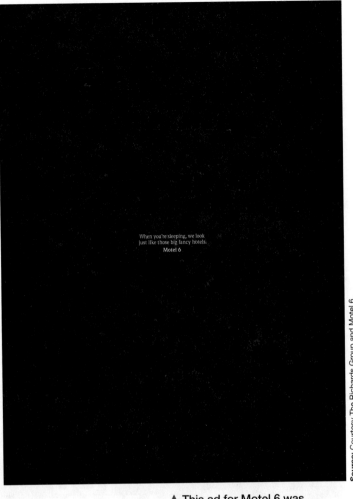

When you're sleeping, we look just like those big fancy hotels.
Motel 6

▲ This ad for Motel 6 was inspired by a focus group and a comment made by one of the participants: "If my eyes are closed, all hotel rooms look alike."

ADVERTISING GOALS

The second step of advertising planning is establishing and clarifying advertising goals, which are derived from the firm's overall communication objectives. Several advertising goals are central to the IMC process. Several of these are listed in Figure 5.9.[15]

6 What are the primary goals of advertising?

Building Brand Awareness

A strong global brand and corporate image should be a key advertising goal. Building a brand's image begins with developing brand awareness. *Brand awareness* means the consumers recognize and remember a particular brand or company name when they consider purchasing options. Advertising can increase brand awareness.

◄ **FIGURE 5.9**
Advertising Goals

• To build brand awareness
• To inform
• To persuade
• To support other marketing efforts
• To encourage action

In business-to-business marketing, brand awareness leads to being considered by members of the buying center, because business customers recognize the brand name of the goods or services the company offers. Brand awareness becomes especially important in modified rebuy situations, when a firm looks to change to a new vendor or evaluates a product that has not been purchased recently. In new buy situations, members of the buying center spend more time seeking prospective vendors than they will for modified rebuys. Consequently, brand equity creates a major advantage for any company with such recognition.

Successful brands possess two characteristics: (1) the top of mind and (2) the consumers' top choice. When consumers are asked to identify brands that quickly come to mind from a product category, one or two particular brands are nearly always mentioned. These names are the **top-of-mind brands**. For example, when asked to identify fast-food restaurants, McDonald's and Burger King almost always head the list. The same may be true for Nike and Reebok athletic shoes, and may occur both in the United States and in other countries.

The term **top choice** suggests exactly what the term implies: A top-choice brand is the first or second pick when a consumer reviews her evoked set of possible purchasing alternatives. Many products become top of mind or top choice due to *brand equity*, the set of characteristics that cause consumers or businesses to believe that a brand is different and better. Advertising can help strengthen brand equity.

Providing Information

Advertising serves other goals, including providing information to both consumers and business buyers. Typical information for consumers includes a retailer's store hours, business location, or sometimes more detailed product specifications. Information may make the purchasing process appear to be simple and convenient, which can entice customers to travel to the store and finalize the purchase.

In business-to-business situations, information from some advertisements may lead various members of the buying center to consider a particular company. Information that reaches members of the buying center during the search stage of the purchasing process will be the most valuable. For high-involvement purchases, in which members of the buying center have strong vested interests in the success of the choice, informative advertisements are the also beneficial. Low-involvement decisions usually do not require the same level of detail.

Persuasion

Persuasion has taken place when an advertisement convinces consumers that a particular brand is superior. Changing consumer attitudes and persuading them to consider a new purchasing choice is a challenging task. Advertisers can utilize several methods of persuasion. One method is to show consumers the negative consequences of failing to use a particular brand. Persuasive advertising is used more in consumer marketing than in business-to-business situations.

Supporting Marketing Efforts

Advertising can be used to support other marketing functions. Manufacturers use advertising to support trade and consumer promotions, such as theme packaging or combination offers. Contests, such as the McDonald's Monopoly game, require additional advertising to be effective.

▼ This advertisement informs consumers that GameStop workers are also players and can provide tips on how to get out of a jam.

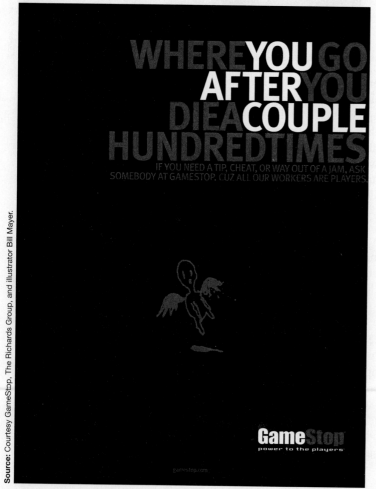

Retailers also advertise to support marketing programs. Any type of special sale (white sale, buy-one-get-one-free, pre–Christmas sale) requires effective advertising to attract customers to the store. Both manufacturers and retail outlets run advertisements in conjunction with coupons or other special offers. Del Monte placed a 30-cent coupon in the advertisement shown in this section. The ad highlights a smaller-size container with a pull-top lid. These features match the advertisement's target market: senior citizens. The first magazine featuring this advertisement was *Modern Maturity*. Manufacturer coupons are regularly redeemed at grocery stores (sometimes at double their face values), and in-store coupons are part of many retail store print advertisements. When ads are combined with other marketing efforts into a larger, more integrated effort revolving around a theme, the program is called a **promotional campaign**.

Encouraging Action

Many firms set behavioral goals for advertising programs. A television commercial encouraging viewers to take action by dialing a toll-free number to make a quick purchase is an example. Everything from ShamWow to Snuggies has been sold using action tactics. Infomercials and home shopping network programs rely heavily on immediate consumer purchasing responses.

Action-oriented advertising may be used in the business-to-business sector. When it is, generating leads becomes the primary the goal. Many business advertisements provide Web addresses or telephone numbers buyers can use to request more information or make a purchase.

The five advertising goals of building image, providing information, being persuasive, supporting other marketing efforts, and encouraging action are not separate from each other. They work together in key ways. For instance, awareness and information are part of persuasion. The key is to emphasize one goal without forgetting the others.

Source: Courtesy of Del Monte Foods.

▲ A Del Monte advertisement directed to senior citizens offering a smaller can with a pull-off lid.

THE ADVERTISING BUDGET

Once the major goals of the advertising campaign have been established, a review of the advertising budget follows. Chapter 4 described the various methods for developing marketing communication budgets. After establishing the total amount of dollars to be allocated to advertising, the challenge becomes choosing the proper media approach to reach the advertising goal. Three basic tactics used to allocate advertising funds are:

7 What are the key elements of an advertising budget?

- Pulsating schedule
- Flighting schedule
- Continuous schedule

A **pulsating schedule of advertising** involves continuous advertising during the year with bursts of higher intensity at specific times (more ads in more media). Companies can also select what is called a **flighting** approach or schedule, whereby ads are presented only during peak times, and not at all during other times of the year.

Firms often advertise more during peak seasons such as Christmas, because this involves sending messages during the times when customers are most inclined to buy, which is termed *being on the hot spot*. Weight Watchers, Diet Centers, and others advertise heavily during the first weeks of January. Many New Year's resolutions include going on a diet.

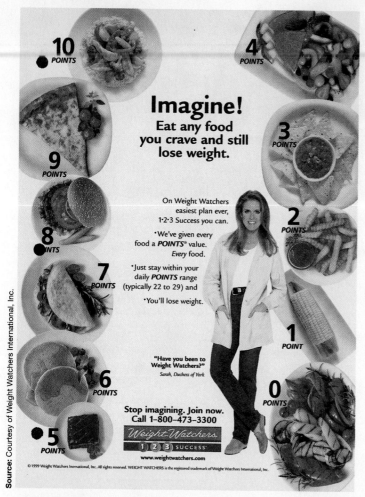

▲ Weight loss companies such as Weight Watchers tend to budget more for advertising after the Christmas Holiday, when individuals make New Year's resolutions to start dieting.

8 What are the issues in the media-selection process?

Advertising during slow sales seasons focuses on "drumming up business" when people do not regularly buy. In retail sales, slow seasons occur during January and February. Some companies advertise more during those periods to sell merchandise left over from the Christmas season and to encourage customers to shop. Manufacturers also realize that many retailers are not advertising and hope that the ads will gain greater attention as a result.

Many marketing experts believe it is best to advertise in level amounts to keep the brand name always in front of consumers, which is a **continuous campaign schedule**. Durable goods, such as washing machines and refrigerators, are purchased on an "as needed" basis. A family ordinarily buys a new washing machine only when the old one breaks down or when they remodel a home. Level advertising increases the odds that the buyer will see an advertisement or remember a given name (Kenmore, Whirlpool, or General Electric) at the right time.

The objective is to match the pacing of advertisements with the message, the media, and the nature of the product. Some media make it easier to advertise for longer periods of time. Contracts for billboards are normally for a month or a year. They can be rotated throughout a town or city to present a continuing message about a company or products. At the same time, budgetary constraints can influence the strategies and tactics used in any advertising program.

MEDIA SELECTION

Selecting the appropriate media requires an understanding of the media-usage habits of the company's target market and then matching that information with the profile of each medium's audience. Volkswagen positioned the Tiguan crossover as a fun vehicle aimed at young, active individuals who love the outdoors. Although television commercials were used in the campaign, the more unique component of the campaign was the outdoor segment. The theme "people want an SUV that parks well with others" was featured in a series of outdoor ads placed at bike racks and trail heads at 150 national parks and resorts. According to Brian Martin, CEO of Brand Connections Active Outdoor, which placed the ads, over 30 million impressions were made with hikers, bikers, and other outdoor-lovers.[16]

The advertising team carefully identifies the media a target market uses. Teenagers surf the Web and watch television. Only a small percentage reads newspapers and newsmagazines. Various market segments exhibit differences in when and how they view various media. Older African Americans watch television programs in patterns that are different from those of older Caucasians. Males watch more sports programs than females, and so forth.

In business-to-business markets, knowing the trade journals or business publications that various members of the buying center most likely read assists in the development of a print advertising campaign. Engineers, who tend to be the influencers, may have different media viewing habits than do vice presidents, who may be the deciders.

Although media buys are guided by the advertising agency and the client company, media companies typically make the purchases. A trend toward involving media companies at an earlier stage in the campaign process has evolved in recent years. Previously, most media companies were contacted after a campaign became ready or was nearly complete, with the specific task of purchasing media space or time. Instead of this approach, Procter & Gamble invited 40 media companies to a conference to solicit ideas about how to market company products and asked for new product suggestions. Companies such as Johnson & Johnson, Clorox, Kimberly-Clark, Verizon, and HP have enlisted media companies as strategic partners in developing advertising and marketing campaigns.[17] Media companies are being invited to participate in the strategy development stage because many have a good understanding of the target audience. They are able to provide valuable information to the creative staff about how to best reach the client's target market employing the primary media that target consumers use.

Source: Courtesy of Chattem, Inc.

▲ Selecting the right media ensures that consumers who are the most likely to purchase Gold Bond Body Lotion will see this advertisement.

THE CREATIVE BRIEF

Typically, creatives work with a document prepared by the client and account executive called the *creative strategy* or *creative brief.* Although various forms exist, the basic components of a standard creative brief are provided in Figure 5.10. The creative takes the information provided to produce advertisements that convey the desired message. A quality creative brief can be extremely helpful. When prepared properly, the brief saves the agency considerable time and effort and results in a stronger advertising campaign for the client.

As mentioned earlier, ineffective communications with clients is a common difficulty agencies experience. The creative brief may part of the problem. A survey of senior executives of advertising agencies suggests that fewer than 40 percent of client briefs are clear.[18] Agency leaders reported that many briefs are weak in the areas of providing competitive information and statements about how the brand should be positioned within the competitive landscape. Consequently, attention should be given to clarifying these issues before creating advertisements.

⑨ How does a creative brief facilitate effective advertising?

The Objective

The first step in preparing the creative strategy is to identify the objective of the ad campaign. Some of the most common advertising objectives include:

- Increasing brand awareness
- Building brand image
- Increasing customer traffic
- Increasing retailer or wholesaler orders
- Responding to inquiries from end users and channel members
- Providing information

The creative reviews the main objective before designing advertisements. The objectives guide the advertising design and the choice of an executional framework. For instance, when increasing brand awareness is the goal, the *name* of the product will be prominently displayed in the advertisement. Building brand image normally results in the *actual product* being more prominently displayed.

◄ **FIGURE 5.10**
The Creative Brief

- The objective
- The target audience
- The message theme
- The support
- The constraints

▲ This advertisement for Playtex used additional target market profile information to help design a message directed to active teenagers and young women.

▼ An advertisement for Sub-Zero illustrating the message theme of keeping foods fresh.

The Target Audience

A creative then examines the target audience. An advertisement designed to persuade a business to inquire about new computer software will be different from a consumer advertisement created for the same company. The business advertisement focuses on the type of industry and a specific member of the buying center. The more detail that is known about the target audience, the easier it becomes for a creative to design an effective advertisement.

Target-market profiles that are too general are not helpful. Rather than specifying "males, ages 20 to 35," more specific information will be needed, such as "males, ages 20 to 35, college educated, and professionals." Other information, including hobbies, interests, opinions, and lifestyles, makes it possible to more precisely target an advertisement. The Playtex advertisement in this section was prepared for young females who enjoy playing sports and have active lifestyles. The additional information helped the creative design an advertisement that appealed to the right group of females.

The Message Theme

The message theme presents an outline of key idea(s) that the advertising program conveys. The message theme represents the benefit or promise the advertiser uses to reach consumers or businesses. The promise, or *unique selling point*, describes the major benefit the good or service offers customers. A message theme for an automobile could be oriented toward luxury, safety, fun, fuel efficiency, or driving excitement. A message theme for a hotel could focus on luxury, price, or unusual features, such as a hotel in Paris, France, noting the ease of access to all of the nearby tourist attractions. The message theme matches the medium selected, the target market, and the primary IMC message.[19]

In the advertisement for Sub-Zero refrigerators in this section, the message theme features the "freshness of food" being kept in the Sub-Zero refrigerator. This message targets consumers, but also may influence managers of restaurants, cafeterias, and catering services.

Message themes can be oriented toward either rational or emotional processes. A "left-brain" ad oriented toward the logical, rational side informs individuals using numbers, letters, words, and concepts. Left-brain advertising should be logical and factual, with a rational appeal. A number of logical features (size, price, special features) are part of the decision to buy a car. At the same time, many cars are purchased for emotional reasons. The right side of the brain contains emotions. It works with abstract ideas, images, and feelings. A car may be chosen for its color, sportiness, or other less rational reasons.

Most advertising focuses on either the right brain or the left brain. Advertising can also be effective by balancing the two sides. Rational, economic beings have difficulty defending the purchase of an expensive sports car such as a Porsche. Many product purchases are based on how a person feels about the good or service, combined with rational information.[20]

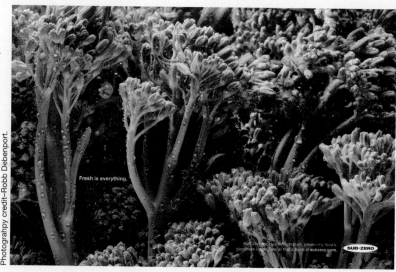

The Support

Support should be provided in the fourth component of the creative strategy. **Support** takes the form of facts that substantiate the message theme. When Aveeno products won "Best of Beauty" awards from *Allure* magazine, the *Allure* "Best of Beauty" seal was placed on the company's products. It was also used in company advertising to support Aveeno's claims of superiority. In the Pearle Vision advertisement in this section, various statements provide support. These include the idea that microTHINS are 30 percent thinner, 40 percent lighter, 4 times more scratch resistant, 10 times more impact resistant, antireflective, and have 99.9 percent UV protection. Supporting evidence allows creatives to design advertisements that attract attention to the materials that substantiate claims made about products.

The Constraints

Constraints are any legal and mandatory restrictions placed on advertisements. Constraints include legal protections for trademarks, logos, and copy registrations. Constraints also include disclaimers about warranties, offers, and claims. For warranties, a disclaimer specifies the conditions under which they will be honored. For example, tire warranties often state that they apply *under normal driving conditions with routine maintenance*, so that a person cannot ignore tire balancing and rotation and expect to get free new tires when the old ones wear out quickly. Disclaimer warranties notify consumers of potential hazards associated with products. Tobacco advertisements must contain a statement from the Surgeon General about the dangers of smoking and chewing tobacco. Disclaimers about offers spell out the terms of financing agreements, as well as when bonuses or discounts apply. Claims identify the exact nature of the statement made in the advertisement. This includes nutritional claims as well as statements about serving sizes and other information describing the product.

After these steps have been completed, the creative brief is ready. From this point forward, the message and the media match, and actual advertisements can be produced. Effective creative briefs take the overall IMC message and tailor it to a specific advertising campaign. This, in turn, gives the company a better chance of reaching customers with messages that return measurable results and help guarantee success. Recent research suggests that campaigns designed in 2 months or less have the greatest likelihood of being "highly effective." Those that take longer tend not to be as effective. The goal is to move forward without rushing. A campaign designed in 2 weeks or less is also likely to be ineffective.[21]

INTERNATIONAL IMPLICATIONS

Advertising management now involves major expenditures overseas. The top 100 global advertisers spent an average of 62 percent of advertising budgets outside

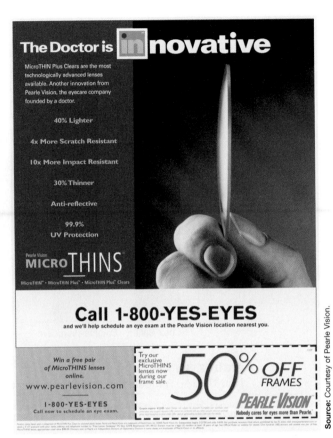

Source: Courtesy of Pearle Vision.

▲ This advertisement for Pearle Vision presents support information to substantiate the message claim.

▼ The Surgeon General's warning is an example of a constraint.

Source: Author Supplied Image.

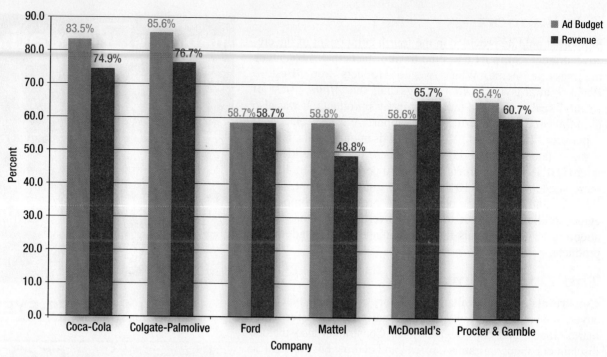

FIGURE 5.11 ▶
Non-U.S. Ad Budgets and Sales Revenues for Major Corporations

Source: Adapted from Laurel Wentz and Bradley Johnson, "Top 100 Global Advertisers Heap Their Spending Abroad," *Advertising Age,* http://adage.com/print?article_id=
140723, November 30, 2009.

the United States. Figure 5.11 compares the non-U.S. advertising budget to non-U.S. sales revenue for six major corporations. As illustrated, Coca-Cola spends 83.5 percent of company advertising dollars outside the United States, where 74.9 percent of its total revenues are generated. Colgate-Palmolive spends 85.6 percent of its advertising dollars on non-U.S. ads and generates 76.7 percent of its revenues outside the United States. Data for Ford, Mattel, McDonald's, and Procter & Gamble are also provided.[22]

Two major differences emerge when advertising management is considered from an international perspective. The first is in regard to the process itself. The second concerns preparing international advertising campaigns.

The general processes used to prepare advertising campaigns are fairly uniform. Some of the most important differences are in the areas of availability of qualified advertising agencies and how those agencies are selected. For example, in many Asian cultures the beginning of a face-to-face meeting would include an exchange of gifts. Also, business cards have differing uses and meanings across cultures. In some countries, cards are only presented to highly trusted allies. In others, they are freely passed out. The marketing team in any company should carefully study the nuances of business meetings, including the use of formal titles, eye contact, who speaks first, and other variables, before beginning a relationship with an advertising agency in another country.

Agencies in other countries might not follow typical procedures such as a shootout or the preparation of a creative brief. Forms of preplanning research may also vary. In some countries, it is not possible to conduct the same types of research as in the United States and other Western cultures.

Advertising campaigns that are designed for an international audience require an understanding of the various languages and cultures that might be involved. In Europe, French, Spanish, Portuguese, Italian, and other languages would require translation and back-translation of advertising themes and messages to make certain the idea can be clearly presented in various countries. Media-selection processes may also require adjustment; some countries have state-run television networks and others place restrictions on what can be shown in an advertisement.

!INTEGRATED CAMPAIGNS IN ACTION

● Oscar Mayer

Jane Hilk, senior vice president of marketing at Oscar Mayer, told the agency team at mcgarrybowen, "Oscar Mayer is everyday food that makes you feel good. It's about real joy, real moments. Living life and loving every minute of it." The ambition of the new campaign was to take Oscar Mayer to a place that is:

● Energetic
● Culturally relevant
● Contemporary
● Iconic
● Able to capture the spirit of the brand

Focus group and consumer research revealed several ideas that impacted the Oscar Mayer brand, which the agency termed the *brand idea*. The consumer insight was that the world is often too negative and uptight. You have to bring your own good times. The product category motivation was that consumers hunger for meal times that do more than just fill them up. That is where Oscar Mayer can make a brand difference. The company offers quality meats that never disappoint and always leave a smile. The brand idea, that Oscar Mayer is "good mood food," was born.

In producing the print ads, the goal of the agency was to capture real moments. The person in each photo never looks directly at the camera. The person should not be perfect. The person's hair may be slightly out of place, there might be a spot of mustard on the chin, and the ketchup on the hot dog looks natural. It was important that the photo not look stock or posed. Instead, it should portray the joy of the moment. The snapshot should capture real life, as people enjoy "good mood food."[23]

Several television commercials were also developed featuring the phrase "It doesn't get better than this," which matched the print and video ads, as well as the digital effort, "Mission to Spread Good Mood Food." The entire multimillion-dollar campaign was launched with three spots and a sponsorship of the *Golden Globes*, which was chosen because of the large number of people who watch the awards show. Jane Hilk

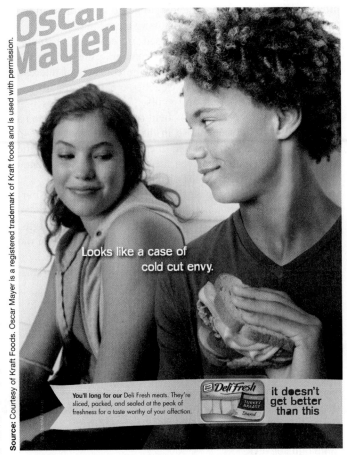

▲ The goal of the Oscar Mayer print ads was to make consumers feel the moment.

noted, "It was an ideal setting to launch Oscar Mayer's new contemporary, energetic, look."[24]

Your instructor has additional information about the ads, visuals, and displays used in this campaign.

66 SUMMARY

Effective advertising requires matching a noticeable message with the appropriate media. This chapter reviews the advertising management process. Effective advertising occurs when the firm has a well-defined mission statement and targets its energies in the direction of creating goods or services to meet the needs of a target market.

Advertising management begins with deciding whether an in-house department should develop advertisements or whether an external advertising agency should be retained. When choosing an external agency, the company's leaders establish clear steps to lead to the optimal agency being selected. The steps include: (1) spelling out and prioritizing organizational goals, (2) carefully establishing quality selection criteria, (3) screening firms based on those criteria, (4) requesting references from firms that are finalists, (5) performing background checks, (6) requesting creative pitches, (7) making an on-site visit to get to know those in the agency, and (8) offering and finalizing a contract.

Common selection criteria used in selecting agencies include: (1) the size of the agency matching the size of the company, (2) relevant experience, (3) no conflicts of interest, (4) production capabilities, (5) quality creative capabilities, (6) suitable media-purchasing skills, (7) other services that can be rendered as needed, (8) client retention rates, and (9) a good chemistry between those in the company and those in the agency. Carefully utilizing these criteria increases the odds of a good match between the company and the agency will exist, which increases the chance of success.

Within the advertising agency, the account manager performs the functions of soliciting accounts, finalizing contracts, and selecting creatives to prepare advertising campaigns. Account executives are go-betweens who mediate between the agency and the client company. Account executives also help client organizations refine their IMC messages and programs.

Creatives prepare advertisements and are guided by the creative brief. This document spells out: (1) the objective of the promotional campaign, (2) the target audience, (3) the message theme, (4) the support, and (5) the constraints. The message theme is an outline of the key idea(s) that the program is supposed to convey. The constraints include logos, warranties, disclaimers, or legal statements that are part of various advertisements.

The creative, account executive, and company should agree about which media to use in a campaign. Media are selected based on costs, types of messages, target market characteristics, and other criteria. The creatives then complete the final elements of the ad, and the campaign is prepared.

Advertising management is an important ingredient in the success of an integrated marketing communications program. A quality ad that garners the attention of people in the target audience, makes a key memorable point, and moves buyers to action is difficult to prepare. At the same time, company officials and market account executives know that designing effective ads with tangible results is a challenging but necessary activity. It is important to go through every step of the process carefully to help the company achieve its marketing goals in both the short and long term.

KEY TERMS

message theme   An outline of key idea(s) the advertising campaign conveys.

leverage point   The key element in the advertisement that taps into, or activates, a consumer's personal value system (a value, idea, or concept).

appeal   The approach used to design the advertisement that attracts attention or presents information to consumers, through the use of humor, fear, sex, logic, or emotions.

executional framework   Method used to deliver the advertising message.

advertising management program   The process of preparing and integrating a company's advertising efforts with the overall IMC message.

crowdsourcing   Process of outsourcing the creative aspect of an advertisement to the public.

advertising campaign management   The process of preparing and integrating a specific advertising program in conjunction with the overall IMC message.

product-specific research   Research that identifies key product characteristics that become selling points.

consumer-oriented research   Research that is used to understand the context of a product's use.

focus group   A set of consumers or businesspeople who are retained to talk about a particular topic, product, or brand.

top-of-mind brands   The brands that quickly come to mind when consumers are asked to identify brands from a product category.

top choice   The first or second pick when a consumer reviews his or her evoked set of possible purchasing alternatives.

promotional campaign   Combining advertisements with other marketing efforts into a larger, more integrated effort revolving around a central idea or theme.

pulsating schedule of advertising   Continuous advertising with bursts of higher intensity (more ads in more media) during the course of the year.

flighting schedule of advertising   A schedule whereby companies present ads only during specific times and not at all during other times of the year.

continuous campaign schedule of advertising   When the company advertises in level amounts throughout the year.

support   The facts that substantiate the unique selling point of a creative brief.

constraints   The company, legal, and mandatory restrictions placed on advertisements. They include legal protection for trademarks, logos, and copy registrations.

REVIEW QUESTIONS

1. Describe the following terms: message theme, leverage point, appeal, and executional framework.
2. Define advertising management. What are the four main steps involved?
3. What four main company activities are involved in the advertising management process?
4. What is the relationship between advertising and the overall IMC process?
5. What factors influence the decision of whether to use an in-house advertising group or an external advertising agency?
6. Besides advertising agencies, what other types of organizations play roles in the communication process?
7. What steps should be taken in selecting an advertising agency?
8. What evaluation criteria should be used in selecting an advertising agency?
9. What is a creative pitch?
10. Describe the role of an advertising agency account executive.
11. Describe the role of the advertising creative.
12. Describe the role of a traffic manager.
13. Describe the role of an account planner.
14. What are the steps of an advertising campaign management process?
15. What are the two main forms of research for the purposes of creating advertisements?
16. What is a focus group, and how can such a group help to create more effective advertisements?
17. Describe the terms top of mind and top choice.
18. What elements are included in a creative brief?

CRITICAL THINKING EXERCISES

Discussion Questions

1. Pick up a magazine that you read on a regular basis. Examine 10 advertisements and identify the major selling point in each. Was the major selling idea clear, or was it difficult to ascertain?
2. Look through the ads in this chapter. Which ad to you like the best? Why? Which ad is the least appealing to you? Why? Discuss what makes a print ad appealing and what creates the opposite effect.
3. Review the responsibilities of each of the jobs under "Roles of Advertising Personnel." Which one is most appealing to you? Why? Which one is least appealing? Why?
4. Print off or open the textbook to Figure 5.9, the list of advertising goals. Create a table with three columns. In the first column, you will record the brand being advertised. In the second column, you will write down which advertising goal you think the ad was designed to meet. In the third column, you will assign a score based on your evaluation of each ad's effectiveness, with 10 being effective and 1 being completely ineffective. Once you have created the table, watch a 1-hour television program and record and evaluate every commercial you see. When you are finished, write a paragraph discussing which goals were used the most and which ads were the most effective at accomplishing their goal.
5. Follow the instructions given in question 4, but instead of a television program gather a group of 20 advertisements from a magazine. Make sure the ads are in a sequence and not ones that you randomly picked or chose.
6. Choose one of the following. Using the information in this chapter, prepare a creative brief. You can pick a brand from within the product category.
   a. Energy drink
   b. Frozen apple juice
   c. Fast-food restaurant
   d. Museum
   e. Dress shoes

INTEGRATED LEARNING EXERCISES

1. Making the decision to use an external advertising agency as opposed to an in-house program for advertising or some other aspect of the advertising function is difficult. Access the American Association of Advertising Agencies Web site at **www.aaaa.org**. From the "News and Views" section, examine articles that might help identify benefits of using an advertising agency. What type of information is available at this Web site?
2. A number of agencies assist business organizations with integrated marketing communication programs. Whereas some firms try to provide a wide array of services, others are more

specialized. Access the following association Web sites. What type of information is available on each site? How would the information provided be useful in building an IMC program?

a. International Social Media Association (**www.ismaconnects.org**)

b. Promotion Marketing Association (**www.pmalink.org**)

c. Outdoor Advertising Association of America (**www.oaaa.org**)

d. Direct Marketing Association (**www.the-dma.org**)

3. Part of a communication marketing analysis includes understanding the media usage habits of consumers and their attitudes toward various media. An excellent source of information in Canada is the Media Awareness Network at **www.media-awareness.ca**. Review the types of information available at the Web site. Examine the news articles. What type of information is available at this Web site and how could it be used in developing an advertising campaign?

4. Many advertisers tend to direct ads toward the right side of the brain and develop advertisements based entirely on emotions, images, and pictures. Companies often advertise auto parts and tools with a scantily clad woman to attract the attention of men. The woman has nothing to do with the product, but garners attention. The rationale for using a sexy woman is that if consumers like her, they will like the product and then purchase that brand. Effective advertisements integrate elements from both the left side of the brain as well as the right. They contain elements that appeal to emotions but also have rational arguments. A laundry detergent can be advertised as offering the rational benefit of getting clothes cleaner but also contain the emotional promise that your mother-in-law will think more favorably of you. For each of the following Internet sites, discuss the balance of left-brain versus right-brain advertising appeal.

a. Pier 1 Imports (**www.pier1.com**)

b. Pig O' My Heart Potbellies (**www.potbellypigs.com**)

c. Volkswagen of America (**www.vw.com**)

d. Discount Cheerleading.com (**www.discountcheerleading.com**)

e. Backcountry.com (**www.backcountry.com**)

5. You have been asked to select an advertising agency to handle an account for Red Lobster, a national restaurant chain. Your advertising budget is $30 million. Study the Web sites of the following advertising agencies. Follow the selection steps outlined in the chapter. Narrow the list down to two agencies and justify your decision. Then choose between the two agencies and justify your choice.

a. The Richards Group (**www.richards.com**)

b. Leo Burnett (**www.leoburnett.com**)

c. BBDO Worldwide (**www.bbdo.com**)

d. Lucas Design & Advertising (**www.aladv.com**)

e. Grey Group (**www.grey.com**)

f. DDB Worldwide Communications Group (**www.ddb.com**)

6. A marketing manager has been placed in charge of a new brand of jeans to be introduced into the market. The company's corporate headquarters are in Atlanta, and the firm's management team has already decided to use one of the local advertising agencies. Two primary objectives in choosing an agency are: (1) the agency must have the capability to develop a strong brand name and (2) the agency must be able to help with business-to-business marketing to place the jeans into retail stores. Type "advertising agencies in Atlanta" into your favorite search engine. Identify an initial list of six ad agencies. Follow the steps outlined in the chapter to narrow the list to two agencies. Then design a project for the agencies to prepare as part of an oral and written presentation to the company's marketing team.

STUDENT PROJECT

Creative Corner

Use the following creative brief for this exercise.

Creative Brief for Ford Motor Company	
Product:	Ford Mustang.
Objective:	To reverse lagging sales.
Target audience:	25- to 35-year-old consumers, split evenly between males and females, college educated, with annual incomes of approximately $40,000. Psychographically, the targeted market is a group known as individualists. They tend not to buy mainstream products. In automobile selection, they place greater emphasis on design elements, distinctiveness, and utility.
Message theme:	An automobile is like a fashion accessory. A car is selected because of the statement it makes to others.

1. As an account executive for an advertising agency, discuss the creative brief in terms of the completeness of the information provided and whether the objective is realistic. What additional information should Ford provide before a creative can begin working on the account?

2. The media planner for the Ford Mustang account suggests a media plan consisting of cable television, print advertising, Internet ads, and network advertising on Fox shows *Family Guy, House, The Wanda Sykes Show, The Simpsons*, and *American Idol*. Evaluate this media plan in light of the creative brief's objectives. Can these shows reach the target audience? What information does a creative and the account executive want from the media planner before starting work on actual commercials?

3. From the viewpoint of the creative assigned to this account, do the creative brief and the media plan (see question 2) contain sufficient information to design a series of advertisements? What, if any, additional information is necessary?

4. Using the information provided in the creative brief, prepare a magazine advertisement. Which magazines might match the target audience?

CASE 1   NAME YOUR HERO

In the Fall 2009 holiday season, the crowded fantasy and gaming world gained several products designed to entice new sets of buyers. The entire Guitar Hero brand faced stiff competition from other gaming products. One highly touted release was the new The Beatles: Rock Band game released early in the season. Other competitors included the Madden NFL product line and the Halo 3: ODST product.

In response, three new Guitar Hero titles were released: Guitar Hero 5, Band Hero, and DJ Hero. Each focused on a specific set of players.

Guitar Hero 5, the most recent version of the original product released in 2005, expands on the innovative technology that allows users to play real songs, real chords, and an almost-real guitar, integrating music, interactivity, and gameplay in a totally new way. The game offers the opportunity to play lead guitar, bass guitar, or drums or to sing the vocals of a variety of tunes. The primary attraction remains the ability to play great guitar riffs from the past. Guitar Hero 5 drew grumbles from Nirvana and Kurt Cobain fans, who did not like the intrusion into the band's well-established image.

Band Hero is a more family-oriented product. The music was selected to attract females and younger "tween" users. At one point, the opening page of the Guitar Hero Web site featured a music video by the youthful Taylor Swift, the most recent CMA Music Awards "Best Artist" winner. Many industry observers believe that Band Hero's design is an obvious response to The Beatles: Rock Band, which has many similar features.

The final new entry, DJ Hero, seeks to capture the hip-hop/rap connoisseur. The game features a turntable. According to Game Hero CEO Dan Rosensweig, "It's really cool. It's got 100 songs and 94 mixes that no one has ever mixed before. This is going to be one of those transformational games. You have this generation's iconic piece of equipment—the turntable—and some fantastic mixes that really give you a chance to release your inner DJ. I think that's going to be one of the hottest selling games this holiday season."

Additional trends should also be considered. When asked about mobile gaming on handheld devices, Rosensweig replied, "We're going to focus on making sure that our consumers can access games wherever it makes sense for them to access it—mobile is one of those environments which is always with you. And obviously, we're taking a look at that."

Part of the challenge in promoting both ongoing and new games is finding ways to capture the attention of the target audience. In the case of the Guitar Hero brand, consumers have somewhat differing viewing and media habits. Guitar Hero 5's audience is likely to be more of a classic music, hard rock crowd; Band Hero needs to reach younger females and families; and DJ Hero should find ways to access the hip-hop crowd.

Rosensweig notes, "Like anything else, we have to continue to remain fresh. You have to really understand that technology makes the game more interesting, more expansive, and more fun." He believes the future is bright. "I think we have an opportunity to redefine the way people interact with music. They want to listen to music, they want to play music, they want to contribute music, they want to create music. The more people and consoles are connected, the more opportunity we have to remain in consumers' lives."

1. Should Guitar Hero retain an advertising agency or develop its own ads in-house? Justify your answer.

2. If Guitar Hero's marketing team retains an advertising agency, what type should it be, and which decision variables should guide the choice?

3. Search online for five advertising agencies that you think would be a good fit for Guitar Hero. Choose the best one. Justify your choice.

4. What type of advertising planning and research should be used for each Guitar Hero product?

5. Should the marketing team develop one set of advertisements for each Guitar Hero product, or an overall campaign for the entire company?

6. Should the company use a pulsating, flighting, or continuous schedule of advertising? Explain.

Sources: Kim Thai, "'Guitar Hero' Amps up for the Holidays," *CNNMoney.com* (http://money.cnn.com/2009/10/23/technology/guitar_dj_hero_activision. fortune/index.ht, accessed November 17, 2009), October 23, 2009; www.guitarhero.com (accessed November 17, 2009); Seth Colter Wells, "Nirvana Heaven and Hell," *Newsweek.com* (www.newsweek.com/id/220978, accessed November 17, 2009), November 3, 2009.

▲ Guitar Hero 5 allows users to play real songs, real chords, and an almost-real guitar.

Source: Getty Images–Thinkstock.

CASE 2 ADVERTISING STEW

Luis Arroyo was about to begin the most exciting job assignment of his life. He had been named the brand manager for the Dinty Moore Beef Stew line of products, which is sold by Hormel Foods. His first assignment was to develop an advertising campaign for the entire line, which would be produced in the summer. The ads were scheduled to run on a pulsating schedule, with the first burst commencing in October.

The Dinty Moore brand has been in existence since 1935. Canned products in the line include Beef Stew, Chicken & Dumplings, Chicken Noodle, Chicken Stew, Meatball Stew, and Turkey Stew. A second, current set of products are microwaveable, featuring Beef Stew (7.5 ounce cup), Beef Stew (10 ounce tray), Chicken & Dumplings (7.5 ounce cup), Noodles & Chicken (7.5 ounce cup), Rice with Chicken (7.5 ounce cup), and Scalloped Potatoes & Ham (7.5 ounce cup).

The Dinty Moore page of Hormel's Web site states that its name is, "Synonymous not only with beef stew, but with a convenient and satisfying meal. Through innovations in packaging, we've made it even easier for you to enjoy by offering cups and trays for microwave cooking. And while convenience is definitely the order of the day, Dinty Moore stew meets the standards of contemporary shoppers because it has no preservatives and only 240 calories per 8-ounce serving."

Health consciousness is a major trend in the food market. Consumers are concerned about the fat, sodium, and calorie content of the foods they purchase. The Dinty Moore line clearly meets standards set by the Food and Drug Administration; however, it is possible that food producers will be required to provide more information about products in the future.

The primary competitors in the canned beef stew marketplace can be placed into four major categories:

- Direct competitors
- Substitute products
- Other foods made at home
- Restaurants

Direct competitors include Castleberry's and Armour. Both companies offer directly competing cans of stew as well as others that might compete with the Dinty Moore line. For example, Armour offers a line of chili and chili beans. Castleberry sells barbeque pork and canned tamales through its American Originals line.

Substitute products are sold by Campbell's and other soup manufacturers. Soup can easily be substituted for stew. Also, a series of private label stews are available.

Home cooking presents an additional source of competition. Many health food trends include cooking at home with natural ingredients. Many consumers now enjoy creating meals at home as a form of social activity and relaxation.

Many restaurants vend products that compete with both homemade and canned stew. The most threatening competitors are restaurants featuring home-style, hearty foods.

Source: Author Supplied Image.

▲ Dinty Moore Stew meets the standards of contemporary shoppers because it has no preservatives and only 240 calories per 8-ounce serving.

Luis decided that he needed more information before moving forward with the advertising campaign. He wanted to know more about the role price plays in purchasing decisions as well as consumers' perceptions of the quality of the Dinty Moore line as compared to Armour and Castleberry's. He also sought information about consumer promotions, especially coupons and price-off programs. He also wanted to investigate possibilities for cooperative advertising with grocery stores as well as tie-ins with other food products. He wanted to begin a new era in his company, where Dinty Moore moved to the strongest position in the marketplace as the top of mind and top choice brand.

1. Should Luis look to hire an external advertising agency or perform most of the tasks in-house? Why?

2. If an external agency is chosen, what relevant experiences would be most helpful to Luis and the Dinty Moore brand?

3. What types of advertising planning and research should be conducted to identify Dinty Moore's most loyal customers and potential new customers?

4. Design a creative brief for the upcoming Dinty Moore advertising campaign.

5. Using the list of advertising agencies provided under question 5 of the Integrated Learning Exercises and the procedure outlined in this chapter, choose an outside advertising agency for the Dinty Moore account. Justify your selection.

Sources: www.hormelfoods.com, www.castelberrys.com, and www.pinnaclefoodscorp.com (accessed January 4, 2008).

6 Advertising Design

Theoretical Frameworks and Types of Appeals

HYUNDAI MOTOR COMPANY

A Small Start-up Becomes a Powerful Player

In 1946, Ju-Yung Chung established the Hyundai Auto Service company in Seoul, South Korea. The name Hyundai translates to "modern" in English. The Hyundai logo has an oval shape designed to express the company's desire to expand globally, with the stylized "H" symbolizing two people (the company and the customer) shaking hands.

Over the next 50 years, the company developed its first domestic model, the Pony. The small automobile was tested, certified, approved, and exported to Europe. Eventually, versions of the Pony, including a pick-up truck, were sold in Canada. The Pony was replaced with an upgraded vehicle, the Hyundai Excel, which met all of the requirements for export into the United States in 1985. Four years later, the Hyundai Sonata was introduced.

At first, Hyundai products met with a great deal of skepticism. The company found its offerings being lumped together with low-quality exports from other countries in the minds of some U.S. consumers. The Yugo, produced in Yugoslavia, had reached U.S. shores at about the same time. At the low point, comedian Jay Leno made a joke about the Hyundai suggesting that buying a tank of gas doubled the value of the car.

In the next two decades, the company earned both respect and market share. The Hyundai Accent replaced the Excel and became especially popular in Australia. Following setbacks due to the financial crisis in Asia in the 1990s, Hyundai began to evolve under the leadership of a new chairman, Mong-Koo Chung, who replaced many top executives in the company with engineers. His goal was to compete with then-industry-leader Toyota on the basis of quality.

Mong-Koo's "zero defect mantra" became a major success. In 1998, Hyundai ranked among the worst in terms of initial defects. The change in quality level was "astounding," says Chance Parker, executive director at J.D. Power, which evaluates product quality. "We really haven't documented that

CHAPTER OBJECTIVES

After reading this chapter, you should be able to answer the following questions:

1 How can the hierarchy of effects model and a means–ends analysis help an advertising creative design better commercials?

2 How can leverage points and taglines increase advertising effectiveness?

3 What roles do visual and verbal images play in advertisements?

4 What are the seven main types of advertising appeals?

5 How can fear be used to create an effective advertisement?

6 How can humor be used to create an effective advertisement?

7 Why does sex play such a prominent role in advertising?

8 How can music, rationality, and scarcity be used to increase advertising effectiveness?

9 What are the primary areas of concern in international advertising?

level of turnaround in that period of time. They've adopted a quality mentality they didn't have before." *Consumer Reports* rated the 2004 Sonata the most reliable car in America for 2004, with only 2 problems per 100 vehicles. Likewise, Hyundai rose to second place in J.D. Power and Associates' 2004 survey of initial car quality, tied with Honda and trailing only Toyota.

These changes meant that by the mid-2000s Hyundai had become an established alternative to other models that were available in the United States. Much of the growth was attributed to the "America's Best Warranty Program," which featured a 10-year, 100,000-mile powertrain protection program, longer than any other company in the industry. The program also carried a 5-year, 60,000-mile new vehicle limited warranty. Both warranties strongly reinforced the company's claims of quality.

In 2008, the company took another turn in response to the dramatic plunge in economic conditions in the United States and worldwide.

Hyundai developed the "Hyundai Assurance Program," which included the warranty program; 24/7 roadside assistance; and, most important, a purchase clause that stated, "If, in the next year you lose your income, we'll let you return it (the car)," in hopes of selling or leasing cars to those worried about job security.

Currently, Hyundai operates two manufacturing plants in the United States, one in Alabama and a second in Michigan. The organization's reach has become global, both in the automotive and in other industries. Potential Hyundai dealers must exhibit high levels of professionalism in the automobile industry and powerful commitments to service. What was once a small start-up in a far away country has become a powerful player in the U.S. auto market and beyond.[1]

OVERVIEW

Which advertising message made the biggest impression on you in the past 5 years? Was it funny, sexy, or emotional? Was it something shown during the Super Bowl? In a recent Adweek Media and Harris Interactive survey, the majority of consumers (55 percent) said that advertisements were somewhat or very interesting. Only 13 percent replied that ads were not interesting at all. When making purchase

I never get bent out of shape over a few vampires. And with fat free milk on my tray, there's a good chance I never will. It has calcium to help prevent osteoporosis. So have a nice tall glass. It's easier to keep your neck out of a vampire's reach if you can stand up straight.

got milk?

SARAH MICHELLE GELLAR © 1998 NATIONAL FLUID MILK PROCESSOR PROMOTION BOARD

▲ By featuring a celebrity, this advertisement seeks to convince consumers of the importance of drinking milk.

decisions, 6 percent of the respondents said advertisements were "very influential," and 29 percent viewed them as "somewhat influential." Contrary to popular opinion, advertising does influence younger consumers. Nearly half of 18- to 34-year-olds in the survey reported that they were influenced in some way by advertising, compared to 37 percent for 35- to 44-year-olds, and 28 percent for consumers age 45 and older.[2]

This poll emphasizes the importance of designing an interesting and influential advertising campaign, which can be one of the most challenging elements of an integrated marketing communications program. A successful advertising campaign results when people do more than just enjoy what they see; it also changes their behaviors and attitudes. At the least, viewers should remember the good or service, so that the next time they make purchases the company or brand comes to mind.

Chapter 5 described the overall advertising management program. The advertising agency is led by an account executive who makes the pitch for the account and works with creatives, media planners, and media buyers. In this chapter, the focus is on the actual message design. This work will be completed by the agency's creative staff.

A message design process will be based on the creative brief that was prepared by the client in conjunction with the account executive. It takes into consideration the media to be utilized. By combining all of these elements, the creative can design effective advertisements.

This chapter covers two major topics. The first part details three theoretical approaches to advertising design:

- The hierarchy of effects model
- Means–end theory
- Visual and verbal imaging

The second part reviews the major advertising appeals. Many of these may seem familiar. The advertising agency's creative team selects the appeal with the best chance of conveying a message that achieves the desired outcome. Several steps are taken before beginning the process of creating an advertising campaign. The activities are summarized by the creative brief.

THE CREATIVE BRIEF

Figure 6.1 outlines the elements of the creative brief, which provides the background for the creative work. An effective advertising message begins with understanding the *objective* of the ad and the *target audience*. The advertising group agrees on the *message theme*, which is the outline of the key ideas the commercial conveys. The account executive or client provides *support* and documentation for the advertising theme or claim. Finally, the creative considers any *constraints* to be included. After completing these steps, the creative prepares the advertisement.

FIGURE 6.1 ▶
The Creative Brief

- The objective
- The target audience
- The message theme
- The support
- The constraints

ADVERTISING THEORY

In developing an advertising campaign, three theoretical approaches might aid in the design process. The hierarchy of effects model and a means–end chain can both assist in developing the leverage point. A *leverage point* moves the consumer from understanding a product's benefits to linking those benefits with personal values. A third theoretical perspective involves the visual and verbal images present in an advertisement.

❶ How can the hierarchy of effects model and a means–ends analysis help an advertising creative design better commercials?

Hierarchy of Effects

The **hierarchy of effects model** helps to clarify the objectives of an advertising campaign. The model outlines six steps a consumer or a business buyer moves through when making a purchase:

1. Awareness
2. Knowledge
3. Liking
4. Preference
5. Conviction
6. The actual purchase

These steps are sequential. A consumer spends a period of time at each one before moving to the next. Thus, before a person develops a liking for a product, she must first know about the product. Once the individual has the knowledge and develops liking for the product, the advertiser tries to influence the consumer to favor a particular brand or company.

The hierarchy of effects approach helps a creative understand how a consumer reaches a purchase decision. Some of the theory's assumptions have been questioned. For one, these six steps may not always constitute the route taken by a consumer. A person may make a purchase (such as an impulse buy) and then later develop knowledge, liking, preference, and conviction. Also, a shopper may purchase products when little or no preference is involved, because a coupon, discount, or purchase incentive caused him to choose one brand instead of another. At other times, the individual might not even remember the name of the brand he purchased. This may be the case with commodity products such as sugar or flour or even clothing purchases such as socks and shirts.

The major benefit provided by the hierarchy of effects model is that it identifies the typical steps consumers and businesses take when making purchases. Building brand loyalty involves all six steps. Logically, a customer cannot be loyal to a brand without first being aware of it. The customer typically also will not be loyal to a brand without sufficient knowledge. Then, the purchaser must like the brand and build a strong preference for it. Finally, the customer experiences the conviction that the particular brand is superior to the others on the market. The components of the hierarchy of effects approach highlight the responses that advertising or marketing communication should stimulate, in both consumers and business-to-business customers.

The hierarchy of effects model features similarities with theories about attitudes and attitudinal change, including the concepts of cognitive, affective, and conative elements. The *cognitive* component is the person's mental images, understanding, and interpretations of the person, object, or issue. The *affective* component contains the feelings or emotions a person has about the object, topic, or idea. The *conative* component consists of the individual's intentions, actions, or behavior. The most common sequence that takes place when an attitude forms is:

Cognitive → Affective → Conative

Any combination of these components is possible, which parallel the six-step hierarchy of effects process. Advertising may follow the steps or be different and highly successful because of how it captures an individual's attention in some unique way. As a general guideline, cognitive-oriented ads work best for achieving brand awareness and brand knowledge. Affective-oriented advertisements are better at inspiring liking, preference, and conviction.

FIGURE 6.2 ▶
Personal Values

• Comfortable life	• Inner peace	• Security
• Equality	• Mature love	• Self-fulfillment
• Excitement	• Personal	• Self-respect
• Freedom	accomplishment	• Sense of belonging
• Fun, exciting life	• Pleasure	• Social acceptance
• Happiness	• Salvation	• Wisdom

▼ This is a conative-oriented advertisement for Campbell's Mega Noodle, because it encourages consumers to try the new soup by offering them a coupon.

Conative-oriented ads are normally best suited to facilitating product purchases or other buyer actions.

Means–End Theory

The second theoretical approach available to creatives is the **means–end chain**, which suggests that an advertisement should contain a message, or *means,* that leads the consumer to a desired end state. These *end* states are personal values (see Figure 6.2). A means–end chain should start a process in which viewing the ad leads the consumer to believe that using the product will help achieve one of the personal values.

Means–end theory forms the basis of the **Means–End Conceptualization of Components for Advertising Strategy (MECCAS)** model.[3] The MECCAS model suggests using six elements in creating ads:

- The product's attributes
- Consumer benefits
- Leverage points
- Taglines
- Personal values
- The executional framework

The MECCAS approach moves consumers through the six elements. The attributes of the product are linked to the specific benefits consumers can derive. These benefits, in turn, lead to the attainment of a personal value. Using the elements in Figure 6.3 and the milk advertisement shown in this section, the product attribute calcium is linked with the benefits of being strong and healthy. The personal value the consumer obtains from healthy bones may be feeling wise for using the product. The leverage point in the advertisement

FIGURE 6.3 ▶
Means–End Chains for Milk

arises from the connection between the benefit of health and the personal value of feeling wise. The white mustache and the text in the advertisement remind the viewer that drinking milk is healthy. In this case, preventing osteoporosis in women becomes the key selling point.

The MECCAS approach can be applied to business-to-business advertisements. Members of the buying center may be influenced by personal values, organizational values, and corporate goals. In the advertisement for Greenfield Online on page 146 and the means–end chain in Figure 6.4, each attribute is linked to the benefits business customers can obtain. Although not explicitly stated, the personal values of members of the buying center choosing Greenfield Online might include job security for making good decisions, self-fulfillment, wisdom, and social acceptance by other members of the buying group.

Leverage Points

Both the hierarchy of effects model and the means–end chain approach include leverage points. A leverage point moves the consumer from understanding a product's benefits to linking those benefits with personal values. To construct a quality leverage point, the creative builds the pathway that connects a product benefit with the potential buyer's value system.

In terms of the hierarchy of effects model, the initial level of awareness begins the process of exposing consumers to product benefits. As the viewer moves through the six stages, she eventually develops the conviction to buy the product. At that point, the benefit has indeed been linked with a personal value. In the milk advertisement used to illustrate the means–end chain, the leverage point presented in the phrase "There's one person I won't be" is tied to the copy message "a woman with osteoporosis." The copy explains that because milk contains calcium (the product attribute), it helps women maintain health bones (the product benefit). Making the decision to drink milk to prevent osteoporosis connects to the personal values of wisdom and seeking a healthy lifestyle.

In the Greenfield Online business-to-business advertisement, the leverage point is the picture of an old-fashioned woman using an old telephone sandwiched between the headline "Are you still buying marketing research done the old-fashioned way?" and the first sentence of the copy explaining that companies can "Do it better on the Internet." The picture presents an excellent mental image of marketing research conducted the old-fashioned way and the opportunities Greenfield Online can provide.

There's one person I won't be.

A woman with osteoporosis. So it's bloody marvelous that fat free milk has the calcium to help prevent it. Thank goodness there's enough to go around.

got milk?

Source: Courtesy of Bozell Worldwide, Inc.

▲ A "Got Milk?" advertisement illustrating the use of a means–end chain.

❷ How can leverage points and taglines increase advertising effectiveness?

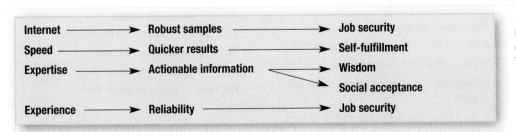

◀ **FIGURE 6.4**
B-to-B Means–End Chain for Greenfield Online

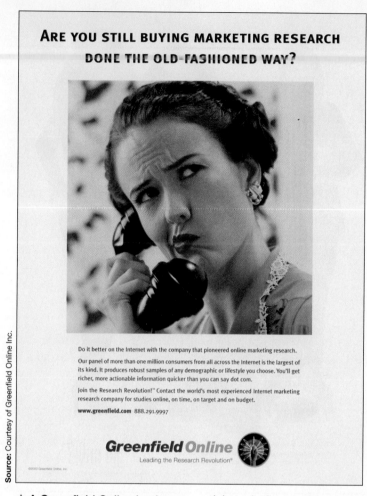

ARE YOU STILL BUYING MARKETING RESEARCH
DONE THE OLD-FASHIONED WAY?

Do it better on the Internet with the company that pioneered online marketing research.

Our panel of more than one million consumers from all across the Internet is the largest of its kind. It produces robust samples of any demographic or lifestyle you choose. You'll get richer, more actionable information quicker than you can say dot com.

Join the Research Revolution!® Contact the world's most experienced Internet marketing research company for studies online, on time, on target and on budget.

www.greenfield.com 888.291.9997

Greenfield Online
Leading the Research Revolution®

▲ A Greenfield Online business-to-business advertisement illustrating the use of a means–end chain.

The means–end chain and MECCAS approaches are based on the product's attributes and its benefits to the consumer. The leverage point message links these attributes and benefits to consumer values. In the ad itself, the executional framework is the plot or scenario used to convey the message designed to complete the linkage. Chapter 7 presents executional frameworks in detail.

An effective leverage point can also be associated with an attitudinal change, especially when the cognitive → affective → conative sequence exists. As the attitude forms, the individual first understands, then is moved emotionally, and then takes action. A leverage point helps the viewer move through these three stages, tying cognitive knowledge of the product to emotional and personal values.

Creatives spend considerable amounts of time designing ads with powerful leverage points. Various types of appeals become the tools creatives use to help consumers make the transition from awareness of a product's benefits to incorporating them with personal values.

Taglines

The key phrase of an advertisement is the **tagline**. It should be something memorable that identifies the uniqueness of a brand or conveys some type of special meaning. "Just Do It" has been Nike's tagline for many years. Other well known taglines are identified in Figure 6.5.

Taglines carry over from one advertisement to others. They provide consistency across various advertising platforms. Consumers often remember taglines and identify them with specific brands. A catchy tagline identifies a brand and then stays with it over successive campaigns. In order to bring freshness to a campaign, company marketers occasionally tweak or modify a tagline. For instance, Allstate's tagline "You're in good hands with Allstate" became "Are you in good hands?" BMW modified the tagline "Sheer driving pleasure" to "The ultimate driving machine."

In other instances, a completely new tagline may be developed. To make the Oscar Mayer brand more contemporary, the company's marketing personnel and its agency, mcgarrybowen, created a new tagline. Oscar Mayer was known for trust, nostalgia, heritage, jingles, bologna, hot dogs, and kids. The image needed to be freshened, made more contemporary, and reach adults as well as kids. The Oscar Mayer marketing team wanted to take the brand to a place that was energetic, culturally relevant, and that captured the

FIGURE 6.5 ►
Taglines Used by Various Brands

- American Express—"Don't leave home without it."
- Avis—"We try harder."
- Bounty—"The quicker picker-upper"
- Capital One—"What's in your wallet?"
- CNN—"The most trusted name in news"
- Energizer—"It keeps going, and going, and going."
- Hallmark—"When you care enough to send the best"
- John Deere—"Nothing runs like a Deer."
- Maxwell House—"Good to the last drop"
- Nokia—"Connecting people"
- Office Depot—"Taking care of business"
- Target—"Expect more. Pay less."
- UPS—"What can Brown do for you?"
- Wal-Mart—"Save money. Live better."

spirit of everyday food making people feel good. Real joy, real moments, real friendship, real emotion, and real people were at the forefront. The idea was that Oscar Mayer is "good mood food." This good mood feeling is visually conveyed in the Oscar Mayer ad in this section, in which marketing brainstorming sessions and music collaboration led to the campaign tagline "It doesn't get better than this."[4]

Verbal and Visual Images

Another theoretical approach to advertising design focuses on the decision the creative makes about the degree of emphasis given to the visual part of an advertisement versus the verbal element. Most major forms of advertising contain both visual and verbal or written elements. A visual ad places the greatest emphasis on the picture or visual element of the ad. A verbal or written ad places more emphasis on the copy.

Visual images often lead to more favorable attitudes toward both the advertisement and the brand. Visuals tend to be more easily remembered than verbal copy. They are stored in the brain as both pictures and words. This dual-coding process makes it easier for people to recall the message. Further, verbal messages tend be stored in the left side of the brain only; images are usually stored in both the left and right sides of the brain.

The advertisement for the Nicole Chair by Thomasville on the next page illustrates the power of visual imagery. Created by The Richards Group, it conveys the chair is "so you" that the design of the chair would be something you would be proud to wear as clothes. The imagery of the chair fabric matching a dress makes the message more powerful.

Visual images range from concrete and realistic to highly abstract. A concrete visual displays something recognizable, such as a person, place, or thing. In an abstract image, the subject becomes more difficult to recognize. Concrete pictures instill a higher level of recall than abstract images. Concrete pictures are dual-coded, allowing the image to be stored in the brain with both a visual and verbal elements. Viewers process an advertisement with a picture of spaghetti as both a picture and as a verbal representation of the restaurant. Ads with concrete images also tend to lead to more favorable attitudes than those with no pictures or abstract pictures.[5]

Radio advertisers often seek to create visual images for the audience. Pepsi produced a commercial in which listeners could hear a can being opened, the soft drink being poured, and the sizzle of the carbonation—an excellent example of creating a visual image. If consumers visualize an image in their imaginations, the effect may be greater than an actual visual. A visual image requires less brain activity than using one's imagination. The secret is getting the person to think beyond the advertisement and picture the scene being simulated.

Visual Esperanto

Visual imagery is widely used in international marketing. Global advertising agencies try to create **visual Esperanto**, the universal language that makes global advertising possible for any good or service. Visual Esperanto advertising recognizes that visual images are more powerful than verbal descriptions. Visual images are more likely to transcend cultural differences.[6] To illustrate the power of a visual image compared to a verbal account, think of the word *exotic*. To some, exotic means a white beach in Hawaii with young people in sexy swimsuits. To others, it may be a small cabin in the snow-capped mountains of Switzerland. To others still, exotic may be a close-up of a tribal village in Africa. The word exotic can vary in meaning. At the same time, a picture of a couple holding hands in front

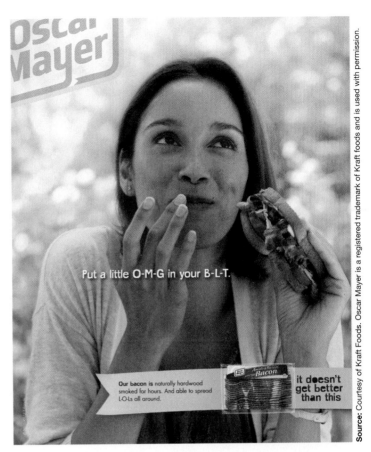

▲ An advertisement for Oscar Mayer using the new tagline "It doesn't getter better than this."

3 What roles do visual and verbal images play in advertisements?

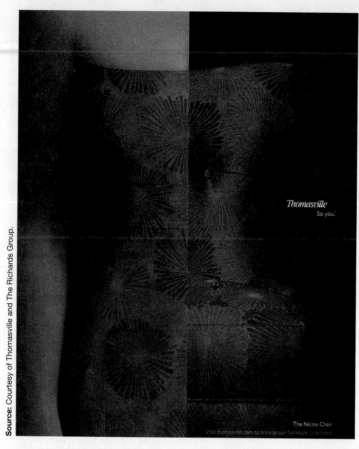

▲ This advertisement for the Nicole Chair by Thomasville illustrates the power of visual imagery.

of Niagara Falls has practically the same meaning across all cultures as does the advertisement for Oscar Mayer shown on page 149. The image of the young couple looking at each other and eating from opposite ends of the hotdog conveys a similar meaning across multiple cultures.

Finding the appropriate image constitutes the most important task in creating visual Esperanto. The creative looks for the image that conveys the intended meaning or message. Brand identity can be emphasized using visuals rather than words. Then the creative uses words to support the visual image. For example, the creative may decide that a boy and his father at a sports event illustrate the priceless treasure of a shared family moment. In Mexico, the setting could be a soccer match instead of a baseball game in the United States. The specific copy (the words) can then be adapted to another country. Identifying an image that transcends cultures is the difficult part of inspiring visual Esperanto. Once a universal image has been found, creatives in each country represented take the image and modify it to appeal to the local target audience.

Business-to-Business

In the past, creatives designing business-to-business advertisements relied heavily on the verbal element rather than on visuals. The basis of this approach was the belief that business decisions are made in a rational, cognitive manner. In recent years, more business ads have incorporated strong visual elements to heighten the emotional aspects of making a purchase.

In summary, the three theoretical models provide useful ideas for the advertising creative. Each suggests a sequence to be followed as during the preparation of an advertisement. The endpoint will be reached when the viewer remembers the products, thinks favorably about it, and looks for that product when making a purchase decision. Various kinds of advertising messages, or appeals, can be utilized to reach such key advertising objectives.

TYPES OF ADVERTISING APPEALS

④ What are the seven main types of advertising appeals?

Throughout the years, advertisers have employed numerous advertising approaches. Of these, seven **advertising appeals** have achieved the most success. Normally one of these types of appeals will be featured in an advertisement (see Figure 6.6).

The type of appeal chosen should be based on a review of the creative brief, the objective of the advertisement, and the means–end chain to be conveyed. A number of factors will be considered, including the product being sold, the personal preferences of the advertising creative and the account executive, as well as the wishes of the client. The team also identifies appeals that are *inappropriate*. Advertising experts know that certain appeals are less successful in certain circumstances. For example, sexual appeals are not very effective for items not related to sex. The advertising team tries to ensure that the appeal represents the

FIGURE 6.6 ▶
Advertising Appeals

● Fear	● Rationality
● Humor	● Emotions
● Sex	● Scarcity
● Music	

best option for the brand, target audience, and the message, to whatever degree is possible.

FEAR

Advertisements featuring fear appeals are commonplace. Life insurance companies focus on the consequences of not having a life insurance policy when a person dies. Shampoo and mouthwash ads invoke fears of dandruff and bad breath, which can make a person a social outcast. Fear is used more often than most realize.

Advertisers employ fear appeals because they work. Fear increases viewer interest in an advertisement and the ad's persuasiveness. Many individuals remember advertisements with fear appeals better than they do warm, upbeat messages.[7] Consumers who pay more attention to an advertisement are more likely to process the information it presents, which makes it possible to accomplish the advertisement's main objective.

The *behavioral response model* explains the way fear works (see Figure 6.7) in advertising.[8] As shown, various incidents can lead to negative or positive consequences, which then affect future behaviors.

Severity and Vulnerability

In developing fear advertisements, the creative includes as many aspects of the behavioral response model as possible. A business-to-business advertiser offering Internet services tries to focus on the **severity** of downtime if a company's Internet server goes down. Another ad describes the firm's **vulnerability** by showing the high probability that a company's server will crash. The Service Metrics advertisement on the next page features a picture of a blindfolded man ready to step into a manhole to illustrate the danger of e-business pitfalls. The advertisement attempts to cause business leaders to believe their companies may be vulnerable. Service Metrics can help them identify these potential problems before they turn into disasters.

Response Efficacy

To further understand the model, consider a young man who has taken up smoking and sees an ad for the Nicoderm CQ patches, which help a person quit smoking. The man

▲ The visual used in this ad contains visual Esperanto, because the meaning easily transfers across other cultures and nationalities.

5 How can fear be used to create an effective advertisement?

◀ **FIGURE 6.7**
The Behavioral Response Model

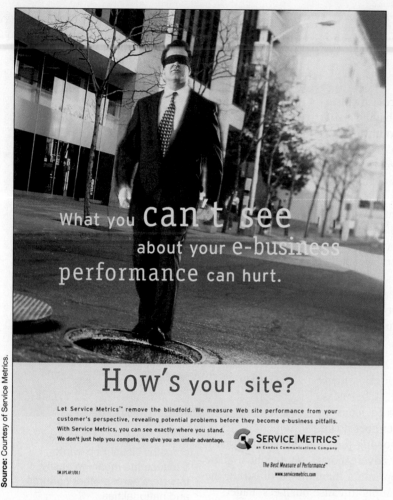

▲ A fear appeal in a business-to-business advertisement.

considers three things in evaluating the advertisement and making a decision to purchase Nicoderm CQ.

Intrinsic and extrinsic rewards are the first factor. Intrinsic rewards come from gaining social acceptance by quitting and feeling healthier. Extrinsic rewards may include saving on the cost of cigarettes as compared to the price for Nicoderm CQ.

Response costs are the second factor considered. When an individual who smokes gains acceptance by his peers, smoking becomes rewarding and there is less incentive to quit. If smoking creates such intrinsic value, then quitting becomes even more difficult. A man who quits smoking becomes more likely to gain weight and lose the friends who continue to smoke. The higher the perceived costs, the less likely the decision to quit smoking becomes.

Self-efficacy constitutes the third factor. In this situation, self-efficacy relates to the man's confidence in his ability to stop smoking. Many individuals have tried and failed. The smoker must believe that Nicoderm CQ can truly help him quit, giving him the final edge needed.

The combination of intrinsic and extrinsic rewards, response costs, and the degree of self-efficacy contribute to the smoker's *response efficacy*. The decision to purchase Nicoderm CQ with the idea of stopping smoking will be based on the conclusion that doing so will have net positive consequences. The person concludes he will fit in with family and friends, feel better about himself, improve his health, and is capable of quitting smoking.

Appeal Strength

When using fear, another factor will be the strength of the appeal. Most advertisers believe a moderate fear level is most effective. A low level of fear may not be noticed, and the fear level may not be convincing in terms of severity or vulnerability. An advertisement with a fear level that is too strong can also backfire, because the message only generates feelings of anxiety. This leads the viewer to avoid watching the commercial, by changing the channel or muting the sound.[9] Consequently a fear appeal's goal should be to make it powerful enough to capture a viewer's attention and to influence her thinking, but not so scary that she avoids the advertisement.

Fear ads match well with certain types of goods and services, especially products that eliminate problems or threats to a consumer's sense of personal security. Account executives, creatives, and company leaders decide when fear represents a good approach or if some other type of appeal offers greater promise.

HUMOR

6 How can humor be used to create an effective advertisement?

Clutter remains a significant problem in every advertising medium. Capturing a viewer's attention is difficult. Even after grabbing the audience's attention, keeping it becomes even more challenging. Humor has proven to be one of the best techniques for cutting through clutter, by getting attention and keeping it. Consumers, as a whole, enjoy advertisements that make them laugh. Something that is funny has intrusive value and attracts attention.[10]

Humor is used in about 30 percent of television and radio advertisements.[11] Humorous ads often win awards and tend to be favorites among consumers. In a *USA Today* consumer survey of the most likeable advertising campaigns for 2006, humor was a key ingredient.[12]

For 27 years, Anheuser-Busch chose humor to advertise the Bud Light brand. Humorous ads included "Spuds McKenzie," "Yes I am," "I love you man," and "Real Men of Genius." As Bud Light's target market began to grow older, the marketing department decided to attract a new set of younger consumers. The decision was made to depart from humorous commercials and show young consumers that Bud Light was not your dad's beer. The "Drinkability" campaign was born. Sales dropped by 3 percent. It was the first decline in Bud Light's 27-year history. As a result, Anheuser-Busch dropped the "Drinkability" theme for Bud Light and returned to humor.[13]

Humorous ads achieve success for three reasons. Humor causes consumers to: (1) watch, (2) laugh, and, most important, (3) remember. In recall tests, consumers most often remember humorous ads. The best results occur when the humor connects directly with the product's benefits. The advertisement should link the product's features with the advantage to customers and personal values in a means–end chain.

Advantages of Humor

Humorous ads pique viewer interest, which makes gaining consumer consideration of the advertisement's message easier. A funny ad captures the viewer's attention, leading to improved comprehension and recall of the advertising message and tagline. Advertising research indicates that humor elevates people's moods. Happy consumers often associate a good mood with the advertiser's products. In essence, humor helps fix the brand in the consumer's cognitive structure with links to positive feelings.

Problems with Humor

Although a funny advertisement can capture the viewer's attention, cut through clutter, and enhance recall, humorous ads can also go wrong. A Snickers commercial that ran during a recent Super Bowl featured two mechanics eating from opposite ends of the same candy bar until they accidentally ended up kissing. The two men responded in disgust by ripping out their own chest hairs. The outcry for some groups was loud enough that it was immediately pulled.[14]

Advertisers should not allow the humor overpower the message. Humor fails when consumers remember the joke but not the product or brand. In other words, the advertisement was so funny that the audience forgets or does not catch the sponsor's name. Humorous advertisements can also fail in terms of accomplishing advertising objectives.

To avoid these problems, the humor used in an advertisement should focus on a component of the means–end chain. The humor should relate either to a product's attributes, a customer benefit, or the personal value obtained from the product. The most effective ads are those in which the humor incorporates all three elements.

International Usage

Some evidence suggests that humor is universal; however, there are particular executions of humor that may not be. Forms of humor are often rooted in various cultures, yet humor may not transfer from one culture to another. Not all audiences experience a humorous ad in the same way. Advertisers should pretest commercials before they are launched in other countries to ensure the message will be liked and will be considered funny rather than offensive.

Humor ads appear in a number of countries. A humorous ad developed for McDonald's in Singapore had the highest recall rate (90 percent) of all other commercials released during the month it ran. In Germany, Ford deviated from traditional ads that concentrated on promoting product quality and value to humor. One advertisement features a pigeon sitting on tree branch with a Ford Ka parked nearby. The bird swoops down to bomb the car, but at the last minute the car hood springs up and knocks the bird out. The advertisement was first shown on Ford's U.K. Web site. Word about the ad quickly spread until more than 1 million people had visited the Web site to see the ad. German dealers

- Captures attention.
- Holds attention.
- Often wins creative awards.
- High recall scores.
- Consumers enjoy ads that make them laugh.
- Evaluated by consumers as likeable ads.

requested the ad so they could show it on television. The feedback and popularity of the ad in the United Kingdom caused Ford's marketing managers to agree to run the ad in Germany. The ad resonated with young, affluent buyers, which Ford had been trying to reach. The new ad was seen as witty, gutsy, and edgy, which worked well with Ford's theme of projecting the Ka as a stylish car.[15]

Humorous ads can be difficult to design. One cynic once noted that there are only 12 funny people in the United States. Humor that doesn't work often creates a negative image for the company. Humor that does work can bring great success to a company and provide great dividends in terms of brand equity. Figure 6.8 summarizes the major reasons for using humor.

❼ Why does sex play such a prominent role in advertising?

▼ An advertisement for Old Orchard featuring a sensuality appeal.

SEX

Sexual appeals are often used to break through clutter. Advertisements in the United States and other countries contain more visual sexual themes than ever. Nudity and other sexual approaches are common. Sexual themes in ads, however, do not sell the way they used to. Sex no longer has shock value. Today's teens grow up in societies immersed in sex. One more sexually oriented ad captures little attention. Currently, many advertisers are shifting to more subtle sexual cues, suggestions, and innuendos.[16] Sexuality has been employed in advertising in the five ways listed in Figure 6.9.

Source: Courtesy: Old Orchard Brands, LLC.

Forever on the lips, never on the hips.

Subliminal Approaches

Placing sexual cues or icons in advertisements in an attempt to affect a viewer's subconscious is the subliminal approach. In an odd paradox, truly subliminal cues are not noticed, which means they do not create any effects. Consumers pay little attention to ads already. A subliminal message that registers only in the viewer's subconscious does not work. If it did, there would be no need for stronger sexual content in advertising.

Sensuality

Many women respond more favorably to a sensual suggestion than an overtly sexual approach. An alluring glance across a crowded room can be sensual and draw attention to a product. Many view sensuality as being more sophisticated, because it relies on the imagination. Images of romance and love can be more enticing than raw sexuality.

Sexual Suggestiveness

A sexually suggestive advertisement hints that sex is about to take place. The Bijan advertisement in this section features Bo Derek. The ad states, "Bo Derek is wearing Bijan Eau de Parfum and nothing else," a sexually suggestive message.

- Subliminal techniques
- Sensuality
- Sexual suggestiveness
- Nudity or partial nudity
- Overt sexuality

Recently, Pine-Sol used suggestiveness to advertise a household cleaner. In several television ads, shirtless, muscular men are shown mopping the floor while the female watches or fantasizes. Diane Amos, who has been featured in Pine-Sol ads for the last 16 years and also appears in this new series of ads featuring men, says "We would all like our husbands to mop. . . . It can be fun, it can be sexy, and women like it clean."[17]

Nudity or Partial Nudity

Products that have sexual connotations, such as clothing, perfume, and cologne, may feature a degree of nudity. Some ads are designed to solicit a sexual response. Others are not. In 1987, underwear companies were first allowed to use live models in television advertisements. The first commercials were modest and informational, emphasizing the design or materials used in the undergarment. The first Playtex bra commercials using live models drew strong criticism from organizations such as the American Family Association. Currently, advertisements for undergarments go much further and involve superstars, such as actress Jennifer Love Hewitt who appeared in television and print ads for the Hanes All-Over Comfort bra and the Perfect Panty. The campaign even included an online element with footage from the photo shoots, a "bad bra toss" game, and a blog about bad bra moments.[18]

Decorative Models

A common sexual approach in advertising is to place **decorative models**, or individuals in advertisements to adorn products as a sexual or attractive stimuli. The models serve no

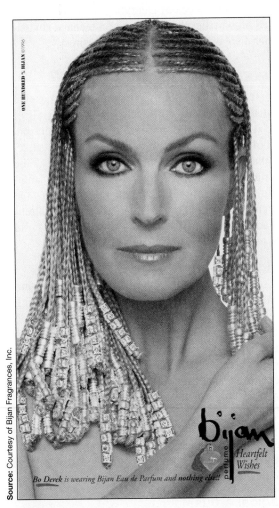

▲ A Bijan perfume advertisement using the sexual suggestiveness approach.

▲ An advertisement for Benetton featuring partial nudity.

FIGURE 6.10 ▶

Factors to Consider
Before Using
Decorative Models

- The presence of female (or male) decorative models improves ad recognition, but not brand recognition.
- The presence of a decorative model influences emotional and objective evaluations of the product among both male and female audiences.
- Attractive models produce a higher level of attention to ads than do less attractive models.
- The presence of an attractive model produces higher purchase intentions when the product is sexually relevant than if it is not sexually relevant.

other purpose than to attract attention. In the past, commercials for automobiles, tools, and beer often used female models dressed in bikinis standing by the products. A number of studies were conducted to determine how effective decorative models are. The basic conclusions are listed in Figure 6.10.[19]

Overt Sexuality

Using overt sexuality in ads for sexually oriented products is normally accepted, but it often becomes controversial when used for other types of products. When Procter & Gamble launched a television advertising campaign for Dentyne, eyebrows were raised. The commercial showed two teens in a living room. The girl pops a piece of Dentyne Fire bubble gum into her mouth and then rips off her blouse and jumps on her boyfriend. At first the parents stare in shock. Then, the mom tries a piece of Dentyne Fire and promptly jumps on the dad. The controversy centered on whether the ad promoted teenage sexuality by suggesting that parents should openly display sexual feelings and desires.[20]

Are Sex Appeals Effective?

Numerous studies have examined the effectiveness of sexual appeals and nudity in advertising. Almost all of them conclude that sex and nudity do increase attention, regardless of the gender of the person in the advertisement or the gender of the audience. Normally, the attention is greater for opposite-sex situations than same-sex situations, for both males and females viewing the opposite gender. To encourage both genders to pay attention to its ads, Guess often features a male and female in a sexually provocative setting in an advertisement.

Attracting Attention

Although sexually oriented ads attract attention, brand recall for ads using a sex appeal is lower than those using other types of appeals. It appears that although people watch the advertisement, the sexual theme distracts them from noticing the brand name.[21]

Sexually oriented advertisements are often rated as more interesting. Those ads deemed to be highly controversial in terms of sexual content are rated as more interesting by both males and females. The paradox, however, is that although the controversial ads are more interesting, they fail to increase the transmission of information. Respondents are less likely to remember any more about the message.[22]

Physiological Arousal

Advertisements using overt sexual stimuli or containing nudity produce higher levels of physiological arousal responses. These arousal responses have been linked to

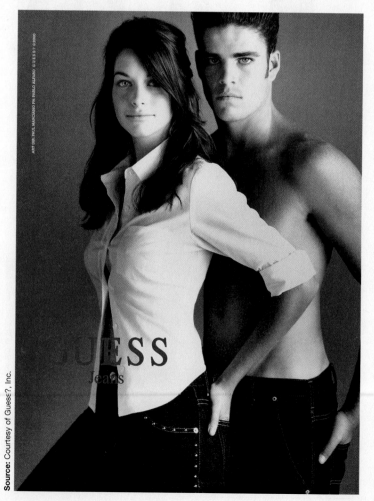

▼ A Guess advertisement with a male and a female model.

Source: Courtesy of Guess?, Inc.

the formation of both affective and cognitive responses. If the viewer is male and the sexual stimulus is female, such as a nude female in an ad for cologne, then the viewer tends to develop a strong feeling toward the ad based on the arousal response his body experiences. Female viewers of male nudity in an advertisement often experience the same type of response, although the arousal response may not be as strong.

Cognitive Impressions

The cognitive impression made on viewers of a sexually oriented ad depends on whether the viewer feels the advertisement is pleasant or offensive. When the viewer likes the ad, it results in a positive impression of the brand. When the viewer thinks the ad is in poor taste, negative feelings and beliefs about the brand often emerge. When sex works, it increases sales. An ad that does not may inspire negative feelings toward the brand.[23]

Societal Trends

In determining the level of sex appeal to feature in an advertisement, the advertising team considers society's view and level of acceptance.[24] Just as economies go through cycles, attitudes toward sex in advertising experience acceptance fluctuate.

The use and acceptance of sexual themes in advertising had swung to a high level of tolerance in the early part of the 2000s, until the Super Bowl of 2004. The public reaction to Janet Jackson's breast-baring halftime show sent ripples all the way to Madison Avenue. Shortly afterward, Victoria's Secret dropped its TV lingerie fashion show. Abercrombie & Fitch killed the company's quarterly catalog, which had been strongly criticized for featuring models in sexually suggestive poses. Anheuser-Busch dropped some of its risqué ads.[25] The trend continued into the next year. When ads for Super Bowl 2005 were unveiled, few used sexual appeals.

The pendulum may now be slowly swinging back toward greater acceptance of sexually oriented ads, but it has not reached the pre-2004 level yet. A recent Calvin Klein ad featuring actress Eva Mendes in the nude in a provocative pose for its Secret Obsession fragrance was rejected by the major networks in the United States, but accepted by television stations in Europe. A less-provocative version had to be created for the United States, and it was not shown until after 9:00 P.M.[26]

The use of sex in advertising will continue. Advertisers should carefully determine the level and the type of sexuality to use and the target audience. What will work at one particular point in time may not work at another.

Disadvantages of Sex Appeals

One major criticism of sexually based advertising is that it perpetuates dissatisfaction with one's body. Females in print advertisements and models in television advertising are often thin. The key to success seems to be the thinner the better. As advertising models have gotten thinner, body dissatisfaction and eating disorders among women have risen. Research indicates that women feel unhappy about their own bodies and believe they are too fat after viewing advertisements showing thin models. Still, ads with thin models are more likely to convince women to purchase a product.[27]

Thin male models have an effect on men, but in reverse. Many men worry they are not muscular enough and are too thin or too fat. It does not make any difference whether the male is viewing a male model or a female model in advertisements.[28]

▼ An advertisement for Stetson directed to women using a sex appeal.

Some companies have begun to feature real women of different shapes and sizes, such as Dove's "Campaign for Real Beauty." The campaign has garnered international attention, won several major advertising awards, and achieved a healthy growth in sales. The approach struck a responsive chord with many women.

Sex Appeals in International Advertising

What is deemed appropriate or acceptable in terms of sexual appeal varies across countries. In Chile, a campaign featuring nude celebrities touting the benefits of drinking milk was launched. The ad's producers stated, "Chile is a country of stuffed shirts, so this campaign is going to shake them up, and at a relatively low cost, thanks to nudity." The Chilean Dairy Federation believed that the ads would promote the idea of rebellion to Chilean youth. As more Chilean kids travel the world and see teens with green and blue hair and body piercings, public nudity will become more associated with freedom. Despite opposition by conservatives, the "naked" milk campaign aroused the attention of Chilean young people, and milk sales grew.[29]

Religions, cultures, and value systems determine the levels of nudity, sexual references, and gender-specific issues that are permitted in a country. Muslim nations tend to reject any kind of nudity and any reference to sexuality and other gender-related issues. They also do not permit any type of advertising for personal goods, such as female hygiene products, contraceptives, or undergarments. Any hint of sexuality or display of the female body is strictly forbidden.

In many Middle Eastern countries, sex and gender issues are taboo subjects. Sexual appeals are not used in advertising, and even sexually related products are difficult to advertise. In response, Procter & Gamble hosted a call-in TV show directed toward young girls in Egypt. The show's panel contained health experts, and topics ranged from marriage to menopause. The call-in show was followed up with a TV talk show called *Frankly Speaking* about feminine hygiene. The goal of the show was to tackle some of the more sensitive issues facing young Egyptian girls. Although the show discussed what happens during puberty, it was P&G's policy not to discuss sexuality. P&G sponsored the show and the primary product advertised was P&G's Always feminine sanitary pads.[30]

In other countries, standards regarding sexually oriented advertising are more permissive but sometimes confusing. In France, sex is everywhere. Advertisers can feature seminude or completely nude models in advertisements if they can be justified; a relationship must exist between the product and the nude model. It does not take much of a justification in France, where sex is viewed as healthy, innocent, and natural. One difference in France, however, is that sex and humor are not mixed. The French do not see sex as silly or funny.[31]

The problem with the stereotyping of females in ads takes a different twist in other countries. For example, in Saudi Arabia and Malaysia women must be shown in family settings. They cannot be depicted as being carefree or desirable to the opposite sex.[32]

In general, the use of sex to make products more appealing is a legitimate tactic for many companies, products, and advertising firms. The goal should be to use sex in an interesting manner that is germane to the product, and within the ethical standards of the region.

▼ An example of an effective sexual appeal promoting milk.

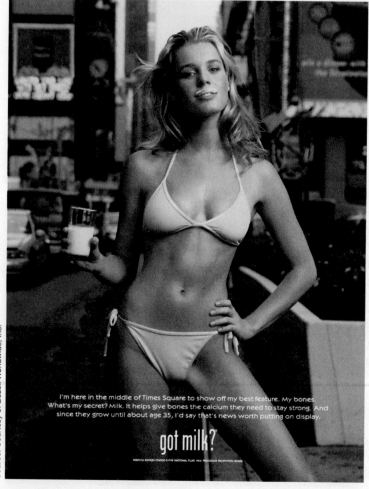

I'm here in the middle of Times Square to show off my best feature. My bones. What's my secret? Milk. It helps give bones the calcium they need to stay strong. And since they grow until about age 35, I'd say that's news worth putting on display.

got milk?

From there, taste and other more personalized standards serve as guides. The U.S. milk industry advertisement shown in this section has been very effective. Although the model is wearing a swimsuit, it is germane to the product. The advertisement seeks to persuade women that milk not only is good for healthy bones, but that it also enhances one's appearance. By telling women that bones continue to develop until the age of 35, the ad reinforces a reason to consume milk.

MUSICAL APPEALS

Music can be an extremely important advertising ingredient. It connects with emotions, memories, and other experiences. Music can be intrusive; it gains the attention of someone who previously was not listening to or watching a program. It may provide the stimulus that ties a particular musical arrangement, jingle, or song to a certain product or brand. As soon as the tune begins, consumers know what product is being advertised because they have been conditioned to tie the product to the music. For example, the Intel "tune" is widely recognized by numerous consumers.

Music gains attention and increases the retention of information when it becomes strongly intertwined with the product. Even when consumers do not recall the ad message argument, music can lead to a better recall of an advertisement's visual and emotional aspects. Music can also increase the persuasiveness of an argument. Subjects who compared ads with music to identical ads without music almost always rated those with music higher in terms of persuasiveness.[33]

Musical memories are often stored in long-term recall areas of the brain. Most people can remember tunes even from their childhood. Figure 6.11 lists some popular songs now being used in commercials. Several decisions are made when selecting music for commercials, including the following:

- What role will music play in the ad?
- Will a familiar song be used, or will something original be created?
- What emotional pitch should the music reach?
- How does the music fit with the message of the ad?

Music plays a variety of roles in advertisements. Sometimes the music is incidental. In others, it becomes the primary theme. An important decision involves selecting a familiar tune as opposed to creating original music. Writing a jingle or music specifically for the advertisement occurs more often. Background or mood-inducing music is usually instrumental, and advertisers often pay musicians to write music that matches the scenes in the ad.

An alternative method used by some advertising agencies is to send the creative brief to interested musicians and ask them to compose and pitch a song. The mcgarrybowen advertising agency used the approach when selecting a song for the new Oscar Mayer campaign. The creative brief was sent to approximately 60 musicians. Each was asked to compose a song he or she felt expressed the emotions conveyed in the brief. Both the Oscar Mayer marketing team and mcgarrybowen decided that the song "It Doesn't Get Better Than This" composed and sung by Joy Williams best brought the emotions of the new Oscar Mayer campaign to life.

8 How can music, rationality, and scarcity be used to increase advertising effectiveness?

- "Revolution" by Beatles (Nike)
- "Real Love" by John Lennon (JCPenney)
- "We're All in This Together" by Ben Lee (Kohl's)
- "Hush" by Deep Purple (Jaguar)
- "Just Fine" by Mary J. Blige (Chevrolet)
- "I'm in the Mood for Love" by Brenda Lee (Victoria's Secret)
- "Thriller" by Michael Jackson (Sobe)
- "Da Ya Think I'm Sexy?" by Rod Stewart (Chips Ahoy)
- "Eyes on Me" by Celine Dion (Celine Dion Sensational)

◀ FIGURE 6.11
Popular Songs Used in Ads

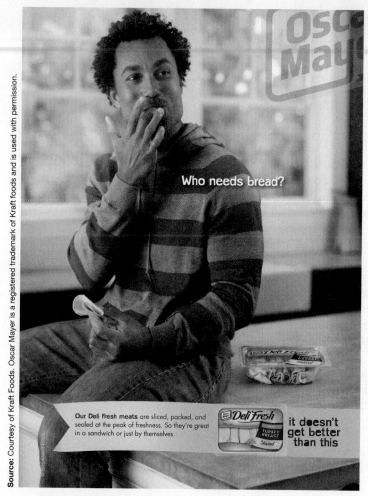

▲ The song "It Doesn't Get Better Than This" was written and sung by Joy Williams for the television ads in the Oscar Mayer campaign.

Advantages of Musical Appeals

Using a well-known song in an advertisement creates certain advantages. The primary benefit is that consumers already have developed an affinity for the song. Brand awareness, brand equity, and brand loyalty become easier to develop when consumers are familiar with the music. This occurs when consumers transfer an emotional affinity for the song to the product. One variation is to purchase an existing song and adapt the ad to the music.[34] Using popular songs may be expensive. The price for the rights to a very popular song can be in the range of six to seven figures.[35] The Internet company Excite paid $7 million for the rights to Jimi Hendrix's song "Are You Experienced," and Microsoft paid about $12 million for "Start Me Up."[36]

Alternate Methods

An alternative method of developing music has emerged, primarily because of the Internet. More cooperation now exists between musicians and marketers. Some musicians view advertisements as a way to get their songs heard. Marketers see an opportunity to tie a new, exciting song to a product. Many consumers are also interested in finding out who performs the music in various ads. The Internet provides the opportunity not only to find out, but also to post it for others to enjoy on sites such as YouTube. When an ad only contains part of the song, many firms place entire tuned on company Web sites or on YouTube so that individuals can download them.

Occasionally, a song written for a commercial will crack Billboard's Top 100 list. Jason Wade, a singer in the band Lifehouse, had never written a song for a commercial before. After viewing a copy of the 60-second commercial for Allstate Insurance produced by Leo Burnett Agency, Wade wrote a song entitled "From Where You Are." The commercial promoted Allstate's safe-driving program for teenagers. After the commercial aired, the song was made available on iTunes. Within 2 weeks, sales were high enough for the song to reach number 40 on Billboard's charts.[37]

RATIONAL APPEALS

A rational appeal follows the hierarchy of effects stages of awareness, knowledge, liking, preference, conviction, and purchase. A creative designs the advertisement for one of the six steps. An ad oriented to the knowledge stage transmits basic product information. In the preference stage, the message shifts to presenting logical reasons that favor the brand, such as the superior gas mileage of an automobile. A rational advertisement should lead to a stronger conviction about a product's benefits, so that the purchase eventually will be made.

Rational appeals rely on consumers actively processing the information presented in the advertisement. The consumer must pay attention to the commercial, comprehend the message, and compare the message to knowledge embedded in a cognitive map. Messages consistent with the current concepts in the cognitive map strengthen key linkages. New messages help the person form cognitive beliefs about the brand and establish a new linkage from her current map to the new product.

A business customer who sees a Kinko's advertisement about videoconferencing services already may have the company in his cognitive structure. The customer may have used Kinko's in the past but was not aware that the company offers videoconferencing.

When Kinko's has been established in this person's cognitive map, creating a new linkage to entice the customer to try its videoconferencing services becomes easier.

Media Outlets

Print media and the Internet offer the best outlets for rational appeals. Print and Internet ads allow readers greater opportunities to process copy information. They can pause and take time to think about the written content. Television and radio commercials are short, which makes it difficult for viewers to process message arguments. Also, if television viewers miss a television commercial they do not have the opportunity to see it until the ad is broadcast again.

Business-to-Business

Print media are used extensively for business-to-business messages. These advertisers take advantage of print's ability to feature rational appeals. Many advertising account executives believe trade publications are the best way to reach members of the buying center. Those in the industry read trade publications carefully. Placing an advertisement in a trade publication means the firm has an excellent chance of hitting its primary target market. Further, trade publications allow advertisers the opportunity to convey more details to potential buyers.

Buying center members who scan trade journals while in the information search stage of the buying process are likely to notice the ad, read it, and process the information. Buying center members who are not looking for information about the particular product will probably ignore the same ad. Magazines do not have intrusion value and readers can easily skip or ignore an advertisement. A rational appeal usually presents a primary appeal with no strong peripheral cues to attract the reader's attention.

Product Attributes

Conventional advertising wisdom suggests that rational appeals are well suited for high-involvement and complex products. High-involvement decisions require considerable cognitive activity, and consumers spend more time evaluating the attributes of the individual brands. Thus, a rational appeal should be the best approach to reach them. For some consumers, however, emotions and feelings even influence high-involvement decisions. For instance, life insurance involves both rational and emotional elements. Various insurance companies can use both in seeking to influence consumers.

In general, rational appeals are effective when consumers have high levels of involvement and are willing to pay attention to the advertisement. Message arguments and product information should be placed in the copy. Consumers can then more fully absorb information.

A rational appeal is superior to other appeals in developing or changing attitudes and establishing brand beliefs. This will be mainly true when a consumer has a particular interest in the product or brand. Otherwise, the consumer often ignores an ad using a rational appeal.

EMOTIONAL APPEALS

Emotional appeals are based on three ideas (see Figure 6.12). First, consumers ignore most advertisements. Second, rational appeals go unnoticed unless the consumer is in the market for a particular product at the time it is advertised. Third, and most important, emotional advertising can capture a viewer's attention and create an attachment between the consumer and the brand.

- Consumers ignore most ads.
- Rational appeals generally go unnoticed.
- Emotional appeals can capture attention and foster an attachment.

◀ **FIGURE 6.12**

Reasons for Using Emotional Appeals

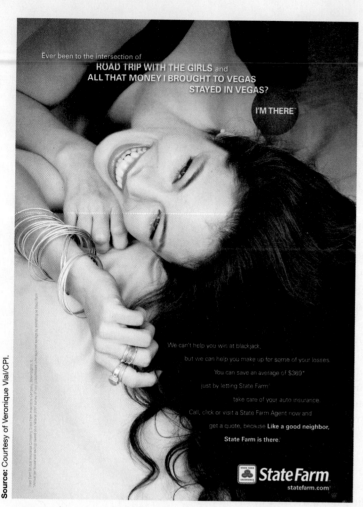

▲ An advertisement for State Farm with an emotional appeal.

Brand Loyalty

Most creatives view emotional advertising as the key to brand loyalty. Creatives want customers to experience a bond with the brand. Visual cues in advertisements are important in emotional appeals. The visual elements of the New Balance ad on the next page contribute to a feeling or mood of serenity. Also, peripheral cues, such as the music and the actor, are crucial. Although individuals develop perceptions of brands based largely on visual and peripheral stimuli, it does not happen instantly. With repetition, perceptions and attitudinal changes emerge. Figure 6.13 displays some of the more common emotions presented in advertisements.

Godiva used an emotional appeal in its latest advertising campaign entitled "the golden moment." Created by Lipman Agency, the campaign focused on the emotional appeal of giving, sharing, or eating Godiva chocolates. According to Laurie Len Kotcher (Chief Marketing Officer and Senior Vice-President for Global Brand Development of Godiva Chocolatier), "When you give the gold box, receive the gold box, eating something from the gold box, there is something special about that moment."[38]

Business-to-Business

Emotional appeals are being used more frequently in business-to-business advertising. In the past, only 5 to 10 percent of all business-to-business ads featured emotional appeals. Today, the figure has risen to nearly 25 percent. A magazine advertisement created by NKH&W Advertising Agency for a product to treat racehorses switched from a rational appeal to an emotional appeal. The target market was veterinarians. In the past, an advertisement would have opened with such ad copy as "For swelling in joints use . . ." The emotional ad shows the horse thinking, "I will prove them wrong. I will run again. I will mend my spirits."[39]

The underlying principle for changing to more emotional business-to-business ads is that emotions can be part of every type of purchase decision. Members of the buying center consider product information in making decisions but, at the same time, they are likely to be affected by emotions. Although a member of the buying center may try to minimize the emotional side of a purchase, the person is still likely to be affected. The affective component of attitudes is just as important as the cognitive component. In the past, business-to-business advertisers tended to ignore the affective element.

FIGURE 6.13 ▶
Emotions Used in Advertisements

● Trust	● Protecting loved ones
● Reliability	● Romance
● Friendship	● Passion
● Happiness	● Family bonds
● Security	● with parents
● Glamour–luxury	● with siblings
● Serenity	● with children
● Anger	● with extended family members

Media Outlets

Television remains one of the best media for emotional appeals. Television offers advertisers intrusion value and can utilize both sound and sight. Models in the ads can be "real people." Facial expressions convey emotions and attitudes. Consumers learn about a particular product and develop attitudes based on these experiences. Television ads also are more vivid, more lifelike, and often create dynamic situations that pull viewers in. Music can be incorporated to make the commercial more dramatic. Peripheral cues are important components of emotional appeals. The cues (such as music and background visuals) also capture the viewer's attention.

Emotional ads are widely featured on the Internet. Many of the same benefits for television are found online. The use of streaming video, animation, and software such as Photoshop make it possible to create engaging emotional ads.

Emotions are tied with humor, fear, music, and other appeals to make a compelling case for a product. The same ad can influence a consumer both emotionally and rationally. The creative selects the most appropriate emotional appeal for the product and company.

I trade sweat for strength.

I trade sleep for sunrises.

I trade doubt for belief.

I trade my walking for nothing.

achieve new balance

▲ New Balance uses visual elements in this advertisement to create an emotional appeal of serenity and peace.

SCARCITY APPEALS

Scarcity appeals urge consumers to buy a particular product because of a limitation. It can be a limited number of the products available or, more often, that the product will be made available for only a limited time. When there is a limited supply of a product, the perceived value of the product may increase. For the Olympics, General Mills introduced USA Olympic Crunch cereal and Betty Crocker Team USA desserts for a limited time.[40] McDonald's, Wendy's, and Burger King offer sandwiches (McRib, Hot N' Spicy Chicken, Dollar Whoppers) for limited-time periods throughout the year. The scarcity concept is also used for musical compilations, encouraging consumers to buy a CD because of its limited availability. By making sure it is not available in retail stores, marketers increase its scarcity value.

A scarcity appeal may be tied to other promotional tools. For example, a manufacturer will advertise a limited price discount offer to retailers who stock up early for Christmas or some other holiday season. Contests and sweepstakes also run for limited times. Encouraging consumers to take action is the primary benefit of a scarcity appeal. Creatives normally receive information about scarcity issues in the creative brief or from the account executive who has consulted with the company.

INTERNATIONAL IMPLICATIONS

Many of the international implications of both advertising theory and the various types of appeals have already been described in this chapter. In summary, leverage points lead to customer values. These values may be influenced by the culture or country in which the consumer lives. Therefore, advertisements should be constructed in ways that express those values.

Advertising appeals should be adapted to cultural differences. As a small example, fear of body odor often sells products in the United States. In other cultures, body odor does not carry the same meaning. Sexual appeals, as noted, must be adjusted to fit the

9 What are the primary areas of concern in international advertising?

! INTEGRATED CAMPAIGNS IN ACTION

Philadelphia Cream Cheese

Sales of Philadelphia Cream Cheese had been stagnant for several years, because most United States consumers only use the product to spread on bagels or as the main ingredient in cheesecake. In other countries, cream cheese is viewed as a more general product that can be spread on crackers, bread, and in cooking other items. Consequently, the opportunity exists to increase U.S. Philadelphia Cream Cheese consumption by suggesting new uses for the product.

To spur sales in the United States, Kraft Vice-President of Marketing Howard Friedman worked with the advertising agency mcgarrybowen to create a new campaign. The primary thrust of the campaign was to expand usage of the product and to increase the buy rate among medium and low users of cream cheese. mcgarrybowen designed a series of ads using an emotion appeal. Television, video, print, and digital ads were produced.

The campaign focused on two target markets: (1) women aged 25 to 44 with some college, incomes over $45,000, and low-skill cooking ability and (2) women older than age 45 with some college, incomes over $75,000, and high-skill cooking ability. In addition to the print and broadcast ads, the campaign focused on providing recipes online submitted by consumers through a contest entitled "Real Women of Philly." The grand prize was $125,000 and an appearance on television on a cooking show.

Your instructor has additional information about the ads, visuals, and displays used in this campaign.

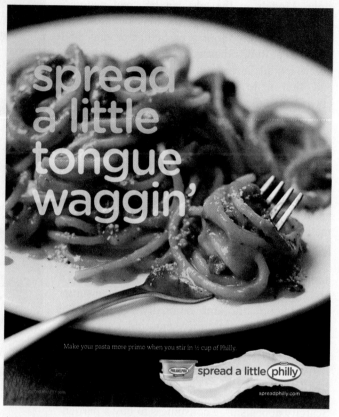

▲ An advertisement for Philadelphia Cream Cheese developed by the mcgarrybowen agency.

laws and customs of a region. Musical tastes vary, as do perceptions of rationality and scarcity. Emotions may be stronger in some cultures, whereas in others people are much more reserved.

An international company or a firm seeking to expand into additional countries should adapt and adjust both the theoretical approach and type of appeal in order to create effective advertisements. Finding universal themes, such as visual Esperanto, may be a great help to the international advertising creative.

❝ SUMMARY

Developing effective advertisements represents a key ingredient in integrated marketing communications efforts. The advertising team should define the objective of the ad, the target audience, the message theme used, the type of support needed, and any constraints that apply. Then, a creative works within the context of key advertising theories in selecting the correct media and designing the leverage point and message appeal that work effectively within each medium.

Three important theoretical approaches drive the development of many advertisements. The hierarchy of effects model

suggests consumers move through a series of stages as they are persuaded to make a purchase: (1) awareness, (2) knowledge, (3) liking, (4) preference, (5) conviction, and (6) the actual purchase. Although the process probably is not a lock-step model that every buyer follows, the hierarchy of effects approach does provide important information about which mental issues to account for in various advertising campaigns. The hierarchy of effects model can be combined with the three main elements present in attitudes: (1) cognitive, (2) affective, and (3) conative components. Ads are designed to influence affective feelings, cognitive knowledge, or conative intentions to act or behave based on an attitude. A means–end chain displays the linkages between a means to achieve a desired state and the end or personal value at issue. Advertisers can select personal values that mesh with the key characteristics of the target market and then construct ads designed to provide them the means to achieve these ends by purchasing the good or service. These ideas help the creative develop a leverage point to move the buyer from understanding the product's benefits to incorporating those benefits with his or her personal values.

Visual and verbal issues should also be considered in the formation of an ad. Concrete visual images are easily recognized and recalled. Abstract images may be linked with values or emotions the product creates or the feeling the buyer should experience that may be associated with the product or company. Visual elements are key components in almost every form of advertising. Verbal elements must reach the more rational, central route of the audience's mental processing procedures.

Beyond these components, advertising creatives must form messages using one (or more) of the seven major appeals: (1) fear, (2) humor, (3) sex, (4) music, (5) rationality, (6) emotions, or (7) scarcity. Just as there are logical combinations of media, there are logical combinations of these appeals for various messages. Often, music provides the backdrop for messages

invoking fear, humor, sex, and emotions. Humor can be linked with sex, music, rationality (by showing how being illogical is silly or funny), and scarcity. Rationality combines with fear in many commercials. Designing a message argument that takes advantage of the various characteristics of these appeals breaks through clutter, and convinces the audience to buy the item involved will be the creative's goal. Mismatches of message tactics are to be avoided, such as combining sex with humor in France, as was mentioned earlier.

Business-to-business ads often appear in print and many times include rational approaches in the copy because the purchase decision variables are more complex. At the same time, many advertisers have recently discovered that emotional ads can be effective, which expands business-to-business advertising into other venues, such as television, radio, and the Internet.

The process of designing ads for international markets is quite similar to that for domestic ads. The major difference is careful consideration of local attitudes and customers, with due care given to the language, slang, and symbols of the area. For example, Sega recently discovered that its product's name is slang for "masturbation" in Italian, after a major advertising campaign had started. These types of mistakes are to be avoided.

KEY TERMS

hierarchy of effects model A marketing approach suggesting that a consumer moves through a series of six steps when becoming convinced to make a purchase: (1) awareness, (2) knowledge, (3) liking, (4) preference, (5) conviction, and (6) the actual purchase.

means–end chain An advertising approach in which the message contains a means (a reasoning or mental process) to lead the consumer to a desired end state, such as a key personal value.

Means–End Conceptualization of Components for Advertising Strategy (MECCAS) An advertising approach that suggests using five elements in creating ads: (1) the product's attributes, (2) consumer benefits, (3) leverage points, (4) personal values, and (5) the executional framework.

tagline A catchy, easy-to-remember phrase in an ad used to make the key point and reinforce the company's image to the consumer.

visual Esperanto A universal language that makes global advertising possible for any good or service by recognizing that visual images are more powerful than verbal descriptions.

advertising appeals Approaches to reaching consumers with ads. The seven major appeals are: (1) fear, (2) humor, (3) sex, (4) music, (5) rationality, (6) emotions, and (7) scarcity.

severity Part of the fear behavioral response model that leads the individual to consider how strong certain negative consequences of an action will be.

vulnerability Part of the fear behavioral response model that leads the individual to consider the odds of being affected by the negative consequences of an action.

decorative models Models in an advertisement whose primary purpose is to adorn the product as a sexual or attractive stimulus without serving a functional purpose.

REVIEW QUESTIONS

1. What are the five main elements of a creative brief? How do they affect the choice of advertising appeals?

2. What are the six stages of the hierarchy of effects model? Do they always occur in that order? Why or why not?

3. How are the three components of attitude related to the hierarchy of effects model?

4. In a means–end chain, what are the means? The ends? How do they affect advertising design?

5. What is a leverage point? How are leverage points related to the hierarchy of effects model, attitudinal changes, and means–end chains?

6. What is a tagline?

7. Why are visual elements in advertisement important? What is the relationship between visual and verbal elements? Can there be one without the other?

8. What is visual Esperanto?

9. What are the seven most common types of advertising appeals?

10. What are the advantages and disadvantages of fear appeals in advertising?

11. When does humor work in an ad? What pitfalls should companies avoid in using humorous appeals?

12. What types of sexual appeals can advertisers use?

13. When are sexual appeals most likely to succeed? To fail?

14. What should international advertisers consider when thinking about using sexual appeals?

15. Name the different ways music can play a role in an advertisement. Explain how each role should match individual appeals, media, and other elements in the design of the ad.

16. What are the advantages and disadvantages of rational appeals? Which media do they best match?

17. How can emotions accentuate advertisements? Why are they being used more often in business-to-business advertisements?

18. What is scarcity? How do scarcity ads lead to buyer action?

CRITICAL THINKING EXERCISES

Discussion Questions

1. Develop a means–end chain similar to the one in Figure 6.3 for each of the following branded products:

   a. Benetton clothes

   b. Stetson cologne

   c. New Balance shoes

   d. Oscar Mayer deli meats

2. Evaluate the balance of visual and verbal elements of five advertisements shown in this chapter. Which is predominant? Which images are considered appropriate for international advertising because they display visual Esperanto characteristics?

3. Watch one of your favorite television shows. Record all of the television commercials in one commercial break (at least seven ads). Identify the appeal used in each one. Were the ads effective? Why or why not?

4. Locate a print ad or television ad that features a fear appeal. Using the behavioral response model in Figure 6.7, identify various elements in the ad that correspond with the components in the model. Some of the elements will require thinking beyond what is visually or verbally present in the ad itself.

5. Hardee's and Carl's Jr. recently used a television commercial featuring a schoolteacher dancing on top of her desk while a room full of guys performed a rap song entitled "I Like Flat Buns." The song seemed appropriate because the ad was for the Patty Melt on a flat bun. Instead, the ad received considerable flack because the sexy blonde schoolteacher was wearing a short, tight skirt. Teachers' associations complained that it was inappropriate because it was a "sexually exploitive assault" on teachers, students, and schools.[41] Do you agree or disagree?

6. Using magazines that you normally read, locate at least one print ad for each of the appeals except music. Discuss the quality of each advertisement and its best and worst aspects. For each ad, present another possible appeal and how it could be used. What personal values and customer benefits does each advertisement present?

7. Locate five television commercials or find five print advertisements that use sex appeals. Identify which of the five ways sexuality was used. Evaluate each ad in terms of the appropriateness and effectiveness of the sex appeal.

8. For each of the following products and target markets, discuss which appeal you think would be the best. Explain why you think it would be effective. Briefly describe a print or television ad that you think would be effective.

   a. Senior citizens—soup

   b. Females, ages 25–40, with children—hot dogs

   c. College students—jeans

   d. Males, ages 25–40, married with children—life insurance

INTEGRATED LEARNING EXERCISES

1. Greenfield Online is one of the leading online research firms. Access the Web site at **www.greenfield central.com**. What types of products does the company offer? How would this information help a creative in developing an advertisement for Greenfield Online? How would this information assist an advertising agency in understanding the target audience for an advertisement?

2. Examine Figure 6.3 and then access the following Web sites for the milk industry. What differences do you see in the Web sites? Who do you believe is the intended audience for each Web site?

   a. **www.gotmilk.com**

   b. **www.whymilk.com**

   c. **www.bodybymilk.com**

3. Visit the following Web sites. Identify which type of appeal each site uses. Evaluate the quality of that appeal. What other appeals can be used to make the site more appealing? Discuss the balance of visual and verbal elements on the Web site and ad.

   a. Service Metrics (**www.servicemetrics.com**)

   b. Hyundai Motors, USA (**www.hyundaiusa.com**)

   c. Skechers (**www.skechers.com**)

   d. Bijan Fragrances (**www.bijan.com**)

   e. Guess (**www.guess.com**)

   f. Oscar Mayer (**www.oscarmayer.com**)

   g. Liz Claiborne (**www.lizclaiborne.com**)

4. Access an online database search engine through your library. Pick one of the appeals listed in the chapter. Find at least three different articles that discuss the appeal. Write a report based on your findings.

STUDENT PROJECT

Creative Corner

It is time to try your creativity with a television advertisement. Borrow a camcorder and develop a 30- or 45-second television spot for one of the following products, using the suggested appeal. Be sure to develop a means–end chain prior to creating the advertisement. If you do not have access to a camcorder, then develop a magazine ad.

a. Denim skirt, sex appeal

b. Tennis racket, humor appeal

c. Ice cream, emotional appeal

d. Vitamins, fear appeal

e. Golf club, rational appeal

f. Spring break trip package, scarcity appeal

g. Restaurant, music appeal

CASE 1 ECKO ENTERPRISES

It is a safe bet to guess that the majority of people over 40 years old have not heard of Marc Ecko or Ecko Enterprises. He was born as Marc Milecofsky and grew up south of New York City in Lakewood, New Jersey. His parents were real estate agents. Ecko has two sisters, one of whom is his twin, Marci. The name Ecko is the result of a family story. When Ecko's mother was pregnant with Marci, the doctor informed her of an "echo" on an ultrasound, which turned out to be Marc.

The world of hip hop belongs to a new generation, one with its own unique form of clothing, known to many as "urban apparel." Ecko Enterprises was formed in 1993 when three friends began creating T-shirt fashions using cans of spray paint. By 2004, the company reported sales of nearly $1 billion. Items from Ecko Enterprises and the Ecko Unlimited brand are sold in more than 5,000 department and specialty stores domestically and in over 45 countries internationally. There are now 30 Ecko Unlimited full-price company annex stores, 16 of which are located outside of the United States. The Ecko Unlimited clothing line often features the stark silhouette of a rhinoceros on T-shirts, baggy jeans, and other products.

Ecko's company competes with firms that rely on the "cred" (credibility) that comes from being a performer, such as the Sean John line featuring P. Diddy, Rocawear from Jay-Z and Damon Dash, and Phat Fashions offered by Russell Simmons. Marc Ecko, in contrast, is simply a fan of the music who grew up living in suburban neighborhoods. Although he is sometimes described as a "former graffiti artist," the reality is that his company was formed while he was studying at Rutgers University to become a pharmacist.

A variety of products are featured through Ecko Unlimited, Marc Ecko Formalwear, and Eckored Kids, including outerwear, footwear, watches, eyewear, underwear, belts, bags, hats, small leather goods, and formal wear. The Marc Ecko Cut & Sew brand is a contemporary menswear line consisting of casual and dress separates designed to blend street-inspired edginess with more sophisticated designs and fabrics. Cut & Sew offers semi-tailored separates, sweaters, urban spa-inspired active wear, woven shirts, and premium denim.

A newer brand, the G-Unit Clothing Company, is an independent venture operated by Ecko and multiplatinum-selling artist 50 Cent. The G-Unit line includes items for men, women, boys, and girls. It features denim, T-shirts, fleece, outerwear, hats, and sportswear. Also, Marc Ecko Enterprises formed an exclusive U.S. and Canadian licensing agreement with Avirex Ltd. to introduce a sportswear collection. The line carries a full collection of apparel, including fashion denim, tees, knits, and outerwear. Other licensing agreements have been formed with Geoffrey Allen, Skechers, Paul D'Avril, Inc., Kid Headquarters, and Viva International.

The company also offers skateboards and skater-influenced clothing and accessories through the Zoo York label. The brand was launched in 1993 and is now part of the MEE line, which is the East Coast's largest action sports company. Ecko also publishes *Complex Magazine*, a bimonthly urban lifestyle publication with a circulation of 325,000. Another new venture is Contents Under Pressure, a game developed in partnership with Atari, Inc. The game features stories and characters in a futuristic universe in which graffiti plays a key role.

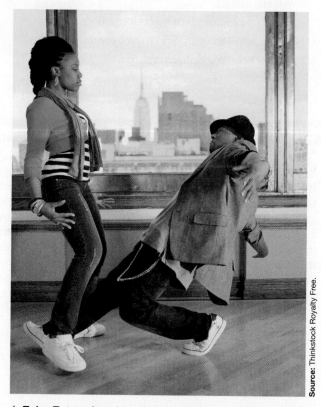

▲ Ecko Enterprises began by selling its unique form of clothing, known as "urban apparel."

Urban apparel can be viewed as a form of "lifestyle merchandising." Ecko was able to translate his own enthusiasm for hip hop into something new and different in the fashion world. By placing ads in hip-hop magazines such as *The Source* and *Vibe,* the Ecko rhino grew based on relationships with a wide range of maverick recording artists, including Talib Kweli and the Beatnuts. Although many retailers feared the urban look, Federated Department Stores, the owner of Macy's and Bloomingdale's, became an enthusiastic seller of Ecko Unlimited.

Russell Simmons, founder of Phat Fashions and the godfather of hip-hop culture, was quoted as saying, "Marc is a very, very creative designer. He's got more edge than most." Simmons describes Ecko's line as having an "alternative" quality or a "more suburban edge." In other words, the Ecko brands were able to gain market among the hip-hop audience. The next issue becomes, as the hip-hop generation ages and new fads and fashions emerge, will Ecko Enterprises be able to continue to grow and succeed?

1. Which of the models presented in this chapter best explains a consumer's purchase of a fashion product created by Ecko Enterprises? Explain.

2. Examine Ecko Enterprises' Web site at **www.marceckoenterprises.com**. Pick one of the brands

and develop a means–end chain that could be used by a creative to develop an advertising campaign.

3. Of the seven advertising appeals, which would work best for Ecko Enterprises' products? Why? Would combinations of appeals be useful for this company? If so, which ones?

4. Pick one of the appeals discussed in the chapter and one of the brands sold by Ecko Enterprises and then develop a print advertisement. Describe your target audience in terms of demographics and psychographics.

Source: Rob Walker, "Cul-de-sac Cred," *New York Times Magazine*, July 10, 2005.

CASE 2   LIGHTING UP KINDLE

The world of book publishing and book reading is currently undergoing radical changes that are largely being driven by new technologies. Authors who previously found themselves shut out of traditional publishing can now use the Internet to distribute their books on topics ranging from self-help to political ideology.

After the initial wave of e-book releases, including one by well-known author Stephen King, changes in consumer book-purchasing patterns slowed. Noted New York literary agent Peter Rubie believed that the secret was mobility. He stated that "as soon as someone can carry an e-book to the beach without needing a laptop, the industry is going to change."

That day may have arrived. In late 2007, Jeff Bezos, the founder and CEO of Amazon.com, announced the release of a revolutionary new product—the Kindle. The Kindle is a wire-less, portable reading device that offers instant access to more than 90,000 books, blogs, magazines, and newspapers. The technology behind the Kindle is the same as that contained in cell phones, which means that users do not need to find a Wi-Fi hotspot to use it. The Kindle weighs 10.3 ounces and can carry 200 books at any time. Readers can download books, magazines, blogs, and newspapers from any location.

The device offered a variety of new features. For example, if a person does not know the meaning of a word in a text, the word can be highlighted and then found in an instant dictionary. Links to other sources, such as Wikipedia, are also available.

The great benefit of Kindle to authors is that their books remain available in perpetuity. No longer will a book go "out of print." Each book download costs the reader about $10.00, and the author receives a royalty, just as in the past. For some authors, an additional benefit is the ability to revise a book over time, because the entire content is digital rather than print.

The Kindle debuted with some buzz, despite its hefty price tag ($400). Bezos appeared on *Charlie Rose*, and several newspaper and magazine articles about the product created some publicity. The company will need to build on that early momentum, because it clearly did not generate the same kind of interest as the MP3 player or the iPhone. Further, competition soon became available in the form of the Sony Portable Reading System.

Author Kevin Maney summarized the Kindle this way: "It's too early to tell whether this is the book's future. The Kindle isn't even set up to do all that just yet. But it is the first e-book reader built to be wirelessly connected to the Internet at all times. It's the first system that shows that living, connected books—some combination of traditional books and Wikipedia—are possible. And, in fact, that's the first reason to think that e-books could evolve into something other than paper books." Consumers will undoubtedly decide the rest.

▼ Portable readers can download books, magazines, blogs, and newspapers from any location.

Source: Shutterstock.

1. As an advertising executive who is working with a creative, which advertising theory do you think best fits the release and subsequent advertising for Kindle?

2. What should be the leverage point in a commercial for Kindle?

3. What type of advertising appeal, or sets of appeals, should be used in promoting Kindle?

4. What should be the headline of a Kindle ad? Why?

5. Design a print ad promoting Kindle. Identify which appeal you used and explain why you chose it.

Sources: www.amazon.com (accessed January 5, 2008); Kevin Maney, "A Book That Never Ends?" *USA Today*, December 6, 2007, p. 19A.

7 Advertising Design
Message Strategies and Executional Frameworks

DOVE

Social and Fashion Advertising

A recent advertisement, titled "Onslaught" was created for Dove products. The commercial opens with the words "A Dove film" and shows a close-up of a smiling, innocent, red-headed girl for nearly 20 seconds. With music featuring a modern sound and the words "Here it comes" frequently repeated in the background, cuts from various pseudo-advertisements display slinky, fashionable, beautiful models. The attributes needed to reach such a status are mentioned, among them "younger, smaller, lighter, thinner, tighter, softer." "It works" is highlighted again and again by the advertising pitchwomen. The inevitable pathway to yo-yo dieting, eating disorders, and various forms of cosmetic surgery follows.

Finally, as a group of young girls around the age of 10 cross a street, the commercial closes with the words, "Talk to your daughter before the beauty industry does." The compelling message does not mention Dove soap or any of its product features. Instead, it offers a strong indictment of the social pressures young girls and young women face.

Advertising and marketing to women and girls may be at a crossroad. Clearly, pressures to grow up more quickly, to look older at a younger age, and to fit in socially drive a great deal of product design and what is called *age-compression marketing.* Some responsible parents and those who offer social commentary are pushing back with the essential message, "Let girls be girls."

Complaints about body image issues are not new. In the 1960s, a young supermodel named Twiggy captured international attention by looking girlish and paper thin. Television programs and a movie remake of *Lolita* stirred additional controversy and debate. The Disney Channel's *Hannah Montana* once again highlighted the mega-power associated with marketing to young girls. The *Hannah Montana* stage show that traveled across the United States resulted in price gouging and

CHAPTER OBJECTIVES

After reading this chapter, you should be able to answer the following questions:

1 How are the three main types of message strategies used to increase advertising effectiveness?

2 How do the main types of executional frameworks help to deliver quality advertising messages?

3 What types of sources or spokespersons can be used in advertisements or commercials?

4 What characteristics are most important when selecting a source or spokesperson?

5 What process is used to create advertisements?

6 What are the principles of advertising effectiveness?

7 How are advertising programs adjusted to fit international circumstances?

CHAPTER 7

Source: Author Supplied Image.

ticket scalping, sending ticket prices into the hundreds of dollars. One side of Hannah, of course, is the glamorous world of a rock star.

Dove's "Onslaught" advertisement sends a competing message. The Dove Web site includes pages called "Campaign for Real Beauty" for young girls and "Dove Pro-Age" for older women. Visitors can make charitable contributions to the Dove Self-Esteem fund through the Web site. Clearly, this division of the company is tapping into an emotion held by many women, especially mothers.

Time cynically notes that Dove is owned by Unilever, which "advertises its Axe Body Spray to men using a lingerie-and-stiletto-clad rock band called Bom Chicka Wah Wahs," and then asks, "What do we tell our daughters about that?"[1]

OVERVIEW

Designing messages to effectively reach a target audience constitutes the essence of integrated marketing communications. Many of these messages are quite personal. They are designed to change or shape attitudes. They should be remembered and lead to a short- or long-term action.

Marketing messages travel in two ways. First, a personal message can be delivered through a personal medium. A sales representative closing a deal, shaking the hand of the buyer, giving a reassuring tap on the shoulder, and smiling while talking delivers a message in an intimate, warm, personal fashion. Clearly, personal media (e.g., sales reps, repair department personnel, customer services representatives) are part of the overall IMC program.

Marketing messages also travel through the various forms of advertising media. Most of these are *impersonal*. Televisions are indifferent as to what appears on the screen. Radios deliver any sound that can be transmitted. Computer screens are nothing more than special-purpose television screens. The challenge to the advertising agency, the company, and especially the creative is to design a personal message, even one being delivered by an impersonal medium. The message should engage the buyer and influence her to recall and purchase the product. Also, many marketers and advertising agencies seek tangible, measurable results.

This chapter first focuses on the main three types of message strategies. Each may be used to help convince the consumer to make a purchase, either through reason, emotion, or an action-inducing advertisement. Second, the major types of executional frameworks are explained. These forms of advertising presentations help the creative prepare original, convincing, and memorable messages. Third, the four types of sources or spokespersons that appear in various advertisements are described and the criteria used to select them are reviewed. Finally, the principles of effective advertising campaigns are presented. Advertisements that are effectively combined with other elements of the promotions mix can lead to a strong company image reflecting a clear IMC theme.

MESSAGE STRATEGIES

❶ How are the three main types of message strategies used to increase advertising effectiveness?

The **message theme** outlines the key ideas in an advertisement. It is a central part of the creative brief. The message theme can be created using a number of message strategies. A **message strategy** is the primary tactic or approach used to deliver the message theme. The three broad categories of message strategies are:[2]

1. Cognitive strategies
2. Affective strategies
3. Conative strategies

The categories represent the components of attitudes, as described earlier. Figure 7.1 identifies the various forms or approaches from each category.

Cognitive Strategies

A **cognitive message strategy** presents rational arguments or pieces of information to consumers. The ideas require cognitive processing. The advertisement's key message describes the product's attributes or benefits. Customers can obtain these benefits by purchasing the product.[3]

A cognitive message strategy advertisement should influence a person's beliefs and/or knowledge structure by suggesting any one of a wide variety of potential product benefits. Foods may be described as healthy, pleasant tasting, or low calorie. A tool can be shown as durable, convenient, or handy to use. A drill press machine used in a manufacturing operation may be portrayed as being more reliable or faster than the competition's machines. Cognitive message strategies clearly present these benefits to customers. The five major forms of cognitive strategies are:

1. Generic messages
2. Preemptive messages

FIGURE 7.1 ▶
Message Strategies

● Generic	● Resonance
● Preemptive	● Emotional
● Unique selling proposition	● Action-inducing
● Hyberbole	● Promotional support
● Comparative	

3. Unique selling proposition

4. Hyperbole

5. Comparative advertisements

Generic Messages

When an advertisement directly promotes the product's attributes or benefits without any claim of superiority, it sends a **generic message**. This works best when a firm is the brand leader and dominates the industry. A generic message makes the brand synonymous with the product category. Campbell's Soups can declare "Soup is good food" without making any claim to superiority. The company leads the industry. When most consumers think of soup, they think of Campbell's, which sells 69 percent of all cans sold each year.[4] Nintendo uses a similar approach because the company dominates the game-console category with a 47 percent market share.[5]

▲ An advertisement for Marion State Bank using a generic message strategy.

Generic message strategies are seldom found in business-to-business advertisements, because few firms dominate an industry to the extent of Campbell's or Nintendo. Intel is the major exception. The company controls 80 percent of the microchip market.[6] The generic message "Intel inside" has been repeated for years.

Generic message strategies can stimulate brand awareness. The advertiser may try to develop a cognitive linkage between a specific brand name and a product category, such as Skechers and sporty footwear. The advertisement may contain little information about the product's attributes. Instead, it attempts to place the brand in a person's cognitive memory and cognitive map.

Preemptive Messages

A claim of superiority based on a product's specific attribute or benefit with the intent of preventing the competition from making the same or a similar statement is a **preemptive message**. Crest toothpaste is known as "the cavity fighter," which preempts other companies from making similar claims, even though all toothpastes fight cavities. An effective preemptive strategy occurs when the company is first to state the advantage. Competitors that say the same thing become viewed as "me-too" brands or copycats.

▼ An advertisement for Bonne Bell featuring a unique selling proposition.

Unique Selling Proposition

An explicit, testable claim of uniqueness or superiority that can be supported or substantiated in some manner is a **unique selling proposition (USP)**. The Bonne Bell advertisement shown in this section features a unique selling proposition aimed at teenagers. The message that Bonne Bell Lipshade is "your 1 and only, 1 handed, sleek sweep flipstick!" stresses a unique product feature.

Hyperbole

An *untestable* claim based on some attribute or benefit is **hyperbole**. When NBC states that it has America's favorite comedies, the claim is hyperbole. It does not require substantiation, which makes this cognitive strategy quite popular.

Comparative Advertising

The final cognitive message strategy, a **comparative advertisement**, allows an advertiser to directly or indirectly compare a product to the competition's. The advertisement may or may not mention the competitor by name. An advertiser can simply present a "make-believe" competitor with a name such as "Brand X." This approach, however, may not be as effective as making a comparison using the actual competitor's name. To provide protection from lawsuits, company leaders make sure any claim concerning the competition can be clearly substantiated.

AT&T and Sprint compare rates. VISA notes that many merchants will not accept American Express. In the business-to-business sector, shipping companies compare delivery times and accuracy rates.

Comparative ads offer the advantage of capturing the consumer's attention. When comparisons are made, both brand awareness and message awareness increase. Consumers tend to remember more of what was said about a brand than when the same information is presented in a noncomparative ad format.

Believability and consumer attitudes represent the negative side of comparative ads. Many consumers consider comparative ads to be less believable. They view the information about the sponsor brand as exaggerated and conclude that the information about the comparison brand probably is misstated to make the sponsor brand appear superior.

Another danger of comparative ads occurs when consumers develop negative attitudes toward the advertisement, which can then be transferred to the sponsor's product. This becomes more likely when the sponsor runs a *negative comparative ad* about the competition's product. Research suggests that negative comparative ads typically result in lower believability of the advertising claim and may result in less favorable attitudes toward the brand.[7] In psychology, the concept of *spontaneous trait transference* suggests that when someone calls another person dishonest, other people tend to consider the speaker to be less than honest. A comparative advertisement that criticizes the competition's brand based on a particular attribute may lead viewers to also attribute the deficiency to the sponsor brand. The transference becomes more likely when the consumer purchases the comparative brand, not the sponsored brand.[8]

Company leaders carefully choose an appropriate comparison firm and are cautious when using a negative comparison format. The comparison brand must be viewed as a viable competing brand. Actual product attributes and customer benefits are noted, without stretching the information or providing misleading information. When actual differences exist, comparative advertising works well. Comparisons consisting of hype and opinion with no substantial differences are less likely to succeed. Misleading comparisons can cause the Federal Trade Commission (FTC) to investigate. The majority of complaints filed with the FTC are about potentially misleading comparison advertisements.

Comparing a brand with a low market share to the market leader works well, because viewers concentrate more carefully on the advertisement's content and message. Comparing a high-market share brand with another high-market share brand may not be as effective. In these cases, a better strategy may be to simply make the comparison without naming the competitor.

Several years ago, Avis was in 10th place in market share in the rental car industry. A series of commercials compared Avis to the market leader, Hertz, mentioning the Hertz name specifically. Most consumers now believe Avis provides the same level of quality as Hertz.[9]

The five cognitive message strategies are based on rational logic. Messages are designed to make sure consumers pay attention to the ad and take the time to cognitively process the information. In terms of attitudes, the sequence of *cognitive → affective → conative* represents the rational approach. The cognitive message strategy first presents consumers with rational information about a good, service, or company, and then leads them to develop positive feelings about the same product or company.

Affective Strategies

Advertisements that invoke feelings or emotions and match those feelings with the good, service, or company use **affective message strategies**. These messages attempt to enhance the likeability of the product, recall of the appeal, or comprehension of the advertisement. Affective strategies elicit emotions that, in turn, lead the consumer to act, preferably by buying the product, and subsequently affecting the consumer's reasoning process.

An emotion such as love can be featured in order to convince consumers that Cheerios is a superior breakfast cereal for loved ones. Consumers can be told that Cheerios offers a rational choice. Company advertisements then mention the cereal's positive effect on cholesterol levels, as shown in the Cheerios ad in this section. The photo of three generations of a family is combined with the words "Your heart has better things to do than deal with heart disease." Family memories and emotions are combined with the product's heart-smart feature. Affective strategies fall into two categories: (1) resonance and (2) emotional.

Resonance advertising connects a product with a consumer's experiences in order to develop stronger ties between the product and the consumer. The use of music from the 1980s takes Echo Boomers back to that time. Any strongly held memory or emotional attachment becomes a candidate for resonance advertising.

Emotional advertising attempts to elicit powerful emotions that eventually lead to product recall and choice. Many emotions can be connected to products, including trust, reliability, friendship, happiness, security, glamour, luxury, serenity, pleasure, romance, and passion.

Emotional appeals are employed in both consumer-oriented and business-to-business ads. Members of the buying center in a business are human. They do not make purchasing decisions based solely on rational thought processes. Emotions and feelings also affect choices. When the product's benefits are presented using an emotional framework, the advertisement will normally be more effective, even in business-to-business ads.[10]

Affective strategies may help develop a stronger brand name. Affective advertisements can cause consumers to like the brand, have positive feelings towards it, and eventually purchase the item. Cognitive beliefs about the brand then follow. This approach relies on the attitude development sequence of *affective → conative → cognitive*. For some products, affective advertisements are effective because there are no real tangible differences among the brands. Skechers Sport Footwear uses an affective strategy in the advertisement in this section. It depicts social acceptance and the idea that Skechers shoes make you a part of the in-crowd, thus trying to create positive feelings toward the Skechers Sport brand.

Conative Strategies

Conative message strategies are designed to lead directly to some type of consumer response. They can support other promotional efforts, such as coupon redemption programs, Internet "hits" and orders, and in-store offers such as buy-one-get-one-free. The goal of eliciting behaviors can be found in any advertisement for old television programs that seeks to persuade viewers to call a toll-free number to purchase the DVDs. These ads typically encourage quick action by stating that the DVD cannot be purchased in stores and will be available for only a limited time.

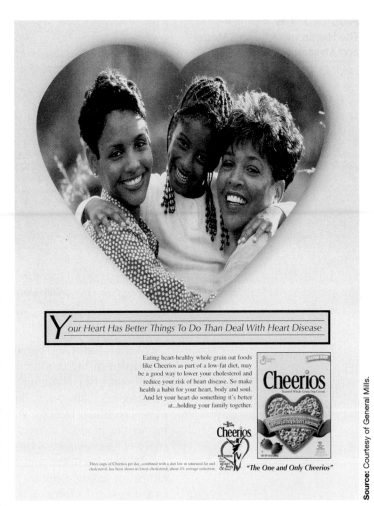

*Y*our Heart Has Better Things To Do Than Deal With Heart Disease

Eating heart-healthy whole grain oat foods like Cheerios as part your low-fat diet, may be a good way to lower your cholesterol and reduce your risk of heart disease. So make health a habit for your heart, body and soul. And let your heart do something it's better at...holding your family together.

Cheerios

"The One and Only Cheerios"

▲ A Cheerios advertisement utilizing a resonance affective message strategy.

▼ An advertisement for Skechers Sport Footwear using an emotional message strategy.

FIGURE 7.2 ▶
The Hierarchy of Effects Model
and Message Strategies

FIGURE 7.2 ▶
The Hierarchy of Effects Model
and Message Strategies

Action-inducing conative advertisements create situations in which cognitive knowledge of the product or affective liking of the product may come later (after the actual purchase) or during product usage. For instance, a point-of-purchase display can be designed (sometimes through advertising tie-ins) to cause people to make *impulse buys.* The goal is to make the sale, with cognitive knowledge and affective feelings forming as the product is used. The attitude sequence for conative message strategies is *conative → cognitive → affective.*

Promotional support conative advertisements are tied in with other promotional efforts, including coupons, phone-in promotions, or a sweepstakes that a consumer enters by filling out the form on the advertisement or by going to a particular retail store.

Cognitive, affective, and conative strategies can be matched with the hierarchy of effects approach, which suggests that consumers pass through a series of stages, from awareness to knowledge, liking, preference, conviction, and, finally, to the purchase. As shown in Figure 7.2, each message strategy can highlight a different stage of the hierarchy of effects model.

Choosing the right message strategy often becomes the key ingredient in creating a successful advertising program. To be effective, the message strategy should match the leverage point and executional framework. These should mesh with the media to be utilized. The creative and the account executive remain in constant contact throughout the process to be certain all of these advertising ingredients remain consistent.

EXECUTIONAL FRAMEWORKS

❷ How do the main types of
executional frameworks help
to deliver quality advertising
messages?

An **executional framework** signifies the manner in which an ad appeal will be presented. It should be chosen in conjunction with an advertising appeal and message strategy. The common types of appeals include fear, humor, sex, music, rationality, emotions, and scarcity. Each can be matched with the appropriate executional framework. Figure 7.3 displays the various frameworks.

FIGURE 7.3 ▶
Executional Frameworks

● Animation	● Authoritative
● Slice-of-life	● Demonstration
● Dramatization	● Fantasy
● Testimonial	● Informative

Animation

Animation has become an increasingly popular executional framework, and its use has risen dramatically. The growing sophistication of computer graphics programs makes new and exciting animation technologies available. Successful films such as *Up* and *Bee Movie* continue to create a great deal of interest in animation advertising. Animation can be featured in television spots and in Internet advertising. It is also used in movie trailers. Single shots of animated characters, such as *Dora the Explorer*, are placed in print ads.

One exciting animation technique, *rotoscoping*, is the process of digitally painting or sketching figures into live sequences, which makes it possible to present both live actors and animated characters in the same frame.[11] The creative can also merge or modify various live scenes. As advertising executive Stan Richards noted, "The opportunities are great, because, we are at a point where, anything that we can think of, we can do. We've never had that before. There is a cost consequence. A lot of that digital production is expensive, but those costs are coming down. Within a few years, those costs will be half of what they are now."[12]

For years, animation was rarely used in business-to-business advertising. Many advertising leaders had negative views of it, believing animation appealed to children but not to businesspeople. These views have changed. Business ads shown on television now take advantage of high-quality graphics to illustrate a product's uses with animation.

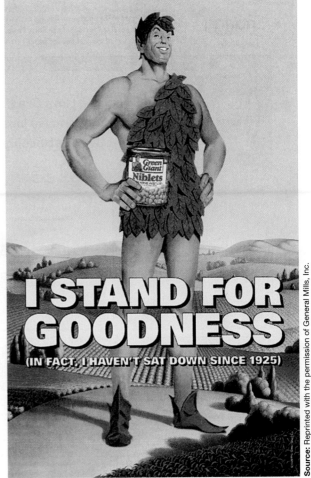

Source: Reprinted with the permission of General Mills, Inc.

▲ A Green Giant advertisement using animation.

Slice-of-Life

In slice-of-life commercials, advertisers provide solutions to the everyday problems consumers or businesses face. The format was made famous by Procter & Gamble during the early days of television advertising. Slice-of-life commercials show the common experiences, and especially the problems, people encounter, and a product is introduced to solve the problem. The most common slice-of-life format has four components: encounter, problem, interaction, and solution (see Figure 7.4). In some ads, the actors portray the dilemma or problem and solve the problems themselves. In others, a voice-over explains the benefits or solution to the problem that the good, service, or company provides.

Slice-of-life executions also appear in business-to-business advertisements, such as the MessageMedia ad shown on page 177. The encounter begins with the potential female customer's problem that the "average single female breaks up with 4.3 men, avoids 237 phone calls, and ignores approximately 79 red lights per year." The interaction occurs through the copy "What are the chances she'll read your e-mail

◄ **FIGURE 7.4**
Components of a Slice-of-Life Ad

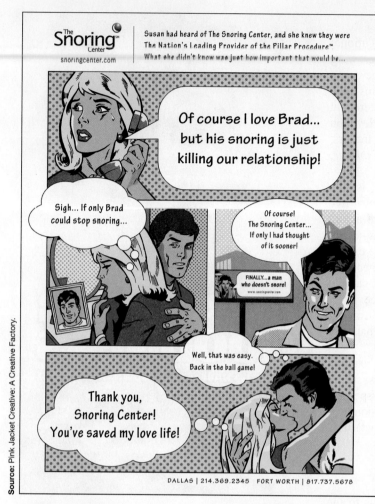

▲ One of a series of advertisements created by Pink Jacket Creative for the Snoring Center using animation characters and a slice-of-life approach.

message?" The solution to this problem is Message-Media's "E-messaging campaign."

Business-to-business advertisements often utilize the slice-of-life method because it allows the advertiser to highlight the ways a product can meet business needs. A typical business-to-business ad begins with a routine business experience, such as a sales manager making a presentation to the board of directors. Then, a projector being used does not have a clear picture. The ad offers the solution: a projector from Sony. The presentation is made with great clarity, and the board of directors accepts the customer's bid for the account. As with all slice-of-life commercials, a disaster has been avoided and a happy ending results instead.

Slice-of-life executions are possible in most media, including magazines or billboards, because a single picture can depict a normal, everyday situation or problem. Finding an image that tells the entire story, with the product being the solution, will be the challenge.

Dramatization

A dramatization is similar to the slice-of-life executional framework. The same format in which a problem is first presented and then a solution appears is used. The difference lies in the intensity and story format. Dramatization presents a higher level of excitement and suspense to tell the story. A dramatization story normally builds to a crisis point leading to a suspenseful climax.

An effective and dramatic advertisement can be difficult to create, because the drama must be completed in either 30 or 60 seconds. Building a story to a climactic moment is challenging given such a short time period. The early "What's in Your Wallet" advertisements for Capital One credit cards did manage to create the appropriate level of excitement. The ads were later replaced with humorous executions. Not all dramatic execution styles can accomplish a high enough level of suspense to make them successful. The slice-of-life framework often offers a better approach.

Testimonials

The testimonial type of executional framework has been successful for many years, especially in the business-to-business and service sectors. When a customer tells about a positive experience with a product, it is a testimonial. In the business-to-business sector, testimonials from current customers add credibility to the claims being made. In many business buying situations, prospective vendors are asked for references. Testimonials provide references in advance. Further, most buyers believe what others say about a company more than they believe what a company says about itself. Testimonials offer greater credibility than self-proclamations.

Testimonials also are an effective method for promoting services. Services are intangible; they cannot be seen or touched, and consumers cannot examine them before making decisions. A testimony from a current customer can be an effective method of describing the benefits or attributes of the service. Most consumers talk to other people when selecting services. Choosing a dentist, an attorney, or an automobile repair shop leads customers to ask friends, relatives, or coworkers. A testimonial advertisement simulates this type of word-of-mouth recommendation.

Testimonials can enhance company credibility. Endorsers and famous individuals do not always have high levels of credibility, because consumers know they are being paid for their endorsements. In testimonials, everyday people, often actual customers, are the main characters. At other times, they are paid actors who look like everyday consumers.

Authoritative

When using the authoritative executional framework, the advertiser seeks to convince viewers that a given product is superior. One form is **expert authority**. These ads employ a physician, dentist, engineer, or chemist to state the particular brand's advantages compared to other brands. Firms also can feature less recognized experts such as automobile mechanics, professional house painters, nurses, and aerobics instructors. These individuals can talk about the brand attributes that make the product superior.

Many authoritative advertisements include some type of scientific or survey evidence. Independent organizations such as the American Medical Association undertake a variety of product studies. Quoting the results generates greater credibility. Survey results are less credible. Stating that four out of five dentists recommend a particular toothbrush or toothpaste is less effective, because consumers do not have details about how the survey was conducted or even how many dentists were surveyed (5 or 500). In contrast, an American Medical Association statement that an aspirin a day reduces the risk of a second heart attack is highly credible. A company such as Bayer can take advantage of the finding by including the information in the company's ads. The same holds true when a magazine such as *Consumer Reports* ranks a particular brand as the best.

Authoritative advertisements have been widely incorporated into business-to-business sector ads, especially when scientific findings support a company's product claims. Independent test results are likely to have a more profound influence on members of the buying center, especially if they are actively looking for rational information to help them make decisions.

The authoritative approach assumes consumers and business decision makers rely on cognitive processes when making purchase decisions and that they will pay attention to an ad and carefully think about the information conveyed in it. The approach works well in print ads, because the buyers take the time to read the claim or findings presented in the advertisement.

Authoritative advertisements perform well in specialty magazines and on specific Web sites. In a hunting magazine, an expert sportsman can discuss the superiority of a particular gun and the readers are individuals with an interest in hunting. Brides observe the endorsements of wedding experts in bridal magazines and Web sites. Readers notice these specialized messages, and the claims have greater credibility. The same will be true in business-to-business magazines. Trade journals in the business world are similar to specialty magazines in the consumer world.

Demonstration

A demonstration execution shows how a product works. A demonstration offers an effective way to communicate the benefits of a product to viewers. One recent advertisement featured a new form of dust cloth that could be attached to a handle or used separately. The demonstration highlighted the product's multiple uses by cleaning a television screen, a wooden floor, a saxophone, and light fixtures. Consumers were being shown how to use the product while at the same time hearing about its advantages.

Business-to-business ads often present demonstrations. They allow a business to illustrate how a product can meet the specific needs of another business. For example,

If...
the average single female
BREAKS UP with 4.3 **men**,
avoids 237 phone calls and *ignores*
approximately **79 RED LIGHTS** per year —
What are the *chances* she'll read
your e-mail message?
...Say something specific.
Contact us for e-messaging
campaigns that *get results.*

messagemedia
e-mail • e-customers • e-business
www.messagemedia.com
888.440.7550

▲ A business-to-business advertisement for MessageMedia containing a slice-of-life execution.

▲ An authoritative execution combined with a humor appeal.

▼ A Jantzen advertisement utilizing a fantasy execution.

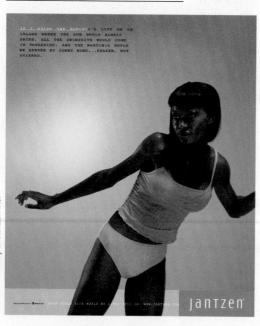

GoldTouch, Inc. can demonstrate the InstaGold Flash System, which deposits a bright and uniform gold surface finish on products, such as jewelry, through a nonelectrical current process of immersion plating. Such demonstrations can be offered via television ads or flash media ads on the Internet.

Demonstration ads are well-suited to television and the Internet. To a limited extent, the print media can feature demonstrations, especially when a series of photos outlines the sequence of product usage.

Fantasy

Fantasy executions lift the audience beyond the real world to a make-believe experience. Some are meant to be realistic. Others are completely irrational. The most irrational and illogical ads are often more clearly recalled. Fantasies can deal with anything from a dream vacation spot or cruise ships to a juicy hamburger or an enticing DiGiorno pizza. The Jantzen ad in this section encourages consumer fantasies. People are encouraged to share their fantasies by contacting Jantzen.

The most common fantasy themes involve sex, love, and romance. According to some marketing experts, raw sex and nudity in advertisements are losing their impact. Instead, advertisers feature a softer, more subtle presentation of sex. Fantasy fits nicely with target audiences that have a preference for a tamer presentation of sexuality. Instead of raw sex and nudity that may be offensive, fantasy takes them into a world of romantic make-believe.

The perfume and cologne industries often employ fantasy executions. In the past, the most common theme was that splashing on a certain cologne caused women to flock to a man. For women, the reverse was suggested. Although used extensively, these ads were not particularly effective because people did not believe them. Currently, perfume advertisers tend to portray the product as enhancing a couple's love life or making a man or woman feel more sensuous.

Television fantasy ads for cruise lines show couples enjoying romantic, sensuous vacations together; swimming; jet skiing; and scuba diving. The cruise becomes more than just a vacation—it is a romantic fantasy trip. Fantasy ads also can show people experiencing the thrill of winning a major sports event or sharing a common product (e.g., beer, pizza) with a beautiful model. The billboard for Kickapoo Casino on the next page uses a fantasy approach by suggesting that hitting the jackpot at the casino will also yield three beautiful girls for the male in the ad. Effective fantasies can inspire both recall and action.

The business-to-business advertising field does not use fantasy a great deal, primarily because of fear that members of a buying center will not take it seriously. Some advertising creatives have been able to feature a fantasy in a business-to-business advertisement by showing a product helping the buyer achieve an unrealistic result or outcome. For example, being promoted from janitor to president because of the correct choice of a cleaning product would be a fantasy aimed at people using or purchasing janitorial supplies.

Informative

Informative advertisements present information to the audience in a straightforward manner. Agencies prepare informative messages extensively for radio commercials, where only verbal communication is possible. Informative ads are less common in television and print, because consumers tend to ignore them. With so many ads bombarding the consumer, it takes more than just the presentation of information to capture someone's attention.

▲ This billboard for the Kickapoo Casino uses a fantasy approach.

Consumers who are highly involved in a particular product category pay more attention to an informational ad. Business buyers in the process of gathering information for either a new buy or a modified rebuy will notice an informative advertisement. If the business is not in the market for a particular product, buying center members pay less attention to the advertisement. Thus, informative ads tend to work best in high-involvement situations. Many advertisers believe that business buyers desire detailed information to make intelligent buying decisions. As a result, the informative framework continues to be a popular approach for business-to-business advertisers.

Correct placement of an informative advertisement is vital. An informative advertisement about a restaurant placed on a radio station just before noon will be listened to more carefully than one that runs at 3:00 P.M. An informative ad about a diet product in an issue of *Glamour* that has a special article on weight control or exercising will be noticed more than if it is placed in the fashion section of the magazine. An informative business ad featuring a new piece of industrial equipment works well next to an article about the capital costs of equipment. Informative ads may have limited uses but become more effective when placed properly.

Beyond these types of executional frameworks, the creative selects the other ingredients, including music, copy, color, motion, light, and the size of a print ad. Almost any of these executional frameworks can be used within the format of one of the various appeals. A slice-of-life can depict fear, as can a dramatization. Informative ads may be humorous, but so can animations. Testimonials or demonstrations are rational or emotional, and so forth. As the advertisement comes together, one element remains: the choice of a source or spokesperson.

SOURCES AND SPOKESPERSONS

One final issue remains for the creative, the company, and the account executive. Selecting the ideal **source and spokesperson** to use in an advertisement will be critical. Figure 7.5 identifies four types of sources and spokespersons.

③ What types of sources or spokespersons can be used in advertisements or commercials?

Celebrity Spokespersons

Of the four types, celebrity spokespersons are the most common, even though their appearances in ads have been declining. According to the research firm Millward Brown, only around 6 percent of advertisements now feature celebrity endorsements.[13]

Companies use a celebrity endorser when the person's stamp of approval enhances the product's brand equity. Celebrities can also help create emotional bonds with brands. Transferring the bond that exists between the celebrity and the audience to the product being endorsed is the objective. A bond transfer will often be more profound for younger consumers. A MediaEDGE survey revealed that 30 percent of 18- to 34-year-olds would try a product promoted by a celebrity. The survey also indicated that younger people are 50 percent more likely than older consumers to recommend a celebrity-endorsed product to others. Older consumers are not as likely to be influenced by celebrity endorsements. Less than 14 percent reported that they would try a celebrity-endorsed product. Still, many advertisers believe that celebrity endorsements improve brand awareness and help define the brand's personality.[14]

▼ This advertisement contains an informative execution to convey the message that products people use every day are made with the petroleum ingredients processed by Calumet.

FIGURE 7.5 ▶
Types of Sources and
Spokespersons

Source ◀ Celebrities / CEOs / Experts / Typical persons

Athletes constitute a significant component of the celebrity endorsers. Some, such as Danica Patrick, earn more from endorsements than they do from their sports. Top athletic endorsers include Phil Mickelson, Dale Earnhardt, Lebron James, Kobe Bryant, Shaquille O'Neal, and Payton Manning, and, until recently, Tiger Woods. The top two female athletic endorsers are Danica Patrick and Maria Sharapova. The two top retired athlete endorsers are Michael Jordan and Cal Ripken, Jr.[15]

Agencies also use celebrities to help establish a brand "personality." The objective is to tie the brand's characteristics to those of the spokesperson. Elizabeth Taylor's love of the finer things in life can be attached to her line of scents and perfumes. A brand personality emerges after the brand has been established. The celebrity helps to define the brand more clearly. Using celebrities for new products does not always work as well as for already established brands.

Additional Celebrity Endorsements

Three additional variations of celebrity endorsements are: (1) unpaid spokespersons, (2) celebrity voice-overs, and (3) dead-person endorsements. *Unpaid spokespersons* are celebrities supporting a charity or cause by appearing in an ad. These types of endorsements are highly credible and can entice significant contributions to a cause. Politicians, actors, musicians, and athletes all appear in these ads. A recent campaign featured a number of musicians plus former Presidents Bush and Clinton in an effort to raise money for Haiti after its devastating earthquake.

▼ The milk industry employs a number of celebrities in the "Got Milk?" campaign.

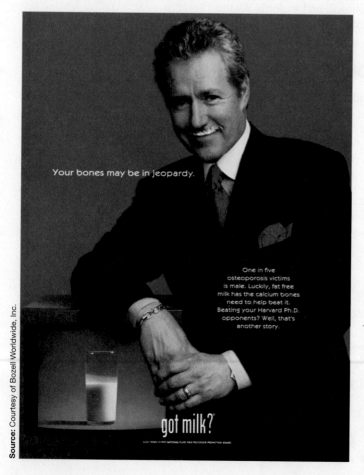

Your bones may be in jeopardy.

One in five osteoporosis victims is male. Luckily, fat free milk has the calcium bones need to help beat it. Beating your Harvard Ph.D. opponents? Well, that's another story.

got milk?

Source: Courtesy of Bozell Worldwide, Inc.

Many celebrities also provide *voice-overs* for television and radio ads without being shown or identified. Listeners often respond to the ads and try to figure out who is reading the copy. This adds interest to the advertisement. Agencies may use a voice-over because the celebrity provides a quality voice to the advertisement even when individuals listening to the ad do not recognize the voice. According to advertising executive Stan Richards, "We use Hollywood actors quite a bit. It's largely not for their celebrity, we're not interested in that. Our voice for Home Depot is Ed Harris, who is a terrific actor. I don't think anybody in the world knows it's him, but he can take a script and bring it to life."[16] One negative of voice-overs is that they can be a distraction if the consumer becomes focused on identifying the speaker rather than hearing the content of the ad.

A *dead-person endorsement* occurs when a sponsor uses an image or past video or film featuring an actor or personality who has died. Dead-person endorsements are somewhat controversial but are becoming more common. Bob Marley, Marilyn Monroe, John Wayne, John Lennon, Elvis Presley, and many others have appeared in ads and have even become spokespersons for products after dying. Michael Jackson may become the next major dead-person endorser.

CEO Spokespersons

Instead of celebrities, advertisers can use a CEO as the spokesperson or source. Michael Dell has appeared as the spokesperson for Dell. A highly visible and personable CEO can become a major asset for the firm and its products. Many local companies succeed, in part, because their owners are out front in small-market television commercials. They then begin to take on the status of local celebrities.

Experts

Expert sources include physicians, lawyers, accountants, and financial planners. These experts are not celebrities or CEOs. Experts provide backing for testimonials, serve as authoritative figures, demonstrate products, and enhance the credibility of informative advertisements.

Typical Persons

Typical persons are one of two types. The first includes paid actors or models who portray or resemble everyday people. The second is actual, typical, everyday people. Wal-Mart has featured store employees in freestanding insert advertisements. Agencies also create "man-on-the-street" types of advertisements. For example, PERT shampoo recently prepared ads showing an individual asking people if they would like to have their hair washed. Dr. Scholl's interviews people about foot problems that might be resolved with cushioned shoe inserts.

Real-people sources are becoming more common. One reason for this is the overuse of celebrities. Many experts believe that consumers have become bored by celebrity endorsers and that the positive impact today is not as strong as it was in the past. One study conducted in Great Britain indicated that 55 percent of the consumers surveyed reported that a famous face was not enough to hold their attention. [17]

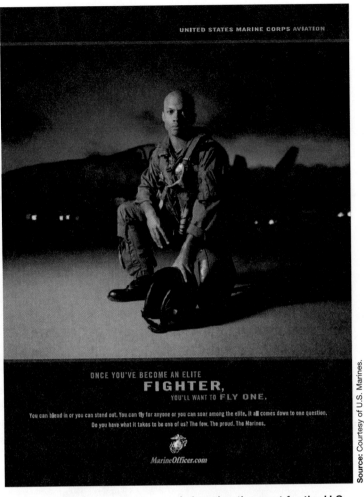

Source: Courtesy of U.S. Marines.

▲ An advertisement for the U.S. Marines with a typical person spokesperson.

Source Characteristics

In evaluating sources, most account executives and companies consider several characteristics. The effectiveness of an advertisement that utilizes a spokesperson depends on the degree to which the person has one or more of the characteristics listed in Figure 7.6.

4 What characteristics are most important when selecting a source or spokesperson?

◀ **FIGURE 7.6**
Characteristics of Effective Spokespersons

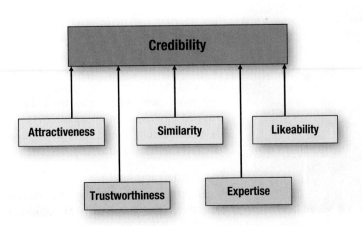

Credibility

Credibility is derived from the composite of attractiveness, similarity, likeability, trustworthiness, and expertise.[18] Credibility affects a receiver's acceptance of the spokesperson and the message. A credible source is believable. Most sources do not score highly on all four attributes, yet they need to score highly on multiple characteristics to be viewed as credible. Celebrities may be more likely to possess at least an element of all characteristics. A CEO, expert, or typical person probably lacks one or more of them.

Attractiveness

Two forms of attractiveness are: (1) physical characteristics and (2) personality characteristics. Physical attractiveness is usually an important asset for an endorser. Bijan used Michael Jordan's and Bo Derek's physical attractiveness to promote lines of menswear, perfume, and jewelry. Advertisements with physically attractive spokespersons fare better than advertisements with less attractive people, for both male and female audiences. At the same time, the attractiveness of the spokesperson's personality will also be important to many consumers. This personality component helps viewers form emotional bonds with the spokesperson. If the spokesperson appears to have a sour personality, even if physically beautiful, consumers are less likely to develop an emotional bond with the individual and the product.

Similarity

Closely related to attractiveness is the concept of similarity. Consumers are more inclined to be influenced by a message delivered by a person who is somehow similar. For example, a "stay-at-home" mom may be more influenced by an advertisement that starts out with a woman saying, "Since I made the decision to stop working and care for my family full-time . . ." Similarity allows the viewer to identify with the spokesperson. Sometimes this may involve the fantasy of identifying with a rich person buying a BMW. At other times *identification* comes from the belief that the source has similar beliefs, attitudes, preferences, or behaviors or faces the same or a similar situation as the customer. Female fans are able to identify with Anna Roberts as the "new face of horse racing" because many females have enjoyed horseback riding and have dreamed of winning a famous horse race. Identification was also gained because most jockeys are males. Anna Roberts immediately gained similarity and identification with female fans.

▼ Attractiveness can be a valuable source characteristic.

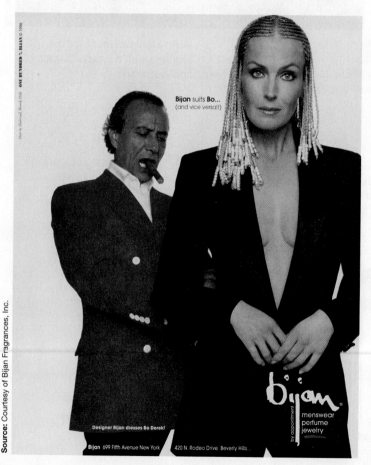

Likeability

Closely related to the personality components of attractiveness and similarity is likeability. Consumers respond positively to spokespersons they like. Viewers may like an actor or the character played by the actor in a movie. An athlete gains likeability if he plays on the consumer's favorite team. Other individuals are likeable because they support the favorite charities of consumers. Consumers who do not like a particular spokesperson are inclined to transfer that dislike to the product. It may not be an automatic transfer, because consumers recognize that endorsers are paid spokespersons. This explains why most companies who used Tiger Woods quickly dropped him as an endorser in 2010. The worry was that his endorsement would have a negative impact on attitudes toward the brand.

Trustworthiness

A celebrity may be likeable or attractive but may not be viewed as trustworthy. Trustworthiness represents the degree of confidence or the level of acceptance consumers place in the spokesperson's message. A trustworthy spokesperson helps consumers believe the message. Likeability and trustworthiness are highly related. People who are liked tend to be trusted, and people who are disliked tend not to be trusted. According to E-Poll Market Research, celebrities ranking the highest in terms of trustworthiness, awareness, and appeal included James Earl Jones, Tom Hanks, and Michael J. Fox.[19] See Figure 7.7 for a complete list.

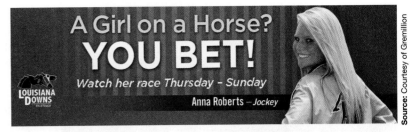

▲ An advertisement for Louisiana Downs featuring the female jockey Anna Roberts.

Expertise

The final characteristic advertisers look for when examining sources is expertise. Spokespersons with higher levels of expertise are more believable. Richard Petty and Jeff Gordon are experts when automobile products and lubricants are advertised. Often when expertise is desired in an ad the advertising agency opts for the CEO or a trained or educated expert in the field. American Express features Maria Barraza, a small-business owner and designer, to promote its Small Business Services. Expertise can be valuable in persuasive advertisements designed to change opinions or attitudes. Spokespersons with high levels of expertise are more capable of persuading an audience than someone with zero or low expertise.[20]

Matching Source Types and Characteristics

The account executive, ad agency, and corporate sponsor, individually or jointly, may choose the type of spokesperson. They can choose a celebrity, CEO, expert, or typical person, and the specific individual should have the key source characteristics.

Celebrities

In terms of trustworthiness, believability, persuasiveness, and likeability, celebrities tend to score well. These virtues increase when the match between the product and celebrity consists of a logical and proper fit. Phil Mickelson endorsing golf merchandise is a good fit, as is Anna Roberts endorsing horse racing. Companies can be creative when making matches. The match of boxer George Foreman to his Lean Mean Grilling Machine has been a great success.[21] Some celebrities have become almost as famous for their advertising appearances as for an acting or athletic career. Danica Patrick has signed endorsement contracts with Honda, Secret, Boost Mobile, Pepsi, and, most recently, Go Daddy, possibly gaining as much notoriety from endorsements as she has from competing in races.[22]

Several dangers exist when using celebrities. Any negative publicity about a celebrity caused by inappropriate conduct may damage credibility. Michael Vick's arrest and conviction for dog fighting created considerable negative press. Hanes brands dropped Charlie Sheen because of domestic violence charges filed against him. Although advertisers like celebrity endorsers because of the potential they have for developing an attraction to their brands, they have to weigh the positive benefits against the potential risks.[23]

The potential for negative publicity has led some advertisers to use deceased celebrities. Companies have concluded that there is no need to risk bringing embarrassment or

◀ **FIGURE 7.7**
The 10 Most Trusted Celebrities

1. James Earl Jones	6. Sally Field
2. Tom Hanks	7. Ron Howard
3. Michael J. Fox	8. Will Smith
4. Mike Rowe	9. Bill Cosby
5. Morgan Freeman	10. Denzel Washington

Source: Adapted from Lacey Rose, "The 10 Most Trusted Celebrities," *Forbes.com* (www.forbes.com/2010/01/25/most-trusted-celebrities-business-intertainment) January 25, 2010.

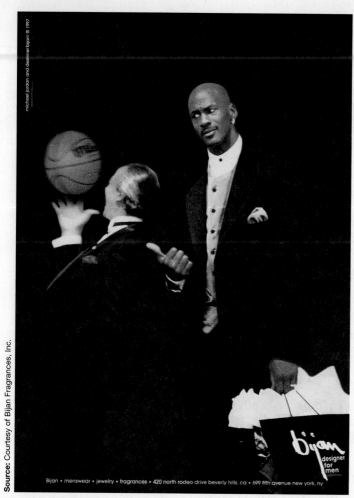

▲ Michael Jordan is a rare celebrity who can endorse multiple products and maintain a high level of credibility.

injury to themselves or the brand. It is also a reason that more ads use cartoon characters. Practically everyone likes cartoons.

A second danger of using celebrities occurs when they endorse too many products, which can tarnish their credibility. Consumers know celebrities are paid, which detracts from believability. When a celebrity endorses a large number of products, consumers' evaluations of that person's credibility decline. Some advertising research indicates that when a celebrity endorses multiple products it tends to reduce likeability as well as consumer attitudes toward the brand.[24]

As a result, careful consideration should be given to the choice of a celebrity. The individual cannot simply be famous. The person should possess as many of the key source characteristics as possible, match the good or service being advertised, not be "spread too thin" or overexposed, and promote a positive image that can be transferred to the good, service, or company.

CEO

A CEO or other prominent corporate official may or may not possess the characteristics of attractiveness and likeability. CEOs should, however, appear to be trustworthy, have expertise, and maintain a degree of credibility. A CEO is not a professional actor or model. It might be difficult for the CEO to come across well in a commercial.

Companies must be aware of the trustworthiness issue. For example, many times the owner of a local auto dealership represents it as the spokesperson. The primary problem is that many consumers view used-car salespeople as untrustworthy. Other local business owners may be highly trustworthy, such as restaurant owners, physicians, and eye care professionals.

Advertising creatives and account executives carefully consider asking a CEO or business owner to serve as a source. They first must be convinced that the individual has enough of the source characteristics to promote the product and gain the consumer's interest and trust.

Experts

First and foremost, experts should be credible. The advertising agency seeks an expert who is attractive, likeable, and trustworthy. Experts are helpful in promoting health care products and other high-involvement types of products. Recent research indicates that experts are more believable than celebrities for high-technology products, and, as a result, the use of an expert reduces a consumer's level of perceived risk in purchasing the product, which means they are the most helpful when consumers or businesses perceive high levels of risk involved in a purchase.[25] When selecting an expert spokesperson, agency leaders should be certain that the person has valid credentials and will be able to clearly explain a product's benefits. Doing so will reduce the level of perceived risk.

Typical Persons

Advertisements with typical persons are sometimes difficult to prepare, especially when they use real persons. Typical-person sources do not have the name recognition of celebrities. Consequently, advertisers often use multiple sources within one advertisement to build credibility. Increasing the number of sources makes the ad more effective. Hearing three people talk about a good dentist will be more believable than hearing it from only one person. By using multiple sources, viewers are motivated to pay attention and process its arguments.[26]

Real-person ads present a double-edged sword. On the one hand, trustworthiness, similarity, and credibility rise when the source is bald, overweight, or has some other physical imperfections. This can be especially valuable when the bald person promotes a hair replacement program or the overweight source talks about a diet program. On the other hand, attractiveness and likeability may be lower.

Special K cereal created a series of ads featuring real women that the company encountered when conducting consumer research into fitness and weight-loss goals. In one spot, the woman "wants to stop using my arms to hide my stomach;" in another the woman wants to hear four little words: "Have you lost weight?" In another ad, the mother wants to show a young daughter "that mommy feels confident," and the voice-over conveys, "Be victorious—take the Special K Challenge." According to Jose Alberto Duenas, Vice-President for Cereal Marketing at Kellogg, "If you want to make a connection, you have to give consumers a chance to take part in the spotlight. Authenticity is what we're looking for."[27]

Using customers in ads can be difficult, because they will flub lines and look less natural on the screen. These difficulties with actual customers and employees lead many ad agencies to turn to professional models and actors to portray ordinary people. Professional actors make filming and photographing much easier. Also, the agency is in the position to choose a likeable, but plain, person. The desired effects (trustworthiness, similarity and credibility) are often easier to create using professional actors and models.

In general, the advertising agency wants to be certain that the source or spokesperson has the major characteristics the advertisement requires. Likeability would be important when creating a humorous appeal. In a rational or informational ad, expertise and credibility are crucial, especially in business-to-business ads. In each case, trying to include as many of the characteristics as possible when retaining a spokesperson will be the goal.

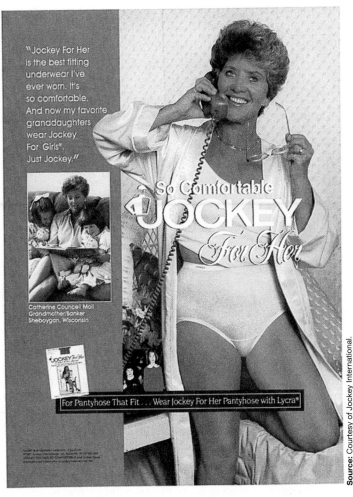

▲ This Jockey advertisement features an older typical-person model.

CREATING AN ADVERTISEMENT

Figure 7.8 illustrates the process a creative uses in preparing an advertisement. The work begins with the creative brief, which outlines the message theme of the advertisement, as well as other pertinent information. Using the creative brief blueprint, the creative develops a means–end chain, starting with an attribute of the product that generates a specific customer benefit and eventually produces a desirable end state. This means–end chain forms the foundation on which all other decisions will be made.

Following the development of the means–end chain, the creative selects a message strategy, the appeal, and the executional framework. The creative suggests or chooses a source or spokesperson at this point, because the choice usually affects other creative decisions. Development of the leverage point that moves the consumer from the product attribute or consumer benefit to the desired end state is usually undertaken after the creative begins work on the advertisement. The type of leverage point depends on the message strategy, appeal, and executional framework.

Although certain combinations tend to work well together, the creative has an almost infinite number of options when preparing an advertisement or campaign. For

5 What process is used to create advertisements?

FIGURE 7.8 ▶
Creating an Advertisement

example, if the creative wants to present a cognitive message strategy, the most logical appeal is rationality. The creative could, however, use fear, humor, sex, music, or even scarcity. An emotional approach would be the one appeal that would not work. The emotional part of the advertisement tends to overpower the cognitive message being sent to the viewer.

When the creative decides to employ humor with a cognitive strategy, other logical and illogical combinations emerge. In terms of an executional framework, the dramatization and authoritative approaches tend not to work as well with humor. The other executional frameworks are viable. This flexibility allows a variety of advertisements to emerge from a single means–end chain. The best combination depends on the creative's expertise and experience as well as her judgment regarding the ideal way to accomplish the client's advertising objectives.

ADVERTISING EFFECTIVENESS

6 What are the principles of advertising effectiveness?

Producing effective ads requires the joint efforts of the account executive, creative, account planner, and media planner. Working independently can produce some award-winning ads, but often they will not be effective advertisements that meet a client's objectives. One major difficulty ad agencies face is producing a commercial that stands out among the thousands of competing messages. An advertisement that breaks through the clutter has won half the battle. Finding ways to lead consumers to react to the ad in the desired manner is what remains.

An effective advertisement accomplishes the client's objectives. Making sure the commercial accomplishes the IMC objectives is the challenge. The seven basic principles of advertising effectiveness, shown in Figure 7.9, should be followed.

FIGURE 7.9 ▶
Principles of Effective Advertising

- Visual consistency
- Campaign duration
- Repeated taglines
- Consistent positioning—avoid ambiguity
- Simplicity
- Identifiable selling point
- Create an effective flow

Visual Consistency

Repeatedly seeing a specific image or visual display helps to embed it in long-term memory. Visual consistency is important because most customers spend very little time viewing an advertisement. In most cases, an individual makes just a casual glance at a print advertisement or a cursory glimpse at a television commercial. Visual consistency leads the viewer to move the message from short-term to long-term memory. Consistently used logos and other long-standing images help place the brand or company in the consumer's mind. People remember Nike because of the visually consistent use of Swoosh. The Prudential Rock emblem is well established in the minds of many consumers.

Campaign Duration

The length or duration of a campaign becomes important because consumers often do not pay attention to advertisements. Using the same advertisement for an appropriate period of time helps embed the message in the consumer's long-term memory. Account executives give careful thought to how long to run an advertisement. The ad should be changed before it becomes stale and viewers become bored with it; however, changing ads too frequently impedes retention. Reach and frequency affect the duration of a campaign. Higher frequency usually leads to a shorter duration. Low reach may be associated with a longer duration. In any case, typical campaigns last about 6 months, but there are exceptions.

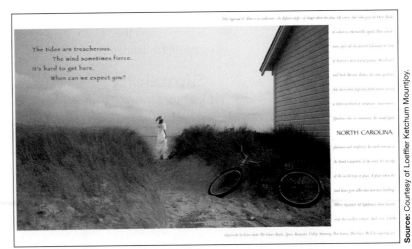

Source: Courtesy of Loeffler Ketchum Mountjoy.

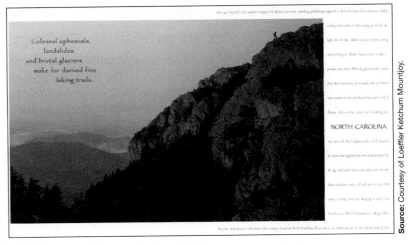

Source: Courtesy of Loeffler Ketchum Mountjoy.

▲ Notice the visual consistency present in these two advertisements for tourism in North Carolina.

Repeated Taglines

Visual consistency combined with consistent taglines can be a powerful approach. The advertisement may change, but either the visual imagery or the tagline remains the same. The U.S. Army has promoted the tagline "Be all that you can be" for many years, and the Marines are known as "The few. The proud. The Marines." Taglines help consumers tie the advertisement into current knowledge structure nodes that already exist in their minds. Figure 7.10 contains some of the more common taglines.

Consistent Positioning

Maintaining consistent positioning throughout a product's life makes it more likely that a consumer will place the product in a cognitive map. When the firm emphasizes quality in every advertisement, it becomes easier to tie the product into the consumer's cognitive map than if the firm stresses quality in some ads, price in others, and convenience in a

1. A diamond is forever.
2. Be all you can be.
3. Can you hear me now?
4. Don't leave home without it.
5. Just do it.
6. Look Mom, no cavities.
7. The ultimate driving machine.
8. What can Brown do for you?
9. We try harder.
10. You deserve a break today.

◄ **FIGURE 7.10**
Which Taglines Can You Identify?

third campaign. Inconsistency in positioning makes the brand and company more difficult to remember. Consistent positioning avoids ambiguity, and the message stays clear and understandable.

Simplicity

Simple advertisements are easier to comprehend than are complex ads. A print ad with a short tagline and limited copy will be much easier to read than one that is overloaded and complex. Consequently, advertisers should resist the temptation to describe all of a product's attributes in a single commercial. Although this practice is more prevalent in business-to-business print advertisements, it should be avoided there as well. Also, consumer ads on radio or television spots can be verbally overloaded, forcing the announcer to talk faster. Doing so is usually ineffective, because the listener receives too much information in a short time period.

The principle of simplicity applies to Internet advertising. The primary reason is load time. Individuals surfing the Internet will not wait more than a few seconds for something to load; if it does not load quickly, they move on to another site.

Identifiable Selling Point

An identifiable selling point places emphasis on three words: (1) identifiable, (2) selling, and (3) point. The advertisement should stress a selling point (price, quality, convenience, luxury) that is easily *identifiable* to the viewer of the ad. The advertisement should *sell* a product's benefits as much as the product itself. Also, the concept is a selling *point,* not selling points. The best advertisements emphasize one major point and do not confuse the viewer by presenting too many ideas. An advertisement's primary goal is to fix the product into the viewer's cognitive map through establishing new linkages or strengthening current linkages. An identifiable selling point helps reach that goal.

Create an Effective Flow

In order to create an effective flow, a print ad should move the reader's eye to all of the key points in the ad. In a television ad, the points to be made should flow in a manner that leads the consumer to the appropriate action or conclusion. Ads without flow confuse the consumer or are simply tuned out.

Beating Ad Clutter

Overcoming clutter constitutes a major challenge when creating an effective advertising campaign. The presence of a competitor's advertisement within the same medium or time slot makes the ad clutter problem worse. A recent survey of television advertising revealed that during prime-time programming 42 percent of the ads shown had one or more competitors advertised during the same hour. Research suggests that an advertisement's effectiveness will be significantly reduced when a competitor's advertisement runs during the same time slot.[28]

One method advertisers use to overcome this brand interference is repetition. Repeating an ad can increase brand and ad recall. In advertising studies, repetition effectively increases recall when no competitor ads are present. When competitor ads are present, repetition does not help the competitive ad interference problem and does not stimulate greater recall.

Variability Theory

Mere repetition of an advertisement does not always work. Some advertisers have begun to emphasize the principles present in **variability theory**,[29] which suggests that variable encoding occurs when a consumer sees the same advertisement in different environments. These varied environments increase recall and effectiveness by encoding it into the brain through various methods. Creatives can generate the effect by varying the situational context of a particular ad. For example, the MasterCard campaign uses various settings to convey the same basic message, "There are some things money can't buy. For everything else, there's MasterCard." Varying the context of the ad increases recall and is an effective method for overcoming competitive ad interference.[30]

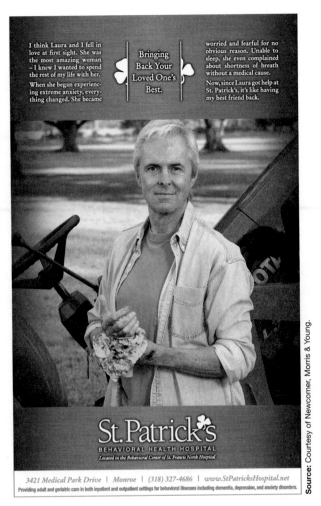

▲ These two advertisements for St. Patrick's use variability theory concepts to help beat clutter.

Using a Second Medium

Using two media to convey a message generally is more effective than repeating an advertisement within the same medium. An advertisement placed in more than one medium reduces competing ad interference. In other words, an ad that appears on television and in magazines works better than one that appears only on television. Consumers seeing an advertisement in a different medium are more likely to recall the ad than if it is always seen in only one medium.

Clutter remains a difficult problem in advertising. Creatives who are able to capture the attention of the audience and transmit messages successfully are in great demand. Companies constantly experiment with various approaches to reach audiences. When a program works, the advertising firm and its client have a great deal to celebrate.

INTERNATIONAL IMPLICATIONS

Many common themes and messages translate well across cultures. The major challenge is making sure that the message strategy and form of executional framework match the tendencies and preferences in a region. For example, some cultures tend to be more rational in their decision-making processes, whereas others favor more emotional approaches. This may, in turn, affect the selection of a message strategy in a given nation.

Comparison ads are less common in other countries, due to both social and cultural differences as well as legal restrictions. Advertisers should be aware of these issues. For example, in many European countries comparative advertising is illegal. In Japan, it is not illegal, but it runs against the society's cultural preferences. In Brazil, the advertising

7 How are advertising programs adjusted to fit international circumstances?

industry is so powerful that any attempt to create a comparative advertisement has been challenged and stopped. Often, international consumers not only dislike the advertisements, but often transfer that dislike to the company sponsoring the ad.[31]

The message strategy chosen affects the execution. For instance, the slice-of-life execution has become popular in Japan in recent years. The slice-of-life style is suited to Japan's soft-sell approach to marketing. A more hard-sell attitude may be used in the United States. Japanese advertising tends to be more indirect, and the slice-of-life approach allows advertisers to present a product in a typical everyday situation. Benefits can be presented in a positive light without making brazen or harsh claims and without directly disparaging the competition.[32]

Other patterns and changes in preferred forms of executions can be discovered by watching local media and reading about trends in magazines and trade journals in the country involved. While maintaining an overall message and idea, the advertiser must adjust to social customs present in a region.

!INTEGRATED CAMPAIGNS IN ACTION

The Soap Opera

The Soap Opera is a one-location laundry that offers 24/7 self-service washers and dryers as well as a fluff and fold service. With the fluff and fold service, customers drop off their laundry and The Soap Opera's staff wash, iron, and fold the clothes. The Soap Opera is located in Ruston, Louisiana, near the campus of Louisiana Tech University.

The owners of The Soap Opera met with Emogen Marketing to discuss the feasibility of a marketing campaign. The objective of the campaign was to increase awareness of the fluff and fold service, particularly among college students. With limited funds, Emogen Marketing crafted a campaign entitled "Why do your own laundry?" that involved a 1-day, on-campus event; creation of a Facebook page; posters on campus bulletin boards; in-store registration for a $50 gift card; and a series of newspaper ads in the student newspaper.

Illustration was a central execution theme in the campaign. It was used in newspaper ads, on the posters, and in displays for the 1-day, on-campus event. One display featured a mannequin dressed as a typical college student doing laundry at the entrance to the student center with the bubble question, "Why do your own laundry?" It was supported by props of a washing machine, a box of laundry detergent, and 20 pieces of clothing strung out on a laundry line. In another display, a mannequin dressed as a Soap Opera employee was rigged with video cameras and a microphone, allowing Emogen staff to interact with students in the style of *Candid Camera*.

During the month following the ad campaign, sales increased by almost 25 percent at The Soap Opera, making it the highest monthly sales in over 20 years of operation. The sales increase held steady for a full year after the promotion. In addition, brand name recognition and brand awareness both increased substantially for The Soap Opera.[33]

Source: Courtesy of Emogen Marketing Group.

▲ Illustration was a key component of The Soap Opera campaign.

Your instructor has additional information about the ads, visuals, and displays used in this campaign.

❝SUMMARY

Advertising is the process of transmitting a personal message through one or more impersonal media. The message should reflect the image that occurs throughout an IMC program. Three types of message strategies are present in advertisements. Cognitive strategies emphasize rational and logical arguments to compel consumers to make purchases. Affective strategies are oriented toward buyer emotions and feelings. Conative strategies are linked to more direct responses, behaviors, and actions. These strategies should be integrated with various types of appeals through the media selected for the campaign.

Executional frameworks tell the story in the ad. Animation has become more sophisticated and provides many new creative approaches in the design of ads. The slice-of-life approach and dramatizations are problem-solving types of ads, leading the consumer to something better by using the product. Testimonials are rendered by individuals who have realized the benefits of a product. An authoritative expert can build consumer confidence in a product or company. Demonstrations show how products can be used. A fantasy takes people away from the real world to a make-believe place. This makes the product more exotic and desirable. Informative ads render basic information about the product. Each execution can be used effectively to persuade consumers and business-to-business buyers to consider a company's offerings.

Celebrities, CEOs, experts, and typical persons can be chosen to be "out front" in the advertisement. Each has advantages and disadvantages. The marketing team selects sources or spokespersons based on the individual's attractiveness, similarity, likeability, trustworthiness, expertise, or credibility. The more of these characteristics that are present, the better off the advertiser will be.

Effective advertising campaigns are based on the seven principles of visual consistency, sufficient campaign duration, repeated taglines, consistent positioning, simplicity, presentation of an identifiable selling point, and creation of an effective flow. Creatives and account executives incorporate these principles into the advertising campaign to enhance the odds of success. Clutter can be overcome by repeating ads and showing them in various media.

Many consider advertising design to be the most glamorous part of the advertising industry, and in many ways it is. The other side of the glamour coin is hard work and the constant pressure to perform. Many people think being a creative is a burnout-type of job. At the same time, those who have proven track records of success are well rewarded for their efforts. Utilizing the principles presented in this chapter can be a key to success in the highly competitive and exciting business of advertising design. ❞

KEY TERMS

message theme The outline of the key idea(s) that the advertising program is supposed to convey.

message strategy The primary tactic used to deliver the message theme.

cognitive message strategy The presentation of rational arguments or pieces of information to consumers.

generic messages Direct promotions of product attributes or benefits without any claim of superiority.

preemptive messages Claims of superiority based on a specific attribute or benefit of a product that preempts the competition from making the same claim.

unique selling proposition (USP) An explicit, testable claim of uniqueness or superiority that can be supported or substantiated in some manner.

hyperbole Making an untestable claim based upon some attribute or benefit.

comparative advertisement The direct or indirect comparison of a good or service to the competition.

affective message strategies Ads designed to invoke feelings and emotions and match them with the good, service, or company.

resonance advertising Attempting to connect a product with a consumer's experiences to develop stronger ties between the product and the consumer.

emotional advertising Attempting to elicit powerful emotions that eventually lead to brand recall and choice.

conative message strategy Advertisements that are designed to lead directly to some type of consumer response.

action-inducing conative advertisements Advertisements that create situations in which cognitive knowledge of the product or affective liking of the product follow the actual purchase or arise during usage of the product.

promotional support conative advertisements Ads designed to support other promotional efforts.

executional framework The manner in which an ad appeal is presented.

expert authority When an advertiser seeks to convince viewers that a given product is superior to other brands in some authoritative manner.

sources and spokespersons Persons in the advertisement who make the actual presentation.

variability theory A theory stating that when a consumer sees the same advertisement in different environments, the ad will be more effective.

REVIEW QUESTIONS

1. Name the three types of message strategies creatives can use. How are message strategies related to the message theme?

2. What types of goods or services best match cognitive message strategies? List the five types of cognitive approaches.

3. When will an affective message strategy be most effective? What two types of affective messages can creatives design? Give an example of each.

4. What is the primary goal of a conative message strategy?

5. How is an executional framework different from an ad appeal? How are they related?

6. List as many uses of animation-based advertisements as possible. What forms of animation are possible with the available technology?

7. How are slice-of-life and dramatization executional frameworks similar? How are they different?

8. How are authoritative and informational executional frameworks similar? How are they different?

9. What types of testimonials can advertisers use? Give an example of each.

10. Which media are best for demonstration-type ads?

11. What kinds of products or services are best suited to fantasy-based executional frameworks? What products or services are poor candidates for fantasies?

12. Identify the four main types of sources or spokespersons. What are the advantages and disadvantages of each?

13. List the key criteria used when selecting a spokesperson.

14. Identify the tactics available to overcome clutter. How does variability theory assist in this process?

15. What issues are present when adapting an advertising program to an international audience?

CRITICAL THINKING EXERCISES

Discussion Questions

1. Select five advertisements from a magazine. Identify the message strategy, appeal, and executional framework in each. Did the creative select the right combination for the advertisement? What other message strategies or executional frameworks could have been used?

2. Watch five television advertisements. Identify the message strategy, appeal, and executional framework each uses. Did the creative select the right combination for the advertisement? What other message strategies or executional frameworks could have been used?

3. Studies involving comparative advertisements as compared to noncomparative advertisements produced the following findings.[34] Discuss why you think each statement is true. Try to think of comparative ads you have seen that substantiate these claims.

   a. Message awareness was higher for comparative ads than for noncomparative ads if the brands were already established brands.

   b. Brand recall was higher for comparative ads than for noncomparative ads.

   c. Comparative ads were viewed as less believable than noncomparative ads.

   d. Attitudes toward comparative ads were more negative than those toward noncomparative ads.

4. The marketing team for Charles Schwab wants to develop an advertisement with the message theme that Charles Schwab understands the needs of individual consumers and can design an investment strategy to meet each person's particular needs. Which type of message strategy should Schwab choose? Why? Based on the message strategy chosen, which executional framework should the company use? Why? What type of source or spokesperson should

Schwab use? Why? Would the type of media being used for the advertisement affect the message strategy choice? Explain your answer.

5. A resort in Florida wants to develop an advertisement highlighting scuba diving classes. The target market will be college students. Discuss the merits of each of the following approaches. In your opinion, which one would be the best? Why? Describe a television ad that could be created using the strategy you chose.

   a. Hyperbole cognitive message strategy, humor appeal, and demonstration execution

   b. Emotional message strategy, emotional appeal, and slice-of-life execution

   c. Conative message strategy, scarcity appeal, and informative execution

   d. Emotional or resonance message strategy, sex appeal, and fantasy execution

   e. Comparative message strategy, fear appeal, and testimonial execution

6. Name three influential commercial spokespersons. For each one, discuss the five characteristics used to evaluate spokespersons and their overall level of credibility. Next, make a list of three individuals who are poor spokespersons. Discuss each of the five evaluation characteristics for each of these individuals. What differences exist between an effective and a poor spokesperson?

7. Find a copy of a business journal, such as *BusinessWeek* or *Fortune,* or a trade journal. Also locate a copy of a consumer periodical such as *Glamour, Time, Sports Illustrated,* or a specialty magazine. Look through an entire issue. What differences between the advertisements in the business journal and consumer journals are readily noticeable? For each of the concepts that follow, discuss specific

differences you noted between the two types of magazines. Explain why the differences exist.

a. Message strategies

b. Executional frameworks

c. Sources and spokespersons

8. Identify an advertisement that uses each of the following executional frameworks. Evaluate the advertisement in terms of how well it is executed. Also, did the appeal and message strategy fit well with the execution? Was the ad memorable? What made it memorable?

a. Animation

b. Slice-of-life

c. Dramatization

d. Testimonial

e. Authoritative

f. Demonstration

g. Fantasy

h. Informative

INTEGRATED LEARNING EXERCISES

1. Current as well as past Super Bowl ads are available at **www.superbowl-ads.com**. Access the site and compare Super Bowl ads for the last several years. What types of message strategies were used? What types of executions were used? Who and what types of endorsers were used? Compare and contrast these three elements of ads.

2. Most advertising agencies provide examples of advertisements on company Web pages. The goal is to display the agency's creative abilities to potential clients. Using a search engine, locate three different advertising agencies. Locate samples of their work. Compare the ads produced by these three agencies in terms of message appeals, executions, and spokespersons. What similarities do you see? What differences do you see? Which agency, in your opinion, is the most creative? Why?

3. Access the following Web sites. For each, identify the primary message strategy used. Does the site use any sources or spokespersons? What type of appeal is being used? For each Web site, suggest how the site could be improved. Explain how the change would improve the site.

a. Georgia–Pacific (**www.gp.com**)

b. Playland International (**www.playland-inc.com**)

c. MGM Grand (**www.mgmgrand.com**)

d. The Exotic Body (**www.exoticbody.com**)

e. CoverGirl (**www.covergirl.com**)

f. Dove (**www.dove.com**)

g. Skechers (**www.skechers.com**)

4. Access the following Web sites. For each, identify and evaluate the primary executional framework used. Is it the best execution, or would another execution work better? Does the site use any sources or spokespersons? What type of appeal is being used? For each Web site, suggest how the site could be improved. Explain how the change would improve the site.

a. Kellogg's Frosted Flakes (**www.frostedflakes.com**)

b. Bonne Bell (**www.bonnebell.com**)

c. MessageMedia (**www.message-media.com.au**)

d. Jantzen (**www.jantzen.com**)

e. Jockey International (**www.jockey.com**)

STUDENT PROJECT

Creative Corner

For a number of years, LendingTree.com used the tagline "When banks compete, you win." In the mid-2000s, when the housing market tumbled, mortgage companies faced financial problems, and consumers defaulted on home mortgages, LendingTree.com changed its approach. The company developed new ads and modified the Web site to educate consumers about "smart borrowing." Other financial and mortgage companies followed suit. JPMorgan Chase asserted "Whether you are saving money, looking for a loan, or managing a business, you can always depend on Chase." Astoria Federal Savings promoted its longevity, telling consumers it had been in business "more than 118 years" and using phrases such as "We're part of your community" and "We're here when you need us."[35]

The marketing department for First National Bank intends to promote its home mortgage business. They are not sure about which creative message strategy to use, which execution would work best, and which appeal to use. They would also like to use some type of spokesperson, but they are not sure which of the four types would be the most effective. They also realize they cannot afford a famous celebrity.

Based on the information provided, design a print advertisement for the local newspaper for First National Bank. Describe a television campaign for the bank. Before launching into these two creative assignments, identify and justify your choice of creative message strategy, executional framework, appeal, and spokesperson.

CASE 1

BLACK-EYED MARKETING

If Black Eyed Peas band member will.i.am wasn't in music, "He'd be the best ad executive on Madison Avenue," says Randy Phillips, president and CEO of the concert promoter AEG Live. "I've never seen anyone more astute at dealing with sponsors' and companies' needs and understanding their brands." The Black Eyed Peas have been able to move beyond the status as a high-energy band into the world of corporate sponsorship without missing a beat.

Marketers love the Black Eyed Peas for the diverse ethnicity of the band's members, writes the *Wall Street Journal*. The band's corporate backers include Coors, Levi's, Honda, Apple, Verizon, and Pepsi. The advertisement featuring the group's song "Hey Mama" and dancing silhouettes that was used to help launch Apple's iTunes store gained almost iconic status.

What makes this group of musicians such an effective set of spokespeople? Part of the appeal is the group's global fan base and the Pea's fetching party anthems, with powerful dance beats, crazy special effects, and repetitive hooks that are integrated into numerous party mixes. As one critic noted, the band achieves the nearly impossible—making both kids and their parents feel cool at the same time.

Beyond the glitz and glitter of the shows, the group gives careful thought to its marketing. Oftentimes, will.i.am pitches concepts to corporate sponsors himself, using "decks" that sum up the Peas' package, frequently in PowerPoint form. He reports, "I consider us a brand. A brand always has stylized decks, from colors to fonts. Here's our demographic. Here's the reach. Here's the potential. Here's how the consumer will benefit from the collaboration."

There was a time when rock and roll was nearly synonymous with rebellion. Bands with corporate ties would be viewed as sell outs. For companies such a move would seem too risky; especially if the band's fans felt betrayed. Over the years, music has become less threatening, as Baby Boomers near retirement age.

The economics of music have also changed. Downloading and pirating CDs is commonplace. Bands can no longer count on record sales to make money. Many younger bands now look for other sources of income and publicity. The Peas were among the fastest learners of the industry's new math. Even now, however, the band hears complaints that they are merely shills. "You have to take the criticism, and sometimes it hurts a lot," says band member Stacy Ferguson, who is also known Fergie.

Currently, many top-name musicians and groups have corporate sponsors. Cooperative advertisements promote the brand, the band, and often a tour. The Rolling Stones began the movement when the group's "Tattoo You" tour was sponsored by Jovan Musk cologne. Even groups that at first resolutely avoided corporate tie-ins, such as U2, have changed. U2 developed a relationship with Apple that included commercials featuring the song "Vertigo." The band helped with BlackBerry commercials and had a sponsored tour with the brand.

The Black Eyed Peas continues to expand their corporate connections. A concert in Times Square promoted Samsung's new line of 3D televisions, which led to a meeting with *Avatar* director James Cameron, who agreed to direct a feature film

Source: Shutterstock.

▲ The Black Eyed Peas use marketing to enhance the band's image and presence.

about the Peas. The 3D film incorporates concerts, travel footage, and narrative themes about technology, dreams, and the brain.

According to will.i.am, all corporate partnerships are equally important. The band lends its music at relatively small charges in exchange for exposure. "It wasn't about the check," says former manager Seth Friedman.

The efforts have paid off. The Black Eyed Peas have performed at an NFL season-kickoff show, New Year's Eve in Times Square, the Grammys, a Victoria's Secret fashion show, and the season opener for *The Oprah Winfrey Show*, for which they summoned a flash mob of synchronized dancers to downtown Chicago. As will.i.am puts it, "I get the credit from the brands. They know. I used to work with the marketing people and the agencies, now I work with the CEOs of these companies."

1. Discuss each of the source characteristics in terms of the Black Eyed Peas serving as a spokesperson for a product. Would it make a difference as to what type of product the Black Eyed Peas were endorsing? Explain.

2. What types of brands or products are best suited to endorsements by the Black Eyed Peas? By rock bands in general? What about country music artists?

3. If you were going to design a television advertisement for a concert for the Black Eyed Peas, what would be your target market? What message strategy and executional framework would you use? Why? Describe your concept of an effective television ad.

4. Suppose the Black Eyed Peas were contracted to perform at your university. Design a print ad for your local student newspaper. Discuss the message strategy and execution you used and why you used it.

5. What types of brands or products would not be suited to endorsements by groups such as the Black Eyed Peas?

Source: John Jurgensen, "The Most Corporate Band in America," *Wall Street Journal Online* (**www.wsj.com**, accessed April 14, 2010).

PEERLESS MARKETING

In the United States, the majority of homes have indoor plumbing. Sinks, faucets, toilets, and other pieces of hardware are largely taken for granted. Only in two circumstances are they prominently in the minds of customers. The first is when a plumbing product is being purchased for the first time, such as when a home is being built or an area is being refurbished. The second is when an item is defective and must be replaced.

The challenge to manufacturers is to make certain that a company's brand is remembered by consumers and preferred by builders and plumbers. The products must be placed in stores such as Home Depot or Lowes in a way that makes them easy to find and always accessible.

One of the major players in the plumbing fixture marketplace is Delta Faucet Company. A strange path brought the company to prominence. In the 1920s, an immigrant named Alex Manoogian founded Masco Company, which provided auto parts. Twenty-five years later, Manoogian was contacted by an inventor who had created the first washerless faucet. Although it was not related to his current business, Manoogian saw the potential and refined the item, which was first sold out of the trunks of salesmen's cars, as the first Delta Faucet. The name was chosen because a key part of the product resembled the shape of the Greek letter delta.

Source: Courtesy of Delta Faucet Company. Photograph by John Welzenbach.

▲ The Delta Faucet Company offers the Peerless brand.

The Delta Faucet Company became a separate part of the original Masco Company and relocated. Over the next two decades, it expanded quickly to an entire line of products. Currently, Delta Faucet Company is a multinational firm with four primary locations: Indianapolis, Indiana; Jackson, Tennessee; London Ontario, Canada; and Panyu, China. It sells over 1 million faucets per month. The overall Masco Company now sells door hardware and locks, cabinets, and glass products in addition to faucets.

The Delta line includes two other names: Brizo and Peerless. Brizo is the high-end line of faucets, Delta is the flagship and primary brand, and Peerless is the lower-end line of items.

The primary advertising challenges appear to exist in four main areas. First, company leaders must make sure that one brand does not cannibalize the others. The brands must remain as distinct products offered to separate sets of consumers. Second, the brands must be viewed as the primary choices and must be remembered by consumers when the time comes to buy a plumbing fixture. Third, there cannot be brand confusion. Builders and plumbers must believe that the fixtures are distinct along several lines, including quality and durability, ease of installation, and strong warranties, but they must also be perceived as being fashionable. Fourth, innovation has become a new part of the plumbing fixture industry. A wide variety of options exist. Delta's products must compete with all the new faucet variations and retain its position as the one of the premier manufacturers.

Complications occur due to differences in markets and customers. Many contractors and builders are simply looking for a low-cost option, especially when lower-end rental properties and similar units are being developed. Plumbers may be willing to install a wide variety of products. They will consider the costs of a product but also want something that will be easy to install and that will be durable. Individual consumers are the most likely to be interested in other product qualities, such as novel features and the look of the product.

1. What type of message strategy should Delta Faucet Company utilize? Should it be the same for all of the brands and in all of the markets (builders, plumbers, consumers)?

2. What leverage point makes the most sense for Delta Faucet Company advertising?

3. What type of executional framework should be used in traditional advertisements aimed at consumers?

4. What type of executional framework should be used for print advertisements aimed at contractors, builders, and plumbers? Why might it be different (or the same) from ads aimed at consumers?

5. Should the company use a spokesperson? If so, which one of the four types should be used? Justify your answers.

Source: www.deltafaucet.com (accessed January 8, 2008).

8 Traditional Media Channels

GODADDY.COM

Super Bowl Buzz

In a period of less than 50 years, the Super Bowl has grown into one of the more iconic life events in the United States. Television audiences totaling around 100 million viewers in the United States and nearly 1 billion people worldwide watch at least part of the game. The 2-week buildup, the 4- to 6-hour pregame shows, and the massive media attention paid to the teams and players have been rewarded with a series of exciting games over the past decade.

At the same time, the Super Bowl has developed into the most watched, analyzed, and discussed *advertising* event of the year. From one of the most famous early commercials, affectionately known as "Mean Joe Green and the Kid" for Coca-Cola, a series of spectacular success stories and monumental moments of failure have been shown during the Super Bowl telecast. Perhaps the most famous is the "1984" commercial for the Apple McIntosh, which only aired a single time but had such a far-reaching effect that it was named the commercial of the decade for the 1980s by *Advertising Age*. Most Super Bowl viewers have their favorite advertising moment as well. They have enjoyed the use of humor, drama, and music in a variety of commercials for beer, chips, cars, sexual dysfunction products, candy bars, and others.

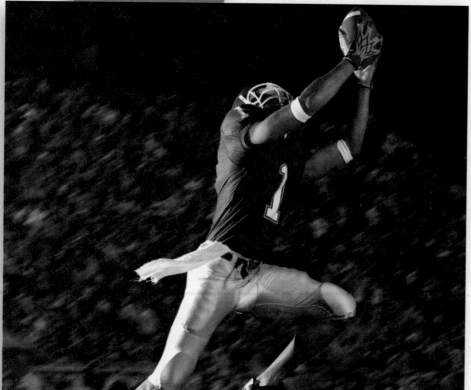

Today's Super Bowl ads generate a great deal of buzz. Of the 38 brands presented during the 2010 Super Bowl, 75 percent experienced nearly twice as many blog posts on the Internet as compared to the average online mentions in the 6 months prior. About one-third of the brands had a threefold increase in online mentions. Doritos enjoyed a 13-fold increase. The additional buzz is not limited to the Internet. One study revealed that 22 percent of word-of-mouth recommendations, whether in person or online, were directly tied to a Super Bowl commercial.

The costs associated with these major events are considerable. A 30-second spot may cost as little as $1 million but can be as high as $3 million. In addition, many companies and advertising agencies spend major amounts of money developing and producing the

CHAPTER OBJECTIVES

After reading this chapter, you should be able to answer the following questions:

1 What is a media strategy?

2 What elements and individuals are involved in media planning?

3 How do the terms used to describe advertising help the marketing team design effective campaigns?

4 What are some of the primary advertising objectives?

5 What are the advantages and disadvantages associated with each of the traditional advertising media?

6 How can the marketing team use the media mix to increase advertising effectiveness?

7 What are the key issues associated with media selection for business-to-business markets?

8 What issues are associated with media selection in international markets?

advertisements. What emerges is a high-stakes investment in what can be a moment of tremendous success or tragic levels of disdain for ads that are deemed failures.

Among the more successful recent Super Bowl advertisers has been Go Daddy (**www.godaddy. com**). The company helps users purchase Internet domain names and performs other Internet domain services. In 2005, the commercial entitled "Proceedings" appeared, the year after Janet Jackson's infamous half-time wardrobe malfunction. "Go

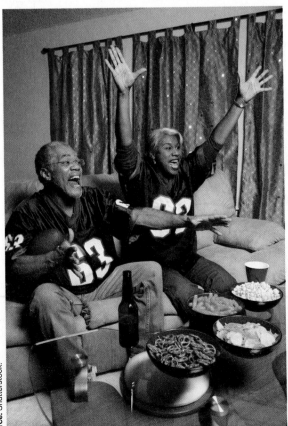

Source: Shutterstock.

Daddy Girl" Nikki Cappelli appears to testify before a shocked Congress, as her tank-top strap keeps breaking. One of the questioners finally has to grab for an oxygen mask.

From the buzz that grew out of that advertisement, plus the one network executives would not allow to be shown, a new form of Super Bowl commercial emerged, because Go Daddy discovered a novel way to create buzz. The company's marketing team submits suggestive and highly provocative advertisements to be shown on the Super Bowl that they know will be banned. Word spreads about the prohibited ads on Web sites and in forums and news articles. This buzz helps drive inquisitive customer to the Go Daddy Web site to watch the banned ads.

Several of the advertisements feature race car driver Danica Patrick. The "Lola" commercial features a former football player who becomes a lingerie designer and makes his fortune with Go Daddy's assistance, with Patrick as the narrator. In another, Ms. Patrick is portrayed in sexy situations as a "Hot Smoking" dancer and entertainer.

To maintain interest, Go Daddy follows up the initial buzz with 30-second spots that tell viewers that to see the entire "unedited" version of the ad they need to visit the Web site.

Over the years, these methods have allowed Go Daddy to benefit from substantial amounts of free publicity, which has undoubtedly increased brand awareness. They also represent a new method of creating Web site traffic through traditional media.[1]

197

OVERVIEW

f a tree falls in the forest and no one is present, does it make a sound? This philosophical question has been posed for many years. In the world of advertising, far too many "trees" fall as unheard and unseen advertisements. Successful marketing involves identifying target markets and then finding media that reach the members of those markets. Once they identify the right media, creatives can design clever, memorable, exciting, and persuasive advertisements.

The third part of this textbook covers the IMC media tools, including both traditional media channels and newer approaches. The concepts of e-active marketing and alternative channels are explained in the upcoming chapters (see Figure 8.1).

Traditional media continue to play an important role in developing a fully integrated marketing program. This chapter explains the various traditional media channels, including:

- The media strategy
- Media planning processes and the roles of the media planner and buyer
- Advertising objectives
- Media choices based on the advantages and disadvantages of each medium
- Media selection in business-to-business and international settings

An advertising campaign should be designed within the framework of the overall integrated marketing communications program. Client companies depend on effective advertisements to attract customers and entice them into purchasing various goods and services. This helps build the firm's image and creates a larger customer base. Advertising media selection is an important element in this process.

THE MEDIA STRATEGY

① What is a media strategy?

The **media strategy** involves analyzing and choosing media for an advertising and promotions campaign. The average consumer examines only 9 of the more than 200 consumer magazines on the market. A radio listener usually tunes in to only three of the stations available in a given market. Television viewers watch fewer than eight of the stations available via cable or satellite. Average network prime-time ratings have declined by more than 30 percent over the last decade. Choosing the best media to speak to potential customers becomes challenging.

FIGURE 8.1 ▶
Overview of Integrated
Marketing Communications

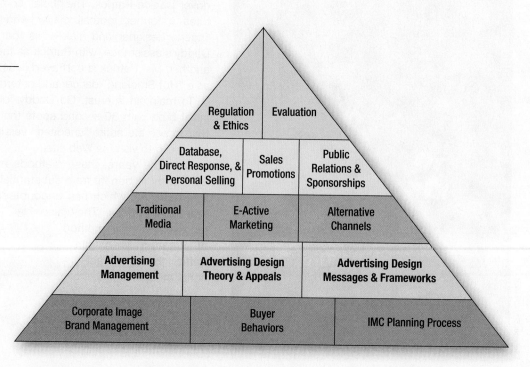

To make the account executive and media buyer's jobs more difficult, prices for advertising time and space have risen. Client budgets for advertising have not risen as quickly, even as stronger demands for results and accountability emerged. The marketing team faces difficulties in locating cost-effective media outlets. After developing a media strategy, other aspects of media selection can proceed.

◀ FIGURE 8.2
Examples of Times Consumers
Are Exposed to Advertisements

- A favorite wake-up radio station or one listened to during the commute to work
- A favorite morning news show or newspaper
- Trade or business journals examined while at work
- A radio station played during office hours at work
- Favorite computer sites accessed during work
- Favorite magazines read during the evening hours
- Favorite television shows watched during the evening hours
- Internet sites accessed during leisure time
- Shopping, dining, and entertainment venues frequented

MEDIA PLANNING

Media planning begins with a careful analysis of the target market. It involves understanding the process customers use in making a purchase and what influences the final decision. One method of addressing media planning is to study the media choices that members of a specific, defined target market might make at different times during the course of a day (see Figure 8.2).

2 What elements and individuals are involved in media planning?

Details of this type are valuable when developing a media strategy. Knowing demographics such as age, sex, income, and education is not enough to understand the media habits of targeted consumers. Information about the listening and viewing patterns of customers helps the marketing team design messages that appeal to them. These can then be placed at the best times and in the best places. No two media plans are alike. The typical components of a media plan include the elements identified in Figure 8.3.

The *marketing analysis* provides a comprehensive review of the marketing program. It includes a statement about current sales, current market share, and prime prospects to be solicited (by demographics, lifestyle, geographic location, or product usage). These elements should reflect a compatible pricing strategy based on the product, its benefits and distinguishing characteristics, and an analysis of the competitive environment.

An *advertising analysis* states the primary advertising strategy and budget to be used to achieve advertising objectives. The *media strategy* spells out the media to be used and the creative considerations. The *media schedule* notes when ads will appear in individual vehicles. The *justification and summary* states the measures of goal achievement. It also explains the rationale for each media choice.[2]

Several individuals are involved in media planning. In addition to account executives, account planners, and creatives, most agencies utilize media planners and media buyers. In smaller agencies, the media planner and media buyer can be the same person. In larger companies, they are usually different individuals. Some agencies will use media firms to handle the media planning and buying, or employ a subsidiary agency.

Media Planners

The **media planner** formulates a media program stating where and when to place ads. Media planners work closely with creatives, account executives, account planners, agencies, and media buyers. The creative should know which media will be used to help

◀ FIGURE 8.3
Components of a Media Plan

- Marketing analysis
- Advertising analysis
- Media strategy
- Media schedule
- Justification and summary

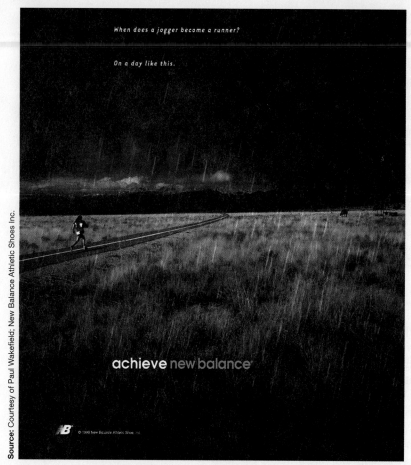

When does a jogger become a runner?

On a day like this.

achieve new balance

▲ An advertisement featuring New Balance shoes that was placed in *Runner's World* magazine.

design effective messages. Television commercials are constructed in different ways than radio or newspaper ads.

Media planners provide valuable services and are in high demand. The issue of accountability for advertising results combined with the need to create a "return on investment" on marketing dollars has caused greater power to be held by the media buying side of an agency.

Media planning impacts strategic planning. Marketing experts at companies such as Procter & Gamble and Unilever consider media planning to be the heart of a communications strategy. In both companies, setting brand priorities and objectives is the first step.[3] The challenge for media buyers in this environment, according to Carl Fremont of the media services company Digitas, is "to integrate marketing messages across a range of media, and sometimes this involves working with several agencies to accomplish the client's goals."[4]

The media planner conducts research to help match the product with the market and media. A target market consisting of 18- to 25-year-old males with college degrees who love the outdoors leads to media that match those characteristics. The New Balance running shoe ad in this section was placed in *Runner's World* near an article about running and was targeted to avid runners.

The media planner also gathers information about various media. This includes newspaper and magazine circulation rates and the characteristics of those who use the medium. The audience for a television show may be quite different from those of a radio station or a magazine. Careful research improves the chances of selecting the appropriate media.

Media Buyers

After the media are chosen, the **media buyer** purchases the space and negotiates rates, times, and schedules for the ads. Media buyers remain in contact with media sales representatives. They know a great deal about rates and schedules. Media buyers also watch for special deals and tie-ins between media outlets (e.g., radio with television, magazines with the same owner, etc.).

Placement in a television show or magazine will be an important consideration, both in terms of price and effectiveness. Recently, the Pink Jacket Creative advertising agency purchased magazine space for the Snoring Center consisting of the outer sides of adjacent pages containing an article. The slender ads on the edges of the two pages bracketed the article. As individuals read the article, they first noticed the ad on the left side of the article and the second half on the right side as they held the magazine open. Not only was the ad space cheaper, it turned out to be more effective in conveying the two-part message.

Some research indicates that there is little connection between the size of an advertising firm and the prices it can negotiate. Differences in media costs are based on the time of the actual purchase (closer to the day the ad is to run) rather than the size of the agency.[5] A media plan costing one firm $10 million can cost another $12 million. Other major factors in cost differences are knowledge of the marketplace and the ability to negotiate package deals.

A **spot ad** is a one-time placement of a commercial in a medium. Rates are negotiated individually by the number of times the ads appear. Spot television prices vary by as much as 45 percent for the same time slot. Radio time slot prices vary by as much as

I said for better or worse...

DALLAS | 214.369.2345
FORT WORTH | 817.737.5678

42 percent and national print ads by as much as 24 percent.[6] Negotiating a price is only one element of an advertising program.

Differences in effectiveness of advertising are related to the quality of media choices, creativity, financial stewardship, the agency's culture and track record, and the relationship between the agency and the medium's sales representative. Advertising effectiveness will be determined by quality of the media selections made combined with the advertisement's content.

ADVERTISING TERMINOLOGY

As with many subjects, advertising has its own unique set of terms and measures. These are listed in Figure 8.4. **Reach** represents the number of people, households, or businesses in a target audience exposed to a media vehicle or message schedule at least once during a given time period, which normally consists of 4 weeks. In other words, how many targeted buyers did the ad reach at least once during a 4-week period?

Frequency

The average number of times an individual, household, or business within a particular target market is exposed to a particular advertisement within a specified time period, again, usually 4 weeks, is **frequency**. It specifies how many times the person saw the ad during a campaign. A regular viewer sees the same ad shown daily on *Wheel of Fortune* more frequently than an ad shown once on *Grey's Anatomy*, even though the program has a greater reach.

Opportunities to See

In media planning, instead of frequency, opportunities to see (OTS) can be used. **Opportunities to see** refers to the cumulative exposures achieved in a given time period. When a company places two ads on a television show that is televised weekly there are 8 OTS (4 shows × 2 ads per show) during a 4-week period.

Gross Rating Points

Gross rating points (GRPs) measure the impact or intensity of a media plan. Gross rating points are calculated by multiplying a vehicle's rating by the OTS, or number of insertions of an advertisement. GRPs give the advertiser a better idea of the odds that members of the target audience actually viewed the ad. By increasing the OTS or frequency, the chances of a magazine reader seeing the advertisement rise. An advertisement featured in each weekly issue of *Time* during a 4-week period is more likely to be seen than one that appears once in a monthly periodical.

Cost

Cost is a measure the overall expenditures associated with an advertising program or campaign. To be able to compare how cost effective one medium or ad placement is to another, a measure called **cost per thousand (CPM)** can be calculated. CPM is the

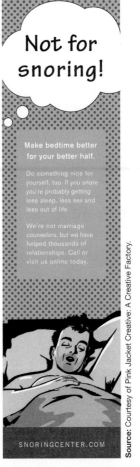

Not for snoring!

Make bedtime better for your better half.

Do something nice for yourself, too. If you snore you're probably getting less sleep, less sex and less out of life.

We're not marriage counselors, but we have helped thousands of relationships. Call or visit us online today.

SNORINGCENTER.COM

▲ Ads for the Snoring Center placed strategically on a two-page article spread on the outer edges.

3 How do the terms used to describe advertising help the marketing team design effective campaigns?

- Reach
- Frequency
- Opportunities to see (OTS)
- Gross rating points (GRP)
- Cost per thousand (CPM)
- Cost per rating point (CPRP)
- Ratings
- Continuity
- Gross impressions

◀ **FIGURE 8.4**
Advertising Terminology

TABLE 8.1 Hypothetical Media Information for Select Magazines

| | Cost Four-Color Full-Page Ad | Total Readership | CPM | Target Market (20 Million) | | | |
				Percent of Readers Fit Target Market	Number of Readers Fit Target Market	Rating (Reach)	Cost per Rating Point (CPRP)
Glamour	$842,658	18,354,000	$45.91	13.51%	2,480,000	12.4	$67,956
National Geographic	$346,080	21,051,000	$16.44	16.25%	3,420,000	17.1	$20,239
Newsweek	$780,180	15,594,000	$50.03	11.93%	1,860,000	9.3	$83,890
People	$605,880	21,824,000	$27.76	6.87%	1,500,000	7.5	$80,784
Southern Living	$11,370	5,733,000	$1.98	10.81%	620,000	3.1	$3,668
Sports Illustrated	$965,940	13,583,000	$71.11	12.96%	1,760,000	8.8	$109,766
Time	$1,324,282	21,468,000	$61.69	11.65%	2,500,000	12.5	$105,943
Travel & Leisure	$183,216	2,205,000	$83.09	12.70%	280,000	1.4	$130,869

dollar cost of reaching 1,000 members of the media vehicle's audience. It is calculated using the following formula:

$$CPM = (Cost\ of\ media\ buy/Total\ audience) \times 1,000$$

Table 8.1 displays cost and readership information for a campaign for a 35 mm digital camera. The first three columns of the table provide the name of the magazine, the cost of a four-color full-page advertisement, and the magazine's total readership. The fourth column contains a measure of the CPM of each magazine. The CPM for *National Geographic* is $16.44. This means that it takes $16.44 to reach 1,000 *National Geographic* readers. The CPM for *Sports Illustrated* is $71.11 and for *Travel & Leisure*, $83.09. The readership of *Travel & Leisure* is the lowest, and yet its CPM is the highest of all eight magazines. In terms of cost per thousand readers, the best buy is *Southern Living*, at only $1.98 per thousand.

Ratings and Cost per Rating Point

A critical concern is the number of readers that fit the target market's profile, in this case for a 35 mm digital camera. **Ratings** measure the percentage of a firm's target market that is exposed to a television show or the number of readers of a print medium. In order to compare media, a measure called the **cost per rating point (CPRP)** may be used. The cost per rating point formula that measures the relative efficiency of a media vehicle relative to a firm's target market is:

$$CPRP = Cost\ of\ media\ buy/Vehicle's\ rating$$

The number of potential buyers of the 35 mm digital camera is 20 million. The table shows the rating for *Glamour* is 12.4, which means that 12.4 percent of the defined target market for 35 mm digital cameras read the *Glamour*. Backing up a step, 13.51 percent, or 2.48 million, of *Glamour's* readership fits the target profile for the 35 mm digital camera. The 12.4 rating is then obtained by dividing the 2.48 million *Glamour* readers that fit the target profile by the 20 million total in the target market. The CPRP for *Glamour* become $67,956. This is the average cost for each rating point, or of each 1 percent of the firm's target audience (35 mm digital camera buyers) that can be reached through an advertisement in *Glamour*. Not all readers of a magazine are part of the firm's target market. The CPRP more accurately measures an advertising campaign's efficiency than does CPM. Notice that the CPRP is the lowest for *National Geographic* and *Southern Living*. It is the highest for *Travel & Leisure*.

CPRP provides a relative measure of reach exposure in terms of cost. It costs $20,239 to reach 1 percent, or 200,000, of the 20 million in this firm's target market using *National Geographic*. It costs $109,766 to reach 1 percent, or 200,000, using *Sports Illustrated*. To reach 1 percent, or 200,000, using *Southern Living* costs only $3,668. *Southern*

	Cost Four-Color Full-Page Ad	Total Readership	CPM	Target Market (20 Million)	
				Number of Readers Fit Target Market	Weighted (Demographic) CPM
Glamour	$842,658	18,354,000	$45.91	2,480,000	$339.78
National Geographic	$346,080	21,051,000	$16.44	3,420,000	$101.19
Newsweek	$780,180	15,594,000	$50.03	1,860,000	$419.45
People	$605,880	21,824,000	$27.76	1,500,000	$403.92
Southern Living	$11,370	5,733,000	$1.98	620,000	$18.34
Sports Illustrated	$965,940	13,583,000	$71.11	1,760,000	$548.83
Time	$1,324,282	21,468,000	$61.69	2,500,000	$529.71
Travel & Leisure	$183,216	2,205,000	$83.09	280,000	$654.34

TABLE 8.2 Calculating Weighted (or Demographic) CPM

Living is the most efficient, which raises the question, "Why wouldn't a media planner just do all of the advertising in that magazine?" The answer lies in *Southern Living*'s rating. Advertising in only that magazine reaches just 3.1 percent (or 620,000) of the target audience; 96.9 percent of the target market does not read *Southern Living* and would not see the ad. Another magazine or media outlet is needed to reach them. This explains why diversity in media is essential to reach a large portion of a firm's target market.

An alternative method of determining whether an ad has reached the target market effectively is a **weighted (or demographic) CPM** value, which can be calculated as:

$$\text{Weighted CPM} = \frac{\text{Advertisement cost} \times 1,000}{\text{Actual audience reached}}$$

Referring to Table 8.2, the cost of an advertisement in *Newsweek* is $346,080. Although it has a readership of 21,051,000, only 1,860,000 of the readers fit the target profile for the 35 mm digital camera. Using the formula for weighted CPM, the cost to reach 1,000 readers of *Newsweek* that fit the target profile is $419.45. As with CPRP, it is now possible to compare across the various magazines to determine which magazines offer the best buy in terms of reaching the target demographic. The difference in the numbers is that CPRP measures the cost of reaching 1 percent of the target market, whereas the weighted CPM measures the cost of reaching 1,000 members of the target market.

Continuity

The exposure pattern or schedule used in a campaign is its **continuity**. The three types of patterns are continuous, pulsating, and discontinuous. A *continuous campaign* uses media time in a steady stream. The Skechers ad shown in this section could be presented on a continuous schedule. The media buys would be for ad space in specific magazines for a period of 1 to 2 years. By using different ads and rotating them, readers will not get bored, because they will see more than one advertisement for the same product.

A retailer such as JCPenney might use a *pulsating schedule* by placing ads in various media throughout the entire

▼ An advertisement promoting the Skechers brand.

year, but then increasing the number of advertisements in small, short bursts around holidays, including Christmas, Thanksgiving, Memorial Day, Labor Day, Mother's Day, Father's Day, and Easter. Pulsating advertising should reach consumers when they are most likely to make purchases or buy special merchandise, such as during the holidays. A Barnes & Noble advertisement just prior to Christmas can encourage consumers to purchase gift cards.

A *flighting (or discontinuous) campaign* schedule would be more likely to be used by a ski resort that runs ads during the fall and winter seasons but none during the spring and summer.

Impressions

The final advertising objective is impressions. The number of **gross impressions** represents the total exposures of the audience to an advertisement. It does not account for the percentage of the total audience that sees the advertisement. Table 8.1 indicates that the total readership of *National Geographic* is 21,051,000. If six insertions were placed in *National Geographic,* multiplying the insertions by the readership would yield a total of 126 million impressions.

ACHIEVING ADVERTISING OBJECTIVES

④ What are some of the primary advertising objectives?

Advertisers consider the number of times a person will be exposed to an ad before it creates an impact. Most agree that a single exposure will not be enough. The actual number inspires a great deal of debate. Some argue it takes three. Others say as many as 10 or more.

The Three-Exposure Hypothesis

With regard to exposures, the basic rule that most media planners have used for years is that it takes a minimum of three for an advertisement to be effective. The three-exposure hypothesis, as developed by Herbert Krugman, suggests that advertisements can make an impact on an audience regardless of individual needs or wants.[7] Further, the **intrusion value** of an advertisement represents the ability of a medium or an advertisement to capture the attention of a viewer without her voluntary effort. Ordinarily it takes at least three exposures to capture and keep a viewer's attention.

Recency Theory

Currently, many advertisers believe that three exposures are not enough to create an impression, primarily because of clutter. Clutter also affects the types of objectives firms try to accomplish.

Recency theory also challenges the three-exposure hypothesis. It suggests that a consumer's attention is selective and focuses on his individual needs and wants. Clutter means that advertisements only have short-term effects and responses dissipate rapidly, with few carryover effects.[8]

Recency theory suggests that consumers have selective attention processes as they consider advertisements. They pay attention to messages that might meet their needs or wants. The closer or more recent an ad is to a purchase, the more powerful the ad becomes. Further, when a consumer contemplates a future purchase of the product being advertised, the consumer will be more likely to notice and react favorably toward an ad. A member of a buying center from a business in the market for a new copier will more readily notice copier advertisements. An individual who is not in the market for a copier ignores the same ad. The same will be true in consumer markets: An individual needing a new pair of jeans notices clothing ads, especially ones that feature jeans.

Recency theory suggests that *one ad exposure* may actually be enough to affect an audience when that person or business needs the product being promoted. Additional exposures may not be necessary. Therefore, companies must advertise almost continually to ensure an advertisement reaches a buyer when she is thinking about making a purchase.

The advertising strategy that matches recency theory would be to spread the message around using a variety of media, each one providing limited exposure per week or time period. In the case of selling supplemental health insurance to the elderly, magazines such as *Senior Living*, televisions spots on local news and weather programs, and newspaper ads can quickly reach the target audience in a cost-effective manner. Such an approach, which maximizes reach, accomplishes more than increasing frequency.

In the business-to-business arena, recency theory argues that ads should appear in a number of outlets and over a longer period of time rather than running a series of ads in one trade journal. Many times, buying centers consist of several members, each with different responsibilities. Making sure each one sees an advertisement would mean placing ads in every journal that might be read by buying center members. To facilitate the purchasing process for a company seeking to acquire an audio-conferencing system, the media buyer purchases space in trade journals, human resource journals, sales journals, and business journals. This increases the odds that the message will reach buying center members. One exposure might be enough for each, because the member is looking for information and is ready to make a decision.

▲ Based on recency theory, a female looking for ski boots is likely to notice this advertisement.

Source: Courtesy of Skis DYNASTAR, Inc.

Effective Reach and Frequency

Seeking to discover the minimum number of exposures needed to be effective may be based on two concepts: effective frequency and effective reach. **Effective reach** suggests the *percentage of an audience* that must be exposed to a particular message to achieve a specific objective. **Effective frequency** refers to the *number of times* a target audience must be exposed to a message to achieve a particular objective. The concept of effective frequency implies that some minimum number of exposures is needed.

Effective frequency and effective reach are crucial. Too few exposures means the advertiser will fail to attain its intended objectives. In contrast, too many exposures waste resources. Discovering the optimal reach and frequency mix to accomplish the intended objectives without experiencing diminishing returns from extra ads is the goal. The optimal mix for an objective dealing with brand recognition will be different than when the objective is brand recall.

Other elements can also enhance effective frequency and effective reach. They include the size and placement of an advertisement. A small magazine advertisement does not create the same impact as a larger ad. If a firm uses 15-second television ads, effective frequency may require six exposures. In comparison, a longer 45-second spot may require only four exposures to be remembered. In television advertising, a spot in the middle of an ad sequence usually has less of an impact than the ads shown at the beginning and end of the series.

The number of different media used in an advertising campaign also influences effectiveness. In general, a campaign featuring ads in two types of media, such as television and magazines, has greater effective reach than a campaign in only one medium, such as magazines only.

▼ Effective reach and effective frequency are important measures to evaluate ads, such as this one for Keepsake.

Source: Courtesy of Keepsake American Achievement Corporation AAC Group Holding Corp.

Objective	Brand Recognition	Brand Recall
Goal	Create or strengthen mental linkages	Place brand in evoked set
Method	Increase reach	Increase frequency (repetition)
Best media	Television	Television
	Billboards	Radio
	Magazines	Newspapers
	Internet	Internet
	Direct mail	

In recent years, numerous media companies have designed computer models to optimize reach and frequency. The programs that evaluate effective reach and frequency are based on probability theory. They are designed to help the marketing team effectively allocate advertising dollars. An interaction of an attention-getting television ad with a magazine ad with copy explaining the product's features may create more potent synergistic effect than would either ad alone.

Brand Recognition

Brand recognition requires an emphasis on the visual presentation of the product and/or logo. The idea is to strengthen or create links between the brand and other nodes of information that exist in the person's knowledge structure. Rather than having the individual recall the brand name from memory, the advertiser wants the person to recognize the brand name and logo at the retail store or in the advertisement. Media that are good at maximizing reach include television, billboards, magazines, the Internet, and direct mail.[9]

▼ By using current advertising software such as Nielsen SAVE or Adware, the marketing team for Celestial Sleepytime Tea can optimize the reach and frequency of an advertisement's exposure.

Brand Recall

To increase brand recall, frequency becomes more important than reach. Repetition helps embed a brand in the consumer's cognitive memory. Repetition increases the odds that a particular brand will come to mind. When the name of a restaurant is mentioned seven times in a 30-second commercial, it becomes easier to remember than if it is stated only once or twice. In terms of media selection, television, radio, newspapers, and the Internet offer the potential for higher frequency.[10] Figure 8.5 compares brand recall with brand recognition.

Once the media buyer, media planner, account executive, and company leaders agree about basic objectives of the advertising campaign, they can select the actual media. The goal is to identify logical media combinations. The next section examines traditional advertising media.

MEDIA SELECTION

Effectively mixing the advertising media is an important part of designing a quality advertising campaign. To do so, the advantages and disadvantages of each individual medium should be understood.

Television

For many years, television held the reputation of being the glamour advertising medium. To some, television advertising

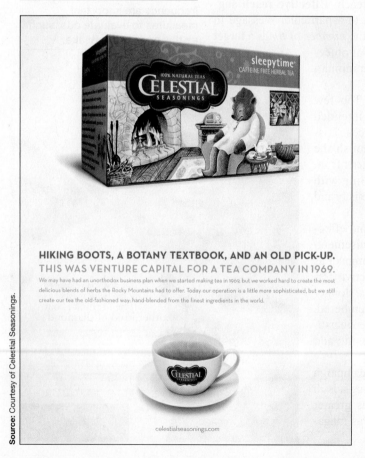

HIKING BOOTS, A BOTANY TEXTBOOK, AND AN OLD PICK-UP.
THIS WAS VENTURE CAPITAL FOR A TEA COMPANY IN 1969.
We may have had an unorthodox business plan when we started making tea in 1969, but we worked hard to create the most delicious blends of herbs the Rocky Mountains had to offer. Today our operation is a little more sophisticated, but we still create our tea the old-fashioned way: hand-blended from the finest ingredients in the world.

celestialseasonings.com

remains the best option. A survey by Nielsen notes that the average consumer watches 31 hours of television per week with only 31 minutes in playback mode by a DVR.[11] Table 8.3 lists the advantages and disadvantages of television advertising.

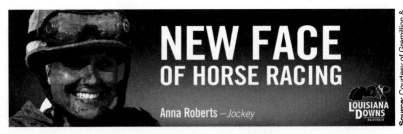

Source: Courtesy of Gremillion & Pou.

▲ In addition to this billboard promoting Louisiana Downs, the advertising agency considers other media that might be used to effectively reach the horse racing target market.

Advantages of Television Advertising

Marketers know that television provides the most extensive coverage and highest reach of any medium. A single commercial may reach millions of viewers. Television also offers a low cost per contact. This justifies spending as much as $3 million for a 30-second spot on the Super Bowl, where a vast audience of over 90 million households may be watching. The cost per person reached by the ad becomes very low.

Television features intrusion value. Television commercials using a catchy musical tune, sexy content, or humor can quickly grab a viewer's attention. Television offers opportunities to be creative in designing advertisements. Visual images and sounds can be incorporated in a commercial. Products and services can be demonstrated on television in a manner not possible in print or using radio advertisements. Segmentation may be achieved by targeting specialty shows and networks, such as *The Food Channel* or *ESPN*.

⑤ What are the advantages and disadvantages associated with each of the traditional advertising media?

Disadvantages of Television Advertising

Clutter continues to be the primary problem with television advertising. It is not unusual for a television program to run 31 commercials per hour, and these take as long as 19 minutes. Four- and 5-minute commercial breaks are common.[12] As a result, many viewers switch channels during commercial breaks. Often, low recall exists, especially for commercials in the middle of an advertising segment. Messages at the beginning or near the end of the break have a better chance at recall. This problem may be made worse by the short amount of copy that can be presented in a 30-second commercial.

Some viewers cope with clutter by using a DVR, recording favorite programs and watching them later. Advertisers fear the DVR users will skip over the commercials. Recent research indicates, however, that fewer than half fast-forward through commercials. Also, the majority watches the television show the same day it is recorded, and 75 percent have watched it by the end of the next day. This means that time-sensitive ads are being seen close to when they first were run. Consequently, the fear that DVRs cause viewers to skip commercials may be somewhat unjustified.[13]

Television airtime is expensive, as is the costs of producing ads. The average cost of production for a 30-second national ad is $358,000. Production fees account for the largest portion of the cost, an average of $236,000. Other costs include director fees ($23,000), fees for editing and finishing the ad ($45,000), and creative/labor fees and music ($34,000).[14]

TABLE 8.3 Television Advertising

Advantages	Disadvantages
1. High reach	1. Greater clutter
2. High frequency potential	2. Low recall due to clutter
3. Low cost per contact	3. Channel surfing during commercials
4. High intrusion value (motion, sound)	4. Short amount of copy
5. Quality creative opportunities	5. High cost per ad
6. Segmentation possibilities through cable outlets	

Ratings

To gain a sense of how well an advertisement fared in terms of reaching an audience, a given program's rating can be calculated. The typical ratings formula is:

$$\text{Rating} = \frac{\text{Number of households tuned to a program}}{\text{Total number of households in a market}}$$

In the United States, approximately 109.7 million households have television sets. To calculate the rating of an episode of *American Idol,* if the number of households tuned to the season finale was 17.8 million, the rating would be:

$$\text{Rating} = \frac{17,800,000}{109,700,000} = 16.2$$

Next, if the advertiser were interested in the percentage of households that actually were watching television at that hour, the program's share could be calculated. If 71 million of the 109.7 million households had a television turned on during the hour in which *American Idol* aired the share would be:

$$\text{Share} = \frac{\text{Number of households tuned to } American\ Idol}{\text{Number of households with a television turned on}} = \frac{17,800,000}{71,000,000} = 25$$

A 16.2 rating would mean that 16.2 percent of all televisions in the United States were tuned to *American Idol.* A 25 share means 25 percent of the households with a television actually turned on were watching the program.

Ratings do not guarantee viewers saw the commercial. Ratings and shares are only indicators of how well the program fared. The figures are used to establish rates for advertisements. The higher a show's rating over time, the more that can be charged. For example in Figure 8.6, the cost of a 30-second ad for *Sunday Night Football* was $339,700 and the Nielsen ratings were 16.8. As the Nielsen ratings decline, so does the cost of a 30-second spot. The *Big Bang Theory* has a Nielsen rating of 12.1 and charges $191,900 for a 30-second spot.[15]

Ratings Providers

ACNielsen is the primary organization that calculates and reports ratings and shares. The company also provides local channel information regarding shares of stations in local markets known as *designated marketing areas* (DMAs). Data-gathering techniques used by ACNielsen include diaries written by viewers who report what they watched, audience meters that record what is being watched automatically, and people meters that allow the viewing habits of individual members of families to be tracked.

These numbers can be further refined to help advertisers understand whether an advertisement reached a target market. Within rating and share categories, viewers can be subdivided by certain demographics, such as age, income, gender, educational level, and race or ethnic heritage. Organizations that prepare this information include Nielsen Media Research; Starch INRA; Hooper, Inc.; Mediamark Research, Inc.; Burke Marketing Research; and Simmons Market Research Bureau. Psychographic information can be then

FIGURE 8.6 ▶
Nielsen Ratings and Cost of a 30-Second Ad

TV Show	Nielsen Rating	Cost of 30-Second Ad
Sunday Night Football	16.8	$339,700
Grey's Anatomy	14.3	$240,462
Desperate Housewives	13.3	$228,851
Two and a Half Men	12.6	$226,635
CSI	14.5	$198,647
The Big Bang Theory	12.1	$191,900

Source: Adapted from Brian Steinberg, "Sunday Night Football Remains Costliest TV Show," *Advertising Age,* http://adage.com/article?article_id=139923, October 26, 2009; "List of Top 20 Prime-time Programs in the Nielsen Ratings for Sept. 28–Oct. 4," *Entertainment Daily,* http://<.com/e/2009/10/06/list-of-top-20-prime-time-programs-in-the-nielsen-ratings-for-sept28-oct4, October 6, 2009.

be added in, such as whether a certain program is mostly watched by active outdoor enthusiasts. This gives the advertiser a sense of whether the program provides the best audience for an advertisement or campaign.

New Trends in Ratings

One approach to ratings that has been growing in use is to provide a rating for the actual commercial time slot rather than the television program. According to Mary Price, a media purchasing expert, We have recently moved from program ratings to *commercial ratings*. At the national level, the measurement standard is called C 3. So it' s a commercial's rating plus any viewing of those commercials three days after the original ran. The next thing we'll see will be an actual commercial rating. For example, we are going to work with the *Discovery Channel*, and instead of C 3 rating, we are going to negotiate our commercial rate based on the *minute* that our commercial airs. That means, if we booked for a .5 rating guarantee and we only get a .3, they owe us an impression. If we get a .7, and we negotiated at a .5, the then next time we only get that .3, because we already made it up.

With commercial ratings, it will tell what commercials are holding viewers and what commercials are driving them away. Ultimately networks will be able to use that information in terms of how much they charge.[16]

Clearly the precision with which advertising exposures are measured will improve with these new techniques.

▲ A storyboard produced by Zhender Communications for a television commercial.

Source: Courtesy of Zhender Communications.

Local and Regional Television Advertising

For local and regional companies, spot TV may be the best television advertising option. In many cases, national brands supplement national commercials with spot TV purchases in select markets. Media planners do this primarily because of the high cost of national ad time and because 75 to 80 percent of prime-time slots are sold out during the spring, shortly after they go on the market. By selecting local early news, late news, and local prime access, a media planner can generate higher GRP at a lower cost than if only national ad time has been purchased.

Effective Television Advertising

Choosing the best television advertising outlets for commercials is challenging. The shows selected should match the firm's target market. Most television programs have well-defined audiences. The media planner looks for the best matches between the product's target market and the television show's audience profile. As described in the Integrated Communications in Action segment in Chapter 5, Oscar Mayer used television to launch the "It doesn't get better than this" campaign on the *Golden Globe Awards*, with supporting print ads. In general, television appeals to advertisers because it can reach a large number of consumers and businesses with a relatively low cost per contact, or per exposure. It also offers advertisers the ability to reach highly segmented markets through the many cable channels that are now available.

Bridgestone's Super Bowl Advertising

Bridgestone purchased the rights to "host" the Halftime Show for the 2010 Super Bowl. The Richards Group was retained to develop the ads. As owner-executive Stan Richards recalls, "For the last 3 years, Bridgestone has had a Super Bowl presence, which, in itself, is very interesting. Any time you have an opportunity to be on the Super Bowl is great,

▲ "Whale of a Tale" was one of Bridgestone's Super Bowl advertisements.

▼ "Your Tires or Your Life," another Bridgestone Super Bowl advertisement, used humor to capture viewer attention.

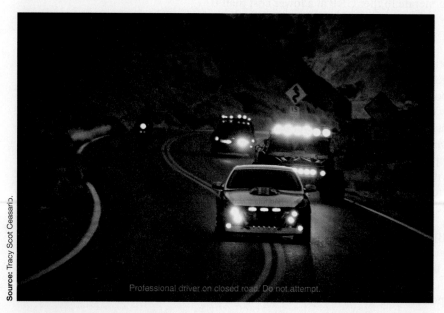

Professional driver on closed road. Do not attempt.

and because of Bridgestone's sponsorship of the Halftime Show, they got a spot in the first quarter and a spot in the second half. We get real excited about that. We work very hard at it. It's the biggest stage in the world. And we want to represent them well.

"We put a lot of teams on it. We probably reviewed upwards of 200 concepts from all the teams. We reduced that to somewhere in the 8, 9, or 10 range, which we took to the client. We wanted to come out of that with the two spots that were going to run in the Super Bowl and one additional spot that would become part of the regular rotation. So, the client then approved three spots for production. As you might imagine, we go all out in terms of production and try to make them as interesting, charming, and endearing as we possibly can."

The three finalists had been sent out for bids to commercial directors and production houses. The three were then scheduled for TV shoots in California and Nevada in late September 2009. After several weeks of editing, the rough cuts were presented to Bridgestone in October. Postproduction editing then occurred, and the final two Super Bowl spots were chosen by Bridgestone in early January. In mid-January 2010, the Bridgestone Facebook Fan Page launched and teasers of the two spots were posted on YouTube to build anticipation for the ads.

The first ad that ran, "Whale of a Tale," employed humor and drama. A whale is hauled by a pickup truck using Bridgestone tires. The truck races to the end of a pier, and the whale is launched into the ocean out of the back of the pickup as the driver slams on the brakes. The punchline "Now that . . . was a bachelor party" follows.

In the second ad, "Your Tires or Your Life," a band of outlaws blockades a driver. The lead henchman proclaims, "Your Bridgestone tires . . . or your life." He becomes confused when, instead of the car's Bridgestone tires being given up as a hostage, a beautiful woman is pushed out of the vehicle. The lead henchman laments, "I said 'life,' not 'wife.'"

Stan Richards is keenly aware of what to expect after the ads run. "You get quick feedback. And happily, we've done exceedingly well in the Super Bowl ad polls." He paused. "I have to tell you, when you go to bed right after the Super Bowl, your last thought is, 'What is it going to say in *USA Today* tomorrow morning?'"[17]

Radio

Despite CDs, iPods, audio books, and other types of audio devices, the vast majority of Americans, approximately 80 percent, still listen to the radio daily.[18] According to Mary Price, "Right now, on a weekly basis terrestrial radio still reaches 93 percent of everybody. It used to be 96 or 97, but it's still up there. As long as they can create a following for local personalities and local events, you can't get that off an iPod. If you want some kind of commentary about the music you're listening to . . . you can't get that on a pre-recorded iPod."[19]

TABLE 8.4 Radio Advertising

Advantages	Disadvantages
1. Recall promoted	1. Short exposure time
2. Narrower target markets	2. Low attention
3. Ad music can match station's programming	3. Few chances to reach national audience
4. High segmentation potential	4. Target duplication when several stations use the same format
5. Flexibility in making new ads	5. Information overload
6. Able to modify ads to fit local conditions	
7. Intimacy (with DJs and radio personalities)	
8. Mobile—people carry radios everywhere	
9. Creative opportunities with music and other sounds	

While radio may not be as glamorous as television, it can be an effective advertising medium. A well-placed, clever ad is a one-on-one message (announcer to driver in a car stuck in traffic). Many smaller local companies rely heavily on radio advertising. Most radio ads are produced locally and with small budgets. Table 8.4 summarizes the advantages and disadvantages of radio advertising.

Advantages of Radio Advertising

Skillful radio advertisers help the listener remember the message by creating powerful images to visualize and by using repetition. This moves the ad from the consumer's short-term to long-term memory. Sound effects and lively tunes assist in this process. Through repetition a person hears an advertisement often enough to assist in recall.

A radio station has definable target markets based on its format, such as talk radio, lite mix, oldies, or country. A firm can advertise on a specific type of station across the country. Radio advertisers can also examine the rating and share of a program as well as the estimated number of people listening to a program. The primary organization that calculates these numbers for local stations is Arbitron. Radio's All-Dimension Audience Research (RADAR) reports ratings for national radio networks.

Radio can create intimacy. Listeners often feel personally close to DJs and radio personalities. The attachment grows over time. Listening to the same individual becomes more personal and intimate, especially if the listener has a conversation with the DJ during a contest or when requesting a song. The bond or intimacy level gives the radio personality a higher level of credibility and an edge to goods and services the radio celebrity endorses.

Beachbody, a fitness brand based in Santa Monica, California, used radio as the prime medium to promote its P90X, a home exercise system that promised total body improvements within 90 days. Fitness and the P90X product require visual images. To create a visual pitch with only audio was challenging. The goal of the campaign was to create enough of a visual in the mind of the listener to drive her to a micro Web site to learn more or place an order.

Robinson Radio from Virginia was contracted to develop and manage the radio campaign. Robinson realized the best approach was to use "radio's secret weapon," the DJs, who used the product, documented their successes, and then described their progress on the air. The DJs also posted their photos on the company's Web site, created chat rooms for listeners, and asked listeners to share their success stories. Early in the campaign it became clear that the micro Web site was a key component of the radio campaign, because it

▼ This advertisement for Mix 95.1 highlights the market niche served by the radio station.

Source: Shutterstock.

▲ Radio enjoys the advantage of intimacy with the local DJ.

allowed communications between the listeners, customers of the product, and the DJs. The other advantage of using radio was that it was easy and inexpensive to make changes to ads as the campaign progressed. The campaign was highly successful in California. Beachbody subsequently expanded the campaign nationally within a few months.[20]

Disadvantages of Radio Advertising

One problem with radio is the short exposure time of an ad. Most radio commercials last 15 or 30 seconds. Listeners involved in other activities, such as driving or working on a computer, may not pay attention to the radio. Further, people often use radio as a background to drown out other distractions, especially at work.

For national advertisers, covering a large area with radio advertisements is challenging. To place a national advertisement requires contacting a large number of companies. Few large radio conglomerates means contacts must be made with multiple stations. Negotiating rates with individual stations based on volume is difficult. Local businesses can often negotiate better rates than national advertisers because of the local company's relationships with the radio stations.

The four main national radio networks in the United States are Westwood One, ABC, CBS, and Unistar. These are joined by a few other strong networks, such as ESPN radio and CNN. Nationally syndicated programs such as those on the Fox radio network offer some opportunities to national advertisers.

In large metropolitan areas, duplication presents another problem. Several radio stations may try to reach the same target market. For instance, Chicago has several rock stations. Advertising on every station may not be financially feasible, yet reaching everyone in that target market will not be possible unless all rock stations are used.

Radio advertising offers a low-cost option for a local firm. Ads can be placed at ideal times and adapted to local conditions. Careful selection of stations, times, and quality construction of the advertisement will be the key. Radio allows local businesses to present remote broadcasts. Remotes can attract attention to a new business (restaurants, retail stores, etc.) or to a company trying to make a major push for immediate customers. Radio promotions can be combined with other media (local television or newspapers) to send more integrated messages.

For business-to-business advertisers, radio provides the opportunity to reach businesses during working hours, because many employees listen to the radio during office hours. Radio can reach businesspeople while in transit to or from work. Both radio and television usage has increased for business-to-business marketing.

Outdoor Advertising

Billboards along major roads are the most common form of outdoor advertising; however, there are other forms. Signs on cabs, buses, park benches, and fences of sports arenas are other types of outdoor advertising. Some would argue that even a blimp flying above a major sporting event is outdoor advertising.

Advances in technology have dramatically changed outdoor advertising. Annual expenditures on outdoor advertisements now total more than $5.5 billion. Global positioning systems, wireless communications, and digital display technology have transformed outdoor advertising. The most popular outdoor technology, LED, is used by companies such as Procter & Gamble and McDonald's. LED technology is used to create video screens for animated videos in locations such as Times Square in New York and the Strip in Las Vegas. It can create both static messages and visuals that change electronically.

TABLE 8.5 Outdoor Advertising

Advantages	Disadvantages
1. Able to select key geographic areas	1. Short exposure time
2. Accessible for local ads	2. Brief messages
3. Low cost per impression	3. Little segmentation possible
4. Broad reach	4. Cluttered travel routes
5. High frequency on major commuter routes	
6. Large, spectacular ads possible	

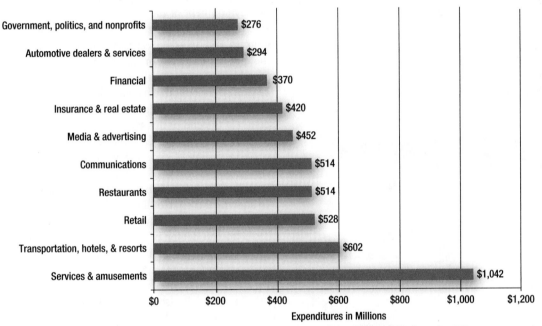

◄ FIGURE 8.7
Expenditures on
Outdoor Advertising

Government, politics, and nonprofits $276
Automotive dealers & services $294
Financial $370
Insurance & real estate $420
Media & advertising $452
Communications $514
Restaurants $514
Retail $528
Transportation, hotels, & resorts $602
Services & amusements $1,042

Expenditures in Millions

Source: Adapted from "Outdoor Advertising Expenditures, 2009 January–June," *TNS Media Intelligence/CMR OAAA*, September 2009.

Table 8.5 lists the advantages and disadvantages of outdoor ads. Figure 8.7 shows a breakdown of outdoor spending.

Advantages of Outdoor Advertising
One primary advantage of billboard advertising is long life. For local companies, billboards are an excellent advertising medium, because the message will primarily be seen by local audiences. It is also a low-cost media outlet in terms of cost per impression. Outdoor advertising offers a broad reach and a high level of frequency if multiple billboards are purchased. Every person who travels past a billboard or sees an advertisement on a taxi has the potential for being exposed to the message. Many billboard companies provide rotation packages in which an ad moves to different locations throughout an area during the course of the year, thereby increasing the ad's reach.

▼ Outdoor advertising in Times Square.

▲ A billboard advertisement for The Snoring Center with the theme "Snoring Kills."

▲ A series of ads for the Unleashed dog park was created by Pink Jacket Creative to gain the attention of motorists, causing them to wonder what the total message would be.

Disadvantages of Outdoor Advertising

A major drawback of outdoor advertising is the short exposure time. Drivers must pay attention to the traffic as they travel by a billboard. As a result, messages must be short. When the ad is placed on a vehicle, pedestrians often get only a quick look. Most either ignore outdoor ads or give them just a casual glance. Ironically, in large cities along major arteries the cost of billboard spots has increased. The reason: traffic jams. People stuck in slow-moving traffic spend more time looking at billboards. If this space is not available, a firm can seek billboard locations where traffic stops for signals or at stop signs.

In the past, outdoor advertising was seldom considered in the planning of an integrated marketing communications program or the development of the media plan. Today, outdoor advertising can be the critical component of an IMC program and, in some cases, the primary medium. The advertisements for the Snoring Center displayed in this section utilized outdoor advertising as the primary medium. The campaign is described in greater detail in the Integrated Campaigns in Action section at the end of this chapter.

The Pink Jacket Creative advertising agency created a feeling of expectancy and mystery with its "Unleashed Dog Park" campaign, which featured the three successive billboards shown in this section. As shown, the first billboard displays a dog on a leash. Next, the dog, now with an unfastened leash, moves to the center of the billboard, and "unlea" appears in the top-right corner. In the final billboard, the dog is on the right side of the billboard, the leash is gone, and the message "Unleashed indoor dog parks" appears. It also displays the services offered, the Web address of the park, and the location of the facility. In addition to billboards, street kiosks and bus wraps were used to get the message out.

Magazines

For many advertisers, magazines have been a secondary choice. Recent research indicates that in some cases magazines can be a quality option. An Affinity Research study suggests that half of magazine readers either take action, such as accessing a Web site, or have more favorable opinions about magazine advertisers. Several studies indicate that magazines are a strong driver of purchase intentions and boost the effectiveness of other media.[21] One study concluded that every dollar a company spends on magazine advertising yields an average of $8.23 in sales. The average return on investment for all other media is $3.52 per advertising dollar spent. The reason for this difference may be magazine advertising's ability to target consumers more efficiently by demographics and lifestyles.[22] Table 8.6 displays the pros and cons of magazine advertising.

Advantages of Magazine Advertising

Magazines can create high levels of market segmentation by topic area. Even within certain market segments, such as automobiles, a number of magazines exist. High audience

TABLE 8.6 Magazine Advertising

Advantages	Disadvantages
1. High market segmentation	1. Declining readership (some magazines)
2. Targeted audience interest by magazine	2. High level of clutter
3. Direct-response techniques (e.g., coupons, Web addresses, toll-free numbers)	3. Long lead time
4. High color quality	4. Little flexibility
5. Availability of special features (e.g., scratch and sniff)	5. High cost
6. Long life	
7. Read during leisure time (longer attention to ad)	

interest constitutes another advantage. An individual who subscribes to *Modern Bride* has an attraction to weddings. People reading magazines also tend to view and pay attention to advertisements related to their needs and wants. Often, readers linger over an ad for a longer period of time because they read magazines in waiting situations, such as in a doctor's office, or during leisure time. The high level of interest, segmentation, and differentiation, when combined with high-quality color, are ideal for products with precisely defined target markets.

Trade and business journals are a major medium for business-to-business marketing. Businesses target advertisements to buying center members. The ad's copy can provide a greater level of detail about products. Interested readers will take more time to study the information provided in the advertisement. Ads can mention toll-free telephone numbers and Web addresses so that interested parties can obtain further information.

Magazines have long lives that reach beyond an immediate issue. An avid magazine reader may examine a particular issue several times and spend a considerable amount of time with each issue. Advertisers know the reader will be exposed to the ad more than once and might be more likely to pay attention. Other individuals may also review the magazine. In the business-to-business sector, trade journals are often passed around to several individuals or members of the buying center. As long as the magazine lasts, the advertisement is still there to be viewed.

Disadvantages of Magazine Advertising

While overall readership of magazines has declined, the trend is less evident among "influential Americans." Individuals with incomes of $100,000 or more read an average of 15.3 publications, and individuals with incomes over $250,000 read an average of 23.8.[23] Magazine advertisements require a great deal of lead time. They are expensive to prepare. They may be less viable for more general consumption products, such as basic necessities.

Magazines continue to be an effective medium for advertising. Although business-to-business marketers increasingly use other media, trade journals and business magazines remain an effective method of reaching their target markets. For both consumer and business

▼ This Treetop advertisement targets new mothers and appears in magazines such as *Parenting*.

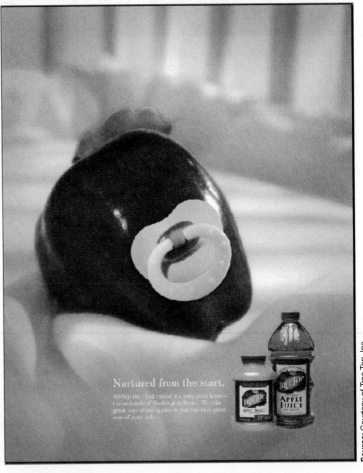

Source: Courtesy of Tree Top, Inc.

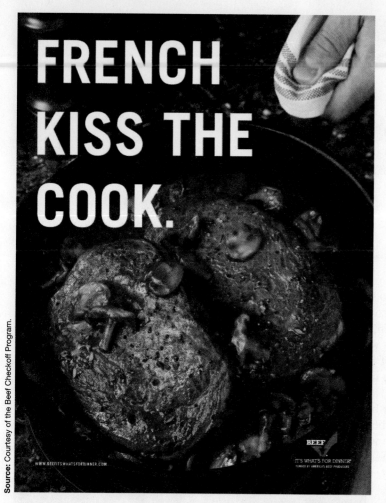

▲ Advertisers can target specific market segments with magazines, making it an attractive medium for ads such as this one for the beef industry.

markets, it appears that magazines, used in conjunction with other media, can enhance the effectiveness of an advertising campaign.

Newspapers

When *USA Today* was launched, few believed a national daily newspaper could succeed. Obviously it has. The nature of news reporting has changed. Many small local papers no longer exist, and conglomerates, such as Gannett, own most major city newspapers. Still, daily readership continues.

For many smaller local firms, newspaper ads, billboards, and local radio programs are the most viable advertising options. Newspapers can be distributed daily, weekly, or in partial form as the advertising supplements found in the front sections of many grocery stores and retail outlets. Table 8.7 displays the advantages and disadvantages of newspaper advertising.

Advantages of Newspaper Advertising

Many retailers rely heavily on newspaper ads because they offer geographic selectivity (local market access). Promoting sales, retail hours, and store locations is easier in a newspaper advertisement. Short lead time allows retailers to change ads and promotions quickly. This flexibility is a major advantage. It allows advertisers the ability to keep ads current. Ads can be modified to meet competitive offers or to focus on recent events.

Newspapers have high levels of credibility. Readers rely on newspapers for factual information in stories. Newspaper readers hold high interest levels in the articles. They tend to pay more attention to advertisements as well as news stories. This increased audience interest allows advertisers to provide more copy detail in ads. Newspaper readers will take more time to read advertising copy, unless simply too much information is jammed into a small space.

Recognizing a match between newspaper readers and its customer base, Starbucks launched a unique newspaper campaign designed by the agency Wieden + Kennedy of Portland, Oregon. Starbucks invited coffee drinkers to stop at a local Starbucks for a free cup of coffee on March 15. Four-page full-color ads were placed in daily newspapers of 11 major markets, including New York, Los Angeles, Chicago, Boston, and Dallas. The ads were placed in the newspapers the week before the giveaway and again the day before. Then, on the day of the giveaway, Starbucks hired street vendors to pass out free copies of the newspapers that contained the Starbucks ad. The newspapers were banded

TABLE 8.7 Newspaper Advertising	
Advantages	**Disadvantages**
1. Geographic selectivity	1. Poor buying procedures
2. High flexibility	2. Short life span
3. High credibility	3. Major clutter (especially holidays)
4. Strong audience interest	4. Poor quality reproduction (especially color)
5. Longer copy	5. Internet competition with classified ads
6. Cumulative volume discounts	
7. Coupons and special-response features	

with the distinctive Starbuck's coffee cup sleeve. The campaign cost $545,000, but resulted in a half-million customers going into a Starbucks store. In some locations lines wrapped around the block. Starbucks estimated the newspaper campaign resulted in 12 million impressions.[24]

Disadvantages of Newspaper Advertising

Newspapers cannot be targeted as easily to specific market segments (although sports pages carry sports ads, entertainment pages contain movie and restaurant ads, and so forth). Newspapers have a short life. Once read, a newspaper normally will be cast to the side, recycled, or destroyed. If a reader does not see an advertisement during the first pass through a newspaper, it probably will go unnoticed. Readers rarely pick up papers a second time. When they do, it is to continue reading, not to reread or rescan a section that has already been viewed.

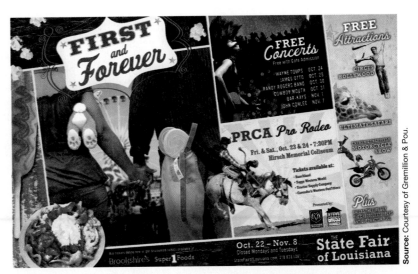

Source: Courtesy of Gremillion & Pou.

▲ Newspapers are ideal for advertising events, such as the State Fair of Louisiana.

Media Mix

Selecting the proper blend of media outlets for advertisements is crucial. As campaigns are prepared, decisions are made regarding the appropriate mix of media. Media planners and media buyers are both excellent sources of information about the most effective type of mix for a particular advertising campaign. Figure 8.8 displays the media mix in the United States for Coca-Cola. Total U.S. spending for advertising by Coca-Cola was $752 million; 63.4 percent went to television advertising. Coca-Cola spent far less on the other media.[25]

Recent studies by Millward Brown and ACNielsen highlight the benefits of combining media.[26] The Millward Brown report states that ad awareness was strongest when consumers were exposed to an advertisement on television and in a magazine. Ad awareness was considerably lower for only those who read the magazine ad and even less for those who only saw the television commercial.

The **media multiplier effect** suggests that the combined impact of using two or more media is stronger than using either medium alone. The British insurance company Churchill discovered that 62 percent of consumers who saw the company's TV commercial and heard its radio ad planned to look into Churchill Insurance, compared to 49 percent who only saw only the television advertisement.[27]

6 How can the marketing team use the media mix to increase advertising effectiveness?

◀ **FIGURE 8.8**
U.S. Advertising Expenditures by Media for Coca-Cola

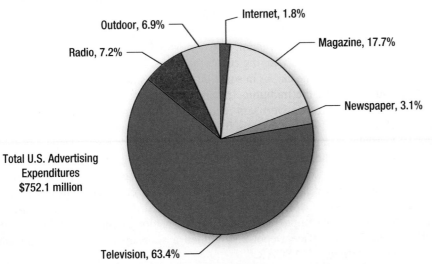

Internet, 1.8%

Outdoor, 6.9%

Radio, 7.2%

Magazine, 17.7%

Newspaper, 3.1%

Total U.S. Advertising Expenditures $752.1 million

Television, 63.4%

Source: Adapted from *Marketer Trees 2009*, **http://adage.com/marketertrees09**, December 28, 2009.

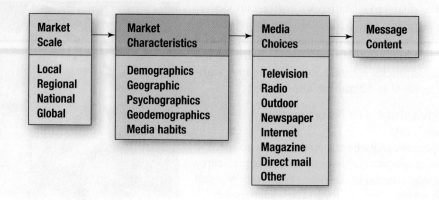

The media multiplier effect is equally important in business-to-business advertising. In a survey conducted by American Business Media, 89 percent of the business respondents indicated that an integrated marketing approach raised their awareness of a company or brand. Seeing advertisements in more than one medium caused the company or brand name to become top-of-mind. It also resulted in more businesses making purchases.[28] Finding effective combinations of media is the key to the media multiplier effect.

Figure 8.9 shows the process for choosing the best media for a particular advertising message. Media experts decide which go best together for individual target markets, goods and services, and advertising messages.

MEDIA SELECTION IN BUSINESS-TO-BUSINESS MARKETS

7 What are the key issues associated with media selection for business-to-business markets?

Identifying differences between consumer ads and business-to-business ads has become more difficult, especially on television, outdoor, and the Internet. In the past, it was easy to spot business-to-business ads. The content was aimed at another company. Television, outdoor, and the Internet were seldom used. Currently, over half of all business advertising dollars are now spent in nonbusiness environments.[29]

Several explanations have been offered regarding the shift to nonbusiness media. First, business decision makers also consume goods and services. The same psychological techniques used to influence and gain consumer attention can be used for business decision makers.

Second, business decision makers are difficult to reach at work. Gatekeepers (secretaries, voice mail systems, etc.) often prevent the flow of information to users, influencers, and decision makers. This is especially true in straight rebuy situations in which orders are routinely placed with the current vendor. Any company that is not the chosen vendor finds it difficult to make contact with buying center members. Business-to-business vendors try to reach them at home, in the car, or in some other nonbusiness venue.

Third, clutter among the traditional business media makes it more difficult to get a company noticed. Business advertisers recognize that a strong brand name is a major factor in making a sale. Taking lessons from major giants such as Nike, Wal-Mart, and Procter & Gamble, business marketers seek to develop strong brands, because the name helps a company gain the attention of members of the buying center.

Office Depot recently launched an advertising campaign directed toward the business buyers that comprise approximately 80 percent of the company's customer base. The campaign, titled "Takin' Care of Business," highlighted the company's commitment to business customers. The campaign included TV spots, along with radio, print, online, and search marketing ads. Office Depot also signed a sponsorship deal to be the official office products partner of NASCAR.[30]

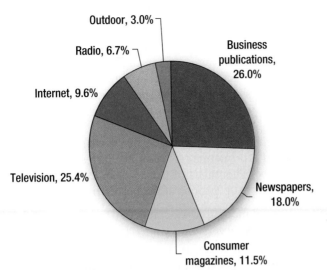

Source: Based on Kate Maddox, "Top 100 B-to-B Advertisers Increased Spending 3% in '06," *B to B* 92, no. 11 (September 10, 2007).

◄ FIGURE 8.10
Business-to-Business
Advertising Expenditures

In the past, business ads were fairly dull. They now are more likely to resemble ads aimed at consumers. Creative appeals and the use of music, humor, sex, and fear are used. The boldest business ads sometimes include nudity or other more risqué material.

Figure 8.10 identifies the ways business-to-business advertising expenditures are divided among the various media. In the past, business publications would account for most of the expenditures, often assuming half of the dollars. Business publications now account for about one-fourth of the more than $14 billion that is spent annually on business-to-business advertising. As more dollars are shifted to nonbusiness types of media, the amount being spent on television, newspapers, and consumer magazines has steadily increased.[31]

Although the use of business publications has decreased, trade journals still provide an excellent opportunity to contact members of the buying center whom salespeople cannot reach. Gatekeepers do not prevent trade journals from being sent to members of the buying center. An advertisement has the best chance of success when a firm makes modified rebuy and the buying center is in the information search stage.

In addition to trade journals, business-to-business advertisers also use business magazines such as *BusinessWeek*. These publications have highly selective audiences, and the ads have longer life spans in print. Business decision makers and members of the buying center spend more working time examining print media than any other medium.

At the same time, buying center members are still more likely to notice the WingspanBank.com ad shown on this page when it is located in a trade journal than they would in a general-audience type magazine such as *Time*. The trade journal's readers are more likely to notice and read the advertisement, because they are more likely to have been working with or thinking about banking or financial services within their companies.

Many goals in business-to-business advertisements are the same as those devoted to consumers. Most of the variables shown in Figure 8.9 apply equally well to business advertising.

▼ An advertisement for Internet banking.

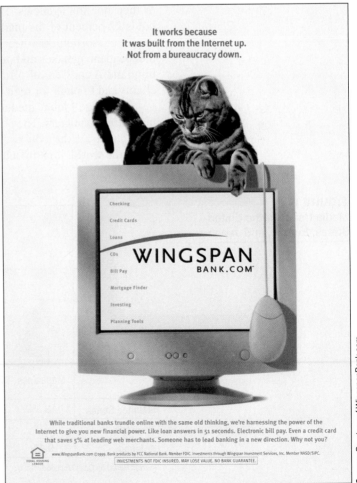

Source: Courtesy of WingspanBank.com.

INTERNATIONAL IMPLICATIONS

8 What issues are associated with media selection in international markets?

Understanding media viewing habits in international markets continues to be an important part of a successful advertising program. In Japan, television is a major advertising tool; in other countries, it is not as prevalent. In Europe, the best way to reach consumers is through print media; magazines and newspapers account for 51.5 percent of total ad spending. Figure 8.11 illustrates differences in media usage in the United States, Europe, and Japan.

For several years, reports have surfaced that teenagers are watching less TV and spending more time on the Internet. A study by Forrester Research contradicted that notion, at least in Europe. Thousands of teenagers in Europe were surveyed about their media usage.[32] The general conclusions of the Forrester study are that:

- European teens spend more time watching TV than they do with any other medium, averaging 10.3 hours per week.
- Average personal time on the Internet is 9.1 hours per week.
- Europeans ages 10 to 17 spend less time on the Internet than individuals 18 and older.
- Only 41 percent of European teens visit social networks at least once a week.
- Teenagers like to multitask—watching TV while texting friends or playing video games while listening to music or TV.
- Younger European teens love video games, playing twice as much as individuals 18 and older.
- Most teenagers do not read the paper. They get news from TV or the Internet.

Although there are a large number of media buying agencies throughout the world, nearly three-quarters of all media buying is conducted by only six large global agencies or their holding agencies. The largest global media company is the WPP Group, which holds 22 percent of the market share.[33] To combat these large media networks, a global media consortium has been formed. The consortium consists of a number of smaller independent agencies and offers services in Europe, North America, the Russian Federation, and Asia. Central offices are located in New York and London to serve business clients and to pitch for regional and national accounts.[34]

The large global media agencies have faced some criticism in recent years from marketing managers. They complain about the inability to provide effective media buys throughout all the countries where the clients operate. Although a few agencies do cover the world, it is difficult to be strong in every country where an agency may have

FIGURE 8.11 ▶
Media Usage in the United States, Europe, and Japan

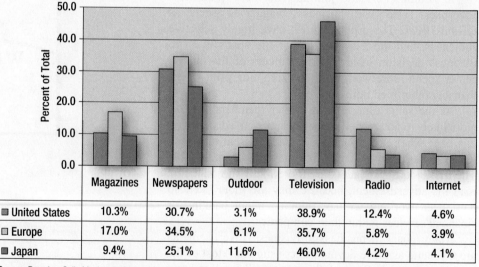

	Magazines	Newspapers	Outdoor	Television	Radio	Internet
▣ United States	10.3%	30.7%	3.1%	38.9%	12.4%	4.6%
▢ Europe	17.0%	34.5%	6.1%	35.7%	5.8%	3.9%
▣ Japan	9.4%	25.1%	11.6%	46.0%	4.2%	4.1%

Source: Based on Colin MacLeod, "Global Adspend Trends," *International Journal of Advertising* 24, no. 2 (2005), pp. 261–62.

a presence. The global agency may not be the best option in every country. For this reason, local media agencies and the consortium of independent agencies believe they have a chance to increase their market share.

In general, the tactics used to develop advertising campaigns and choose appropriate media in the United States apply to other countries throughout the world. What differs is the nature of the target markets, consumer media preferences, and the processes used to buy media. Company representatives carefully attend to cultural mores to make sure the buying process does not offend the cultural and religious attitudes in any given region. The goal is to fully understand the target market as a company purchases advertising time or space and prepares advertising campaigns.

! INTEGRATED CAMPAIGNS IN ACTION

The Snoring Center

In the past decade, the Pink Jacket Creative advertising agency, led by co-owners Bill Breedlove and Elena Baca, helped develop a highly successful advertising program for a medical company—The Snoring Center. According to Breedlove, "When we first started working with The Snoring Center, a physician had an office here in Dallas. He decided he wanted to start treating snoring and sleep apnea. Did you know that 46 percent of adults snore? 25 percent snore habitually? Of that, 23 percent of married couples regularly sleep apart because of sleep apnea."

To develop brand awareness for The Snoring Center, the central component of the advertising program was billboards, with television and print ads as support media. Bill Breedlove recalls, "It was a really simple outdoor campaign. We put up branded billboards that said simply, 'Snoring Kills . . . ,' and then underneath it would have something that it kills, such as 'it kills careers' or 'it kills your love life,' or 'it kills your mojo,' or 'your morning quickies,' or 'your afternoon delight,' and so on.

"We ran a 26 week outdoor campaign, where we changed every Monday what snoring kills by just supplying a snipe (a banner), which kept the budget down. We able to take a branding commodity like a billboard and turn it into a direct response vehicle.

"The phones started ringing after about 6 weeks. And while getting patients to come in and get treatment was our objective, there was also really fun stuff. We would have people call and say 'I'm going to be on vacation next week, and I can't stand it. Can you tell me what snoring is going to kill this week?' It was just a really simple and fun campaign. We like breaking rules and making billboards lead to phone calls, that sort of thing."

Within a year and a half, the physician shut his ENT practice down and had two locations of The Snoring Center. Within 24 months, The Snoring Center became the world's leading provider of minimally invasive snoring treatment. The company now performs more procedures than any other provider in the world.[35]

Your instructor has additional information about the ads, visuals, and displays used in this campaign.

Source: Courtesy of Pink Jacket Creative: A Creative Factory.

▲ Billboard ads were the central component of the campaign for The Snoring Center.

SUMMARY

In traditional advertising, the roles of media planners and media buyers have grown in importance. According to Bob Brennan, chief operating officer of Chicago-based Leo Burnett Starcom USA, in the past "Ninety-five percent of your success was great creative and 5 percent was great media. Now it's much closer to 50–50."[36]

A media strategy is the process of analyzing and choosing media for an advertising and promotions campaign. Media planners and buyers complete much of this work. The media planner's primary job is to formulate a program stating where and when to place advertisements. Media planners work closely with creatives and account executives. Media buyers purchase the space, and they negotiate rates, times, and schedules for the ads.

The goals of reach, frequency, opportunity to see, gross rating points, effective rating points, cost, continuity, and gross impressions drive the media selection process. Reach is the number of people, households, or businesses in a target audience exposed to a media vehicle or message schedule at least once during a given time period. Frequency is the average number of times an individual, household, or business within a particular target market is exposed to a particular advertisement within a specified time period. Gross rating points (GRPs) measure the impact or intensity of a media plan. Cost per thousand (CPM) is one method of finding the cost of the campaign by assessing the dollar cost of reaching 1,000 members of the media vehicle's audience. Cost per rating point (CPRP) is a second cost measure, which assesses the efficiency of a media vehicle relative to a firm's target market. Ratings measure the percentage of a firm's target market that is exposed to a show on television or an article in a print medium. Continuity is the schedule or pattern of advertisement placements within an advertising campaign period. Gross impressions are the number of total exposures of the audience to an advertisement.

The three-exposure hypothesis suggests that a consumer must be exposed to an ad at least three times before it has the desired impact; other experts believe even more exposures are necessary. In contrast, recency theory suggests that ads truly reach only those wanting or needing a product and that the carryover effects of advertising diminish rapidly. It is necessary, therefore, to advertise on a continuous basis to ensure that the message is noticed by consumers when a purchase decision is made.

In addition to these basic concepts, advertising experts often utilize the concepts of effective frequency and effective reach. Effective frequency is the number of times a target audience must be exposed to a message to achieve a particular objective. Effective reach is the percentage of an audience that must be exposed to a particular message to achieve a specific objective.

In seeking advertising goals, marketing experts, account executives, and others assess the relative advantages and disadvantages of each individual advertising medium. Thus, television, radio, outdoor, magazines, and newspapers should all be considered as potential ingredients in a campaign. Other new media can be used to complement and supplement the more traditional media outlets. Logical combinations of media should be chosen.

In business-to-business settings, companies can combine consumer media outlets with trade journals and other business venues (trade shows, conventions, etc.) to attempt to reach members of the buying center. In many cases, enticing ads using consumer appeals such as sex, fear, and humor have replaced dry, dull, boring ads with an abundance of copy.

International advertising media selection is different in some ways from that which takes place in the United States, because media buying processes differ as do media preferences of locals in various countries. At the same time, the process of media selection is quite similar. Marketing experts choose media they believe will reach the target audience in an effective manner.

KEY TERMS

media strategy The process of analyzing and choosing media for an advertising and promotions campaign.

media planner The individual who formulates the media program stating where and when to place advertisements.

media buyer The person who buys the media space and negotiates rates, times, and schedules for the ads.

spot ad A one-time ad placed on a local television station.

reach The number of people, households, or businesses in a target audience exposed to a media vehicle or message schedule at least once during a given time period.

frequency The average number of times an individual, household, or business within a particular target market is exposed to a particular advertisement within a specified time period.

opportunities to see (OTS) The cumulative exposures to an advertisement that are achieved in a given time period.

gross rating points (GRPs) A measure of the impact or intensity of a media plan.

cost per thousand (CPM) The dollar cost of reaching 1,000 members of the media vehicle's audience.

ratings A measure of the percentage of a firm's target market that is exposed to a show on television or an article in a print medium.

cost per rating point (CPRP) A measure of the efficiency of a media vehicle relative to a firm's target market.

weighted (or demographic) CPM A measure used to calculate whether an advertisement reached the target market effectively.

continuity The schedule or pattern of advertisement placements within an advertising campaign period.

gross impressions The number of total exposures of the audience to an advertisement.

intrusion value The ability of media or an advertisement to intrude upon a viewer without his or her voluntary attention.

effective reach The percentage of an audience that must be exposed to a particular message to achieve a specific objective.

effective frequency The number of times a target audience must be exposed to a message to achieve a particular objective.

media multiplier effect The combined impact of using two or more media is stronger than using either medium alone.

REVIEW QUESTIONS

1. What is a media strategy? How does it relate to the creative brief and the overall IMC program?
2. What does a media planner do?
3. Describe the role of media buyer in an advertising program.
4. What is reach? Give examples of reach in various advertising media.
5. What is frequency? How can an advertiser increase frequency in a campaign?
6. What are gross rating points? What do they measure?
7. What is the difference between CPM and CPRP? What costs do they measure?
8. What is continuity?
9. Describe the three-exposure hypothesis.
10. How does recency theory differ from the three-exposure hypothesis?
11. What is effective frequency? Effective reach?
12. What are the major advantages and disadvantages of television advertising?

13. What are the major advantages and disadvantages of radio advertising?
14. What are the major advantages and disadvantages of outdoor advertising?
15. What are the major advantages and disadvantages of magazine advertising?
16. What are the major advantages and disadvantages of newspaper advertising?
17. Is the strong intrusion value of television an advantage? Why or why not?
18. What special challenges does media selection present for businesses? What roles do gatekeepers play in creating those challenges?
19. What special challenges does media selection present for international advertising campaigns? What differences and similarities exist with U.S. media selection processes?

CRITICAL THINKING EXERCISES

Discussion Questions

1. To be effective, multiple media should be chosen and integrated carefully. Individuals who are exposed to advertisements in combinations of media selected from television, radio, magazines, newspapers and outdoor are more inclined to process the information than when only a solitary medium is used. For each of the media, what is the probability of you being exposed to an advertisement? The percentages should add up to 100 percent. Discuss which media are most effective in reaching you. Explain.

2. Billboard advertising in Times Square is so popular that space has already been sold for the next 10 years. Coca-Cola, General Motors, Toshiba, Prudential, NBC,

Budweiser, and *The New York Times* are paying rates in excess of $100,000 per month to hold these spaces. Why would companies pay so much for outdoor advertising? What are the advantages and disadvantages of purchasing billboards at Times Square?

3. The Super Bowl is the most watched program on television. Many tune in just to watch the ads. Interview 10 individuals of various ages, genders, and ethnicities. Ask each what they thought of last year's Super Bowl ads. Summarize what you were told. Based on these interviews, how effective is Super Bowl advertising? Is it worth paying $1 to $2 million for 30 seconds? What about for business-to-business ads? Do you think the Super Bowl is a good venue for business-to-business advertising?

4. Xerox offers a color printer that sells for $1,200. The goal is to market it to business buyers. What media mix would you suggest for a $20 million advertising campaign? Justify your answer.

5. Use the Internet or phone directory to identify all of the radio stations in your area. What type of format does each have (i.e., talk, country, hip hop, rock, etc.)? Is radio a good advertising medium to reach college students at your university? Why or why not? Which of the radio stations on your list would be the most effective in reaching college students?

6. As you drive to school (or home) make a list of all of the billboards and outdoor advertising you see. Which are the most effective? Why? Which are the least effective? Why? How effective are billboards at reaching you with an advertising message?

7. Pick five different magazines on a wide range of topics. For each, describe the types of ads and the number of ads in the issue. Did you see any business-to-business ads? What similarities did you see in the ads across the five magazines? What differences did you notice? Which would be most effective at reaching people in your demographic?

INTEGRATED LEARNING EXERCISES

1. Go to the Life Section of *USA Today* (**www.usatoday.com /life/default.htm**) and locate the Nielsen ratings. What were the top five television shows last week? What other information is available at the Web site about Nielsen ratings?

2. The table below provides the population of the top 10 demographic marketing areas (DMAs). The target market for a particular company is yuppie boomers, or those 35 to 54 years old who are professionals or managers. Based on the percentage of adults in each DMA that fits the target market profile, calculate the size of the target market in each DMA. Washington, D.C. has been completed for you. If you had funds to advertise in only 5 of the 10 DMAs, which five would you choose? Why?

3. In Canada, a valuable source of information is BBM (Bureau of Broadcast Measurement). Access this Web site at **www.bbm.ca**. What type of information is available on the site? What media does the BBM cover? How can it be used to develop a media plan for Canada?

4. A trade organization for magazines is the Magazine Publishers of America. Access the association's Web site at **www.magazine.org**. What type of information is available?

How could it be used by a company wanting to advertise in magazines?

5. Two Web sites that are important for radio advertising are the Radio Advertising Bureau at **www.rab.com** and the top 100 radio sites at **www.100topradiosites.com**. Access both sites. What information is available on each site? Discuss how the information can be used to develop an advertising plan using radio.

6. A major company for outdoor advertising is Lamar Advertising Company. Access its Web site at **www.lamar.com**. Access the outdoor advertising component of the company and locate the rates for your area or another area of interest to you. What type of outdoor advertising is available? What other products does Lamar offer? What services does Lamar offer? Write a short report on what types of advertising Lamar can provide for a company.

7. One of the best sources of information for business-to-business advertisers is *BtoB* at **www.btobonline.com**. What type of information is available at this Web site? How can it be used? What benefits would a business-to-business advertiser derive from the Web site?

DMA	Population	DMA Percent	Number in Target Market
Washington, D.C.	3,965,200	18.4%	729,600
San Francisco–Oakland	4,824,600	14.2	
Boston	4,495,600	13.6	
Dallas–Ft. Worth	3,669,900	13.3	
Houston	3,251,100	13.1	
New York	14,432,500	12.0	
Chicago	6,483,800	11.7	
Philadelphia	5,655,800	11.6	
Los Angeles	11,391,200	11.3	
Detroit	3,549,600	11.1	

STUDENT PROJECT

Creative Corner

Coca-Cola has created its own Digital Network, a group of 28 electronic billboards in 27 different markets. Although Coca-Cola leases the outdoor space, it owns the 14- by 48-feet LED screens. This allows Coca-Cola to advertise its products 24 hours a day, 7 days a week. It provides greater flexibility in changing ads and also in partnering with retail grocery stores, such as Kroger. By controlling the message on the LED billboards, Coca-Cola is also able to test different billboard ads and determine the optimal number of times an ad should change on the screen and how long it should be used before motorists tune it out.[37]

Design an advertising campaign for Coca-Cola for the Digital Network. Carefully explain how you intend to use this medium. Match it with an executional framework that can take advantage of the technology. Create a new tagline for Coca-Cola to be used in all the Digital Network advertisements.

CASE 1 AUTO INSURANCE: MIXING MEDIA AND MESSAGES

In 2009, over 136 million cars were being driven in the United States and there were more than 240 million vehicles on the roads. Each one requires some form of insurance to protect the driver, other drivers, and the vehicle itself. The massive marketplace for auto insurance that results has induced a great number of companies to try to gain a share of the market.

Two major auto insurance providers include GEICO and Allstate. Both feature well-recognized advertising campaigns. The approaches used by these companies are quite different.

GEICO has developed two major continuing themes along with streams of other types. The first major theme features the GEICO Gecko, with an Australian accent, that has a major following among viewers. In 2010, many of the advertisements were humorous interactions between the Gecko and a company executive. The ads used mild humor and featured the tagline, "15 minutes could save you 15% or more on car insurance."

The second major theme is the GEICO "Caveman" series of commercials, which also use humor. Each ad in the series notes that GEICO is so simple that "even a caveman" can see the advantages GEICO offers. The theme has been tied to many campaigns, including one as a sponsor of NHL hockey. Actor Ben Wilson has played the primary caveman role over the years.

Other GEICO approaches have featured celebrities, including Little Richard, Joan Rivers, James Lipton, and Peter Frampton, making fun of themselves. A recent campaign began with spokesperson Mike McGlone, who has a highly distinctive voice, asking, "Could switching to GEICO really save you 15% or more on car insurance? Does Charlie Daniels play a mean fiddle?" Other similar rhetorical questions are posed about other situations, including Elmer Fudd and "Does a 10-pound bag of flour make a really big biscuit?"

In contrast, Allstate employs the same spokesperson, actor Dennis Haysbert, in all of its ads. Allstate presents a new aspect of the company's insurance in each campaign. One campaign noted that the company has a "first-accident forgiveness" policy that does not penalize drivers for being involved in a fender bender.

Another campaign reminds car owners that Allstate gives discounts to good drivers. Allstate shrinks the deductible for each year that a driver goes without an accident. A new campaign features a safe driver bonus, in which the price of renewing Allstate insurance goes down every 6 months that the drive goes without an accident.

Following the 2009 recession, the "Back to Basics" campaign noted that Allstate opened during the Great Depression and has survived 12 recessions. Haysbert states, "Protect the good things. Put them in good hands." In another ad he states that this could be "The recession that made us great."

Both GEICO and Allstate campaigns are supported by other media, including billboards, print, and others. Both companies spend a great deal of money developing high-

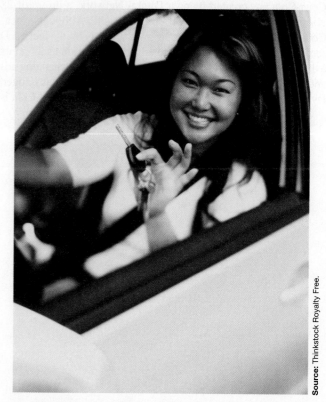

▲ GEICO and Allstate use different advertising approaches to lure customers.

quality, memorable advertisements. Both have large numbers of policyholders.

1. Which approach do you believe is most effective at creating intrusion value? Which approach is best at creating brand recognition and recall? Brand loyalty?

2. Why does GEICO use a humor approach? Why does Allstate use a more serious approach?

3. Which support media work best for these two companies? Which would be less valuable?

4. When purchasing insurance, which is more important, effective reach or effective frequency? Why?

5. Compare the advertising of GEICO and Allstate to that of other insurance companies. In your opinion, which company has the most effective advertising? Why? Which company has the worst advertising? Why? Finally, does advertising make an impact on what insurance company is used?

MAINSTREAMING HEAD SHAVING

CASE 2

Todd Green's hair history features a common story. At a relatively young age, he began to experience male-pattern baldness, a development that affects nearly 20 million men in the United States. Todd considered the options, including hair plugs, medicines, and creams, and of course, a rug. Eventually he decided to go with the flow and became a head shaver.

Inspiration then met the situation. Todd's frustrations were twofold. First, traditional razors are hard to manage because the handle moves awkwardly when cropping the day's growth. Other products, such as clippers, electric shavers, and depilatories, just didn't suit his needs. Second, being a night shaver meant that he was often faced with a five o'clock shadow the next afternoon. While pondering the dilemma, Todd did the natural thing and rubbed his head. Inspiration arrived. He concluded that it would be much easier to shave his head if he could just put the blade above his finger.

Not long after, the HeadBlade was born. Todd first tried selling the innovation to companies such as Gillette and Schick. When they showed no interest, he formed his own company with money he borrowed from his father and his friends. He quit his job and worked for 2 years to develop the first version (go to **www.headblade.com** to see an actual photo).

The HeadBlade was first sold through an e-commerce program. A great deal of free publicity followed, with features in a wide variety of magazine articles and mentions on television programs. The HeadBlade received several awards for innovation, including prizes from Summit Creative, *Time*, *I.D. Magazine*, and eventually the Museum of Modern Art.

The HeadBlade Company now offers the basic product for about $13.00, plus HeadShed Lotion and HeadShade Sunscreen, as well as fashion merchandise, most notably T-shirts. The company sells travel kits and other methods to carry the product.

Green does not believe his product is just a fad. His company's sales have reached $10 million annually. He has developed ties with the International Fight League, with comedian Howie Mandel, and with former NBA player John Amaechi. As he put it, "We're going after both the X Games demographic and the average guy who shaves his head. We want to be the Home Depot of head care." From a marketing perspective, The HeadBlade faces two challenges. The first is

Source: Author Supplied Image.

▲ The HeadBlade provides an excellent alternative to shaving with a traditional straight-edge razor.

the likelihood of being copied by similar products, possibly from larger, mainstream companies. The second is finding ways to advertise the company's product on a national and international scale. This will undoubtedly include greater use of traditional media.

1. Discuss the concepts of reach and frequency as they would apply to advertising the HeadBlade.

2. Would the three-exposure hypothesis or the recency theory best explain the purchase of a HeadBlade?

3. Which traditional media are best suited to advertising the HeadBlade? Which do not fit?

4. Design a national and an international advertising program for the HeadBlade, identifying the target markets and methods to reach them.

Sources: **www.headblade.com** (accessed January 10, 2008); "First Person: A Cut Above: Todd Green Makes a Business out of Baldness," *BusinessWeek* (**www.businessweekonline.com**, accessed January 10, 2008), December 2007.

9 E-Active Marketing

MARKETING ZEN

Imagine a situation in which a person walking down a very busy street is suddenly handed a bullhorn. The person may or may not have been encouraged to say something and really has no idea what to say. In essence, this is the dilemma many companies face. In the past decade, new megaphones named Facebook, Twitter, Yahoo!, Google, YouTube, MySpace, the blogosphere, and others have emerged, and company leaders wonder if they should use them and, if so, how.

Marketing Zen offers solutions to the social media dilemma. Founder and owner Shama Kabani has been described as one of the "10 Most Influential and Powerful Women in Social Media." She notes, "We take over online marketing for companies; we handle everything from soup to nuts. We handle their Web site, their SEO [search engine optimization], their social media, their e-mail marketing, everything. We are their online marketing department. About 80 percent of our business is essentially taking over online marketing and handling that department for them."

Shama believes that a considerable amount of misunderstanding about social media exists and that it creates confusion about how a business can use it effectively. She states that one of the biggest misconceptions about social media is "That it's a magic bullet. Companies think or want to believe that social media works differently than offline marketing. They think, 'People are going to find my profile on Twitter and call me and give me their business.' No. It's not a direct route."

Social media also shifts the nature of the communication process. Shama reports, "I did my thesis on why people visit social networking sites and how they utilize their time on those sites. Some interesting results came out of that one. What we found was that people use these sites, more than anything, like a water cooler. Especially for virtual workers."

Consequently, it is not merely a company presenting a message to potential customers. Instead, "People don't really want to be on social networks to be fans of something—they don't really care about what a company does. The

▼ Shama Hyder Kabani

CHAPTER OBJECTIVES

After reading this chapter, you should be able to answer the following questions:

1 What is e-active marketing?

2 How has Web 2.0 affected the field of marketing communications?

3 How can e-commerce programs and incentives build a stronger customer base and overcome consumer concerns at the same time?

4 What makes e-commerce a crucial part of business-to-business commerce?

5 How can interactive marketing and online advertising increase brand awareness, sales, and customer loyalty?

6 How can brand spiraling and blogs generate positive outcomes for the marketing department?

7 Why have online social networks, consumer-generated advertising and reviews, e-mail, and viral marketing become key components of market communications programs?

8 How can e-active marketing be conducted successfully in international markets?

number one reason why people use social networks, I found in my research, was to showcase their own identities. The companies that are really successful can play into people's identities. So if I say, 'I love Coca-Cola,' that is saying a lot more about me than it is about the company. It takes a certain person to like Coca-Cola and be a fan of their page. If I say, 'I like Pepsi,' that says something about me. I don't really have to care about the brand. I care just about how it tastes, and I'm sticking to it. Companies have to figure out, how can we play into someone's identity? What can we do that is different?"

She continues, "Social media is a megaphone; it's an amplifier, but what are you going to amplify? We talk to most companies about creating their own content. We talk to B2B [business-to-business] companies in terms of, 'How do you establish expertise?' In B2B, the customers want expertise. For B2C [business-to-consumers], the difference is people want free stuff. So, you need something to attract people. There's so much stuff out there."

To assist companies in understanding the nuances of social media, Shama formed Marketing Zen. What at first was primarily a consulting business has evolved into a more full-service company. The organization grew from 4 to over 20 employees in less than a year.

Any new client of Marketing Zen is advised to make sure there is a bonafide reason for becoming involved with social media. In fact, Shama has written and published an article about the 10 reasons why a company should not use the forum. She says, "You use social media when you have something to say. It is a means to an end. If all your customers are on the Web, or people are looking for you on the Web . . . then you should be on the Web."

The company uses two types of metrics to assess the effectiveness of a social media program. "There is a quantitative metric and a qualitative metric," Shama reports. "With social media, often the qualitative can be heavier, because you're

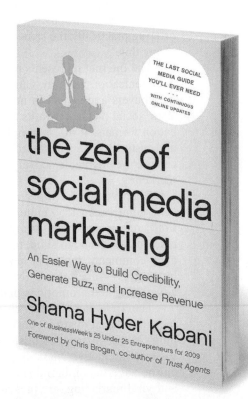

▲ Shama's book *The Zen of Social Media Marketing*.

looking at what people are saying about the company, and what are they saying about the brand. How are they responding? Are they talking to their friends about it? It's being on the Internet to see what people are saying about them."

"The quantitative metrics really depend on what the goals were. We measure things like traffic to the Web site and new visitors. Because social media is a great tool to attract people, we try to send them to the Web site. We try to send them to the hub of what's going on. You look at visitors; you look at how much time they spend on the site. You look at Twitter followers; you look at Facebook fans, and any other tool that we can utilize. We look at how many people left comments on the blog, we look at how many bloggers are talking about them."

In the end, the bottom line is greater traffic to a company's Web site, longer visits while on the site, and ultimately making sales while building loyalty. Marketing Zen stays with a client to update and improve social media efforts over time. Shama notes, "Our business is more than sales. It's relationship-building and networking and marketing and follow up and keeping in touch." By keeping true to its principles, Shama believes Marketing Zen has a bright future, even as the Internet, social media, and other forms of communication continue to evolve.[1]

OVERVIEW

❶ What is e-active marketing?

The Internet has changed the ways individuals communicate and how the world conducts business. Web 1.0 transformed traditional retailing by selling goods and services over the Internet. A company in practically any location could compete globally, and the size of an organization's operation made little difference. The Internet was an open environment, just a click away. A buyer could locate numerous sellers offering practically the same merchandise at comparable prices and with similar offers at any time.

The Internet represents more than a means to conduct business transactions. It is a communication highway. Currently, Web 2.0 helps create online communities that connect buyers and sellers in new ways. It includes interactive company and brand Web sites; social media networks, such as Facebook and Twitter; blogs; and other communication formats. It offers a multichannel communication system that allows businesses and customers to speak to each other and listen to a myriad of voices. Today's businesses can use the Internet to actively interact with customers. The result is a new term: e-active marketing.

E-active marketing combines two major components of Internet marketing: (1) e-commerce and (2) interactive marketing. Both activities are vital to an organization's online presence. Many of today's consumers rely heavily on the Internet to research products, to shop, to make comparisons, to read both favorable and unfavorable comments by other consumers, and to interact with other consumers and businesses. An effective IMC program incorporates these new elements into the advertising and promotions plan.

The first part of this chapter examines e-commerce programs, including the incentives used to attract customers as well as consumer concerns with Internet shopping. Next, business-to-business e-commerce programs are described. Finally, the various interactive marketing methodologies being used by companies, including online advertising, brand spiraling, blogs, online social networks, e-mail campaigns, and viral marketing, are presented. Each may be designed to increase the company's brand presence and influence purchase decisions. International challenges are also described.

WEB 2.0

A recent study revealed that many companies are slashing traditional media marketing budgets and moving the funds to online communication. Many marketing experts believe that online searches, e-mail, social media, Web display ads, and mobile marketing will soon become a significant portion of marketing expenditures. Web 2.0 changes the ways consumers communicate and interact with companies.

Online communication channels are pushing companies into "real-time" communications. When actor Ed Norton was interviewed in a Times Square studio as part of a Diet Coke promotion, the event was shown live on billboards in Times Square and on the Diet Coke Web site as well as on banner placements on Web sites at E! Online, Cosmopolitan, and Hello. Burger King and Adidas have also presented live feeds. Burger King featured NASCAR driver Tony Stewart, and Adidas ran an online campaign on Justin.tv with Chicago Bulls' star Derrick Rose.[2]

Instant communication means consumers want instant customer service. Apple, Bank of America, and Overstock.com provide live customer service on company Web sites. Verizon offers live chat to contact consumers who access the company's Web site. The marketing team knows that when a person spends more than 2 minutes on a step while signing up, the person almost always quits. Verizon can "ping" the customer and offer a live chat with a service rep to guide him through the process.

Consumers also expect instant responses to negative events. When an Internet video showed two Domino's employees doing disgusting things to food, Twitter lit up with chatter and demands that the company address the matter. When Ford's legal department sent a legal notice to a Ford Ranger blogger to surrender his URL, Scott Monty, Ford's social media leader, jumped in and quickly resolved the issue before it went viral.[3]

Many companies now employ people to monitor Twitter and other social media sites and to develop a Web presence. These activities are not cheap. According to one analyst, a company with 500,000 customers will probably invest about $1.2 million in social networks and online monitoring over the first 3 years.[4]

> **2** How has Web 2.0 affected the field of marketing communications?

> **3** How can e-commerce programs and incentives build a stronger customer base and overcome consumer concerns at the same time?

E-COMMERCE

Selling goods and services on the Internet is the focus of **e-commerce** programs. Many types of e-commerce programs exist, ranging from click-only operations that sell entirely online to bricks-and-clicks that supplement physical store operations with an online presence. E-commerce involves both businesses selling to consumers (B2C) and businesses selling to other businesses (B2B). Mega-retailers such as Wal-Mart as well as mom-and-pop operations vending merchandise from home engage in e-commerce. Online sales account for nearly 8 percent of all retail activity.[5]

▼ Many companies now employ individuals to monitor Twitter and social media sites.

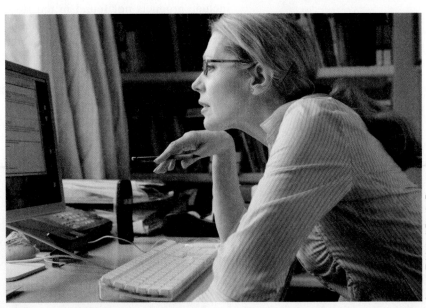

Many luxury shoppers prefer to purchase online. Forty-five percent of ultra-affluent households, those with annual incomes of more than $250,000, reported that they prefer to buy online. Fifty-six percent of households with annual incomes greater than $1 million reported that they prefer online shopping. The primary drivers of this preference include convenience, selection, and the perceived value of merchandise.[6]

Further, many consumers may make purchases at retail stores but first use the

Source: Thinkstock Royalty Free.

i want everything at my party to be yellow. i want yellow balloons, yellow cups, and yellow icing on my cake because yellow is the prettiest color ever. except for pink. i want everything at my party to be pink.

www.iparty.com > birthdays > basics > pink > cups/plates/napkins/favors > order

i want. i click. iparty.com

aol keyword: iparty

▲ iParty.com offers consumers a wide array of products, which makes online purchasing easy and convenient.

Internet to collect information. A Pew Research Center survey revealed that 80 percent of Americans have researched a product online before making a purchase.[7] In Australia, half of the consumers first conduct online research. The number of men shopping online is greater than the number of Australian women shopping online. A similar pattern has emerged in Great Britain and other countries.[8]

E-Commerce Components

Figure 9.1 lists the features that are part of a successful e-commerce operation. Previously, Web sites only needed a catalog, shopping cart, and payment system to conduct business. These are no longer sufficient.

Catalogs

A catalog may display only a few items or provide a complex presentation of thousands of products. The nature of the firm's operation determines the type of catalog. Customers should be able to easily locate products of interest. Photos, streaming videos, and product information can help create an appealing online catalog. When the company offers a printed catalog or has a retail store, the printed catalog or store will be tied to the Web catalog. Victoria's Secret features a "catalog quick order" system that allows customers to enter the product number from the print catalog and then go straight to checkout. The program saves considerable time in trying to find and buy a product on the Web.[9]

Sears Holdings developed an online shopping experience called "Shop Your Way" that assists customers by letting them shop in the ways they feel most comfortable. The customer can access Sears.com, Kmart.com, LandsEnd.com, The-GreatIndoors.com, or the new mobile application site Sears2Go. Each offers the consumer the ability to select a product from any retail operation in the manner desired.

To encourage online shopping, Sears Holdings expanded its online offerings to include products not found in the stores or in catalogs. Customers can choose how they shop online: the Web, mobile phone, or at an in-store terminal. A community Web site, MySears.com, presents unbiased customer reviews and assists individuals in getting or giving ideas and sharing knowledge. Online tools such as Quickview, Save for Later, and Wish Lists make the shopping experience easier for customers. Sears Holdings helps customers purchase products from all of its companies as a single transaction. Sears Holdings provides an excellent example of how an online catalog has been changed into a communication and interaction tool.[10]

FIGURE 9.1 ▶
E-Commerce Web Site Components

- Catalog
    - Product information
    - Product navigation
- Shopping cart
    - Save or wish basket
- Payment system
    - Easy, quick, convenient checkout

- Store locator
- Customization functionality
- Customer reviews or feedback applications

Shopping Carts

The shopping cart aids consumers as they select products. A shopping cart can range from checking a circle for an item to more complicated systems that are designed to keep records of multiple purchases. Most shopping carts provide a "save" or "wish" basket that allows consumers to save choices for later purchases.

Many online retailers find that shoppers abandon shopping carts prior to checkout. The reasons vary, but the most common include hidden charges, difficulty in checking out, and requiring customers to register at the site in order to pay. Greg Hintz of Yahoo! Shopping offers these suggestions to keep customers from abandoning a shopping cart:

- Show any additional costs, such as shipping and handling, upfront, so there are no surprises when the customer reaches checkout.
- Make checkout easy and allow customers to make purchases without registering a user name and password.
- Make it easy for customers to enter discount codes from coupons, gift certificates, and other promotions.
- Provide a checkout procedure that is safe and that the customer feels can be trusted.[11]

Payment Methods

Methods of payment should be easy, quick, and convenient. It may be a credit card system or a payment service such as PayPal, Google Checkout, eBillme, or online banking payments. E-retailers that offer multiple methods of payment have experienced greater increases in sales than those providing fewer options. Currently, online retailers offer an average of 2.6 payment options, up from 2.1 in 2005.[12] For businesses, a voucher system or computerized billing system can directly invoice a purchase. In more trusting relationships, the invoice can be added to the customer's records without mailing a physical bill.

Store Locators

The store locator assists customers who want to pick up an item rather than having it shipped. Home Depot and Target store locators tell consumers where the nearest store can be found. Sears Holdings offers curbside pickup and even allows someone else to pick up the merchandise for the buyer. For manufacturers such as Skyjacker, a store locator shows the address of the nearest retail store that sells the company's products.

Customization

Most customers want the convenience customization provides. Shoppers do not want to take time to sift through details. They prefer sites that remember them and the merchandise they prefer. Customization features also include the ability to:

- Locate the nearest retail store on a Web site or via mobile phone
- Print coupons or other promotions from the Web site or use a mobile phone to access discounts at the retail store
- Access information on the Web site or via a mobile phone that an item is in stock prior to making a purchase[13]

Customer Reviews and Feedback

Many companies are hesitant about adding reviews and feedback options due to the potential for negative comments, but they represent an emerging trend in the

▼ A store locator provides an important function on the Skyjacker Web site by directing customers to the nearest retail store that sells Skyjacker products.

Web 2.0 environment. These venues provide opportunities for active interactions with customers and generate more honest relationships. They encourage customers to become brand advocates and provide insights into customer thoughts and lifestyles.[14]

Review and feedback pages also provide a level of confidence for new customers visiting the site. Sears Holdings utilizes MySears.com. Best Buy and other retailers provide customer reviews on company Web sites regarding the various brands in stock. These programs present opportunities for customer feedback, comments, and interaction. Some e-commerce sites have also added another feature, a "tell a friend" function that encourages positive word-of-mouth recommendations.

New Trends

As e-commerce moves into real-time communication and active interactions with customers, businesses are scrambling to make Web sites relevant to today's consumers. Some suggestions for the developing the next generation of e-commerce sites are offered in Figure 9.2.

FIGURE 9.2 ▶
Building the Next Generation
of E-Commerce Sites

▼ E-commerce retailer Bluefly often provides financial incentives to encourage online purchases.

- Consider how users will interact with the brand and then develop means of brand engagement.
- Allow for drill-down of search results by grouping products around brands and common parameters.
- Maximize traffic through effective search engine optimization.
- Encourage consumer interaction via blogs, feedback applications, or customer reviews.
- Develop a simple, secure checkout procedure.

Source: Adapted from Mike Fletcher, "How to Create the Perfect E-Commerce Website," *Revolution*, March 2009, pp. 6–63.

tuesday, 11:15 p.m.
buying a new dress.

bluefly

www.bluefly.com
the outlet store in your home

Women's, men's and kid's designer fashions.
Save up to 75%. 90-day money back guarantee.

E-COMMERCE INCENTIVES

Cyberbait is any lure or attraction that brings people to a Web site. The various forms include incentives designed to encourage consumers (or businesses) to visit a Web site and to make online purchases. Cyberbait incentives can be classified into three categories:

- Financial incentives
- Convenience incentives
- Value-based incentives

These features do not appear separately; they are normally combined into an overall approach.

Financial Incentives

Financial incentives can persuade an individual or business to make a first-time purchase via e-commerce and encourage former customers to return. The incentive may take the form of a reduced price, free shipping, or an e-coupon. These financial incentives can be offered because conducting business online provides cost savings through:

- Reduced shipping costs, because the costs are passed along to the buyer
- Decreased labor costs, because shelves do not have to be restocked or not stocked at all if merchandise is shipped directly from the producer
- Lower personnel costs (sales force), because in-store salespeople are not needed

Once the individual or company takes advantage of the financial incentive and makes the switch, continuing the incentive may not be necessary. At that point, the convenience and added-value features help keep the customer.

Bluefly (**www.bluefly.com**) is a New York–based upscale apparel and home furnishings discounter. The Bluefly ad in this section states that the company is "the outlet store in your home." The company's marketing team believes that greater site traffic leads to more business. Bluefly uses cyberbait to drive traffic to the company's Web site in order to collect names for its database as well as to boost sales.

Bluefly sells hard-to-get fashion accessories that even celebrities and socialites have waited months to purchase. An online sweepstakes named "30 Bags in 30 Days" focused on this advantage. Customers could enter once per day. The sweepstakes increased site traffic by 100 percent compared to the same month from the previous year. Half of the visitors asked Bluefly to send them a daily reminder to play the sweepstakes. Forty percent referred friends to the site and the sweepstakes. A 62 percent increase in sales from the new customers that the sweepstakes brought in was the result. Existing customers continued to make purchases after the sweepstakes ended.[15]

Typically, the most effective financial incentives offer something free or at a discount. A survey by BizRate Research suggests that the most popular online promotion is free shipping.[16] Two things should be kept in mind for financial incentives. First, the incentive should be meaningful to individuals visiting the site. Second, the incentive should be changed periodically to entice new visitors to buy and to encourage repeat purchases by current visitors.

BOOK A TRIP

Travelocity.com
Powered By SABRE

WITHOUT MAKING ONE

Too busy to book your hotel room, air travel, car rental?
Book your next trip on-line with Visa.
It's fast. It's safe. It's a four-star destination for travelers.

VISA

Worldwide. Webwide. Visa.® It's everywhere you want to be.®

© 1999 Visa U.S.A. Inc.   www.visa.com

▲ This advertisement offers the convenience of making travel arrangements online and paying for them with a credit card.

Convenience Incentives

Making the shopping process easier creates an incentive that can encourage customers to visit a Web site. Instead of traveling to a retail store, a consumer can place the order in the office or at home. The order can be made at any time, day or night. The convenience and speed of purchasing merchandise online drives many consumers to e-retailers.

Convenience becomes an additional advantage when the consumer seeks specific product information. Using the Internet is quicker and easier than reading *Consumer Reports* or talking to a salesperson. The majority of consumers research major purchases online before going to a store. Most shoppers have looked at least once at an online peer review before finalizing a purchase, and roughly 40 percent have compared product features and prices across outlets online before buying.[17] The most frequently employed site for information searches is Google. It is accessed in about two-thirds of all information searches. No other source is used more than 14.5 percent of the time. Figure 9.3 lists the top search providers. For each, the most frequently given reasons for selecting the method was that it was easier, more convenient, and quicker.[18]

Value-Added Incentives

Value-added incentives lead consumers to change purchasing habits over the long term. They can make the difference between an ordinary and an exemplary site. The added value may be personalized shopping, whereby the software system recognizes patterns in customers' purchasing behaviors. The same specialized software informs customers about special deals. These offers are matched to past purchasing behaviors or search patterns. A consumer going through the mystery section of an online bookstore might see a banner pop up advertising a special deal on a new mystery novel. In addition to

FIGURE 9.3 ▶
Top U.S. Online Search Providers

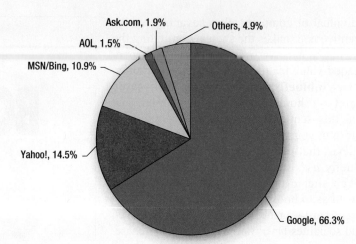

Ask.com, 1.9%

Others, 4.9%

AOL, 1.5%

MSN/Bing, 10.9%

Yahoo!, 14.5%

Google, 66.3%

Source: Adapted from "Top 10 U.S. Search Providers, Home & Work," *Nielsen Internet* (**http://en-us.nielsen.com/rankings/insights/ rankings/internet**, accessed February 22, 2010).

▼ WeddingChannel.com uses various incentives to attract consumers to its Web site.

I remember her in blue jeans and a T-shirt in high school. I remember her in a thrift store leather jacket in college. I remember her in a rain jacket in Oregon. I remember her in a swimsuit on the beach in Florida. I remember her without a swimsuit on the beach in Greece. I remember her in a sleeping bag in a tent in Yellowstone, refusing to come out. But I can't say that I remember ever seeing her in a dress like that.

Date set: *May 20th*

Plan your wedding | Buy a gift | Find your dress | Book your honeymoon | More

Thousands of gowns. And everything else you need to plan the perfect wedding.

WeddingChannel.com™

instant banners, consumers and businesses may also receive e-mails offering new information and other special deals.

Many e-retailers offer merchandise on the Web site that is not available in a print catalog in order to add value. Design Within Reach, a modern furniture retailer, advertises, "Our Web site offers numerous products not always included in the catalog, as well as weekly features of new items."[19] Sears Holdings uses the same approach.

Frequently, a combination of incentives makes the difference. The cyberbait may include a discount or special price on a pair of jeans (a financial-based incentive) and at the same time offer the freedom to place an order at 3:00 A.M. (a convenience-based incentive). The same site may feature a game or offer a weekly fashion tip on some topic (value-added incentive). This combination entices consumers and businesses to return to the site. E-shoppers find it easy to surf the Internet and search competing sites. When they do so, brand names and particular Web sites are not as important. Consumers need reasons to regularly return to sites.

CONSUMER CONCERNS WITH E-COMMERCE

Some consumers are still wary of purchasing products via the Internet. The primary reasons are highlighted in Figure 9.4.[20] Although these concerns are not as widespread as they were 10 years ago, they still exist for some individuals.

- Seller opportunism
- Security concerns
- Information privacy issues
- Brick-and-mortar purchasing habits

◀ **FIGURE 9.4**

Reasons Consumers Are Wary of Purchasing Products on the Internet

Seller Opportunism

One of the major economic benefits of the Internet also results in one of consumers' worst fears. The Internet allows a company from anywhere to conduct business with an individual or another business anywhere in the world. This freedom of access also creates apprehension when buyers wonder whether a business is legitimate or if the Web site is attempting to make illegal gains through fraud, identity theft, or some other activity. Trust remains the key issue.[21]

Security Issues

Consumer concerns about security are based on past incidents in which credit card numbers have been stolen as well as from cases of identity theft. A Javelin Strategy & Research study estimates retailers lose approximately $21 billion in online sales due to fears about identity and data theft.[22] Although still a concern, worries are declining as more consumers become accustomed to using the Web. Fears about giving out credit card information are no greater now than they are for telephone orders or in-store credit card sales. Consumer confidence in e-commerce Web site security has risen. A recent survey revealed that three-fourths of online shoppers have faith in Web security.[23]

Privacy Issues

Beyond apprehensions about identity theft and fraud are concerns that unscrupulous firms will sell sensitive personal information. Once this information becomes readily available, the individual loses control over who sees it and how it is used. A person might not wish to have his shopping patterns known, especially when the individual buys personal care products such as those for baldness, sexual dysfunction, weight loss, or other private matters.

Further, many consumers are frustrated by being bombarded with advertising and marketing messages. Consumers also strongly express the desire to maintain control over personal information. They believe they should decide who should use it and how it should be used.

Company leaders should be extremely careful about the types of data and information that are collected from Web site visitors. This goes back to the issue of trust. Successful online retailers gain the confidence of browsers who visit a Web site.

Purchasing Habits

Many consumers are still most comfortable when they buy merchandise at retail stores. At the retail store, consumers can view and touch the merchandise. They can inspect it for defects and compare brands. Clothes can be tried on to make sure they fit. The customer can see how the clothing item looks while being worn. It takes time to change this habit, especially the preference for retail shopping. Doing so requires the right kinds of incentives.

To reach reluctant consumers, retailers rely on several tactics. Some allow consumers to purchase a product online but then pick the item up at the retail store. To complete these types of sales, retailers send text messages and e-mails informing customers that the product has arrived at the store.[24]

Some purchase habits are already changing. Many consumers are far more comfortable with e-commerce purchases, especially during busy times of the year, such as the Christmas shopping season. Clearly e-commerce will not replace brick-and-mortar stores. At the same time, it has become a vital supplement for many retail chains and stores.

BUSINESS-TO-BUSINESS E-COMMERCE

4 What makes e-commerce a crucial part of business-to-business commerce?

E-commerce represents a key part of many business-to-business operations. In many buying situations, purchasing agents use the Internet to compare prices and product information. Once a business account has been established, the customer finds it easy to place an order, and the price may be lower than those offered by traditional outlets. Consequently, competing in e-commerce requires an effective e-commerce site and a strong, distinct brand name.

The number of hits on a business-to-business Web site directly relates to the amount spent on advertising and sales promotions. Recently, one large business-to-business company went from 20,000 visits per month to 80,000 visits per month during a 6-month period by doubling the company's annual advertising budget for print, direct mail, and trade shows. A small company went from 2,000 to 6,000 hits per month by increasing the company's budget for print ads from $25,000 to $65,000 per year.[25]

5 How can interactive marketing and online advertising increase brand awareness, sales, and customer loyalty?

Financial, convenience, and value-added incentives can also be offered to business buyers. The iGo Internet advertisement shown in this section offers a 10-percent discount as a financial incentive for orders placed via the Internet at **www.igo.com** or by telephone.

For businesses, ordering merchandise, supplies, and materials using the Internet can save purchasing agents considerable time. Businesses can also check the status of an order, shipment information, and billing data online. In most cases, obtaining information about a purchase online will be considerably quicker than making a telephone call. Convenience represents a highly attractive incentive for many companies.

▼ An Internet advertisement for iGo featuring financial incentives to encourage business-to-business purchases.

E-commerce programs offer other benefits for business-to-business companies. A growing form of e-commerce in the business-to-business sector is online exchanges and auctions. These exchanges allow business buyers to purchase a variety of commodities and goods at lower prices. The Internet enables vendors to speed up time to market, to sell directly to other businesses, and to cut transaction and inventory costs. Buyers can find both nonproduction goods, such as office supplies, as well as production-related supplies, raw materials, and equipment. Sites offering oil, natural gas, electricity, coal, chemicals, steel, and other raw materials also are available. Many online markets are operated by intermediary companies that match buyers and sellers.

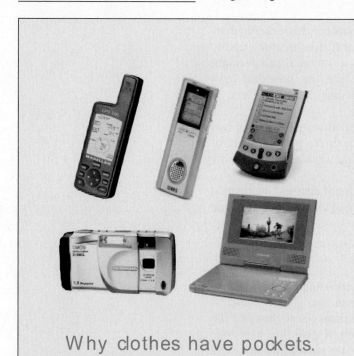

Why clothes have pockets.

What good is a pocket if it's empty? iGo offers over 7,900 mobile technology products from hard-to-find batteries, chargers and adapters to the coolest cell phones and digital cameras. To receive a 10% discount, visit us at www.igo.com/esvp or call 1-888-205-0065 and mention code IGOESVP.

iGo
Mobile Technology Outfitter™

10% discount on any product or service purchased through employeesavings.com

| Batteries and Power Gear | Laptop Gear | Cellular Gear | PDA and Handheld | Hot Products | Travel Gear |

INTERACTIVE MARKETING

Interactive marketing is the development of marketing programs that create interplay between consumers and businesses rather than simply sending messages to potential customers. The programs feature two-way communication and customer involvement.

The Internet offers the ideal medium for interactive marketing because of the ability to accurately track browser activities and translate the information into instant reactions. Software such as the Relationship Optimizer and Prime Response by NCR uses powerful data analysis techniques to personalize marketing messages. The NCR software analyzes customer interactions such as click-stream data traffic—any type of customer interaction with the firm—and combines it with demographic information from external or internal databases. As the

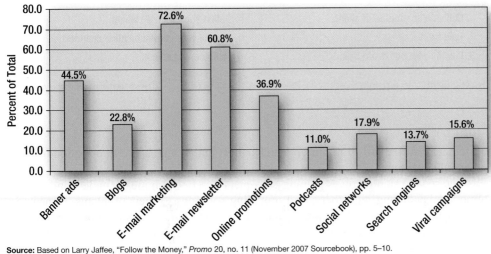

Source: Based on Larry Jaffee, "Follow the Money," *Promo* 20, no. 11 (November 2007 Sourcebook), pp. 5–10.

data are being processed, the software can launch complex interactive and personalized marketing materials in real time.

Interactive marketing emphasizes two primary activities. First, it assists marketers in targeting individuals, specifically potential and current customers, with personalized information. Second, it engages the consumer with the company and product. The consumer becomes an active participant in the marketing exchange rather than a passive recipient. Figure 9.5 lists online interactive tactics used by companies and the percentage of companies that utilize each method.

Figure 9.6 identifies marketing objectives and the percentage of companies that use interactive marketing campaigns to accomplish them. As shown, interactive marketing can achieve a wide variety of objectives and serve many purposes, such as branding, building loyalty, generating sales, and driving individuals to Web sites.

Marketing Zen's Shama Kabani describes the steps involved in developing an effective interactive marketing strategy (see Figure 9.7).[26] It starts with cultivating an attitude of giving. To engage customers with a brand, they must believe something of value is being presented to them in exchange for their engagement. In this two-way interaction, both sides must receive something of value. The quickest way to capture the attention of

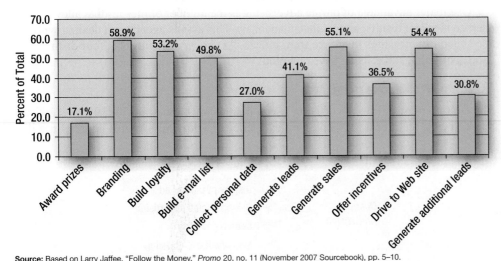

◀ **FIGURE 9.6**
Interactive Marketing Objectives

Source: Based on Larry Jaffee, "Follow the Money," *Promo* 20, no. 11 (November 2007 Sourcebook), pp. 5–10.

Source: Adapted from Shama Hyder Kabani, "Online Marketing Plan," The Marketing Zen Group (**www.marketingzen.com**), pp. 9–13.

FIGURE 9.7 ▶
Steps in Developing an
Interactive Marketing Strategy

1. Cultivate an attitude of giving.	4. Define your ultimate vision.
2. Gain trust.	5. Choose your communication channels.
3. Identify your one-word brand.	6. Evaluate and adjust.

customers is a free gift. It might be merchandise, but it can also be information or some other valuable item.

The second step involves gaining customers' trust, which means understanding customers, empathizing with them, and providing solutions to their problems. Consumers will engage with companies and brands they trust. The company should be honest, upfront, and cannot pull surprises or use trickery to gain a sale. Otherwise it will become a one-time transaction.

Shama suggests that companies should synthesize the company or brand down to the one word that best describes what the company offers or stands for. It might be "feminine" or "quality" or "communication" or "innovator" or "passionate." Tied closely with the one-word brand is an ultimate vision. What is the outcome the company delivers? For FedEx, it is "overnight delivery." For Burger King, it is "Have it your way."

Choosing the best communication channels to deliver the message and to interact with customers and prospects will be the next step. As shown in Figure 9.5, a number of options are available. The best choices depend on the target audience and the message.

Evaluation and adjusting constitute the final step. These activities are especially important for interactive marketing programs, because the field changes so rapidly. Current channels may not exist in 5 years, or even by next year. Different, and perhaps better, channels may arise.

The next few sections of this chapter examine the primary interactive methods currently being used by companies. Bear in mind that this field continues to evolve: What is presented in this chapter may be outdated by the time the book is published.

ONLINE ADVERTISING

Online advertising represents a highly effective method for reaching today's consumers, especially the younger, more Internet-savvy market. Consequently, budgets for online advertising have steadily increased. Funds devoted to online advertising have become a larger portion of overall advertising and marketing budgets.

One major advantage of online advertising is the number of metrics that allow advertisers to measure results, almost instantaneously. This assists agencies in dealing with the accountability pressures they face from clients. As shown in Figure 9.8, four distinct categories of online advertising have emerged.

Banner Advertising

The first form of online advertising was a display, or banner, ad. In 1994, AT&T ran one carrying the message "Have you ever clicked your right mouse here? You will."

FIGURE 9.8 ▶
Types of Online Advertising

This very basic form of advertising has generated billions of dollars in advertising revenues. Today, banner ads account for 32 percent of online advertising.[27]

Currently, banner ads can be embedded with videos, widget applications, or targeted display ads to increase the chances viewers will see and click the icon. The newest online technology, which has been taken from paid search auction systems, allows advertisers to display a banner ad to only individuals the company chooses. This system is built on a vast warehouse of user Internet data and automated auction advertising exchanges, such as Google's Double-Click, Yahoo!'s Right Media ad exchange, and Microsoft's AdECN. Advertisers develop messages for specific audiences and set the price they are willing to pay to reach that audience with a banner ad. When a consumer, such as a 20- to 25-year-old female, accesses a particular Web site with this technology, in a microsecond the software searches the ad auction exchange for advertisers matching the profile of the woman who just logged onto the page. Once an advertiser has been located, a banner ad instantly flashes on the computer screen. It may be an advertisement for L'Oreal or Liz Claiborne. If a male with an interest in fishing logs on, an advertisement for a boat, fishing supplies, or fishing attire may appear. The automated exchange system grants precise targeting of ads to specific consumers.[28]

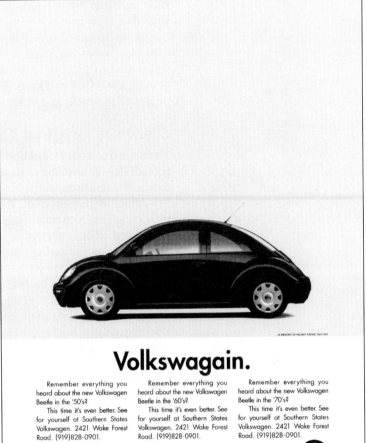

Source: Courtesy of Volkswagen.

▲ Google's Double-Click technology targets advertisements to consumers most interested in a product such as a Volkswagen.

Widgets

Widgets are mini-applications embedded in a banner ad that permit a consumer access to some form of dynamic content that is provided by an external source other than the company where the ad resides. Widgets provide individuals with personalized access to Web information or functionality from any device connected to the Internet.

Boxcar Creative developed a widget application for ConocoPhillips using RICH expandable banners to create interactive polls, fun facts, and a carbon calculator. Both the poll and the calculator collected and produced results without the user ever leaving the banner advertisement. Only when an individual clicked "learn more" was she taken to a micro-site landing page with additional content and data collection opportunities.

Geo-target ads are another version of banner advertising that have increased in popularity. These ads are presented only to individuals who log onto a Web site in a particular region. It is ideal for retailers and smaller businesses seeking to reach a specific region of the country.

Classified and Media/Video Advertising

Online classified ads comprise a significant percentage of online advertising budgets. Media/video ads have become the fastest-growing format. This growth may rise as mobile phones and other handheld devices develop increased video display capabilities.

An Eyeblaster study revealed that online videos performed best when they appear next to online content or in an e-mail, compared to social network or gaming sites. Eyeblaster examined two metrics: dwell rate and dwell time. **Dwell rate** measures the proportion of ad impressions that result in users clicking an ad or mousing over it. **Dwell**

time measures the amount of time individuals spend engaged with an advertisement. Both dwell rate and dwell time were higher for video ads placed beside content and in an c-mail as compared to social networks and gaming sites. Ariel Geifman of Eyeblaster explains, "What we found is that people browse social networks really quickly. People spend a lot of time in social networks, but it's not on the same Web page." In terms of gaming sites, Geifman said, "People are more focused on the game" and as a result less interested in watching a video ad.[29]

Search Engine Optimization

The largest category of online expenditures is for spots on search engines. These are the text ads that appear next to search results when a specific word is keyed in. Funds devoted to search engines constitute nearly 41 percent of online advertising expenditures.

About 80 percent of all Web traffic begins at a search engine.[30] Therefore, one key marketing goal is to make sure that a company's name or brand becomes one of the first ones listed when a person performs a search. **SEO**, or **search engine optimization**, is the process of increasing the probability of a particular company's Web site emerging from a search.

Optimization can be reached in one of three ways. First, a *paid search insertion* comes up when certain products or information are sought. Companies can speed this process by registering with various search engines in order to have the site indexed and also by paying a higher placement fee for top positions. The placement of the ad on a search page depends on the price the company pays and the algorithm a search engine used to determine the advertisement's relevance to a particular search word or phrase.

Second, a company can increase identification through the *natural* or *organic emergence* of the site. This method involves developing efficient and effective organic results that arise from a natural search process. Each search engine uses a slightly different set of algorithms to identify key phrases that match what was typed into the search box. To be listed first in an organic search requires time and effort. When a Web site is first built, it probably will not emerge at the top of the search results. It takes time for the search engine to locate the site.

Some studies suggest that the impact of organic listings can be impressive. For sites that come up on the first page of a search or within the top 10, Web traffic increases ninefold. For second- and third-page listings, Web traffic increases sixfold. In terms of sales, being a top 10 listing has resulted in a 42 percent increase in sales the first month and a 100 percent increase the second month.[31]

The third optimization method, *paid search ads,* includes small text boxes that pop up when a particular word is typed in or it can be paid link boxes at the top or side of a search result. A comScore study suggests that search ads have a strong positive impact on brand awareness, perception, and purchase intentions, even if consumers do not click the paid search ad.[32] The study revealed that for brands in the top search positions:

- The paid search ads generated a 160 percent increase in unaided awareness.
- Consumers were 20 percent more likely to have a positive perception of the brands.
- Consumers were 30 percent more likely to consider purchasing the brand.

Many dollars are being spent on search engine optimization. The typical click-through rate for online advertising is around 0.2 percent; for search advertising it is

▼ Search engine optimization leads consumers using search engines to find a company's products and information on the Internet.

around 5 percent.[33] Although the early results are impressive, remember that search engine optimization should be considered a long-term investment. The effects do not occur quickly. Getting into the top 10 listings of a search can take months or years. It requires optimizing content, programming, and finding the codes that will be picked up by search engines.

The Impact of Online Advertising

As more dollars shift to online advertising, concerns have arisen about the impact of the ads. Web users, just like television viewers, are becoming immune to advertisements. The percentage of people who respond to banner ads steadily shrinks. The click-through rate on major Web destinations has declined to less than 1 percent. A recent measurement showed a response rate of 0.27 percent.[34] For this reason, advertisers have begun banking on new technologies to increase response rates and to deliver targeted messages to individuals most likely to respond.

BRAND SPIRALING

To build a brand's reputation and brand loyalty, online advertising should be integrated with offline branding tactics that reinforce each other to speak with one voice. This process, **brand spiraling**, involves the use of traditional media to promote and attract consumers to a Web site. Television, radio, newspapers, magazines, and billboards can be designed to encourage consumers to visit the firm's Web site in an effort to maintain a uniform brand presence and advertising message.

One recent study indicated that after viewing a magazine advertisement nearly half of the consumers polled said they might access a Web site or conduct an online search for the product. Over 40 percent are more inclined to visit a Web site after seeing a television or newspaper advertisement.[35] Traditional media can be the driving force behind online branding efforts.

Currently, tailor-made Web sites can be used with direct mail and e-mail campaigns. These sites are accessed through **personalized URLs**, called **PURLs**, such as the hypothetical **www.kenclow.offer.officedepot.com**. A PURL is a personalized Web page that is preloaded with the customer's personal data, contact information, purchase behavior, and previous interactions with the company. A company such as Ford could display the customer's current vehicle, maintenance record, and other interactions with the company. The PURL creates a one-on-one dialogue with a customer and can engage her with the company and provide messages, offers, and incentives tailored to her past data and history.[36]

Although many companies continue to utilize online advertising, a movement into more interactive technologies has taken place. Blogs, e-mail marketing programs, podcasts, social networks, and consumer-generated content are emerging as effective new advertising channels.

6 How can brand spiraling and blogs generate positive outcomes for the marketing department?

▼ Off-line advertising is an important part of building an online presence.

BLOGS

The term *blog* is derived from the phrase "Web logs." **Blogs** are essentially online musings. They cover a wide range of topics. Some blogs permit visitors to post comments; others are just the ramblings of an individual. What makes blogs powerful is that one consumer dissatisfied with a particular brand can now tell thousands, and in some cases millions, of others. Previously, a bad shopping experience meant that 12 to 15 people would hear about it. Now an individual's complaint can be sent to more than just friends and

Imagine a Place Like No Other

Shirlock's Inside Out

Specializing in Re-Design, Fluffing, Home Decor, Gifts, Crabtree & Evelyn and More

3300 East Zora (Just 1 block E. of Range Line) — 417-624-7538 — Tues.-Fri. 10-5, Sat. 10 'til 2

Source: Courtesy of Joplin Globe.

family. A discontented consumer can speak to anyone who is willing to listen (or read about it) via the Internet.

The power of online buzz has grown at an exponential rate. Several unique methods of communication between individuals have emerged. Advertisers now look for ways to tap into these venues. A recent American Marketing Association survey illustrates the growth of these intrapersonal online communication channels. An online survey of 1,174 people revealed that:

- 47 percent go to a social network site to download coupons or to search for information about a product.
- 45 percent go to a social network site to find out about upcoming sales in retail stores and discounts on particular brands of products.
- 22 percent read or write a product review on a blog.[37]

Company-Sponsored Blogging

Some marketing experts have begun looking for ways to use blogs to promote products or to get closer to customers. This includes setting up company-sponsored blogs that can emulate word-of-mouth communication and can engage customers with a company. The online retailer Bluefly regularly updates customers with fashion news through its Flypaper blog (**http://flypaper.bluefly.com**). The blog encourages customers to visit the site to enjoy postings on new styles, upcoming designers, and fashion *faux pas*. In the past, Bluefly customers may have relied on magazines such as *Vogue* for fashion information. Now they can get information quicker, and, more important, it is interactive. This allows the marketing team to engage customers and develop a two-way channel of communication.

▼ Skyjacker hosts a company-sponsored blog where consumers can discuss suspension systems and lift kits.

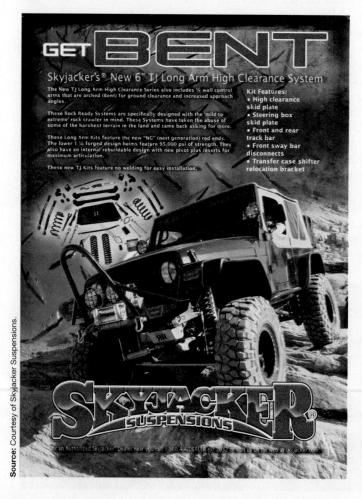

Research by comScore revealed that shoppers who visit blogs spend more than the average shopper. For Bluefly, the individuals who access the Flypaper blog are the company's very best customers. In addition to spending more money, the study indicated that the average visitor to a blog spends nearly 23 hours online per week, compared to 13 hours per week for the average Internet user.[38]

A company-sponsored blog can provide a number of benefits; however, analysts stress the importance of identifying a specific reason for the blog before launching it. It may be to make the company more open (Dell), to humanize the company (Microsoft), or to show a fun-and-happy company (Southwest Airlines).[39] When Coca-Cola acquired 40 percent of the Honest Tea company, many customers were unhappy about the move and voiced opinions on the blog. Seth Goldman, CEO of Honest Tea, took time to answer each one. While some customers still did not like the idea, "The blog at least helps people see how we think about it," Goldman said.[40]

The methods used to respond to negative comments are important. CEO Bill Marriott of Marriott International hosts a blog for customers and employees. About 20 percent of the blog's readership consists of employees. Marriott's comment section is monitored, and no comment is posted until it has been approved. Comments are not removed simply because they are negative. Only those not germane to the discussion or blog are taken down. The remaining are left up and addressed by Bill Marriott, which gives credibility to the blog by being willing to hear negative feedback.

For small businesses, blogs provide a relatively inexpensive way to communicate with customers. Robb Duncan began a blog for his Georgetown gelato shop, Dolcezza. When a second store was opened in Bethesda, Maryland, he announced an ice cream giveaway on opening night through the blog. Over 1,000 individuals showed up.[41]

ONLINE SOCIAL NETWORKS

Online social networks have become extremely popular with people and with companies seeking to communicate with consumers. According to Forrester Research, 75 percent of Internet users participate in some type of social media.[42] A growing percentage of consumer activity on the Internet takes place on social networking or blogging sites.

7 Why have online social networks, consumer-generated advertising and reviews, e-mail, and viral marketing become key components of market communications programs?

Facebook

Facebook is the largest social media site, with over 310 million users worldwide. It presents the largest source of display ads of all social networks, with 14.7 percent share.[43] According to *Adweek*, Facebook's popularity comes from a blend of "sheer size of fan base, record of publishing useful content, and the extent of consumer interaction that is offered." The companies with the most successful Facebook presence, according to *Adweek*, are Starbucks, Coca-Cola, Best Buy, Starbucks, and Microsoft. Starbucks has 3.7 million fans, compared to 3.5 million for Coke. Best Buy has almost 900,000, and Microsoft has just over 300,000.[44] An independent study by WetPaint and the Altimeter Group notes that these companies and others that have high levels of social media activity tend to increase revenues more than companies that lack a social media presence.[45]

Companies that successfully use social media offer some type of discount or special promotion to fans. Of the consumers who follow a brand on Facebook, over one-third cited special deals as the main reason they became fans. When developing a social media strategy, the marketing team attempts to provide content that will lead consumers to make purchases and spread word about the brand.[46]

▼ Facebook has become popular with people of all generations.

When Little Debbie, the snack cake company, set up its original Facebook account, the company posted updates, uploaded TV ads, presented other marketing materials, and then waited for fans to appear. There was very little response. Consequently, the marketing team developed an engagement advertisement directed toward 21- to 49-year-olds. The commercial publicized a sweepstakes with a Smart car as the prize. The sweepstakes included the option to become a fan. Within 12 hours, Little Debbie's fan base grew from 5,000 to over 125,000. The company also received over 6,000 comments from fans who said they love Little Debbie snack cakes.[47] The next challenge Little Debbie faces will be keeping the fan base interested. New deals, promotions, and offers appear to be the key.

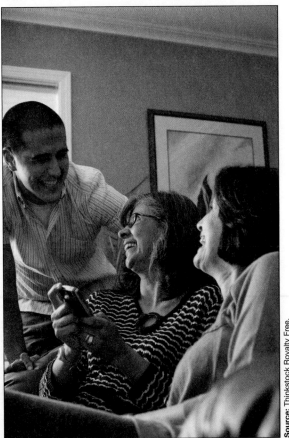

Twitter

The Twitter micro-blogging service allows individuals and companies to send out tweets, currently a maximum of 140 characters per message. Twitter can be an effective method of reaching out to customers. It can also help monitor what customers are saying about a company or brand. Software, such as Tweetscan or Summize, can locate a brand or company name mentioned in tweets. Company officials can then respond or gather the information for future use or evaluation. It provides valuable information on how customers feel about the brand and what they are saying.

JetBlue, Comcast, H&R Block, and Southwest Airlines are just a few companies that monitor tweets. Christopher Hoff tweeted his displeasure with Southwest when his flight was delayed and his luggage was lost. The next day he received a message from Southwest stating, "Sorry to hear about your flight—weather was terrible in the NE. Hope you give us a 2nd chance to prove Southwest = Awesomeness."[48] For

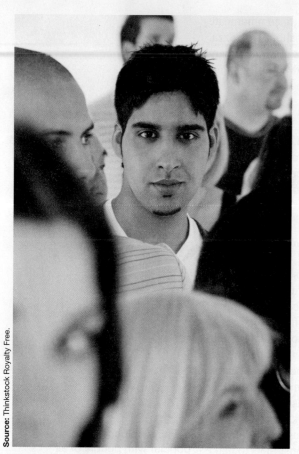

▲ The challenge for companies is finding ways to use social media to reach consumers.

some consumers; however, it may be unnerving to discover that companies can monitor name mentions.

Three weeks after Curtis Kimball opened his crème pastry cart in San Francisco, he noticed a stranger in line to purchase some of his desserts. When quizzed, the man said he heard about the pastry cart from Twitter. Kimball created a Twitter account and now has a fan base of 5,400 customers who wait for him to post his location and list the flavor of the day.[49]

When KFC first developed its line of grilled chicken, the new product was unveiled on the Oprah Winfrey show with details of a voucher on her Web site for a free grilled chicken meal. The link was placed on Twitter and was quickly forwarded to millions of users. The rush to print the voucher was so great it crashed the Web site, and KFC franchises were overwhelmed with demand for the free grilled chicken meal.[50]

Combined Social Media Programs

Recently, Ford identified 100 top bloggers and gave them a Ford Fiesta for 6 months. The only stipulation was that they were required to upload a video on YouTube about the car. They were also encouraged to talk about the car, with no restrictions, on their blogs and also on Facebook and Twitter. When asked about this unique marketing approach, Scott Monty, Ford's chief blogger, said, "It's about culture change and adapting to this ongoing way of communicating. The bloggers are fully free to say what they want."[51]

Coca-Cola developed Expedition 206, which involved sending three individuals in their 20s on a 275,000-mile trip to 206 countries where Coca-Cola was sold. Equipped with laptop computers, video cameras, and smartphones the trio set off on their journey, which was tracked on Facebook, Flickr, YouTube, and Twitter. In addition to reading and hearing about the journey, fans could offer suggestions on what the trio should see at each destination.[52]

The future of social media is still being written. Before the next edition of this textbook, the landscape likely will change. Although the names of major social media sites or who participates may be different, it is clear that social media has become a major part of the integrated marketing landscape. The challenge for a company is making the best use of the technology to advance its brand.

CONSUMER-GENERATED ADVERTISING

Crowdsourcing involves soliciting ideas from individuals for a commercial or actually obtaining an entire advertisement that has been created by an outside person. It offers an alternative to creating commercials in-house or using an external advertising agency. The goal of using crowdsourcing is to create a viral buzz as users view advertisements online, recommend or send favorites to friends, and post links.[53]

Consumer-generated ads are not always created for television. Travelers at the Liverpool Street Station in London were greeted one January morning by several hundred commuters who started dancing instead of getting onto the train. The dance was captured by hidden cameras. A day later it was played during a commercial break on the *Celebrity Big Brother* television show. The entire episode was an event sponsored by T-Mobile for its "Life for Sharing" campaign. The ad was shown only that one time on television, but it spread via e-mail messages, blogs, social networks, and Twitter until it had been watched more than 15 million times on YouTube.[54]

Consumer-generated advertising can be powerful. Nick Haley, an 18-year-old student, was an Apple computer loyalist who received his first Macintosh at the age of 3. He felt inspired to make a commercial about the Apple iPod Touch after hearing the song "Music Is My Hot, Hot Sex." A lyric in the song was, "My music is where I'd like to touch." Using the song as a background, Haley created a fast-paced tour of the abilities of the iPod Touch. He uploaded the video to YouTube. He received four stars out of a possible five and comments such as "That's awesome" and "Makes me want to buy one."

Among the viewers of Haley's commercial was an Apple employee, who asked the staff to contact the company's advertising agency TBWA/Chiat/Day. The agency liked the commercial, contacted Haley, and invited him to make a high-definition version of it.[55]

Nick Haley's story is beginning to be repeated as companies and advertising agencies realize the power of consumer-generated advertising. In the words of Haley, "That's the whole point of advertising; it needs to get to the user. If you get the user to make ads, who better?" According to Lee Clow, chairman and chief creative at TBWA Worldwide, consumer-generated ads are part of a new world. "It's an exciting new format for brands to communicate with their audiences. People's relationship with a brand is becoming a dialog, not a monolog."[56]

CONSUMER-GENERATED REVIEWS

Word-of-mouth endorsements have changed. In the past, a satisfied or dissatisfied consumer would tell friends and relatives about a purchasing experience. Now, many companies that vend multiple goods or services solicit consumer-generated reviews of those products.

Amazon.com stands at the forefront of consumer-generated reviews. Each book offered online holds a space where individual customers can write reviews, both with words and a one- to five-star rating. The site informs the shopper of the number of reviews, the average star rating, and notes if the reviews are written by anonymous critics or those who provide their real names. A person wishing to place his name on a review must authenticate it by presenting Amazon.com with a credit card number. Customers benefit by reading the reviews before making purchases. The system may not be perfect, because an author may use a pseudonym to write a highly favorable review and encourage friends and family members to do the same. At the same time, the author cannot control the outside reviews that are posted.

Best Buy has incorporated consumer feedback into online retailing. The company hosts a blog section for consumers to read about and discuss various topics. In each product category, such as cameras, Best Buy provides a discussion forum on a variety of related topics. In the digital camera discussion forum, consumers can post photos they have taken with various cameras. Best Buy posts customer reviews of each product, both positive and negative. The reviews may have a considerable influence on which brands consumers consider and eventually purchase. By providing blogs, discussion forums, and consumer reviews, Best Buy offers consumers ways to search for and evaluate products and to make purchase decisions without leaving the company's Web site.

Consumer-generated reviews and discussions can be important vehicles for reaching early adopters of products. They provide a forum that allows for the dissemination of information among consumers.

Customer-generated reviews should be carefully considered. Too many negative reviews and low-star ratings can harm the company. The marketing team should carefully monitor them to see what is being said. Also, reviews stress the importance of consistent, high-quality products and services. Reviews provide important information about how company products are evaluated by customers and how the brand compares to the competition. This information becomes critical when developing marketing plans, product modifications, and service strategies.

The use of consumer-generated reviews continues to rise. The marketing challenge will be managing this aspect of consumer word-of-mouth endorsements in ways that enhance brand equity and increase sales.

▼ Best Buy's Web site provides consumer reviews of numerous products, such as video cameras.

Source: Courtesy of Summer Bradley.

E-MAIL

E-mail can be another important part of a company's interactive marketing strategy. To be successful, an e-mail marketing program should be integrated with other channels. It cannot simply be a program where addresses are purchased and mass e-mails are sent to individuals on the list. Most people resent spam, and response rates are extremely low.

Response rates increase when e-mail messages resemble the information on the company's Web site and in its advertisements and direct mail messages. When Data Inc. introduced new project management software, the marketing team integrated e-mail with a Webinar, direct mail, social media, and telemarketing. The Webinar explained how the new software tool worked. Direct mail, telemarketing, and e-mail were used to reach 600 influential decision makers. For e-mails that were returned undeliverable, Data, Inc. used LinkedIn to locate the contact's correct information. The e-mail integrated approach resulted in a 3 percent response rate.[57]

Using Web Analytics to Direct E-Mail

Web analytics is the process of analyzing where consumers went at a brand's Web site, what they did within the Web site, and what other sites were visited. An individual who spends 10 minutes examining merchandise within a particular section of a site becomes an excellent target for an e-mail about the products examined. When an individual visits several Web sites to look at similar merchandise, the person has reached the latter stages of the purchase process and is close to making the purchase decision or actual purchase. Web analytics allows a company to develop e-mail campaigns that offer the greatest chance of response.

E-mail campaigns can also be directed at consumers who abandon shopping carts without making purchases. About 40 percent of online shoppers abandon the shopping cart just prior to the checkout. Only about 30 percent of these shoppers return to complete the transaction. The IT department can identify the individuals who abandon a shopping basket. Sending an e-mail to these individuals offering free shipping, a discount if they complete the order, or a simple reminder that they have items in their shopping basket can lead to greater sales. Converting these individuals to customers is much easier and more lucrative than sending mass e-mails. Targeted e-mails have a conversion rate 5 to 10 times higher than mass e-mails sent to the firm's customers. In addition, revenues from these follow-up e-mails are three to nine times higher.[58]

E-Mail Newsletters

E-mail newsletters can help to create brand awareness, drive traffic to a Web site, and spur sales. Newsletters are especially beneficial when consumers sign up to receive them. The newsletter must be constructed to offer value to recipients. It must go beyond product information. The more valuable the content is to the recipients, the more likely the newsletter will yield results.

Thrillist (**thrillist.com**) and UrbanDaddy (**urbandaddy.com**) send out e-mail newsletters to 1.1 million subscribers. Most subscribers are college graduates with median incomes of $88,000. The UrbanDaddy newsletter emphasizes an exclusive and luxurious approach, advising men on where to shop and how to fit in. The Thrillist newsletter features a fun and relaxed tone. Both organize free, heavily-sponsored events for subscribers of the newsletters. The newsletter becomes a means of engaging the subscribers with the Web sites.[59]

▼ Haik Humble can employ various Web analytics to develop a direct e-mail campaign.

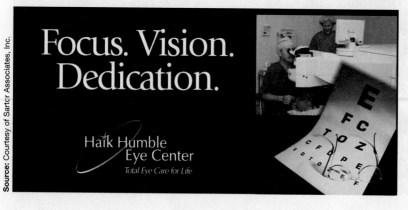

Focus. Vision. Dedication.

Haik Humble Eye Center
Total Eye Care for Life

VIRAL MARKETING

Viral marketing is preparing a marketing message that is passed in some way from one consumer to another through digital means. A viral campaign can take the form of an e-mail or it can be a video that is posted to a personal blog and passed to other blogs or Web sites such as YouTube. It can become a form of advocacy or word-of-mouth endorsement. Viral marketing occurs when one customer passes a message to other potential buyers. The term *viral* is derived from the image of a person being "infected" with the marketing message and then spreading it to friends, like a virus. The difference is that the customer voluntarily sends the message to others.

Viral marketing messages may include advertisements, hyperlinked promotions, online newsletters, streaming videos, and games. For instance, about a dozen videos were posted on YouTube of a man claiming to be the "world's fastest nudist." He streaks through various locations in New York City wearing only tennis shoes, tube socks, and a fanny pack positioned strategically in front. The links to the videos were e-mailed from individual to individual. They were posted on popular blogs such as The Huffington Post and Gawker. One appeared on CNN on *Anderson Cooper 360*. The campaign turned out to be a viral video campaign for Zappos, an online shoe and apparel store. The viral campaign highlighted that Zappos was selling clothes, because additional videos were posted that showed a van screeching up to the "fastest nudist" and several people jumping out wearing Zappos T-shirts. As the van leaves, the video shows the nudist dressed in pants and a shirt.[60]

Figure 9.9 provides some suggestions on how to create successful viral campaigns. The viral message should focus on the product or business. In the Zappos videos, the nudist is given clothes by a Zappos team. The marketing team determines why an individual would want to pass the message along or tell friends about it.

OfficeMax created a viral campaign close to the Christmas holiday season that centered around a quartet of dancing elves with cutout photos pasted on their bodies. Visitors to the special micro-site were encouraged to paste their pictures on the elves and pass it along to friends. The viral campaign drew more than 10 million visitors, because it was unique and it provided something that people wanted to pass along to others. Later, the *Today Show* and *Good Morning America* created their own dancing holiday greetings for viewers.[61]

Individuals should receive an incentive to pass the message along. A message with entertainment value offers one incentive. The incentive can be financial, such as free merchandise or a discount if the message is passed along to friends who make a purchase, log onto a Web site, or register for an e-newsletter. The incentive could also just be the campaign's uniqueness. A message that can be personalized has a great chance of being sent on.

With so many forms of interactive marketing available to companies, viral marketing has lost some of its luster. Some consumers have lost enthusiasm and are less willing to pass along messages. The advantage to the marketing team is that it can track the results of a viral campaign and analyze the resulting data to determine what works and what does not.

• Focus on the product or business.	• Offer an incentive.
• Determine why individuals would want to pass the message along.	• Make it personal.
	• Track the results and analyze the data.

◀ **FIGURE 9.9**
Keys to Successful Viral Marketing Campaigns

INTERNATIONAL IMPLICATIONS

8 How can e-active marketing be conducted successfully in international markets?

The ability to reach customers worldwide represents one of the major advantages e-commerce holds over brick and-mortar retail stores. Some online companies are still forced to turn away international orders because they do not have processes in place to fill the orders. This means that while the Internet makes it possible to sell items in an international marketplace, some companies are not prepared to go global. Obstacles to selling across national boundaries include communications barriers, cultural differences, global shipping problems due to a lack of sufficient infrastructure, and varying degrees of Internet capabilities in other countries.[62] Also, Internet companies must follow local exporting and importing laws.

Source: Thinkstock Royalty Free.

▲ International shipping is an important component of a global e-commerce business.

Shipping Issues

One key to the effective launch of a global e-commerce site is preparing to make international shipments. Air transport is affordable for smaller products; DHL Worldwide Express, FedEx, and UPS offer excellent shipping options. Larger merchandise normally can be shipped by a freight forwarder that finds the best mode of delivery, from ships to trucks to rail. Air transport companies and freight forwarders both offer specialized logistics software and provide the proper documentation and forms to meet importing and exporting regulations in every country served.

Payment Methods

Shipping arrangements are not the only concern. Payment mechanisms must also be addressed. Each country has a different currency, and methods of payment also vary. For example, in Europe debit cards are preferred to credit cards. Europe also has a high rate of credit card theft, which increases the risks associated with accepting them.

Communication Issues

Developing a Web site that appeals to the audience in each country will be a key task. It includes adding information that someone in another country would require, such as the country code for telephone numbers. It also requires removing or changing any colors, words, or images that might be offensive to a particular group of people in another country.

New globalization software has been developed for companies expanding into other countries. One software package translates an English-language Web site into a large number of foreign languages. Another valuable feature that the software offers is "cultural adaptation," which adjusts a Web site's terminology, look, and feel to suit local norms. The software also has a feature in which the content developed in one location can easily be deployed to all sites around the world. This provides a more consistent look to the Web sites, without someone spending time modifying each foreign site. The software makes it easier to prepare a Web site in the proper native language and also conform to local customs.[63]

Technology Issues

The technical side of international e-commerce remains challenging. Software compatibility remains an unresolved technical issue. Ideally, these various technologies will eventually be merged into a single system. Currently, the bandwidth for handling Internet traffic varies considerably. Information technology staff are involved in every step of an internationalization process in order to overcome the potential technical glitches.

A coherent IMC strategy utilizes local input from the various countries involved. The brand on an Internet site must be consistent from one country to the next. Each site should also consistently present the company's primary marketing message. For IBM, this meant using local companies in each country to design individual Web sites and provide the information used on each site. To ensure consistency, IBM designs the main marketing messages at its central office, but then local companies translate the messages and add reseller contact and pricing information.

In the future, the growth of international e-commerce will continue to rise. Firms that get in on the ground floor are likely to enjoy a major marketing advantage.

! INTEGRATED CAMPAIGNS IN ACTION

● Interstate Batteries

Interstate Batteries employed its internal marketing department to launch a geo-targeted online media plan for all company Battery Centers that are located in cities throughout the United States. The objectives of the campaign were to:

- Increase awareness of all Interstate Battery Centers
- Drive traffic to all Interstate Battery Centers
- Create awareness of key brand messages

Source: Courtesy of Interstate Battery.

▲ Interstate Batteries launched a geo-targeted online advertising campaign to build awareness of all company Battery Centers and to drive traffic to geo-specific landing pages.

Interstate Batteries used online display advertising to create awareness and provide information about the location of its stores. The campaign was geo-targeted by each store's market zip codes. Consumers who clicked on the ads were taken to a geo-specific landing page that provided information about the closest All Battery Center. The campaign targeted the 25 to 54 age group with the selected zip codes surrounding each of the battery stores.

Online metrics to measure the success of the campaign were determined prior to the launch. Metrics included click-through, coupon redemption, changes in sales, and the number of transactions at the retail stores. Additional online metrics included the number individuals who enlarged the map, submitted information by e-mail, and printed the coupon.

Your instructor has additional information about the ads, visuals, and displays used in this campaign.

❝ SUMMARY

Increased usage of the Internet by both consumers and businesses has led many marketing teams to develop an Internet presence. E-active marketing combines the two major components of Internet marketing: e-commerce and interactive marketing. Web 2.0 changes the ways consumers communicate and interact with companies. The key is to integrate e-marketing strategies with the overall integrated marketing communications plan.

An e-commerce Web site includes a catalog, a shopping cart, a payment collection method, and a store locator. In e-commerce and other Internet ventures, customers should believe the process is secure and be enticed to change buying habits. Three incentives that help people alter buying patterns are financial incentives, greater convenience, and added value.

Interactive marketing is the development of marketing programs that create interplay between customers and businesses. It assists marketing in targeting potential customers with personalized information and engages the consumer with the product and company.

Online advertising reaches young, more Internet-savvy consumers. It includes banner advertising, classified and media/video advertising, search engine optimization, and paid search ads.

Brand spiraling may be used to combine the Internet program with advertising in traditional media. Blogs create a new form of word-of-mouth advertising. Blogs can be company-sponsored or posted by individual Internet users.

Online social networks include Facebook, Twitter, and others. Social media have become a major part of the integrated marketing landscape. Consumer-generated advertising includes crowdsourcing and other methods. They represent a new method for engaging customers with a brand or company. Consumer-generated reviews offer the opportunity to create forums for customers to discuss product benefits and problems.

E-mail may be used to supplement an integrated program. Web analytics assist in directing e-mail blasts to the most viable markets. E-mail newsletters can help create brand awareness, drive traffic to a Web site, and spur sales.

Viral marketing is preparing a marketing message that will be passed along by consumers. Effective viral programs spur consumer interest and provide rewards for passing messages to others.

International markets may also be served by e-commerce enterprises, especially when cultural differences, shipping problems, and Internet capability problems can be solved. Information technology departments play a key role in solving the Internet problems. Shipping issues and language differences also require attention in this lucrative and growing marketplace.

❞

e-active marketing   Term used to describe the two major components of Internet marketing: e-commerce and interactive marketing.

e-commerce   Selling goods and services on the Internet.

cyberbait   Some type of lure or attraction that brings people to a Web site.

interactive marketing   Individualizing and personalizing Web content and e-mail messages for various consumers.

widgets   Mini-applications embedded in a banner ad that permit a consumer access to some form of dynamic content that is provided by an external source other than the company where the ad resides.

dwell rate   Measures the proportion of ad impressions that resulted in users clicking an ad or mousing over it.

dwell time   Measures the amount of time individuals spend engaged with an advertisement.

search engine optimization (SEO)   The process of increasing the probability of a particular company's Web site emerging from a search.

brand spiraling   The practice of using traditional media to promote and attract consumers to a Web site.

personalized URLs (PURLs)   A personalized Web page that is preloaded with the customer's personal data, contact information, purchase behavior, and previous interactions with the company.

blogs   Online musings by an individual or group; the term is derived from "Web logs."

viral marketing   An advertisement that is tied to an e-mail or other form of online communication in which one person passes on the advertisement or e-mail to other consumers.

REVIEW QUESTIONS

1. Define e-active marketing.
2. How has Web 2.0 influenced the field of marketing?
3. What is e-commerce? What are its main components?
4. What is cyberbait? What are the three main forms of cyberbait?
5. What concerns do some consumers still have about e-commerce?
6. What benefits do e-commerce programs offer to business-to-business operations?
7. What is interactive marketing?
8. What primary forms of online advertising are used by marketing teams?
9. What is meant by the term search engine optimization (SEO)? How can it be accomplished?
10. What is brand spiraling?
11. What is a blog? How can blogs be used in marketing communication programs?
12. How can online social networks be used to supplement advertising and communication tactics?
13. Describe consumer-generated advertising.
14. How can a marketing team take advantage of customer-generated reviews?
15. Identify and describe the elements of an effective e-mail campaign in marketing.
16. What is viral marketing? What is the goal of a viral marketing program?
17. What challenges must be overcome to establish an international e-commerce operation?

CRITICAL THINKING EXERCISES

Discussion Questions

1. What types of goods or services have you purchased online during the past year? Have your parents or grandparents purchased anything online? If so, compare your purchases and attitudes toward buying via the Internet with theirs. If neither you, your parents, nor your grandparents have used the Internet to make purchases, why not?

2. For what type of products do you conduct Internet searches for information? What factors determine whether you conduct online searches for information? When searching for information, what sites do you use? How effective are each of the following search results in your decision on what sites to access?

   a. Paid search insertions

   b. Organic search results

   c. Paid search ads

3. Examine the four issues people have with purchasing over the Internet in Figure 9.4. Interview five people of various ages and genders. Which issues were a concern? Which issues were not a concern? Does gender or age make a difference in how individuals feel about the issues of seller opportunism, security, privacy, or purchasing habits?

4. Are you on Facebook? Why or why not? If you are on Facebook, how much time do you spend online at Facebook? Do you use Twitter? Why or why not? Based on your experience with Facebook and Twitter, how can companies use them to reach you? Are you a fan of any company on Facebook? If so, why did you become a fan? If not, why did you choose not to become a fan?

5. Interview five individuals of different ages about blogs. What percent have read, launched, or participated in blogging on the Internet? What was each person's motivation?

6. Do you use consumer-generated reviews in making purchase decisions? How valuable do you think they are to consumers? What are your thoughts about consumer-generated ads? Is that a trend for the future where

companies will use more consumer-generated ads and fewer agency-produced ads? What are the pros and cons, from your perspective, of consumer-generated materials?

7. Have you ever participated in a viral marketing campaign? If so, discuss why you participated and your evaluation of the viral campaign from the company or brand's perspective. If you have not participated in a viral campaign, what type of incentive would it take for you to participate? How effective do you think viral campaigns are with consumers in your market segment?

INTEGRATED LEARNING EXERCISES

1. Best Buy was a late e-commerce entrant, but it has developed a strong e-commerce component. The key to Best Buy's success, according to Barry Judge, vice president of marketing, is, "We do a lot of one-to-one marketing. We're not overly focused on where the consumers buy." The Web site carries every product that Best Buy stocks. It uses personalized services, along with convenient pickup and fair return policies to entice consumers to shop. Consumers can purchase items on the Internet and either have them shipped directly to them or pick them up at the closest store. Shoppers can use the Internet to see if Best Buy stocks a particular item, to determine what the item costs, and to gather product information. What is the advantage of this strategy? Access the Web site at **www.bestbuy.com**. Evaluate it in terms of ease of use and product information, and then locate the Best Buy closest to you. Next, access Circuit City's Web site at **www.circuitcity.com**. Compare it to Best Buy's site. Select a product, such as a camcorder, to compare the two Web sites.

2. Pick one of the following product categories and access the Web sites of two companies that sell the product. What types of financial incentives are offered on each company's Web site to encourage you to purchase? What about the other two types of incentives, greater convenience and added value? What evidence do you see for them? Compare and contrast the two companies in terms of incentives offered.
   a. Contacts or eyeglasses
   b. Water skis
   c. Clothes
   d. Cameras
   e. Camping supplies

3. The three main companies businesses use to ship small packages either overnight or 2-day delivery are FedEx, UPS, and the U.S. Postal Service. Access the Web sites of each shipping solution provider: **www.fedex.com**, **www.ups.com**, and **www.usps.gov**. What delivery guarantees does each offer? Which site is the most user-friendly? Which site appears to offer the best customer service?

4. Figure 9.1 identifies the components of an e-commerce site. Access each of the following Web sites and evaluate each along the six components of a good e-commerce site.
   a. Travelocity (**www.travelocity.com**)
   b. Wells Fargo Bank (**www.wellsfargo.com**)
   c. WeddingChannel.com (**www.weddingchannel.com**)
   d. Bluefly (**www.bluefly.com**)

5. Customer interactive software is an important part of many Web sites. Access the following two companies that sell interactive software. What capabilities does each software package offer? What other services are available?
   a. Escalate Retail (**www.escalate.com**)
   b. Convergys (**www.convergys.com**)

6. Blogs provide opportunities for both individuals and businesses to share information, thoughts, and opinions. Go to Google Blog Search at **http://blogsearch.google.com**. Type in a topic that you are interested in exploring that is related to advertising and marketing communications, such as "advertising to children." Locate three blogs on the topic you chose. Discuss who initiated the blog and the value of the information on the blog.

7. Access each of the following search engines. For each one, discuss how it handles paid search advertising when you type in a search, such as "running shoes." What ads do you see as display ads and what ads are part of the search results? Discuss the differences among the five search engines. Which one do you like the best? Why?
   a. Google (**www.google.com**)
   b. Yahoo! (**www.yahoo.com**)
   c. AltaVista (**www.altavista.com**)
   d. AOL Search (**http://search.aol.com**)
   e. Bing (**www.bing.com**)

STUDENT PROJECT

Creative Corner

Bluefly's marketing team wants to enhance the company's brand name and Internet presence. They have asked you to be an Internet advertising consultant. Access the Bluefly Web site at **www.bluefly.com**. Once you feel comfortable with the company, prepare the following creative material and information for Bluefly.

1. Bluefly wants to use brand spiraling to increase brand awareness and enhance the brand name. Outline a media plan that you believe will accomplish this objective.

2. The company is interested in placing an advertisement on a social network, such as YouTube or Facebook. Other than Facebook, what other social networks would you advise? Which site or sites would you recommend? Design the display ad that should be placed on Facebook or another social network site.

3. The company believes a viral marketing campaign would be effective in drawing new visitors to the site. Design a viral marketing campaign.

4. Search engine optimization seems to be an effective tool for driving individuals to the company's site. Which search engine should be used? Identify five key words that you believe Bluefly should advertise. Design the display or listing ad that should be used.

CASE 1 · BING CHALLENGES GOOGLE'S SEARCH ENGINE DOMINANCE

Every once in awhile, a product or a company's name becomes so famous it gets added to the national vocabulary. A generation ago, employees started making "xerox" copies. Before that, people started taking "aspirins" instead of "pain medicine" and covering wounds with "band aids" rather than "adhesive strips." Today, it is common to hear someone say she "googled" something.

The basic Google business model is to organize a vast amount of information into a system that can be easily accessed using the Web. Google provides information to users for free. The company sells advertising that is linked to the free information. One primary advantage held by Google is that the firm has been able to expand indexing and retrieval searches into nearly 100 languages. Using tools from Basis Technology, Google is able to offer searches in Asian languages as well as other challenging languages. The net result is a global company with a worldwide reach.

The year 2004 was especially significant at Google. The company sold stock for the first time, raising $1.67 billion in capital. The stock price then soared. Many major firms have learned that advertising on a search engine like Google provides a targeted audience with profitable results. Naturally, advertising dollars are quick to follow, and in this case they moved to Google, the market leader in search engine use. One industry leader commented that Google has created almost a "new world order" in advertising.

Google's management team remains acutely aware of competitors. Microsoft and Yahoo! are two main search engine providers that could affect Google's share. New competitors emerge every day. In June 2009, Microsoft introduced the search engine Bing in an effort to challenge Google.

Bing replaced Microsoft's Live Search engine. It was started after more than a year of research showing that although users said they were generally satisfied with Web search services there were times when searches became too difficult. In the beginning, Bing received praise from many influential reviewers, increasing the possibility that it could shake up the dynamics of the search business, which is worth $12 billion in the United States alone.

In July 2009, Microsoft and Yahoo! announced a partnership in Internet search and advertising intended to build on the introduction of Bing and close the gap with Google; however, Google still held 65 percent of the search market, compared with 10 percent for Microsoft. Then, the competition with Google became more direct.

Bing began running television commercials designed to indirectly hint that Google searches were too complicated, turning users into data-spewing zombies. Bing was offered as the easy-to-use alternative.

Then, Microsoft CEO Steve Ballmer allegedly offered to pay Rupert Murdoch's News Corp. to remove all its content from Google. This would include content from *The Wall Street Journal*, the *New York Post*, and *The Times* of London. The idea was that if Web surfers could not find News Corp. content when they did a Google search, they would be more inclined to use Bing. There were reports that Microsoft offered the same deal to other publishers.

News providers have long been frustrated that stories and materials they create are posted without the news company receiving any compensation, whereas Google and Bing are able to sell advertising right beside the stories. Google responded by saying any organization was free to pull content at any time, apparently unfazed by Bing and Microsoft's effort.

Other search engines have also emerged. Still, Google's power in the marketplace makes company leaders optimistic about the future. Time will tell if Bing can make inroads on what is practically a cultural icon: Google.

1. What tactics should Microsoft and Bing use to gain market share?

2. As an advertiser, does Bing hold an advantage due to lower clutter on the site, or does Google's wider reach offset that advantage?

3. Which site would facilitate a faster search engine optimization effort? Why?

4. Which site, Google or Bing, would be most useful to an international company? Why?

5. Design an advertisement for Bing that would appear in a magazine. Which magazine would you use for the ad? Why?

Sources: Heidi Gautschi, "Search in Any Language," *EContent* 28, no. 5 (May 2005), p. 29; "Google Is Standing on the Brink of Global Dominance," *Marketing Week* (April 28, 2005), p. 31; Thomas Claburn and Tony Kontzer, "Google Wants a Piece of the Business Market," *InformationWeek,* no. 1040 (May 23, 2005), p. 29; Mathew Creamer and Kris Oser, "Google Breaks Down and Decides to Advertise," *Advertising Age* 76, no. 18 (May 2, 2005), p. 3; Daniel Lyons, "Google This: The Tech Giants Duke It Out—Again" (www.newsweek.com/id/224597/page/1, accessed March 29, 2010), November 28, 2009; "Microsoft Corporation" (http:// topics. nytimes.com/top/news/business/companies/microsoft_corporation/ index.html?scp=1&sq=bing%20versus%20google&st=cse, accessed March 29, 2010).

▲ Will Bing be able to challenge Google when it comes to search engine dominance?

CASE 2 SOMETHING SALTY FOR THE HOT TUB MARKET

Bernie Johnson was about to begin a new business venture. After working for years in the pool and spa industry as a salesperson in a local store, he decided to launch his own line of products, a series of hot tubs with the brand name Salt Spa.

Bernie was convinced that the future of the hot tub marketplace was in selling saltwater systems, actually saline-based ones, rather than traditional tubs using chemicals and chlorine. Saltwater systems work by creating their own chlorine. An electric current passes through saltwater in a chlorinator cell, which splits the salt into sodium and chloride. It then releases a chlorine gas that dissolves in the water. This process not only sterilizes the water, it prevents the growth of algae.

Saline-based systems offer a number of benefits. First, the water is not as harsh, so it does not hurt a person's eyes. It is also less irritating to the skin. It feels softer and does not create drying effects on the skin after the person leaves the tub. People who have reactions to chlorinated tubs are generally reacting not to the chlorine, but to other chemicals and by-products. They generally do not encounter the same problem lounging in a saline hot tub. Also, swimming suits worn in salt-based hot tubs last much longer than do those exposed to chlorine.

A saline-based system means the consumer does not have to buy expensive and dangerous chemicals. Instead, the maintenance process is adding common salt to the system, and it is not added often, because the system recycles the salt. Sometimes it requires adding acid to balance the pH levels. In essence, saline hot tubs are more environmentally friendly. In general, a saltwater tub is safer, less expensive to maintain over time, healthier, and better for the environment.

▲ Many consumers are now switching pools and hot tubs to salt water.

The major disadvantage of a saline-based tub is the cost. The price of installing a saline system to an existing chlorine hot tub is high. Doing so also voids any factory warranty. When running salt through a hot tub filter, the consumer must be very conscientious about cleaning the filter. Also, the consumer must also watch out for any corrosion, which is the primary problem when trying to maintain a saltwater hot tub. It is similar to what happens to a car after several winters. The salt from the road is like acid on the hull of a new car.

Bernie intended to sell both salt-based hot tubs and conversion kits. His primary markets were going to be: (1) online buyers through his Web site, (2) any retail outlets that would carry his line, and (3) spas and other places offering hot tubs to clients.

The challenges to his new business would be to build a recognizable brand, make inroads with retailers, and find ways to reach business-to-business clients. Hot tubs are sold as primarily luxury items, which means that the people who buy them have higher incomes and live in nicer homes. Finding ways to reach them was one key.

Bernie had to make sure that retail salespeople did not say that a saltwater hot tub system is chemical free—a myth perpetuated on many Web sites. Salt is a chemical compound. It is not on the periodic table. When the electrodes separate the salt, it becomes two chemicals, which means the tub is not chemical free.

Attracting spas and other businesses to buy saline-based systems would require both an Internet presence and a small sales force to make calls, possibly one or two salespeople at first. Still, he was excited, because Bernie believed he was getting in on the ground floor of a major change in the marketplace.

1. Can Salt Spa products be sold through a traditional e-commerce program?

2. What should be the major features of the Salt Spa Web site?

3. Describe how a blog, social network, or e-mail program could be used to drive traffic to the Salt Spa Web site.

4. Should the company expand into converting chlorine-based swimming pools to salt water? Why or why not?

5. What types of relationships must Bernie build to make sure his products are sold in any new home being built with a spa room? How can his Internet program help him in this area?

Sources: Anne Clark, "Saline Versus Chlorine: Which Is Better for Your Pool or Hot Tub?" (www.ezinearticles.com, accessed January 15, 2008). http://www.repair-home.com/Saltwater_Hot_Tubs.html, accessed August 31, 2010.

Source: Author Supplied Image.

10 Alternative Marketing

THE VIDEO GAME MARKET REACHES A NEW NICHE

Video games offer marketers a popular medium to reach younger consumers as they relax and enjoy free time. Video game marketing is a multimillion dollar marketplace. Some companies focus on selling the devices that play the games. Others concentrate on developing new games. More recently, advertisements and product placements represent a lucrative new method for reaching this valuable target market.

Traditionally, video games were developed for teen and young adult males. Today IDC Research estimates that 40 percent of gamers are females. One recent estimate suggests that more than 130 million females play video games. Another study notes that the growth in the number of female gamers is worldwide. In India, females make up over 20 percent of all gamers.

The introduction of new games for females has drawn more girls and women into gaming. Electronic Arts (EA) introduced *Littlest Pet Shop* for young girls and *Charm Girls* for older girls. Sony has created a *Hannah Montana* game. Ubisoft Entertainment launched *Your Shape* and *Just Dance*, and Nintendo offers *Wii Fit Plus*. EA's *Sports Active* became a top 10 title for 3 consecutive months, according to research firm NPD Group. Ubisoft's *Imagine* video game series features games in which girls can play the role of a ballerina or explore female-dominated professions. Ubisoft sold 14 million *Imagine* video games in 3 years.

An entire Web site, Women Gamers.com (**www.womengamers. com**), is devoted to women who enjoy video games. The site offers reviews of games and posts various types of commentary articles. One asks why females who are in a room with men playing a virtual shootout war-type game feel relegated to spectator status. Another questions why the most recent list of top 50 game developers did not include one female name.

Some argue that more can be done to entice women into the market. Courtney Simmons, public relations director for Sony Online Entertainment (SOE), recently spoke to an invitation-only crowd at the Game Developers Conference in San Francisco. Simmons was joined by several other women from SOE to announce the details of the Gamers in Real Life (G.I.R.L.) program at the

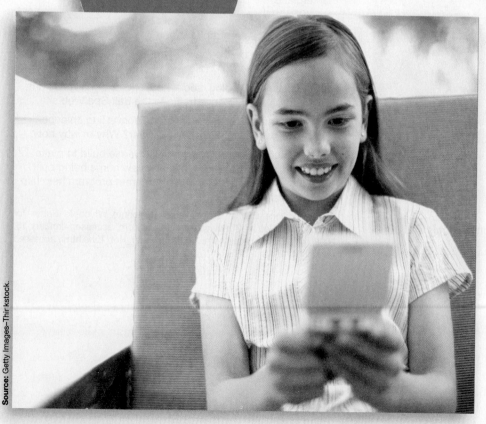

CHAPTER OBJECTIVES

After reading this chapter, you should be able to answer the following questions:

1 How can buzz marketing, guerrilla marketing, lifestyle marketing, and experiential marketing enhance a marketing communications program?

2 What methods can be used to effectively employ product placements and branded entertainment?

3 Why has the use of alternative media venues, especially video game advertising, grown in marketing communications programs?

4 How have in-store marketing and point-of-purchase displays evolved into even more effective communication and sales tools?

5 How can brand communities enhance brand loyalty and devotion?

6 What methods are used to adapt alternative marketing programs to international marketing efforts?

company's San Diego headquarters. The program, which emerged from a partnership with The Art Institutes, was the first of its kind. Participants, who were female students currently enrolled at an Art Institute school, engaged in a game-building contest. The winner received $10,000 toward her tuition and a paid internship at one of SOE's development studios.

Simmons enjoys playing video games with her three children. She argues that women are being "gamed down to," because, she says, "there is a lack of understanding about how women play." Simmons wants "more women making games," she says, "making more games that women want to play."

Studies and sales data have shown that women are more likely to play handheld casual games, such as the Nintendo DS, along with more socially-oriented games, such as *The Sims*, where women are more than 55 percent of players. Although the number of women who play games is high and growing, just under 12 percent of video game developers are women, according to the International Game Developers Association. By diversifying the workforce, developers believe they can create products that appeal to a wider audience.

Some progress has been made. Prior to the release of the *Littlest Pet Shop*, EA conducted extensive market research about what female users want in a game. The company's marketing team discovered that girls like it better when the pets make eye contact with the player. After testing the game with girls, EA added accessories for the pets and gave players the ability to customize them. The *Littlest Pet Shop* became EA's best-selling game in its market.

From a marketing communications perspective, gaming appears to offer great potential for all three aspects of the marketplace. As more females purchase gaming devices and play games tailored to them, sales may grow exponentially. Further, the ability to reach girls, young women, and mature women with products placed in the games or advertising messages embedded in them presents a potentially powerful new method to develop brand awareness and brand loyalty in an alternative medium.[1]

▲ Females are now a prime target for video games.

CHAPTER 10

OVERVIEW

Traditional mass media advertising faces many challenges. Although advertisers are not ready to abandon radio, television, magazines, newspapers, and outdoor programs, they know that many new and valuable media outlets have emerged. As a result, alternative marketing programs and alternative media are on the rise. Increasing numbers of dollars are spent finding ways to reach potential customers in new and innovative formats. Successful advertising and promotional programs that utilize alternative approaches can be developed.

In this chapter, four main topics are presented. First, the four main types of alternative marketing programs are identified: buzz marketing, guerrilla marketing, product placements and branded entertainment, and lifestyle marketing. Next, a series of marketing tactics associated with alternative media are described. Third, in-store marketing will be examined. Finally, brand communities are discussed. The international implications of these new forms of alternative media are also presented.

ALTERNATIVE MARKETING PROGRAMS

① How can buzz marketing, guerrilla marketing, lifestyle marketing, and experiential marketing enhance a marketing communications program?

Developing alternative marketing programs requires creativity and imagination. Marketers seek to identify new places where a consumer's path intersects with a brand's presence, or create a new intersection point. Then, attention-getting marketing messages can be developed for those points of contact. This means a firm can supplement or replace mass media advertising with more targeted options.

In essence, the goal remains the same as for traditional media. Marketing professionals continue to look for innovative ways to reach a target audience. Alternative marketing programs and alternative media venues have become widely accepted options. Figure 10.1 lists some of the more common alternative marketing choices. These programs seldom operate independently. A guerrilla marketing campaign might also include buzz and lifestyle marketing components. The same campaign may contain e-active components and traditional media.

Alternative marketing relies on buzz, word-of-mouth, lifestyles, and times when consumers are relaxing and enjoying hobbies and events. Integrating these venues using one coherent integrated marketing program that speaks with a clear voice and message is the goal.

BUZZ MARKETING

Buzz marketing has become one of the fastest-growing areas in alternative marketing. Estimated expenditures for these programs are now at $1 billion annually. **Buzz marketing**, or *word-of-mouth marketing*, emphasizes consumers passing along information about a product. A recommendation by a friend, family member, or even an acquaintance carries higher levels of credibility than does an advertisement. It can be more powerful than the words of a paid spokesperson or endorser. Buzz, or word-of-mouth, can be generated in the following ways: (1) consumers who truly like a brand and tell others, (2) consumers who like a brand and are sponsored by a company to tell others, and (3) company or agency employees who tell others about the brand.

Consumers Who Like a Brand

The ideal situation occurs when a consumer truly likes a particular brand and tells others. These messages can be delivered in person or via the Internet in chat rooms,

FIGURE 10.1 ▶
Forms of Alternative Marketing

- Buzz marketing
- Guerrilla marketing
- Lifestyle marketing
- Experiential marketing
- Product placement and branded entertainment

blogs, or e-mails. Many musical groups have gained fame and fortune through this type of word-of-mouth support by those who have seen the bands in bars or as part of a small concert or tour.

Sponsored Consumers

Many companies sponsor individuals as agents or advocates to introduce new products. It works best when these individuals, or ambassadors, also like the brand. An alternative type of sponsorship is using house parties.

Brand Ambassadors

Brand ambassadors, or customer evangelists, are typically individuals who already like the products that they are asked to sponsor. The company offers incentives and rewards in exchange for advocacy. Companies select these ambassadors based on their devotion to the various brands and the sizes of their social circles. Once recruited, they are expected to deliver messages to their families, friends, reference groups, and work associates. Some are asked to develop grassroots, no- or low-cost marketing events and to promote the brand on the Internet through blogs or on social networks such as Facebook. Brand advocates are told to be upfront and honest about their connections with the brand.

Sony used buzz marketing and brand advocates to launch its GPS camera. The product featured an emerging technology. Sony's marketing department believed it was important to get people to physically try the product.

Sony's marketing team selected 25 ambassadors from a pool of 2,000 applicants. The individuals chosen displayed high levels of interest in cameras, taking pictures, and also had plans to either travel or participate in sporting events. Each ambassador was given a free camera and lessons on how to use it. The Sony ambassadors were encouraged to hand out discount coupons, show the cameras to anyone who asked, and blog weekly about their adventures on a Sony micro-site.

One of the ambassadors, Cheryl Gillet, described and photographed her trip to Australia, adding a map of her journey. Juxtaposed with destinations on the map were photos of beach scenes and her tanned friends in swimsuits. Even those applicants who were not selected were pleased because each was rewarded with a 20-percent discount coupon for the GPS camera.[2]

Procter & Gamble used a similar approach for a series of products. Justin Breton was a student at Boston University. He spent about 15-hours per week talking about PUR, a water filtration system from Procter & Gamble. Justin was just one of 100 college "ambassadors" hired by P&G to pitch items ranging from PUR to Herbal Essences hair products. The students created their own marketing plans and earned up to $2,500 per semester. They were required to submit regular reports and were monitored by P&G and RepNation.[3] This approach helped Procter & Gamble place products in the hands of consumers and provided students with opportunities to create unique marketing ideas.

House Parties

Brand ambassadors can also host house parties. Nestlé Purina spent $50,000 on 1,000 house parties to market a new line of dog food, Chef Michael's Canine Creations. Purina identified childless individuals with household incomes greater than $60,000, who love to pamper their pets. House Party, a firm that matches brands with party hosts, located the homes for Purina. Dianna Burroughs

▼ The House of Blues in New Orleans benefits from the buzz generated by customers who tell their friends about the music and atmosphere.

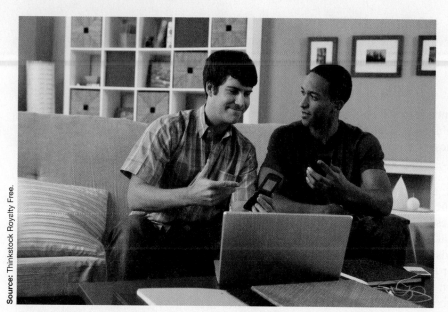

▲ Many companies employ college students to pitch products ranging from air filtration systems to cell phones to computer software.

hosted a party in her Manhattan West Village condo. Fourteen guests and their dogs arrived to sample the filet-mignon-and-potato-flavored kibbles from Chef Michael's Canine Creations. House Party's other clients include Avon, Procter & Gamble, Kraft, Mattel, Hershey's, and Ford.[4]

Pepsi utilized a similar approach to launch its lemon-lime soft drink Sierra Mist Ruby Splash. Through Grow Marketing, a nontraditional marketing and publicity company, influencers who loved lemon-lime beverages and who had deep and robust relationships within their social circles were recruited. They needed to be 18 to 34 years old and enjoy holding barbeques and other types of parties.

Pepsi delivered free ice cold drinks to about 300 parties. Each had 16 to 45 people in attendance. The marketing team also placed 45 custom-designed refrigerators in lifestyle venues where the target market consumers shop, such as sneaker and bike shops, surf shops, and skateboard stores. One party was held at graduation celebration for a college student. It included a backyard barbeque and pool party. Another individual hosted a party for his softball team. The owner of Rider Skate Board Shop hosted an outdoor movie night and invited his friends. The key to all of these events was that the host was an influencer among his or her friends and associates.[5]

Company Employees

A final group of advocates includes company employees. The company or agency decides whether they should pose as customers or identify themselves as being affiliated with the company. According to the Word of Mouth Marketing Association (WOMMA), individuals should be upfront and clearly identify themselves as being with the company.

A few years ago, Wal-Mart featured a blog about two ordinary people, Laura and Jim, trekking across the Unites States in an RV and staying in Wal-Mart parking lots. The blog appeared to be written by a couple who were avid customers of Wal-Mart. The blog received considerable attention after *BusinessWeek* exposed Jim as a professional photojournalist employed by Edelman, Wal-Mart's public relations firm. Both Wal-Mart and Edelman received considerable criticism regarding the program because of the lack of transparency.[6]

The Word of Mouth Marketing Association provides guidelines for companies seeking to generate word-of-mouth communications through employees, agency employees, or even sponsors or agents. It encourages:

- Honesty of relationship—be honest about the relationship between consumers, advocates, and marketers.
- Honesty of opinion—be honest in presenting opinions about the brand, both good and bad.
- Honesty of identity—identify honestly who you are.[7]

Buzz Marketing Stages

As shown in Figure 10.2, buzz marketing can be compared to how a virus replicates, which consists of three stages: inoculation, incubation, and infection.[8] The inoculation stage corresponds to the product being introduced. During incubation, the product will be tried by a few innovators or trendsetters. In the infection stage, widespread use of the product occurs.

Only a few companies have been successful with buzz marketing during the inoculation stage, or product introduction. In most cases, buzz marketing will not be successful

- Inoculation—the product is introduced.
- Incubation—the product is used by a few innovators or trendsetters.
- Infection—widespread use of the product occurs.

Source: Adapted from Jim Matorin, "Infectious 'Buzz Marketing' Is a Smart Way to Build Customer Loyalty at Your Operation," *Nation's Restaurant News*, Vol. 41, no. 18 (April 30, 2007), pp. 18–20.

at this stage unless brand agents or brand ambassadors are employed. Otherwise, generating word-of-mouth communication can be virtually impossible. Previous research suggests that the true customer-generated buzz occurs only after awareness of the product has developed. That awareness typically requires advertising through traditional channels.[9]

Buzz Marketing Preconditions

Advertising and buzz communication programs from actual customers cannot create a successful buzz by themselves. Other preconditions should be met (see Figure 10.3). First, the product must be unique, new, or perform better than current brands. The brand should stand out and have distinct advantages over current products on the market. Although not essential, memorable advertising helps to generate buzz. Intriguing, different, and unique advertising captures attention and can generate talk among people. Getting consumers involved can enhance the creation of word-of-mouth communications.

Stride Sugarless Gum developed a Web site to complement the company's traditional advertising. The campaign used the tagline "Stride gum lasts a ridiculously long time." Consumers were invited to share what they would like to do for a ridiculously long time and to post photographs of these activities on the Stride micro-site developed for the Sugarless Gum.[10]

Buzz marketing works for two primary reasons. First, as noted, people often trust someone else's opinion more than paid advertising. Second, people like to render their opinions. They like to share their thoughts. Humans have an innate desire for social interaction and are concerned about the welfare of others. Sharing an opinion can build a person's ego and sense of self-worth, especially when the opinion leads to happiness or satisfaction with a particular product.

- Product must be unique, new, or superior.
- Brand must stand out.
- Advertising should be
  - Memorable
  - Intriguing
  - Different
  - Unique
- Consumer involvement with the brand

Stealth Marketing

A special form of buzz marketing, **stealth marketing**, uses surreptitious practices to introduce a product to individuals or fails to disclose or reveal the true relationship with the brand. Someone posing as a tourist can ask people to take a photo with a new camera and then talk to them about the camera. An attractive model ordering a beer or soft drink can tell everyone about how great it tastes. In both instances, someone is being paid to extol the product's benefits.

One stealth marketing ploy that received national attention was a 6-minute video entitled "Bride Has Massive Hair Wig Out" featuring a young bride-to-be who was

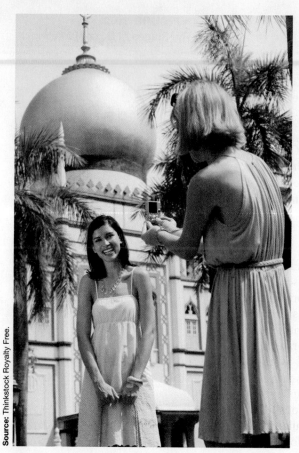

▲ After asking someone to take her picture, this individual can then talk about the camera.

unhappy with her haircut. In the video, she starts hacking off her hair just prior to the wedding ceremony. Her friends try in vain to stop her. It turns out she was just acting. It was a cleverly produced video ad for Unilever's Sunsilk Haircare brand produced by its advertising agency.

Thinking it was a real bride and real situation, the "Wig Out" video attracted millions of online viewers, was tweeted to thousands, appeared on blogs, was featured on CNN, and was the subject of talk shows before the truth about it being Unilever's stealth marketing campaign was revealed.[11]

Stealth marketing thrives in the online world, especially with social media sites where it is easy to create videos and offer brand endorsements. Most people are not likely to pass on traditional advertisement and clips. The result has been a rise in stealth approaches.

Some argue that stealth marketing represents a shrewd way to reach consumers and generate buzz. At the same time, the Word of Mouth Marketing Association has clearly stated the importance of honesty of relationship and honesty of identity. The Federal Trade Commission (FTC) has issued an opinion letter supporting the Word of Mouth Marketing Association regarding the full disclosure of any paid individuals in ads. There is, however, still an enticement to create stealth marketing campaigns that generate buzz. The debate over the ethics of this approach is likely to continue.

GUERRILLA MARKETING

Guerrilla marketing programs are designed to obtain instant results using limited resources. It was developed by marketing guru Jay Conrad Levinson. Historically, guerrilla marketing has been one of the most successful alternative media marketing programs. Its tactics rely on creativity, quality relationships, and the willingness to try unusual approaches. These programs were originally aimed at small businesses; however, now guerrilla marketing tactics are used by a wide array of firms. Guerrilla marketing emphasizes a combination of media, advertising, public relations, and surprises to reach consumers.

Guerrilla marketing utilizes alternative tactics and venues and focuses on finding creative ways of doing things. To be successful, the thinking process in the marketing department has to change. Discovering "touch points" with customers is the first step. Touch points include the places where the customers eat, drink, shop, hang out, and sleep. Next, the marketing team identifies ways to reach consumers that are unique and memorable at one of those touch points. To do so requires creativity, imagination, and unorthodox thinking.

Figure 10.4 compares guerrilla marketing to traditional marketing. Guerrilla marketing tends to focus on specific regions or areas. It is not a national or international campaign, and instead features personal communication. Creating excitement that will spread to others by word-of-mouth is the objective. Guerrilla marketing often involves interacting with consumers, not just sending out a message. Building relationships with customers should be the outcome. By getting consumers to react or to do something, the program enhances the chance that the message will hit home. Advertisements are made accessible to consumers, where they live, play, and work, in ways that are noticed. The eventual relationships that evolve help create brand loyalty and positive recommendations to other consumers.

Guerrilla marketing requires an aggressive, grassroots approach to marketing. It should promote a one-to-one relationship with consumers through innovative, alternative means of branding. It should also produce considerable buzz. When done properly,

◄ **FIGURE 10.4**
Traditional vs. Guerrilla Marketing

Traditional Marketing	Guerrilla Marketing
• Requires money	• Requires energy and imagination
• Geared to large businesses with big budgets	• Geared to small businesses and big dreams
• Results measured by sales	• Results measured by profits
• Based on experience and guesswork	• Based on psychology and human behavior
• Increases production and diversity	• Grows through existing customers and referrals
• Grows by adding customers	• Cooperates with other businesses
• Obliterates the competition	• Aims messages at individuals and small groups
• Aims messages at large groups	• Uses marketing to gain customer consent
• Uses marketing to generate sales	• "You Marketing" that looks at how can we help "You"
• "Me Marketing" that looks at "My" company	

◄ **FIGURE 10.5**
Reasons for Using Guerrilla Marketing

• To find a new way to communicate with consumers	• To impact a spot market
• To interact with consumers	• To create buzz
• To make advertising accessible to consumers	• To build relationships with consumers

Source: Based on Lin Zuo and Shari Veil, "Guerrilla Marketing and the Aqua Teen Hunger Force Fiasco," *Public Relations Quarterly* 51, no. 4 (Winter 2006–2007), pp. 8–11.

guerrilla marketing has the potential to be a powerful marketing weapon. Figure 10.5 identifies six reasons why companies should use guerrilla marketing.

In the Engobi case described in the Integrated Campaigns in Action segment at the end of this chapter, Pink Jacket Creative generated buzz about Engobi, a caffeine-enhanced snack chip, during the inoculation stage of the buzz process, which can be extremely difficult. As shown in the photo in this section, "Engobi Girls" were employed to distribute free samples of the chips and to generate interest in prospective customers as part of an ingenious guerrilla marketing campaign.

LIFESTYLE MARKETING

Another program that can be used to make contacts with consumers in more off-beat and relaxed settings is **lifestyle marketing**, which involves identifying marketing methods associated with the hobbies and entertainment venues of the target audience. Lifestyle marketing includes contacting consumers at places such as farmer's markets, bluegrass festivals, citywide garage sales, flea markets, craft shows, stock car races, and other places where large concentrations of potential customers are found.

A wide range of consumer lifestyles can be found, from relatively standard habits to more edgy and extreme behaviors. The energy drink Red Bull and the producers of the energy snack PowerBar offered free samples to people attending sports events, including football and baseball games. The simple concept was that people who watch sports might be most inclined to give the product a try.

▼ "Engobi Girls" were a central component of the guerilla marketing campaign created by Pink Jacket Creative for a new form of snack chips.

Source: Pink Jacket Creative.

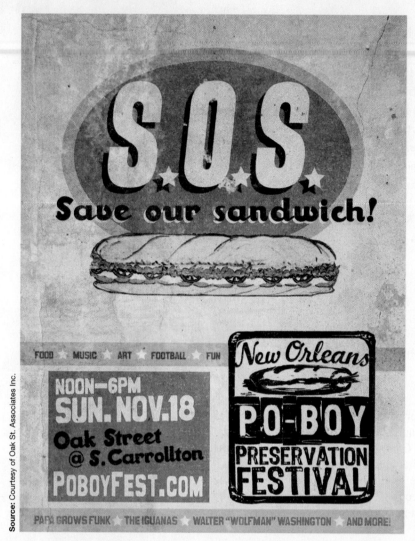

▲ The Po-boy Preservation Festival is an excellent venue for lifestyle marketing.

A|X Armani Exchange reaches young, hip, urban consumers through sponsored events at music festivals and fashion shows in college towns, such as Austin, Texas.[12] In all cases, the purpose of a lifestyle marketing program is finding a venue where the target market goes for relaxation, excitement, socialization, or enjoyment.

EXPERIENTIAL MARKETING

A newer form of alternative marketing, **experiential marketing**, combines direct marketing, field marketing, and sales promotions into a single consumer experience. It typically involves direct marketing through interactive means such as special events and free samples. Experiential marketing seeks to engage consumers with the brand, rather than just providing a free sample. According to Bruce Burnett, chief executive of i2i Marketing, experiential marketing "gives consumers the opportunity to question as well as gain hands-on experience with a brand, allowing them to be more intimate with it, leading to a higher conversion rate."[13]

Nickelodeon used an experiential marketing approach in its Nickelodeon's Slime Across America tour. The 15-city tour was developed by the experiential marketing agency Oasis. It featured a fully interactive 18-wheel slimemobile equipped with five sliming stations. Free, live entertainment was provided by Sony BMG artists The Naked Brothers Band, Tiffany Evans, and Menudo. In addition to enjoying the slime stations, kids could use the slime mobile's virtual sliming zone to digitally capture their personal sliming moments and download them from the Nickelodeon Web site.

The tour reached over 30,000 kids and used 345 gallons of slime. Over 3,000 user-generated videos were recorded, and 37 percent were retrieved once the kids got home. Nearly half of the videos were then forwarded to friends. The campaign also resulted in 3,000 spots on local cable television stations where the tour went and generated about 20 million impressions on television, on the Internet, and in print sources, such as the *Chicago Tribune*.[14]

Jack Morton Worldwide created an experiential marketing campaign for Cotton, Inc. aimed at 18- to 34-year-old women. The traveling mall exhibit featured the songs "The Fabric of Our Lives" and "Dixie" sung by contemporary artists Zooey Deschanel (indie-rock), Miranda Lambert (country), and Jazmine Sullivan (R&B). Mall shoppers were able look into the singers' closets, which were filled with cotton clothes. Shoppers could also record a personal version of "The Fabric of Our Lives." The campaign's budget was $500,000 to $1 million. The exhibit was designed to provide mall shoppers with tangible contacts with cotton fabrics.[15]

To increase the probability that a positive experience will occur from an experiential marketing event, companies should follow these steps:

Step 1 Choose a clear, concise market segment to target.

Step 2 Identify the right time and place to involve consumers with the brand. Choose opportunities that fit with consumers' lives and when they can engage with the brand emotionally and logically.

Step 3   Make sure the experience reveals clearly the brand's promise and represents the brand well to consumers.

The key to experiential marketing is letting consumers enjoy the benefit of a good or service before actually making a purchase.[16]

PRODUCT PLACEMENTS AND BRANDED ENTERTAINMENT

Most marketers believe that getting a product noticed has become increasingly difficult. In response, many firms have increased expenditures on product placements and branded entertainment. Each couples the popularity of an entertainment venue with a product or company.

Product Placements

A **product placement** is the planned insertion of a brand or product into a movie, television show, or program in some other medium with the purpose of influencing viewers. Product placements have been a part of motion pictures since the beginning of the industry in the 1890s. Lever Brothers placed the company's soap brand in some of the early films. In the 1930s, Buick created a 10-picture deal with Warner Brothers for placements. Several tobacco companies paid actors to endorse and use the brands. Early television programs, such as the *Colgate Comedy Hour,* were sponsored by brands.

The biggest surge in product placement may have occurred in 1982, when Reese's Pieces were used to lure E.T. out of hiding as part of the plot of the movie. The placement of the Reese's Pieces spurred a 65 percent increase in sales following the movie's release.[17]

Advertisers believe product placements can lead to increased awareness and more positive attitudes toward the brand. In a few isolated cases, sales of a brand have increased. In most instances, however, no immediate impact on sales occurs. Research by Nielsen has revealed the following about product placements:

- Brands placed within "emotionally engaging" television programs were recognized by 43 percent more viewers.
- Brand recognition increased 29 percent for brands placed in highly enjoyed programs.
- Positive brand feelings increased by 85 percent for brands placed in popular programs.[18]

One key advantage of brand placement is the low cost per viewer, especially for movies. After a movie has finished at the cinema, it will usually be converted to a DVD for movie rental. From there, the movie may be converted to television for viewing on syndication outlets or one of the premium movie channels. It might also be made available on TV through video-on-demand. This expands a movie's reach beyond the cinema screen to other venues where it may be seen multiple times by individuals.

Harley-Davidson hired Davie Brown Entertainment to locate appropriate product placement opportunities in movies, television, music, and video games. This became the first time in Harley-Davidson's history that product placement was the core marketing strategy. According to Dino Bernacchi, director of advertising and promotions for Harley-Davidson, "We want to use [product placement] to socialize Harley-Davidson motorcycling . . . Entertainment can sensationalize the excitement and thrill of riding to the point of moving people to check it out." Only 3 percent of American consumers own a motorcycle, but another 15 to 20 million have the desire to buy one. Harley-Davidson believes that using strategic product placements will encourage those on the edge to go ahead and make the purchase.[19]

Source: Thinkstock Royalty Free.

▲ Tracy is passing out samples of a new drink at a farmer's market.

❷ What methods can be used to effectively employ product placements and branded entertainment?

Source: Getty Images–Thinkstock.

▲ Harley-Davidson emphasized product placements in television shows, movies, music, and video games in a recent marketing campaign.

Branded Entertainment

Branded entertainment is the integration of entertainment and advertising by embedding brands into the storyline of a movie, television show, or other entertainment medium.[20]

For instance, in an episode of the CTV drama *The Eleventh Hour*, Nicorette was integrated into a story about a character trying to quit smoking. In the movie *Up in the Air* starring George Clooney, American Airlines and Hilton Hotels were displayed prominently. The movie's plot involves Clooney's character logging 10 million miles on American so he can have his name emblazoned on the plane and ride along with American Airlines' chief pilot. Actual American Airlines planes were used in the film. Many of the hotel scenes were filmed at Hilton locations. Integrating the brands into the story made them much more noticeable to the viewing audience.[21]

The use of branded entertainment has increased sharply with the rise of reality television shows that the focus on creating "real-world" situations. The success of branded entertainment in reality shows has led to its use in scripted television shows. Branded entertainment may also be found in novels, plays, songs, and movies.

Achieving Success with Individual Consumers

Figure 10.6 identifies the major factors that influence the success of brand placements and branded entertainment. The media used has an impact on effectiveness. Some television programs have lost clout due to placement clutter. For instance, 4,349 product placements were used during Fox's *American Idol* show from January to May in one season.[22] Only the prominent brands, such as the red plastic cups of Coca-Cola in front of the judges, were noticeable. Most were lost in the clutter of other brands appearing on the show.

Product placements and branded entertainment work because no "call to action" appears. Instead, increasing brand awareness and generating positive feelings toward the brand are the goals. When a consumer's favorite actor uses a particular brand or her favorite show contains a particular brand, it becomes more likely that the individual will transfer those positive feelings to the brand.

Some consumers are more receptive to brand placements than others. People between the ages of 15 and 34 are more likely to notice brands placed in a movie or show. Also, individuals in North America and the Asia-Pacific area are more receptive than viewers in Europe.

When a consumer sees a brand placement of a product that he has purchased, it may reinforce that idea that a wise decision was made, further validating the original purchase decision.[23]

Company Tactics

The actual manner in which a brand is placed into a movie or show is important. Brand insertions work best when they seem logical. In other words, the most effective placements

FIGURE 10.6 ▶
Key Factors Influencing the Effectiveness of Product Placement and Branded Entertainment

- Media
- Supporting promotional activities
- Consumer attitudes toward placements
- Placement characteristics
- Regulations

Source: Based on Simon Hudson and David Hudson, "Branded Entertainment: A New Advertising Technique or Product Placement in Disguise?" *Journal of Marketing Management* 22, no. 5/6 (July 2006), pp. 489–504.

are those woven into the program in such a way that it appears to be a natural part of the story. Brands shown in the background that seem to be artificially inserted are not nearly as effective.

For some companies, an advantage to product placement in movies is that it bypasses most of the legislation and guidance that is intended to control advertising to children and young adults. A study of the top 25 box office movies revealed that 32 percent were rated for viewing by adolescents and contained prominent brand placements for tobacco products. If these companies would have tried to advertise directly to teens, they would have encountered with numerous regulations and severe penalties.[24]

Many companies buy advertising spots on television programs that feature product placements of the brand. Additional promotional incentives may also be offered. This helps move the consumer beyond recognition and liking to the actual purchase.

Budgets for product placements and branded entertainment have been increasing for several reasons. First, a brand's appeal may be stronger when it appears in a nonadvertising context. Second, the perception of what others think of a brand is important to consumers. For many, it can be more important than how the consumer views the brand. Seeing the brand being used in a television show, a movie, or a book makes the brand look acceptable and even desirable. Third, seeing the brand used by others provides postpurchase reassurance for individuals who already bought the item.

Fourth, for individuals who place little value in brand names and branded products, having a brand placed in a program can provide evidence of the brand's advantages. The evidence may be strong enough for them to consider purchasing the brand. In these cases, the brand does not have to directly persuade the consumer of its merits. It does so through the acceptance and use of the brand by the actor or program.

The Media's Perspective

For moviemakers and television producers, money is the primary motivation behind product placements and branded entertainment. In the past, brand mentions were incidental or used by movie producers to create realism in a film. They now generate additional income. Martha Stewart charges $10,000 for a 30-second placement on her show. For a one-time mention in the show with a product close-up, the price goes up to $100,000. For a 2-minute branded entertainment segment with two or three talking points, the price rises to more than $250,000.[25]

In summary, brand placements offer an excellent method to increase share of mind and build brand awareness. Although some are concerned that programs are becoming saturated with product placements, they continue to be utilized. If clutter becomes too severe, usage will be likely to decline, but only if the impact on consumer responses and attitudes also declines.[26]

ALTERNATIVE MEDIA VENUES

The fast-food restaurant KFC donated $15,000 to two different Indiana cities to paint the face of Colonel Sanders on fire hydrants and fire extinguishers as part of a campaign to promote its "fiery" chicken wings. "Similar alternative marketing efforts have been used as people become immune to advertising in print, outdoors, and on television," said Allen Adamson, managing director of the branding firm Landor Associates of New York. Laura Ries, president of the marketing consulting firm Ries & Ries, adds, "People ignore advertising, they try to get away from it whenever possible. So hitting them in unusual and unlikely places, at least initially, is likely to get some attention." Figure 10.7 identifies some of the many alternative forms of media that can be used.

③ Why has the use of alternative media venues, especially video game advertising, grown in marketing communications programs?

Mobile Phone Advertising

Currently, mobile phone advertising is considered an alternative form of advertising. The graph shown in Figure 10.8 indicates that mobile advertising continues to grow rapidly. With the development of new apps, it may soon evolve into a mainstream form of advertising.

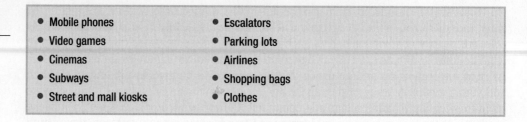

- Mobile phones
- Video games
- Cinemas
- Subways
- Street and mall kiosks
- Escalators
- Parking lots
- Airlines
- Shopping bags
- Clothes

Total mobile advertising may reach $1.56 billion by 2013, from $320 million in 2008. Mobile advertising consists of three principal formats: messaging, display, and search.[27]

Mobile phone advertising is in its infancy. Only about 23 percent of U.S. mobile phone users have seen advertising on their phones. That percentage increases steadily each month. According to Nielsen, about one-third of mobile phone users are open to advertising if it will lower their monthly bills.[28]

Most mobile phone advertising consists of small banner ads in the corner of a Web page or text messaging ads that resemble spam. *Click-to-call advertising* has emerged as a new form. Rather than dialing a number, a user can tap the number featured in an ad to be connected. This technology has increased the response rate to ads. *Search ads* that appear on mobile phones that have the phone number of a local business use a similar format. Someone looking for a pizza restaurant on a trip can search on a mobile phone and see a search ad with the name and phone number of a local pizza place.

Many of the top brands have developed apps for mobile phones in an effort to engage consumers. Brands including Coca-Cola, Nike, Procter & Gamble, Amazon.com, Target, Disney, and Wal-Mart all offer mobile phone apps. Most banks now have apps that allow consumers to conduct banking transactions on mobile phones.

Sports Illustrated recently promoted its annual Swimsuit issue using bar codes that were available in print ads in magazines such as *People, Time,* and *Sports Illustrated.* Users who took a photo of the bar code with their mobile phones could view photos of the "rookie" models who would appear in the new Swimsuit issue. Those who purchased the special issue could access bar codes to view behind-the-scenes mobile videos of the models' photo shoots.[29]

Video Game Advertising

Product placements in video games have become common. Products can be part of a stand-alone game purchased at a retail store and played on the computer or they can be placed in an Internet video game. In-game brand placement enjoys all of the advantages

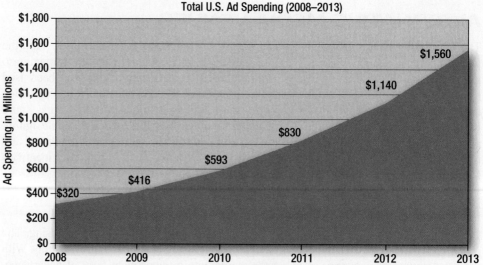

Source: Adapted from "Mobile Ad Spending Trends Upward," *Adweek* (**www.adweek.com/aw/content_display/news/agency/ e3if5f773e59310e059c43c9851**, January 7, 2010).

• In-game advertisements	• Game-related Web sites
• Rotating in-game advertising	• Advergames
• Interactive ads	• Sponsored downloads

◀ **FIGURE 10.9**
Video Game Advertising

of brand placements and branded entertainment. Video game advertising reaches young people, who have become difficult to contact through traditional media. In addition, it has the added feature of interactivity. Advertisers spend approximately $1 billion per year on in-game advertising. It is an attractive market for the following reasons:

- 75 percent of all U.S. Internet users spend at least 1 hour a month playing online games.
- 27 percent average 30 hours a month playing games.
- The primary game-playing market segment is 16- to 34-year-old males.
- The fastest-growing video game market segment is females.[30]

Video game advertising takes several forms (see Figure 10.9). The original and most widespread form of video game advertising involves locating a brand placement in the game. It can take the form of a billboard in a racing game, a Coke vending machine, or a McDonald's that is permanently integrated into the game. With the cost of producing a game now in the $20 to $30 million range, game producers welcome product placement advertising as a source of revenue.

The number of game-related Web sites has exploded in recent years. Rather than placing ads in the game itself, advertisers can place ads on these gaming Web sites. Although the exact number of gaming Web sites has not been identified, estimates are that there are in excess of 6,000. Some of these sites receive as many as 7 million visits per year.[31]

A number of companies have developed video games to be played on branded Web sites. These branded video games are called **advergames**. Axe, a brand of men's deodorant, offers an online game for men. The game allows the individual to test their "pickup" skills with 100 different "hot" women. Players collect and use pickup moves to try to woo the various women featured in the game.

Other companies that have created advergames include Maxwell House, Holiday Inn, Baskin-Robbins, and Suave. Instead of creating a special micros-site for the game, the advergames can be placed on free gaming portals, such as Kewlbox (**www.kewlbox.com**), where 90 percent of the games are advergames, which are offered for free. They are played 500,000 to 700,000 times per day.[32] Research by Blockdot.com suggests that consumers have positive feelings about brands that sponsor advergames. More specifically, 83 percent of consumers think positively about companies that underwrite advergames and 70 percent are more likely to buy products from companies that sponsor the games.[33]

Sponsored downloads for games offer a new option that has become especially popular with automotive manufacturers. The games include video downloads for racing games that insert automaker's brand as the cars driven by each player.

Benefits of Video Game Advertising

IGA Worldwide research indicates that the majority of gamers like seeing ads in video games, if they are done well and fit in the scene. The study revealed that 82 percent of gamers find the games to be just as enjoyable when ads were present. A 44 percent increase in recall of brands resulted from ads being presented in games when compared to awareness prior to exposure in the video game. Positive brand attribute associations also increased.[34]

Online video games offer advertisers the luxury of using high-quality Web metrics. Advertisers can track the length of ad exposure in an online game. In most cases, the company can tie in demographic information to find out who views the in-game ad, how long they play, and how often. These metrics then make it possible to target ads specifically to the consumer, demographic group, location profile, or type of player.[35]

Disadvantages of Video Game Advertising

The primary disadvantage of a product placement within a game is that the ad soon becomes static and the player no longer notices it. To combat this problem, Massive, a new media company, has pioneered a technology that rotates or changes ads in online video games in real time. Advertisers are able to insert new ads and products into the online game each time the person plays it. By changing the ads, the marketing team delivers time-sensitive promotions. Advertising can be current rather than using messages that were prepared a year in advance. Massive can make the advertisement interactive, allowing the player to click on it for additional information.[36]

Cinema Advertising

Prior to a movie, patrons now watch more than just promotional trailers and offers for concession stand products. Most theaters run advertisements during prefeature programming. Some products may have direct relationships with the movie, others are totally unrelated. Although clutter exists in the sense that the commercials may run consecutively and be mingled with new movie previews, they are being shown to what is essentially a "captive" audience waiting for the feature to start.

Cinema advertising rarely appears at the center of an integrated ad campaign, but that was the case with HP's launch of the Photosmart Premium printer with TouchSmart Web. According to Tariq Hassan, HP's vice president of marketing, "We had to create more awareness; we had to touch the consumer. The theater was a natural fit." The cinema campaign included a 30-second spot in the prefeature programming at 17,300 theaters and 2,600 plasma screens in theater lobbies. It also executed an interactive "lobby domination" strategy in 15 theaters in New York, Chicago, San Francisco, San Diego, Miami, and Houston. Theater lobbies were turned into branded events with banners, signage, holographic 3-D kiosks, and large manned booths where the printer was demonstrated. The campaign delivered 50,000 product demonstrations averaging 6 minutes in length and a total of 700,000 lobby impressions.[37]

Other Alternative Media

In addition to mobile phones, video games, and cinema, a number of other media alternatives are available. Advertisers continue to search for new ways to reach consumers in media that are not currently being used for advertising. Ads now appear on subways and other public facilities as local and state governments struggle to balance budgets. Parking lots, stairs, and escalators all feature advertising displays. Airlines increase revenues by presenting advertisements on flight-ticket jackets and using in-plane signage. Shopping bags, clothes, and restaurant menus provide additional advertising venues.

Alternative media was an important component of the advertising campaign for Unleashed Dog Parks created by the Pink Jacket Creative advertising agency. As shown in the two photos in this section, Pink Jacket added a bus wrap ad and a street kiosk ad to reinforce the billboards that were running. The objective was to reach people during routine moments in their daily lives.

In summary, the popularity of using nontraditional formats to deliver advertising messages continues to increase. Each time an innovative marketing professional identifies a new venue, a certain segment of the advertising community jumps on board.

▼ A bus wrap advertisement for Unleashed Dog Parks created by the Pink Jacket Creative advertising agency.

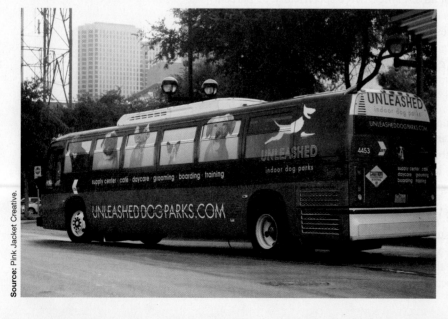

Source: Pink Jacket Creative.

These methods make it possible to send messages that either cut through or go around clutter to reach people in moments when they may be more receptive to an advertisement's content.

IN-STORE MARKETING

Approximately 60 percent of all purchase decisions are made in the retail store.[38] Except for point-of-purchase (POP) displays, in-store marketing has not received much attention. Funds devoted to it represent a small percentage of advertising and marketing budgets. This may mean companies are missing a genuine opportunity.

To understand the potential of in-store advertising, consider what affects consumers as they purchase clothing. In a survey of about 600 consumers, 52 percent said that in-store signage, displays, or point-of-purchase displays influenced their decisions. This far outdistances print advertising and even word-of-mouth communications.[39] Figure 10.10 displays a complete list of these influences.

Source: Pink Jacket Creative.

▲ A street kiosk advertisement for Unleashed Dog Parks created by the Pink Jacket Creative advertising agency.

In-Store Marketing Tactics

The in-store shopping experience has a major impact on purchase decisions. In a survey of shoppers, 69 percent called the in-store time the "make or break" experience. "Understanding high potential shopper strike zones has become increasingly critical given the intensified battle for consumer loyalty and share of mind in-store," says D'Anna Hawthorne, strategic director at Miller Zell, a retail consulting firm. Companies now try to engage consumers, not just merchandise items on a shelf. According to consumers, end-aisle displays and merchandise displays are the most engaging. Ceiling banners and overhead mobiles are the least engaging.[40]

The use of color, light, and sound has long been a part of in-store marketing. Retailers brighten and soften products using displays and photos often featuring the current and most popular colors. Music, from the elevator-type to popular new forms for trendy stores, has long been a part of retail shopping.

Now retailers can add *motion*. Placing and using video screens and television monitors to present messages represents the newest and most expensive in-store marketing

 4 How have in-store marketing and point-of-purchase displays evolved into even more effective communication and sales tools?

◀ **FIGURE 10.10**
Types of Advertising That Most Influenced Clothing Purchases

Source: Adapted from Amy Johannes, "Snap Decisions," *Promo* 18, no. 11 (October 2005), p. 16.

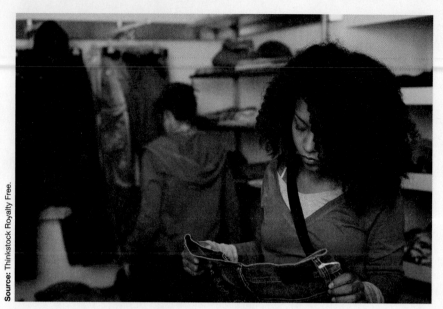

Source: Thinkstock Royalty Free.

▲ Approximately 60 percent of all purchase decisions are made in the retail store.

tactic. Many static signs have been replaced with high-technology mediums. Also, shopping carts with static signs that are broken or unreadable are being replaced with video screens. Spending on digital signage may double to $2.8 billion annually by 2011. Digital media within the store offers retailers the opportunity to customize messages to fit the store and the aisle where the display is located.[41]

Airplay America produces The Salon Channel, a retail television channel and digital signage network for beauty salons. Programming consists of human interest and lifestyle stories. Beauty shop patrons spend an average of 30 to 45 minutes per salon visit. The Salon Channel provides entertainment, including features about nationally recognized stylists and the latest hairstyles, along with advertisements for products and services, many of which are related to beauty and fashion.[42]

Wal-Mart is following the same path. In the past, Wal-Mart's ads appeared on all in-store televisions at the same time. Using new technologies, the marketing department distributes ads geared to each department within a store and for specific aisles. Wal-Mart uses the approach in 1,200 stores on more than 100,000 television monitors. Television monitors are no longer hung from the ceiling. The new flat-screen panel monitors are placed at eye level in the aisles, because it leads to greater recall of ads. Digital monitors are also being installed at end-caps and at point-of-purchase displays. These television monitors contain advertising pertinent to the end-cap or POP display.[43]

Unilever tested the Wal-Mart in-store network system. Unilever's advertising team created a commercial specifically to be shown in Wal-Mart. The ad was part of Unilever's "real beauty" campaign. Instead of using young and slinky female models posing in underwear, an elderly Wal-Mart employee talks about how pretty she feels, even with her wrinkles.[44]

To fully appreciate the potential impact of this new form of in-store advertising, consider this: Each week 68 million viewers watch the combined national television newscasts of Katie Couric, Brian Williams, and Diane Sawyer. The number of shoppers at Wal-Mart each week is 127 million. The potential audience for a commercial on the Wal-Mart television system will be nearly twice as large as an advertisement on the three national newscasts.[45] In addition, the Wal-Mart ad reaches consumers as they shop and as they make purchase decisions.

A final in-store tactic relies on the other senses, *taste* and *smell.* Using scents to enhance a shopping experience is not new. New methods include releasing pheromones into the store's air to make customers feel aroused and sexy. Others retailers rely on less controversial approaches, such as baking and selling pastries and offering specialty coffees and teas. High-end retailers often present patrons with hot tea as part of the shopping experience. This personalizes the shopping experience and makes it more pleasant, which may cause the customer to return.

POINT-OF-PURCHASE TACTICS

Traditionally, one of the most important components of in-store marketing has been **point-of-purchase displays (POP)**, which include any form of special display that advertises merchandise. Point-of-purchase displays are located near cash registers in retail stores, at the end of an aisle, in a store's entryway, or any other location where they will be noticed. Point-of-purchase advertising includes displays, signs, and devices used to identify, advertise, or merchandise an outlet, service, or product. POP displays can serve as an important aid to retail selling.

Point-of-purchase displays remain highly effective tools for increasing sales. Nearly 50 percent of the money spent at mass merchandisers and supermarkets results from unplanned, impulse buys. For food purchases, 88 percent of the decisions about brands are made in the store at the time of the purchase. Overall, 67 percent of purchase decisions are made in the store. In many instances, point-of-purchase materials and other in-store advertising enticements influenced the decision.[46]

Coca-Cola reports that only 50 percent of soft drink sales are made from the regular store shelf. The other 50 percent results from product displays in other parts of the store. American Express discovered that 30 percent of purchases charged on the American Express card came from impulse decisions by customers seeing the "American Express Cards Welcome" sign.

Research indicates that an average increase in sales of about 9 percent occurs when one POP display is used. Although only about half of POP displays actually impact sales, those that do increase purchases by an average of nearly 20 percent. Consequently, point-of-purchase advertising remains attractive to manufacturers.[47]

Currently, manufacturers spend more than $17 billion each year on point-of-purchase advertising materials. The largest users are restaurants, food services, apparel stores, and footwear retailers. The fastest-growing categories are fresh, frozen, or refrigerated foods and professional services.[48]

Manufacturers view point-of-purchase displays as an attractive method of getting a brand more prominently displayed before customers. Many retailers have a different perspective. Retailers believe that POP materials should either boost sales for the store or draw customers into the store. Retailers are not interested in the sales of one particular brand, but instead want to improve overall sales and store profits. Retailers prefer displays that educate consumers and provide information. As a result, retailers are most inclined to set up displays to match the retailer's marketing objectives.

▲ Point-of-purchase displays help sell products such as cosmetics, perfume, or cologne.

Designing Effective Point-of-Purchase Displays

▼ Point-of-purchase displays are often located near cash registers.

To be effective, POP displays should clearly communicate the product's attributes. Pricing and other promotional information should be included. The display should encourage the customer to stop and look, pick up the product, and examine it. A customer who stops to examine a product on display is more likely to buy that product.

The display should make a clear, succinct offer that the customer immediately understands. In most cases, a display only has three-tenths of a second to capture the customer's attention. If it fails, the customer simply moves on to other merchandise. Colors, designs, merchandise arrangements, and tie-ins with other marketing messages are critical elements of effective POP displays.

The best point-of-purchase displays are integrated with other marketing messages.

FIGURE 10.11 ▶

Effective Point-of-Purchase (POP) Displays

- Integrate the brand's image into the display.
- Integrate the display with current advertising and promotions.
- Make the display dramatic to get attention.
- Keep the color of the display down so the product and signage stand out.
- Make the display versatile so it can be easily adapted by retailers.
- Make the display reusable and easy to assemble.
- Make the display easy to stock.
- Customize the display to fit the retailer's store.

Logos and message themes used in advertisements should appear on the display. A study by the Saatchi & Saatchi advertising agency revealed that consumer purchase decisions are made in just 4 seconds. On average, a consumer only looks at a display or signage for 3 to 7 seconds.[49] Tying a POP display into current advertising and marketing increases the chances of it being noticed. The display should present any form of special sales promotion that the company is currently offering. Customers quickly recognize tie-ins with current advertising and promotional themes as they view displays. Figure 10.11 lists some additional pointers for point-of-purchase advertising.

Measuring Point-of-Purchase Effectiveness

Both manufactures and retailers seek to measure the effectiveness of POP displays. By linking the POP display into a point-of-sale (POS) cash register, results can easily be gathered. Items on the display are coded so that the POS system picks them up. Then individual stores measure sales before and during a point-of-purchase display program by using cash register data. The data also helps the retailer decide when it is time to withdraw or change a display as sales begin to decline. This technology enables retailers to identify the displays that generate the largest impact on sales. A retailer might use this method to test different types of POP displays in various stores. The most effective displays can then be expanded to a larger number of stores.

From the manufacturer's viewpoint, using point-of-sale data helps to improve POP displays. The data may also be used to strengthen partnerships with retailers. These bonds help the manufacturer weather poor POP showings. Retailers are more willing to stay with a manufacturer that tries to develop displays that benefit both parties.

BRAND COMMUNITIES

⑤ How can brand communities enhance brand loyalty and devotion?

Brand communities are the ultimate demonstration of brand loyalty and brand devotion. In most cases, a symbolic meaning behind the brand links individuals to the brand community and other owners of the brand. The identity and belonging are formed through interactions between customers and with the product. A set of shared values and experiences that integrate with feelings about the brand becomes the result.

Brand communities do not form around every brand. They cannot be created by the brand itself; however, a marketing department can facilitate and enhance the community experience. A company with a strong brand community maintains a positive image, has a rich and long tradition, occupies a unique position in the marketplace, and enjoys a group of loyal, dedicated followers.[50] Figure 10.12 highlights some of the reasons that brand communities exist. Most brand communities require some type of face-to-face interactions, although the Internet does provide a venue for members to contact each other and to blog about the product.

Jeep, Harley-Davidson, and Apple are firms with loyal brand communities. In each case, the brand owners are diverse. This can be seen in the Jeep Jamborees and Camp Jeep events,

FIGURE 10.12 ▶

Reasons Brand Communities Form

- Affirmation of the buying decision
- Social identity and bonding
- Swap stories
- Swap advice and provide help to others
- Feedback and new ideas

which are events sponsored by Jeep. Both allow Jeep owners the opportunity to share driving experiences, tell stories, and share ideas. Most of the interactions among customers occur during the company-sponsored barbecue. They also take place during roundtable discussions hosted by a Jeep engineer or other Jeep employee.

Many, if not most, of the attendees at a Camp Jeep event have no experience driving their Jeep off-road. Among those who have driven their Jeep off-road, some have a "tread lightly" ethos, whereas others have mud-covered vehicles from heavy off-road use. First timers at the camp are often timid and afraid they won't fit in, but soon find they do as repeaters fully welcome anyone and everyone to the Jeep community. The vehicle provides the common bond that brings individuals together regardless of demographic and psychographic differences.

Perhaps Harley-Davidson represents the best example of a brand community. The company's leadership team has done an excellent job of creating a unique brand community spirit. An organization called HOG has formed around the Harley brand. In return, Harley-Davidson offers benefits, such as information about community gatherings along with special marketing offers for accessories, to HOG members. The benefits are only available to the HOG group. This encourages new Harley-Davidson owners to join the HOG brand community.

Marketers seek to facilitate and enhance the community in which owners can interact. Figure 10.13 provides information on ways a marketing team can assist in creating a brand community.

Building a brand community begins with sponsoring events that bring product owners together. Jeep sponsors both the jamborees and a camp. Harley-Davidson sponsors rides, rallies, and even local events. These events are critical for the creation of a brand community spirit and allow for bonding between owners. Eventually this produces a sense of social identity.

Company representatives should become involved in club events. Jeep engineers always attend Jeep events and mingle with customers. They provide advice and encouragement to any new owner who is taking his or her vehicle off-road for the first time. Harley managers, including the CEO, ride Harleys to rallies to talk with owners.

In addition to company-sponsored events, other venues for interaction can be encouraged. The Internet offers another place for owners to talk. They can visit through blogs, chat rooms, or social network micro-sites. The company can become involved in these exchange venues. Employees should openly identify themselves. Brand communities enjoy company involvement and want an honest exchange of comments.

While providing venues and means for developing a brand community spirit, the company continues other advertising and marketing programs. A brand community normally grows around a brand with a strong image. That image should be maintained. The pride of owning the brand should be featured in advertisements, making its uniqueness and position in the marketplace clear.

Source: Courtesy of Skyjacker Suspensions.

▲ Skyjacker has a brand community consisting of off-road enthusiasts.

- Create member benefits to encourage new customers to join a group.
- Provide materials to the group that are not available anywhere else.
- Involve firm representatives in the groups.
- Sponsor special events and regular meetings.
- Promote communications among members of the group.
- Build a strong brand reputation.

◀ **FIGURE 10.13**
Ways to Enhance a Brand Community Spirit

Source: Based on "Brand Communities," *Bulletpoint*, no. 133 (July 2006), pp. 12–16.

INTERNATIONAL IMPLICATIONS

6 What methods are used to adapt alternative marketing programs to international marketing efforts?

Alternative marketing can be used to reach minority groups within the United States. An example of buzz marketing occurred when a company called Clamato sought to increase brand awareness among U.S. Latinos. The company gave 2,000 agents a 32-ounce bottle of Clamato and 10 coupons. The agents reached 34,000 potential customers, and positive opinions of the drink rose from 32 to 78 percent.[51]

Alternative marketing methods are being tried in other countries. Starbucks and Pepsi combined efforts to produce a movie series called *A Sunny Day*. The film follows a girl from the Chinese countryside to the big city, where she discovers love, blogging, and Starbucks. The series was tailored for Shanghai's subway and the 2.2 million who ride it each day. The story was made into a soap opera-style script featuring short daily segments. A Web site featured story snippets each day for those who missed seeing it on the subway and wanted to know what happened. The Shanghai subway has a network of 4,000 flat-screen monitors that provide train information, clips of soccer highlights, entertainment news, and advertising. Marketers pay to run ads, just like they would on television. *A Sunny Day* was the system's first venture into a short miniseries, with episodes each day for 40 weeks.[52]

Brand communities are developing in other countries. Jeep is using the brand community concept to build a brand presence in China. The first Jeep was introduced in China in 1983 by American Motors through a joint venture in Beijing; however, recent sales of Jeep have slowed. In response, the first 3-day Camp Jeep in China was created. It attracted 700 Jeep owners and 3,000 participants. The event included off-road courses, bungee jumping, a hiking course, wall climbing, a soccer field, and an off-road ATV course. Musical entertainment and time slots for karaoke enthusiasts were provided.[53] The purpose of the event was to renew Jeep's strong brand name and to create a strong sense of community among current Jeep owners in China. Through these individuals, Jeep hopes to generate word-of-mouth, or buzz, for the Jeep brand, driving new customers to the Jeep brand.

The clutter problems that plague U.S. advertisers are present around the world. The tactics being used to overcome it domestically will be adapted to international operations. Firms from other nations will adapt alternative media tactics. International conglomerates will also respond with new and creative alternative marketing programs.

! INTEGRATED CAMPAIGNS IN ACTION

● Engobi

A notable example of guerrilla marketing is provided by the Engobi campaign created by the Pink Jacket Creative advertising agency. Engobi, the world's first caffeine-infused snack chip, was developed by Rudolph Foods Company. Due to a limited media budget, traditional media were not feasible for the product launch.

Engobi needed to get consumers to both hear about and try the product. This required a unique approach. Pink Jacket Creative formed a cross-functional team and gave it the task of coming up with an idea that would hit on all aspects of a full marketing campaign—branding, design, new media, public relations, and events.[54]

The team quickly realized that guerrilla marketing was the way to go. A strong device was needed to anchor the brand and portray it as a snack that "hip" individuals would eat. The "Engobi" girl was born. She had cinnamon-and-lemon-colored beehive hair, nerdy glasses, and a sexy lab coat with fishnet stockings. She was impossible to ignore.

The next step was to develop all of the components of the campaign. A company Web site was created to provide

Source: Pink Jacket Creative.

▲ The Engobi girl was part of the street team in New York City.

consumers with information about the product and the new product category, caffeinated chips. The Web site promoted a contest, "Don't Be a Piano Hero," which started with people sending in videos of themselves playing the *Guitar Hero* video game. The best performer would win a Fender Stratocaster guitar. It was a great idea, but company attorneys determined that copyright restrictions meant that the name *Guitar Hero* video game could not be used. The contest continued, but no one could mention the name of the game. Instead, the site pointed out that it wasn't *Piano Hero*.

The most dramatic part of the campaign took the form of human vending machines. The venue was New York City. Small signs advertising the event and stating that Engobi girls would be passing out free samples were posted in stair risers of the New York City subway system. Next, Engobi girls were placed inside "vending machines" and provided free samples of the chips.

People flocked to the human vending machines to see what was going on. They took pictures and videos along with the samples and quickly spread them across the Internet through blogs and e-mails. The typical sampling approach lasts only about 1 second. In this instance, the average sampling time surged to between 18 and 26 seconds.

For this and other guerrilla marketing campaigns, Pink Jacket Creative operates under a different philosophy— "the right size idea." The right size idea fits the client perfectly. It speaks to the brand's audience, reaches the

▲ The Engobi human vending machine was so captivating it resulted in an average sampling time of 18 to 26 seconds.

client's goals and overcomes obstacles, and can take many different forms. For Engobi, the guerrilla marketing campaign created a great deal of buzz ideally suited to the cutting-edge new product.

Your instructor has additional information about the ads, visuals, and displays used in this campaign.

SUMMARY

Alternative media has many success stories. Well-known brands, such as Ben & Jerry's and Starbucks, have emerged using very little traditional advertising. Each found new methods to establish a brand presence, including alternative media and alternative marketing methods. Starbucks built a community of coffee lovers through local involvement and word-of-mouth.

The four forms of alternative marketing programs are buzz marketing, stealth marketing, guerrilla marketing, and product placements. Buzz marketing, or word-of-mouth marketing, places the emphasis on consumers passing along information about a brand. The consumers can be those who like a brand, sponsored consumers, or company insiders. Some consider using company insiders to be unethical.

Stealth marketing uses surreptitious practices to introduce a product to individuals or fails to disclose or reveal the true relationship with the brand. It also draws some ethical criticism.

Guerrilla marketing programs are those designed to obtain instant results with limited resources through creativity, high-quality relationships, and a willingness to try unusual approaches. Lifestyle marketing involves the use of marketing methods associated with the hobbies and entertainment venues of the target audience. Experiential marketing combines direct marketing, field marketing, and sales promotions into a single consumer experience.

Product placements are planned insertions of a brand or product into a movie, television program, or some other media program. Branded entertainment is the integration of entertainment and advertising by embedding brands into the storyline of a movie, television show, or other entertainment medium.

Numerous alternative media venues are available. They include mobile phone advertising, video game advertising and advergames, cinema advertising, airline in-flight advertising, and others. Use of these media has been on the increase as the impact of traditional media and the Internet continue to decline.

In-store marketing programs take two forms. New tactics include the use of high-tech video screens and television monitors in new and more visible places. This also includes tailoring messages to individual parts of the store. Traditional point-of-purchase advertising continues to be widely utilized. Recently, POP advertising has been combined with newer technologies to increase its effectiveness.

Brand communities evolve when consumers feel a great deal of brand loyalty and devotion. They form around events, programs, and exchanges of information. A company with a strong brand and a devoted marketing team can assist in the formation and continuance of brand communities.

Alterative media choices are being utilized to reach minority groups in the United States in unique new ways. They are also expanding into international markets. As advertising clutter increases, the use of these media is likely to grow, and will likely become cluttered as well.

KEY TERMS

buzz marketing   Emphasizes consumers passing along information about a product to others; also known as *word-of-mouth marketing*.

stealth marketing   The use of surreptitious practices to introduce a product to individuals without disclosing or revealing the true relationship with the brand.

guerrilla marketing   Programs designed to obtain instant results through the use of limited resources by relying on creativity, high-quality relationships, and the willingness to try new approaches.

lifestyle marketing   Marketing methods associated with the hobbies and entertainment venues of the target audience.

experiential marketing   Combining direct marketing, field marketing, and sales promotions into a single consumer experience.

product placement   The planned insertion of a brand or product into a movie, television show, or some other media program.

branded entertainment   The integration of entertainment and advertising by embedding brands into the storyline of a movie, television show, or other entertainment medium.

advergames   Branded video games.

point-of-purchase displays (POP)   Any form of special display that advertises merchandise.

brand communities   A link that forms due to an association between the brand, a consumer, and others who own or purchase the brand.

REVIEW QUESTIONS

1. What are the main alternative media programs described in this chapter?
2. What is buzz marketing?
3. What three types of consumers can pass along buzz marketing messages?
4. Why is buzz marketing effective? What preconditions should be met to ensure its effectiveness?
5. What is stealth marketing?
6. What is guerrilla marketing? How does it differ from traditional marketing?
7. What is lifestyle marketing? What types of locations are suited to lifestyle marketing?
8. What is experiential marketing?
9. What are product placements and branded entertainment? What do they have in common?

10. Identify the alternative media venues described in this chapter.
11. Describe the forms of video game advertising, including advergames.
12. What is in-store marketing? Why is it important?
13. What new in-store marketing tactics are being utilized?
14. What is point-of-purchase advertising? Why is it important?
15. How have new technologies changed some forms of point-of-purchase advertising?
16. What is a brand community?
17. What should a company's marketing team do to assist in the development and growth of brand communities?
18. Is the use of alternative media growing or declining in international markets? Explain why.

CRITICAL THINKING EXERCISES

Discussion Questions

1. Consider a set of products to which you have a high level of loyalty. Would you consider being a brand advocate, ambassador, or evangelist for a brand? Pick the brand where your loyalty is the highest. What type of offer would it take from the company for you to become a brand ambassador? What would you do to be an effective advocate for that brand?

2. Consider a recent purchase you made at the recommendation of someone else. Why did you trust that person's recommendation? How important is the recommendation of others in your purchase decisions?

3. Can you think of a lifestyle marketing program or an experiential marketing campaign that you experienced? What was your reaction? Was the approach effective with you? Why or why not? What about with other consumers? If you

have not experience lifestyle or experiential marketing, think of a situation and brand where you think it would be effective. Explain why.

4. Suppose you were approached by a local small business owner of a small clothing boutique. She has heard about guerrilla marketing and wants to try it. First, why should she use guerrilla marketing? What are the pros and cons? Second, what guerrilla marketing techniques would you suggest?

5. Find a movie that you have already watched and enjoyed. Watch it again, but this time make a list of all of the product placements you see. Identify if it was a prominent placement, if the actor used the brand, or if it was just in the background. When you finish, discuss the product placements that were the most effective and those that were the least effective. What made the placement effective? What made it ineffective?

6. Do you play video games? If so, approximately how many hours a month do you play games (including online games)? What advertising have you noticed in the games? How effective was the advertising?

7. Go to a nearby retail store. Examine the point-of-purchase displays in the store. Which ones were the most impressive? Why? Which ones did not succeed at getting your attention? Why not? Go back to the store a week later. How many of the displays have changed? What is your overall evaluation of the point-of-purchase displays used by the retailer?

8. Go to a nearby retail store and talk to the manager or one of the employees. Ask them about the store signage, including point-of-purchase displays. Ask the employee to discuss what signage is effective and why. As a customer, did you agree with the manager's or employee's viewpoint? Why or why not?

INTEGRATED LEARNING EXERCISES

1. Access **www.womengamers.com**. Locate and read two recent articles of interest to you. Summarize the primary message or findings of each article. What is your overall opinion of this Web site? How can it be beneficial to a marketing manager?

2. Access Ugg's Web site at **www.uggaustralia.com**. Evaluate the Web site in terms of its effectiveness, freshness, and the use of alternative marketing methods. What traditional marketing methods did you see? Do you think Ugg has effectively merged traditional and nontraditional advertising methods? Why or why not?

3. Access the Word of Mouth Marketing Association Web site at **www.womma.org**. List the alternative names used for word-of-mouth marketing. Do you think these are good synonyms for word-of-mouth communications? Why or why not? What features did you find on the site? What benefits does the site provide? What value would the site be to a business? Is there any value for a consumer?

4. Type "buzz marketing" into an online search engine. Find two advertising agencies or marketing agencies that offer buzz marketing expertise. Which company do you think offers the best buzz marketing program? Why?

5. Type "guerrilla marketing" into an online search engine. Find two agencies that offer guerrilla marketing services. Describe what type of services each offers. Go to an article database and type in "guerrilla marketing." Find two articles about guerrilla marketing that are of interest to you. Summarize the articles.

6. Online gaming has become very popular, especially with the 16- to 34-year-old demographic. Access the Kewlbox Web site at **www.kewlbox.com**. Discuss the various games that are available. Locate some advergames. Who were the sponsoring brands? What is your evaluation of the game site?

7. Point-of-purchase displays should be an important component of a firm's IMC program. Research indicates that effective displays have a positive impact on sales. Access the following firms that produce point-of-purchase displays. Which firm's site is the most attractive? Which firm would be the best from the standpoint of developing displays for a manufacturer? Explain.

   a. Acrylic Designs, Inc. (**www.acrylicdesigns.com**)

   b. Vulcan Industries (**www.vulcanind.com**)

   c. Display Design & Sales (**www.displays4pop.com**)

STUDENT PROJECT

Creative Corner

Ugg is the brand name for an Australian company that sells big, bulky sheepskin boots. The company's marketing team wondered if it would be possible to get fashion-conscious consumers to even consider the boots. Instead of advertising to the fashion-conscious consumer, Ugg's marketing team targeted high-profile fashion influencers. They successfully contacted and convinced Kate Hudson and Sarah Jessica Parker to wear the items. Then Oprah Winfrey praised Uggs on one of her shows. At that point, the boots became fashionable, and retailers couldn't keep them in stock.[55]

Ugg became successful using unique alternative marketing methods. Access Ugg's Web site at **www.uggaustralia.com** to learn about the company's products and the company itself. Suppose Ugg wanted to initiate a buzz marketing campaign at your university and that they contacted you for marketing advice. First, they would like to recruit some brand ambassadors as advocates for their brand. Your first task, therefore, is to design a flyer to post around campus announcing that Ugg wants to hire brand ambassadors. But, before you can design the flyer, you must decide on the relationship the ambassador will have with Ugg and the type of reward or payment she will receive. After you design the flyer, your second task is to design a buzz marketing program that you believe Ugg and the new brand ambassador should use on your campus.

CASE 1 AFTER THE RUSH: WHAT'S NEXT FOR RED BULL?

In today's active world, people need help. At least, that would be the position presented by any of the companies that sell energy drinks. Red Bull and other products are designed to jolt a consumer into action.

Red Bull's ingredient list begins with taurine, which occurs naturally in the human body. Red Bull helps to replace the taurine that is lost during conditions of high stress or physical exertion, which, in turn, helps the person recover more quickly. The carbohydrate glucuronolactone, which also is found naturally in the human body, is added to help with detoxification processes as well as support the body in eliminating waste substances. The amount of caffeine in a serving of Red Bull is nearly double the amount present in Mountain Dew, which is perceived by many as the highest-energy soft drink. Red Bull also contains acesulfame K, sucrose, glucose, B vitamins, and aspartame, which is well-known as the key ingredient in NutraSweet. The company's marketing materials emphasize that the formula took 3 years to develop. The 8.3-ounce canned drink was first launched in Australia in 1984. Red Bull tastes sweet and lemony, and, as one fan put it, "like a melted lollypop." The price of a single can is typically much higher than a 16-ounce bottle of soda.[56]

When Red Bull was introduced into the United States, the product clearly struck a chord in some markets. Those pulling all-nighters for school, work, or partying, as well as those engaged in extreme sports, quickly gravitated to Red Bull. By 2010, the drink continued to hold a 60 to 70 percent share of the U.S. market for similar drinks and annual sales.

Red Bull's entry into the United States has been viewed by many marketing experts as one of the first and classic uses of alternative and buzz marketing. Red Bull's brand management team began by identifying a target audience—those who would most likely want the buzz created by an energy drink. One key constituent group would be college students. Consequently, the company gave free samples of the drink to college and university students, who were encouraged to throw big parties where cases of Red Bull would be provided.

Red Bull's marketing team created a group of "consumer educators" who traveled to various locations giving out free samples. The brand managers also organized and sponsored extreme sporting events, such as skateboarding and cliff diving, for consumer educators to attend. The concept was that the participants and fans of these types of sports had buzz-seeking desires and an interest in products that were positioned as "sleek, sweet, and full-throttle."[57] From the parties and the extreme sports, word-of-mouth communications about the brand spread. The buzz-seeking target audience became Red Bull's first customer base.

The traditional soft-drink companies were slow to react. Eventually, Pepsi created a competing product called Adrenaline Rush; Coca-Cola entered the market with KMX; and Anheuser Busch developed 180, which is supposed to turn a person's energy level around by 180 degrees. Pepsi may be less concerned with Red Bull due to its ownership of Gatorade. Still, both Coke and Pepsi have concentrated efforts on garnering shelf space in convenience stores and superstores.

▲ Red Bull used alternative marketing to establish a presence in the United States.

Source: Author-Supplied Image.

More recently, Red Bull's marketing efforts have been expanded to include more traditional forms of advertising. At the same time, endorsers tend to be edgier figures, such as famed kayaker Tao Berman, and the commercials themselves remain offbeat. Red Bull creator Dietrich Mateschitz summarized it best, "If we don't create a market, it doesn't exist." And $1.6 billion later, it is clear that he has a point.

Two challenges have begun to emerge. First, Red Bull has been banned in some countries, including France and Canada. Other nations have examined the product and express fears about its impact on health. The second is keeping Red Bull on the cutting edge. A series of new energy formulas are available, including the heavily advertised 5-Hour Energy drinks. Can Red Bull maintain its edgy marketing presence over a sustained period of time?

1. What alternative marketing methods does Red Bull use?

2. Visit Red Bull's Web site (**www.redbull.com**) and identify the alternative media venues used by Red Bull's marketing team.

3. What role should traditional media play in Red Bull's future, especially when compared to alternative media?

4. Are there ways to build brand communities around Red Bull? What role might Twitter, Digg, or Facebook play in supporting such communities?

5. Red Bull believes that staying with alternative approaches best fits its image. As you think about all of the alternative marketing methods and alternative media, what suggestions would you make to Red Bull for the future? Describe a campaign for Red Bull using one or more alternative methods.

TANNING AND VOLLEYBALL: REVITALIZING A LIFESTYLE

Jessica Jones faced a difficult challenge as she took control of the Sun Products, Inc., account. As a relatively new account executive, Jessica knew it was important to establish measurable results when conducting various marketing communication campaigns. Sun Products sells items oriented toward beach-related activities, the most successful of which is the company's line of sunscreen products.

The tanning industry faces a unique set of challenges as a new generation of consumers emerges. First, consumers are now more aware of the dangerous long-term effects of tanning than ever before. These include more wrinkles and vastly increased chances of developing skin cancer in later life. In Australia, where the ozone layer is the most depleted, exposure to the sun is even more hazardous. More important, however, is a potential shift in cultural values regarding appearance.

As the new millennium commences, it is possible that a certain set of consumers will begin to believe that tanning is equal to foolishness—or at least that a suntan is no longer as "sexy" as it has been for many years. Beach bums and bunnies continue to run counter to this trend. The question remains, however, whether being bronze is a good idea.

One way to counter this problem is by developing new products designed to screen out the sun rather than enhance the sun's tanning properties. Lotions with higher SPF (sun protection factor) values generally sell at higher prices. Higher-quality sunscreens do not wash off in a pool or while swimming. Further, items containing herbal ingredients and new aromas are designed to entice new interest. Products with aloe vera and vitamin E may help reduce the pain of and heal sunburns more quickly. Products that "tan" without exposure to the sun are being developed for those who want the beach look without doing time in the sand.

At the same time, to promote more "traditional" products to college students on spring break and others who still enjoy a deep, dark tan requires careful promotion. Advertisements often stress the "fun" aspects of being outdoors.

Hawaiian Tropics, one of the chief competitors in the tanning industry, has taken a unique approach to the promotion of its products. The company holds an annual contest in which the Tropics team of beach girls is chosen to represent the firm. Contestants are female, beautiful, and have good tans. Those who win the contest tour the country promoting Hawaiian Tropics products and appear on television programs. At individual events held at beaches across the United States and in other locations, free samples of Hawaiian Tropics are given out, along with coupons and other purchase incentives. Giveaways of beach towels and other beach equipment are used to heighten interest in the product at various stores.

Beach Volleyball Magazine notes that it features not a sport, but a lifestyle. The activity has the benefit of being included as part of the Summer Olympics. Some women, such as Misty May-Treanor and Kerri Walsh, have recognizable names on the national stage and enjoy immense popularity within the women's volleyball fan base. In addition, there are professional beach volleyball tournaments across the United States each year.

Promotion of women's beach volleyball tends to focus on tans, bikinis, and the sexy, athletic competitors. Many of the marketing materials available online, on posters, and in other places feature photos of beach volleyball players in skimpy swimsuits. Fans also tend to attend events wearing outfits designed to show off a fit body and a great tan.

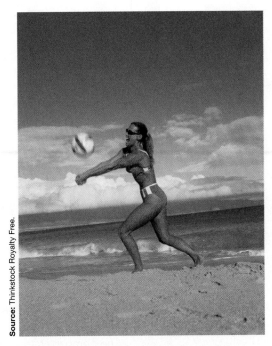

Source: Thinkstock Royalty Free.

▲ Beach volleyball is a natural tie-in with sun tanning products.

Jessica suspects there is a natural tie-in available with beach volleyball, especially on the women's side. Instead of tanning for its own sake, getting a tan while doing something healthy seems like a great appeal. The primary issue is whether the appeal can move beyond volleyball fans to the larger public. The secret would be to find a theme for a tie-in that would appeal to a larger audience.

An entire range of promotional items is possible. Items include coupons, premiums and giveaways, contests, samples, bonus packs (with various ranges of SPF values in the same pack), and refunds for higher-priced lotions.

Jessica knows the key is to maintain a consistent message and theme for her company. It must stand out in the crowd of Coppertone, Bain de Soleil, and Hawaiian Tropics. She realizes that to succeed she needs Sun Products' point-of-purchase displays placed prominently in as many places as possible, from drugstores to swimming specialty stores.

1. Is a buzz marketing program possible for Sun Products? Why or why not?

2. Design a complete lifestyle marketing program for Sun Products based on a tie-in with women's beach volleyball. Include both traditional and nontraditional advertising venues.

3. Name any opportunities you can identify for product placements or brand entertainment for Sun Products.

4. How could Sun Products use guerrilla marketing? Describe a possible guerrilla marketing campaign.

5. Is there a potential overlap between the brand community that loves beach volleyball and a brand community for Sun Products? Describe the ways that Sun Products' marketing department could build and enhance a connection between the two.

11 Database and Direct Response Marketing and Personal Selling

LEVI STRAUSS & CO.

Using Quality Information to Build Relationships

Levi Strauss & Co. has been in business since 1853, when a Bavarian immigrant by the name of Levi Strauss opened a clothing operation. Since that time, the firm has continued to operate, guided by four principles: empathy, originality, integrity, and courage. The goal of integrity has led to a strong emphasis on social responsibility. Empathy and originality fit with designing innovative clothing and knowledgeable customers. Courage represents the desire to take bold steps that company leaders believe are right, such as the move toward providing health insurance to same-sex domestic partners.

The company's three primary brands are Levi's, Dockers, and Levi Strauss Signature. The Dockers brand targets older customers. The Dockers line features pants that are comfortable, fashionable, and acceptable in many workplaces, at least on casual days. Dockers are sold at Sears, JCPenney, and slightly more upscale clothing stores that target a broad market. The Levi Strauss Signature brand is emphasized in Europe and other parts of the world.

For many years, the original Levi's brand was a dominant force in the U.S. teen and young adult marketplace. In the past two decades, however, brand erosion has taken place. Many younger buyers began to express the sentiment that Levi's were the jeans worn by their parents. Firms such as Old Navy, Calvin Klein, and other brands were gaining sales at Levi's expense, because younger customers didn't view Levi's as a hip brand.

The company responded to these challenges by developing a strong database marketing program. Levi's marketing team recognized that to be effective a company's database must be much more than a collection of names and addresses. Levi's reacted by emphasizing relationship marketing, with a goal of understanding what consumers wanted and giving them a voice that would be heard by company leaders. To meet these objectives, the firm used a survey to identify five consumer groups. These groups became part of a pilot program.

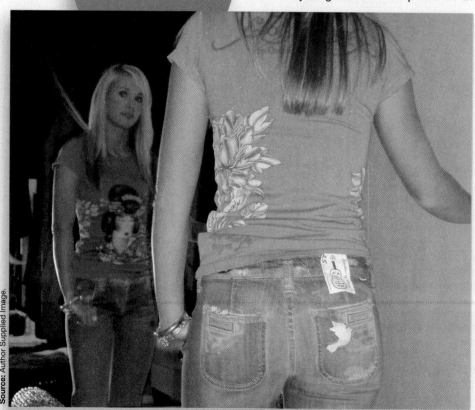

CHAPTER OBJECTIVES

After reading this chapter, you should be able to answer the following questions:

1 What role does database marketing, including the data warehouse, data coding and analysis, and data mining, play in creating and enhancing relationships with customers?

2 How can database-driven marketing communication programs help personalize interactions with customers?

3 How do database-driven marketing programs create sales and build bonds with customers?

4 When should direct response marketing programs be used to supplement other methods of delivering messages and products to consumers?

5 What are the tasks involved in developing successful personal selling programs for consumers and businesses?

6 How should database marketing and personal selling programs be adapted to international settings?

Using the existing database, the company's marketing team contacted various shoppers and enticed them to fill out questionnaires. In total, nearly 100,000 consumers completed questionnaires, which were distributed at stores, colleges, the Lilith Fair, and via customer service lines. Levi's carefully recorded the "doorway" each respondent used and tied it to other information, which eventually yielded the five major groups of shoppers. Each of the five groups expressed differing needs when it came to jeans.

Next, Levi's targeted the groups individually. Promotions were structured to match the nature of the customer profile that emerged. For example, one group, known as Valuable Shoppers, represented individuals who were willing to spend $60 or more on a pair of pants. These patrons received thank-you gifts following purchases of custom-fit jeans. The gift was a planter with flower bulbs and a card signed by the sales clerk who took the fitting. Responses from this group were impressive. A Valuable Shopper who was sent a gift purchased, on average, 2.3 more pairs of jeans within the next few weeks.

Online shoppers, a group identified as Generation Y consumers, were between 18 and 25 years old and did not receive the same premium. Instead, the marketing team delivered fashion messages to them. Thus, the promotional approach matched the buyer group's characteristics.

By contacting consumers through questionnaires, gifts, promotions, and service lines, Levi's marketing team believed it was able to establish a more intimate form of communication with the company's clientele. This, in turn, helped combat declining interest in Levi's products.

Levi's success started with having a fairly well-established database to begin the program, enhancing the database, and listening to what consumers had to say. Any organization that is willing to utilize the talents and programs made available from an effective database management team may be in the position to reap similar rewards.[1]

OVERVIEW

Successful businesses continually acquire new customers and work to retain them. Repeat customers purchase more frequently and spend more money. Maintaining repeat business is far less expensive than constantly replacing those who turn to other companies.

This fourth section reviews a variety of promotional tools that are used to acquire and retain customers, as displayed in Figure 11.1. Database programs, direct response marketing, and personal selling are examined in this chapter. Sales promotions, both consumer and

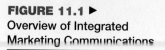

FIGURE 11.1 ▶
Overview of Integrated
Marketing Communications

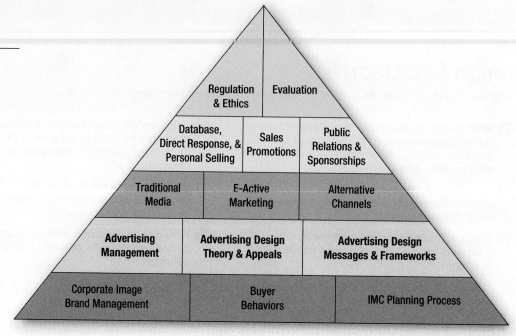

trade promotions, are examined in Chapter 12, followed by public relations and sponsorship programs in Chapter 13.

Database marketing provides a new communication link with customers. This, in turn, helps to produce higher levels of customer acquisition, customer retention, and customer loyalty. Database marketing has become increasingly crucial. New technologies associated with the Internet and computer software make it easier to build and develop strong database programs.

The first part of this chapter examines database marketing, including data warehouses, data coding, and data mining, as well as data-driven communications and marketing programs. Three data-driven marketing programs are described: permission marketing, frequency programs, and customer relationship management systems. Databases are also used for direct response marketing techniques, including direct mail, television programs and traditional media, alternative media, and telemarketing. Finally, databases are a key component of personal selling.

Today's customers clearly value personalized marketing efforts. Creating programs that individualize messages and marketing materials is the core of successful database marketing, direct response efforts, and personal selling.

DATABASE MARKETING

① What role does database marketing, including the data warehouse, data coding and analysis, and data mining, play in creating and enhancing relationships with customers?

Database marketing involves collecting and utilizing customer data for the purposes of enhancing interactions with customers and developing customer loyalty. Successful database marketing emphasizes (1) identifying customers and (2) building relationships with them. This includes understanding the lifetime values of various customers and the development of customer-retention efforts, especially for the best customers. Enhancing customer loyalty represents the primary benefit of database marketing. Although database marketing can be used for selling products, retention and relationships remain the primary focus.

Mitchell's of Westport is a high-end clothing store. When shoppers visit the store, the sales staff can access data regarding their preferences, sizes, previous purchases, and other information. Purchases are followed up with thank-you notes. Customers receive notices when new shipments of clothes arrive and are given invitations to special events. Loyalty to the store remains high. Some customers who have moved to new cities return to buy clothing.[2] One vital ingredient stands out: Data are used to make customers feel special and to develop relationships with them. Although selling occurred, it did not drive the database program.

- Building a data warehouse
- Database coding and analysis
- Data mining
- Data-driven marketing communications
- Data-driven marketing programs

The tasks associated with database marketing are displayed in Figure 11.2. Of these, building the data warehouse and data coding are the two key activities that are described next.

BUILDING A DATA WAREHOUSE

Successful database marketing requires a quality data warehouse. The **data warehouse** holds all of the customer data. In building one, the IT department and marketing team first distinguish between an operational database and the marketing database. The *operational database* contains the transactions individuals have with the firm and follows accounting principles. The marketing department manages the *marketing database*, which contains information about current customers, former customers, and prospects. Examples of data and analyses found in a standard marketing data warehouse include:

- Customer names and addresses
- E-mail addresses and the cookies that record visits to the company's Web site
- History of every purchase transaction
- History of customer interactions, such as inquiries, complaints, and returns
- Results of any customer surveys
- Preferences and profiles supplied by the customer
- Marketing promotions and response history from marketing campaigns
- Appended demographic and psychographic data from sources such as Knowledge Base Marketing or Claritas
- Database coding, such as lifetime value and customer segment clusters

Collecting customer names and addresses is the easiest part of developing the database. Collecting the other information that turns the data warehouse into a powerful marketing and communication tool can be more challenging.

The marketing team typically employs a system for updating addresses, because approximately 20 percent of Americans move each year. When individuals fill out a change of address form with the U.S. Postal Service, the information is sent to all of the service bureaus authorized to sell the information to businesses. A company that sends database names to one of these service bureaus receives address updates for only a few cents per hit, or per individual that moves. Updating mailing addresses should occur at least once each year, depending on how often the database is used and the frequencies of contacts.

E-Mail and Internet Data

E-mail addresses are essential elements of a quality database. The Internet and e-mail provide cost-effective channels of communication to be used in building relationships with customers. Most database programs take advantage of cookies to register and store Web site visits and browsing patterns. This information makes it possible to personalize the firm's Web site for each customer. When someone logs onto the site, a greeting such as "Welcome back Stacy" can appear on the screen. The cookie technology makes it possible for the system to recognize that Stacy, or at least someone using her computer, is accessing the Web site. If Stacy has purchased products or browsed the catalog, then the content of the pages can be personalized to contain the products she has an interest in purchasing.

Purchase and Communication Histories

Effective database programs maintain detailed purchase histories of customers. The database records every interaction the company has with a customer. When a customer sends an e-mail to tech support, this information should be placed in the database. Any person who returns a product or who has called customer service with a complaint has the information documented. Purchases and interaction histories determine future communications with customers and assist the marketing team in evaluating each customer's lifetime value, and other customer value metrics.

Personal Preference Profiles

Purchase and visit histories do not provide sufficient information. Quality database marketing programs include profiles with specific information about each customer's personal preferences. These profiles and personal preference files may be constructed in various ways, including customer surveys. Others companies gather information on the Web site or in retail stores.

Every time the company initiates contact with customers, the information should be placed in the database, along with the customer's response. This information provides a rich history of what works and what does not. It further allows for customization of communication methods for each customer, which leads to the highest probability of success.

Customer Information Companies

Oftentimes, demographic and psychographic information are not available through internal company records. In these cases, the information can be obtained by working with a marketing research firm that specializes in collecting customer data. Knowledge Base Marketing, Donnelly, Dialog, and Claritas are four of the many companies that market this type of information.

▲ Purchase and communication histories provide important database information for a company such as Scott, which sells and rents power-line and utility equipment.

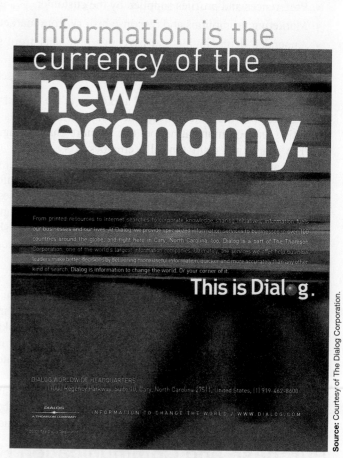

▲ Dialog is a marketing research firm that supplies companies with customer information.

Another approach used by companies operating online Web sites, such as Gap and Victoria's Secret, is to combine online information about customers with offline information provided by firms such as Acxiom and Datran Media. Once merged, this information can then be stored in cookies to allow for customization and personalization of Web sites and communications with customers. For instance, based on income level and past purchasing habits, two women in adjoining offices can access the same cosmetics Web site; one might see a $300 bottle of Missoni perfume and the other might see the $25 house brand.[3]

Geocoding

The process of adding geographic codes to each customer's record so that customer addresses can be plotted on a map is called **geocoding**. Geocoding helps decision makers finalize placements of retail outlets and can be used to direct marketing materials to specific geographic areas. Geocoding also allows for combining demographic information with lifestyle data. This assists the marketing team in selecting the best media for advertisements.

One version of geocoding software is named *CACI Coder/Plus*. The software identifies a cluster in which an address belongs. A group such as Enterprising Young Singles in the CACI system contains certain characteristics, such as enjoying dining, spending money on DVDs and personal computers, and reading certain magazines. A retailer could then target this group with mailings and special offers.[4]

DATABASE CODING AND ANALYSIS

Database coding and analysis provide critical information for the development of personalized communications. They also assist in creating marketing promotional campaigns. Common forms of database coding are lifetime value analysis and customer clusters.

Lifetime Value Analysis

One calculation that may be used is the lifetime value of a customer or market segment. The **lifetime value** figure represents the present value of future profits a customer will generate over his or her life in a relationship with a brand or firm.[5] Some companies calculate the value for individual customers. Others calculate it for customer segments. Many marketing experts believe the latter value provides more accurate information, because it sums costs across a market segment. Individual lifetime value calculations normally only contain costs for single customers.

The key figures in calculating the lifetime value of a consumer or set of consumers are revenues, costs, and retention rates. Revenue and costs are normally easy to obtain, because many companies record these numbers for accounting purposes. Retention rates require an accurate marketing database system.

An important figure is the cost of acquiring a new customer. It can be calculated by dividing the total marketing and advertising expenditures in dollars by the number of new customers obtained. As an example, when $200,000 dollars are spent and the company acquires 1,000 new customers as a result, the acquisition cost is $200 per customer ($200,000 divided by 1,000).

Another key amount is the cost of maintaining the relationship. This involves all costs associated with marketing, communicating, and maintaining the database records. These records are more difficult to obtain because such costs are usually for a campaign, which makes allocating costs to a single customer difficult. Computer and database technology can average or allocate a portion of these costs to individual customer records or to a lifetime value segment.

The end product for either individual customers or a customer segment is a lifetime value figure. For instance, when the lifetime value of a customer segment is $1,375, the figure represents the amount, on average, that each customer will generate over his or her lifetime. By communicating with and marketing to the customer segment, the lifetime value may be increased. Lifetime value analysis also notifies customer contact and service personnel about a customer's worth to the company.

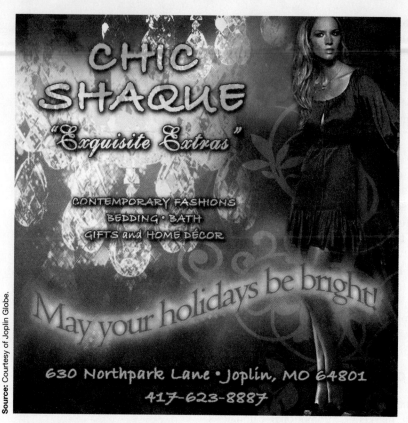

▲ Knowing the lifetime value of customers helps the marketing team develop useful databases for retailers such as Chic Shaque.

Customer Clusters

Coding can be used to group customers into clusters based on a wide variety of criteria. A bank may group customers based on the number of accounts, types of accounts, and other relationships a customer may have with the organization. For example, customers with a home mortgages above $100,000 with a balance of 30 to 60 percent remaining may be targeted for a home equity loan. A clothing retailer can group customers by the type of clothing each group purchases and then develop marketing programs for the various groups. For instance, teenagers who like Western wear would be in a different cluster than teenagers who like hip, trendy fashions.

Unified Western Grocers is a wholesale cooperative association serving 3,000 grocery stores. The company used customer cluster analysis to reduce 19 different advertising campaigns and programs for the various stores it served down to 4, based on customer commonalities. The four clusters that emerged from the analysis were: affluent urban and suburban households; mid-downscale rural seniors; large, low-income urban households; and unacculturated Hispanics. Advertisements and shelf allocations of brands were then designed for each of the four customer clusters. Advertising design costs were reduced and more effective ads were created.[6]

DATA MINING

Data mining involves using computer data analysis software to mine data for meaningful information and relationships. Data mining includes two activities: (1) building profiles of customer segments and/or (2) preparing models that predict future purchase behaviors based on past purchases.

Data mining helps the marketing team build profiles of the firm's best customers. These profiles, in turn, help identify prospective new customers. They can be used to examine "good" customers to see if they are candidates for sales calls that would move them from "good" to a higher value. Companies offering different types of goods and services develop multiple profiles. These profiles are used to target sales calls and to look for cross-selling possibilities.

The marketing team at First Horizon National Bank used data mining to expand the company's wealth management business by studying consumer groups. Data about existing customers from the mortgage side of the firm's business made it possible to locate the best prospects for investment services. Linking the data mining program with cross-selling resulted in an increase in company revenues from $26.3 million to $33.8 million in just 1 year.[7]

Retailer American Eagle used data mining to study how consumers responded to price markdowns. The information helped the marketing team determine when to cut prices and by how much in order to optimize sales. Markdown programs were geared to individual stores, because consumers responded differently in each outlet.[8]

The second data mining method involves developing models that predict future sales based on past purchasing activities. Staples, Inc. used a modeling program to examine the buying habits of the company's catalog customers. The program identified the names of frequent buyers. Customized mailings were sent to those customers.

The method used to mine the data will be determined based on the specific information that is needed. Once the data have been mined for information, individual marketing programs can be designed. Profiles and models assist in designing effective marketing programs. A direct-mail program to current customers is different from one designed to attract new customers. The data provide clues about the best approach for each customer segment.

Data coding and data mining serve three purposes. First, they can be used to develop marketing communications. The marketing team utilizes the information to choose types of promotions, advertising media, and the message to be presented to each group of customers. Second, they can be helpful in developing marketing programs. Third, companies that employ salespeople can use the information to qualify prospects and make personal sales calls on those individuals or businesses that have the most potential. These activities are discussed in the following sections.

DATABASE-DRIVEN MARKETING COMMUNICATIONS

The primary reason for building a database, coding the information, and performing data mining is to use the output to establish one-on-one communication with each customer. Personalized communications build relationships and lead to repeat business and customer loyalty. They may help move the company and its products from brand parity to brand equity. A database marketing program provides the tools to personalize messages and keep records of the types of effective and ineffective communications.

> **②** How can database-driven marketing communication programs help personalize interactions with customers?

The Internet is the key technology for database-driven communications. Figure 11.3 highlights reasons why the Internet is important in customer interactions. The Internet enables instant communications, quick analyses, and targeted messages.

Identification Codes

A database-driven marketing program starts with assigning individual customers IDs and passwords that allow them to access components of the Web site that are not available to those who simply visit the site without logging on. The IDs and passwords are tied to cookies in order to customize pages and individual offers. When the system works properly, the customer does not have to log in each time. Instead, the cookie automatically does it for the user. For example, each time a user accesses Barnes & Noble, he receives a personalized greeting, such as "Welcome, Jim." Next, when an order is placed, the user does not have to type in address or credit card information. It is in the database and comes up automatically. This saves the customer time and effort and increases the probability he will make a purchase.

Specialized communications should be sent after the sale. Each time a purchase is made a series of communications follows. First, an e-mail confirming the order and thanking the buyer for making the purchase is sent. An estimate of shipping date will be included. When the order is pulled and shipped, another e-mail containing the tracking number follows. Some companies include an e-mail in the interim stating that the order is at the warehouse and is being pulled and made ready for shipment.

- It is the cheapest form of communication.
- It is available 24/7.
- Metric analysis reveals that the customer read the message, the time it was read, and how much time was spent reading it.

- Customers are able to access additional information whenever they want.
- It can build a bond with customers.

◄ FIGURE 11.3
Why the Internet Is Important in Customer Communications

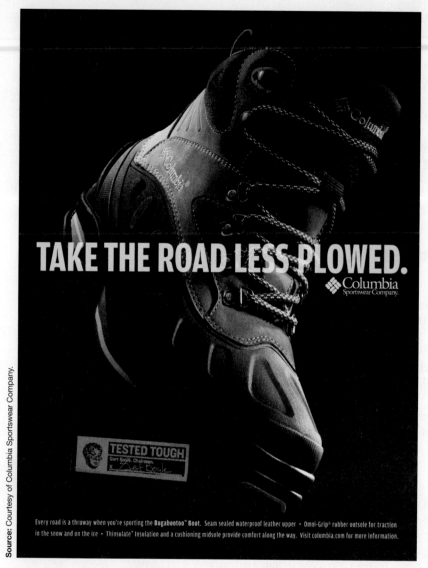

TAKE THE ROAD LESS PLOWED.

Columbia
Sportswear Company.

TESTED TOUGH

Every road is a thruway when you're sporting the **Bugabootoo™ Boot**. Seam sealed waterproof leather upper • Omni-Grip® rubber outsole for traction in the snow and on the ice • Thinsulate™ insulation and a cushioning midsole provide comfort along the way. Visit columbia.com for more information.

▲ Through customer profile information, Columbia can identify individuals with high levels of interest in hiking.

Customer Profile Information

An effective database-driven communication program relies on customer profiles and any other information about customer preferences to help individualize messages. Bluefly and other online clothing operations send e-mails about new fashions that have arrived. These e-mails do not go to every person in the database. E-mails are sent only to those individuals who have indicated a desire to receive the information or who have indicated they have an interest in fashion news. Customers should feel they are receiving special "inside" information.

Customer profiles can also be used to send birthday greetings to loyal customers. Recently, a steak and seafood restaurant sent a card and offered a $10 birthday discount to 215,600 customers who had provided their birthdates. The cost of mailing the birthday card and discount was $90,000. Approximately 40 percent of the cards were redeemed. Each birthday customer brought about 2 other people with them, and those individuals paid full price for their meals. The result was $2.9 million in revenues derived from the program.[9]

The profiles, cookies, and ID numbers are also critical when the customer initiates contact with the company. When a customer contacts the company on the Web or through e-mail, the company already knows something about the individual. Responses can then be created that are tailored to that particular individual.

In-Bound Telemarketing

Contacts made by telephone work the same way as Internet contacts. The service-call operator knows immediately the identity of the person calling. Customer data appears on the screen in front of the in-bound telemarketer. The operator can then treat the caller in a more personal way. When the company calculates a lifetime value code, the operator also knows the customer's value and status. The operator can ask about a recent purchase or talk about information provided on the customer's list of preferences or a customer profile. This means the operator can greet and treat each customer as an individual, not as just some random person making a call.

Trawling

Database marketing includes a procedure called **trawling**, which is the process of searching the database for a specific piece of information for marketing purposes. Home Depot uses trawling to locate individuals who have recently moved. Home Depot's marketing team believes that when people buy new homes they will often need home improvement merchandise. Most of the time, these items include merchandise sold at Home Depot.

Other marketers trawl a database to find anniversary dates of a special purchase, such as purchasing a new car. Some car dealerships send a correspondence on each year's anniversary of a car purchase to see if the customer is satisfied or is interested in trading for a new vehicle. It can be used to locate individuals who have not made a purchase within the last 3 months or who purchased a lawnmower last year. Trawling can be used in a wide variety of ways to communicate with specific individuals who meet a particular criterion.

DATABASE-DRIVEN MARKETING PROGRAMS

❸ How do database-driven marketing programs create sales and build bonds with customers?

Database-driven marketing programs take many forms. They may be used in conjunction with other marketing activities. Some of the more common programs include permission marketing, frequency programs, and customer relationship management efforts.

Permission Marketing

A strong backlash by consumers against spam and junk mail exists. Consequently, many marketing departments have turned to **permission marketing**, a program in which promotional information will be sent to only those consumers who give the company permission to do so. Permission marketing programs can be offered on the Internet, by telephone, or through direct mail. Response rates are often higher in permission programs, because customers only receive requested marketing materials or those for which permission was given. Results are enhanced when permission marketing programs utilize database technology and segment customers; however, not everyone who signs up for permission marketing becomes a valuable customer.

Figure 11.4 lists the steps of a permission marketing program. Permission can be obtained by providing an incentive for volunteering. Information, entertainment, a gift, cash, or entries in a sweepstakes are common incentives. The information provided is primarily educational and focuses on the company's product or service features.

Reinforcing the relationship involves an additional new incentive beyond the original gift. Relationships can be enhanced when more in-depth information about a consumer, such as hobbies, interests, attitudes, and opinions, is known. This information can be used to entice additional purchases by offering special deals.

Quris, Inc., of Denver, Colorado, solicited travelers and frequent fliers for an e-mail permissions marketing program. The permission marketing e-mails were opened and read regularly by 54 percent of the program's enrollees. In one year, nearly two-thirds made online purchases that were tied directly to the permission program. Frequent fliers who participated in the e-mail permission program spent an average of an extra $1,210 per year.[10]

Keys to Success in Permission Marketing

For a permission marketing program to succeed, the marketing team ensures that the recipients have agreed to participate. Unfortunately, some consumers have been tricked

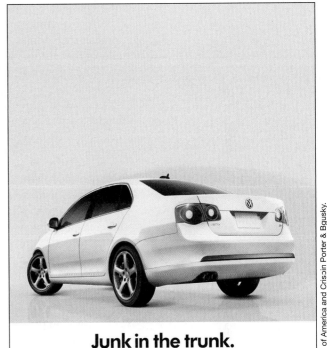

Junk in the trunk.

This Volkswagen is carrying an extra burden.

Several hundred actually. We're not talking weight, or the various awards Jetta has won—most recently Autosite.com's Best Car for the Environment—or even the responsibility of being North America's best-selling Volkswagen.

Those aren't exactly tough burdens to bear.

We're talking about the hundreds of German-engineered advancements we've wedged inside it over the years.

Features like uni-body construction, 8-speaker sound system, 6 standard airbags, traction control and ABS brakes.

Not to mention an extra large trunk. Each one adds a level of performance to the Jetta. But each one can also add weight to its price—if we're not careful.

Lucky for us, we are. Introducing the jam-packed Jetta at a new low price. Because an award-winning car that's gotten expensive isn't much of an achievement in our book.

The world has come to expect more from a Volkswagen. The 2008 Jetta. Priced for the people at $16,990.

Source: Courtesy of Volkswagen of America and Crispin Porter & Bgusky.

▲ A company such as Volkswagen can use trawling to correspond with buyers on each yearly anniversary of their car purchases.

---

1. Obtain permission from the customer.
2. Offer the consumer an ongoing curriculum that is meaningful.
3. Reinforce the incentive to continue the relationship.
4. Increase the level of permission.
5. Leverage the permission to benefit both parties.

◀ **FIGURE 11.4**
Steps in Building a Permissions Marketing Program

into joining permission marketing programs. One common tactic is to automatically enroll customers in a permission marketing program when they complete an online survey or make an online purchase; opting out of the program requires the individual to un-check a box on the site. Although this approach increases the number of individuals enrolled, the technique often creates bad feelings.

The marketing material should be relevant to the consumer receiving it. Far too many people have joined permission marketing programs that have turned into situations where they provide no input and are bombarded with extraneous marketing messages. This does not create loyalty and runs counter to the purpose of a permission program.

One recent survey revealed that 80 percent of consumers stopped reading permission e-mails from companies because they were shoddy or irrelevant. Another 68 percent said the e-mails came too frequently, and 51 percent said they lost interest in the goods, services, or topics of the e-mails. On the whole, consumers delete an average of 43 percent of permission e-mails without ever reading them.[11]

To overcome these challenges, the marketing team monitors responses and customizes the permission program to meet individual customer needs. Database technology allows for customization by tracking responses. When a customer regularly accesses a Web site through a link in an e-mail sent by the company to read the latest fashion news, the behavior can trigger e-mail offers and incentives on fashions related to the news stories. An individual who does not access the Web site and does not appear to be interested in fashion news receives a different type of e-mail offer. By capitalizing on the power of database technology, a company can enhance the permission marketing program and make it beneficial to the company and the customer.

Permission Marketing Enticements

Figure 11.5 lists the top reasons for opting into e-mail programs. Winning a sweepstakes is at the top of the list. Also, when the individual is already a customer of the company, the person feels favorably predisposed to the company's products.[12] It is normally much easier to entice current customers into the permission marketing program than it is to attract new customers.

Figure 11.6 provides a list of motives that help retain customers in a permission marketing relationship. As shown, consumers remain with such programs for a variety of reasons.[13]

Permission marketing programs have the potential to build strong, ongoing relationships with customers when the program offers something of value to the customer. To optimize permission marketing, firms feature empowerment and reciprocity.[14] **Empowerment** means consumers believe they have power throughout the relationship and not just at the beginning when they agreed to join the program. They can make decisions and have choices about what is received.

To maintain positive attitudes, consumers should be given rewards along the way, not just at the beginning. This creates feelings of **reciprocity**, or a sense of obligation

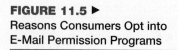

FIGURE 11.5 ▶
Reasons Consumers Opt into E-Mail Permission Programs

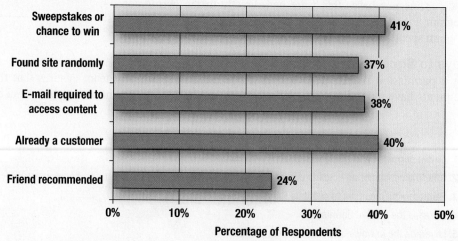

Source: Joseph Gatti, "Most Consumers Have Reached Permission E-mail Threshold," *Direct Marketing* (December 2003), pp. 1–2.

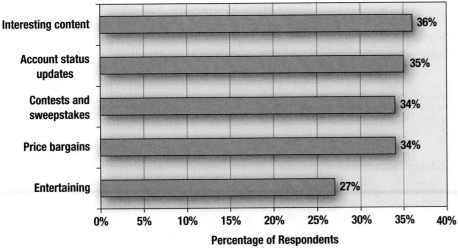

◀ **FIGURE 11.6**
Reasons Consumers Remain in a
Permission Marketing Program

Source: Joseph Gatti, "Most Consumers Have Reached Permission E-mail Threshold," *Direct Marketing* (December 2003), pp. 1–2.

toward the company. One common mistake is only rewarding consumers for joining the program. Empowerment and reciprocity lead the customer to believe the company values the relationship. This increases the chances the consumer will continue to be an active participant.

Frequency Programs

With a **frequency program** or **loyalty program**, a company offers free merchandise or services for a series of purchases. These efforts encourage customers to make repeat purchases. In the airline industry, frequent-flyer programs offer free flights after a traveler accumulates a certain number of miles. Grocery stores offer special discounts when purchases reach a certain amount within a specified time period.

According to research by the Chief Marketing Officer (CMO) Council, two-thirds of consumers belong to loyalty programs. On the average, households are enrolled in 14 programs, but only actively participate in about 6. Figure 11.7 provides a list of benefits of such programs cited by customers.[15]

Goals

Various reasons for developing frequency programs are provided in Figure 11.8. Frequency programs were first developed to differentiate one brand from its competition. Now, however, they now tend to be common across all competitors in an industry (credit cards, airlines, grocery stores, hotels, restaurants, etc.).

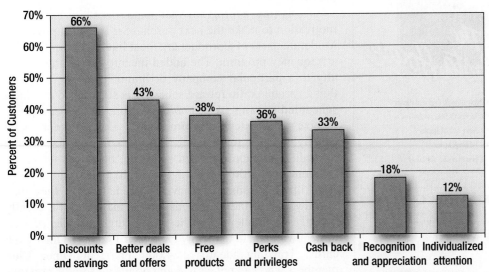

◀ **FIGURE 11.7**
Benefits of Loyalty Programs
Cited by Customers

Source: Adapted from Mark Dolliver, "Gauging Customer Loyalty," *Adweek* (**www.adweek.com/aw/content display/news/agency/ e3i4a73f5d7451749a37c7fca20**, February 16, 2010).

FIGURE 11.8 ▶
Goals of Frequency or Loyalty Programs

- Maintain sales, margins, or profits.
- Increase loyalty of existing customers.
- Preempt or match a competitor's frequency program.
- Induce cross-selling to existing customers.
- Differentiate a parity brand.
- Preempt the entry of a new brand.

Source: Grahame R. Dowling and Mark Uncles, "Do Customer Loyalty Programs Really Work?" *Sloan Management Review* 38, no. 4 (Summer 1997), pp. 71–82.

FIGURE 11.9 ▶
Principles in the Development of Frequency or Loyalty Programs

- Enhance the value of the product.
- Calculate the full cost of the program.
- Maximize customer motivation to make additional purchases.

Principles

As shown in Figure 11.9, three principles guide the development of a loyalty program. The first suggests that the program should add value to what the product offers or provide a unique new feature. Miller Brewing offers a loyalty program. The Miller High Life Extras loyalty program allows consumers to earn points by purchasing specially marked 12-packs and 30-packs. The points can be redeemed for merchandise ranging from High Life screensavers to branded fire pits. Most of the merchandise offered reinforces the Miller brand. The company's name is featured prominently on branded apparel, including Miller High Life deliveryman shirts, boxer shorts, hooded sweatshirts, and baseball caps.[16]

The more effort a customer expends to participate in a frequency program, the greater the value of the reward should be. Many consumers are willing to put forth greater effort to obtain luxury rewards as opposed to necessity rewards. Shoppers at a grocery store are more likely to put forth a higher level of effort in order to receive a free overnight stay at a nearby local resort or a free meal at nice restaurant than they would for a $25 gift certificate for food.[17]

To determine the full cost of the program, the marketing team should also consider the expenses associated with record keeping. Many times, the cost of maintaining a frequency account is greater than any potential additional profits.

Designing a program that maximizes the customer's motivation to make the next purchase is the third principle. Moderate users of a product are most likely to be enticed by a frequency program. The added incentive encourages loyalty to a particular company or brand. Research suggests that a variable ratio reward schedule is superior to regularly scheduled rewards. A *variable ratio* means that customers receive intermittent reinforcements. They do not know exactly when a reward will be given or the size of the reward. The random reward schedule, however, should be frequent enough to encourage them to make purchases.[18]

Although consumers have frequency cards, they may not always use them. The marketing manager of a locally owned restaurant noticed he had a large number of customers who had not recently used their Frequent Diner Club cards. Trawling identified 4,000 Frequent Diner Club members who had not earned any points during the previous 3 months. The restaurant sent a letter to each of the 4,000

▼ Many restaurants, such as The Pasta House, have frequency or loyalty programs for diners.

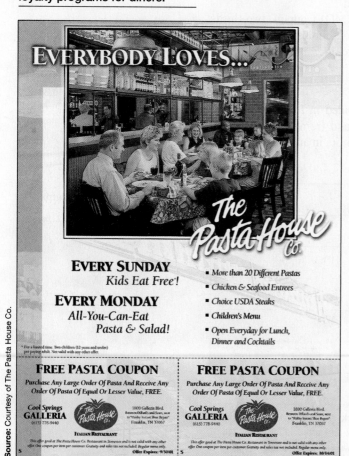

offering a $5 discount on dinner. The offer was good for 35 days and the mailing cost $1,800. The results were as follows:

- The average number of member visits per day increased from 25 to 42 during the promotion and to 29 per day after the promotion ended.
- Average visits by individual members holding cards increased both during and after the promotion.
- Incremental sales increased by $17,100 during the promotion and by $4,700 after the 35-day promotion.

By spending $1,800, this promotion led to reactivations by about 600 people who had not dined at the restaurant in 3 months. Of the nearly 600 who came back during the promotion, 147 dined at the restaurant after the promotion was over.[19]

Customer Relationship Management

Customer relationship management programs (CRM) generated a great deal of interest in the 1990s. Several companies invested significant dollars in CRM software, employee training, and implementation. **Customer relationship management (CRM)** programs allow companies to use databases to customize products and communications with customers, with the goals of higher sales and profits. Unfortunately, however, most CRM endeavors were not successful. Several reasons have been given for the poor results; the central one seems to be that CRM programs focused on making sales rather than on enhancing relationships.

The basic tenets of customer relationship management programs are sound. The objectives of CRM and its implementation are the ingredients that are usually flawed. Successful programs build long-term loyalty and bonds with customers through the use of a personal touch, facilitated by technology. Customer relationship management programs were designed to go beyond the development of a database and traditional selling tactics to the mass customization of both communications and products.

Two primary CRM metrics are the lifetime value of the customer and share of customer. The lifetime value concept has already been discussed in an earlier chapter. The second metric, share of customer, is based on the concept that some customers are more valuable than others and that over time the amount of money a customer spends with a firm can increase. **Share of customer** refers to the percentage of expenditures a customer makes with one particular firm compared to total expenditures in that product's category. Share of customer measures a customer's potential value. The question becomes, "If more is invested by the company in developing a relationship, what will the yield be over time?" When a customer makes only one-fourth of his or her purchases of a particular product with a specific vendor, increasing the share of the customer would mean increasing that percentage from 25 percent to a higher level, thus generating additional sales revenues. The ultimate goal would be leading the customer to make 100 percent of his or her purchases with one vendor.[20]

Assuming the tenets of CRM are sound, the question revolves around why so many programs failed. The Gartner Group, a research and advisory firm, identified four factors that contributed to these failures. First, the program was often implemented before a solid customer strategy was created. Market segments should be identified first so

▼ Glaxo Pharmaceutical's CRM program includes a product information hotline.

Instead of talking to some automated answering service, you'll speak to one of our pharmaceutical professionals employed specifically to answer your questions about Glaxo products.

These professionals are available by phone Monday through Friday, 8am to 4:30pm EST. And then can be reached any hour of any day in an emergency.

Most information can be provided on the spot. And if requested, we make every effort to send follow-up documentation within ten days.

Just call us toll free at 1-800-334-0089, or write us at the address below. You'll get a response that's not only fast, but personal.

HERE'S WHO YOU WON'T BE TALKING TO WHEN YOU CALL OUR PRODUCT INFORMATION LINE.

Glaxo Drug Information Services, 5 Moore Drive, Research Triangle Park, North Carolina 27709

that customization programs can then proceed. Failing to understand market segments resulted in a "ready, fire, aim" approach.[21]

Second, rolling out a CRM program before changing the organization to match it creates problems. A CRM program affects how customers are viewed as well as the methods used deliver goods and services. A new management philosophy becomes essential. Failing to educate the entire staff about this new perspective and approach quickly leads to problems.

Third, some CRM programs failed because they were technology-driven rather than customer-driven. Technology can only assist in record keeping and some aspects of order fulfillment. The rest is the responsibility of the employees, who must understand the customer and develop customized approaches.

Fourth, CRM programs fail when customers feel like they are being "stalked" rather than "wooed." Trying to build a relationship with a disinterested customer will be more annoying to the customer than helpful. For example, the *Dallas Morning News* discovered that its telemarketing program to gain subscribers was annoying people rather than winning them over. These problems have led many marketing departments to abandon CRM programs and to search for new and different ways to build relationships with customers.

In general, database-driven marketing programs should be designed to enhance customer loyalty. When a hotel's check-in person knows in advance that a business traveler prefers a nonsmoking room, a queen-size bed, and reads *USA Today*, these items could be made available as the guest arrives. Training hotel clerks and other employees to use the database helps them to provide better service, thereby building loyalty from regular customers. Any organization's marketing department can adapt these techniques to fit the needs of its customers and clients.

In addition to permission marketing, frequency programs, and CRM systems, other marketing programs can result from database analysis. Internet programs, trade promotions, consumer promotions, and other marketing tactics can be facilitated by carefully using the database.

4 When should direct response marketing programs be used to supplement other methods of delivering messages and products to consumers?

DIRECT RESPONSE MARKETING

One program that is closely tied to database marketing is direct response marketing. **Direct response marketing** (or **direct marketing**) is the targeting of products to customers without the use of other channel members. Figure 11.10 identifies the most

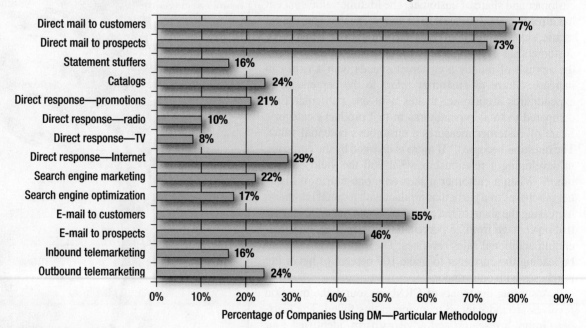

FIGURE 11.10 ▲
Methods of Direct Marketing

Source: Richard H. Levey, "Prospects Look Good," *Direct* 16 (December 1, 2004), pp. 1–5.

typical forms of direct marketing and the percentages of companies using them. Notice that direct marketing can be targeted at customers as well as prospects. According to the Direct Marketing Association, about 60 percent of a typical direct marketing budget is used for prospecting for new customers; the other 40 percent is spent retaining current customers.[22]

Direct response advertising, especially television and magazine advertising, is used extensively by pharmaceutical companies. A recent study revealed that this direct response approach works. Ads for prescription medications by pharmaceuticals prompted almost one-third of Americans to ask their doctors about a particular brand of medicine and 82 percent of those who asked their doctors received some type of prescription. The prescription was for the advertised brand 44 percent of the time; for another drug, 56 percent of the time. Sometimes doctors prescribed both the advertised brand as well as another brand.[23]

Individuals and companies can respond to a direct marketing piece in a number of ways, such as by telephone, e-mail, visiting a retail location, or using a PURL, or personalized URL, as described in an earlier chapter. PURLs offer the advantage of preloading all of the individual's personal data to the site, which can then be used to personalize the information and any offer. It also assists in tracking the individual's onsite activities and can be used to make real-time changes in offers.[24]

Direct Mail

As shown in Figure 11.10, mail remains the most common form of direct marketing. Direct mail can be targeted to both consumers and business-to-business customers. The success of a direct mail program will be determined by the quality of the mailing list. Companies have two sources when compiling a mailing list: the firm's internal database or a commercial list.

When the company's internal list is used, the marketing department carefully parses the list and separates active members from inactive members. A different direct mail piece will be sent to prospective new customers as compared to a piece designed to entice repeat purchases. Mailing direct offers to individuals (or businesses) who have not purchased recently but who have purchased in the past often yields a better response rate than cold-call mailing lists from brokers.

Types of Commercial Lists

Purchasing a commercial list, either a response list or a compiled list, is the most common approach. A **response list** consists of customers who have made purchases or who have responded to direct mail offers in the past. Brokers selling these lists provide information about the composition of the list and how much was spent by buyers on the list. In addition, a "hot list" can be requested. It contains the names of individuals who have responded within the past 30 days. Individuals on the hot list are the most likely to make purchases. This type of list is more costly: as much as $250 per thousand names. A regular response list may sell for $100 per thousand names.

The second form, a **compiled list**, provides information about consumers who meet a specific demographic profile. The disadvantage of a compiled list is that although someone might fit a demographic category, only about one-half of Americans purchase items by mail.

Caterpillar's marketing team wanted to reach potential buyers in the Southwest as part of its "Eat My Dust" campaign. The company purchased 1,700 names of individuals who had purchased industrial loaders during the past 5 years from Equipment Data Associates, a Charlotte, North Carolina, firm that compiles detailed purchasing histories of more than 870,000 U.S. contractors. Rea & Kaiser's Nichols agency designed a sweepstakes to win a new Cat 414E. An eye-catching direct mail piece urged contractors to sign up either online, by mail, or at a local Caterpillar dealer. Standard response rates are 1 to 3 percent; the response rate for the "Eat My Dust" direct mailer was 18 percent.[25] Using a highly targeted list provided the key difference.

▲ A direct mail piece sent by Diamond Security & Communications.

Advantages of Direct Mail

Direct mail can be easily targeted to various consumer and business groups. The impact is easily measurable. The marketing team compares the number of mailings to the number of responses. The team can test every component of a direct-mail campaign, including the type of offer, the copy in the ad, graphics used, color, and the size of the mail packet. For business-to-business marketing, direct mail will be superior to e-mail and other direct marketing methods, especially when a company seeks to introduce itself to prospects and needs to break through multiple layers of gatekeepers.

Direct mail drives online sales. A recent Pitney Bowes study revealed that direct mail remains the primary tool for promoting company Web sites. Direct mail was used to advertise a firm's Web site by 70 percent of firms with annual sales of at least $1 million. In addition, 43 percent of Internet sales were driven by some type of direct mail.[26]

The technology of direct marketing has greatly improved. Mailings can be customized to the individual recipient through **digital direct-to-press**, a software program that instructs the computer to send a tailor-made message. Digital direct-to-press may be especially useful in the business-to-business sector, where there are fewer total customers to contact than in consumer markets. Sending a customized message to each business customer may increase the chance that the message will be viewed. The expense of the software limits the number of companies that can afford it.[27]

Catalogs

Many consumers enjoy catalogs, and they view them at their leisure. Catalogs have a longer-term impact because they are kept and shared. Catalogs are a low-pressure direct response marketing tactic that allows consumers time to consider goods and prices. Many marketers believe that online shopping has replaced catalog mail-order shopping; however, research by the U.S. Postal Service reveals that although the number of consumers purchasing online has increased, consumers continue to prefer to receive catalogs by mail. In many cases, receiving a catalog is the first step in the buying cycle.[28]

Successful cataloging requires an enhanced database. Many catalog companies, such as L.L.Bean and JCPenney, create specialty catalogs geared to specific market segments. The items have a lower cost and a higher yield, because they target individual market segments.

Catalogs are essential selling tools for many business-to-business marketing programs. They provide more complete information to members of the buying center as well as prices for the purchasing agent. When combined with the Internet, a catalog program can provide a strong connection with individual customers.

Direct Response Mass Media

Television, radio, magazines, and newspapers are additional tools for direct response advertising. Direct response commercials can be presented on many channels and stations. Often, these commercials are slightly longer (60 seconds), which allows a potential buyer time to find a pen to write down a toll-free number, an address, or a Web site. Catchy, easy-to-remember contact information is often used, such as "1-800-Go-Green" or "**www.gogreen.com**." Repeating the response format helps customers remember how to respond. Often a "call-now" prompt concludes the ad.

Television also features infomercials for various types of products, such as exercise equipment and cooking tools. Cable and satellite systems have led to the creation of numerous direct response channels. The Home Shopping Network is one of the most successful. The channel is, in essence, a 24-hour infomercial station. Other channels feature jewelry, foods, and shoes.

Direct response techniques also are used on radio stations and in magazines and newspapers. Radio does not have the reach of television, but it can be targeted by the type of station format. Radio ads repeat the response number or Web site frequently so consumers can make contacts.

Print media can be sent to various market segments. Newspaper advertisements may feature Web site information and other quick-response formats. The same holds true for magazines. Both provide Web site information and toll-free numbers.[29]

Internet

The Internet has become a valuable form of direct marketing. Not only can consumers respond directly to ads placed on a Web site, direct response advertisements can be placed on search engines and used in e-mails.

As was shown in Figure 11.10, e-mail is a frequently used form of direct response marketing. E-mail provides a cost-effective method of reaching prospects. It helps build relationships with current customers through personalization of communications and by providing marketing offers tailored to each consumer's needs, wants, and desires. For business-to-business marketers, e-mail works better than postal mail and other direct marketing forms when the recipient is familiar with the company.[30]

By placing ads on search engines and using search engine optimization, firms can make direct response offers directly to individuals and businesses in the market for particular products. A direct response ad for fruit trees that appears when a person types in "apple trees" will be more effective than one that appears when a person searches on "iPad." The same is true when a purchasing agent types in "computer furniture."

Direct Sales

In the consumer sector, companies such as Amway, Mary Kay, and Avon use direct sales. The salesperson contacts friends, relatives, coworkers, and others and provides them with small catalogs or marketing brochures. Alternatively, individuals may host parties and invite friends and relatives to see products.

In launching a new line of cosmetics, Mark, for teenagers and women under 30, Avon brought direct selling into the digital and social media age. More than 40,000 "Mark Girls" work in the United States. They are primarily women between the ages of 18 and 24 who use grassroots methods to sell Mark cosmetics and fashion accessories in dorms, through sororities, and via Facebook. The brand offers personalized e-boutiques, iPhone apps, and a Facebook e-shop. Kristi-auna Mangum is a marketing major at Ohio State University. She is also a sales manager for Mark and manages 155 other Mark girls, earning commissions that range from 20 to 50 percent of the product's price.[31]

▼ More than 40,000 "Mark Girls" work in the United States for Avon.

Source: Thinkstock Royalty Free.

Telemarketing

Telemarketing takes place in two ways: inbound or outbound. *Inbound telemarketing* occurs when an individual initiates a call to a company. When a customer places an order, cross-selling can occur by offering other products or services. Many times inbound calls take place because the customer has a complaint or problem. Direct response marketing can be used to offer the customer a method to solve the problem. For example, when a customer calls a mortgage company because of a late fee, the person can be encouraged to sign up for a direct pay program, which means the customer does not have to worry about possible mail delays.

The least popular method for direct marketing is *outbound telemarketing*. Cold-calling of consumers yields few buyers and alienates many people. No-call list legislation, whereby a person or organization can designate a telephone number that may not be contacted by business organizations using telemarketing programs, has been passed. Many people even object to calls from companies with which they do business.

Outbound direct response telemarketing will be more successful when it is tied into a database and either customers or prospects are being contacted. An outbound telemarketing program that contacts customers who have not purchased in a year can help bring those customers back. A company that purchased a copy machine can be called to see if it is interested in paper and toner. A vendor can also learn why a client has not purchased recently.

⑤ What are the tasks involved in developing successful personal selling programs for consumers and businesses?

▼ Building relationships with customers is an important component of personal selling.

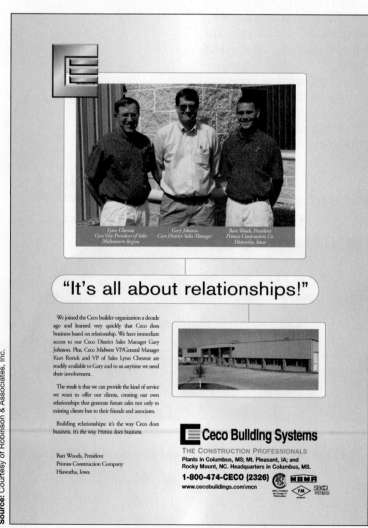

PERSONAL SELLING

Personal selling offers a face-to-face opportunity to build relationships with consumers. It takes place in both consumer and business-to-business transactions. Personal selling may result in the acquisition of new customers in addition to influencing current customers to increase levels of purchases. It is also used to service and maintain existing relationships. The goal of personal selling should not be limited to simply making sales. An additional objective should be to develop longer-term relationships with customers. In **relationship selling**, the goal is to create a customer for life, not for a single transaction.

Figure 11.11 identifies the standard steps in the selling process. A quality data warehouse accompanied by effective database technologies provides key tools that assist in personal selling.

Generating Leads

The first task in personal selling, especially for business-to-business relationships, is producing quality leads. Figure 11.12 identifies some of the most common methods. Making personal sales calls is costly, which makes generating quality leads crucial.

Referrals are ideal leads, because most recommendations are made by satisfied individuals. Referrals give the salesperson a head start. Making contact with purchasing agents or buyers in business organizations is often difficult. Using the name of the person who gave the referral can help the salesperson get past any gatekeepers. Also, if someone has given a referral, then the potential lead becomes more receptive to the sales call and has a more positive attitude toward the salesperson. The best referrals are from current customers.

• Generating leads	• Handling objections
• Qualifying prospect	• Sales closing
• Knowledge acquisition	• Follow-up
• Sales presentation	

◄ **FIGURE 11.11**
Steps in the Selling Process

• Referrals	• Directories
• Database-generated leads	• Cold calls
• Networking	

◄ **FIGURE 11.12**
Methods of Generating Sales Leads

Referrals from other channel members, vendors, and acquaintances can also be good because they allow the salesperson to get a foot in the door with a potential prospect.

For generating leads, databases provide quality leads, especially internal databases. Most of these leads are generated through some type of advertising or inquiry. Direct response ads in various media, such as television, radio, magazines, or newspapers, can generate leads. Online ads on various Web sites or search engines may also generate leads. Individuals may send an e-mail inquiry or request additional information through the company's Web site.

Databases also provide quality leads through trawling and analytical techniques, such as data mining. A company may trawl its database for customers who have not made purchases within the last 6 months or for companies that purchased a particular type of equipment and have not ordered additional parts or supplies. Data mining helps the company's marketing team create a profile of the best customers. Then lists of leads consisting of customers who are not high purchasers may be created. Trawling and data analysis techniques provide leads with higher sales potential.

Other less desirable means of generating sales leads are networking, directories, and cold calls. Although these methods may produce some leads, most are time consuming and not very productive. Networking in civic and professional organizations allows salespeople to make personal contacts. Directories may be obtained from the federal government, professional organizations, or research firms that provide the names of companies that purchase specific products or those in a given industry. The challenge is locating quality leads from the list. Cold calls are the worst method of generating leads. The salesperson has no idea if the company or individual has any interest in the product.

Qualifying Prospects

Every name or prospect may not be viable. Also, prospects are not of equal value. With this in mind, qualifying prospects means evaluating leads on two dimensions: (1) the potential income the lead can generate and (2) the probability of acquiring the prospect as a customer. Based on the outcomes of these evaluations, determinations can be made regarding the best methods of contact and what happens with the lead. The high cost of making personal sales calls means that only the best leads warrant personal visits. Some prospects receive telephone calls or e-mails from an inside salesperson. Others may be mailed or e-mailed marketing materials but are not contacted directly by a salesperson.

Once the leads are analysed using the two categories, sales potential and probability of acquisition, they are then placed into categories, or buckets, with the leads high on both dimensions as being the best, or "A" leads. These leads normally receive a sales call from the sales staff. The second best group, or "B" leads, often will be contacted by a telemarketer or through e-mail. The third best group, the "C" leads, will be sent marketing materials and encouraged to make inquiries if they are interested. Leads that score low on both dimensions may be kept in a database and monitored for future action if the lead's situation changes.

FIGURE 11.13 ▶
Knowledge Acquisition
Information

- Understand the prospect's business.
- Know and understand the prospect's customers.
- Identify the prospect's needs.
- Evaluate the risk factors and costs in switching vendors.
- Identify the decision makers and influencers.

Knowledge Acquisition

During the knowledge acquisition phase, salespeople or individuals within the sales organization gather information about the prospect in preparation for a sales call. Figure 11.13 identifies typical information to be gathered. The more a salesperson knows about a prospect before making the sales call, the higher the probability of making a sale or gaining permission to demonstrate the company's prospect.

Understanding the prospect's business, customers, and needs will be extremely helpful. In selling janitor supplies to a commercial cleaning company, understanding the commercial cleaning company's customers provides information about the type of cleaning chemicals needed. Cleaning heavy, greasy industrial areas requires chemicals that are different from those used to clean medical offices or office buildings. A manufacturer that supplies electronic components for high-tech aerospace customers has needs that are different from a company supplying electronics for automobile engines or for televisions and radios.

Changing vendors involves risk and switching costs. From the prospect's perspective, it helps to understand those risks and costs. When switching costs are low and risk is also perceived to be low, convincing a company to change vendors becomes easier.

The final valuable piece of information is a list of the names of any decision makers or decision influencers. The names of these individuals are often difficult to obtain prior to the sales call, but getting them should be a high priority during the first meeting. Understanding who will be involved in the decision process is important as the sales process proceeds.

The Sales Presentation

The initial sales call can be used to gather information, discuss bid specifications, answer questions, or to close the deal with a final pitch or offer.[32] The exact nature of the first sales call depends on the information gathered prior to the call. Also the stage of the buying process affects the presentation. The types of sales presentations used typically fall into one of these categories: (1) stimulus-response, (2) need-satisfaction, (3) problem-solution, and (4) mission-sharing.[33]

A **stimulus-response** sales approach, often called a "canned" sales pitch, uses specific statements (stimuli) to elicit specific responses from customers. The salesperson normally memorizes the stimulus statement (the pitch). Telemarketers, retail sales clerks, and new field sales reps often rely on this method.

The **need-satisfaction** sales approach strives to discover a customer's needs during the first part of the sales presentation and then provide solutions to those needs. The salesperson should skillfully ask the right questions. She should understand the customer's business and customers. Once a need has been identified, the rep then shows how the company's products meet that need.

▼ Understanding customer needs provides the basis for the need-satisfaction sales approach.

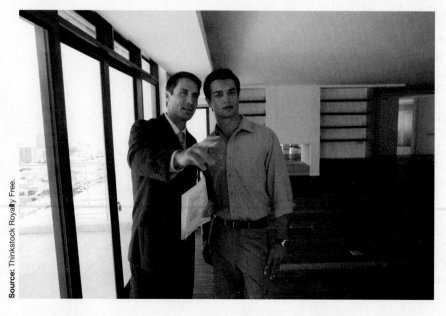

Source: Thinkstock Royalty Free.

The **problem-solution** sales approach requires employees from the selling organization to analyze the buyer's business. It usually involves a team of individuals, such as engineers, salespeople, and other experts. The team investigates a potential customer's operations, its problems, and then offers feasible solutions.

In the last approach, **mission-sharing**, two organizations develop a common mission. They then share resources to accomplish that mission. This partnership resembles a joint venture as much as a selling relationship.

• Head-on method   • Compensation method
• Indirect method   • "Feel, felt, found"

◀ **FIGURE 11.14**
Methods of Handling Objections

Handling Objections

Companies and individuals seldom make purchases after a sales presentation without raising some objections or concerns. Salespeople anticipate objections and should carefully answer them. The most common methods of handling objections are listed in Figure 11.14.

With the *head-on approach*, the salesperson answers the objection directly. Doing so, however, indicates that the customer or prospect is wrong. The salesperson should use tact. No one likes being told they are wrong. The salesperson uses care to not offend the customer.

To avoid a confrontation, some salespeople employ an *indirect approach*. This method allows the salesperson to never really tell the customer he is wrong. Instead, the salesperson sympathizes with the customer's viewpoint and then provides the correct information.

When the customer's objection is partially true, then salesperson may utilize the *compensation method*. With this approach the salesperson replies "yes, but . . ." and then explains the product's benefits or features that answer the customer's objection.

Some customers do not have specific objections, but are anxious or worried about the consequences of switching to a new vendor. For this situation, a sales rep can use a *feel, felt, found* method. The salesperson allows the customer to talk about her fears or worries. In response, the salesperson can relate personal experiences or experiences of other customers who had the same fears and worries and how the product resulted in a positive experience.

Closing the Sale

It may be that the most important part of the sales call is the closing, and it may also be the most difficult part. Salespeople often fear feelings of rejection or failure when prospects or customers say "no." Successful salespeople are masters at making the close. Figure 11.15 identifies some of the most common sales-closing methods. The one to be used depends on the personality of the salesperson, the personality of the prospect, and the situation surrounding the sales call.

With the *direct close*, the salesperson asks for the order outright. This approach may be used when objections have been answered and the salesperson feels confident that the prospect is ready to buy.

When the salesperson is not sure if the prospect is quite ready, the *trial method* can be used. With this approach, the salesperson solicits feedback that provides information regarding the customer's reaction, without asking directly for the sale. If the reaction is positive, the salesperson will ask for the order. If not, then the salesperson returns to the sales presentation. Another alternative is to *summarize* the product's benefits and how it meets the customer's needs prior to asking for the order.

• Direct close   • Continuous "yes" close
• Trial close   • Assumptive close
• Summarization close

◀ **FIGURE 11.15**
Methods of Closing Sales

Sometimes a salesperson asks a serious of questions along the way, ensuring the customer will *continuously* respond "yes." By answering "yes" to smaller questions about the benefits of a product, when it comes time to ask for the order the customer may be more likely to respond with a "yes."

A salesperson can also *assume* the customer will say yes. He might ask, "How many cases do you want?" or "How would you like this to be shipped?"

Follow-Up

Keeping a customer happy after the purchase will result in repeat business, customer loyalty, and positive referrals. Quality follow-up programs are cost-effective ways to retain customers, which is much cheaper than continually finding new ones. Unfortunately, following-up may be neglected by the sales staff, especially if the salesperson receives commission on new sales but not on follow-up activities. In this situation, the company must designate other employees to follow-up to ensure that customers are satisfied with their purchases.

INTERNATIONAL IMPLICATIONS

6 How should database marketing and personal selling programs be adapted to international settings?

Database marketing faces the same challenges as other aspects of an IMC program when a firm moves into the international arena. These include differences in technology, which make data collection and analysis more difficult due to issues such as language and Internet availability. Further, local laws may limit the methods by which information can be collected as well as the types of information a company seeks and/or shares with other companies.

In many parts of the world, customers may only live a few miles apart yet reside in different countries. For example, the European Union consists of many nations in close proximity. Therefore, decisions must be made as to whether data will be country specific.

Programs such as permission marketing, frequency, and CRM are subject to legal restrictions as well as cultural differences. In some instances, they may be highly accepted. This is the case for permission marketing in Japan. In many Asian cultures, the giving of gifts takes on added meaning. This may include stronger bonds between customers and companies and is important in personal selling.

Direct marketing programs also must be adapted to local conditions. Mail delivery systems may be easier to access in some countries than others. The same is true for telephone systems, Internet access, and other technologies. Infomercials may not be possible in countries with state-run television systems. A company's marketing team should consider all local legal, social, cultural, technological, and competitive conditions before embarking on an international database-driven marketing program or direct marketing program.

❝SUMMARY

Database marketing has become a vital element of a complete IMC program. The two key activities involved at the most general level, identifying customers and building relationships with them, have an impact on numerous other IMC tasks. It is clearly more cost-effective to retain customers than to continually seek out new ones. Further, the actual message may change when communicating with long-time, loyal customers.

Building a data warehouse begins with collecting data to be used by the marketing department. Beyond basic information, such as a customer's name, address, and e-mail address, other key data include the customer's purchase history and preferences. Geocoding is the process of adding geographic codes to customer records, which assists in selecting media and creating messages targeted to specific groups.

Database coding and analysis leads to either lifetime value analysis of customers or the clustering of customer groups based on customer spending patterns. Data mining programs involve building profiles of customer segments and/or preparing models that predict future purchase behaviors based on past purchases. The information gathered from data coding and data mining leads to the development of data-driven marketing communications and marketing programs.

Database-driven marketing communication programs are facilitated by effective identification codes that allow for personalization of messages and interactions. An effective database-driven communication program relies on customer profiles combined with other information available regarding specific customers. In-bound telemarketing programs, trawling, advertising, and lifetime value segment programs can be fine-tuned for individual customers.

Database-driven marketing programs include permission marketing, frequency programs, and CRM systems. Permission marketing is a selling approach in which the customer agrees to receive promotional materials in exchange for various incentives. Frequency programs are incentives customers receive for repeat business. Both are designed to create customer loyalty over time. CRM is designed to build long-term loyalty and bonds with customers through the use of a personal touch facilitated by technology.

Closely related to database marketing is direct response (or direct) marketing. These marketing efforts may be made by mail, catalog, phone, mass media, the Internet, or e-mail. Direct mail programs remain popular as outbound telemarketing programs continue to diminish.

In the new age of marketing communications, a case can be made that individual consumers desire greater intimacy with the companies that serve them. They are drawn to firms that take the time to build relationships through quality, customized communications and marketing programs. It seems likely that this trend will continue and that successful marketing teams must continue to emphasize methods for identifying customers and personalizing relationships with them.

KEY TERMS

data warehouse   The place where customer data are held.

geocoding   Adding geographic codes to customer records to make it possible to plot customer addresses on a map.

lifetime value   The present value of future profits a customer generates over his or her life in a relationship with a brand or firm.

data mining   The process of using computer data analysis software to mine data for meaningful information and relationships.

trawling   The process of searching the database for a specific piece of information for marketing purposes.

permission marketing   A form of database marketing in which the company sends promotional materials to customers who give the company permission to do so.

empowerment   Consumers believe they have power throughout the seller–consumer relationship, not just at the beginning when they agreed to join a frequency program.

reciprocity   A sense of obligation toward a company that results from receiving special deals or incentives such as gifts.

frequency (or loyalty) program   A marketing program designed to promote loyalty or frequent purchases of the same brand (or company).

customer relationship management (CRM)   Programs designed to build long-term loyalty and bonds with customers through the use of a personal touch facilitated by technology.

share of customer   The percentage of expenditures a customer makes with one particular firm compared to total expenditures in that product's category.

direct response (or direct) marketing   Vending products to customers without the use of other channel members.

response list   A list of customers who have made purchases or who have responded to direct mail offers in the past.

compiled list   A list consisting of information about consumers who meet a specific demographic profile.

digital direct-to-press   Software that instructs the computer to create a tailor-made direct mail message to a customer.

relationship selling   Developing long-term relationships with customers rather than focusing on a single transaction.

stimulus-response   A sales approach, often called a "canned" sales pitch, that uses specific statements (stimuli) to elicit specific responses from customers.

need-satisfaction   A sales approach in which the salesperson strives to discover a customer's needs during the first part of the sales presentation and then provides solutions to those needs.

problem-solution   A sales approach that requires employees from the selling organization to analyze the buyer's operations and offer ways to solve their problems.

mission-sharing   A sales approach in which two organizations develop a common mission and then share resources to accomplish that mission.

REVIEW QUESTIONS

1. What two activities are part of a successful database marketing program?

2. What is a data warehouse? What is the difference between an operational database and a marketing database?

3. List the steps involved in building a data warehouse.

4. What is geocoding?

5. Define lifetime value. How is it determined?

6. What are the two primary functions of data mining?

7. Explain how identification codes are used in database-driven marketing communications.

8. Explain how consumer profile information is used when sending communications to customers.

9. Describe a permission marketing program. What are the key benefits of this approach?

10. What are the keys to an effective permission marketing program?

11. Describe a frequency program. What three principles should guide the development of a loyalty program?

12. What is customer relationship management? Explain why most CRM programs have not been successful.

13. What is meant by the term share of customer?

14. What is direct response marketing?

15. Explain how response lists and compiled lists are used in direct mail programs.

16. Why is digital direct-to-press popular in business-to-business direct marketing?

17. Explain the two ways infomercials are presented as parts of a direct response program.

18. What is relationship marketing?

19. What steps are involved in the personal selling process?

20. Identify the four types of sales presentations typically used by sales reps.

21. What types of closing methods are available to salespeople?

CRITICAL THINKING EXERCISES

Discussion Questions

1. Assume that you are the account executive at a database marketing agency. A music retailer has asked you to develop a database for the company. How would you go about building a data warehouse? What information should be in the databases? Where and how would you obtain the data?

2. Hickory Outdoor is a retail store that sells fishing, hunting, camping, and other outdoor equipment and supplies, including various items for a number of outdoor sports. The company has built a database of its customers over the last 5 years. The marketing team can use data mining to improve their marketing efforts. Suggest ways data mining can be used. What type of marketing programs would you suggest based on data mining? What other types of marketing programs can be developed from the database?

3. Karen's Formal Dress is a retailer specializing in formal and wedding wear. She has a database with over 3,000 names of individuals who have purchased or rented formal wear. She would like to develop a permission marketing program. How can the marketing team encourage individuals to give permission to receive marketing materials? Once the company has the customer's permission, how can the relationship be continued to make it beneficial to both the consumer and to Karen's Formal Dress? Describe the methodology Karen should use in her permissions marketing program, including the types of materials, methods of distribution, and incentives.

4. A primary reason for developing a frequency program is to encourage customers to be loyal to a business or brand. For each of the following products, discuss the merits of a frequency program. What types of incentives would individuals need to join the frequency club and then to continue participation in the program?

   a. Local restaurant
   b. Auto repair service
   c. Printing service
   d. Clothing retailer

5. Examine the forms of direct response marketing shown in the graph in Figure 11.10. Which ones have you responded to in the past? Which ones are most likely to influence a purchase decision? Which ones are the least likely? Discuss the type of direct response offer and ad that influences your purchase decision.

6. The marketing team for Hickory Outdoor (see question 2) is seeking to use direct response advertising to accomplish two goals: (1) to sell specific merchandise and (2) to encourage individuals to visit the store or its Web site. Which types of direct response advertising would be the most effective? Why? What type of direct response offers should Hickory Outdoor make?

7. Examine the direct marketing methods highlighted in Figure 11.10. Evaluate each method for the following types of businesses. Which ones would be the best? Which ones would not work as well? Justify your answers.

   a. Shoe store
   b. Sporting goods retailer
   c. Internet hosiery retailer (sells only via the Internet)
   d. Manufacturer of tin cans for food-processing companies

8. Interview five individuals. Ask each person to list the catalogs they have received during the past month. Have each person discuss why he or she receives certain catalogs. Ask how often each person orders something out of a catalog and how the order is usually placed. Is anyone accessing the Internet for information offered in a catalog or ordering from a catalog after accessing a Web site? Discuss how important the catalog market is today and what you see as the future of catalog marketing.

INTEGRATED LEARNING EXERCISES

1. Pick one company that sells clothing. Go to the company's Web site. What evidence do you see of database marketing and of personalization of the Web site? Describe a database marketing program that the company could use.

2. Go to Web site for Scotts Miracle Gro at **www.scotts.com/ smg**. What evidence do you see of database marketing and of personalization? Review the concepts presented in the section "Database-Driven Marketing Communications." What steps should Scotts take to develop data-driven communications with visitors to the Web site as well as individuals who make purchases?

3. A number of companies specialize in database marketing. You are the manager of a small chain of 25 restaurants. Review the Web site of each of the following companies. Outline what each company offers. Which one would be the best for your company? Why?

   a. Database Marketing Group (**www.dbmgroup.com**)

   b. Advanced Marketing Consultants (**www.marketing principles.com**)

   c. Dovetail (**www.dovetaildatabase.com**)

4. *DMNews* is a trade journal for database marketing and CRM programs. Access the Web site at **www.dmnews.com**. What types of information are available on the site? How could this help companies with database marketing and CRM programs? Access and read one of the articles from the journal. Write a paragraph about what you learned.

5. CentricData is a database marketing firm that specializes in mid-size to large retailers. Access the Web site at **www.centricdata.com**. What types of services does CentricData offer? How could this company help a retail store develop a database marketing program?

6. The Direct Marketing Association (DMA) is a global trade association of business and nonprofit organizations that use direct marketing tools and techniques. Access the trade organization's Web site at **www.the-dma.org**. What services does the DMA provide its members? What value would this be to a business in developing a direct marketing program?

7. A primary key in successful direct marketing is the quality of the list that is used. One company that specializes in compiling lists is US Data Corporation. Access the company's Web site at **www.usdatacorporation.com**. What types of lists does the company offer? Access one of the lists and describe how that list can be compiled. Discuss how a company could use US Data Corporation for a direct response marketing campaign.

8. Almost all hotels have some type of frequency or loyalty program. Examine the loyalty programs of the following hotels. Critique each one. Which ones are best? Why?

   a. Best Western (**www.bestwestern.com**)

   b. Days Inn (**www.daysinn.com**)

   c. Doubletree Inn (**doubletree.hilton.com**)

   d. Marriott (**www.marriott.com**)

   e. Radisson (**www.radisson.com**)

   f. Wyndham Hotels & Resorts (**www.wyndham.com**)

STUDENT PROJECT

Creative Corner

Lilly Fashions sells fashionable, trendy clothes. Its primary target customer is 20 to 30 years old, female, has an average income of $40,000, and has some college. Lilly's marketing team wants to capitalize on the concepts of database marketing and direct response marketing. Design a newspaper advertisement that encourages females in the company's target market to visit the retail store and join Lilly's database program. In addition, design a direct mail piece that would go to individuals who are currently in the database but who have not made a purchase within the last 3 months. Design an e-mail that can be sent to members in the database on the person's birthday offering them a free meal at a local restaurant, if they come to the store to pick up the meal voucher. This promotion is a joint promotion with the restaurant, which shares in the cost, which means the restaurant must also be part of the e-mail.

CASE 1   ANHEUSER-BUSCH: DATABASE MARKETING AND PERSONAL SELLING

Margie Washburn was about to begin an exciting new era in her life. She had purchased the distributorship rights for Anheuser-Busch InBev products in the Denver/Aurora, Colorado, area. Even though her company would be standing in the shadow of the Coors Brewing Company, she believed that through effective database marketing and personal selling tactics Budweiser and Busch products would be widely accepted in the region.

As a distributor, Margie's primary customers are other businesses, specifically, bars, taverns, and restaurants that serve beer to patrons; retail outlets such as grocery stores, convenience markets, and liquor stores; and entertainment venues, including the arena housing the Denver Nuggets. She did not expect to make in-roads selling beer at Coors Field, home of the Denver Broncos.

Anheuser-Busch competes in a highly fragmented market. Major vendors include Miller/Coors, Heineken, Corona, and Guinness. Recently, other beer companies had created buzz and captured some market share, including Dos Equis, Stella Artois, and Samuel Adams. The microbrewery trend that expanded quickly in the 1990s had slowed; however, several popular local companies were doing well in the Denver area.

Anheuser-Busch InBev had endured some negative publicity in the past decade, when the former Anheuser-Busch, owned and operated from the United States, was acquired by Belgian brewer InBev. Some customers feared that popular products such as Budweiser and Bud Light would somehow be changed by an international company.

Advertising and promotional efforts targeted at individual consumers continue. Budweiser's "King of Beers" approach, including commercials featuring the Clydesdales, maintained a strong brand presence. Bud Light's use of comedy had also created positive reactions. A recent campaign emphasizing the romance and marriage of Bud Light with wheat had been used to kick off another variation of Anheuser products, Bud Light Golden Wheat. Anheuser-Busch produces lower-end beers, including Natural Light, as well as the higher-end Michelob line of beers.

One of Margie's challenges was finding out how each type of customer related to her products and brands. She needed to know how many restaurants and drinking establishments prominently displayed her beers. She also was interested in finding out whether her products received good, fair, or poor shelf space in off-sale outlets. From there she might be able to find ways to create bonds with individual consumers that would "pull" Anheuser-Busch brands to the forefront in these locations.

Margie also knew that her competitors employed brand ambassadors, especially on-campus at the universities in the Denver area. The ambassadors were college students who pitched Miller/Coors products to fellow students and local watering holes. Miller/Coors also sponsored a variety of events targeting college-age students with music and sports.

To compete, the new Anheuser-Busch InBev distributorship required an extensive, coordinated marketing communications

▲ Margie faced a number of challenges with her distributorship.

program. The objective would be to tie brand loyalty and positive relationships with individual consumers to database programs use personal selling tactics to reach all of the business-to-business customers in the area. Margie looked forward to getting started.

1. What types of data should the distributorship collect about individual consumers? How can it be used?

2. What types of data should the distributorship collect about business customers? How can it be used?

3. Can the distributorship build any frequency or loyalty programs in the area? If so, describe what would work. If not, why not?

4. What sales approach should the sales staff use for the various businesses that sell Anheuser-Busch products, such as nightclubs?

5. What type of sales approach should the company use to entice liquor vendors to carry and emphasize Anheuser-Busch products in both on-sale and off-sale venues?

CASE 2 FOLLOW THE BEST

George Coffman's entrepreneurial adventure began in a pattern that was similar to many other start-ups. He had grown increasingly tired of answering to a supervisor he did not respect and believed simply lacked the knowledge to manage his department. At the same time, an idea continued to preoccupy his mind: What if he started a company that was essentially a male version of Lillian Vernon? After all, Lillian Vernon had been named to the Direct Marketing Hall of Fame in 1994 and continued a successful run to the present day.

Rather than using a person's name, George chose to brand his company Maximus. He believed the name conjured up images of maleness and virility. The range of products offered by Lillian Vernon includes personalized gifts, holiday items, home and office products, garden and outdoor items, bags, jewelry and accessories, and toys. Maximus would offer many of the same products, with an emphasis on masculine products for home and office and sportswear fashions.

The evolution of Lillian Vernon was of particular interest to George. Ms. Vernon had begun her company by personalizing items for women out of her garage. Initially, she solicited business with magazine advertisements. Eventually, her company grew to the point where a full catalog was developed. A large number of the sales came from call-in orders. As new technologies emerged, Lillian Vernon expanded into Web sites, some retail stores, and Internet communications.

Maximus would follow a similar route. The first items to be offered would be personalized sportswear, with a focus on hunting, fishing, and other outdoor activities. George believed that many hunters and fishermen would enjoy seeing their initials embossed on boots, coats, super-warm socks, and other items. He would begin by advertising in *Field and Stream* and similar magazines. He would also try look for ways to reach the women who might wish to buy these items as gifts for Father's Day, Christmas, and birthday celebrations.

The idea was to expand into other lines as the brand gained recognition. The first target market, male sportsmen, would eventually expand into men who preferred other activities, such as gardening. Also, those with home offices who wanted to personalize some space would be targeted.

George had pitched his idea to several investment capital companies. He had struck a chord with some investors. They had bought in, which provided Maximus with start-up funds and monies for his original advertising and promotions. The

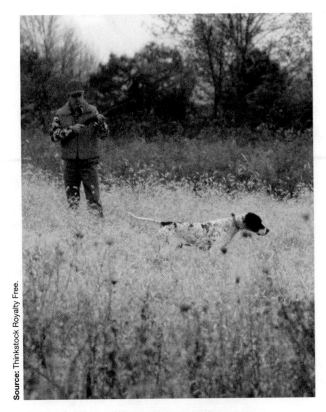

Source: Thinkstock Royalty Free.

▲ The first items Maximus focused on were personalized hunting and fishing sportswear.

investors insisted that George consider building a database marketing program as part of his start-up.

1. How can George gather names, addresses, and e-mail addresses of potential customers?

2. What types of database-driven marketing communications will be most successful for Maximus?

3. Can Maximus utilize a permission marketing program or a frequency program? If so, how?

4. Using the Lillian Vernon Web site as a guide (**www.lillianvernon.com**), construct the opening screen of a Web site for Maximus.

12 Sales Promotions

SALES PROMOTIONS AND MORE HOOK FANS

"What is your favorite word?" This question was posed by baseball executive Jay Miller at a recent marketing conference. "If you think about it, it might be that one of your favorite words is your own name," he said with a smile. Miller continued, "When you come to our ballpark, we are going to know your name." In truth, Jay Miller is talking about two ballparks, one in Corpus Christi, Texas, and the other in Round Rock, Texas. The ballparks are home to minor league professional baseball teams.

The Corpus Christi team, the Hooks, continues to be a stellar success. The organization, an affiliate of the Houston Astros, averages more than 7,000 fans per game over 72 home dates each summer. This ranks among the top franchises at the Double-A level of professional baseball. Beyond the statistics, however, is the sense of civic pride that permeates the team, the fans, and the entire organization. In a city with a large Hispanic community, the term *la familia* clearly applies. The Hooks are a family that hosts a large number of guests at each game.

Professional baseball thrives on consumer promotions. For fans, numerous discounts and giveaways are part of the scene. In 2010, the Hooks staged over 30 promotional nights. The free gifts included bobbleheads, baseball card sets, duffle bags, blankets, photos, autographed souvenirs, and more. In addition, the team offers "One Dollar Hot Dog and Soda Night," "Half-Price Group Night," "Thirsty Thursdays," and "Friday Fireworks."

Sponsorships and trade promotion tie-ins are widely utilized. The ballpark is named "Whataburger" field, due to the sponsorship of the popular hamburger chain. Whataburger hosts its own fan day. Other sponsors place advertising on the scoreboard, field, walls, and other places. Special corporate box seats are available for entertaining clients and rewarding employees. Various business organizations are featured on the video board and on items given to fans. In addition, the Hooks have created ties with several local charities and civic organizations, including the "Get Hooked on Reading" program for young fans.

CHAPTER OBJECTIVES

After reading this chapter, you should be able to answer the following questions:

1 What are the differences between consumer promotions and trade promotions?

2 How can the various forms of consumer promotions help to pull consumers into the stores and push products onto the store shelves?

3 How do different types of customers respond to consumer promotions?

4 What types of trade promotions can help push products onto retailers' shelves and eventually to end users?

5 What concerns exist for manufacturers considering trade promotions programs?

6 What issues complicate international sales promotions programs?

All of these sales promotions serve to enhance the rest of the organization's marketing efforts. Jay Miller and CEO Reid Ryan strongly emphasize the importance of "awesome customer service." At a Hooks game, everyone from parking attendants to the ticket takers to the ushers and concessions personnel focuses on friendly, first-name care. Miller and Ryan routinely circulate through the stands to mingle with fans, solve any problems, and provide an occasional extra thrill. One of their favorites is finding a family sitting in the cheapest (most distant) seats in the stadium and moving them to the owner's box next to the field.

The team also hosts a "postgame catch" in which many lucky kids are brought down to the field to play catch with the players. On Sundays, or "Kids Day," fans are allowed on the field prior to the game. Many times disadvantaged children, Little Leaguers, and others are paired with a player to go on the field as the game is about to begin to stand during the national anthem. Other attendees participate in the "Dizzy Bat Race" or in races with the Hooks mascot. Even those who stay in the stands may find themselves featured in "Kiss Cam" or "Fan Cam" on the 16-by-22-foot video screen between innings.

Reid Ryan's father is Hall of Fame pitcher Nolan Ryan, who is one of the principle owners of the team. Reid believes the success of the organization, known as Ryan Sanders Baseball, results from promoting a summer-long experience rather than a single event. Instead of focusing on wins and losses or even on players, the enjoyment of attending a series of games in a low-cost, family friendly environment remains the key to long-term fan loyalty. Players come

▲ Reid Ryan

and go, teams win and lose, but a fun summer evening with family and friends creates a long-lasting impression. The Hooks' advertising tagline, "Catch a Memory-Hooks Baseball," expresses this feeling.

Jay Miller has been associated with professional baseball for over 24 years. He has been named "Executive of the Year" on more than one occasion. He proudly reports that sales of memorabilia for the Hooks are higher than the majority of minor league teams, an indication of the strong loyalty in the community. A walk down the streets of Corpus Christi or a visit to the ballpark confirms the devotion fans show by proudly wearing caps, T-shirts, and jerseys with the Hooks insignia and logo.

▲ Jay Miller

Both Miller and Ryan stress the importance of brand and image building. In a marketplace where a wide variety of summertime activities are possible, they emphasize the goal of being top-of-mind, or the family's first choice. A stadium full of happy customers for every home game provides all the evidence they need that their approach is working.[1]

1 What are the differences between consumer promotions and trade promotions?

OVERVIEW

It may be tempting to think that a high-quality advertising program completes the task of promotion. It does not. A fully integrated marketing communications program includes additional key activities. This chapter describes sales promotions programs. **Sales promotions** consist of all of the incentives offered to customers and channel members to encourage product purchases.

Sales promotions take two forms: consumer promotions and trade promotions. **Consumer promotions** are the incentives that are directly offered to a firm's customers or potential customers. Consumer promotions are aimed at those who actually use the product, or end users. They may be individuals or households. Another end user may be a business that consumes the product, and the item is not resold to another business. In other words, consumer promotions are offered in both consumer markets and business-to-business markets.

Trade promotions are used only in the distribution channel. **Trade promotions** consist of the expenditures or incentives used by manufacturers and other members of the marketing channel to purchase goods for eventual resale. Trade promotions provided to other firms help push products through to retailers.

In the past, some marketing experts believed that any type of sales promotion, whether consumer or trade, eroded brand equity. They suggested that the incentives simply encouraged customers, businesses, and the distribution channel to focus on price. Recently, however, that view has changed. Many company leaders recognize that promotions can differentiate a brand from the competition, which helps build brand awareness and can improve a brand's image.[2]

The marketing team carefully designs promotional programs to help the company reach its IMC objectives and that support a brand's position. In the early stages of a product's life cycle, promotions are typically designed to match advertising and other efforts focused on brand awareness, creating opportunities for trial purchases and stimulating additional purchases. Later, the goal often shifts to strengthening a brand, increasing consumption, fending off competition, or finding new markets.

This chapter examines consumer promotions first, followed by trade promotions. Although the presentations are separate, the marketing team designs both at the same time. The adjustments made to sales promotions programs in international markets are also described.

CONSUMER PROMOTIONS

2 How can the various forms of consumer promotions help to pull consumers into the stores and push products onto the store shelves?

Enticing a consumer to take the final step and make the purchase constitutes a primary goal for a consumer promotions program. Advertising creates the interest and excitement that brings the consumer into the store. Marketers then use other tactics. In addition to leading to the final decision to buy an item, consumer promotions programs can be highly effective in generating store traffic and enhancing brand loyalty.

- Coupons
- Premiums
- Contests and sweepstakes
- Refunds and rebates
- Sampling
- Bonus packs
- Price-offs

◄ **FIGURE 12.1**
Types of Consumer Promotions

During the last two Super Bowls, Denny's offered free breakfast to anyone who came into the restaurant from 6:00 A.M. to 2:00 P.M. the Tuesday following the game. In 2010, roughly 2 million Americans took advantage of the offer. Some had to wait in line for hours for a free breakfast. The promotion's goal, according to CEO Nelson Marchioli, was to "re-acquaint America with Denny's." He added, "We've never been thanked this much—and folks are saying they'll come back." The cost of the entire promotion, including food, labor, and the Super Bowl commercial, was about $5 million. In exchange, Denny's earned something money alone cannot buy; a powerful positive public relations blitz. The promotion garnered as much as $50 million in free, positive media news coverage. The company also received 40 million hits on its Web site in the week following the Super Bowl,[3] suggesting a highly successful consumer promotions program.

Figure 12.1 identifies the most common consumer promotions. Each of these forms of promotions is described next.

COUPONS

A coupon offers a price reduction to the consumer. It may be a percentage off the retail price, such as 25 or 40 percent, or an absolute amount, such as 50 cents or $1. In one year, nearly 188 billion coupons were printed and 1.6 billion were redeemed. The 0.85 percent redemption rate represents approximately $2.25 billion in savings for consumers, or about $1.41 per coupon.[4] Nearly 80 percent of all U.S. households use coupons, and almost two-thirds are willing to switch brands with coupons.[5] Figure 12.2 provides a more detailed breakdown of coupon usage.

Coupon Distribution

Manufacturers issue approximately 80 percent of all coupons. Figure 12.3 identifies the various forms of coupon distribution. Most coupons are sent through print media. The vast majority are distributed through **freestanding inserts (FSIs)**, which are sheets of coupons distributed in newspapers, primarily on Sunday. FSIs represent almost 90 percent of all coupons distributed. The percentage has been steadily declining as consumers switch to digitally-delivered coupons. Other methods of distribution include in-store, on-shelf, and coupons attached to free samples of a product. The remaining coupons are distributed in or on product packages; by direct mail; by mass print media, such as magazines and newspapers; and by company employees.[6]

◄ **FIGURE 12.2**
Percentage of Consumers Who Use Coupons

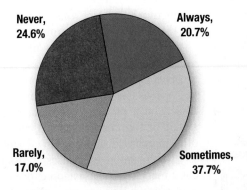

Never, 24.6%

Always, 20.7%

Rarely, 17.0%

Sometimes, 37.7%

Source: Karen Holt, "Coupon Crimes," *Promo* 17, no. 5 (April 2004), pp. 23–29.

FIGURE 12.3 ▶
Methods of Distributing Coupons

- Print media
  - Freestanding inserts (FSIs)
- Direct mail
- In- or on-package

- In-store
  - Scanner delivered
- Digital
- Employee delivered

FSIs and print media remain popular for several reasons. First, the consumer makes a conscious effort to clip or save the coupon. Second, coupons create brand awareness. The consumer sees the brand name on the coupon even when it is not redeemed. Third, FSIs encourage consumers to purchase brands on the next trip to the store. Consumers are more likely to purchase a couponed brand and remember the name when they redeem a coupon, which helps move the brand to a consumer's long-term memory.

Digital coupons are rapidly growing in popularity. About 15 percent of the U.S. population, or 45 million consumers, redeem digital coupons. Digital coupon users tend to be more affluent and better educated. The average household income for a digital coupon user is $97,000. One-third of them have earned a college degree. Sites such as coupons.com make it easy for consumers to find and print coupons, download them onto mobile devices, or transfer them to a loyalty card. Retail stores, including JCPenney, Kroger, and Safeway, feature technologies that allow consumers to redeem coupons from cell phones. CVS Pharmacy lets customers scan a loyalty card at a kiosk inside the store entrance to receive instant coupon offers and in-store specials based on their purchase histories. This ease of use spurs the growth of digital coupons.[7]

▼ A manufacturer's coupon for 50 cents off the new Snax Stix.

Source: Courtesy of Keebler Company.

Types of Coupons

Coupons are distributed in retail stores, offered digitally from the Internet or in a store, such as CVS, and can be placed on or near packages. In each instance, the consumer can immediately redeem the coupon at the store. This form of distribution is an *instant redemption coupon* program. The coupons often lead to trial purchases and purchases of additional packages of a product. Many grocery stores permit a company to cook a food product and offer free samples along with coupon giveaways, which represents another form of instant redemption couponing.

Coupons can be placed inside packages so that customers cannot redeem them quite as quickly. This encourages repeat purchases. The coupons are called *bounce-back coupons*.

Some coupons are issued at the cash register. *Scanner-delivered coupons* are triggered by an item being scanned on the register. The coupon being delivered is often for a competitor's product, thereby encouraging brand switching the next time a consumer makes a purchase.

To encourage purchases of additional products, sometimes manufactures use *cross-ruffing coupons*, which involves placing a coupon on one product for another product. For example, a coupon for French onion dip may be placed on a package of potato chips. Cross-ruff coupons should be for products that logically fit together and that are often purchased and consumed simultaneously. Occasionally, a manufacturer uses cross-ruffing to encourage consumers to purchase another one of its products. Kellogg's may place a coupon on a Rice Krispies box for another cereal, such as Frosted Flakes or an oatmeal product. This type of couponing tactic encourages consumers to purchase within the same brand or family of products.

Disadvantage of Coupons

Customers who already have a brand preference redeem approximately 80 percent of all coupons.[8] Some believe that offering price discounts through coupons to customers who are willing to pay full price does not make sense. Manufacturers, however, argue that these consumers may be willing to stock up on the item, which means they do not buy from the competition. In essence, manufacturers recognize that these brand-preference customer redemptions are a "necessary evil" when using mass distribution. To send fewer coupons to current customers, firms may use direct mail to distribute them primarily to customers who are not brand loyal, thereby targeting nonusers and the competitor's customers.

PREMIUMS

Premiums are prizes, gifts, or other special offers consumers receive when purchasing products. The consumer pays full price for the good or service with a premium. In contrast, coupons grant price reductions.

Types of Premiums

Four major types of premiums are identified in Figure 12.4. *Free-in-the-mail premiums* are gifts individuals receive for purchasing products. To receive the gift, the customer mails in a proof of purchase to the manufacturer, who then mails the gift to the customer. More than one purchase may be required to receive some gifts. A premium offer appears in the Fisher Boy advertisement shown in this section. Consumers collect points from the front of Fisher Boy packages to be redeemed for "cool" prizes. To further encourage sales, the advertisement also carries a coupon.

Credit card companies use premiums to entice individuals to sign up for credit cards. Instead of providing a proof of purchase, the consumer activates the card to receive an incentive, which can range from cash back on a purchase to merchandise and frequent-flier miles.

In- or *on-package premiums* are usually small gifts, such as toys in cereal boxes. The gift may be disguised or packaged so the consumer must buy the product to see the premium. At other times, the gift is attached to the package, such as a package of blades with the purchase of a razor.

Store or *manufacturer premiums* are gifts given by either the retail store or the manufacturer when the customer purchases a product. Fast-food restaurants offer children a toy with the purchase of a child's meal. Hyundai recently offered a unique premium. With the purchase of a new Hyundai Equus, with the suggested retail price of $50,000, customers received a free Apple iPad loaded with the 300-page owner's interactive manual. The iPad included a leather slipcase with the car's service appointments preloaded and scheduled.[9]

The fourth type, a *self-liquidating premium* requires the consumer to pay a small amount of money for the gift or item. The premium may be offered for only $4.99 plus

Source: Courtesy of Betty Crocker and Tyson.

▲ A cross-ruffing coupon for Tyson and Betty Crocker.

| ◀ **FIGURE 12.4** |
| Types of Premiums |

- Free-in-the-mail
- In- or on-package
- Store or manufacturer
- Self-liquidating

▲ A free-in-the-mail premium by Fisher Boy for "cool" prizes and a coupon for 55 cents off.

shipping and handling and two proofs of purchase from boxes of Cheerios. The premium is called *self-liquidating,* because the $4.99 covers the premium's cost. The manufacturer may also receive money for shipping and handling so that consumers are paying most or all of the expense of the item.

Keys to Successful Premium Programs

Successful premium programs have several common elements (Figure 12.5). First, the premium should match the target market. A target market consisting of older, high-income individuals can be reached with a premium such as china or fine crystal. If the market is children, a cartoon figure or a character from Disney or Sesame Street becomes more attractive.

The best premiums reinforce the firm's image. They should not be low-cost trinkets. Offering cheap merchandise insults customers and damages the firm's image. Premium programs succeed when they tie in with the firm's products to enhance the image of the product and the brand.[10]

Premiums are integrated with the other components of the IMC program. Premiums provide an excellent means of adding value to a product instead of slashing prices or using coupons. Premiums can serve as a "thank you" to current customers or to attract new customers. *Sports Illustrated* has a rich history of premium programs, from DVDs to watches to phones, which are presented for either renewing a subscription to the magazine or ordering one for the first time.

Some marketing experts believe overusing coupons damages a brand's image. Conversely, premiums might actually enhance an image. Picking the right type of premium becomes the key. Premiums can be used to boost sales; however, they usually are not as successful as coupon sales. Nevertheless, premiums remain a valuable consumer promotional tool.

In the United States, approximately $24 billion is spent on premiums each year.[11] Although premiums add value and enhance the brand, they are not as effective at increasing profits. Therefore, a clear relationship between the premium's intention and IMC goals should be established. Logically, the goal should be more about image than profit.

CONTESTS AND SWEEPSTAKES

Contests and sweepstakes are popular consumer sales promotions. Companies spend approximately $1.9 billion on various games, contests, and sweepstakes each year, which appear in both consumer markets and business markets.[12] The prize list determines the success or failure of these appeals. Members of the target market for the contest or

FIGURE 12.5 ▶
Keys to Successful Premium Programs

- Match the premium to the target market
- Carefully select the premiums (avoid fads, try for exclusivity)
- Pick a premium that reinforces the firm's product and image
- Integrate the premium with other IMC tools (especially advertising and POP displays)
- Don't expect premiums to increase short-term profits

Source: Based on Don Jagoda, "The Seven Habits of Highly Successful Premiums," *Incentive* 173, no. 8 (August 1999), pp. 104–105.

sweepstakes must desire the prizes in order to entice them to participate. A prize with a low or zero value will not succeed.

Contests

The words *contest* and *sweepstakes* tend to be used interchangeably, yet there are some differences, primarily legal. *Contests* normally require the participant to perform some type of activity. The winner will be selected from the group that performs best or provides the most correct answers. Often, contests require a participant to make a purchase to enter. In some states, however, forcing consumers to make a purchase to enter a contest is illegal. In developing contests, the marketing team first investigates the state and federal laws that apply.

Contests range from the controversial bikini or suntan contests at local nightclubs to popular television shows such as *Jeopardy* or *American Idol* in which contestants must answer questions or win competitions to earn prizes. Although some contests are mostly chance, others require skill. For example, Ryan Leer won a contest held by Quiznos for creating a video clip that featured a fake rocket-launcher shooting Quiznos' "Toasty Torpedo" sandwiches. He won $10,000 and a year's supply of sandwiches. Customers were able to go online to vote on winning videos, which gave Quiznos additional exposure. In addition, the company added 68,000 customers to Quiznos' marketing database.[13]

Sweepstakes

No purchase is required to enter a sweepstakes. Consumers can enter as many times as they wish, although it is permissible for firms to restrict customers to one entry per visit to the store or location. Probability dictates the chances of winning a sweepstakes. The odds of winning must clearly be stated on all point-of-purchase (POP) displays and advertising materials. In a sweepstakes, the probability of winning each prize must be published in advance.

Components of Prizes

People enter contests and sweepstakes that they find interesting or challenging. Consumers do not enter every contest or sweepstakes they encounter. Instead, they selectively choose. The decision will be based on the perceived value of the contest or sweepstakes prize combined with the odds of winning. The greater the perceived odds of winning, the more likely it becomes that a person will participate.

The perceived value of a prize consists of two components: extrinsic value and intrinsic value. The *extrinsic value* represents the actual attractiveness of the item (a car versus a free sandwich). The greater the perceived and extrinsic values, the more likely people will become involved.

Intrinsic values are those associated with participating. A contest requiring the use of a skill, such as the one with recipes or an essay contest, entices entry by individuals who enjoy demonstrating that skill. Extrinsic rewards become secondary. Instead, participants enjoy competing and demonstrating their abilities. This, in part, explains the popularity of fantasy football and baseball leagues and "pick the winner" sports contests.

Sears recently launched a national "More Green Across America" contest that encouraged individuals to nominate baseball fields, playgrounds, and other community green spaces. The contestants sent photos and wrote short essays about why the area deserved a makeover.

▼ This advertisement for fantasy fishing by Bassmaster is designed to appeal to outdoorsmen.

Source: Courtesy of Newcomer, Morris & Young, Inc.

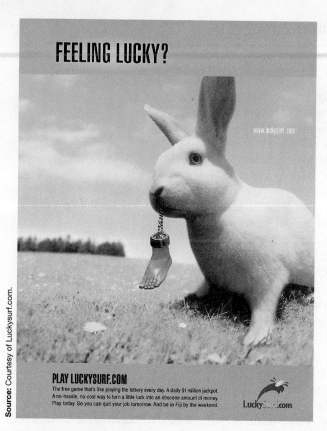

FEELING LUCKY?

www.luckysurf.com

PLAY LUCKYSURF.COM
The free game that's like playing the lottery every day. A daily $1 million jackpot.
A no-hassle, no-cost way to turn a little luck into an obscene amount of money.
Play today. So you can quit your job tomorrow. And be in Fiji by the weekend.

LuckySurf.com

▲ The Internet provides a new medium for offering contests and sweepstakes.

Baseball Hall-of-Famer Mike Schmidt was the campaign's spokesperson. Sears narrowed the list down to 10 worthy projects and then had the public vote for the winner. The grand prize winner received a new yard tractor, mower, line trimmer, edger, and blower as well as a visit from the Sears Blue Lawn & Garden Crew to bring the beautification project to fruition.[14]

To encourage consumers to continue participating in a contest, the extrinsic values of prizes can be increased by allowing small, incremental rewards. A consumer who wins a soft drink or a sandwich in a sweepstakes at Subway may be more likely to continue participating. Scratch-and-win cards tend to be effective because the reward is instant.

A mobile phone promotion developed by Hip Cricket, a mobile marketing and event company, provided instant notification of winning via text messaging. Hip Cricket developed a sweepstakes for Miller Brewing Company's Icehouse brand. The sweepstakes was the first to be conducted live, during a rock concert. Music fans, 21 years old or older, entered the sweepstakes by text messaging the words "Pick Me" during the concert. At 10:00 P.M., one concertgoer, Melissa Hasty, received word via text message that she had won the grand prize, a 5-day, 4-night Caribbean cruise on the "Rock Boat." Other fans won secondary prizes throughout the night, again, receiving notification via their mobile phone's instant messaging system. Winning is always fun. For Melissa and others at the concert, winning instantly was even more exciting.[15]

The Internet and Social Media

The Internet has become a popular location for contests and sweepstakes. It provides opportunities for individuals to see a prize's intrinsic value by creating interactive games to challenge a contestant's ability. The Internet offers promoters data-capturing capabilities. Internet contests are less costly to set up and run than other types of promotions.

The newest trends in contests and sweepstakes include using social media. Microsoft, Sephora, NASCAR, Comcast, Chic-fil-A, and McDonald's have created Twitter sweepstakes or have used Twitter and social media sites to enlist participants for a contest or sweepstakes. The intention is to use the sweepstakes or contest to ignite a viral buzz around the brand.[16]

Goals of Contests and Sweepstakes

Contests and sweepstakes encourage customer traffic and can boost sales. Although contests and sweepstakes routinely increase customer traffic, the question remains as to whether they actually boost sales. Some do, others do not. Marketers recognize that intrinsic rewards tend to draw consumers back. This means online games are exciting prospects, because they can be structured to create intrinsic value.

REFUNDS AND REBATES

Refunds and rebates are cash returns offered to consumers or businesses following the purchase of a product. Consumers pay full price for the product but can mail in some type of proof of purchase. The manufacturer then refunds a portion of the purchase price. A *refund* is a cash return on what are called "soft goods," such as food or clothing. *Rebates* are cash returns on "hard goods," which are major ticket items such as automobiles and appliances.

Only about 30 percent of all rebates are claimed. For rebates valued at $50 or more, the percentage of claims rises to about 65 percent. The inconvenience associated with getting the rebate is the primary reason for low response rates. Too many steps or long waiting times because of "snail mail" are common complaints about rebates. Many consumers wait 2 to 3 months to receive a rebate check.[17]

Many rebate programs suffer from diminished effectiveness, because consumers have come to expect them. For example, car dealers often find that customers wait until rebates are offered. As a result, no new purchase activity is associated without the rebate, but rather it delays the purchase process. Further, increasing the amount of a rebate no longer seems to spur additional sales, yet discontinuing or reducing rebate levels tends to have an immediate negative impact.

Refunds and rebates achieve the greatest successes when they are perceived as being new or original. When they become an entrenched part of doing business, they are expected discounts. To be effective, rebates and refunds should change the buyer's behavior, either by leading to a more immediate purchase or by causing the customer to change brands.

SAMPLING

Sampling is the actual delivery of a product to consumers for their use or consumption. In business-to-business markets, samples of products may be provided to potential clients. Sampling also can be featured in the service sector. For example, a tanning salon may offer an initial visit free to encourage new customers to try its facilities. Dentists and lawyers use sampling when they offer an initial consultation free of charge.

In a survey of 1,800 consumers, more than one-third of those who tried a sample purchased the product during the same shopping trip. Fifty-eight percent indicated they would buy the product again. Nearly one-fourth said they bought the product being sampled instead of the brand they had intended to purchase.[18]

▲ This advertisement for Skyjacker offers a $35.00 rebate on four Skyjacker Hydro or Nitro shocks.

Sample Distribution

Figure 12.6 lists various ways samples are distributed. The most common consumer method, *in-store distribution*, delivers the sample in the store, such as when a food product is cooked and given to customers on site. *Direct sampling* means items are mailed or delivered door-to-door to consumers. In the business-to-business sector, salespeople often deliver direct samples to prospects or to current customers when they are featuring a new product.

Response samples are made available to individuals or businesses responding to a media offer on television, on the Internet, from a magazine, or by some other source. *Cross-ruffing* sampling plans provide samples of one product on another. A laundry detergent with a free dryer sheet attached to the package is a cross-ruffing sample.

Media sampling means the sample is included in the media outlet. Recently, samples for Dr. Scholl's Her Open Shoes insoles were affixed to heavy-stock paper in magazines such as *In Style*, *All You*, *Shape*, and *Glamour*. Women could remove the insole and test it on one foot and compare it to the other foot that did not have an insole. Approximately 3 million were distributed. One month after the run, 11 percent of subscribers had

• In-store distribution	• Media sampling
• Direct sampling	• Professional sampling
• Response sampling	• Selective sampling
• Cross-ruff sampling	

◀ **FIGURE 12.6**
Methods of Distributing Samples

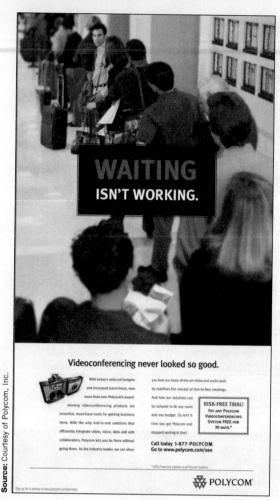

Videoconferencing never looked so good.

▲ This business-to-business Polycom advertisement offers a free 30-day, risk-free trial.

purchased insoles and nearly 60 percent said they planned to make purchases. Approximately 57 percent had peeled the sample insole out of the magazine and 37 percent said they actually tested it.[19]

Professional samples are delivered to professionals, such as doctors, who may then provide patients with the free drug samples. *Selective samples* are distributed at a site such as a state fair, parade, hospital, restaurant, or sporting event. For instance, many times Power Bars are given to people attending football or basketball games. There is a tie-in between the product (nutrition) and the event (athletics).

In recent years, marketers have increased usage of freestanding inserts to distribute samples. A variety of products have been distributed in newspapers, including breakfast bars, coffee, shampoo, snacks, tea, and automotive cleansers. Companies using newspapers employ the FSI insert method because it breaks through the clutter and captures attention. The newspaper is an "invited medium." Therefore, consumers are often more receptive when samples are included in the paper.[20]

Benefits of Sampling

Product sampling offers an effective way to introduce a new product, generate interest in that product, and collect information about consumers. Internet-based response sampling programs have become popular with both consumers and manufacturers. Bristol-Myers/Squibb was one of the first companies to utilize the Internet for product sampling. The company offered a free sample of Excedrin to individuals who requested one. They had to be willing to provide their names, addresses, and e-mail information. In addition to the 12-pack sample of Excedrin, consumers received coupons for additional purchases, along with the quarterly *Excedrin Headache Relief Update Newsletter*. The advantage of this form of response sampling is that only consumers who requested the product received it. Also, companies normally can gather additional information to be added to a database. Seventy percent of consumers who requested a sample online were willing to complete a survey to receive the item.[21]

Successful Sampling Programs

As with the other consumer promotions, sampling should be a central part of the IMC plan. Sampling encourages a trial use by a consumer or a business. It will be most effective when it introduces a new product or a new version of a product to a market. Samples also help to promote a current product to a new target market or to new prospects.

Successful sampling means targeting the right audience at the right venue. Mass sampling will not be nearly as cost-effective as targeted sampling. Recently, Mars Petcare introduced a line of dog food with a cross-country sampling tour called "Share the love." Cesar Canine Cuisine Bistro brand samples were given to pet owners at 125 dog parks and beaches. Coupons were made available online in order to capture information and build the company's database.[22]

BONUS PACKS

When an additional or extra number of items are placed in a special product package, it is a bonus pack. Offering four bars of soap for the price of three is a bonus pack promotion. Recently, Rayovac attached three free AA batteries in a bonus pack containing nine batteries. Typical bonuses range from 20 to 100 percent of the normal number of units in a package. A 30 percent bonus is the most common.

Types of Bonus Packs

Figure 12.7 identifies the major objectives of bonus packs. Increasing the size or quantity of the package can lead to greater product use. When a package that contains eight small

- Increase usage of the product
- Match or preempt competitive actions
- Stockpile the product
- Develop customer loyalty
- Attract new users
- Encourage brand switching

candy bars is increased by four more bars, consumers are likely to eat more, because they are readily available. This will not be true for products with more constant consumption rates. If Colgate offers a bonus pack with an additional tube of toothpaste, consumers do not use more of the product. In effect, this delays the next purchase. Manufacturers offer these types of bonus packs because they preempt the competition. A consumer with a large quantity of the merchandise on hand becomes less likely to switch brands.

Keys to Successful Bonus Packs

Bonus packs reward customer loyalty by offering, in effect, free merchandise. Bonus packs can lead to brand switching if the consumer has used the brand previously. Facing purchase decisions, consumers may opt for brands that offer more product at the regular price. The packages present an advantage that competitive brands are not offering.

Bonus packs tend to be popular with manufacturers, retailers, and customers. A retailer can build a positive relationship with a manufacturer that uses a bonus pack to increase brand switching and stockpiling. Retailers gain an advantage because the bonus pack is a "bargain" or "value" offered through the retail outlet. Customers enjoy bonus packs because it feels like they are getting free merchandise. For ongoing products with high levels of competition, the bonus pack approach can help maintain brand loyalty and reduce brand switching at a minimal cost.

▼ A bonus pack offer for two packages of Lean Slices by Carl Buddig.

Bonus packs rarely attract new customers, because they have not previously purchased the brand. Obtaining an extra quantity does not reduce the purchase risk. In fact, it adds to the risk, especially when the customer does not like to waste a product by throwing it away if he is dissatisfied with it. Marketing research indicates that when the bonus is small (20 to 40 percent), consumers often believe the price has not truly changed. Unfortunately, when the bonus is large, such as a two-for-the-price-of-one sale, consumers tend to believe that the price was first increased to compensate for the additional quantity. In that instance, increasing the size of a bonus captured the consumer's attention but did not convey the desired message.[23]

PRICE-OFFS

A price-off is a temporary reduction in the price of a product to the consumer. A price-off can be physically marked on the product, such as when a bottle of aspirin shows the regular retail price marked out and replaced by a special retail price (e.g., $6.99 marked out and replaced by $5.99). Producing a label with the price reduction premarked forces the retailer to sell the item at the reduced price. This ensures the price-off incentive will be passed on to consumers. At other times, the price-off will not be printed on the actual item, but instead on a point-of-purchase display, sign, or shelf.

Benefits of Price-Offs

Price-offs are excellent at stimulating sales of existing products. They can entice customers to try new products, because the lower price reduces the financial risk of making

Talk About Light... Only 1 gram of fat per package!*

*On any Lean Slices turkey product

Buddig
Where Taste, Quality and Value All Meat.

MANUFACTURER'S COUPON   EXPIRES 5-31-00

SAVE 60¢ on any 2 packages of Lean Slices by Carl Buddig

151526

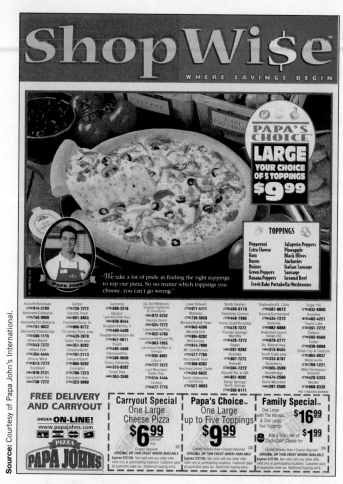

▲ A price-off and coupon offer for Papa John's pizza.

the purchase. They can encourage customers to switch brands in brand parity situations or when no strong brand loyalty exists. In cases where consumers do have a brand preference, a price-off on a favorite brand encourages stockpiling of the product and possibly increased consumption of the item.[24] A consumer who purchases additional breakfast bars because of a price-off tends to consume more breakfast bars. Again, this will not be true for products such as deodorant or toothpaste. Stockpiling for those types of products only delays the next purchase and does not increase consumption. Similar effects occur in the business-to-business arena when price-offs are used.

Price-offs have proven to be successful consumer promotions for two reasons. First, the price-off has the appeal of a monetary savings. Second, the reward is immediate. Unlike rebates, refunds, contests, sweepstakes, and other promotional incentives, consumers do not have to wait for the reward.

Problems with Price-Offs

Although price-offs are easy to implement and can have a sudden impact on sales, they can also cause problems. Sales may increase, but the program can have a negative impact on a company's profit margin. It normally takes at least a 20 to 40 percent increase in sales to offset each 5-percent price reduction.

Another danger of price-off programs is that they encourage consumers to become more price sensitive. In the same way that customers respond to rebates, they can either wait for a price-off promotion or choose another brand that happens to be on sale. In addition, when used too often, price-offs can have a negative impact on a brand's image. As always, price-off programs should be incorporated into the firm's overall IMC program.

OVERLAYS AND TIE-INS

At times companies combine two or more consumer promotions activities into a single campaign, called an *overlay*. To attract Chinese consumers in Canada, Tropicana combined sampling with coupons. Free samples (50,000 cups of orange juice) were given out along with 30,000 coupons at a Chinese New Year's celebration in Vancouver. Asians who live in the United States and Canada are not typically large users of coupons; however, Tropicana Canada's research indicated that the Chinese consider oranges to be harbingers of good luck. A few weeks after the promotion, 40 percent of the coupons were redeemed, and sales of Tropicana orange juice among the Chinese community in Canada increased considerably.[25]

Developing a consumer promotion with another product or company is another common strategy, called a *tie-in*. *Intracompany tie-ins* are the promotion of two different products within one company using one consumer promotion. An alternative method is partnering with another company, which is an *intercompany tie-in*. Fast-food restaurants often use tie-ins with movies and toys to create attractive children's promotions. Whether a promotion is a stand-alone, overlay, or tie-in program, careful attention will be given to planning the event to maximize its effect.

PLANNING FOR CONSUMER PROMOTIONS

3 How do different types of customers respond to consumer promotions?

In planning the consumer promotions component of the IMC, the promotions should support the brand image and the brand positioning strategy. To ensure this occurs, marketers carefully consider the target audience. Research will be conducted to identify the core values present in the target audience, as well as opinions regarding the firm's products, especially as they relate to the competition. After gathering this information, the marketing team finalizes the consumer promotions plan. In terms of promotions, consumers can be divided into four general categories: promotion-prone, brand-loyal, brand-preferred, and price-sensitive. (see Figure 12.8).

Promotion-prone consumers regularly respond to various consumer promotions and like to purchase products that are on-deal. They tend to clip coupons on a regular basis, enter contests and sweepstakes, purchase bonus packs, and respond to other promotional offers. In contrast, for **price-sensitive consumers**, price remains the primary, if not only, criterion used in making a purchase decision. Brand names are not important, and these individuals do not pay more for a brand name. They take advantage of any type of promotion that reduces the price.

Brand-loyal consumers purchase only one particular brand and do not substitute, regardless of any deal being offered. They make whatever effort is necessary to purchase their chosen brand. More common is brand preference. **Brand-preference consumers** have a small set of brands for which they have a strong preference. When promotions are offered for one of their chosen brands, it becomes the one to be purchased. When the promotion is for a brand not in the brand-preferred set, it will be ignored regardless of the size or type of promotion being offered.

Consumers do not fit into one of the four categories for all purchases. They may tend to be one of the four types, but promotion or brand preferences will change across product and service categories. A beer drinker may be extremely promotion prone; a wine drinker may be quite brand loyal. The same beer drinker may be extremely loyal to a pizza brand, and the same wine drinker may be price sensitive when it comes to buying potato chips.

In planning promotions, the marketing team understands that promotion-prone consumers purchase the brand that is on-deal. Price-sensitive consumers purchase whichever brand is cheaper, regardless if it is on-deal or off-deal. Therefore, these two types of consumers are not highly attractive to pursue with consumer promotions, unless the promotional goal is to increase sales, market share, or customer traffic. There will be little or no future allegiance to the brand.

Brand-loyal consumers only use a promotion when it is for their favored brand. Offering a promotion to this group makes little sense, because they will buy the brand anyway. The ideal group to target is the brand-preferred consumer, especially if the promotion features a brand in their preference set. This can enhance loyalty toward the brand and prevents them from purchasing a competing brand. It may also move the consumer closer to brand loyalty.

Manufacturers should understand retailer objectives in using promotions. It does little good to create a promotion that will be popular with consumers if retailers are not willing to work with the manufacturer to enhance the promotional offer. Retailers prefer promotions that benefit them. The primary reasons retailers support manufacturer consumer promotions programs are to:

- Increase store traffic
- Increase store sales
- Attract new customers
- Increase the basket size[26]

You have been prudent with your finances. Why let the economy determine your lifestyle? Enjoy the luxury you deserve.

PLATINUM MOTORCARS

Platinum Motorcars 4514 Cole Avenue, Suite 600 Dallas, Texas 75205 1(888)5-PLATINUM 469.374.9090 469.533.6492 fax platinummotorcars.net

MENTION THIS AD AND RECEIVE 20% OFF A 2 DAY RENTAL

▲ A price-off promotion by Platinum Motorcars offering 20 percent off on a 2-day rental if the consumer mentions seeing the promotion in the ad.

▼ Brand-preferred consumers are the ideal group to target.

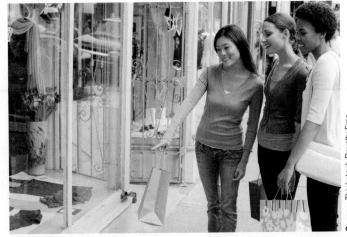

FIGURE 12.8 ▶

Types of Consumers in Relation
to Consumer Promotions

- Promotion-prone
- Brand-loyal
- Brand-preferred
- Price sensitive

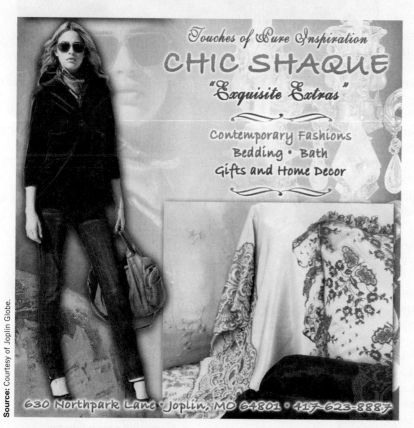

Source: Courtesy of Joplin Globe.

▲ When developing promotions, Chic Shaque's marketing team first seeks to understand the type of consumers that shop at its retail store.

❹ What types of trade promotions can help push products onto retailer shelves and eventually on to end users?

The promotions program should be tied to the theme of the IMC program while keeping in mind where the promotions will be seen by the consumer. Specific goals associated with the product, the target market, and the retail outlets are first formulated. Building-brand is more of a long-term goal; generating sales is more short range. Price-based offers normally are designed to attract new customers or to build sales. Other consumer promotions such as high-value premiums can be used to enhance a firm's image over time.

TRADE PROMOTIONS

Trade promotions are incentives members of the trade channel use to entice another member to purchase goods for eventual resale. Trade promotions are aimed at retailers, distributors, wholesalers, brokers, or agents. A manufacturer can offer trade promotions to convince another member of the trade channel to carry its goods. Wholesalers, distributors, brokers, and agents use trade promotions to persuade retailers to purchase products for eventual resale.

Trade promotions account for a significant percentage of a supplier's or retailer's gross revenues. Twenty years ago they may have only accounted for about 25 percent of a manufacturer's marketing budget; today it is nearly 70 percent. Trade promotions are often the second-largest expense for a manufacturer after the cost-of-goods-sold. Trade promotions account for 17.4 percent of gross sales revenues for manufacturers.[27]

Trade promotions are an integral part of an IMC program. Unfortunately, in many companies, the individual handling trade promotions may not be involved in the IMC planning process. Leaders in these firms often view trade promotions as being merely a means for getting products onto retail shelves or satisfying a channel member's request. As a result, little consideration may be given to matching the IMC program when trade promotions programs are developed.

A variety of trade promotions tools exist. Individual companies select trade promotions techniques based on several factors. These factors include the nature of the business (manufacturer versus distributor), the type of customer to be influenced (e.g., selling to a retailer versus selling to a wholesaler), company preferences, and the objectives of the IMC plan. The primary types of trade promotions are listed in Figure 12.9.

FIGURE 12.9 ▶

Types of Trade Promotions

- **Off-invoice allowance:** A per-case rebate paid to retailers for an order.
- **Slotting fees:** Money paid to retailers to stock a new product.
- **Exit fees:** Money paid to retailers to remove an item from their SKU inventory.

Trade Allowances

Trade allowances provide financial incentives to other channel members to motivate them to make purchases. Trade allowances can be packaged into a variety of forms, including the ones described in Figure 12.10. Each makes it possible for the channel member to offer discounts or other deals to customers.

Off-Invoice Allowances

Off-invoice allowances are financial discounts given for each item, case, or pallet ordered. They encourage channel members to place orders. Approximately 35 percent of all trade dollars are spent on off-invoice allowances, making them the largest expenditure among trade promotions tools.[28] As with refunds, rebates, and price-offs in the consumer sector, many retailers are reluctant to purchase merchandise unless some type of trade allowance is given. In addition, there is tremendous competitive pressure to offer trade allowances, as companies selling the same type of products compete for limited shelf space.

Slotting Fees

The most controversial form of trade allowance, **slotting fees**, are funds charged by retailers to stock new products. Retailers justify slotting fees in various ways.[29] First, retailers spend money to add new products to inventories and to stock merchandise. An unsuccessful product means the retailer's investment in inventory represents a loss, especially when the retailer has stocked the product in a large number of stores. Slotting fees recover some of the loss.

Second, adding a new product in the retail store means providing shelf space. Shelves are already filled. Adding a new product means either deleting brands or products or reducing the amount of shelf space allocated to them. In both cases, the retailer spends both time and money on creating space for a new product.

Third, slotting fees make it easier for retailers to finalize decisions about new products. A typical supermarket carries 35,000 SKUs (stock-keeping units). The supermarket's managers must evaluate at least 10,000 to 15,000 new products per year. Most will fail. Consequently, retailers believe charging slotting fees forces manufacturers to weed out high-risk product introductions. The average total cost in slotting fees for a nationally introduced product ranges from $1.5 to $2 million.[30] Consequently, retailers contend that slotting fees force manufacturers to conduct careful test marketing on products before introducing them. Such testing limits the number of new products offered each year. This, in turn, drastically reduces the number of new product failures.

Finally, slotting fees add to the bottom line. Many products have low margins or markups. Slotting fees provide additional monies to support retail operations. It has been estimated that between 14 and 27 percent of trade promotion monies given to retailers go directly to the retailer's bottom line.[31]

The other side of the argument comes from manufacturers, who claim slotting fees are practically a form of extortion. Many manufacturers believe slotting fees are too costly and are unfair in the first place. These fees compel manufacturers to pay millions of dollars to retailers that could be used for advertising, sales promotions, or other marketing efforts.

▼ A new product, such as a new flavor of Ott's salad dressing, will often be charged slotting fees.

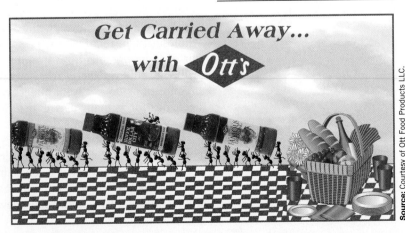

Get Carried Away...
with Ott's

Source: Courtesy of Ott Food Products LLC.

Slotting fees can prevent small manufacturers from getting products into stores simply because they cannot afford them. Some large retail operations have small-vendor policies; however, placing merchandise remains extremely challenging.

Exit Fees

Instead of paying a slotting allowance, some retailers ask for **exit fees,** which are monies paid to remove an item from a retailer's inventory. This approach may be used when a manufacturer introduces a new size of a product or a new version, such as a 3-liter bottle of Pepsi or Pepsi Diet Vanilla. PepsiCo already has products on the retailer's shelves. Adding a new-sized container or new variety of the product involves lower risk and is not the same as adding a new product. Rather than charging an up-front fee, such as a slotting allowance, retailers request exit fees if the new version of the product fails or if one of the current versions must be removed from the inventory. Four percent of retailers use exit fees, compared to the 82 percent using slotting fees.[32]

Trade Allowance Complications

In offering trade allowances to retailers, manufacturers assume that a portion of the price reduction will be passed on to consumers. This occurs only about half of the time. When a portion of the price allowance is passed on to consumers, retailers often schedule competing brands, so they can have at least one special offer going at all times. It is not an accident that one week Pepsi offers a reduced price and the next week Coke offers a discount. The two products are rarely promoted on-deal at the same time. By offering only one on-deal at a time, the retailer always has a reduced priced brand for the price-sensitive consumer. The retailer also can charge the brand-loyal consumer full price 50 percent of the time. While accomplishing these goals, the retailer receives special trade allowances from both Pepsi and Coke.

In an effort to increase profit margins, retailers often engage in two activities: forward buying and diversion. *Forward buying* occurs when a retailer purchases extra amounts of a product while it is on-deal. The retailer then sells the on-deal merchandise after the deal period ends, saving the cost of purchasing the product at the manufacturer's full price. *Diversion* occurs when a retailer purchases a product on-deal in one location and ships it to another location where it is off-deal. For example, a manufacturer may offer an off-invoice allowance of $5 per case for the product in France. Diversion tactics mean the retailer purchases an excess quantity in France and has it shipped to stores in other European countries. To do so, retailers first examine the potential profits to be earned, less the cost of shipping the product to other locations. Shipping costs tend to be relatively high compared to trade allowances offered. Consequently, retailers do not use diversion nearly as much as forward buying.

Trade Contests

To achieve sales targets and other objectives, channel members sometimes use trade contests. Winners receive prizes or cash, which is known as **spiff money**. A contest can be held at any level within the channel. It can be between brokers or agents, wholesalers, or retail stores. To prevent undue influence of contests on buyers, a number of large organizations prohibit employees from participating in vendor contests. Although this is exactly what a contest is designed to accomplish, many large retail organizations do not want buyers participating, because these buyers make purchase decisions for as many as 500 to 2,500 stores and participating in a contest may result in poor buying decisions.

In the mid-2000s, demand for cruise ship vacations steadily increased. Intense competition took place between the cruise lines. Some cruise ship companies used a combination of advertising, consumer promotions, and trade promotions to attract patrons. Royal Caribbean International offered travel agents cooperative advertising programs featuring TV commercials, newspaper ads, as well as an e-mail template to contact potential travelers.

Norwegian Cruise Lines enrolled 5,500 agents in a "Sale of All Sails" promotional contest. Prizes were based on bookings. Each agent that set up a Holland America cruise was enrolled in the trade contest. The prizes offered included a free cruise with five veranda staterooms. The Princess Cruise line offered booking agents the chance to win a West Coast sailing cruise with a mini-suite. One cruise was awarded each week during a 90-day period. Offering travel agents the chance to win prizes and cruises for themselves likely caused them to be highly motivated to book cruises for the lines holding the contests.[33]

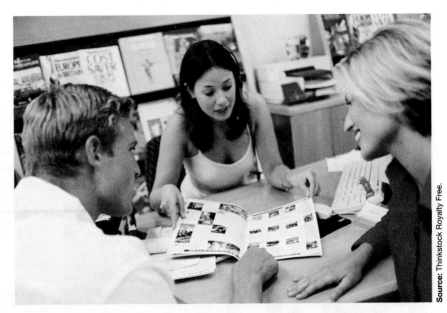

▶ Trade contests were held among travel agents to increase cruise ship bookings.

Trade Incentives

Trade incentives are similar to trade allowances. The difference is that **trade incentives** involve the retailer performing a function in order to receive the funds. The purpose, however, remains the same as for trade allowances: to encourage retailers either to push the manufacturer's brand or to increase retailer purchases of that brand. The three major types of trade incentives are identified in Figure 12.11.

Cooperative Merchandising Agreements

The most comprehensive trade incentive, a cooperative merchandising agreement (CMA), is a formal agreement between the retailer and manufacturer to undertake a two-way marketing effort. The CMA can be for a wide variety of marketing tasks. A CMA can feature the manufacturer's brand as a price leader in an advertisement. A cooperative agreement can be made to emphasize the manufacturer's brand as part of an in-house offer made by the retail store or a by using a special shelf display featuring a price incentive.

Cooperative merchandising agreements are popular with manufacturers because the retailer performs a function in order to receive the allowance or incentive. The manufacturer retains control of the functions performed. Also, if price allowances are made as part of the CMA, the manufacturer knows that the retailer passes a certain percentage or the entire price discount on to the consumer. CMAs allow manufacturers to create annual contracts with retailers. These longer-term commitments reduce the need for last-minute trade incentives or trade allowances.

CMAs also benefit retailers. The primary benefit, from the retailer's perspective, is that the program allows them to develop *calendar promotions*, which are promotional campaigns the retailer plans for customers through manufacturer trade incentives. Signing an agreement means a retailer can schedule the weeks a particular brand will be on sale and offset the other weeks with other brands. Calendar promotions allow the retailer to always have one brand on sale while the others are off-deal and to rotate the brands on sale. By arranging sales through trade incentives, the margins for the retailer are approximately the same for all brands, both on-deal and off-deal, because they rotate. Retailers can effectively move price reductions given to the customer to the manufacturer rather than absorbing them. A store may feature Budweiser on-deal one week and Heineken the next. Loyal beer drinkers stay with their preferred brand, while price-sensitive consumers can choose the on-deal brand, and the store retains a reasonable markup on all beers sold.

Trade Incentive
→ Cooperative merchandising agreement
→ Premium or bonus pack
→ Co-op advertising programs

◀ **FIGURE 12.11**
Types of Trade Incentives

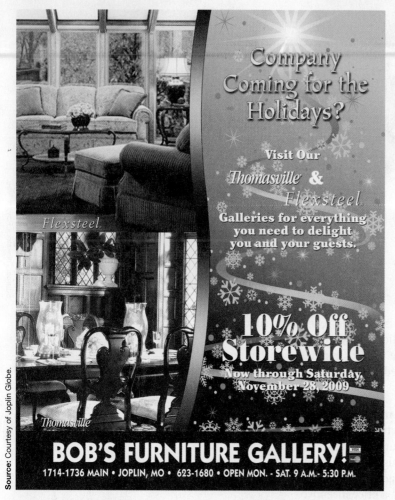

▲ A co-op advertisement for Bob's Furniture Gallery featuring both the Flexsteel and Thomasville brands.

Premiums and Bonus Packs

Instead of offering the retailer a discount on the price, the manufacturer offers free merchandise in the form of a premium or bonus pack. For example, a manufacturer can offer a bonus pack of one carton for each 20 purchased within the next 60 days. The bonus packs are free to the retailer and are awarded either for placing the order by a certain date or for agreeing to a minimum-size order. Often, to receive the free merchandise the retailer must meet both conditions: a specified date and a minimum order size.

Cooperative Advertising

The final trade incentive, a cooperative advertising program, is used when the manufacturer agrees to reimburse the retailer a certain percentage of the advertising costs associated with advertising the manufacturer's products in the retailer's ad. To receive the reimbursement, the retailer follows specific guidelines concerning the placement of the ad and its content. In almost all cases, no competing products can be advertised. Normally, the manufacturer's product must be displayed prominently. There may be other restrictions on how the product is advertised as well as specific photos or copy that must be used.

In most cooperative advertising programs, retailers accrue co-op monies based on purchases, normally a certain percentage of sales. B.F. Goodrich, a manufacturer of automobile tires, offers a 4.5 percent co-op advertising fund on all purchases made by the retailer of Goodrich tires. The money can accrue for 1 year, and then it starts over again. B.F. Goodrich pays 70 percent of the cost of an approved advertisement. Any of the media can be used for the advertisement, including radio, newspaper, magazines, television, and outdoor advertising.

Unlimited media choices are not offered by all manufacturers. Dayton, another tire manufacturer, does not allow co-op dollars to be used for magazine advertising. B.F. Goodrich allows group ads for co-op monies; Dayton does not. Further, Dayton requires preapproval for some of the media buys and advertisements; B.F. Goodrich does not require any preapprovals. Thus, each manufacturer has a unique set of restrictions to be followed by retailers seeking to qualify for co-op monies.[34]

Co-op advertising programs allow retailers to use the manufacturer's dollars to expand advertising programs. In a co-op ad, the retailer gains additional advertising coverage at minimal cost. Retailers also benefit from the image of a national brand, which can attract new or additional customers to the store. Wal-Mart recently expanded co-op advertising efforts with major manufacturers, who contributed over $400 million toward Wal-Mart's annual advertising budget. In Wal-Mart's system, manufacturers have considerably more creative input into the ads and are prominently displayed in the ad instead of taking minor roles.[35]

Manufacturers also benefit from co-op ads. By sharing advertising costs with retailers, the manufacturer gains additional exposure at a reduced cost. More important, almost all co-op advertising programs are tied to sales. The retailer accrues co-op advertising dollars based on a certain percentage of sales. Thus, to get the co-op money, the retailer must not only promote the brand prominently, but must also purchase the product for resale. As a result, a wide variety of cooperative advertisements appear regularly in every medium, for both consumer and business-to-business products.

► **FIGURE 12.12**
Five Categories of Buyers
Attending Trade Shows

- **Education seekers** Buyers who want to browse, look, and learn but are not in the buying mode
- **Reinforcement seekers** Buyers who want reassurance they made the right decision in past purchases
- **Solution seekers** Buyers seeking solutions to specific problems and are in the buying mode
- **Buying teams** A team of buyers seeking vendors for their business; usually are in the buying mode
- **Power buyers** Members of upper management or key purchasing agents with the authority to buy

Trade Shows

Trade shows are used extensively in business-to-business marketing programs. They benefit both manufacturers and retailers. From a manufacturer's standpoint, a trade show offers the opportunity to discover potential customers and sell new products. Also, relationships with current customers can be strengthened at the show. A trade show often provides the chance to investigate what the competition is doing. Many times, trade shows present a situation in which the manufacturer's sales team can meet directly with decision makers and buyers from business-to-business clients. A trade show can strengthen the brand name of a product as well as the company's image.

From the retailer's perspective, a trade show allows buyers to compare merchandise and to make contacts with several prospective vendors in a short period of time. In some cases, the retailer can negotiate special deals. Trade shows represent an ideal place for buyers and sellers to meet in an informal, low-pressure setting to discuss how to work together effectively.

Some national and international trade shows are attended by thousands of buyers. To be sure a trade show will succeed, manufacturers seek out key buyers and try to avoid spending too much time with nonbuyers. Figure 12.12 identifies five categories of buyers who attend trade shows. Many marketers try to weed out the education seekers who are not interested in buying. Manufacturer's agents concentrate efforts on three groups: solution seekers, buying teams, and power buyers. Asking the right questions identifies solution seekers and buying teams. The power buyers are more difficult to find because they do not want to be identified. They often do not wear badges at trade shows, which means vendors are never sure who they are.

In the United States, few deals are finalized during trade shows. Buyers and sellers meet, discuss, and maybe even negotiate, but seldom are buys completed. Instead, manufacturers collect business cards as leads to be followed up later. This procedure varies for international customers. International attendees tend to be senior executives with the authority to make purchases. They fit into the power-buyer category listed in Figure 12.12. American manufacturers know that the international attendee often wishes to conduct business during the show, not afterward. The international attendees spend more time at each manufacturer's booth. They stay longer in order to gather and study information in greater detail. The international guest, who pays more for travel expenses, wants more in-depth information than an American counterpart requires.

The number of international trade show visitors has increased as competition continues to expand globally.

▼ A trade show provides an excellent opportunity for companies to locate potential customers.

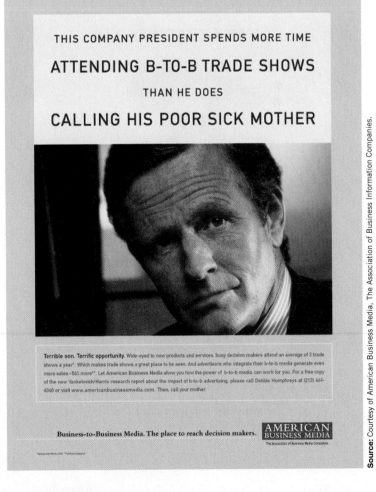

THIS COMPANY PRESIDENT SPENDS MORE TIME

ATTENDING B-TO-B TRADE SHOWS

THAN HE DOES

CALLING HIS POOR SICK MOTHER

Business-to-Business Media. The place to reach decision makers.

The increase in international participants has caused trade show centers to set up more meeting spaces, conference centers, and even places to eat where buyers and sellers can meet and transact business.

Trade shows have changed in other ways. Large national and international shows are being replaced by niche and regional shows. For example, in the 1990s many megasports trade shows were attended by everybody in the sporting goods business. The National Sporting Goods Association World Sports Expo in Chicago attracted in excess of 90,000 attendees during the mid-1900s. The number has dwindled to fewer than 40,000 today. Now manufacturers and retailers attend specialty trade shows that focus on only one sport or regional shows that focus on one section of the country. Smaller shows are cheaper to set up. Many company leaders believe they provide higher-quality prospects, better opportunities to bond with customers, and offer more quality one-to-one time with customers and potential customers. In contrast, it is relatively easy to get lost in the crowd at a bigger show.[36]

CONCERNS WITH TRADE PROMOTIONS

5 What concerns exist for manufacturers considering trade promotions programs?

The marketing team should incorporate trade promotions into the overall IMC effort. In many companies this does not occur, primarily because of employee pay structures. Sales and brand managers face quotas, and when sales fall behind the easiest way to boost them is to offer retailers a trade deal. Further, brand managers are often evaluated based on the sales growth of a brand. Offering trade deals becomes the easiest way to ensure continuing growth. The pattern of using trade deals to reach short-term quotas rather than long-term image and theme-building will not change until top management adopts a new approach. The IMC process only succeeds when a long-term horizon is emphasized and compensation structures change to match.

A strong brand image causes retailers to stock the product even when fewer trade deals are offered, because a strong brand by itself can help pull customers into retail stores. A customer who believes Sony is a strong brand in the stereo marketplace will ask for the brand in an electronics retail store. This makes stocking Sony an advantage, even when limited trade promotions are available.

The cost of trade promotions represents another concern. Manufacturers spend billions of dollars each year on them. These costs are often passed on to consumers in the form of higher prices. Estimates suggest that 11 cents out of every dollar spent for a consumer product goes directly for the cost of trade promotions.[37] The goal should be to keep the cost at a reasonable level. Money should be spent wisely, rather than simply getting into "bidding wars" with competitors. Trade promotions dollars are best used when they build relationships and help achieve other key IMC goals.

Another concern is that the use of trade promotions has led to a situation in which merchandise does not move until a trade promotion incentive has been offered. In the grocery industry, the majority of all purchases made by retailers are on-deal with some type of trade incentive in place. The constant use of deals has trimmed manufacturer margins on products and created competitive pressures to conform. If a manufacturer tries to halt or cut back on trade promotions, retailers replace the manufacturer's products with other brands or trim shelf space to allow more room for manufacturers offering better deals.

▼ Trade promotion expenditures are a major component of the marketing budget for products such as Pennant's pesticides.

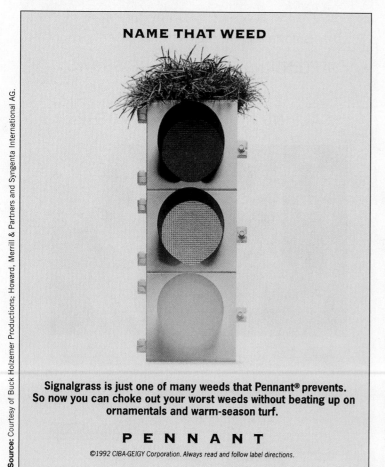

NAME THAT WEED

Signalgrass is just one of many weeds that Pennant® prevents. So now you can choke out your worst weeds without beating up on ornamentals and warm-season turf.

P E N N A N T

©1992 CIBA-GEIGY Corporation. Always read and follow label directions.

The best way to correct these problems would be to spend more on advertising focused on building or rebuilding a brand's image. Also, the marketing team should be certain promotions fit the brand's image. "If it doesn't fit," writes Brian Sullivan in *Marketing News,* "don't use it."[38] Unfortunately, to spend more on advertising means cutting trade promotions incentives. The risk becomes that other competitors will move in by offering better trade promotions to retailers, and shelf space is lost as a result. Then, the cycle begins again.

Managing trade promotions programs represents a challenging part of the marketing planning process because such a large percentage of the marketing budget is trade promotions. Effective IMC programs achieve a balance between all elements of the promotions mix and identify clear goals and targets for trade promotions programs. Only then will the company be able to compete on all levels and not just through a cycle of trade promotions bidding wars.

INTERNATIONAL IMPLICATIONS

Consumer promotions are adapted to the countries in which they are offered. There are two complications: legal and cultural. Any coupon, premium, contest, sweepstakes, or price change must fit with local legal regulations. The marketing team should investigate any potential legal problems before launching an international consumer promotions program.

Culturally, citizens in some countries may take a dim view of some promotions. For instance, in some cultures those who redeem coupons may be viewed as being of lower socioeconomic status, which may dissuade some from using them. Participation in contests or sweepstakes may violate religious norms in other nations.

The same holds true for trade promotions. Laws will vary regarding discounts, spiff money, slotting fees, and exit fees. These issues may also be reflected in cultural values. And, as previously noted, the ways in which managers in companies around the world participate in trade shows varies.

Finally, the emphasis placed on sales promotions will be different, depending on the company involved and the country in which that company operates. Both small companies seeking to do business in foreign countries and large international conglomerates will need to adjust to local conditions when employing these marketing tactics. At the same time, the goal remains to be certain that the efforts match the company's image and overall approach to marketing communications.

6 What issues complicate international sales promotions programs?

INTEGRATED CAMPAIGNS IN ACTION

Wayport Austintatious

The company Wayport is the world's largest Internet hotspot provider. According to Pink Jacket Creative advertising agency executive Bill Breedlove, "If you're in a Marriott hotel, or a McDonald's, they even have Starbuck's now, you're logging onto their site. They specialize in verticals that are health care, such as regional hospitals and major hospital chains as well hospitality, and QSRs [quick-service restaurants]."

Pink Jacket Creative was able to provide a combination of buzz marketing and trade show expertise in one event. According to Breedlove, "There was a trade show in Austin, Texas. It was for the hospitality industry. They came to us with a challenge. Like any trade show challenge, they wanted to get the top executives from the top hotel chains away from the floor of the trade show and in their own environment, so that their salespeople can work on them, and everybody wants that."

"The way that we did it for Wayport is that we identified all of the executives that we were targeting, and we wanted to have something that had a little feel of what Austin is about, because some people who attend the trade shows want an opportunity to enjoy the town. Austin is a big music and party town, particularly on 6th Street, where all of the bars and music venues are.

"We first made an invitation card with a custom sound chip that was shaped like a guitar case and branded with the campaign. I should back up and say the campaign was called Austintatious. Everything is over the top about Austin. We mailed that out. We went into a recording studio and wrote a little song that invited them to this Austin music fun thing. The event was a party on 6th Street.

(Continued)

▲ A Willie Nelson impersonator was one of the entertainers at the Austintatious nightclub takeover event.

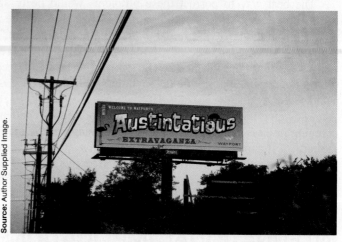

▲ This Austintatious billboard was seen by trade show attendees at the Austin airport.

"We physically went into one of the bars, one of the most popular night spots, and we rented it for the evening. We sent a team down before the event started and we gutted the entire place. We took everything that they had out of there. We redesigned it in our Austintatious theme, threw a 3-hour party, took it all down, and put it back the way it was, except that they liked some of the things that we had put up, so they kept a few.

"We sent some invitations and an email blast that drove people to a microsite to register to attend the party. We rented a billboard space, right at the exit of the airport, and we put up a big Austintatious extravaganza billboard that was only intended for 200 people who were flying in. We thought Austintatious was a cool, fun word.

"Then we took the folks to this bar that we had redecorated and had a little shindig, and their salespeople got to mingle, and it was quite successful. They were making appointments right and left with their marketing people and technology folks. So it was fun." And highly successful.[39]

Your instructor has additional information about the ads, visuals, and displays used in this campaign.

 # SUMMARY

An IMC program should incorporate all four elements of the promotions mix. Advertising may be considered to be the main "voice" of the IMC message. At the same time, the sales promotion part of the mix, including trade and consumer promotions, plays a crucial role in the success or failure of the overall marketing program.

This chapter reviewed the techniques available to attract customers by using consumer promotions. These tactics include coupons, premiums, contests and sweepstakes, refunds, rebates, samples, bonus packs, and price-off deals. These items should be combined with specific promotional goals to have the right impact on customers.

Consumer promotions are often used to boost sales. They can be an excellent short-term method to increase sales or a firm's market share. They can also be an excellent means of introducing new products. Often, a consumer promotion prompts consumers to at least try the product, where selling it at the regular price will not. Coupons and contests have been successful tactics for attracting new customers. Consumer promotions can

boost sales of a particular brand, and evidence suggests that they increase sales of the overall product category rather than just take sales away from competitors.

Trade promotions complement consumer promotions. The use of trade allowances, trade contests, trade incentives, and participation in trade shows helps the manufacturer or member of the marketing channel maintain positive contact with other organizations and moves products toward the retailer. Trade promotions work best when they are integrated into other IMC efforts rather than being viewed as a necessary evil or simply as a short-term tool to increase sales.

Internationally, sales promotions can be used when they are chosen based on the characteristics, attitudes, laws, regulations, and cultural nuances of a given geographic region. The primary objective of any promotions program must always be to enhance the message sent forth in other aspects of the IMC program in a manner that helps the company reach its long-term marketing objectives in a cost-effective and positive fashion.

KEY TERMS

sales promotions   All of the incentives offered to customers and channel members to encourage product purchases.

consumer promotions   Incentives directly offered to a firm's customers or potential customers.

trade promotions   Expenditures or incentives used by manufacturers and other members of the marketing channel to purchase goods for eventual sale.

freestanding inserts (FSIs)   Sheets of coupons distributed in newspapers, primarily on Sunday.

promotion-prone consumers   Consumers who are not brand loyal and regularly respond to promotions, such as coupons, price-off plans, or premiums, only purchasing items that are on-deal.

price-sensitive consumers   Consumers for whom price is the primary, if not only, criterion used in making a purchase decision.

brand-loyal consumers   Consumers who purchase only one particular brand and do not substitute, regardless of any deal being offered.

brand-preference consumers   Consumers who prefer a small set of brands.

trade allowances   Financial incentives to other channel members to motivate them to make purchases.

slotting fees   A form of trade allowance in which are funds charged by retailers to stock new products.

exit fees   Monies paid to remove an item from a retailer's inventory.

spiff money   Rewards given as contest prizes to brokers, retail salespeople, stores, wholesalers, and agents.

trade incentives   Funds given that require the retailer to perform a function in order to receive the dollars.

REVIEW QUESTIONS

1. Define sales promotion. What are the two main categories of sales promotions?

2. Name and describe the types of coupons. Which is the most popular with manufacturers? Which has the highest redemption rate?

3. What problems are associated with coupon programs?

4. What is a premium? What types of premium programs can companies use?

5. What are the keys to successful premium programs?

6. What is the difference between a contest and a sweepstakes?

7. What are the two main components of prizes rendered in contests and sweepstakes?

8. What role does the Internet and social media play in offering contests and sweepstakes?

9. How is a refund different from a rebate?

10. What are the primary types of samples?

11. What benefits and problems are associated with sampling?

12. What are the benefits of offering bonus packs?

13. What benefits and problems are associated with price-off tactics?

14. What is an overlay? A tie-in?

15. What four categories of consumers can be associated with consumer promotions?

16. What are the major types of trade allowances?

17. What is a slotting fee? An exit fee?

18. What is meant by the term on-deal?

19. What complications are associated with trade allowances?

20. How does the spiff money relate to trade contests?

21. What are the main types of trade incentives?

22. Describe a cooperative merchandising agreement.

23. How are premiums or bonus packs used as trade incentives?

24. How can a cooperative advertising program benefit both a manufacturer and a retailer?

25. Name ways in which trade shows have changed in recent years.

26. Describe how to effectively utilize trade promotions.

27. What problems must be overcome when developing international sales promotions programs?

CRITICAL THINKING EXERCISES

Discussion Questions

1. According to Kim James, sales promotion manager for Eckerd Drug, "The teen and preteen segments are important because they (teens) are developing buying habits and loyalties during these ages and are our future loyal consumers." In addition to established brands such as Cover Girl and Maybelline, Eckerd Drug now stocks brands such as Bonne Bell, Jane, and Naturistics.[40] Which consumer promotions would be the best to attract teens and preteens to the cosmetics department of Eckerd Drug? What tie-ins or overlays would you recommend?

2. Refer to the list of consumer promotions in Figure 12.1. Discuss each one in terms of your personal usage. Which ones do you use? How often? Why?

3. Design a magazine advertisement with a detachable coupon or premium for one of the following products.

Compare your offer with those of other students in your class. Discuss the differences between the offers.

a. SunBright Tanning Salon

b. Dixie Printing

c. Hamburger Haven

d. Blue Bell Ice Cream

4. The Rawlings Sports Equipment Company plans to increase sales of baseball gloves this season. The company intends to use a coupon program. Discuss the pros and cons of each method of coupon distribution listed in Figure 12.3 for Rawlings. Which method should Rawlings use? Why?

5. To maintain a strong brand image, Revlon's marketing team decides to use a premium for each of its lipstick products. What type of premium would you suggest for Revlon for each of the target markets listed here? Which premium would you use? Justify your answers.

a. Females, ages 60+

b. Teenagers, ages 14 to 19

c. College students, ages 18 to 25

d. Professional females, ages 30 to 50

6. Interview five people. Ask each person to identify the last contest and the last sweepstakes he entered. What was the enticement to enter? What was the extrinsic reward? What was the intrinsic reward? Summarize your findings.

7. Video games generate major revenues for many companies. One manufacturer decided to use sampling as a method to reach the primary target market—males between the ages of 15 and 30. The sampling could have been distributed in one of two ways. First, the actual game could be loaded on a computer for targeted individuals. Second, potential customers could be sent an abbreviated version of the game. Which sampling method would be best? Using Figure 12.6, discuss the pros and cons of each sampling method in terms of this new video game. Which type and method of sampling would you recommend? Why?

8. Consumers can be divided into four broad categories in terms of how they respond to consumer promotions: (1) promotion prone, (2) brand loyal, (3) price sensitive, and (4) brand preference. Identify two services or goods that would fit into each category for you personally. For example, you may be promotion prone when you buy soft drinks (your favorite brand is "What's on Sale"), but be very brand loyal when you buy shoes (Nike, Reebok). What determines which type of category you fit into for the various products you discussed?

9. Interview three people who have lived in another country about the use of consumer promotions in those countries. Make a list of those promotions that are heavily used and those that are not used. Present your findings to the class.

10. As with the other consumer promotions, international expansion requires understanding the laws and customs of each country and culture. In Saudi Arabia and other Muslim countries, Clinique had to modify its sampling techniques. In the United States and Western cultures, Clinique provides cosmetics samples in retail outlets for customers to try. In the United States, women normally sell retail cosmetics; in Saudi Arabia, men do. At the same time, Muslim custom prohibits a man from touching a woman whom he is not related to. Female customers must either apply the cosmetics themselves or bring their husbands to the store with them.

Asking a female customer "What color are your eyes?" constitutes a grave offense in Saudi Arabia, because the eyes are believed to be the gateway to the soul. Asking her about skin tone does not make sense because women keep their faces covered. Sampling is very important for Clinique in Saudi Arabia.[41]

How would you organize a sampling program in light of these cultural factors? What other consumer promotions could be used? If you have someone in your class from a Muslim country, ask your classmate to discuss the use of consumer promotions in her home country.

INTEGRATED LEARNING EXERCISES

1. Coupons are a popular form of consumer promotions. Access three of the following Web sites. What are the advantages and disadvantages of each to a consumer? How do the Web sites impact manufacturers? How do they impact retailers?

a. Coupon Country (**www.couponcountry.com**)

b. CoolSavings (**www.coolsavings.com**)

c. SmartSource (**www.smartsource.com**)

d. Coupons.com (**www.coupons.com**)

2. Sweepstakes and contests are excellent methods for building customer traffic to a retail outlet and interest in a brand. Certain firms assist in the development of sweepstakes and contests. This is important due to a variety of legal restrictions imposed by different states. Access the following Web sites. What types of services does each offer? How do the companies assist in developing a

contest or sweepstakes? Which firm would you choose if you were responsible for developing a contest or a sweepstakes program?

a. Promotion Activators, Inc. (**www.promotionactivators. com**)

b. Centra Marketing & Communications (**www.centra marketing.com**)

c. Ventura Marketing & Promotion (**www.sweepspros.com**)

3. Examine the following Web sites. What types of promotions are available? What are the objectives of the various consumer promotions? Do the promotions on the Web sites mesh with the company's advertising and consumer promotions at retail outlets?

a. Taco Bell (**www.tacobell.com**)

b. Hershey's (**www.hersheys.com**)

c. Quaker Oats (**www.quakeroats.com**)

d. Papa John's (**www.papajohns.com/index.shtm**)

4. One widely read journal featuring promotional marketing is *Promo*. Access the Web site at **www.promomagazine.com**. Examine the table of contents and access the various areas. After exploring the site, write a short report about what is available at the Web site and how it can be used to assist companies wanting to develop various promotions.

STUDENT PROJECT

Creative Corner

Reread the opening vignette that featured the Corpus Christi Hooks. From the following list of special days, pick two and then design two different ads. Make sure that each advertisement features a consumer promotion that is either mentioned in the vignette or that you come up with on your own.

Opening Day	Cinco de Mayo
Mother's Day	Father's Day
Fourth of July	Labor Day
Play-off Games	Championship Celebration

CASE 1
NEWMAN'S OWN ORGANICS: SALES PROMOTIONS AND RETAIL RELATIONSHIPS

Jason David had recently been promoted to Director of Sales Promotions for Newman's Own Organics. He was excited to find ways to expand product offerings into a wider variety of retail stores. His assignment was to fine-tune both the consumer and trade promotions that would be offered in various markets.

Newman's Own Organics is a spin-off from the original Newman's Own company. In the 1980s, celebrity actor Paul Newman and his friend, writer A. E. Hotchner, decided to concoct a batch of salad dressing to be given to their friends for the Christmas holiday season. The dressing became so popular that the two created the Newman's Own company to sell the item. The two agreed that proceeds and profits would be given to charity.

Newman's Own sold over 10,000 bottles of the salad dressing in its first 2 weeks on the market. In the first year, Newman's Own made a profit. The company slowly expanded to a wider variety of salad dressings, and then to salsa, marinara, steak sauce, pizza, and even wine.

Among the more famous charities supported by Newman's Own are the Hole in the Wall Camps, which bring together children with serious and terminal illnesses for a free summer-camp experience. The Newman's Own Foundation had given over $250 million to various charities prior to Paul Newman's death. The figure now approaches $300 million. The company's mission statement reads "Shameless Exploitation in Pursuit of the Common Good."

Newman's Own Organics was founded by Nell Newman, Paul's daughter, in 1993. She became the sole proprietor in 2001. The product line for Newman's Own Organics includes pretzels, chocolate bars, "Fig Newmans," Champion Chip Cookies, Chocolate Cups, Newman O's, Pop's Corn, Alphabet Cookies, coffee, dried fruit, olive oil and balsamic vinegar, dried fruit, pet food, mints, tea, and soy crisps.

The company's products are certified to be genuinely organic by Oregon Tilth. This means that the ingredients are grown on farms that have not used artificial fertilizers or pesticides for 3 years or more. The farms and processors have been certified by an independent third party. Kosher certification is made by the Union of Orthodox Jewish Congregations.

Newman's Own Organics is described as the "second generation." The company is for a profit, with a royalty paid to the Newman Foundation based on sales and profits. In this way, the organization is able to capitalize on the popularity of Paul Newman, the strong relationship to charitable giving, and the niche market of organic foods.

Jason's responsibility was to find and develop retail outlets for Newman's Own Organics products. Large retailers that sell food products, such as Target and Wal-Mart, constitute one major marketplace. Small grocery stores that are more upscale and feature organic foods are a second. Third would be any specialty stores that offer organic products.

Prospects might be developed by identifying the stores that carry Newman's Own products. Further, the Internet offers the potential to sell products directly to consumers without a retail store but also to direct consumers to stores that carry the items. Various types of promotions for the products and various charities, including the Hole in the Wall Camps, could be promoted on the Newman's Own Organics Web site.

Source: Jupiter Images—Thinkstock Images Royalty Free.

▲ Jason's challenge was to find and develop retail outlets for Newman's Own Organics.

Jason knew that he had the advantage of a strong brand, plus connections to the original company that would give him in-roads into meeting with prospective retail customers. He also knew that it would take more than a name to persuade retailers to make room on the shelves for the products. Beyond simple placement, the ultimate goal was to develop bonds and relationships that would lead retailers to feature the products in advertisements and promotions over time.

1. What types of consumer promotions would be best suited to end users of Newman's Own Organics products?

2. What types of trade promotions should Jason offer to retailers?

3. Would you expect Newman's Own Organics products to sell at a higher price than competitors, to match competitor prices, or to compete by lowering prices in various ways, including using sales promotions?

4. Should Jason explore placing Newman's Own Organics in restaurants to gain brand recognition? Why or why not?

5. Can you envision any types of trade shows that Jason should attend on behalf of Newman's Own Organics? Access the Trade Shows News Network at **www.tsnn.com** and BizTradeShows at **www.biztradeshows.com** for specific trade shows and locations.

6. Now that Paul Newman has passed away, what challenges will be present as the "second-generation" companies move forward and memories of Paul Newman begin to fade away?

Sources: Lenora Chu, "Newman's Own after Paul," **CNNMoney.com** (http://money.cnn.com/2008/09/27/smallbusiness/paul_newman.smb/), September 27, 2008; Newman's Own (http://newmansown.com, accessed May 10, 2010); Newman's Own Organics (www.newmansownorganics.com/funfacts.html, accessed May 10, 2010).

BEN'S COMPLETE LAWN CARE SERVICE

Ben Folds had turned a part-time college job into a full-time business. As a student, he maintained a solid client list of people using his lawn-mowing service. Following graduation, he knew the type of business that best matched his skills and personality: a complete lawn care service.

Lawn care is typically divided into three main types of companies: (1) those that mow lawns and provide trimming; (2) firms that provide fertilizers, insect control, and weed control; and (3) sod and seeding companies. Ben's idea was to provide every single aspect of lawn care, from the first spring feeding to mowing, trimming, weeding, leaf removal, and even a winter fertilization program. He would also offer sod and seed services for lawns with bare spots or brand new lots.

Ben's vision was to service two main types of customers: (1) residential homeowners who do not want to do lawn work, either because they don't enjoy it or because they do not have the time, and (2) businesses requiring lawn care, including any construction contractors and house builders that want to subcontract the grass-growing part of finishing a home.

Companies that provide lawn-mowing services tend to compete with price and quality. Most offer free bids for a residential mowing job. The more successful firms are those that make a lawn look as good as possible, including trimming around hard-to-reach spots.

Fertilization, weed control, and insecticide providers normally offer a full price and then discount in a variety of ways. Prepayment discounts are given for those who pay in advance. Quantity discounts are given for customers who use the services more frequently, such as a price-per-treatment for eight summertime treatments that is substantially lower than the price-per-treatment for a customer who only schedules four. Referral discounts are given when a customer finds a new client for the company. Specials are run for extra services when needed. The major national companies will also offer larger price discounts to those customers who decide to terminate services. A follow-up call is made or a coupon is sent to the customer, proposing substantial price discounts to get the reluctant customer to reestablish a relationship with the company.

Sod and seeding companies charge what the market will bear. A customer with only a few options pays more for sod and seed than one who lives where there are more competitors. Many sod companies primarily service wealthy homeowners and contractors.

Ben knew his company faced several challenges. First was brand-name awareness. He had to reach a wide audience of

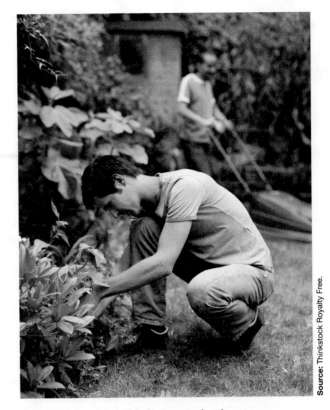

Source: Thinkstock Royalty Free.

▲ Ben took pride in his lawn care business.

potential buyers. Second would be convincing homeowners to use his services rather than those of national chains. His biggest advantage was being a full-service lawn care company, offering more than just one or two types of services. Ben's Complete Lawn Care Service began operations in Minneapolis in the winter. The company had four employees. Ben knew that he had to build a strong client list quickly and keep those clients happy so that word-of-mouth referrals would help his firm grow in the future.

1. What kinds of promotions are used by Ben's competitors?

2. Design a consumer promotions campaign for Ben's Complete Lawn Care Service.

3. What types of advertisements should be used in conjunction with the company's consumer promotions campaign?

13 Public Relations and Sponsorship Programs

PLATINUM MOTORCARS

Benny Black drove up to his Platinum Motorcars location to begin another day's work in his 1997 Mercury Sable with 198,000 miles on the odometer. He calls the car, which he purchased on craigslist, "Goldie." Benny doesn't believe in using his own money to buy and drive fancy cars.

At the same time, he wore a high-end black suit. As he explained, "I'm always going to be dressed to the nines. I always have the matching pocket square with the same color tie. I'm letting you know where my brand is. I'm not going to be cheap. You know that right from the get-go. You know it's going to be expensive, but you're going to get the value in what it is that you're trying to do."

Platinum Motorcars grew out of a unique entrepreneurial experience. Benny said, "I had 2 years' experience in the limo business. I told the wife one day that I wanted to start a limo company. I always had the affinity of wanting to serve people of wealth, with means, because I thought, 'If you can serve the masses, great, but if you can find a niche, and just reach a certain type of clientele, I always thought the easy one would be people with money.' My motto has always been 'a rich man will always be rich.' That's the ones you want to try to get to."

▼ Benny Black

He continued, "I had that (limo service) for 2 years. I had already built a clientele base, but I thought there was too much competition, because I wasn't using my own limousine. What I was doing was to borrow a limo from my friends, pay them for the limo, get paid for my time, and then just try to give that great service to the client.

"I had to figure out a different way. I could utilize the same clientele but in something that nobody else is doing. So that's where I had the idea that I needed to figure out how I can drive nice cars and not have to pay for them.

"My biggest catalyst for that was that I got a call from one of the larger hotels, and they had a ballplayer in town that wanted to be driven around in a limousine. I picked him, and while I was driving I actually said to him, 'If you ever need a nice

CHAPTER OBJECTIVES

After reading this chapter, you should be able to answer the following questions:

1 What is the relationship between public relations and the marketing activities performed by a company?

2 How can the public relations functions help to build better relationships with all internal and external stakeholders?

3 How can the positive, image-building programs that are commonly used by companies as part of the public relations effort build customer loyalty and brand image?

4 What steps can companies take to prevent or reduce image damage when negative events occur?

5 How can sponsorships be tied to public relations efforts to strengthen a customer base?

6 What role can event marketing play in creating customer excitement and brand loyalty?

7 Can public relations programs, sponsorships, and event marketing be adapted to international settings?

car while you're in Dallas, let me see what I can do for you.'

"And he said, 'Can you get me a Bentley tomorrow after the game?' This was in 2000.

"So I said, 'Yeah, I think I can make that happen.' I just got on the phone with some of the clients I'd been servicing, I called one client in particular and I said, 'I need to borrow one of your Bentleys.'

"They said, 'What have you got going on?'

"I said, 'I've got an athlete that wants to rent one to drive tomorrow after the game.'

"He said, 'What will you give me?'

"I said, 'I'll give you a thousand.'

"He said, 'Give me a thousand and an autographed jersey, and it's yours.'"

Benny completed the deal, making a handsome profit.

From there, Black developed the business model that has expanded to include rental services for high-end luxury vehicles, chauffeur services, and sales/leasing arrangements. His exotic rental cars include Aston Martin, Bentley, Rolls Royce, Ferrari, and Lamborghini. Sports cars are also available, with Mercedes, BMW, Porsche, and Maserati vehicles for rent.

Renters must meet high standards, including a $1,000 hold on a credit card, a $250 nonrefundable reservation fee, proof of insurance, and a significant charge for cancellation. Drivers must be 25 years old for some cars and over 30 for others. Platinum Motorcars serves an impressive client list, including major sports stars, celebrities, local business leaders, and even foreign dignataries and

tourists. As Black puts it, "I became 'The Exotic Car Guy.' I'm the guy you call when you come into Dallas. My tagline is 'We provide the lifestyle you deserve.'"

Recently, the company featured a major event that included sponsorships from several sources. It was a party at the Platinum Motors primary location. "It was last year, July 23; we picked the 23rd because it was 7 days before our 10-year anniversary. We knew we could get least 250 people, because I had that in my clientele base. Between my party planner, Jackson, who also takes care of my concierge services for my clientele and Susan who takes care of my P.R., we figured if we could get 250, we're good.

"Probably 3 days before the actual party, we used Facebook to put the word out there, and then *FD Lux* and *Paper City* (local print media) wanted to be exclusive media sponsors of the party. We figured our brand was strong enough that if we could get a media sponsor, we could also get a liquor sponsor. And then we got a high-end restaurant that wanted to sponsor the food. So we ended up getting all these things for free for the party." Benny asked all of the sponsors to invite their guests and clients.

"The place looked like a club, but you're sitting with a bunch of exotic cars and pretty people. It was phenomenal. There's pictures of it still on Facebook. We had Moet (champaigne) in the front and Belvedere [liqueur] in the rear. We had a DJ. We had strobe lights. Each light changed to the beat of the music. And every car in my parking lot was spotlighted.

339

"The party swelled to 600 people in this building. We made the *Dallas Morning News*, because the party started at 6:30 and by 6:45 there was a line a half mile long, down to the Royal Lane stop light. We had people who parked in the parking lot and just walked down, because the parking line wasn't moving fast enough, even with our valet. That was the most amazing part. The fact that so many people could fit in here, and the fact that they stayed.

"With our social media, there's where we got people to start talking about it and seeing us more. Most people don't ever get to touch a Mercedes. When we had our party, I let you sit in it. I let the car sell itself. People had their pictures taken inside the car and put them on Facebook. They changed their profiles to having people seeing them sitting in a Lamborghini or a Bentley. So they get asked, 'Where did you get a Bentley?' And they say, 'I was at Benny Black's party,' and then I became viral over Facebook.

"We have people still saying it was one of the best parties they've been to, mainly because of the mix of people. In Dallas, certain people only go to certain scenes that they travel and move around to. But somehow, because I had so many different people that were helping me to market, we had people from all different grades of parties and events, which I hadn't seen before. I thought that was the best. We had young and old. We had old money that I didn't think even got out to events, including some socialites that had been around Dallas for a long time."

The party created both an immediate and a long-term buzz for the company. Through these types of connections, innovations, and effective combinations of the Internet, social media, word-of-mouth, and exciting events and offers, the future looks bright for Benny Black and Platinum Motorcars.[1]

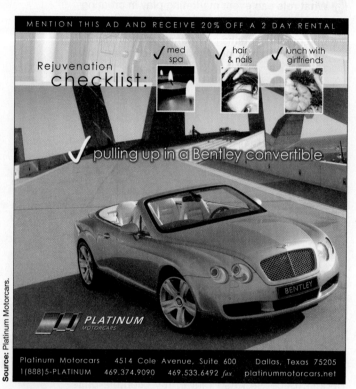

MENTION THIS AD AND RECEIVE 20% OFF A 2 DAY RENTAL

Rejuvenation **checklist:**
✓ med spa   ✓ hair & nails   ✓ lunch with girlfriends

✓ pulling up in a Bentley convertible

PLATINUM MOTORCARS

Platinum Motorcars   4514 Cole Avenue, Suite 600   Dallas, Texas 75205
1(888)5-PLATINUM   469.374.9090   469.533.6492 *fax*   platinummotorcars.net

Source: Platinum Motorcars.

▲ An advertisement for Platinum Motorcars promoting a Bentley convertible.

OVERVIEW

The traditional promotions mix consists of advertising, sales promotions, personal selling, and public relations efforts. At this point in the textbook, the first three elements in the mix have been presented. This chapter covers the fourth element—public relations. Sponsorship and event programs are also examined.

Public relations efforts, sponsorships, and event programs are part of the overall IMC approach. The same unified message appears in every marketing endeavor, from the appearance of the company's letterhead and stationery to advertisements, promotional items, information in press releases, and in any sponsorship program. Making sure that each component of a firm's IMC plan speaks with one voice remains the goal. Extending this objective to public relations and sponsorships will be an important task for the marketing team.

This chapter begins with a discussion of the nature of a public relations function within an integrated marketing plan. Second, sponsorship programs and event marketing tactics are outlined to show how the company can make quality contacts with existing customers, new prospects, vendors, and others. Successful positive public relations and sponsorship programs enhance the firm's image and its brands become better known, because they are perceived more favorably in the marketplace.

PUBLIC RELATIONS

In Hollywood, one well-worn phrase is "There's no such thing as bad publicity." This may be true for a bad-boy actor trying to get his name out to the public; however, in the world of marketing and communications bad publicity is *worse* than no publicity. Many business organizations spend countless hours fending off negative press while trying to develop positive and noticeable messages and themes.

The **public relations (PR) department** manages publicity and other communications with every group in contact with the company. Some of the functions performed by the public relations department are similar to those provided by the marketing department. Others are quite different. Often, the public relations department stays separate from the marketing department. The two may cooperate with and consult each other, yet each has a unique role.

Some marketing experts argue that public relations should be part of the marketing department, just as advertising, trade promotions, and consumer promotions are under the jurisdiction of the marketing manager. Others suggest that public relations activities are different and cannot operate effectively within a marketing department. Instead, a member of the public relations department should serve as a consultant to the marketing department. Still others contend that a new division, called the "department of communications," should be created to oversee both marketing and public relations activities.

Internal Versus External Public Relations

The first major decision company leaders make concerning public relations is who will handle the various activities. They can be managed by an internal public relations officer or department. Other companies hire public relations firms to complete special projects or all public relations functions. When a company retains a public relations agency, normally an internal company employee takes charge of internal public relations, because most public relations firms deal only with external publics.

The decision criteria used in selecting advertising agencies can be applied to selecting a public relations firm. Developing a trusting relationship with the public relations agency and carefully spelling out what the firm expects from the agency are high priorities.

Public Relations Tools

A number of tools are available to the public relations department. These include company newsletters, internal messages, public relations releases, correspondences with stockholders, annual reports, and various special events. Even the bulletin board in the company's break room can convey messages to internal stakeholders.

Capturing hits will be one common goal of a public relations firm. A **hit** is the mention of a company's name in a news story. Hits can be positive, negative, or neutral in terms of the impact on a firm. Each hit improves that chance that consumers will see the name of a company in a news-related context, which can increase brand or company awareness. This may be true; however, the agency also considers the type of image being portrayed. It may be a more prudent strategy to seek fewer hits and to make sure that each one projects the company in a positive light that also reinforces the firm's IMC theme.

When employing a public relations firm, the agency's personnel should be familiar with the client's IMC approach.

1 What is the relationship between public relations and the marketing activities performed by a company?

▼ A major decision company leaders make is who should handle the public relations activities.

Source: Getty Images–Thinkstock.

FIGURE 13.1 ▶
Public Relations Functions

- Identify internal and external stakeholders
- Assess the corporate reputation
- Audit corporate social responsibility
- Create positive image-building activities
- Prevent or reduce Image damage

Then, members of the public relations firm can work on ideas that reinforce the theme. Special events, activities, and news releases may be developed to strengthen the company voice.

❷ How can the public relations functions help to build better relationships with all internal and external stakeholders?

PUBLIC RELATIONS FUNCTIONS

Public relations activities are not standard marketing functions. The marketing department concentrates on customers and the channel members en route to those customers, such as wholesalers and retail outlets. In contrast, the public relations department focuses on a variety of internal and external stakeholders, including employees, stockholders, public interest groups, the government, and society as a whole.

Figure 13.1 displays five key public relations functions. These tasks are completed by public relations personnel, whether they are internal employees or members of a public relations company hired to perform those functions.

IDENTIFYING STAKEHOLDERS

Every recipient of a company communications is important. Any constituent who makes contact with a company should receive a clear, unified response. A **stakeholder** is a person or group who has a vested interest in the organization's activities. Vested interests include:

- Profits paid as common stock dividends
- Loan repayments that a lending institution seeks to receive
- Sales to the company or purchases made from the company
- Wages paid to employees
- Community well-being
- A special-interest topic

In essence, a wide variety of items can cause people or other companies to believe they hold a stake in the firm's activities. Stakeholders become targets for public relations communications.

To understand the nature of public relations programs, the public relations agency begins by identifying the publics that make contact with the company. Figure 13.2 identifies the primary internal and external stakeholders that the public relations department monitors.

Communications to each of these stakeholder groups are crucial. To ensure consistency, the company develops a clear communication strategy that fits with the IMC plan and corporate image. The overall message to each stakeholder should be the same. Then, each message can be tailored to meet the different expectations of the various audiences. By customizing the content, style, and channel of communication, each stakeholder group receives a message that best resonates with it, yet it remains consistent with other messages.

FIGURE 13.2 ▶
Stakeholders

- Employees
- Unions
- Shareholders
- Channel members
- Customers
- Media
- Local community
- Financial community
- Government
- Special-interest groups

In addition to sending communications to individual stakeholders, the public relations department closely monitors the actions and opinions of each group. When changes in attitudes, new views, or serious concerns develop, the public relations department should be ready to respond. The public relations department will be responsible for making certain all communications to each of these publics remain consistent with the firm's message and image.

Internal Stakeholders

Company leaders know the value of quality internal communications. Employees provide a powerful channel of communication to people outside the organization. They can either enhance or damage a firm's reputation. What employees say to others has a much higher level of credibility than what a company says about itself. Word-of-mouth communications, even informal statements by employees, impact purchasing and investing decisions.[2]

Employees receive a constant stream of information from the company. The same holds true for other internal stakeholders, such as corporate shareholders and labor unions. Many of these individuals are away from the marketing and public relations departments. They should still be aware of what the company seeks to achieve with the IMC program, even if this means presenting only basic information. Those closest to the marketing department, such as employees serving customers, will be more acutely aware of the nature of the IMC plan, including how the company's message theme should be transmitted to constituents.

The Motorola advertisement shown in this section states that the company's "Wireless Communications Centers help you stay connected." Employees who are aware of Motorola's theme communicate the same message when dealing with customers, vendors, and other publics.

To communicate effectively with employees, the public relations department works closely with the human resource (HR) department. Publications and communications aimed at employees should be consistent with the image and message that the firm espouses to customers and others. When a firm advertises that its employees are always ready to assist customers, the public relations team makes sure employees are aware of the message. Employee behaviors should be consistent with the advertising theme being conveyed to customers. The HR department looks for and hires workers who are attracted to that approach. Performance appraisals and rewards can be structured to favor those who buy into the company's IMC approach. This emphasis on providing quality information about company activities extends to every public relations event and sponsorship program.

External Stakeholders

Overseeing external communications continues to be a daunting task, because the company has little or no influence over how publics perceive organizational activities. External stakeholders include groups such as the media, the local community, the financial community, the government, and special-interest groups. The company has no control over what these groups say or how information about the company will be interpreted. The public relations agency continually disseminates positive information and quickly reacts to any negative publicity or complaints.

A totally integrated communications program accounts for all types of messages that an organization delivers to internal and external stakeholders. Every contact point provides the opportunity for a quality message to be sent. The marketing department tends to create contact points with customers and potential customers. To complement this effort, the public relations department deals with the myriad of contact points that are not created or planned, yet may be just as critical. An unplanned contact point such as a news

Source: Courtesy of Motorola, Inc./Personal Communications Sector. © 1999.

▲ Communications by the employees of Motorola should match the message conveyed in its advertising.

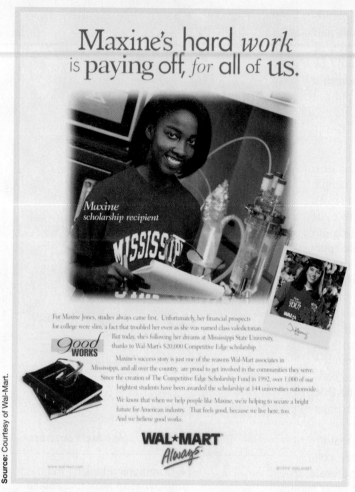

▲ A Wal-Mart advertisement directed to employees, the local community, and other stakeholders.

story or an individual talking to an employee of the firm at a social gathering allows the firm to build a positive image or minimize the impact of any negative messages that are circulating. Dealing with unplanned contact points will be challenging. They cannot always be anticipated. Constant monitoring of what goes on around the firm is one key to keeping constituents as satisfied as possible while insulating the firm from negative publicity.

ASSESSING CORPORATE REPUTATION

A corporation's reputation is both fragile and valuable. Well-received corporate and brand names can enhance businesses during the good times and protect them when a crisis or problem occurs. Consumer decisions regarding which brands to purchase are influenced by a company's reputation. People also decide where to invest based on corporate reputations. Potential employees choose where to apply and work based on an organization's reputation.

In one survey, two-thirds of those who responded believed that most businesses would take advantage of consumers if they thought they would not get caught.[3] Corporate scandals, accounting fraud, and the recent economic and financial crisis have reduced the confidence consumers have in businesses. A *McKinsey Quarterly* survey reported that 82 percent of senior executives said public trust in corporations has deteriorated.[4]

People remain leery of big business, suspicious of business motives, and continue to distrust most companies. Perceptions of corporate reputations by external publics are at an all-time low. As one homemaker stated, "I'm very disappointed in how money can rob the goodness in people." She went on to state that putting money under her mattress would be a safer place than investing in today's corporations.[5]

Assessing and managing a company's reputation will be as important as promoting its products. Yet, with all that is at stake, fewer than half of the companies in the United States have someone assigned to monitor corporate reputation. This means that many company leaders have little idea what consumers, investors, employees, and the public think about the firm. A company cannot effectively pursue a public relations program when company leaders do not know what people believe about the organization.

Assessment begins when surveys and interviews are conducted to reveal perceptions of an organization. These efforts can be completed internally or performed by an outside company, such as a public relations firm. Internal views of the corporation's reputation as well as opinions held by those outside the company are examined.

AUDITING CORPORATE SOCIAL RESPONSIBILITY

Corporate social responsibility is the obligation an organization has to be ethical, accountable, and reactive to the needs of society. Figure 13.3 outlines some of the general areas in which firms can become more ethical and reactive to society's needs. Globalization and increased pressures from the public for corporate transparency have led to an increasing emphasis on social responsibility in some circles. According to Bradley K. Googins, director of the Boston College Center for Corporate Citizenship, "Quality used to be the difference between brands, then it was technology. Now, it really comes back to

> **Image-Destroying Activities**
> - Discrimination
> - Harassment
> - Pollution
> - Misleading communications
> - Deceptive communications
> - Offensive communications
>
> **Image-Building Activities**
> - Empowerment of employees
> - Charitable contributions
> - Sponsoring local events
> - Selling enviromentally safe products
> - Outplacement programs
> - Supporting community events

◀ **FIGURE 13.3**
Examples of Activities that Affect a Company's Image

reputation. It's really the question of who you want to do business with and that relationship with the consumer and the product."[6]

Business experts agree that socially responsible firms are more likely to thrive and survive in the long term. Companies engaged in positive activities generate quality publicity and engender customer loyalty. Firms that work to eliminate unfair practices, pollution, harassment, and other negative activities are more likely to stay out of court, and the company suffers fewer negative word-of-mouth comments by unhappy employees or consumers. Managing these activities properly can lead to a more positive corporate image.

A corporate social responsibility audit is usually undertaken by the organization's management team in conjunction with department managers. Often, external agencies provide guidelines. A social responsibility audit should be designed to make sure the organization has clear-cut ethical guidelines for employees to follow and that the company serves the interests of all publics. Guidelines include use of a corporate or professional code of ethics, specifying activities that would be construed as being unethical, and statements about the positive activities a company can pursue. Many firms also offer access to "ethics hotlines," where employees can call or e-mail to discuss specific ethical dilemmas.

A firm found to be deficient during a social responsibility audit should take clear steps to resolve the problems. Firms without codes of ethics start by setting up committees or groups to develop them. Companies without other ethical guidelines move quickly to establish them.

The public relations department makes sure internal publics are aware of a corporation's social responsibility efforts. The department then informs the general public about these activities while seeking to enhance the firm's image.

3 How can the positive, image-building programs that are commonly used by companies as part of the public relations effort build customer loyalty and brand image?

▼ This General Mills advertisement thanks both customers and employees.

CREATING POSITIVE IMAGE-BUILDING ACTIVITIES

In an effort to positively influence the views that consumers and other stakeholders have about a company, many firms engage in cause-related marketing and green marketing. These planned events draw positive attention to the organization as a solid corporate citizen, one committed to social responsibility. The public relations department then sends out messages in the form of press releases and holds press conferences to highlight these positive, image-building activities.

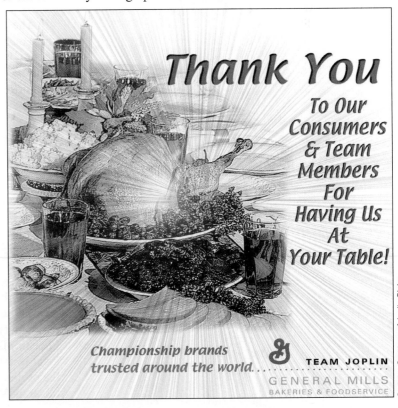

Source: Courtesy of Joplin Globe.

Cause-Related Marketing

Cause-related marketing is a program whereby a firm ties a marketing program to a charity in order to generate goodwill. American businesses pay over $1.5 billion each year for the right to use a nonprofit organization's name or logo in company advertising and marketing programs.[7] This type of partnership agreement between a nonprofit cause and a for-profit business assumes that consumers will purchase from companies that seek to support a good cause.

Many times brand parity exists for goods and services. Customers perceive that there are few notable differences between products and the companies that sell them. Marketers engage in cause-related marketing to develop stronger ties and to move consumers, as well as businesses, toward brand loyalty. A survey by Cone Communications and Roper Starch Worldwide revealed that:

- 78 percent of consumers are more likely to purchase a brand associated with a cause they care about.
- 54 percent would be willing to pay more for a brand that is associated with a cause they care about.
- 66 percent would switch brands to support a particular cause.
- 84 percent indicated that cause-related marketing creates a more positive image of a company.[8]

In the past, some companies donated to causes with little thought to the impact or benefit of such gifts. These philanthropic efforts were expected of big business. Today, most companies want some type of benefit. Although company leaders believe a charity is worthwhile, supporting that charity ought to, in some way, result in a tangible benefit. Otherwise the company should not give support. Possible benefits include:

- Additional customers
- Increased profits
- Consumer goodwill for the future
- Better relations with governmental agencies
- Reduced negative public opinion

These benefits lead companies to get involved. Relationships that do not yield positive benefits to the business sponsor do not last long. In choosing a cause, the marketing team focuses on issues that relate to the company's business. Supporting these efforts makes the activity more credible to consumers. When the company supports an unrelated cause, consumers may feel that the business is merely trying to benefit from the nonprofit's reputation. This may lead some consumers to stop buying the company's products or to believe the company wishes to cover up unethical behaviors. Many consumers have become even more skeptical about the motives behind giving to various charities. Even though most people understand that a business must benefit from the relationship, they still tend to develop negative views when they believe that the business exploits a relationship with a nonprofit.

When a fit exists, positive reactions emerge. Recently, Kraft Foods' Triscuit brand crackers partnered with the nonprofit Urban Farming to create 50 community-based home farms. The first garden opened in Los Angeles, with additional community farms located in Dallas, Detroit, Philadelphia, Phoenix, Tampa, and other cities. The farms are maintained by local residents and community volunteers. Information about the projects and tips for starting home gardens can be found at the brand's microsite (**www.triscuit.com/homefarming**).

▼ A Wal-Mart advertisement highlighting a social cause.

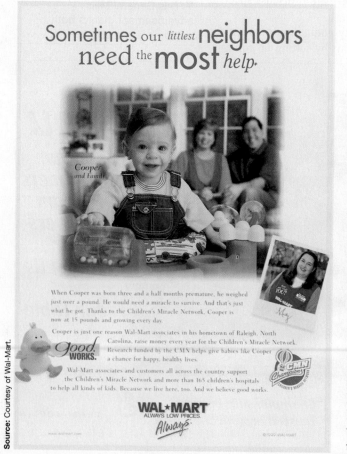

Sometimes our *littlest* neighbors need *the* most *help.*

Cooper and family

When Cooper was born three and a half months premature, he weighed just over a pound. He would need a miracle to survive. And that's just what he got. Thanks to the Children's Miracle Network, Cooper is now at 15 pounds and growing every day.

Cooper is just one reason Wal-Mart associates in his hometown of Raleigh, North Carolina, raise money every year for the Children's Miracle Network. Research funded by the CMN helps give babies like Cooper a chance for happy, healthy lives.

Wal-Mart associates and customers all across the country support the Children's Miracle Network and more than 165 children's hospitals to help all kinds of kids. Because we live here, too. And we believe good works.

good WORKS.

WAL★MART
ALWAYS LOW PRICES.
Always

The Web site provides information about what vegetables and herbs to plant and the best planting dates based on a consumer's ZIP code. In addition to promoting the community farms by printing the program's Web site address on Triscuit boxes, Kraft Foods also attached free basil and dill herb seed cards to 4 million boxes of Triscuits. Kraft Foods supported the Triscuit home farming initiative with public relations releases, print ads, banner ads about gardening on women's general interest Web sites, messages on packages, blogs, and tweets through the Kraft Foods Twitter account.[9]

Benefits to Nonprofit Organizations

Cause-related marketing also assists nonprofit organizations. Competition has increased in both the business world and the nonprofit world. An increasing number of nonprofit organizations compete for contributions and gifts. Strategic relationships with businesses can boost contributions to a nonprofit organization considerably. A General Mills Yoplait campaign raised over $10 million for the Susan G. Komen Breast Cancer Foundation. Featuring the slogan, "Save Lids to Save Lives," General Mills donated 10 cents for each Yoplait lid that was returned by consumers.[10] The relationship resulted in direct increases in revenues for Yoplait and positive publicity for the foundation.

Most of the time corporations select the nonprofits they want to support. Occasionally, the reverse occurs. Alice Berkner, founder of the International Bird Rescue Research Center, obtained a small grant to test major dish soaps for cleaning birds harmed by oil spills. Procter & Gamble's Dawn detergent worked the best. When first approached by Berkner about supporting the cause, P&G turned her down. Then, during the 1989 Exxon Valdez oil spill, volunteers used Dawn on the oil-covered birds to remove the black crude. Media coverage was extensive. Now Dawn donates around $100,000 annually to the research center. A television commercial created by Kaplan Thaler Group shows a baby duck, penguin, and seal being washed by Dawn. There is no voice-over, just the song "Wash Away" sung by Joe Purdy. The copy on the screen states that Dawn has helped save thousands of animals caught in oil spills.[11]

A complex linkage exists between public relations and cause-related marketing. To benefit from cause-related marketing, company leaders want publicity. Yet, if the company publicizes too much, people think the cause is only being used for commercial gain. In a survey of British consumers, the vast majority said a company should spend funds on communications about cause-related efforts. The same survey indicated that two-thirds also said the amount spent should not be significant. The majority of those surveyed said their purchase decisions are influenced by the causes a company supports. This makes informing people about what a company is doing important; however, doing so involves walking a thin line between publicizing and what might be viewed as corporate self-aggrandizement.[12]

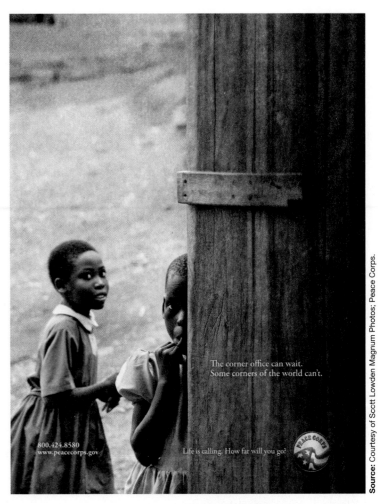

The corner office can wait.
Some corners of the world can't.

800.424.8580
www.peacecorps.gov

Life is calling. How far will you go?

PEACE CORPS

Source: Courtesy of Scott Lowden Magnum Photos; Peace Corps.

▲ The Peace Corps is a social cause supported by a number of companies.

Green Marketing and Pro-Environmental Activities

Green marketing is the development and promotion of products that are environmentally safe. Most consumers favor green marketing. One recent survey indicated that 58 percent of Americans try to save electricity, 46 percent recycle newspapers, 45 percent return bottles or cans, and 23 percent buy products made from or packaged in recycled materials.[13]

Your daily work will be anything but a chore.

800.424.8580
www.peacecorps.gov

Life is calling. How far will you go?

▲ This Peace Corps advertisement asks young adults to join the organization.

Although consumers support green marketing and environmentally safe products, actual purchases of such products only occur when all things are considered equal. Most consumers are not willing to sacrifice price, quality, convenience, availability, or performance for the sake of the environment. According to a recent study, about 40 percent of consumers said they did not purchase green products because they believed they were inferior.[14]

To benefit from green marketing, the company identifies market segments that are most attracted to environmentally-friendly products. In the U.S., consumers can be divided into five segments based on their propensity to use green products and their attitudes about environmental issues. Only 9 percent of American consumers are classified as "True Blue Greens," and another 6 percent are classified as "Greenback Greens." The True Blue Greens are active environmentalists who support environmentally safe products and shop for green brands. The Greenback Greens purchase environmentally safe products, but are not politically active. The other three groups, Sprouts, Grousers, and Basic Browns, are less committed or not committed to environmental protections.[15]

Company leaders carefully choose the green marketing strategy that matches the target market. In making the decision about the degree of emphasis to place on green marketing, managers ask three questions. First, what percentage of the company's customer base fits into the green marketing segments? Second, can the brand or company be differentiated from the competition along green lines in such a way that it can become a competitive advantage? Third, will the company's current target audience be alienated by adopting a green marketing approach?

Promoting Green Activities

Almost all firms say they are pro-environment and provide information on company Web sites about environmental activities. The amount of effort given to publicize these activities varies widely.[16] For example, Coca-Cola tries to protect the environment, but most people are unaware of the company's efforts. Coca-Cola has invested in various recycling programs and recyclable package designs. The activities are not publicized, because of concerns that doing so might reduce the product's appeal to some of the company's audience or hurt sales.

Promoting the direct, tangible benefits of a product first, with the environmental benefits presented as secondary factors, can be an alternate approach. The Toyota Prius was launched with an emphasis on fuel efficiency. Consumers were told they would spend less on gas. The fact that the Prius was an environmentally advanced, fuel-efficient hybrid vehicle was mentioned, but not stressed. The idea was that strong environmentalists would believe buying a hybrid car is important. For those who were not strong environmentalists, it did not matter, because the car delivered fuel efficiency.

Starbucks offers another example. Renewable energy now accounts for about 20 percent of the power used in its company-owned stores. For this initiative, Starbucks was named one of the Environmental Protection Agency's Top 25 Green Power Partners. The citation is posted on Starbucks' Web site, but it is buried deep in the social responsibility section.[17]

For some companies, environmental activities are fully integrated into the company's business design and marketing approach. This occurs when the primary customer base consists of True Blue Greens and the Green-back Greens. Examples of these types of companies include The Body Shop, Patagonia, Honest Tea, and Seventh Generation. For Honest Tea, social responsibility is embedded in every company activity, from the manufacturing process to the marketing of products. Honest Tea uses biodegradable tea bags, organic ingredients, and community partnerships. Honest Tea's marketing program focuses on concern for and support of environmental and social issues.

Seventh Generation has produced natural-ingredient cleaning products for 21 years. Although the company is well known among environmentally conscious shoppers, including its 27,000 fans on Facebook, few people had ever heard about the brand. To increase awareness, Seventh Generation hired Minneapolis-based Carmichael Lynch to develop a series of print and television commercials about the brand's safety and green ingredients. Print ads appeared in *Good Housekeeping* and *Parents*. TV ads were aired on Bravo, the Food Network, the USA Network, as well as on the *Today Show* and *Ellen*. Video preroll and banner ads appeared on Web sites such as Hulu, iVillage, Yahoo!, Facebook, Lifetime, and Good Housekeeping. The campaign's goal was to educate consumers about the products and the importance of protecting the environment.[18]

Source: Thinkstock Royalty Free.

▲ Companies such as Honest Tea and Seventh Generation have demonstrated a concern for the environment.

Greenwashing

Most business leaders believe their companies should be involved in protecting the environment and creating green products; however, the marketing emphasis varies. Some companies that have claimed to make green products have been exposed by bloggers who point out that the efforts are not truly green. Faking green, called **greenwashing**, can damage a company's reputation when such information is posted on blogs and communicated to consumers. Each company's marketing team decides whether green marketing will be a central part of the IMC message and how to position the company in terms of the environment. Honesty and transparency are important.

PREVENTING OR REDUCING IMAGE DAMAGE

 4 What steps can companies take to prevent or reduce image damage when negative events occur?

One important public relations function, **damage control**, is reacting to negative events caused by a company error, consumer grievances, or unjustified or exaggerated negative press. Corporate and brand images are quickly damaged by negative publicity and events. A strong company image that took years to build can be quickly destroyed. ExxonMobil continues to suffer from the negative publicity surrounding the1989 *Exxon Valdez* accident. British Petroleum (BP) is likely to suffer the same fate from the 2010 spill in the Gulf of Mexico.

Bad news travels quickly and hits hard. The Jet Blue incident in which passengers were essentially forced to sit in a plane on the ground for many hours due to bad weather quickly damaged the company's reputation for quality customer service. Company leaders tried to quickly respond in order to limit the harm to Jet Blue's image.

Not all negative publicity is generated by the media. Sometimes negative publicity comes from word-of-mouth communication from customers, employees, or other individuals connected with the company. With the Internet, bad experiences and negative comments can be posted and spread to thousands in a very short time through social networks, blogs, and Twitter.

FIGURE 13.4 ▶
Damage-Control Strategies

- Proactive Strategies
  Entitlings
  Enhancements

- Reactive Strategies
  Internet Interventions
  Crisis management programs
  Apology strategy
  Impression management techniques

Damage control applies to two situations. The first occurs when the firm has made an error or has caused legitimate consumer or public grievances. The second takes place when unjustified or exaggerated negative press appears. Defending an organization's image and handling damage control takes two forms: (1) proactive prevention strategies and (2) reactive damage-control strategies (see Figure 13.4).

Proactive Prevention Strategies

Proactive prevention means that rather than waiting for harmful publicity to appear and then reacting, many firms charge certain employees with minimizing the effects of any future bad press in advance. These approaches may prevent negative publicity from emerging in the first place. Two proactive prevention techniques are entitlings and enhancements.[19] **Entitlings** are attempts to claim responsibility for positive outcomes of events. **Enhancements** are attempts to increase the impact of the desirable outcome of an event in the eyes of the public.

Entitling is being used when a firm associates its name with a positive event. For example, being the official sponsor of a U.S. Olympic team that wins a gold medal attaches the company's name to the athletic achievements of people who do not work for the firm, yet the firm can claim responsibility for some aspect of their successes.[20]

Enhancements occur when the marketing or public relations department suggests that something relatively small is a big deal. Many products that are fat free create the impression that they are diet foods. In fact, many fat-free products have just as many calories as do those that contain fat. Still, a fat-free label might convince customers that the company is trying to help them by offering healthy food that will allow them to watch their weight.

Reactive Damage-Control Strategies

Company leaders often must react to unforeseen events. They cannot anticipate every possible contingency. In these instances, managers work diligently to blunt the effects of unwanted bad publicity by every means possible. Crisis management and other techniques can help the firm cope with circumstances that threaten its image. Reactive damage-control strategies include Internet interventions, crisis management programs, apology strategies, and impression management techniques.

Internet Interventions

It is possible to combat negative online word-of-mouth with **Internet interventions**. Many new forums for consumers to share negative word-of-mouth and spread bad experiences have emerged, including e-mail, social networks, blogs, and Twitter. Consumers from around the world can share horror stories about companies or products. Individuals can say anything online, even when it unfairly portrays various industries, companies, or brands.

These outlets create many venues for people to vent emotions, which can be devastating to a company's reputation. Companies such as Ford, Pepsi, and Southwest Airlines use software and assign employees to monitor Internet postings, blogs, and tweets. Even with these technological tools, monitoring everything said about a company remains a daunting task. It can involve hundreds of posts per day. Employees must quickly decide which to investigate further. Marcus Schmidt, a senior marketing manager for Microsoft suggests, "If you start seeing a lot of people retweeting it, then you know to pay attention."

Last year, Coke's software identified a Twitter post by a frustrated consumer who was not able to redeem a prize from the MyCoke rewards program. The consumer's profile indicated that he had more than 10,000 followers. Adam Brown, Coke's head of social media, posted an apology on the individual's Twitter profile and offered to help. The consumer received the prize. He later changed his Twitter avatar to a photo of himself holding a bottle of Coke. According to Brown, "We're getting to a point if you're not responding, you're not being seen as an authentic type of brand."[21]

Not every activity warrants a formal reaction. Still, monitoring the Internet keeps the company's leadership informed about what people are saying and thinking.

Crisis Management

A company can either accept the blame for an event or offer an apology or refute the charges in a forceful manner in a **crisis management** program. A crisis may be viewed as a problem or an opportunity. Oftentimes, a crisis contains the potential to improve the firm's position and image.

When PepsiCo encountered claims that hypodermic needles were being found in its products, the management team quickly responded with photographs and video demonstrating that such an occurrence was impossible, because the bottles and cans are upside down before being filled with any soft drink. Next, footage of a con artist slipping a needle into a bottle was shown. This fast and powerful answer eliminated the negative publicity, and Pepsi was able to make a strong statement about the safety of its bottling methods.

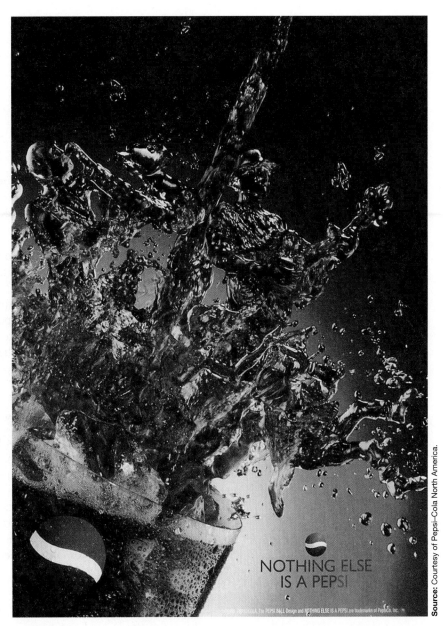

NOTHING ELSE IS A PEPSI

Source: Courtesy of Pepsi-Cola North America.

▲ When reports surfaced of hypodermic needles in Pepsi products, Pepsi quickly reacted by showing the public how cans and bottles are filled.

Unfortunately, some company leaders manage only to make matters worse, as was the initial reaction of Toyota to quality problems with its vehicles. Continual denials of quality problems were not received well when new problems kept emerging. Many consumers became angry when it was revealed that Toyota was aware of the problems for a long time without seeking to correct them. Eventually, the president of Toyota Motors, Akio Toyoda, was summoned to Washington to testify before the House Committee on Oversight and Government Reform.

Realizing its image was quickly eroding and the outcry against the company was building, Toyota launched a full-scale public relations campaign using print, television, and social media networks. Full-page newspaper ads and several television spots were quickly created in which Toyota announced a temporary halt in production followed by an apologetic, but reassuring, message that Toyota would pull through the crisis.

Toyota's errors in handling mainstream media were apparent to many marketing experts. The company did manage social media outlets more effectively. Toyota created a social media response room staffed with individuals who monitored online conversations and responded to consumer concerns. Consumers received answers on Toyota's four Facebook pages and Twitter. Finding brand loyalists online, Toyota asked if they could repost their tweets, blogs, and videos on the Toyota social media outlets. The company

FIGURE 13.5 ▶
Elements of an Apology Strategy

1. An expression of guilt, embarrassment, or regret

2. A statement recognizing the inappropriate behavior and acceptance of sanctions for wrong behavior

3. A rejection of the inappropriate behavior

4. Approval of the appropriate behavior and a promise not to engage in inappropriate behavior

5. An offer of compensation or penance to correct the wrong

then created a series of videos with customers and employees telling their stories that were posted to its YouTube channel and other social media sites. The social media PR effort may have helped save Toyota's brand image, at least in the online world.[22]

Apology Strategies

An **apology strategy** is another reactive form of crisis management and damage control. When an investigation reveals that the firm was at fault, an apology should be offered quickly. An apology contains the five elements shown in Figure 13.5.[23]

Apologies are most often used in situations in which the violation is minor or in which the firm or person cannot deny responsibility. It can become an effective strategy for creating a strong emotional bond with the public. Consumer may not remain angry with a company that admits a mistake. When customers believe the apology was sincere and heartfelt, they normally forgive the company and feel more positively toward the company afterward.

Impression Management

Trying to project a certain type of image is **impression management**, or "the conscious or unconscious attempt to control images that are projected in real or imagined social interactions."[24] In order to maintain or enhance an image, individuals and corporations attempt to influence the identities they display to others. Each can be projected in a manner that maximizes positive characteristics while minimizing any negative elements.

Any event that threatens a person's image or a company's desired identity creates a predicament. When faced with one, concerted efforts are made to reduce or minimize the negative consequences. When the predicament cannot be avoided or concealed, then an individual or company engages in any remedial activity that reduces the potentially harmful consequences, including:

- Expressions of innocence
- Excuses
- Justifications
- Other explanations

An *expression of innocence* approach means company leaders provide information designed to convince others (clients, the media, and the government) that the company was not associated with the event that caused the predicament. In other words, they say, "We did not cause this to happen. Someone (or something) else did."

Excuses are explanations designed to convince the public that the firm and its leaders are not responsible for the predicament or that it could not have been foreseen. Thus, they should not be held accountable for the event that created the predicament. They say, "It was an act of God. It was totally unavoidable. It was the random act of an individual."

Justifications involve using logic designed to reduce the degree of negativity associated with the predicament. Making the event seem minor or trivial is one method. Making the argument that the firm had to proceed in the way it did ("We pollute because if we don't we'll be out of business, and our employees will lose their jobs") is another form of justification.

Other explanations may be created to persuade individuals that the cause of the predicament does not truly represent what the firm or individual is really like. In other words, the case was the exception rather than the rule, and customers should not judge the firm too harshly. You will hear comments such as "This was a singular incident, and not indicative of the way we do business."[25]

Each company's management team, marketing department, and public relations specialist should be acutely aware of the speed with which events can cause great damage to a firm's image. Both proactive and reactive measures should be taken to make sure the firm survives negative publicity without major damage.

SPONSORSHIPS

To build brand loyalty and other positive feelings toward a company, many marketing leaders utilize sponsorships and event marketing. These programs make it possible to meet with prospects, customers, vendors, and others in unique situations. People who attend sponsored activities or special events already have favorable feelings about the activity taking place. These positive attitudes are easily transferred to a company that has provided funding.[26]

Sponsorship marketing means that the company pays money to sponsor someone, some group, or something that is part of an activity. A firm can sponsor a practically unending list of groups, individuals, activities, and events. For years, firms sponsored everything from local Little League baseball and soccer teams to national musical tours, NASCAR drivers, and sports stadiums.

Forms of Sponsorships

In North America, approximately $16.3 billion is spent each year on sponsorships and events.[27] Figure 13.6 provides a breakdown of the spending. Sports represent just over 71 percent of all sponsorships. Sporting events are highly popular and often attract large crowds. In addition to the audience attending the game or competition, many more watch on television. Popular athletes can be effective spokespersons for various products. If possible, the firm should be the exclusive sponsor of the person or team, which makes it easier to remember than when there are multiple sponsors.

Sponsorships were a major part of Ford's integrated advertising and marketing push for the Ford F-Series Super Duty pickup trucks. Although the integrated campaign includes television ads, print ads, and online chats, the central component of the campaign was the sponsorship of Toby Keith's concert tour, entitled "America's Toughest Tour." The Ford F-Series trucks were highly visible at the concerts, with truck-themed set pieces on stage and at least one F-Series truck actually on the stage. In addition to the concert tour, Ford also sponsored a Monster Jam truck show and individual professional bull riders. The company sponsors the Future Farmers of America, the American Quarter Horse Association, and the Dallas Cowboys.[28]

> **5** How can sponsorships be tied to public relations efforts to strengthen a customer base?

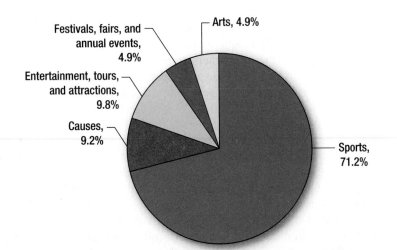

Festivals, fairs, and annual events, 4.9%
Arts, 4.9%
Entertainment, tours, and attractions, 9.8%
Causes, 9.2%
Sports, 71.2%

◀ **FIGURE 13.6**
Marketing Expenditures on Sponsorships and Events

Source: Allison Enright, "Events & Sponsorships," *2008 Marketing FactBook, Marketing News*, 42, no. 12 (July 15, 2008), p. 26.

At 24, I became the second youngest champion in NASCAR history. Here's another little-known fact. Of the 42 drivers who chase me at more than 200 mph, most don't get enough calcium. My advice? Drink three glasses of milk a day. Preferably while standing still.

MILK
Where's *your* mustache?"

▲ In addition to milk, notice all of the corporate sponsors on Jeff Gordon's NASCAR uniform.

Speedo used sponsorships to build customer loyalty and capture over 60 percent of the competitive swimwear market in the United States. Swimmers wearing Speedo's revolutionary LZR Racer swimwear design broke 38 world records. The full-body suit was created with the help of NASA and is worn by competitive swimmers all over the world. By sponsoring the U.S. Olympic trials and athletes, including Michael Phelps, Speedo's market share grew rapidly until it became the swimwear brand of choice for even noncompetitive swimmers.[29]

Some organizations have moved away from sports sponsorships toward more cultural events, such as classical music groups and jazz bands, visual art exhibits by noted painters, dance troupes, and actors for various theater performances. Cultural sponsorships are not the best match for every firm. They are most effective for products sold to affluent consumers. Consequently, financial institutions are primary sponsors of these types of performers and performances. In the past, many institutions provided funds without receiving much recognition. Now these philanthropic efforts are being leveraged by having the name of the company strongly associated with the cultural activity. This includes printing the name of the firm on programs and regularly mentioning the brand or corporate name as being responsible for arranging for the artist to be present at the cultural event. Also, sponsors usually receive choice seats at performances that can be given to key clients.

Rather than sports or the arts, Coca-Cola, Ford, and AT&T chose to sponsor the popular television show *American Idol.* Each company paid $35 million for the right to be part of one of the most watched TV shows, to post online content, and to run off-air cobranded marketing programs. Ford featured its vehicles in music videos sung by the final 12 contestants. Ford also gave away a Ford Escape Hybrid to the top two finalists. Coca-Cola placed branded cups in the center on the judges' table. Coke graphics were also visible behind the contestants when they were being interviewed. AT&T benefited greatly from the sponsorship by being responsible for the text-message voting tabulations each week. AT&T also featured *Idol* downloads, ring tones, and videos of bad auditions and poor performances.[30]

The newest format is sponsoring bloggers. Colleen Padilla, a 33-year-old mother of two and author of the popular Web site Classy Mommy (**www.classymommy.com**), has reviewed nearly 1,500 products, including microwave dinners, Nintendo Wii, and baby clothes. Her site attracts 60,000 unique visitors every month. Companies are eager to send her products to test and, if she likes them, to post positive comments on the Web site. When she does not like an item, nothing will be posted. When a review is provided, Padilla tells her readers if the brand was sent to her. She also includes videos of brands, including Healthy Choice, which are labeled as "sponsored posts."

For some bloggers, such as Drew Bennett, product sponsorships have become a lucrative business. Bennett began with a photo-a-day blog that mushroomed into sponsored products at his site BenSpark.com. He has written more than 600 posts for companies such as X-Shot, a telescope camera extender. Bennett typically earns between $5.35 and $10 per post. Most product sponsors pay Bennett between 11 and 68 cents each time a reader moves from his site to the brand's site.

K-Mart used a similar approach to generate positive buzz. Through 800 blog posts and 3,200 Twitter messages, K-Mart reached 2.5 million people. The campaign began with six popular bloggers receiving a $500 gift card to shop at K-Mart and then writing about their experiences.[31]

Choosing Sponsorships

In choosing a sponsorship, the marketing team matches the event's audience profile with the company's target market. A firm sponsoring a singer at a music show attended mainly by women works best when the company's primary customers are female music lovers. Marketing executives also consider how the individual participant or group image relates to the firm's image. A contestant in an upscale event, such as a piano competition, may be sponsored by a tuxedo or formal gown company.

To maximize the benefits of a sponsorship effort, the company first defines the program's primary goals. These are integrated with the firm's overall IMC theme, so that the public can easily see the link between the person or group being sponsored, the activity, and the company involved. To achieve the maximum impact for the sponsorship, the message will be combined with other advertising and promotional efforts, such as a sampling program or a giveaway (T-shirts, caps, etc.). A sponsorship supported by additional marketing efforts has the best chance of accomplishing its objectives.

Sponsorship Objectives

It may be hard to measure the direct impact of a sponsorship program. Sponsorships can be designed to accomplish a variety of objectives. They can be designed to:

- Enhance a company's image.
- Increase a firm's visibility.
- Differentiate a company from its competitors.
- Showcase specific goods and services.
- Help a firm develop closer relationships with current and prospective customers.
- Sell excess inventory.

The Green Turtle restaurant built visibility and a positive image through the use of a sponsorship. The company sponsored Amelia's Ace of Hearts Ride to raise money for breast cancer. Approximately 200 of the 400 bike riders registered at the restaurant, and 300 people celebrated at an after-party in the restaurant. The event raised $28,000 for the charity. According to Leho Poldmae of The Green Turtle, "These events and sponsorships put the human aspect into marketing. They are much more powerful than ads in touching and reaching customers."[32]

The best sponsorship programs include methods of assessment. The marketing department follows up to make sure that the goals were achieved. In each sponsorship program, an attempt should be made to gather tangible evidence that the sponsorship was worthwhile.

Source: Courtesy of Newcomer, Morris & Young, Inc.

▲ Matching the audience profile with the company's target market is important when selecting sponsorships.

EVENT MARKETING

Event marketing is similar to sponsorship marketing. The major difference is that sponsorship marketing involves a person, group, or team. **Event marketing** involves a company in supporting a specific event. Event marketing and lifestyle marketing are closely related. Both typically include setting up a booth or display and maintaining a physical presence at an event.

Sponsoring the right event can provide a company with brand-name recognition and help develop closer ties with vendors and customers. Events can also help boost morale

6 What role can event marketing play in creating customer excitement and brand loyalty?

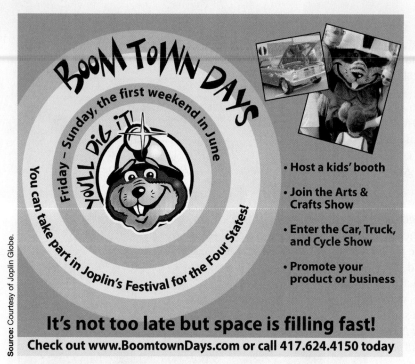

BOOM TOWN DAYS

Friday – Sunday, the first weekend in June

YoU'LL DiG iT!

You can take part in Joplin's Festival for the Four States!

• Host a kids' booth

• Join the Arts & Crafts Show

• Enter the Car, Truck, and Cycle Show

• Promote your product or business

It's not too late but space is filling fast!

Check out www.BoomtownDays.com or call 417.624.4150 today

▲ An advertisement for Boomtown Days seeking corporate sponsors.

for the employees who participate in or attend them. Sponsoring local events such as the Special Olympics provides a company with the potential to generate free publicity. These events can also be used to enhance the company's image in the local community.

As is the case with sponsorships, many event marketing programs feature sports. Other events are more related to lifestyles. A rodeo sponsored by Lee Jeans, a music concert put on by a local business, or a health fair conducted by a local hospital are all examples of event marketing.

Event marketing has proven to be especially successful with Hispanic consumers. It can be an excellent method of building brand awareness and building brand loyalty. According to Renata Franco of Cox Communications, "Hispanics are much more community-centered. Events do really well." When Cox Communications sponsors a Hispanic event, the company employs bilingual brand ambassadors who can personally speak to attendees.[33]

Several key steps are involved in preparing an event. Therefore, to ensure the maximum benefit from event sponsorships, companies should:

• Determine the objective(s) of the event.
• Match the event with the company's customers, vendors, and employees.
• Promote the event.
• Make sure the company is included in all event advertising and brochures.
• Track results.

Determining Objectives

Communication objectives should be outlined before becoming involved in an event. When rewarding customers is the objective, marketers look for events that major customers would enjoy. Some objectives are more internally oriented, especially those designed to increase employee involvement or to boost morale. These can be achieved by finding events internal members will like. Externally oriented objectives include helping the firm maintain its market share, building a stronger brand presence, enhancing the product or firm's image, or increasing sales.

Matching the Event to Publics

The event should match the firm's customers, vendors, or employees. Different companies have customers who are more likely to attend certain events. Vendors and employees may also favor different events.

Promoting the Event

Events are promoted through advertising and public relations releases. Special effort will be given to contacting interest groups that would benefit from the event. An event such as a local Special Olympics requires commercials, contacts with the press, and finding ways to reach parents and relatives of those who might participate.

Advertising at the Event

Event sponsors should insist on placement of the company's name and logo and other product information in every advertisement and brochure for the event. Many attendees of special events keep programs as souvenirs. Placing the sponsor's name and message on the program generates an advertisement with a longer lifespan. The sponsoring business can maximize brand-name exposure by connecting the firm's name with the event's marketing program. The marketing team works closely with the event management team to make sure the company's name receives prominent attention in all materials associated with the occasion.

Tracking Results

Some events turn out better than others for the sponsor. To determine the best events, the marketing team tracks results. In addition to sales, employees can monitor how many pieces of literature were given to attendees, the number of samples distributed, or the number of visitors to the sponsor's display booth. Further, marketing research can measure brand awareness before and after the event to see if any new level of awareness emerged.

Tracking results allows the business to evaluate the investment in the event. Company leaders and marketing managers then decide if sponsoring a particular event was beneficial and whether to sponsor the event or similar events in the future.

When Victoria's Secret launched the brand Pink, it was coupled with a unique event marketing promotion during spring break. The goal was to reach 18- to 24-year-old females. The event began with a three-story pink box set up on a beach in Miami. Advertisements, Internet postings, street teams of employees giving out fliers, aerial signs, posters in nearby hotels, and public relations press releases built excitement during the 5-day countdown. Many spring breakers showed up at the pink box. They were treated to a fashion show and a live concert by No Mercy. After the concert, Victoria's Secret Pink gift cards were passed out and the company hosted nightclub parties. The unique marketing event spurred sales of both the new Pink brand and other Victoria's Secret brands. The Victoria's Secret marketing team completed the evaluation stage and discovered a big increase in Pink brand sales in the Miami area and that the other Victoria's Secret brand sales also rose dramatically.[34]

An Advertising Research Foundation study revealed that intentions to purchase a branded product increased from 11 to 52 percent among consumers who attended a brand-sponsored event. Further research suggests that purchase intentions translate into sales about half the time. The Advertising Research Foundation study investigated events sponsored by Frito-Lay, State Farm, and Coca-Cola. As with sponsorships, sports-related events tended to have the best results.[35]

▲ Note the sponsors of the Louisiana Fair listed at the bottom of the Web page screen.

Source: Courtesy of Gremillion & Pou.

Cross-Promotions

Cross-promotions with the event sponsor or other companies involved are often used to boost the impact of an event marketing program. A **cross-promotion** is a marketing event that ties together companies and activities around a specific theme. Recently, eBay partnered with Sony and Baskin-Robbins to create a unique event called "Camp eBay." During the summer months, consumers are typically outdoors enjoying the warm weather and are not logged onto the Internet, so eBay decided to go to consumers. Camp eBay was eBay's first attempt at event marketing. The aim was to create awareness in and to educate people who do not use eBay. The program was also designed to encourage existing buyers and sellers to be more active in the summertime.

The Camp eBay program began with the purchase of a refurbished school bus that was sent out on a mobile marketing tour to six high-traffic areas: the Indy 500, CMA Fan Fest, eBay Live, Taste of Chicago, the Ohio State Fair, and the Minnesota State Fair. The school bus classroom drew 52,000 people who attended 30-minute sessions on how to use eBay.

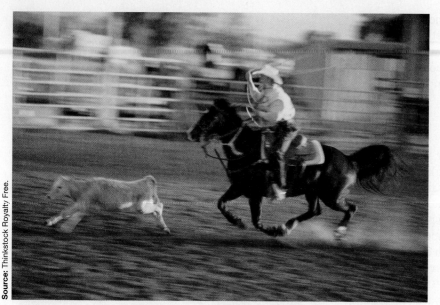

▲ Sponsoring events such as a rodeo allows companies to reach consumers in a less cluttered environment.

7 Can public relations programs, sponsorships, and event marketing be adapted to international settings?

Participants earned badges redeemable for prizes that were furnished by Sony and Baskin-Robbins. The prizes were worth a total of $85,000. In addition, eBay pitched tents at 20 Clear Channel Entertainment venues that hosted nearly 400 concerts. The impact of the event marketing program was that 45 percent of existing users increased purchases, leading to an overall increase in sales of 2 percent during the promotion and 9 percent after the event.[36]

Sponsorship programs and event marketing have increased in popularity during the past decade due to their potential to reach consumers on a one-to-one basis. In the future, sponsorships and event marketing tie-ins with other media, especially the Internet, will rise. Rock concerts, boat shows, music fairs, and a wide variety of other, more specialized programs are likely to be featured by various companies. Many marketing experts believe that making contact with customers in personalized ways that do not directly involve a sales call are valuable activities. Event marketing and sponsorship programs create that type of contact.

INTERNATIONAL IMPLICATIONS

The public relations function has become increasingly valuable in the international arena for several reasons. First, the growing number of international firms creates the need to make sure the company will be viewed in a positive light in every country in which it does business.

Second, the impact of terrorism and war over the past decade has heightened sensitivities between many nations. Any company conducting business in a foreign land will have a public relations officer in charge of monitoring news stories and other events so that the firm can react to negative press.

Third, whenever there are differences among cultures, the potential exists to offend without intending to do so. In 2008, when Rocco Mediate was involved in a valiant effort to win a playoff in the U.S. Open golf tournament, sportscaster Johnny Miller made a joke that Mediate looked more like "the guy that would clean your pool" than a professional golfer. A number of Italians took offense, believing it was an ethnic slur. Miller apologized, stating he was referring to the "every man" quality Mediate possessed.

Corporate social responsibility also has no national boundaries. Many heated debates have taken place regarding outsourcing. Critics argue that nations other than the United States have enjoyed the advantages of unfair wage rates and the ability to pollute freely, thereby cutting costs and attracting businesses to them. Any multinational corporation or company conducting business in foreign lands should be aware of these criticisms and find effective ways to respond.

Many sponsorships now contain an international flavor. Some of the more visible ones are found in sports, most notably automobile racing and soccer. Sportswear brand Adidas signed an agreement with the NBA to be the league's official supplier in Europe and worldwide. The sponsorship is huge for Adidas because NBA merchandise is sold in more than 100,000 stores in 100 countries on six continents.[37]

The principles that guide the development of sponsorships domestically apply equally well to any international involvements. To fully prepare an effective sponsorship program in an international setting, the marketing team will employ a cultural assimilator to make sure that any foreign language is being used correctly, that the sponsorship is legal, and that it does not violate any local cultural norms. As the world continues to become smaller, with increasing interactions between countries, companies, and individuals, the growth of multinational sponsorships should be expected to continue.

INTEGRATED CAMPAIGNS IN ACTION

Curb It

Pratt Industries makes cardboard boxes from recycled paper. The company invested $160 million in a wastepaper recycling mill in Shreveport, Louisiana. Demand was not a problem for Pratt Industries. Wal-Mart, Target, and other large retailers were willing to purchase recycled boxes almost as fast as Pratt could make them. The problem was that Pratt needed recycled materials with which to make the cardboard boxes.

Pratt Industries hired the Gremillion & Pou advertising agency to create an integrated marketing campaign to encourage citizens of Shreveport to recycle their trash. Research showed that people did not like sorting trash and were not willing to go out of the way to drop trash off. The challenges Gremillion & Pou faced were:

- To communicate the ease of curbside recycling
- To leverage environmental concerns to create a desire to recycle materials
- To teach the public how easy it was to recycle

To meet these challenge, the agency created an animated green frog named "Curb It." This character was used in ads, in PSAs, and on recycling bins. The campaign caught the interest of city officials and the town's citizens. Soon recycling became the easy and popular thing to do.

Your instructor has additional information about the ads, visuals, and displays used in this campaign.

Source: Courtesy of Gremillion & Pou.

▲ An advertisement encouraging people to recycle.

❝ SUMMARY

The public relations department plays a major role in an integrated marketing communications program, whether the department is separate from marketing or combined as part of a communications division. Public relations efforts are oriented to making sure that every possible contact point delivers a positive and unified message on behalf of the company.

Many stakeholders exist inside and around a company. Any person or group with a vested interest in the organization's activities is a stakeholder. Internal stakeholders include employees, unions, and stockholders. External publics include members of the marketing channel, customers, the media, the local community, financial institutions, the government, and special-interest groups.

To reach all intended audiences, the public relations department has a series of tools available. These include company newsletters, internal messages, public relations releases, correspondence with stockholders, annual reports, and various special events. Even the bulletin board in the company's break room can be used to convey messages to internal stakeholders.

In the attempt to build a favorable image of the company, the public relations department develops special events such as altruistic activities and cause-related marketing programs. Care must be taken to make certain that these acts are not perceived with cynicism and skepticism. This means being certain that any good deed matches with the company's products and other marketing efforts. A natural fit between an altruistic event and the company's brand is more readily accepted by various members of the public.

The public relations team is also responsible for damage control when negative publicity arises. Both proactive and reactive tactics are available to maintain a positive image for the company. Damage control tactics include Internet interventions, crisis management programs, and impression management techniques.

Sponsorship programs enhance and build the company's image and brand loyalty. A sponsorship of an individual or group involved in some kind of activity—whether a sporting event, a contest, or a performance by an artistic group—can be used to link the company's name with the popularity of the player involved. Sponsorships should match with the firm's products and brands.

Event marketing occurs when a firm sponsors an event. A strong physical presence at the event is one of the keys to successfully linking an organization's name with a program. To do so, the firm determines the major objective of the sponsorship, matches it with company customers and publics, and ensures that the firm's name is prominently displayed on all event literature.

Managing public relations, sponsorships, and event marketing programs requires company leaders to assess the goals and the outcomes of individual activities. A cost–benefit approach may not always be feasible, but the marketing team should be able to track some form of change, whether it is increased inquiries, the number of samples passed out at an event, or a shift in the tenor of news articles about the organization. The primary task of public relations is to be the organization's "watchdog," making sure those who come in contact with the company believe the firm is working to do things right and to do the right things.

KEY TERMS

public relations (PR) department A unit in the firm that manages items such as publicity and other communications with all of the groups that make contact with the company.

hit The mention of a company's name in a news story.

stakeholder A person or group with a vested interest in a firm's activities and well-being.

corporate social responsibility An organization's obligation to be ethical, accountable, and reactive to the needs of society.

cause-related marketing Matching marketing efforts with some type of charity work or program.

green marketing The development and promotion of products that are environmentally safe.

greenwashing Activities that are presented as being green or environmentally friendly that are not.

damage control Reacting to negative events caused by a company error, consumer grievances, or unjustified or exaggerated negative press.

entitlings Attempts to claim responsibility for positive outcomes of events.

enhancements Attempts to increase the impact of a desirable outcome of an event in the eyes of the public.

Internet interventions Confronting negative publicity on the Internet, either in Web site news releases or by entering chat rooms, blogs, or social networks.

crisis management Either accepting the blame for an event and offering an apology or refuting those making the charges in a forceful manner.

apology strategy Presenting a full apology when the firm has made an error.

impression management The conscious or unconscious attempt to control images that are projected in real or imagined social situations.

sponsorship marketing When the company pays money to sponsor someone or some group that is participating in an activity.

event marketing When a company pays money to sponsor an event or program.

cross-promotion A marketing event that ties together companies and activities around a specific theme.

REVIEW QUESTIONS

1. Describe the role of the public relations department. How is it related to the marketing department? Should both departments be called the "department of communications"? Why or why not?

2. What is a stakeholder?

3. Name the major internal stakeholders in organizations. Describe each one's major interests in the company.

4. Name the major external stakeholders in organizations. Describe each one's major interest in the company.

5. What is corporate social responsibility? How is it related to public relations activities?

6. What is cause-related marketing? How can company leaders create effective cause-related marketing programs?

7. What is green marketing? How do different companies promote environmentally-friendly activities?

8. What reactive damage-control techniques are available to the public relations team?

9. What four forms of impression management are used to combat negative events?

10. What is sponsorship marketing? Name a pro athlete, musician or musical group, or performer of some other type who has been featured in a sponsorship program. Was the program effective or ineffective? Why?

11. Describe an event marketing program. What must accompany the event in order to make it a success?

12. What are cross-promotions? How are they related to event marketing programs?

13. How are public relations programs and sponsorship adapted to international companies?

CRITICAL THINKING EXERCISES

Discussion Questions

1. Watch the news on television or read a local news story about a local or national business. Was the report positive or negative toward the firm? Did the news report or article affect your attitude toward the company? Watch one of the many special investigative shows, such as *60 Minutes*. What companies did it investigate? If your firm was being featured, what would you do to counteract the bad press?

2. One of the vice presidents of a small but highly respected bank in a local community was charged with sexual harassment by a female employee. What type of communications should be prepared for each of the constituencies listed in Figure 13.2? Which of the constituencies would be the most important to contact?

3. Is the local community important to a manufacturing firm that sells 99 percent of its products outside the area? Does it really matter what the local people say or believe about

the manufacturer as long as the firm's customers are happy? Explain.

4. What causes do you support or are special to you? Do you know which corporations sponsor or support the causes? If not, see if you can find literature or Web sites that contain that information. Why do you think the corporations choose a particular cause to support? What benefits do corporations receive from sponsorships?

5. When Starbucks opened its first coffee shop inside a public library, 10 percent of all proceeds from coffee sold there went to support the operation of the library. Do you think a public library should allow a for-profit organization such as Starbucks to sell products inside the building? Is this a conflict of interest for government-sponsored organizations, such as libraries? What if the local doughnut shop wanted to sell doughnuts at the library? Should it be allowed to do so? How does a head librarian decide?

6. Managers often are the most difficult group for the public relations department to reach. To entice employees to reach departmental goals, managers often communicate using memos or verbal messages. These messages may conflict with the IMC theme. For example, in an effort to trim costs a manager may send a memo to all employees telling them to use only standard production procedures. Through verbal communications, employees learn that anyone caught violating or even bending the policy to satisfy a customer will be immediately reprimanded. The manager's action suggests that even though he wants employees to provide customer service, in actuality they had better not do anything that is not authorized. Employees soon get the message that management cares only about costs, not the customer. Employees will perceive any advertising message about customer service as a big joke. Write a memo to employees that supports the IMC goal of high customer service, yet alerts them to the need to follow standard operating procedures. Is there anything else you would do to ensure that employees do not receive conflicting messages?

7. Sponsorships are now a major component of professional sports. Football, basketball, baseball, and golf all have sponsors. Many stadiums are now named for companies. Why do you think companies spend millions on these sponsorships? What impact does it have on you? What sponsorships do you notice? Which ones do you not notice? Why?

INTEGRATED LEARNING EXERCISES

1. Although some firms handle public relations activities internally, many firms retain public relations firms to work on special projects and to handle unique situations. The Public Relations Society of America (PRSA) is one of the major associations for PR practitioners. In Canada, the primary association is the Canadian Public Relations Society (CPRS). Access the Web sites of these two organizations at **www.prsa.org** and **www.cprs.ca**. What types of information does each provide? What types of services are offered? How would these organizations be beneficial to various companies?

2. *PRWeek* is an excellent publication. Access the online version at **www.prweek.com**. What type of information is available? How would this site be valuable to a PR practitioner? How could it be used by a firm seeking a public relations agency? How could it be used by a marketing manager?

3. The American Institute of Philanthropy ranks the various charities. Access the Web site at **www.charitywatch.org**. How does the Institute rate the charities? How can this information be used by a company to determine which charities to support?

4. A number of companies offer services to help firms plan and develop sponsorships. One company is IEG. Access its Web site at **www.sponsorship.com**. Review the Web site. Identify the various services offered by IEG. If you were the marketing manager for a company that wanted to develop a sponsorship program, how could IEG help? Be specific.

5. Event marketing is used by many organizations to accomplish various objectives. Access the following companies that assist firms with event marketing. What type of services does each offer? What is your evaluation of each of the companies? If you were hosting an event, which company would you hire? Why?

   a. Advantage International, LLC (**www.advantage-intl.com**)
   b. Fuse Youth Marketing Agency (**www.fusemarketing.com**)
   c. RPMC Event and Promotion Agency (**www.rpmc.com**)

6. Corporate sponsorships are important to nonprofits. Without the financial assistance provided, many nonprofits would not exist. Look up two organizations from the following list of nonprofits. Who are their corporate sponsors? What benefits do the profit-seeking companies receive from these sponsorships?

   a. American Cancer Society (**www.cancer.org**)
   b. Arthritis Foundation (**www.arthritis.org**)
   c. Multiple Sclerosis Society (**www.mssociety.org.uk**)
   d. United Cerebral Palsy (**www.ucp.org**)
   e. Alliance for the Wild Rockies (**www.wildrockiesalliance.org**)
   f. National Wildlife Federation (**www.nwf.org**)
   g. Trout Unlimited (**www.tu.org**)

STUDENT PROJECT

Creative Corner

Circle K Ranch has been selling, training, and boarding horses for almost 20 years. With the recent downturn in the economy, however, Circle K has experienced a decline in all facets of its business. In talking with some marketing students at the local university, the owner of Circle K Ranch, Kathy Kroncke, wondered about using cause-related marketing, sponsorships, and even event marketing to boost the awareness and image of her business. She recently added horseback riding to her list of services and developed a 10-mile ride that goes through a local state park. So far, business has not been what she expected, despite research that indicated a high level of interest in riding, especially by 15- to 40-year-old females. Design a cause-related marketing program, a sponsorship program, and an event marketing program for Circle K Ranch. After you have designed each of the programs, choose the one you think would be the best for Circle K Ranch. Design a newspaper ad featuring the program. What other methods would you use, both traditional and nontraditional, to publicize the program you chose?

CASE 1   OLIVE GARDEN: MEET THE GIRLS NEXT DOOR

Public relations challenges come in many forms, some expected and others that could never be imagined. The Olive Garden has developed a strong brand and corporate image focused on family, friends, and fun. The company was launched as a subsidiary of General Mills as an entry into the casual Italian restaurant marketplace. The initial success and growth led to a spin-off, and Darden Restaurants has directed the chain since the early 1990s.

Olive Garden restaurants are distinctive, featuring a casual Italian decor. The menus have been upgraded to move beyond more basic dishes to include items such as Mediterranean Garlic Shrimp and Capellini Pomodoro. Chefs continue to look for ways to treat regular customers to new and exciting dishes to accompany old favorites. All the while, endless bowls of salad and servings of breadsticks, along with tasty servings of soup, are part of the regular fare.

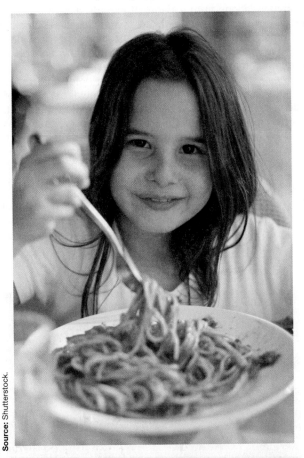

Source: Shutterstock.

▲ **The Olive Garden has communicated an image of being a "wholesome family restaurant."**

The wholesome family atmosphere projected by Olive Garden's marketing communications includes the term "Hospitalino," which suggests the commitment to a warm, comfortable environment for dining. Commercials and advertisements carrying the tagline "When you're here, you're family" have helped Olive Garden establish a strong brand presence in a highly competitive marketplace.

The Girls Next Door has become a popular television program on E! Entertainment Television. The show features three beautiful young women who live in Hugh Hefner's exotic Playboy Mansion. In 2008, over 1.4 million viewers watched the antics of the young women in various stages of dress and settings. One of the three, Kendra Wilkinson happens to be a genuine fan of the Olive Garden. During one program, she mentioned how much she loved the artichoke dip and breadsticks. She quickly became known as practically a "new spokesperson" for the company.

Without question, Kendra's affection for the Olive Garden was sincere. As she noted, "I love the Olive Garden, because I grew up going there. That used to be the place we would go for Mother's Day, for birthdays. My grandpa just died, and right after his funeral, we went to the Olive Garden." She pointed out when asked that she received no compensation for mentioning the restaurant on *The Girls Next Door*.

Ms. Wilkinson did, however, convince Hefner to create a contest. Women were invited to compete for a chance to become one of the "Sexiest Girls of Olive Garden." The winner was to receive a Playboy photo shoot conducted by Kendra Wilkinson for an upcoming edition of the magazine.

Olive Garden's management and marketing team faced a dilemma. On the one hand, a surprising overlap exists between the types of individuals who dine at the Olive Garden and those who watch *The Girls Next Door*. Many are college educated, affluent, and enjoy upscale dining. More women watch the television program than men, and more women dine at the Olive Garden than men.

At the other extreme, protests have been lodged against the television show. The Florida Family Association had encouraged advertisers to stop buying spots for the show. Playboy has long been a source of controversy in the United States.

From the Olive Garden's perspective, the publicity generated by the linkage between the two organizations could have been viewed as a blessing or a curse. At first, the company did not make official statements about the contest. Undoubtedly, the marketing and public relations teams believed the company was navigating through some very choppy waters.

1. Who are Olive Garden's internal and external stakeholders that have been affected by this turn of events?

2. For casual observers of media, would the "Sexiest Girls of Olive Garden" appear to be a sponsorship?

3. Is this event an instance in which damage-control programs were in order? If so, which one(s)?

4. Kendra Wilkinson said she believed Olive Garden could afford to appear to be a little "edgy" without detracting from its family-friendly brand. Do you agree or disagree? Why?

5. If you were the public relations agency for the Olive Garden, how would you handle this situation? What steps would you take and what tactics would you use to ensure Olive Garden's image is not adversely affected.

Sources: R. Dana, "When You're Here, You're Family—But What About a Playboy Model?; Olive Garden Has Mixed Feelings About Its Biggest Celebrity Fan," *Wall Street Journal* (August 13, 2008). p. A.1; "Playboy.com features 'The Girls of Olive Garden,'" The Bryant Park Project, National Public Radio (www.npr.org/templates/story/story.php?storyId=92544599, accessed May 13, 2010); Korin Miller, "Playboy Dishes up 'Girls of Olive Garden,'" *New York Daily News* (http://www.nydailynews.com/gossip/2008/07/16/2008-07-16_playboy_dishes_up_girls_of_the_olive_gar.html, accessed May 13, 2010), July 16, 2008; www.olivegarden.com (accessed May 13, 2010).

CASE 2 · NEW DRUG FACES PUBLIC RELATIONS AND MARKETING CHALLENGES

It is unusual for a new product to create a vehement public response with both supporters and detractors. One such product, which was approved by the FDA in 2006 and made widely available in 2007, is Gardasil. The drug was developed by Merck and Company.

Gardasil is provided in the form of a vaccine. It was developed to prevent cervical cancer by blocking infection from human papillomavirus, which is spread through sexual contact. The Food and Drug Administration permits Gardasil to be used by females ages 9 through 26, with the goal of inoculating girls before they become sexually active. Although the vaccine does not prevent every form of papillomavirus, it does treat four of the most common, including 100 percent prevention of the most common type and 70 percent of the four most common types combined.

Nearly half a million women are diagnosed with cervical cancer each year. According to some experts, Gardasil might make it possible to eliminate cervical cancer within a generation. It is also a victory for Merck, the fourth-biggest U.S. drug maker, which has focused increasingly on vaccines and may generate $3 billion in annual sales from Gardasil alone. "It's important from a public health perspective because you're eliminating a cancer," said Les Funtleyder, an analyst in New York for Miller Tabak & Co. "The subtle point is these guys are creating new drugs for important health problems, which is what a pharma is supposed to do."

Gardasil requires three doses to be given over 6 months. In 2007, each dose cost around $120. Consequently, affordability may determine how effective the drug is in quelling cervical cancer. About 80 percent of cases are in poorer countries. "Critical to success will be ensuring that women in the world's poorest countries—where cervical cancer hits hardest—have rapid and affordable access to this lifesaving new tool," said Gabriel N. Hortobagyi, a physician at the University of Texas M.D. Anderson Cancer Center in Houston and president of the American Society of Clinical Oncology, in a statement. Human papillomavirus, or HPV, is one of the most common sexually transmitted viruses in the world, and it causes genital warts as well as cancer. About 20 million people in the United States are infected, according to the U.S. Centers for Disease Control and Prevention (CDC).

Why the controversy? Many social conservatives fear that providing the vaccine may provide subtle approval for young women to engage in sex, much in the same way as providing birth control information and condoms are sometimes condemned. Some of the response was in regard to the recommendations from a panel of experts assembled by the CDC. The panel issues widely followed guidelines, including recommendations for childhood vaccines that become the basis for vaccination requirements set by public schools. The panel recommended that the vaccine be required.

Merck company officials and others noted that research indicates the best age to vaccinate would be just before puberty to make sure children are protected before they become sexually active. The vaccine would probably be targeted primarily at girls, but could also be used on boys to limit the spread of the virus. "If you really want to have cervical cancer rates fall as much as possible as quickly as possible, then you want as many people to get vaccinated as possible," said Mark Feinberg, Merck's vice president of medical affairs and policy, noting that "school mandates have been one of the most effective ways to increase immunization rates." That is the view being pushed by cervical cancer experts and women's health advocates.

Source: Thinkstock Royalty Free.

▲ **Many young girls could benefit from the HPV virus vaccine Gardasil.**

Not surprisingly, a major clash emerged, mostly notably when the state of Texas made it a requirement to have the vaccine in order to be admitted to school. The battle lines were primarily drawn over girls being forced to take a medicine, with or without parental consent, along with the concerns expressed about sexual activity.

Company officials from Merck worked carefully with both governmental agencies and other groups to reduce concerns. In 2008, the company began advertising Gardasil in television commercials entitled "One Less" and "Guard Yourself." A powerful point is made: by taking the medicine, one less person will become infected.

1. Describe the stakeholders and the positions of each group involved in this controversy.

2. Outline the positive public relations opportunities available to promote Gardasil.

3. Describe how Merck should respond to negative publicity and complaints about the product.

4. Could Merck use cause-related marketing effectively, or would it be construed as a means of marketing the drug?

5. What sponsorships and event marketing programs should be used to promote Gardasil?

Sources: Angela Zimm and Justin Blum, "FDA Approves Merck's Cervical Cancer Vaccine," *Boston Globe* and *Bloomberg News* (**www.boston.com/business/healthcare/articles**, accessed January 28, 2008), June 9, 2006; Rob Stein, "Cervical Cancer Vaccine Gets Injected with a Social Issue," *Washington Post* (**www. washingtonpost. com/wp-dyn**, accessed January 28, 2008), October 31, 2005.

14 Regulations and Ethical Concerns

A SALTY SITUATION

How much sodium should an adult consume per day? According to the National Research Council of the National Academy of Sciences, 1,200 to 1,500 milligrams per day is sufficient. The body needs sodium for a number of key functions, including regulation of blood pressure and blood volume as well as muscle and nerve functioning. A tablespoon of table salt, which is 40 percent sodium, contains 2,300 milligrams of sodium.

Many health care professionals are concerned with the amount of sodium in food products, especially processed foods. Overconsumption of sodium is related to numerous health problems, including high blood pressure, which can lead to strokes and heart attacks. Further, excess sodium is connected to fluid build-up, which aggravates cirrhosis and kidney problems, and can contribute to congestive heart failure.

These concerns have been well known for many years, yet the food industry has been slow to respond. Why? Essentially, there are two answers. First, salt gives food flavor. Everything from meats, such as bacon, sausage, and ham, to canned soups and vegetables use salt to add taste. A serving of Van Camp's Baked Beans contains over 390 milligrams of sodium (a 15-ounce can contains more than three servings of sodium). Products such as Worcestershire sauce, soy sauce, and bouillon cubes also contain high levels of salt. Typical diet-food frozen dinners average between 510 and 590 milligrams per serving. Even cookies and cakes contain surprisingly large amounts of sodium.

The second reason for high sodium content is food preservation. Salt placed into food draws away moisture so that bacteria do not grow. Salt also kills existing bacteria that might cause spoilage. At one time, salting was one of the only methods available to preserve food. Currently, many other methods are available, which leads back to the taste issue.

Fast-food companies and other restaurants are notorious for using high levels of sodium in the items sold. For example, a McDonald's Big Mac contains 1,040 milligrams of sodium (the number rises if a soft

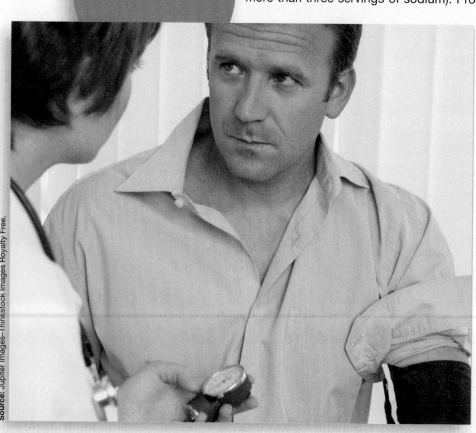

CHAPTER OBJECTIVES

After reading this chapter, you should be able to answer the following questions:

1 What agencies and laws regulate marketing communications?

2 Why is it that puffery is legal and deception is not? What role does substantiation play in differentiating between the two?

3 What legal remedies can be used to correct deceptive communications practices?

4 How do the three major industry regulatory agencies help keep advertising and business practices from injuring customers or other businesses?

5 What ethical criticisms have been registered against advertising and marketing practices?

6 What marketing tactics raise ethical concerns?

7 How can marketers apply the various ethical frameworks and ethics programs to their activities and actions?

8 What international issues influence the discussion of legal and ethical marketing activities?

drink and fries are added). A Burger King Whopper contains nearly 1,500 milligrams.

The net result is that consumers, unless they are very careful, typically consume as much as 3,000 milligrams of sodium per day. The negative health effects of sodium overconsumption are well documented. Yet Congress and the Food and Drug Administration do little more than require the amount of sodium contained in products to be reported, with no attempts to limit amounts.

Some companies have begun to respond. In 2008, Lays launched a new line of products with the label "Pinch of Salt." A 1-ounce serving of these potato chips contains 75 milligrams of sodium (a bag is typically 12 ounces). In contrast, a 1-ounce serving of regular Lays chips contains 270 milligrams of sodium.

In 2006, Campbell's began selling soup flavored with sea salt, which reduces the sodium content. Campbell's is also looking for ways to reduce sodium in V8 drinks. Numerous companies specialize in low-sodium foods.

The sodium content of food products provides an example of the intersection between what is legal and what is ethical. Time will tell if various organizations respond in ways that benefit profits or society, and whether the government will respond with legislation.[1]

OVERVIEW

The final level of an IMC program includes making certain the communications program meets ethical and legal requirements and is properly evaluated. These topics are examined in this part of the text. Figure 14.1 displays the completion of an IMC program.

The fields of marketing and marketing communications have long been the subject of scrutiny from the general public, special interest groups, and the government. This is not surprising. In marketing and sales, money is involved as people make purchases. Many people and organizations are concerned about the public trust and the well-being of the community. When goods and services are sold that can injure people or cause harm in some other way, criticisms and legal actions are likely to follow.

FIGURE 14.1 ▶
Overview of Integrated
Marketing Communications

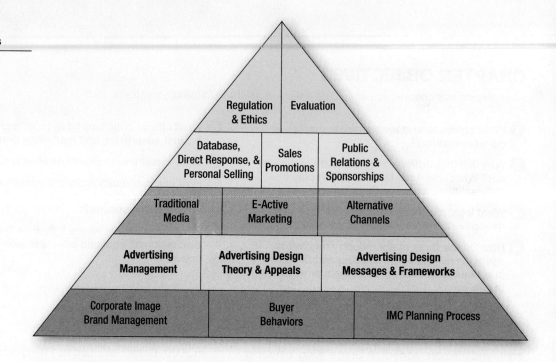

FIGURE 14.1 ▶
Overview of Integrated
Marketing Communications

This chapter examines two interrelated topics. The first is a description of the legal environment surrounding marketing and marketing communications. The second part features views of ethics, morals, and social responsibility as they relate to marketing, advertising, and promotions.

In essence, those who are involved in marketing programs should consider both the letter of the law—regulations and other legal limitations—as well as the spirit of the law. Guided by both personal principles and organizational guidelines, marketing professionals can try to ensure that their actions are both legal and ethical.

❶ What agencies and laws regulate marketing communications?

MARKETING COMMUNICATIONS REGULATIONS

The U.S. federal government has passed considerable legislation designed to keep companies from taking advantage of consumers and other businesses. Various states also regulate for-profit companies and other organizations. Many of these federal and state laws are enforced by regulatory agencies. In this section, governmental actions are reviewed in the areas of legislation and regulation of company marketing practices.

Governmental Regulatory Agencies

Numerous governmental agencies serve as watchdogs to monitor for potential violations of the law, some of which are only partially related to marketing. For example, the Food and Drug Administration (FDA) regulates and oversees the packaging and labeling of products. The FDA also monitors advertising on food packages and advertisements for drugs, yet its primary responsibilities are ensuring food quality and drug safety.

The Federal Communications Commission (FCC) regulates television, radio, and the telephone industry. The FCC grants (and revokes) operating licenses for radio and television stations. The FCC also has jurisdiction over telephone companies. The FCC does not have jurisdiction over the content of advertisements transmitted by mass media. Further, the FCC does not control which products may be advertised. The organization is, however, responsible for monitoring advertising directed toward children. Under FCC rules, TV stations are limited to 12 minutes per hour of children's advertisements during weekdays and 10 minutes per hour on weekends. Recently, Viacom agreed to pay $1 million for programming on Nickelodeon that violated the time limitation 600 times in the span of 1 year.[2]

- Food and Drug Administration (FDA)
- Federal Communications Commission (FCC)
- U.S. Postal Service (USPS)
- Bureau of Alcohol, Tobacco and Firearms (ATF)
- Federal Trade Commission (FTC)

◄ **FIGURE 14.2**
Government Regulatory
Agencies

The U.S. Postal Service (USPS) has jurisdiction over all mailed marketing materials. The USPS also investigates mail fraud schemes and other fraudulent marketing practices. The Bureau of Alcohol, Tobacco and Firearms (ATF) rules when the sale, distribution, and advertising of alcohol and tobacco are at issue. Ordinarily, the governmental agency that examines incidents involving deceptive or misleading marketing tactics is the Federal Trade Commission (FTC). These agencies are listed in Figure 14.2.

The Federal Trade Commission

The **Federal Trade Commission, or FTC**, which was created in 1914 by the passage of the Federal Trade Commission Act, presides over marketing communications. The act's original intent was to create a federal agency to enforce antitrust laws and protect businesses from one another. It had little authority over advertising and marketing communications except when an advertisement was considered to be unfair to the competition, thereby restricting free trade.

Unfair and Deceptive Marketing Practices

In 1938, Congress passed the Wheeler–Lea Amendment to Section 5 of the Federal Trade Commission Act to increase and expand the authority of the FTC and to prohibit false and misleading advertising. The agency was given the authority to stop unfair or deceptive advertising practices and to levy fines when necessary. The law also granted the FTC access to the courts to enforce the law and ensure that violators abide by FTC rulings.

A firm can violate the act even when the company did not expressly intend to deceive. An advertisement or communication is deemed to be deceptive or misleading when:

1. A substantial number of people or the "typical person" is left with a false impression or misrepresentation that relates to the product.
2. The misrepresentation induces people or the "typical person" to make a purchase.

Consumers may be misled by advertisements, mailings, corporate literature, labels, packaging, Web site materials, and oral and written statements made by salespeople. This gives the government a great deal of latitude in dealing with deceptive practices.

Deception Versus Puffery

Advertising can include puffery in advertisements and messages. **Puffery** exists when a firm makes an exaggerated statement about its goods or services. The key difference, in terms of the FTC and the courts, between puffery and a claim is that puffery is not considered to be a *factual statement*. In contrast, a *claim* makes a factual statement that can be proven true or false. Firms are entitled to offer puffery statements without proving them; claims must be substantiated or proven in some manner.

Terms normally associated with puffery include words such as *friendliest, best, greatest*, and *finest*. A firm can advertise "our brand is the best" or "our signature dishes use only the finest ingredients." Courts and the regulatory agencies view these statements as puffery and believe that consumers expect firms to use them routinely in their advertisements. The advertisement by Flair Jewelers in this section states that "Nobody does 'I do' like we do," which is a form of puffery. No statement of fact that can be proven true or false is offered.

The word *best* will normally be accepted as puffery. The word *better* has been construed to imply a comparison. The term has recently been tested through the FTC, the National Advertising Division of the Better Business Bureau, and the courts. Papa John's use of the phrase "Better Ingredients, Better Pizza" was found to be puffery, as was the phrase "Only the best tomatoes grow up to be Hunt's."

❷ Why is it that puffery is legal and deception is not? What role does substantiation play in differentiating between the two?

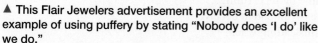

▲ This Flair Jewelers advertisement provides an excellent example of using puffery by stating "Nobody does 'I do' like we do."

▲ Yamaha uses puffery in this advertisement stating that its boats are "engineered like no other."

▼ Cruex states that nothing else stops itching better or faster than Cruex, which would be considered a claim by the FTC and therefore would require substantiation.

In another situation, Progresso made the statement "Discover the Better Taste of Progresso" in company advertisements. The slogan was challenged by Campbell's Soup Company, which argued that Progresso's "better taste" phrase was not puffery. Campbell's representatives argued that taste tests can be used to determine if one food product tastes better than other brands. The courts agreed and ordered Progresso to either modify the phrase or prove that Progresso soups do taste better.[3]

Substantiation of Marketing Claims

The concept of substantiation applies to claims that are not puffery. **Substantiation** means that an advertising claim or promise must be proven with data, facts, or through competent and reliable evidence. Failure to do so can result in a lawsuit or governmental action.

An advertisement featuring an endorser must contain truthful statements that represent the person's experiences or opinions. When a commercial uses an expert endorsement, the statements must be based on legitimate tests performed by professionals in the field.

All marketing claims must reflect the typical experience that a customer would expect to encounter from the use of a good or service, unless the advertisement clearly and prominently states otherwise. A few years ago a Kleenex Cottonelle ad made the claim that the product was softer. Kleenex provided actual touch tests by consumers as evidence. The company then used engineering and lab tests to show that Kleenex tissue consists of 24 percent more cottony, soft fiber. Thus, Kleenex was able to substantiate the claim.

Substantiation may not be easy. To increase the probability the substantiation will be accepted by the FTC and courts, company leaders use the following principles:[4]

1. The federal government assumes consumers read ads broadly and do not pay much attention to fine print and qualifying language. Thus, hiding a qualifier at the bottom of the ad or using words such as *usually, normally*, or *under typical situations* somewhere in the ad is not normally accepted as substantiation.

2. The evidence has to be for the exact product being tested, not for a similar product, regardless of the similarity.

3. Evidence should come from or be accepted by experts in the relevant area of the product and would be considered valid and reliable by the experts. Studies conducted by the company or something found on the Internet is not acceptable.

4. The FTC and courts will consider the totality of the evidence. If the company has one study that supports the claim but there are four studies by other independent organizations that indicate something different, then the evidence will not be accepted as valid substantiation.

Regardless of the type of communication, the FTC prohibits unfair or deceptive marketing communications. Marketers must be able to substantiate claims through competent and reliable evidence. Unfortunately, a great deal of gray area exists between puffery and a claim that must be substantiated. Consequently, lawsuits are filed and governmental agencies are forced to address complaints and suspected violations of the law. These agencies and their rulings strongly affect individual marketing practices as well as company actions.

How Investigations Begin

Many companies have been cited for illegal activities, including deception. In each case, various types of complaints triggered an FTC investigation. These include problems noticed by:

- Consumers
- Businesses
- Congress
- The media

Each can raise questions about what appears to be an unfair or deceptive practice. Most investigations by the FTC are confidential at first, which protects the agency and the company being investigated.

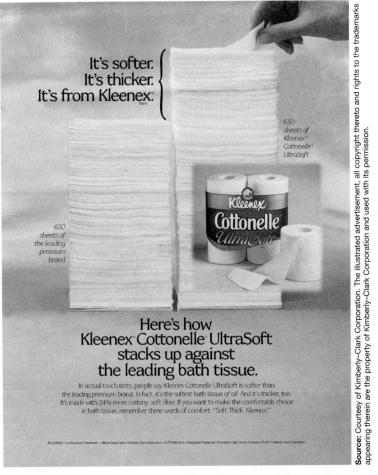

It's softer.
It's thicker.
It's from Kleenex.

650 sheets of Kleenex Cottonelle UltraSoft

650 sheets of the leading premium brand

Here's how
Kleenex Cottonelle UltraSoft
stacks up against
the leading bath tissue.

In actual touch tests, people say Kleenex Cottonelle UltraSoft is *softer* than the leading premium brand. In fact, it's the softest bath tissue *of all*. And it's thicker, too. It's made with 24% more cottony, soft fiber. If you want to make the comfortable choice in bath tissue, remember three words of comfort: "Soft. Thick. Kleenex."

▲ An advertisement for Kleenex Cottonelle with a claim that must be substantiated.

3 What legal remedies can be used to correct deceptive communications practices?

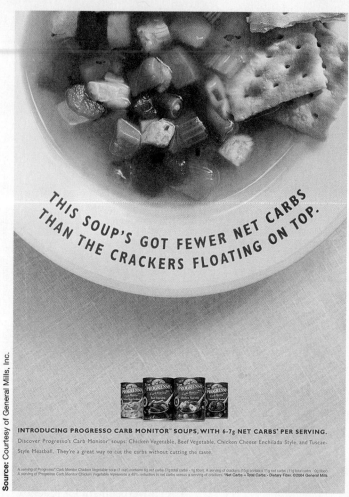

THIS SOUP'S GOT FEWER NET CARBS THAN THE CRACKERS FLOATING ON TOP.

INTRODUCING PROGRESSO CARB MONITOR™ SOUPS, WITH 6-7g NET CARBS* PER SERVING.

Discover Progresso's Carb Monitor™ soups: Chicken Vegetable, Beef Vegetable, Chicken Cheese Enchilada Style, and Tuscan-Style Meatball. They're a great way to cut the carbs without cutting the taste.

A serving of Progresso™ Carb Monitor Chicken Vegetable soup (1 cup) contains 6g net carbs (7g total carbs − 1g fiber). A serving of crackers (15g) contains 11g net carbs (11g total carbs − 0g fiber). A serving of Progresso Carb Monitor Chicken Vegetable represents a 45% reduction in net carbs versus a serving of crackers. *Net Carbs = Total Carbs − Dietary Fiber. ©2004 General Mills.

Source: Courtesy of General Mills, Inc.

▲ An advertisement for Progresso Soup with a testable claim that must be substantiated.

Consent Orders

When the FTC believes a law has been violated, a **consent order** will be issued. When company leaders sign the consent order, they agree to stop the disputed practice without admitting guilt.

Kentucky Fried Chicken (KFC) signed consent agreements with the FTC concerning two ads the FTC investigated and concluded were not adequately substantiated. In the first, the FTC held that KFC made false claims in an advertisement that stated eating two Original Recipe fried chicken breasts had less fat than the Burger King Whopper. It was true that the chicken did have slightly less total fat and saturated fat than the Whopper; however, the chicken had more than three times the trans fat and cholesterol, more than twice the sodium, and more calories. Thus, the FTC ruled the claim was inadequately substantiated.

In the second ad, KFC claimed that one Original Recipe chicken breast had only 11 grams of carbohydrates and 40 grams of protein, compatible with a "low-carbohydrate" weight-loss program. The FTC found the ad misleading, because the "low-carbohydrate" weight-loss programs such as the Atkins Diet and the South Beach Diet specifically recommend against eating breaded, fried foods.[5]

Administrative Complaints

Most FTC investigations end with the signing of a consent order. When a consent agreement cannot be reached, the FTC issues an **administrative complaint**. At that point, a formal proceeding similar to a court trial will be held before an administrative law judge. Both sides submit evidence and render testimony. At the end of the administrative hearing, the judge makes a ruling. When the judge concludes a violation of the law has occurred, a *cease and desist order* may be issued. The order requires the company to stop the disputed practice immediately and refrain from similar practices in the future. A company that is not satisfied with the decision of the administrative law judge can be appeal the case to the full FTC commission.

The *full commission* holds hearings similar to those before administrative law judges. Rulings are made after hearing evidence and testimony. Companies that are dissatisfied with the ruling of the full FTC commission can appeal the case to the U.S. Court of Appeals and further, to the highest level, the U.S. Supreme Court. The danger for companies that appeal cases is that consumer redress can be sought at that point. This means companies found guilty of violating laws can be ordered to pay civil penalties.

Courts and Legal Channels

Occasionally, the FTC uses the court system to stop unfair and deceptive advertising and communications practices. This occurs when a company violates previous FTC cease and desist orders or when the actions of a company are so severe that immediate action is needed. The latter occurred in a case involving the National Consumer Council (NCC), a debt reduction and negotiation firm based in Santa Ana, California. The FTC investigation found that the National Consumer Council encouraged consumers to stop paying their debts once they signed up with NCC for debt reduction. At the same time, NCC did not normally start negotiation with debtors for 6 months. By then, the customer's debtors were irate and not willing to negotiate. In the meantime, the NCC customer had been making payments into a fund at NCC. Charges and monthly fees were being withdrawn for payment to NCC. Many customers did not know NCC was making the charges. Eventually, the customers discovered that not only did NCC ruin their credit ratings, but they were also deeper in debt than when they signed on. Almost all of them were forced to declare bankruptcy. Due to the severity of NCC's activities, the FTC obtained a restraining order from a federal court to immediately close NCC's operation. The FTC also obtained a restraining order against the London Financial Group, which provided telemarketing, accounting, and management services to NCC.[6]

The FTC also works with other legal entities, such as state and federal attorneys general. The FTC, Orange County (CA) district attorney, and the California State Attorney investigated Body Wise International, Inc., for false and deceptive advertising and for violating a consent agreement between Body Wise International and the FTC that was made in 1995. The complaint against Body Wise involved the alleged medical benefits of a product called "AI/E-10." Body Wise International advertised that AI/E-10 could prevent, treat, and cure diseases such as cancer, HIV/AIDS, and asthma. Body Wise supported these claims through the expert testimony of a physician, Dr. Stoff. The FTC investigation revealed that Stoff was receiving royalties from every bottle that was sold and that he could not provide medical substantiation for any of the claims. The FTC order banned Body Wise International from making the claims and prohibited Stoff from misrepresenting the tests and studies of AI/E-10. In the final settlement, Body Wise International agreed to pay $2 million to the FTC in civil penalties and $1.5 million in civil penalties. The final agreement also contained a $358,000 monetary judgment against Dr. Stoff.[7]

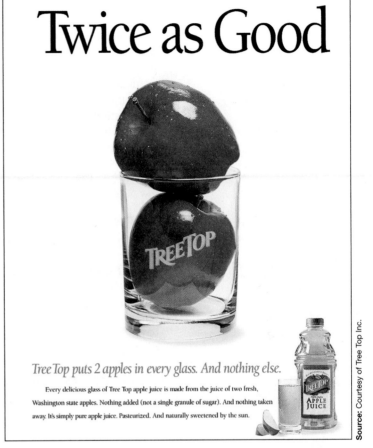

Tree Top puts 2 apples in every glass. And nothing else.

Every delicious glass of Tree Top apple juice is made from the juice of two fresh, Washington state apples. Nothing added (not a single granule of sugar). And nothing taken away. It's simply pure apple juice. Pasteurized. And naturally sweetened by the sun.

▲ The FTC and courts would consider the statement "Twice as Good" to be puffery, but the statement "Tree Top puts 2 apples in every glass. And nothing else." would have to be substantiated.

Corrective Advertising

In the most severe instances of deceptive or misleading advertising, the FTC can order a firm to prepare **corrective advertisements**. These rare situations occur only when the members of the FTC believe that discontinuing a false advertisement will not be sufficient. When the FTC concludes that consumers believed the false advertisement, it can require the firm to produce corrective ads to bring consumers back to a neutral state. Consumers should return to the beliefs they had prior to the false or misleading advertising.

The FTC ordered corrective advertising for the Novartis Corporation. The judgment was based on false and deceptive advertisements of a product called Doan's analgesic. During the investigation, members of the FTC concluded that Doan's claim of greater efficiency than competing products was not substantiated. The FTC ordered Novartis to immediately cease comparative advertising and to make this statement in corrective ads: "Although Doan's is an effective pain reliever, there is no evidence that Doan's is more effective than other pain relievers for back pain." Novartis was ordered to spend $8 million advertising the statement and include it for 1 year in all advertisements, except for 15-second broadcast ads. Unhappy with the order, leaders at Novartis filed a lawsuit in federal court against the FTC, but the federal court upheld the FTC order.[8]

Trade Regulation Rulings

The final type of action the FTC takes is a **trade regulation ruling**, which applies to an entire industry in a case of unfair or deceptive practices. Normally, the commission holds a public hearing and accepts both oral and written arguments. The commission then makes a ruling that applies to every firm within an industry. As with other FTC rulings, decisions can be challenged in the U.S. Court of Appeals.

The recent rise in personal blogs led to an explosion of product reviews by bloggers. Often bloggers are paid or received free merchandise to post positive comments. Blogger Jessica Smith was given a Ford Flex to use for 1 month plus a free gas card in exchange for a positive review. Microsoft sent bloggers a free laptop loaded with the newest Microsoft operating system. After investigating these practices, the FTC issued a ruling that bloggers who review products must disclose any connection with the advertiser or product, whether the product provided was free or if they were compensated in any way. The ruling also applies to celebrities who promote products on talk shows or on Twitter.[9]

A similar industry trade ruling occurred with gift cards issued by retailers. Many retailers were charging dormancy fees for cards that were not used immediately and many had expiration dates. This information was not conveyed to consumers at the time of purchase. The FTC issued a ruling that any merchant issuing a gift card must "boldly" display any fees or expiration dates on the card.[10]

④ How do the three major industry regulatory agencies help keep advertising and business practices from injuring customers or other businesses?

INDUSTRY OVERSIGHT OF MARKETING PRACTICES

Federal regulatory agencies cannot handle all industry activity. Although industry regulatory agencies have no legal power, they can reduce the load on the FTC and the legal system. The three most common and well-known industry regulatory agencies are all a part of the Council of Better Business Bureaus: (1) the National Advertising Division, (2) the National Advertising Review Board, and (3) the Children's Advertising Review Unit (Figure 14.3).

Council of Better Business Bureaus

The Council of Better Business Bureaus provides resources to consumers and businesses. Consumers and firms can file complaints with the bureau about unethical business practices or unfair treatment. The bureau compiles a summary of all charges leveled against individual firms. Customers seeking information about the legitimacy of a company or its operations can contact the bureau. The bureau gives them a carefully worded report containing any complaints against the company and reveals the general nature of customer concerns. The Better Business Bureau helps individuals and businesses make sure they are dealing with a firm with a low record of problems.

National Advertising Division

Complaints about advertising or some aspect of marketing communications are referred to the National Advertising Division (NAD) of the Council of Better Business Bureaus for review. The NAD reviews the specific claims. NAD lawyers collect information and evaluate data concerning the complaint to determine whether the advertiser's claim is substantiated. If it is not, the NAD negotiates with the advertiser to modify or discontinue the ad. When the firm's marketing claim can be substantiated, the complaint is dismissed.

Individuals and companies both can file complaints about unfair ads. Many cases referred to the NAD result from disputes between two rival brands. Recently, H-E-B Grocery, a chain in Texas, filed a complaint with the NAD about a Wal-Mart ad that featured a scene of individuals shopping for groceries. The voiceover says that consumers could save $700 per year if they shopped at Wal-Mart. The final 4 seconds of the ad state that the claim was based on a Global Insight, Inc., study. After investigating the complaint, the NAD ruled against Wal-Mart and said that the claim was not sufficiently substantiated. Although Wal-Mart disagreed with the NAD ruling, the company accepted the request and

FIGURE 14.3 ▶
Regulatory Agencies of the Council of Better Business Bureaus

- National Advertising Division (NAD)
- National Advertising Review Board (NARB)
- Children's Advertising Review Unit (CARU)

discontinued the ad. Wal-Mart's leaders did respond, however, stating, "We firmly believe that the claim is well-supported by the Global Insight study, and that the advertising clearly communicates the claim and the basis for the claim."[11]

The Wal-Mart decision illustrates the power of the NAD and is typical of NAD recommendations. In 95 percent of the cases when the NAD recommends an ad be discontinued or modified, the company voluntarily complies with the decision. The NAD is not a legal entity, which means companies do not have to abide by a decision.[12]

National Advertising Review Board

When a complaint cannot be resolved by the NAD or the advertiser appeals the NAD's decision, it goes to the National Advertising Review Board (NARB). The NARB is composed of advertising professionals and prominent civic individuals. When the NARB rules that the firm's advertisements are not substantiated, it orders the firm to discontinue the advertisements in a manner similar to a consent order by the FTC. The NARB is a private board. When the business or firm being accused refuses to accept the NARB ruling, the matter will be turned over to the FTC or an appropriate federal regulatory agency.

The NARB has been involved in numerous business-versus-business disputes. Minute Maid was recently ordered to modify ads because the copy claimed that consumers preferred Minute Maid orange juice to Tropicana by a 2:1 margin. Tropicana lodged a complaint and won when it was heard by the NAD. Minute Maid disagreed with the NAD ruling and appealed to the NARB. Minute Maid complained that the decision by the NAD placed an unnecessary and unfair burden on comparative advertising, because all claims relative to a competitor must be substantiated. The NARB supported the NAD and issued an order for Minute Maid to comply with the ruling.[13]

The NARB seldom refers a case to the FTC. Such an action has been taken only four times in the past 25 years. The last was a case dealing with Winn-Dixie, which made direct price comparisons with competitors. The NARB found that Winn-Dixie was using prices that were up to 90 days old. The NARB ruled that any price comparisons made in an advertisement by Winn-Dixie must use prices that are no more than 7 days old. The decision to forward the case to the FTC was made when Winn-Dixie refused to modify the ads and accept the NARB ruling.[14]

Children's Advertising Review Unit

The Children's Advertising Review Unit (CARU) investigates and monitors all forms of advertising in all media directed toward children younger than 12 years of age. It also monitors online privacy practices of Web sites targeted at children younger than 13 years of age. The CARU operates in a manner that is similar to the NAD.

In addition to handling complaints about advertising to children, CARU began prescreening ads directed to children in 2005. CARU now examines more than 300 ads per year. The prescreening allows CARU to highlight any potential problems with an advertisement before it goes into production. CARU has also issued a series of guidelines to help advertisers prepare ads for children. Figure 14.4 highlights these guidelines.[15]

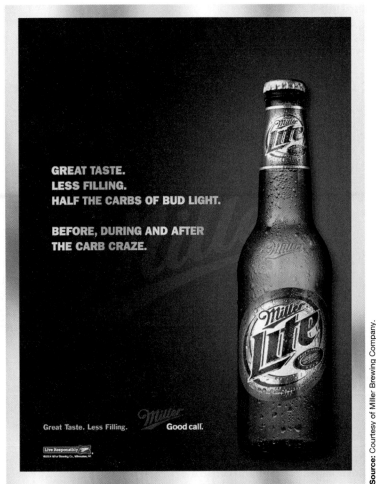

Source: Courtesy of Miller Brewing Company.

▲ Most of the cases reviewed by the NAD are from comparative ads, such as this one by Miller Lite claiming it has "Half the Carbs of Bud Light."

FIGURE 14.4 ▶
CARU Guidelines for Advertising
to Children

FIGURE 14.4 ▶
CARU Guidelines for Advertising
to Children

- Ads for toys should not create unreasonable expectations. Toys shown in ads should look and act as they would if a child were playing with it.
- Ads should not blur the line between fantasy and reality.
- Ads should have clear and visible disclosures about what items come with a toy and what items do not.
- Items that require adult supervision must be shown with adults supervising the child.
- Products and ad content should be appropriate for children.

Children younger than age 12 do not have the same reasoning abilities as adults. Consequently, the CARU stresses the importance of advertisers acting responsibly. Advertisements must show a toy as if a child were playing with it. It must convey the difference between any fantasy used in an ad and the reality when the child plays with the toy. When accessories are shown, the commercial must clearly state that the accessories do not come with the original toy so the child will not be disappointed. If an item such as a trampoline is advertised, then adult supervision must also be shown in the advertisement.

These industry-based actions are designed to control the marketing communications environment and limit legal actions that will be required by the courts or a governmental agency. As highlighted in Figure 14.5, industry regulatory agencies offer several benefits over FTC and legal remedies. The cases are normally heard sooner and are less costly for the companies involved. Further, complaints are heard by attorneys and business professionals with experience in advertising. Although FTC judges may have knowledge of the advertising industry, it is not normally as extensive as the individuals involved in the CBBB's agencies.

Effective management, however, will be proactive rather than reactive. Company leaders can work to create an image of a socially responsible firm. This is a far better approach than reacting to the constant scrutiny of angry consumers and regulatory agencies.

FIGURE 14.5 ▶
Advantages of Using the CBBB's
Industry Regulatory Agencies

- Lower cost
- Faster resolution
- Heard by attorneys and business professionals with experience in advertising

⑤ What ethical criticisms have been registered against advertising and marketing practices?

IMC AND ETHICS

In many instances, an advertising or marketing practice may be deemed legal but be ethically suspect. In this section, various marketing and advertising tactics are considered. Then ethical frameworks and responses are described.

Ethics and morals are key principles that can be used to guide a person's activities in the world of commerce. **Morals** are beliefs or principles that individuals hold concerning what is right and what is wrong. **Ethics** are moral principles that serve as guidelines for both individuals and organizations. Marketing and marketing communications activities are affected by ethical and moral concerns. Ethical issues are present in advertising decisions and actions. At the most general level, several major ethical concerns and criticisms have arisen. They include the items shown in Figure 14.6.

FIGURE 14.6 ▶
Concerns and Criticisms
Regarding Advertising

1. Advertisements cause people to buy more than they can afford.
2. Advertising overemphasizes materialism.
3. Advertising increases the costs of goods and services.
4. Advertising perpetuates stereotyping of males, females, and minority groups.
5. Advertisements often make unsafe products, such as alcohol and tobacco, seem attractive.
6. Advertisements often are offensive.
7. Advertising to children is unethical.

ETHICS AND ADVERTISING

Some critics complain that advertisements cause people to *buy more than they can afford.* It is closely connected to the comment that advertising *overemphasizes materialism.* A case can be made that many commercials do indeed stress luxury, social standing, and the prestige of being first to purchase an item. At the same time, the messages are still just commercials. Those who defend advertising point out that consumers should be responsible for spending money wisely.

Advertising has been alleged to *increase the costs of goods and services.* This debate has been waged for many years. Advertising professionals note that without consumer awareness, products would not be purchased, because consumers would not know of their existence. Further, advertising widens the base of potential customers and may increase repeat business. Additional sales lead to economies of scale and lower, rather than higher, prices.

Perpetuating Stereotypes

Many social commentators have suggested that advertising and other forms of media perpetuate stereotyping of men, women, and minority groups. This leads to several questions. For instance, is segmentation the same as stereotyping? In an era in which the term *political correctness* routinely appears, debate defining "acceptable" continues. In marketing, some of the categories in which market segments are identified include age, race, gender, social status, and income. When marketing to or portraying individuals from these categories, do advertisers use clichés that are no longer appropriate?

Advertisements often depict teenagers in one-dimensional ways rather than reflecting the complexities of young adulthood. Teens are often depicted as rebellious, carefree, and sexually starved. For baby boomers, the images are presented of white, well-educated, well-off people living in spacious homes and driving expensive cars, which stands in contrast to the complex makeup of multiple nationalities of all income levels. From a marketing perspective, it is much easier to group people into smaller subgroups with common interests. Is it unethical, bad business, or simply a practical matter to represent or misrepresent consumers in these ways?

Advertising Unsafe Products

Marketing has been associated with unsafe products, such as alcohol, cigarettes, and other potentially harmful items. By the age of 18, the average American teen has viewed more than 100,000 beer commercials. The use of sexuality and social acceptance combined with humor makes the products in commercials appear desirable. Critics of the brewing industry and marketing agree: Many beer commercials encourage underage drinking and build brand loyalty or brand switching in a population that should not even use the product. Occasional underage drinking can lead to an addiction in a few months, because underage drinkers are less developed mentally, physically, and emotionally. The question becomes: Do a few public relations advertisements represent a real attempt to reduce underage drinking, or are they designed to placate the government and critics?

The same holds true for tobacco products. Many charges have been made arguing that tobacco companies focus on reaching young people through characters such as Joe Camel. Any marketing professional entering the field should consider his or her comfort level with such tactics.

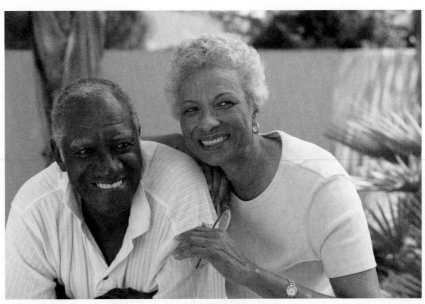

▼ Elderly people are sometimes stereotyped in advertising.

Source: Getty Images–Thinkstock.

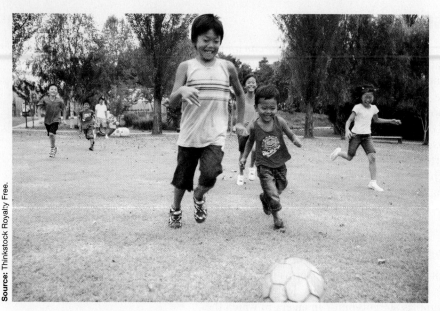

▲ From a social perspective, advertising to children remains a controversial issue.

After tobacco advertising on television was banned by the government, marketers created a series of tactics to make certain company products are mentioned on the air. Sponsorships of the Virginia Slims Tennis Tournament and Marlboro Cup Racing have come under scrutiny, because sportscasters state the names of the products while reporting scores and results. Is this ethical?

Offensive Advertisements

Many adult products require tasteful advertising and marketing programs, even when they are free to be shown through any medium. Feminine hygiene products, condoms, and other personal adult products may be featured in practically any venue. It is the responsibility of the marketing professional to select media that are appropriate as well as to create ads that will not be offensive.

In the international arena, this responsibility becomes even greater. In many Islamic countries, advertisements for personal hygiene or sexually related products would be highly offensive. Company leaders should explore cultural differences before undertaking any kind of marketing campaign.

Another ethical issue that has arisen concerns the use of nudity and sexuality featuring children. In recent years, an increase in sensitivity to issues of child molestation, child pornography, and related sexual issues has emerged. Marketing professionals must carefully consider what the limits should be. Suggesting that sex sells is simply not enough, nor is making a defensive claim about freedom of speech or freedom of expression. Ethics, morals, and a clear conscience should serve as additional guides when a company pushes the limits of sexuality when using young people as models.

Advertising to Children

A continuing controversy in the field of marketing is the ethical acceptability of advertising to children. Children represent a tremendous level of spending and buying power, over $20 billion annually. Critics question the tactics used to reach them.

Mary Pipher, clinical psychologist and author of *The Shelter of Each Other*, suggests that "No one ad is bad, but the combination of 400 ads per day creates in children a combination of narcissism, entitlement, and dissatisfaction."[16] Ads targeted to children employ multiple tactics, including building brand awareness through images and logos, featuring toys and collectibles, and developing tie-ins with television programs and movies, including the recent *Hannah Montana* phenomenon. Characters such as Barney, Ronald McDonald, and Harry Potter vend everything from food to toys to clothes.

With so many potential venues to sell directly to children and to put pressure on their parents, many company leaders believe it is best to "get them while they're young." From a societal perspective, however, the question remains as to whether such impressionable young minds should be subjected to so many messages.

6 What marketing tactics raise ethical concerns?

MARKETING AND ETHICS

Ethical dilemmas are present in places other than advertisements. Many times, however, a connection exists between a marketing program and what takes place in the marketing communications area. A review of some of these issues follows (see Figure 14.7).

- Brand infringement
- Professional services marketing
- Gifts and bribery
- Spam and cookies
- Ambush marketing
- Stealth marketing

◀ **FIGURE 14.7**
Ethical Issues in Marketing

Brand Infringement

Numerous ethical challenges have been associated with brand management. One continuing problem, **brand infringement**, occurs when a company creates a brand name that closely resembles a popular or successful brand, such as when the Korrs beer company was formed. In that case, the courts deemed the brand an intentional infringement, and the name was abandoned. Another brand-infringing company that was ordered by the courts to give up the name was Victor's Secret.

The brand infringement issue becomes more complex when a brand is so well established that it may be considered a generic term, such as a Kleenex tissue or a Xerox copy. Band-Aid encountered the problem in the 1970s, forcing the marketing team to make sure the product was identified as "Band-Aid Brand Strips" rather than simply "band aids," to keep the competition from being able to use the name. The most vulnerable new brand name may be Google, as in "I Googled myself" or "I Googled it."

A newer form of unethical behavior, *domain squatting* or *cyber squatting* on the Internet, is the controversial practice of buying domain names (barnesandnoble.com, kohls.com, labronjames.com, etc.) that are valuable to specific people or businesses in the hopes of making a profit by reselling the name. At the extreme, whitehouse.com was a pornographic Web site. Any new company trying to build a presence in the marketplace may find itself stifled by domain squatters. Names matter, and cyber squatters are willing to take advantage of these activities to make profits at some else's expense.[17]

Marketing of Professional Services

Is it ethical to advertise a physician's services or new drugs? For many years, attorneys, dentists, and physicians did not advertise for fear of being viewed as "ambulance chasers." Recently the trend has gone in the opposite direction. In some instances, a dermatologist will advertise a "skin rejuvenation" practice with only a bare mention that it is also part of a medical practice. Critics argue that this takes medicine into the area of merchandising and suggest that doing so is deceptive.

People injured by accidents, poor medical care, or bad medications are encouraged to call a toll-free number for information on how they can obtain compensation. Other ads encourage people to get rid of bad debts by filing bankruptcies. Critics of medical advertising have suggested attorneys are now chasing the same ambulances, hoping for large settlements of which they receive a substantial portion.

Pharmaceutical companies now spend millions advertising new drugs. A great deal of discussion has taken place with regard to sexual dysfunction products. The unfortunate reality is that many young men are buying and using the drugs for recreational purposes. Some marketing critics complain that advertising and promotional tactics encourage this type of misuse.

▼ Attorneys, dentists, and physicians who advertise have been criticized as "ambulance chasers."

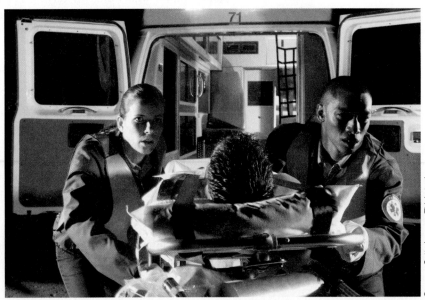

Source: Getty Images–Thinkstock.

The marketing of herbs, supplements, and other untested products has also created concern. Claims are made regarding their contributions to energy level, sexual stamina, and mental acuity. Other products are marketed using unsubstantiated reports about weight loss.

Physicians, pharmaceutical companies, and attorneys have the right to market their services. The ethical questions deal with how these services are presented to the public.

Gifts and Bribery in Business-to-Business Marketing Programs

When marketing to other businesses, close personal contacts are often common, both in personal sales calls and in other venues such as trade shows. Among the more serious ethical issues are gifts and bribery.

To influence sales, purchasing agents and other members of the buying company are often the recipients of gifts, meals, entertainment, and free trips. From a personal ethics standpoint, many concerned leaders question accepting personal gifts that are designed to influence business decisions. The International Olympics Committee wrestled with this issue when Salt Lake City hosted the 2002 Winter Olympics. Exorbitant gifts may have swayed the selection process.

Closely tied with the issue of receiving gifts is offering or accepting bribes. These can be related to gaining governmental contracts or making business contacts. Without them, permits may not be granted or can be very difficult to obtain. In Germany and France, the government actually allows companies to write off bribes as tax deductions.

Spam and Cookies

Technology creates a double-edged sword in the area of marketing. On the one hand, it leads to ingenious new ways to quickly reach a set of consumers with a key message and to keep in continuous contact with those customers. On the other hand, it can be invasive and intrusive and presents ethical dilemmas for those working on the Web.

Many long and loud complaints about spamming have been raised. Even with anti-spam legislation, individuals continue to receive unwanted e-mails. One university in the Midwest receives about 100,000 e-mails a day, of which approximately 98,000 are spam. Should this be considered an ethical issue or simply a practical matter? Either way, the marketing team should assess the viability of spam programs.

Cookie technology allows a company's Web site to track a browser's activities and other Web sites a consumer has visited. The technology allows a firm to customize and personalize Web content to match a consumer's interest. A Harris Interactive survey revealed that 95 percent of consumers believe it is at least somewhat important that companies know "who I am, my buying history, past problems or complaints, preferences, and billing record."[18] At the same time, many consumers are concerned about privacy issues and what firms do with the information collected. Primary questions that are raised are:

- Should an Internet company be allowed to gather this information?
- Should the company be allowed to sell the information to other companies?

Answers fall into two categories: (1) legal and (2) moral. Although it may be legal to collect and transfer consumer information in this manner, the ethical issue remains. Marketing professionals will continue to face the need for quality information. They should balance the need with the ethical ramifications of invading privacy rights. Failure to do so may have long-term implications for both the company and those who use the Internet to shop for products.

Ambush Marketing

The rise of dollars spent on sponsorships of sports and the use of athletes as endorsers has been accompanied by a rise in **ambush marketing**, which is "a brand's attempt to associate itself with a team or event without buying the rights to do so."[19] Official sponsorships

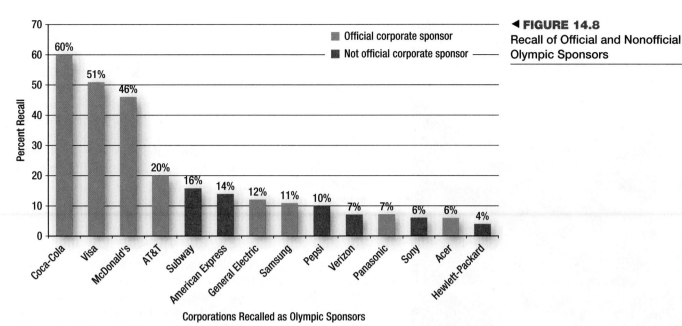

Source: Adapted from Aaron Baar, "Olympics Sponsors Benefit, As Do Competitors," *Marketing Daily* (**www.mediapost.com/publications/ ?fa=Articles.printFriendly&art aid=122665),** February 17, 2010.

often cost millions, so firms have looked at alternative methods of capitalizing on a major sporting event without paying for the rights to be an official sponsor.

To appreciate the potential impact of ambush marketing, consider Figure 14.8. Chadwick Martin Bailey of Boston surveyed individuals asking them to recall the official sponsors of the 2010 Winter Olympics. In Figure 14.8, the bars in blue represent the $40 million companies paid to become official sponsors. The companies indicated by red were not official sponsors, but consumers thought they were. Some of this confusion was deliberately created. Figure 14.9 identifies the primary categories of ambush marketing.

Direct ambush marketing occurs when firms intentionally design advertising or marketing campaigns to capitalize on a major sporting event. The firm seeks to appear to be an official sponsor without stating whether it is or is not a sponsor. VISA was the official credit card sponsor of the Olympics. American Express was not; however, during, and after the Olympics American Express ran television commercials with scenes of Barcelona, Spain (the site of the Summer Olympics) and a message that said, "You don't need a visa" to visit Spain.

Verizon was also not an official sponsor of the Olympics, but the company ran ads stating that it was a sponsor of the U.S. speed skating team. The result of the campaign was that 7 percent of viewers of the Olympics thought Verizon was a sponsor, more than some of the companies that paid the $40 million sponsorship price tag.[20]

Indirect ambush marketing occurs when a firm suggests or hints it is associated with a sporting event when it is not. With **allusion ambushing**, an organization creates an impression that is a sponsor, when it is not. During a recent Summer Olympics, Nike ran a series of ads centered on the number 8, which is a symbol of good luck in China, where the games were being held. Nothing was said about the Olympics or even the athletes competing in the events. **Distractive ambushing** occurs when a company designs a promotion or event near a major sporting event. During a recent

DIRECT AMBUSH ACTIVITIES	
INDIRECT AMBUSH ACTIVITIES ⟶	Allusion ambushing Distractive ambushing Saturation ambushing
INCIDENTAL AMBUSH ACTIVITIES	

◀ **FIGURE 14.9**
Types of Ambush Marketing

Source: Adapted from Simon Chadwick and Nicholas Burton, "Ambushed!" *The Wall Street Journal* (**http://online.wsj.com/article/SB10001424052970204731804574391102699362862.html**). January 25, 2010.

▲ Stealth marketing involves pitching the benefits of a product without revealing you are paid to do so.

Winter Olympics, MasterCard, which was not an official sponsor, sent two catering trucks to busy intersections in Vancouver every day to distribute cups of coffee and cocoa. As a result, MasterCard's logo was seen all over downtown Vancouver on cups and napkins. **Saturation ambushing** occurs when a firm increases advertising and marketing during a major event, such as the NCAA basketball tournament. No mention is made of the event, but the brand will be seen numerous times by viewers of the event not only during but also before and after the event. This method works best when an event lasts several days, such as the NCAA basketball tournament or the Olympics.[21]

Incidental ambushing occurs when a brand is associated with an event without any intentional or indirect effort on the part of the company. At recent collegiate swimming events as well as the Olympics, announcers have mentioned Speedo's LZR Racer swimsuit worn by swimmers. Speedo gained considerable brand exposure, but it was incidental and not planned by Speedo's marketing team.

None of these ambushing strategies are illegal; however, some question whether such approaches are ethical. Clearly, direct and indirect ambush marketing approaches capitalize on the popularity of the event without paying the price to be an official sponsor.

Stealth Marketing

Some companies have used the buzz method of **stealth marketing** to overcome clutter. The approach entices consumers to look at a product through a personal contact without them realizing the person making the pitch is actually being paid or compensated in some way.

Jonathan Margolis, CEO of the Michael Alan Group and co-author of the book *Guerilla Marketing for Dummies*, believes the risks of stealth marketing outweigh the benefits. He says, "It might work if the product is good enough, but ultimately the consumer is being duped. It's risky to stage something that people think is a natural occurrence. There is a potential for backlash. Consumers don't like being deceived, and brands don't want to look bad."[22]

A recent event illustrates why Margolis believes stealth marketing borders on being unethical. An attractive 26-year-old woman was paid by BlackBerry to go to nightclubs and bars and flirt with well-dressed men. She enticed the men to pay attention her, handed them her BlackBerry, and asked them to put their phone numbers in the phone, with the promise she would call. She had no intention of calling; rather she sought to show them the phone, get them to hold it, and use it while she talked about how much she loved it. Many view that level of deception as unethical.

Not all marketers agree. According to Jason Van Trentlyon, president of Street Guerilla Marketing, "Stealth marketing has a greater potential to make a more sincere impact on the public as opposed to a TV or billboard ad. People are inundated with so many blatant advertisements on TV and in magazines that they don't pay attention anymore. This is a way of creating buzz, and any buzz is good buzz."[23]

❼ How can marketers apply the various ethical frameworks and ethics programs to their activities and actions?

RESPONDING TO ETHICAL CHALLENGES

The foundation and frameworks for ethical guidelines are derived from several sources. These include philosophy, law, religion, and common sense.

One *philosophy of life* involves maximizing pleasure and minimizing pain. This idea represents **hedonism**. Critics note that life is often more than the simple pursuit of pleasure and avoidance of pain. **Homeostasis** is the natural craving for balance. People balance a variety of urges throughout life.

The **law** offers guidelines regarding right and wrong as well as what is acceptable and what is not within a geographic area. Legal systems are designed to tell people what they can and cannot do. Remember, however, that not all legal systems are the same.

Many **religions**, or belief systems, profess a version of the philosophy that is summarized by the *Golden Rule*: Do unto others as you would have them do unto you. Acting in a morally acceptable manner starts with treating others well. Still, specific religious ideologies vary widely. Many disagreements about what is right or wrong exist. Respect, tolerance, discussion, compromise, and accommodation should become ethical guidelines when the religious views of others contradict your own.

At the end of the day, one overriding constant may be that ethical actions, moral correctness, and social responsibility all boil down to *common sense.* Two processes can be used to analyze an ethical concept. The first is logic and reasoning, which leads to common sense conclusions. One's conscience may become muted over time if it is continually ignored; however, most people know when they are doing something right or wrong. The second element of common sense is gut instinct. Deep down inside, most people know when something is appropriate or inappropriate. A person's inner thoughts and gut reaction should never be ignored in an ethical-reasoning process.

Ethical Frameworks

The building blocks and personal ethical systems noted in the previous sections help to define various approaches to ethical reasoning. As shown in Figure 14.10, several frameworks have been proposed for the analysis of ethical issues, including utilitarianism, individualism, the rights approach, and the justice approach.

Utilitarianism is a means of making decisions based on what is the greatest good for the greatest number of people. Utilitarianism is referred to as the "calculus of pain," because it tries to minimize pain and maximize pleasure for the greatest number of people.

Unfortunately, utilitarianism perspectives may overlook the rights or needs of the minority. As an extreme example, the use of slaves may create greater well-being for a vast majority of slaveholders, but at the same time the rights of the few, the slaves, are being destroyed.

Ethicists may conclude that utilitarianism involves a judgment call as to what is "good" as well as considering that "good" in light of its effects on both the majority and the minority. Care should be given in deciding how much "pain" to others is acceptable.

Individualism represents the degree to which a society values personal goals, personal autonomy, privacy over group loyalty, commitments to group norms, involvements in collective activities, social cohesiveness, and intense socialization. Therefore, ethical decisions are based on personal self-interests, so long as one's actions do not harm others.

The individualism approach may cause the weakest members of society to suffer the most. In health care, individualists favor systems in which those with money are able to retain the best medical professionals. The individualist position has been used to criticize programs such as socialized medicine. It suggests that those who do not contribute to society's well-being, by being employed and paying taxes, have not earned equal access to health care.

The **rights approach** is a means of making decisions based on the belief that each person has fundamental rights that should be respected and protected. These rights include freedom of speech, privacy, and access to due process, plus the right to a safe and healthy environment at work and at home. Rights to free speech include the rights of companies to advertise any kind of product, even those that make people uncomfortable or ones they object to.

The difficulty with the rights approach is that many times the rights of one group, or a certain type of right, may impede on others. For example, conflict between rights to privacy versus freedom of speech arises when the issue is a job reference. Someone who

• Utilitarianism	• Rights approach
• Individualism	• Justice approach

◀ **FIGURE 14.10**
Ethical Frameworks

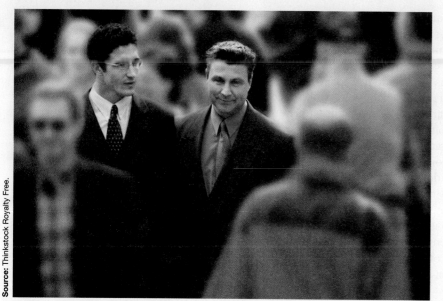

▲ The rights approach is based on the belief that each person has fundamental rights that should be protected.

has been fired for being incompetent, unreliable, or unethical may wish to keep that information confidential. Freedom of speech, however, should protect the rights of a former employer who simply tells the truth about why the person was terminated. As an ethical framework, the balancing act is present in defining what rights apply to a situation and which rights take precedent.

The **justice approach** is a method of decision making based on treating all people fairly and consistently. *Distributive justice* concentrates on the fairness of rewards, punishments, and outcomes. *Procedural justice* focuses on fair and consistent application of rules and protocols.

The justice approach suggests that when someone is hurt by another's actions, as an individual or collectively, there should be consequences. These consequences are supposed to punish the perpetrator for the misdeeds and serve as a deterrent to others. Also, when one's actions help others or lead to a greater good, the consequences should be in the form of a reward. In both circumstances (harm or good), the methods by which rewards are granted or negative sanctions are imposed should be based on an impartial, reasonable, and constant program of judgment and justice.

One problem with the justice approach is that what one person considers a proper reward or punishment may not seem fair to another. Many people believe that capital punishment is a just outcome for some crimes. Others believe it is never justified. The same holds true regarding those who make the judgments. What may seem like a fair procedure to one could appear to be totally biased to another.

ETHICS PROGRAMS

Various individuals and groups have responded to the need for a more ethical environment by creating ethics training programs, codes of ethics, and ethics consulting systems. These attempts are designed to assist individual employees, managers or supervisors, and others within a company facing ethical challenges or dilemmas.

Ethics Training Programs

Ethics training can take place at several points. Early moral training occurs in many families as part of growing up, both in secular settings and in religious organizations. Those attending college receive further instruction. The Association to Advance Collegiate Schools of Business (AACSB), which is a major accrediting body for schools of business, has placed a strong emphasis on ethics instruction for over a decade.

Many corporations now add ethics topics into new-employee training programs as well as manager training systems. Some are self-created; others are developed in conjunction with professional organizations and nearby colleges and universities.

Codes of Ethics

Codes of ethics are created in two ways. The first is within professional organizations. In marketing, two key organizations are the American Marketing Association (AMA) and the American Academy of Advertising (AAA). The AMA code of ethics may be found on the organization's Web site (**www.marketingpower.com**).

The second way ethical codes are developed is within business organizations. Many firms have written and revised ethical codes. Some of the more common components of codes of ethics are displayed in Figure 14.11.

- The purpose of the code, including (1) regulation of behavior and (2) inspiration to employees.
- A statement of aspirations often included in a preamble that outlines the ideals a company aspires to for its employees. The statement should include the values and principles of the organization.
- A list of principles.
- A list of rules, if needed.
- A statement regarding how the code was created.
- How the code will be implemented.
- How the code will be publicized internally to employees.
- How the code will be publicized externally to constituents and publics.
- How the code will be enforced.
- A statement regarding how and when the code will be revised.
- Most of the time, values, principles, and rules are listed in order of importance.

◀ **FIGURE 14.11**
Components of Codes of Ethics

Ethics Consulting Systems

Numerous individuals and organizations are willing to provide counsel regarding ethical dilemmas. Some employ "ethics hotlines" through which a concerned employee can make contact to discuss an ethics problem. The services offered by such organizations vary. Some provide additional instruction, whereas others offer ethical consultations designed to build in-house ethics advisors as well as formulate codes of ethics.

Ethics and social responsibility concerns all boil down to the actions and decisions made by individuals and groups. Any person entering the fields of marketing and advertising should carefully consider what he or she considers to be acceptable and unacceptable acts prior to taking a position as well as while working within any role. The term *whistle-blower* describes an individual who is willing to go public with charges about an organization doing something that is illegal or unethical. Making the choice to be a whistle-blower is difficult; it can cause a career setback and make the individual vulnerable to lawsuits and other retaliatory actions. Failure to take action is also a choice. One's conscience and belief system provide the ultimate guides as to when and how to respond to moral issues.

INTERNATIONAL IMPLICATIONS

❽ What international issues influence the discussion of legal and ethical marketing activities?

Each individual country has its own set of laws regarding what is legal and what is not in the areas of marketing, promotions, and advertising. The role of the marketing department is to make sure these laws and regulations are clearly understood. The company should make every effort to comply with them.

Legal systems vary. In the United States and many Western countries, *common law* is based on local customs, traditions, and precedents. Legal history, previous cases, and national customs serve as guides, and judges typically have more discretion in making legal decisions.

Civil law, which is present in many European countries, is based on a broad set of legal principles, and decisions are made based on legal codes that have been written over time. This gives judges less flexibility.

Theocratic law is based on religious teachings. The most common form of theocratic law, Islamic law, is based on the *Koran* and *Sunnah*. In many Islamic countries, transactions are regulated in different ways. For instance, charging interest is not permitted in the Islamic system.

Moral reasoning follows a similar pattern in international marketing. One cannot assume that a given system of ethics and morals is completely acceptable in another country. For example, views of the roles of men and women in society vary widely. Any marketing program with an international outreach should employ a cultural assimilator to help individuals understand ethical principles present in other nations.

❝❝ SUMMARY

To enforce fair standards in the areas of advertising and marketing communications, a number of governmental agencies are ready to take action when needed. These include the Federal Trade Commission, the Food and Drug Administration, the Federal Communications Commission, and others. Each tries to keep unfair marketing activities from taking place.

The FTC is the primary agency regulating marketing communications, and it makes special efforts to stop instances of unfair or deceptive practices. In conjunction with the courts, the FTC and other governmental agencies regulate the majority of companies and industries in the United States. The FTC regulates cases of fraudulent practices targeted at individual consumers as well as conflicts between businesses. Through the use of consent orders, administrative complaints, cease and desist orders, and full commission hearings, the FTC is able to make its findings and rulings known to the parties concerned. Court actions and corrective advertising programs are utilized in more severe cases. Trade regulation rulings apply when an entire industry is guilty of an infraction.

Ethics and morals are key principles that can be used to guide a person's activities in the world of commerce. Morals are beliefs or principles that individuals hold concerning what is right and what is wrong. Ethics are moral principles that serve as guidelines for both individuals and organizations.

Marketing and marketing communications activities are affected by ethical and moral concerns.

Some of the more common complaints about advertising include issues of materialism and overconsumption. Also, there are criticisms that advertising perpetuates stereotypes, features unsafe products, sends out offensive messages, is deceptive, and unfairly targets children. Each of these issues requires consideration by anyone entering the profession.

Marketing programs are also subject to ethical concerns. Brand infringement, questionable medical marketing and advertising programs, business-to-business tactics, and Internet marketing programs have all come under scrutiny. Responses to these criticisms are the responsibility of top management, the marketing department, and those associated with public relations.

A number of ethical frameworks and guidelines are available. Those in the field of marketing may be guided by concepts regarding social responsibility. Also, ethics programs consisting of ethics training, codes of ethics, and ethics consulting systems are available to those facing dilemmas or wishing to pose questions.

The issues of legality and morality are present in the international arena as well. Each is complicated by different bodies of law and views of ethics in various nations. Companies seeking to expand internationally should be aware of these differences in order to find ways to respond to them.

❞❞

KEY TERMS

Federal Trade Commission (FTC) A federal agency that presides over marketing communications.

puffery When a firm makes an exaggerated claim about its products or services without making an overt attempt to deceive or mislead.

substantiation Firms must be able to prove or back up any claims made in their marketing communications.

consent order A directive issued when the FTC believes a violation has occurred.

administrative complaint A formal proceeding similar to a court trial held before an administrative law judge regarding a charge filed by the FTC.

corrective advertisements Ads that bring consumers back to a neutral state, so consumers once again hold beliefs they had prior to being exposed to a false or misleading advertisement.

trade regulation ruling Findings that implicate an entire industry in a case of unfair or deceptive practices.

morals Beliefs or principles that individuals hold concerning what is right and what is wrong.

ethics Moral principles that serve as guidelines for both individuals and organizations.

brand infringement Occurs when a company creates a brand name that closely resembles a popular or successful brand.

ambush marketing A brand's attempt to associate itself with a team or event without buying the rights to do so.

direct ambush marketing When a firm intentionally designs advertising or marketing to capitalize on a major sporting event without becoming a sponsor.

indirect ambush marketing When a firm suggests or hints that it is associated with a sporting event when it is not.

allusion ambushing When a firm creates an impression that it is a sponsor, when it is not.

distractive ambushing When a firm designs a promotion or event near a major sporting event without sponsoring the event.

saturation ambushing When a firm increases advertising and marketing during a major event without mentioning or sponsoring the event.

incidental ambushing A brand is associated with an event without any intentional or indirect effort on the part of the company.

stealth marketing A tactic in which consumers are enticed to look at a product through a personal contact without them realizing that the person making the pitch is being paid or compensated.

hedonism Maximizing pleasure and minimizing pain.

homeostasis The natural craving for balance.

law Governmental guidelines for what is right and wrong as well as what is acceptable and what is not within a geographic area.

religions Belief systems.

utilitarianism A means of making decisions based on what is the greatest good for the greatest number of people.

individualism The degree to which society values personal goals, personal autonomy, privacy over group loyalty, commitments to group norms, involvements in collective activities, social cohesiveness, and intense socialization.

rights approach A means of making decisions based on the belief that each person has fundamental rights that should be respected and protected.

justice approach A method of decision making based on treating all people fairly and consistently.

REVIEW QUESTIONS

1. Name the governmental agencies that oversee marketing programs.
2. What role did the Wheeler–Lea Amendment play in regulating advertising practices?
3. When does an ad or message become false or misleading?
4. What is puffery? When is puffery legal?
5. What does substantiation mean? How does a company know that the substantiation test has been passed?
6. What four groups can trigger an investigation by the FTC?
7. What are the steps of the process when the FTC investigates a claim of false or misleading advertising?
8. What is a consent order?
9. What is an administrative complaint?
10. What is the purpose of a corrective advertisement?
11. What is a trade regulation ruling? How does it differ from other Federal Trade Commission rulings?
12. What is the relationship between the Council of Better Business Bureaus and the National Advertising Division?
13. What is the primary function of the National Advertising Review Board?
14. How does the Children's Advertising Review Unit operate?
15. Define *ethics* and *morals*.
16. Identify the types of ethical complaints that are raised regarding advertising.
17. What is brand infringement?
18. What types of ethical issues have been raised regarding medical marketing and advertising?
19. Describe the ethical issues associated with Internet marketing.
20. Describe all of the forms of ambush marketing.
21. What is stealth marketing? How does it create an ethics debate?
22. Describe four ethical frameworks noted in this chapter.
23. Name the three types of ethics programs that can be used to help marketing professionals cope with moral challenges.

CRITICAL THINKING EXERCISES

Discussion Questions

1. In labeling of food products, companies walk a fine line between promoting the product and truth in content. Phrases such as "low sodium," "fat free," "no sugar added," and "light" may give the impression that a food is healthful, but not reveal the entire truth. How often do you read package labels and make purchases based on their content? On your next trip to the grocery store, examine various labels that have one of the words identified earlier in this question and compare them to other brands. Do those brands actually contain less than competing brands?

2. Reread the section "Deception Versus Puffery." Find three advertisements that you think are examples of either deception or puffery. How difficult is it to differentiate between the two? When does an ad cease to be puffery and become deceptive?

3. One of the industries closely watched by the FTC is the weight-loss industry. Find three advertisements from magazines, newspapers, or television that deal with weight loss. What claims were made? Do you believe the claims are truthful and legitimate? How do you, as a consumer, distinguish between what is truthful and what is deceptive?

4. Advertising directed toward children remains a hot topic among parents and educators. Many feel that advertising unfairly targets children and creates materialistic desires. By the time a child is 3 years old she already knows many brands of products, such as McDonald's. What is your opinion of advertising to children? Is the current regulation enough, or should it be more stringent?

5. One of the criticisms of advertising is that it causes people to buy more than they can afford. Each year a large number of people in United States declare bankruptcy, often because they have overspent. Do you agree that advertising causes people to buy more than they can afford, or is advertising just responding to the materialistic desire of individuals? Defend your response.

6. Advertising does increase the cost of goods and services, but a common defense is that advertising provides people with knowledge about availability of products, which allows consumers to make more intelligent decisions. Do you think this is a valid defense of advertising? Why or why not? What other defense could you offer to support why advertising is important?

7. Think about advertisements you have seen or heard recently and identify one that you believe is offensive. Why was it offensive? Why do you think the advertiser ran the ad if it is offensive? Do you think offensive ads can be effective? Why or why not?

8. What is your opinion of alcohol and tobacco advertising? Should alcohol and tobacco companies have the same freedom to advertise as other product manufacturers? Do you think it is a danger for children to see alcohol or tobacco ads? Does it influence their desire to use these products?

9. Using sex to sell products is another area that many consumers find offensive. Locate two print ads or television ads that are highly sexual in nature, one that you consider offensive and one that you consider is appropriate. What makes the difference? Are there too many ads that use sexual themes?

10. You undoubtedly have seen advertisements by attorneys and medical professionals. Discuss your opinion about these advertisements? Do you think ads by attorneys just increase the number of lawsuits and bankruptcies? Why do medical professionals such as doctors and dentists advertise? Does it affect your opinion of their professionalism? Why or why not?

11. Figure 14.10 identifies four ethical frameworks. Although each framework has its merits, which one do you lean toward or believe in the most? Why? Discuss the other three frameworks in terms of your own personal philosophy of life.

12. Do you believe that ethics can be learned, or is it something an individual has internally? What can companies do, if anything, to make their employees more ethical? Why has America seen so much corruption in the corporate world? What steps would you suggest to curb this corruption?

INTEGRATED LEARNING EXERCISES

1. The Federal Trade Commission (FTC) is the primary federal agency that oversees advertising and other marketing-related communications. Access its Web site at **www.ftc.gov**. What type of information is available on the Web site for consumers? For businesses? Pick one of the headlines and write a brief report about the article's contents.

2. The FTC's Bureau of Consumer Protection works for the consumer to prevent fraud, deception, and unfair business practices in the marketplace. Access the FTC's Web site at **www.ftc.gov** and go to the Consumer Protection section of the site. What information is available? Find an article or recent event from the Web site and write a short report. How does the FTC's Bureau of Consumer Protection safeguard consumers?

3. Access the FTC's Web site at **www.ftc.gov**. Access each of the following components of the Web site. What type of information does each section contain? Why is it important?
   a. Competition
   b. Economics
   c. Policy

4. One of the primary functions of the FTC is to investigate possible false and deceptive advertising and marketing practices. Access the FTC Web site at **www.ftc.gov**. Go to the "Actions" section of the site. Read through the list of recent actions. Find two that are interesting. Review the cases and write a brief report on each case. What were the results of the FTC investigation?

5. Access the FTC Web site at **www.ftc.gov**. Go to the "News" section of the Web site. Read through the list of recent actions. Find two that are interesting. Review the cases and write a brief report on each case. What were the results of the FTC investigation?

6. The Council of Better Business Bureaus is an important industry organization for businesses as well as consumers. Access the Web site at **www.cbbb.org**. What types of information are available on the Web site? How can the CBBB assist consumers? How can it be beneficial to businesses?

7. Access the Web site of the Council of Better Business Bureaus at **www.cbbb.org**. Go to the "Business" section of the Web site. What types of information are available? Briefly describe each component of the "Business" section of the Web site and how it is beneficial to businesses.

8. The National Advertising Division (NAD) of the Council of Better Business Bureaus can be found at **www.nadreview.org**. Access the site. Look through the recent cases the NAD has investigated. Find two of interest to you. Write a report about each case, discussing the issues and the findings of the NAD.

9. The Children's Advertising Review Unit (CARU) of the Better Business Bureau can be found at **www.caru.org**. Access the site. Look through the recent cases the CARU has investigated. Find two of interest to you. Write a report about each case discussing the issues and the findings of the CARU.

10. Protecting the privacy of children is an important function of the Children's Advertising Review Unit (CARU). Access the CARU Web site at **www.caru.org**. Go to the "Privacy Program" component of the site. Discuss the information that is available on the site. How does this protect children? How is it beneficial to parents?

STUDENT PROJECT

Creative Corner

Solidax ADX was developed in the United States in 2005 and was recently rated by the Weight Loss Institute to be the best weight-loss product on the market. Solidax ADX is based on synephrine, chromium picolinate, and pyrovate and is designed to suppress appetite and increase metabolism and calorie expenditure. Unlike other diet pills, it does not have negative central nervous effects.

The ingredients found in Solidax have been proven to be effective in controlled, laboratory-based human weight-loss studies.[24]

Concerned about recent FTC investigations of false and deceptive advertising of competing brands, the makers of Solidax ADX want a print ad that will be effective but not subject to FTC investigation. Based on the information provided, design a print advertisement for Solidax ADX.

CASE 1   ASSESSING SMART CHOICES

One continuing trend in the United States is an interest in the content of food products. Many consumers want to buy foods that promote good health and nutrition. One recent effort that generated a substantial amount of controversy was the Smart Choices Program, which was created by the nonprofit American Society of Nutrition. Ten large food manufacturers enrolled in the program, including Kellogg's and Kraft.

Under the system, a food product had to meet a specific set of guidelines to qualify for the Smart Choices endorsement. The system was based on the federal Dietary Guidelines for Americans developed by a conglomerate of food industry leaders, academics, nutritionists, and public interest organizations. Accepted products received permission to print a front-of-package or front-of-box label, in the form of a large green checkmark, with the phrase "Smart Choices Program and Guiding Food Choices" underneath. The logo clearly suggested an endorsement of a nutritional program, and many critics believed consumers would interpret the label as carrying a governmental stamp of approval.

Any company wishing to place the Smart Choices label and logo was required to pay up to $100,000 per year for the right to do so. Quickly, manufacturers of a series of foods, including sugary cereals, snacks, and sandwich spreads, paid the money. Among the products that featured the endorsement were Fruit Loops, Kid Cuisine Cheeseburgers, Teddy Grahams, and Kraft Macaroni and Cheese. And as one industry observed noted, the more products receiving the label, the greater the amount of money the American Society of Nutrition was able to collect from a food producer.

▲ The Smart Choice endorsement suggested a nutritional, healthy product.

It did not take long for the reactions to grow strong. Following a *CBS Evening News* report and other exposures in various media, companies began to withdraw support for the Smart Choices Program logo. Charges were raised that conflicts of interest could not be avoided using the system as it had been implemented. The Food and Drug Administration (FDA) issued a Guidance for Industry letter in October of 2010. The agency announced that it would analyze food labels with the intent of identifying any that might be misleading. The FDA also announced it would develop a universal front-of-packaging labeling system that all food manufacturers must follow. The FDA did not name the Smart Choices Program specifically in the letter, but the program subsequently decided to suspend the use of the logo.

The Friedman Sprout, which is the official student newspaper for the Friedman School for Nutrition Science and Policy, published an article wondering if the school's reputation had been damaged by the involvement of the school's dean with The American Society of Nutrition.

The American Society of Nutrition continues operations. Its chief officer remains with the organization. The organization has announced intentions to follow new FDA guidelines for labels on packages and to become re-involved with the food manufacturers that had originally participated in the program.

1. Why would the FDA become involved in this situation? What legal standard might have been violated?

2. What actions could the FDA have taken beyond writing a Guidance for Industry letter?

3. Do you believe the American Society of Nutrition violated any ethical standards? If so, which ones?

4. Do you believe the food manufacturers that sold sugary cereals and junk food carrying the Smart Choices Program label violated any ethical standards? If so, which ones? Explain.

5. Should the food manufacturers continue associating with the American Society of Nutrition? Why or why not?

6. Do you believe the dean of the School for Nutrition Science and Policy violated any ethical standards? If so, which ones? Explain.

Sources: Kelly Dumke and Rachel Zavala, "The Controversy Surrounding Smart Choices," *The Friedman Sprout* (http://friedmansprout. wordpress.com/2009/12/02/the-controversy-surrounding-smart-choices/), December 2, 2009; Randall Pinkston, "Experts Say Industry Food Labels Deceptive," *CBS Evening News* (www.cbsnews.com/ stories/2009/09/06/eveningnews/main5291352.shtml), September 6, 2009; "Smart Choices?" *CBSNewsOnline* (www.youtube.com/ watch?v=dWMVcURE-eE, accessed May 18, 2010); Rebecca Ruiz, "Eight Puzzling Food Labels," *Forbes* (www.forbes.com/2009/09/23/ food-labels-healthy-lifestyle-health-smart-choices-nutrition.html), September 23, 2009.

CASE 2   CRAIGSLIST: COMMUNITY AND CONTROVERSY

In 1995, Craig Newmark, an enterprising software engineer, created an e-mail list for friends and coworkers. At the time, he was employed by Schwab after stints with several other companies in IT departments. In 1999, Craig Newmark retired and began working full time on the Craigslist Web site.

The original intention of the page was to help people to locate jobs, housing, goods, services, romance, local activities, and advice—just about anything. Today, the site provides local classified ads and forums for over 450 cities worldwide. By 2008, Craigslist had over 9 billion visitors per month.

In 2000, the organization was headed by a new CEO, Jim Buckmaster. Buckmaster has been described as a communist, a socialistic anarchist, and an anti-establishment leader. He has been condemned by many, including now-deceased minister Jerry Falwell on a national Fox television broadcast.

Why such a high level of antipathy toward an organization linked with eBay (25 percent ownership)? Why the frustration with a forum for finding a house or getting a job? The answer may be with the community itself.

Although Craigslist is careful to avoid illegal activities, such as cyber-stalking, identity theft, and prostitution, it has been used to facilitate some of these crimes. For example, one woman used Craigslist to find a contract killer to execute her husband. In 2010, Craiglist deleted one page of the Web site that offered adult services with the word "Censored" over the listing. Some viewed the action as a form of protest more than the attempt to slow adult solicitation of sexual activity.

Even after these events had been addressed, many complain that some of the content on Craigslist is explicitly sexual, scatological, offensive, graphic, tasteless, and/or not funny. The site acknowledges that this is the case.

At the same time, Craigslist is involved in community work, makes charitable contributions, and serves as a resource for nonprofit organizations. The company's mission includes a statement regarding "helping people help."

1. How might laws and regulations associated with marketing affect an organization such as Craigslist?

2. Should any additional laws be created to deal with social community Web sites such as Craigslist? If so, what type?

3. What are the moral implications of a Web site that hosts arrangements for ethically questionable activities, such as sexual encounters among married people with nonspouse partners?

4. How do the concepts regarding social responsibility apply to an organization such as Craigslist?

15 Evaluating an Integrated Marketing Program

SANDS RESEARCH, INC.

Neuromarketing on the Cutting Edge

If any one theme emerges from the interviews with members of the various advertising agencies featured in this textbook, it would be that companies demand clear and convincing evidence that marketing and advertising actually work. Tangible measures such as increases in store traffic, Web site hits, coupons redeemed, and sales provide behavioral evidence. Many times, of course, other factors influence these outcomes, and a time lag, from when the ad ran to when the behavior occurred, also be involved.

Advertising agencies continue to look for methods to refine the development and delivery of marketing messages. Many techniques are available, including day-after-recall tests and studies of brand perceptions and loyalty. What remains is finding real-time data suggesting that an advertisement has captured and kept a viewer's attention.

Sands Research, Inc., led by its chairman and chief science officer, Dr. Steve Sands, is a leading neuromarketing firm. The company is a pioneer in developing applications that use cognitive neuroscience technology to provide unique insights into consumer responses to television and print advertisements, product packaging, and digital media. By combining its technology with before and after questionnaires, Sands Research provides a comprehensive, objective analysis of the viewer's engagement in the marketing material being presented by an advertiser.

Recently, Dr. Sands announced a breakthrough in the rapidly growing area of applying neuroscience to market research. Sands Research uses high-density arrays of EEG (electroencephalograph) sensors to capture brainwave activity across the full brain at 10,000 times a second, per sensor. In essence, this means the firm has the ability to study the impact a message has on capturing a person's attention and track times of peak interest as the person stays engaged with that message.

Traditional methods of analyzing the impact of an advertisement use rating statements and open-ended questions that tend to be verbally

▼ Sands Research uses EEG sensors to study brain activity created by viewing advertisements or marketing materials.

Source: Shutterstock.

CHAPTER OBJECTIVES

After reading this chapter, you should be able to answer the following questions:

1 What are the three broad categories of evaluation tools that can be used to evaluate IMC systems?

2 How do marketing teams match evaluation methods with IMC objectives?

3 What forms of message evaluations can be conducted to assess IMC programs?

4 Which evaluation criteria are suggested by the positioning advertising copytesting (PACT) system?

5 How do online evaluation systems assist advertising managers in assessing the quality of a firm's Internet activities?

6 What types of behavioral evaluations can be employed to assess IMC programs?

7 What criteria should be used to assess the overall IMC program?

8 How are evaluation programs adjusted to match international operations?

biased. They may also fail to completely measure the impact of the nonverbal components of commercials, including music and visuals. Creative people have long suspected that traditional research approaches, such as day-after-recall testing, unfairly reward overly rational advertising and penalize emotional executions.

Research suggests that when commercials quickly capture attention, they tend to generate more "peak" moments during the run. Peak moments of attention increase positive feelings toward commercials and potentially influence recall. Peaks are likely to occur when:

- Important news, such as the announcement of a strong price promotion, is provided.
- Inciting incidents, typically involving a moment strongly charged with negative emotion to set up a joke or storyline, appear.
- Surprising moments or turning points in stories take place.
- The delivery of climatic moments or punch lines occurs.

The value of these new techniques may be enhanced through the understanding that three different memory systems may be involved in developing a person's view of a brand: knowledge memories, emotion or episodic memories, and action or procedural memories of bodily

Pummelos • Lemons • Navel Oranges • Moro Blood Oranges • Grapefruit

Cara Cara Oranges • Satsuma Mandarins • Minneola Tangelos • Meyer Lemons

Persian Limes • Key Limes • Clementine Mandarins • Fairchild Tangerines

MASTER THE YIN & YANG OF ASIAN FLAVORS.

With Sunkist. citrus, you'll have them eating right out of your chopsticks!

Sunkist

For an inspirational spin on Asian menuing, ask for our new *Flavors of Asia Wheel*. Developed by Chef Robert Danhi, these new recipe concepts make it easy to add exotic, patron-pleasing flavor to any menu. To request your wheel and for more citrus recipes, visit foodservice.sunkist.com

SUNKIST and Design are registered trademarks of ©2008 Sunkist Growers, Inc. All rights reserved.

Source: Courtesy of Sunkist Growers.

▲ Through cognitive neuroscience, Sands Research better understands how consumers process the information and visuals contained in this Sunkist advertisement.

experiences and physical sensations. Evidence from these studies suggests that these memories might be stored in different parts of the brain.

393

Consequently, a rational and verbal memory might be reported but emotional or episodic memories may not. This would explain the under-reporting of the impact of musical and visual cues in advertisements.

The full impact of these new technologies has yet to be realized. At the least, Sands Research suggests the company can help an advertiser create an advertisement with the greatest potential for capturing attention from storyboard to the run of the commercial. And,

an exciting new era in marketing measurement may be well underway.[1]

❶ What are the three broad categories of evaluation tools that can be used to evaluate IMC systems?

▼ This advertisement for the Lafayette House could be evaluated using either a message evaluation or a respondent behavior technique.

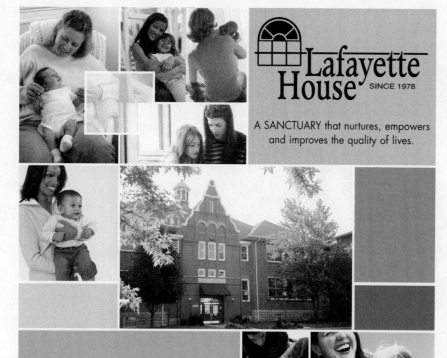

Lafayette House SINCE 1978

A SANCTUARY that nurtures, empowers and improves the quality of lives.

Working to end domestic violence and substance abuse in our communities.

A United Way/United Fund member agency

Supported by the Domestic Violence Shelter Tax Credit Program, through the Missouri Department of Public Safety

Source: Courtesy of Joplin Globe.

OVERVIEW

John Wanamaker, a well-known nineteenth-century department store owner, was one of the first to use advertising to attract customers to his store. He once remarked, "I know half the money I spend on advertising is wasted, but I can never find out which half." Evaluating the effectiveness of advertising has become increasingly difficult. In today's environment, company executives demand measurable results because of the high costs of advertising campaigns. The challenge for advertising account executives and others who prepare ads is offering evidence that those campaigns are successful.

To meet the growing insistence for accountability, research and media experts spend time and energy seeking to develop new and accurate measures of success. These measures, known as **metrics**, should accurately portray the effectiveness of a marketing communications plan, which is not an easy task.

This final chapter considers the various methods available for evaluating components of an IMC program. Three broad categories of evaluation tools can be used to evaluate IMC systems: message evaluations, online evaluations, and respondent behavior evaluations.

Message evaluation techniques examine the message and the physical design of the advertisement, coupon, or direct marketing piece. Message evaluation procedures include the study of actors in advertisements as well as the individuals who speak in radio ads. A message evaluation program considers the cognitive components associated with an ad, such as recall and recognition, as well as emotional, attitudinal, and behavioral intention responses.

Online evaluation metrics examine online advertising and marketing campaigns. The Internet provides a unique set of metrics not available with traditional media. In addition to click-throughs, companies can track such metrics as dwell rate and dwell time. The Internet provides highly accurate, real-time measures of consumer reactions.

Respondent behavior evaluations address visible customer actions, including store visits, inquiries, or actual purchases. This category contains evaluation techniques that are measured using numbers, such as the number of coupons redeemed, the number of hits on a Web site, and changes in sales.

The emphasis on providing compelling proof that advertising actually works has led to a greater emphasis on respondent behaviors. Higher sales, increases in store traffic, a greater number of daily Internet hits on a Web site, and other numbers-based outcomes appeal to many managers. At the same time, message evaluations, online metrics, and behavioral responses help the marketing manager and advertising team build short-term results and achieve long-term success.

MATCHING METHODS WITH IMC OBJECTIVES

Methods of evaluation are chosen to match the objectives being measured.[2] An advertising campaign with the objective of increasing customer interest in and recall of a brand will be measured using the level of customer awareness as the metric. Normally, this means the marketing team measures awareness before, during, and after the ads have run. At other times, objectives vary. Redemption rates measure the success of a campaign featuring coupons, which means behaviors (purchasing) rather than cognitive processes (recall) are being tested. Redemption rates reveal the number of items purchased, with and without coupons.

Several levels are used to analyze an advertising or IMC program. They include the following:

- Short-term outcomes (sales, redemption rates)
- Long-term results (brand awareness, brand loyalty, or brand equity)
- Product-specific awareness
- Awareness of the overall company
- Affective responses (liking the company and a positive brand image)

The temptation may arise to overemphasize the first factor, short-term outcomes, without considering the long-term impact of a campaign or marketing program. The company endeavors to maintain a voice that carries across campaigns over time. Consider Budweiser's advertising. Many ads achieved short-term success because they were funny. Over time, Anheuser-Busch has maintained a strong and consistent voice by using humor to promote products, from the Budweiser frogs and lizards to the "Whazzup" team, the "True" campaign, and more recent radio ads glorifying odd habits and occupations.

In light of the overall marketing and advertising goals, the marketing manager then considers the various options for evaluating advertising. Evaluation procedures are selected prior to launching a campaign. An ad placed in a trade journal can contain a code number, a special telephone number, or a special Internet microsite to track responses. For coupons, premiums, and other sales promotions, code numbers are printed on each item to identify the source.

In general, careful planning prior to initiating an IMC program makes evaluation of the campaign easier and more accurate. At the same time, the evaluation of a specific advertisement or marketing piece may be difficult, because many factors affect the outcome being measured. For instance, a retailer may run a series of newspaper and radio ads to boost store traffic. In order to measure the impact of the ads, the retailer keeps records of store traffic before, during, and after the campaign. Unfortunately, the traffic count may be affected by other factors, even something as simple as the weather. If it rains for 2 days, the traffic count will probably be lower. Further, the store's chief competitor may

2 How do marketing teams match evaluation methods with IMC objectives?

▼ Careful planning prior to launching a campaign can help a company such as A.G. Edwards better evaluate the effectiveness of advertising.

YOU CAN'T RIDE OFF INTO THE SUNSET IF YOUR NEST EGG WON'T CARRY YOU. We're big believers in a long-term retirement plan based on objective financial advice. And in having a financial consultant who can help you every step of the way. To see whether your nest egg could benefit from such Midwestern horse sense, visit agedwards.com or call 866-379-4243.

A.G. EDWARDS.
FULLY INVESTED IN OUR CLIENTS.

Source: Courtesy of A.G. Edwards, Inc.

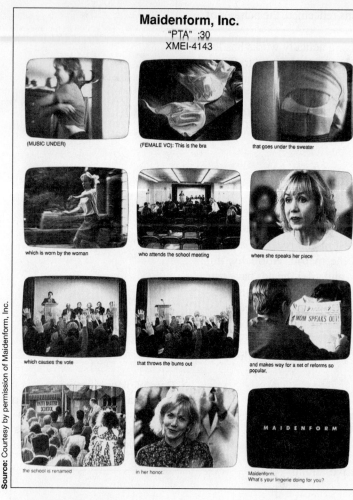

▲ A storyboard for a
Maidenform TV advertisement.

③ What forms of message
evaluations can be
conducted to assess IMC
programs?

run a special sale during the same time period, which also affects traffic. A TV program, such as the season finale of a major series, or even a special program at the local high school (commencement, school play), could have an impact. In other words, many extraneous factors might affect results. When reviewing an advertising program, these factors should be considered.

Performing one specific analysis normally does not adequately assess the influence of the impact of an advertisement on a company's image. Even though store traffic was low, the ad may have been stored in the buyer's long-term memory, which may make a difference later. Conversely, the same ad may have been awkward or in some way offensive. The store owner may believe the weather affected the outcome instead of a poor advertising design. Consequently, company leaders consider short- and long-term implications when assessing an IMC program.

MESSAGE EVALUATIONS

Evaluation or testing of advertising communications occurs at every stage of the development process. This includes the concept stage before an advertisement is produced. Testing at that stage often involves soliciting the opinions of a series of experts or from "regular" people. Ads can be tested after the design stage is complete but prior to development. Television commercials can be designed using a **storyboard**, which is a series of still photographs or sketches outlining the structure of the commercial. Print ads can be analyzed using artist sketches.

Although ads and marketing pieces can be tested prior to production, most advertising agencies perform a small amount of pretesting, primarily due to the lack of reliable test results. According to Elena Petukhova from The Richards Group advertising agency, "We really don't trust the results of pretests using boards because the format makes a difference. Consumers are used to seeing the finished product, so when you show them a mockup or sketch they tend not to see it very positively. It is difficult for them to make the transition to what the ad will look like after production, and in their minds they compare it to finished ads, which produce low evaluation scores. Whenever possible, we wait until after production to test ads."[3]

As shown in Figure 15.1, the primary methods used by companies and advertising agencies to evaluate advertising and ad campaign messages are advertising tracking

FIGURE 15.1 ▶
Evaluating Advertising Messages

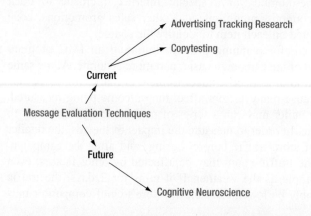

research and copytesting. Each fits with different circumstances, advertising methods, and IMC objectives.

Advertising Tracking Research

A common method of evaluation involves tracking an advertisement by one of the advertising research firms, such as Nielsen IAG or Millward Brown. Tracking research examines ads that have launched. It is an in-market research method that monitors a brand's performance and advertising effectiveness. Tests can be performed at specific times or intervals or continuously. Ad tracking provides a general measure of the effect of the media weight (i.e., spending level), the effectiveness of the media buys, and the quality of the ad's message and execution. By using ad tracking, the relative impact of a message compared to the competition and over time can be examined.

Nielsen IAG provides ad tracking. The company offers a syndicated database of real-time brand and ad performance tracking based on more than 210,000 program television episodes and 250,000 commercials. In addition to television ads, the service can be used to evaluate Internet ads and in-cinema campaigns. Nielsen conducts thousands of surveys daily measuring viewer engagement with TV programs and the effectiveness of each advertisement on network and cable television channels.[4]

Ad Tracking Methodology

With ad tracking, research respondents are usually shown a brief portion of an advertisement or a few stills from a TV ad with the brand name removed or not visible. Respondents are asked if they recognize the company, which measures brand and ad recognition. They are then asked to identify the brand being advertised, which measures unaided brand awareness. When they are unable to correctly identify the sponsor, they are given a list of brands and asked to identify the correct brand, which measures aided brand awareness. In addition to recognition and unaided and aided brand awareness, tracking research also measures:

- Memorability
- Likability
- Unaided and aided message recall
- Unaided and aided campaign recall

Similar techniques are now available for magazines. Mediamark Research & Intelligence's AdMeasure tracks recall and response to advertisements in every issue of 200 magazine titles. Affinity has produced a competing service, the American Magazine Study Print Ad Ratings, which tracks ad measurements across 125 magazine titles.[5]

The Richards Group employs Nielsen IAG to provide ad tracking research for television ads for its clients, which include Motel 6, Home Depot, Chick-fil-A, and Bridgestone. IAG tracks every ad for The Richards Group's clients as well as for each brand's major competitors. This allows for comparisons with the competition and tracks performance over time.

▼ Tracking measures can now be used to evaluate print ads in magazines, in addition to television and the Internet.

Report Cards and Benchmarks

According to Dave Snell of The Richards Group, the tracking by Nielsen IAG offers a continuous "report card" as well as a "benchmark." Within the second or third week of a new campaign, the ad tracking research provides two types of information about a new advertisement's performance. First, it shows how the new ad performs in comparison to the brand's competitors. Second, it

Show Your True Colors.

Flair
J·E·W·E·L·E·R·S
Monroe • West Monroe

Source: Courtesy of Newcomer, Morris & Young, Inc.

indicates show how well the advertisement performed in relation to those from previous campaigns.

Nielsen IAG also builds a benchmark for a company as it measures ad performance over months and years. These benchmark data are extremely valuable when a new campaign launches. New ads are compared to previous ones along various dimensions to ensure the ads performed as expected. Using the benchmark from previous ads provides a better indicator of performance than would comparisons with competitors or ads for similar products.

The tracking service can also "help us to know when wear-out is beginning to set in," says Dave Snell. Measuring the ads' effectiveness on a biweekly basis and graphing those measures indicates when an advertisement starts to lose its impact. At that point, the agency and client can switch to a new campaign, bring back a previous ad, or modify the current commercial.

According to The Richards Group's Elena Petukhova, the one disadvantage of ad tracking services is that they do not provide any diagnostics. The data indicate how the ad performs in relation to the competition, against previous ads, and over time. They do not provide information about why an advertisement did not perform well. Other types of research are used to find out why an advertisement failed. In essence, ad tracking research indicates when an advertisement has worn out or is not performing, but it does not tell the agency what to do.

Copytesting

The second form of message evaluation, copytesting, assesses the finished marketing piece or one in the final stages of development. **Copytests** elicit responses to the main message of the ad as well as the format used to present the message.

Three common copytesting techniques are portfolio tests, theater tests, and online tests. A **portfolio test** displays of a set of print ads, one of which is the ad being evaluated. A **theater test** displays of a set of television ads, including the one being evaluated. The individuals who participate do not know which piece is under scrutiny. Both techniques mimic reality in the sense that consumers normally are exposed to multiple messages, such as when a radio or television station plays a series of commercials in a row or when a set of newspaper ads appears on a single page. The tests also allow researchers to compare the target piece with other marketing messages. For these approaches to yield the optimal findings, all of the marketing pieces shown must be in the same stage of development, such as preproduction ads or finished ads.

The use of the Internet is quickly replacing both the portfolio and theater tests for copytesting. Online copytesting costs less and produces more immediate results. Millward Brown is one of several advertising research firms that use online testing procedures, including copytesting. Typically, an agency client will perform copytests five to eight times per year. Copytests provide an advertising agency with the in-depth potential of an ad under ideal circumstances. When tests are conducted online, consumers pay more attention to the ad than they would for a television show, radio program, or while reading a magazine. Therefore, copytesting results offer a measure of the ad's potential when it receives the viewer's complete, 100 percent attention.

▼ Copytesting provides valuable input for advertising agencies and clients such as 3M about the effectiveness of ads.

Copytesting are used for finished ads that have already been launched. Millward Brown typically copytests the ad using 150 respondents. Quantitative questions that are asked address issues such as:

- Breakthrough ability
- The brand message and image
- How memorable the ad and brand are
- How enjoyable the ad is
- What the ad communicates
- How well it communicates the intended message
- Potential responses (i.e., likelihood of making a purchase)
- Persuasive power of the ad
- Engagement of the viewer with the ad and brand

Testing Emotional Reactions

In addition to these measures, Millward Brown provides a second-by-second emotional reaction chart that shows how viewers feel about an advertisement to be shown on television. As they watch the ad on a computer screen, respondents move the computer mouse to indicate their feelings, one direction for positive feelings the other direction for negative feelings. By superimposing these 150 emotional reaction tests onto one graph, the client sees how the feelings and emotions of the respondents change throughout the advertisement. This information is quite valuable, because it indicates when emotions change. Although the test does not measure the level of emotion but rather changes in emotion, these data provide sufficient evidence for the agency to develop hypotheses or best practice ideas to assist in making future advertisements.

Verbatim Comments

The final piece of information provided to clients by Millward Brown and other agencies is the verbatim comments of the respondents. Each respondent is asked to present, in his or her own words, thoughts about the advertisement. According to The Richards Group's Dave Snell, "These verbatim comments are extremely valuable to us because it provides a written commentary on what people think about the ad and what thoughts are foremost from watching the ad."[6] Millward Brown asks a number of open-ended questions to engage respondents and gain a deeper understanding of their thought processes. The research team also asks respondents to tell the story of the ad, which provides additional valuable insights. According to Elena Petukhova, "It can tell you a lot about the ad, both positive and negative. It tells you what the customer sees and thinks and how the ad story came across to them."[7]

As noted, ad tracking does not generate information about why an ad did not perform well or what to do to correct it. Copytesting procedures can provide some of this information. Advertising creatives can then determine what to do next. By using continuous ad tracking and copytesting, an agency can build a benchmark for a particular client on an advertisement's performance. The agency can also gain ideas on what works and what does not for consumers for that particular product category and brand.

Copytesting Controversies

Some controversy regarding copytesting remains. A number of advertisers and marketers strongly believe that copytesting favors rational approaches over affective and

▼ Verbatim comments obtained through copytesting can be valuable when evaluating advertisements featuring celebrities, such as Spike Lee.

conative (action-inspiring) methods. To correct this potential deficiency, some research firms have added emotional tests to copytesting procedures.

Further, some marketers believe copytesting prior to production stifles the creativity needed to produce ads that will stand out in the clutter. Recently, creatives working for brands including Nike, Volkswagen, Budweiser, and Target have been allowed to skip the copytesting phase of advertising design and move straight into production. Unless the client insists on preproduction copytests, a few agencies move directly into production and perform copytests after the ad launches. Many advertisers believe copytests are likely to lead to ad messages about the product benefits that are believable and understandable to members of a focus group or copytest panel. Most consumers in focus groups will know little, if anything, about how to create an effective advertisement. It does not make sense to have them serve as final judges of an ad's quality.

Although a number of marketing professionals do not favor using copytests at all, the majority believe they are necessary, primarily due to accountability issues. When the time comes to support a decision for a high-dollar advertising campaign, advertising agency and company executives want evidence that supports the investment. Also, advertising agencies can use the results of copytesting to perfect future ads and campaigns by understanding what works and what does not work in a given marketplace.

Emotional Reaction Tests

Many ads are designed to elicit emotional responses from consumers. Emotional ads are based on the concept that ads eliciting positive feelings are more likely to be remembered. Also, consumers who have positive attitudes toward ads develop more positive attitudes about the product. This, in turn, should result in increased purchases.[8]

Measuring the emotional impact of an advertisement can be difficult. The simplest method involves asking questions about an individual's feelings and emotions after viewing a marketing communication piece. An alternative method, a **warmth monitor**, relies on the concept that feelings of warmth are positive when they are directed toward an ad or a product. To measure warmth, subjects are asked to manipulate a joystick or the mouse on a computer while watching a commercial, moving one direction for warmer and another for cooler.[9]

The warmth meter was developed at the University of Hawaii. Individuals viewed advertisements in a theater-type lab featuring a big-screen television. Those who felt negatively about what they were watching pulled a joystick downward. Those who felt more positively pushed the joystick in the opposite direction. As they watched a commercial, the subjects constantly moved the joystick, thereby conveying their feelings during every moment of the ad. The results of the 20 participants were tallied into one graph and then placed over the commercial. This technology allowed the advertiser to see the parts of the ad that elicited positive emotions and which parts elicited negative emotions.[10]

A similar technology has been developed by Reactions & Opinions, Inc., for use on the Internet. The company can poll 1,000 or more people who view an advertisement online. As individuals watch the ad on streaming video, the participants use a mouse to move a tab on a sliding scale from 1 to 10. When they like what they see, they slide the tab toward the 10. Those who do not like what they see slide the tab toward the 1. After the data have been collected, a graph can be superimposed over the advertisement. This shows the advertiser the likable and dislikable parts of the commercial. A major advantage of using the Internet is that subjects provide ratings at their convenience. If the agency needs a focus group to discuss the ad, subjects can be selected from the participants. The focus group session can even be held online.[11]

Most of the time, emotions are associated with a shorter-term event, such as a reaction to an advertisement. At the same time, emotions are strongly

▼ Conducting emotional reaction tests would help *Family Circle* ensure that this advertisement will accomplish its objectives.

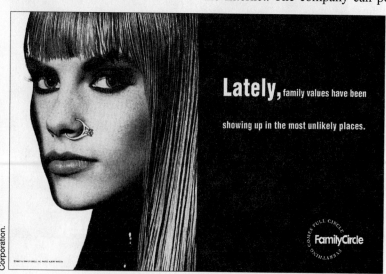

Lately, family values have been

showing up in the most unlikely places.

FamilyCircle

held in the memories of most people. A commercial that made a viewer angry may be retrieved, along with the accompanying anger, every time the individual remembers either the ad or the company. Advertisers can lessen the potential for a problem by examining emotional responses to ads before they are released.

Emotional advertising based on a substantial amount of pretesting led to a highly successful antismoking campaign in Minnesota. Using opinions generated from focus groups, ads were structured to show the devastating effects of smoking (lost vocal chords) and of secondhand smoke on children. The images were shown to groups of smokers and nonsmokers before being released because they were so dramatic and graphic. The net result was much stronger attitudes favoring smoke-free environments and additional calls to the state's quit-smoking hotline.[12]

Cognitive Neuroscience

In recent years, significant advances have occurred in **cognitive neuroscience**, a brain-image measurement process that tracks brain activity. As noted in the opening vignette for this chapter, it tracks the flow and movement of electrical currents in the brain. One study using cognitive neuroscience (psychophysiology) demonstrated that the currents in a subject's brain indicated a preference for Coke or Pepsi that are the same as for the product a person chooses in a blind taste test. According to neuroscientist Justin Meaux, "Preference has measurable correlates in the brain; you can see it." Richard Siberstein, an Australian neuroscientist, used physiological measurements of the brain to show that successful ads tend to generate higher levels of emotional engagement and long-term memory coding.[13]

Consider a sexually provocative advertisement under development. Members of a focus group may enjoy the ad but cover up these feelings by saying it was sexist and inappropriate. These responses may be due to the desire for social acceptance. In a copytest for the same ad, a respondent may also offer socially acceptable answers even though he is not face-to-face with the researcher. The individual may not move the computer mouse to report his true feelings in a study using an emotional monitor. The negative stigma attached to sex in advertising often affects self-reported reactions. A physiological arousal test, such as cognitive neuroscience, may be a better indicator of a person's true response. Many advertising researchers believe physiological arousal tests are more accurate than emotional reaction tests because physiological arousal cannot easily be faked.[14]

The most recent research in this area has been by companies such as EmSense, Neuro-Focus, Sands Research, and OTX Research. These companies are experimenting with portable devices that measure both brain waves and biologic data. Coca-Cola used this methodology to select ads to run on the Super Bowl. Coke produced a dozen ads that were evaluated by the EmSense device. The EmSense device measures brain waves and monitors breathing, heart rates, blinking, and skin temperatures as consumers watch ads. Through these physiological measurements, Coca-Cola researchers were able to determine which ads to use during the Super Bowl. Some Super Bowl ads were modified to produce higher levels of emotions.[15]

Frito-Lay used neuroscience to test product packaging. The company discovered that matte beige bags of potato chips picturing potatoes and other healthier ingredients did not trigger anterior cingulated cortex activity (the area of the brain associated with guilt) as much as shiny potato chip bags.

Frito-Lay's chief marketing officer, Ann Mukherjee, said, "Brain-imaging tests can be more accurate than focus groups." After a focus group rejected a Cheetos advertisement, Frito-Lay tested the commercial using neuroscience methods. The ad featured a woman taking revenge on someone in a Laundromat by putting orange snack food in a dryer that was full of white clothes. The focus group participants felt the prank made Frito-Lay look mean-spirited. The neuroscience test showed women loved the commercial.[16]

The power of cognitive neuroscience is that it reveals physiological reactions to a message. It shows where brain activity occurs and, to some extent, the level of activity. It can identify times when a test subject becomes enthralled with a message. It also indicates when the person merely focuses on the logo or an attractive woman in the commercial. The methodology

▼ Cognitive neuroscience tests can be used to study the impact of this advertisement for Maidenform.

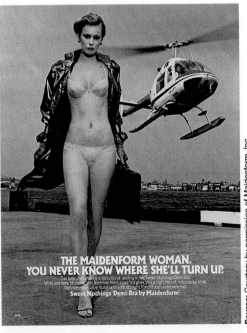

THE MAIDENFORM WOMAN.
YOU NEVER KNOW WHERE SHE'LL TURN UP.

identifies positive and negative emotions and the intensity of the emotions by the amount of neurons firing. This methodology enables scientists (and marketers) to understand the information being processed, where it is being processed, and how the individual reacted to the ad or marketing piece. Although still in its infancy, cognitive neuroscience offers great potential for evaluating advertising and marketing.

4 Which evaluation criteria are suggested by the positioning advertising copytesting (PACT) system?

EVALUATION CRITERIA

Each of the evaluation programs mentioned thus far require quality evaluation criteria. One helpful program, **positioning advertising copytesting (PACT),** was created to evaluate television ads. It was formulated by 21 leading U.S. advertising agencies.[17] Even though PACT examines the issues involved in copytesting television ads, the principles can be applied to any type of message evaluation system and all types of media. Figure 15.2 lists the nine main principles to follow when testing a written or verbal marketing communication piece.

First, no matter which procedure will be used, it should be *relevant to the advertising objective being tested.* For a coupon promotion designed to stimulate trial purchases, marketers should evaluate coupon's copy in order to determine its ability to stimulate those purchases. An evaluation of attitudes toward a brand requires a different instrument.

Researchers should agree on how the results are going to be used when selecting test instruments. They should also agree on the design of the test in order to obtain the desired results. This will be especially true during the preparation stage in an advertisement's development, because many tests are used to determine whether the advertisement eventually will be created.

The research team should also select a *cutoff score* to be used following the test. This prevents biases from affecting findings about the ad's potential effectiveness. Many advertising agencies use test markets for new advertisements before they are launched in a larger area. A recall method used to determine if people in the target market remember seeing the ad should have a prearranged cutoff score. In other words, the acceptable percentage may be established so that 25 percent of the sample should remember the ad in order to move forward with the campaign. When the percentage is not reached, the ad has failed the test.

Using multiple measures allows for more precise evaluations of ads and campaigns. A well-designed ad may fail one particular testing procedure yet score higher on others. Consumers and business buyers who are the targets of marketing communications are complex human beings. Various people may perceive individual ads differently. As a result, advertisers usually try to develop more than one measure to be certain greater agreement can be reached about whether the ad or campaign will succeed and reach its desired goals.

The test to be used should be *based on some theory or model of human response to communication,* which makes it more likely that the test will accurately predict the human response. Enhancing the odds that the communication will produce the desired

FIGURE 15.2 ▶
Copytesting Principles of PACT

- Testing procedure should be relevant to the advertising objectives.
- In advance of each test, researches should agree on how the results will be used.
- Multiple measures should be used.
- The test should be based on some theory or model of human response to communication.
- The testing procedure should allow for more than one exposure to the advertisement, if necessary.
- In selecting alternate advertisements to include in the test, each should be at the same stage in the process as the test ad.
- The test should provide controls to avoid biases.
- The sample used for the test should be representative of the target sample.
- The testing procedure should demonstrate reliability and validity.

Source: Based on PACT document published in the *Journal of Marketing* 11, no. 4 (1982), pp. 4–29.

results (going to the Web site, visiting the store, or making a purchase) when an ad launches becomes the objective.

Many testing procedures are based on a single exposure. Although in many cases this may be sufficient for research purposes, sometimes *multiple exposures* are necessary to obtain reliable test results. For complex ads, more than one exposure may be needed. The human mind only comprehends so much information in one viewing. The marketing team should make sure a person can and will comprehend the ad to determine whether the ad will achieve its desired effects.

Often ads are tested in combination with other ads to disguise the one being examined. Placing the test marketing piece in with others means the test subjects do not know which ad is being evaluated. This prevents personal biases from affecting judgments. To ensure valid results, *the alternative ads should be in the same stage of process development.* When ad copy is being tested prior to ad development, then the alternative ads should also be in the ad copy development stage.

Next, adequate controls are put in place to *prevent biases and external factors from affecting results.* To help control external factors, experimen-

▲ Following the principles of PACT will ensure a better evaluation of this ad for Chic Shaque.

tal designs are often used. When conducting experiments, researchers try to keep as many things as constant as possible and manipulate one variable at a time. With a theater test, the temperature, time of day, room lighting, television program, and ads shown can all be the same. Then, the researcher may display the program and ads to an all-male audience followed by an all-female audience. Changing a single variable (gender) makes it possible to see if the ad, in a controlled environment, was perceived differently by men as opposed to women.

This does not mean that field tests are ineffective. Testing marketing communications in real-world situations can be extremely valuable because they approximate reality. When conducting field tests, such as mall intercepts, those performing the testing seek to control as many variables as possible. Thus, the same mall, same questions, and same ads are shown. Then, age, gender, or other variables can be manipulated one at a time.

As with any research procedure, sampling procedures are important. The *sample being used should be representative of the target population.* A print ad designed for Spanish-speaking Hispanic Americans should be tested using a Spanish questionnaire or interview format.

Finally, researchers continually try to make tests *reliable and valid.* Reliable means "repeatable." In other words, if the same test is given five times to the same person, the individual should respond in the same way each time. If a respondent is "emotional" on one iteration of a warmth test and "neutral" when the ad is shown a second time, the research team will wonder if the test is reliable.

Valid means "generalizable." Valid research findings can be generalized to other groups. For instance, when a focus group of women finds an ad to be funny, and then a group of men reacts in the same way, the finding that the humor was effective becomes more valid. This would be an increasingly valuable outcome if the results were generalizable to people of various ages and races. Many times an ad may be reliable, or repeatable in the same group, but not valid or generalizable to other groups of consumers or business buyers.

The PACT principles are useful when designing tests of short-term advertising effectiveness. They are also helpful when seeking to understand larger and more long-term issues such as brand loyalty and identification with the company. The goal is to generate data that document what a company is doing works. When this occurs, the company and its advertising team have access to valuable information.

FIGURE 15.3 ▶
Methods of Measuring
Effectiveness of Interactive
Marketing

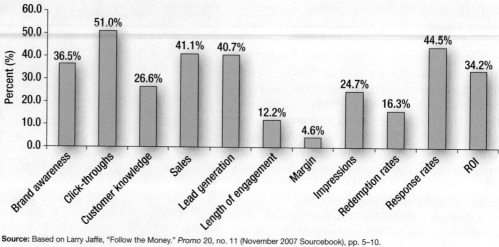

Source: Based on Larry Jaffe, "Follow the Money." *Promo* 20, no. 11 (November 2007 Sourcebook), pp. 5–10.

⑤ How do online evaluation systems assist advertising managers in assessing the quality of a firm's Internet activities?

▼ By using technology such as MarketingMatch Planner, the McCormick company tracks who went to the Web site to see the recipes.

YOUR CLIENT CUT YOUR DEADLINE.
AT LEAST DINNER CAN GO ON AS PLANNED.

CHICKEN DIJON

Delicious Dijon sauce. Savory chicken breasts. All the makings of a mouth-watering meal, in just 25 minutes. So no matter what they do at work, it won't hurt your dinner plans. Look for it in our color-coded Meal Idea Center. For more chicken ideas, look for the yellow packages or click to www.mccormick.com.

McCormick
The taste you trust™

ONLINE EVALUATION METRICS

To evaluate interactive marketing communications from the Internet, a number of metrics are available that provide hard and soft data. Figure 15.3 identifies methods of measuring interactive marketing and the percentage of companies using each method.

Click-throughs remain the primary method used to measure the impact of online advertising. The number of click-throughs provides an idea of how many people who see an online ad click it and go to the Web site. Once there, additional metrics, such as length of engagement, dwell rate, dwell time, redemption rates, response rates, and sales, become available. Redemption rates and response rates occur when visitors to the site take an action. Sales occur when the individual makes the purchase online. *Dwell rate* measures the proportion of ad impressions that resulted in a user engaging with the ad, such as clicking it or just mousing over it. *Dwell time* measures the amount of time users spend engaged with a particular ad. *Length of engagement*, a newer metric, measures how long the person stays at a Web site. It represents a surrogate of a person's interest in the product and the site being visited.

AdKnowledge introduced an online management tool called MarketingMatch Planner to evaluate Internet advertising campaigns. MarketingMatch Planner software includes two components: Campaign Manager and Administrator. Campaign Manager records traffic to a site and performs postpurchase analysis. Administrators integrate Web ad-buy data and performance analysis with the firm's accounting and billing systems. In addition, MarketingMatch Planner can integrate third-party data, including audience demographics, from the following sources:

- MediaMetrix for basic demographics
- NetRatings for gross rating points (GRP) and other ratings instruments
- Psychographic data from SRI Consulting
- Web site ratings and descriptions from NetGuide
- Web traffic audit data from BPA Interactive[18]

Interactive data should be evaluated carefully. Results are viewed in light of the company's IMC objectives. An IMC objective of building brand awareness requires something other than Internet sales data to be assessed. An Internet ad might bring awareness to a brand but not lead to an online purchase. This occurs, for example, when a consumer or business uses the Internet to gather information but then makes the actual purchase at a retail store or by telephone. In that situation, the analysis of an Internet advertising campaign may not reflect all of the brand awareness or sales that the campaign generated.

One of the newest forms of online evaluations is measuring and monitoring *Web chat*. Web-scanning software allows marketers to gauge consumer reactions to a new advertising campaign, whether it is through traditional media or online.

Harrah's, a gaming and hospitality company, worked with the Ogilvy advertising agency to evaluate comments made on consumer reviews on the travel site TripAdvisor. com. Ogilvy also scanned reviews and comments on social media sites such as Facebook and Twitter to better understand people's views of casinos, hotels, and spas in general. Harrah's learned that travelers tended to chat about the view from their rooms, such as the view of the Las Vegas strip from the Paris Las Vegas hotel. The scan revealed that travelers also chatted about hotel amenities, including the size of the room, menu offerings, and other services. In response to this information, Harrah's changed the photo on the Paris Las Vegas hotel Web site to the Las Vegas strip. Information and photos on rooms, menus, and other services was also provided. These changes resulted in a notable increase in sales. In addition, Harrah's developed a TV, print, radio, and Web advertising campaign based on what was learned from Web chatter.[19]

BEHAVIORAL EVALUATIONS

6 What types of behavioral evaluations can be employed to assess IMC programs?

The first part of this chapter regarding message evaluations focuses on insights into what people think and feel. Some marketers contend that the only valid evaluation criterion is *actual sales*. An advertisement may be fun and enjoyable, but if sales do not increase sales, it was ineffective. The same reasoning applies to other marketing communication tools, such as consumer promotions, trade promotions, and direct marketing tactics.

It may be true that tangible results should be the bottom line of any marketing program; however, not all communication objectives can be measured using sales figures. Leaders of companies with low brand awareness may be most interested in the visibility and memorability aspects of a communication plan, even though a marketing program designed to boost brand awareness does not result in immediate sales.

Measuring the results of a consumer promotion campaign featuring coupons using sales figures is easier than measuring the results of a television advertising campaign. Consequently, effective promotions evaluations involve the study of both message and behavioral elements. In this section, various behavioral measures are discussed (see Figure 15.4).

Sales and Response Rates

Measuring changes in sales following a marketing campaign is relatively simple. Universal product codes (UPCs) and scanner data are collected by many retail outlets. These data are available on a weekly and, in some situations, daily basis. They are available for each store. Many retail outlets have access to real-time sales information that can be accessed at any point during the day.

◀ **FIGURE 15.4**
Behavioral Measures

- Sales
- Response rates
- Redemption rates
- Test markets
- Purchase simulation tests

Scanner data make it possible for companies to monitor sales and help both the retailer and the manufacturer discover the impact of a particular marketing program. At the same time, extraneous factors can affect sales. In a multimedia advertising program, it would be difficult to know which ad moved the customer to action. A company featuring a fall line of jackets may be affected by a cold snap. If so, what caused the customer to buy—the ad or the weather? Firms utilizing trade and consumer promotion programs must account for the impact of both the promotion and the advertising when studying sales figures. Sales are one indicator of effectiveness; however, they may be influenced by additional factors.

As highlighted in Figure 15.5, advertisements are probably the most difficult component of the IMC program to evaluate, for several reasons. First, as just noted, it is difficult to distinguish *the effects of advertising from other factors.* Advertisements create short- and long-term effects, and consumers and businesses see them in many different contexts. The direct impact of one ad or one campaign on sales will be difficult to decipher.

Second, *advertising often has a delayed impact.* Many times consumers encounter ads and are persuaded to purchase the product, but will not actually make the buy until later, when they actually need the item. A woman may be convinced that she wants to buy a new pair of jeans in response to a sexy and effective advertisement by Calvin Klein. Still, rather than buying them herself, she leaves several well-placed hints for her husband before her next birthday, which could be several months later. The problem is that her husband may have purchased another brand or a different gift. So, she either waits for another special occasion for her husband to purchase the jeans or she makes the purchase herself at a later time.

Third, many times consumers may decide to make purchases based on an advertisement but *change their minds when they arrive at the retail store.* A competing brand may be on sale, the store could be out of the desired brand, or the salesperson could persuade the customer that another brand is better. In each case, the ad was successful on one level but another factor interfered before the purchase was made.

Fourth, *the brand being advertised may not be part of the consumer's evoked set.* Upon hearing or seeing the ad, however, the brand is moved into the evoked set. Thus, even when the brand is not considered at first, it will be in the future when the need arises or when the consumer becomes dissatisfied with a current brand.

Fifth, advertising is an essential component of building brand awareness and brand equity. Although sales may not be the result immediately, *the ad may build brand equity,* which, in turn, will influence future purchases.

Measuring the effects of trade and consumer promotions, direct marketing programs, and personal selling on actual sales is easier. Manufacturers can study the impact of trade promotions by observing changes in sales to the retailers at the time the promotions are being offered. The same holds true for consumer promotions, such as coupons, contests, and point-of-purchase displays. Many manufacturers' representatives push hard to get retailers to use the company's POP displays. At the same time, the retailer will be more interested in the effects of the display on sales. Using scanner data, both the retailer and the manufacturer can measure the impact of a POP display. Retailers normally use POPs that have demonstrated the ability to boost sales.

POPAI

To track the impact of POP displays, Anheuser-Busch, Frito-Lay, Procter & Gamble, and Warner-Lambert joined together as initial sponsors of a program developed by Point-of-Purchase Advertising International (POPAI). In the initial study, POPAI tracked 25

FIGURE 15.5 ▶
Reasons Advertising Is Difficult to Evaluate

- Influence of other factors
- Delayed impact of the ads
- Consumers changing their minds while in the store
- Whether the brand is in the consumer's evoked set
- Level of brand equity

◀ **FIGURE 15.6**
Responses to Marketing
Messages That Can Be Tracked

- Changes in sales
- Telephone inquiries
- Response cards
- Internet responses
- Direct-marketing responses
- Redemption rate of sales promotion offers—coupons, premiums, contests, sweepstakes

different product categories in 250 supermarkets nationwide. Sponsors paid between $50,000 and $75,000 to receive customized data about the POP displays featuring particular brands. One advantage of using POPAI data is that each firm sees the impact of the POP for its brand and also receives comparative data showing how well the display fared against other displays. The POPAI program features a low cost. Sponsors of the POPAI program attained valuable data at a much lower cost than if they had sought the information on their own.[20]

A wide variety of responses to marketing communications programs are available besides sales. Figure 15.6 lists some of the responses that can be tracked.

Toll-Free Numbers

One method of measuring the impact of an advertisement, direct mailing piece, TV direct offer, or price-off discount to a business customer is assigning a toll-free number to each marketing piece. A great deal of information can be collected during an inbound call. Sales data can be recorded and demographic information gathered. Psychographic information then can be added by contacting various commercial services.

In business-to-business situations, a toll-free number provides contact names to help the vendor discover who performs the various functions in the buying center. As a result, a toll-free number provides sales data to determine which marketing program would be best and also can be used to generate valuable information that can be tied to the sales data. Knowing who responds to an offer helps a firm better understand its customers and the right approach for each target group.

Response Cards

Response cards collect customer information as the forms are filled out at the time of an inquiry. The primary disadvantage of response cards is that less data are obtained. Consequently, commercial sources are needed to obtain additional demographic and psychographic information, because response cards solicited from current customers contain information the firm may already have in its database.

Internet Responses

Internet responses are excellent behavioral measures. By using cookies, a marketing team obtains considerable information about the person or business making the inquiry. In addition, many times the person or business responding voluntarily provides a great deal of helpful information. Responses to direct advertising through Internet views may also be tracked.

The Canadian Tourism Commission tested direct-response ads that were placed on television, radio, direct mail, and online. Each ad used a different URL for viewers to access for additional information. To the tourist, there was no perceivable difference, because each URL took the person to the designated Canadian Tourism site. The Tourism Commission could easily track which ad the person viewed and which URL the person used. This made it possible to count the number of visitors from each of the direct-response advertisements.[21] The next section of this chapter presents more detail about online evaluation methods.

▼ One measure of effectiveness of this advertisement is the increase in the number of phone calls made to schedule a consultation.

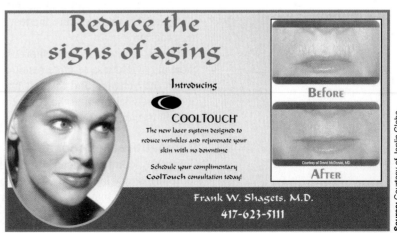

Source: Courtesy of Joplin Globe.

Redemption Rates

Various kinds of redemption rates are used as behavioral effectiveness measures. Coupons, premiums, contests, sweepstakes, and direct-mail pieces can be coded to record redemption rates. Comparing a current campaign with previous campaigns makes it possible for a firm to examine changes made in the design or execution of an ad. The results are reviewed in light of positive or negative changes in redemption rates.

Immediate changes in sales and redemptions are one form of behavioral evaluation. An advertiser or company may use them and fail to see "the forest for the trees." One campaign, advertisement, or promotions program should be viewed in the context of all other marketing efforts. Behavioral measures are best when the team sees them as part of the bigger picture.

Test Markets

Test markets allow company leaders to examine the effects of a marketing effort on a small scale before launching a national or international campaign. An organization can examine several elements of a marketing communication program in one setting. If the test market is successful, the likelihood that the national campaign also will be effective increases. Test markets measure the effects of a campaign in a new country before launching a full-scale international effort. Test market programs are used to assess:

- Advertisements
- Consumer and trade promotions
- Pricing tactics
- New products

Test markets are cost-effective methods to analyze and make changes in marketing efforts before millions of dollars are spent on something that will not accomplish its objectives. Ads can be modified, promotions revised, and pricing policies revisited before undertaking a more widespread program. For example, McDonald's tested new ads that touted cleaner restaurants and friendlier service. The goal of the commercials was to test a campaign emphasizing McDonald's effort to improve in-store and drive-through service. Two television spots and one radio spot were produced and aired in Tampa and Seattle. Reactions from the test markets provided McDonald's marketing team and the advertising agency information about the impact of the ad campaign, the parts of the message that should be modified, and whether the campaign should be launched nationally.[22]

One major advantage of a test market is that it resembles an actual situation more than any of the other tests discussed thus far. Making sure that the site selected for the test market strongly resembles the target population will be the key. A product targeted toward senior citizens should be studied in an area with a high concentration of seniors.

The test market campaign should resemble the national or full marketing plan, if possible. A lengthy time lapse may cause a company to experience differing results. Marketers try to make sure the test market provides a mirror image of the actual marketing program.

A test market can be as short as a few days or as long as 2 to 3 years. A test that is too short may yield less reliable results. If the test market is too long, the national market situation may change and the test market may no longer be a representative sample. The greater drawback is that the competition can study what is going on. This gives them time to react to the proposed marketing campaign.

Competitive Responses

Competing companies can respond to a test market program in one of two ways. First, some firms may introduce a special promotion in the test market area in order to confound the results. This may reduce sales for the product, making the campaign appear to be less attractive than it actually was. The second approach involves not intervening in the test market, but instead using the time to prepare a countermarketing campaign. Firms that use this tactic are ready when the national launch occurs, and the impact may be that the test market results are not as predictive of what will happen.

Scanner Data

Scanner data make it possible for results from test market campaigns to be quickly available. The figures can be studied to determine if test market results are acceptable. A firm also can design several versions of a marketing campaign in different test markets. Scanner data assist marketers in comparing the sales from each test market to determine which version works best. For example, in one test market the firm may present an advertising campaign only. In the second test market, coupons may be added to the ad program. In the third test market, a premium can be combined with advertising. The results from each area help the marketing team understand which type of marketing campaign to use.

▲ Marketers can use scanner data to measure the results of a test market.

Source: Getty Images–Thinkstock.

Testing Prices

Other test markets examine different prices in different regions in order to determine the price to charge and the elasticity associated with that price. The marketing team might vary the size of the coupon or premium to discover the impact. Rather than making a change at the national level, company leaders modify the consumer promotion in selected markets.

Test markets provide the opportunity to test communication ideas in more true-to-life settings. Test markets can be used for trade and consumer promotions, direct marketing, and other marketing communication tools. They are not quite as accurate when assessing advertising, because changes in sales take longer and the test market program may not be long enough to measure the full impact. In any case, test markets are valuable instruments to use when examining specific marketing features and more general communications campaigns.

Purchase Simulation Tests

Instead of test markets, marketing researchers can employ purchase simulation tests. One cost-effective approach to examine purchase behaviors is the *simulated purchase test*. Research Systems Corporation (RSC) specializes in purchase simulation studies. RSC tests the impact of commercials by studying consumer behaviors in a controlled laboratory environment.

Consumers can be asked if they would be willing to buy products in a variety of ways, using various methods. They might be asked about purchase intentions at the end of a laboratory experiment. In this situation, however, intentions are self-reported and tend not to be an accurate predictor of future purchase behaviors. RSC does not request consumer opinions, ask them to describe their attitudes, or even ask if they plan to purchase the product. Instead, RSC creates a simulated shopping experience. Subjects are able to choose from a variety of products they would see on a store shelf. After completing a simulated shopping exercise, the subjects are seated and watch a television preview containing various commercials. The participants are asked to view the TV program as they would watch any TV show at home. The test ad is placed in with other ads, and the subjects do not know which ad is being tested.

▲ Rather than field test markets, researchers can use simulated shopping exercises.

After completing the preview, the subjects participate in a second shopping exercise. Researchers then compare the products chosen in the first shopping trip to those selected in the second. Shifts in brand choices are at least partly due to the effectiveness of the advertisement, because it was the only variable that changed.

A major advantage of this methodology is that the test procedures do not rely on opinions and attitudes. Among other things, this means that RSC's procedure can be used in international markets as well as domestic markets.[23] In some cultures, subjects tend to seek to please the interviewer who asks questions about opinions and attitudes. As a result, the answers are polite and socially acceptable. The same subjects may also seek to provide answers they think the interviewer wants to hear. By studying purchases instead of soliciting opinions, subjects are free to respond in a more accurate fashion.

Any methodology designed to tap into behaviors rather than emotions and feelings has a built-in advantage. Opinions and attitudes change and can be quickly affected by other variables. Observing behaviors and changes in behaviors gets more quickly to the point of the experiment, which is whether the buyer can tangibly influenced by a marketing communications tool.

In summary, the systems designed to examine respondent behaviors are response rates, online metrics, test markets, and purchase simulation tests. Many of these programs are used in conjunction with one another and also with the message evaluation techniques described earlier. None of these approaches is used in a vacuum. Instead, the data generated and findings revealed are tested across several instruments and with numerous groups of subjects. In that manner, the marketing department manager and the advertising agency can try to heighten the odds that both short- and long-term goals can be reached through the ads, premiums, coupons, and other marketing communications devices used. Even then, the job of evaluation is not complete.

❼ What criteria should be used to assess the overall IMC program?

EVALUATING THE OVERALL IMC PROGRAM

As has been noted throughout this textbook, the huge expenditures companies make on marketing communications has led CEOs and other executives to continue to push for greater accountability. These individuals, as well as stockholders and boards of directors, want to know what type of return results when a firm spends a large sum of money on an advertising campaign or other marketing activity. The idea is to try to discover the *return on investment (ROI)* of an advertising and promotions program.

One problem is that there is no agreement about what the ROI means when it is applied to a marketing program. No consensus exists regarding how to measure marketing ROI. In one study, more than 70 percent of marketers said it would be difficult to measure the impact of advertising and marketing on sales. The same number predicted that it would be extremely difficult for the marketing industry to reach any agreement on what constitutes ROI for marketing.

Table 15.1 lists some of the potential definitions of marketing ROI. The most common are behavioral responses, such as incremental sales, total sales, and market share. Notice that the measures used to set prices for advertising time and space, such as gross rating points delivered and reach/frequency achieved, are not often considered the best definition of ROI.[24]

TABLE 15.1 Definitions of ROI for Marketing

Definition of ROI	Percent Using
Incremental sales from marketing	66%
Changes in brand awareness	57
Total sales revenue from marketing	55
Changes in purchase intentions	55
Changes in market share	49
Ratio of advertising costs to sales	34
Reach/frequency achieved	30
Gross rating points delivered	25
Post-buy analysis comparing the media plan to its delivery	21

Source: Paul J. Cough, "Study: Marketers Struggle to Measure Effectiveness," *Shoot* 45, no. 29 (August 20, 2004), pp. 7–8.

This confusion will likely continue, even as company executives try to justify advertising and marketing expenditures. This means those in the marketing profession will keep trying to identify ways to measure the impact of marketing communications, ultimately in dollars and cents.

Many years ago, Peter Drucker outlined a series of goal areas that are indicative of organizational health. These goals match very well with the objectives of an IMC program and are listed in Figure 15.7.[25] As marketers struggle to find a way to measure ROI of marketing communication expenditures, understanding the various measures of overall health of an organization can provide valuable insight on how marketing communications contributes.

Market share has long been linked to profitability. It demonstrates consumer acceptance, brand loyalty, and a strong competitive position. The IMC planning process should help the marketing team understand both market share and the relative strengths and weaknesses of the competition. IMC programs are designed to hold and build market share.

Innovation includes finding new and different ways to achieve objectives. This applies to many marketing activities, including new and unusual trade and consumer promotions, public relations events and sponsorships, e-commerce and e-active programs, and the firm's advertising efforts.

Productivity reflects the industry's increasing emphasis on results. IMC experts are being asked to demonstrate tangible results from IMC campaigns. Both short- and long-term measures of the effects of advertisements and promotions demonstrate the "productivity" of the organization in terms of gaining new customers, building recognition in the marketplace, determining sales per customer, and through other measures.

Physical and financial resources are also important to an IMC program. Physical resources include the most up-to-date computer and Internet capabilities. The firm must provide sufficient financial resources to reach this goal. Scanner technologies and other devices that keep the firm in contact with consumers are vital elements in the long-term success of an IMC plan.

- Market share
- Level of innovation
- Productivity
- Physical and financial resources
- Profitability
- Manager performance and development
- Employee performance and attitudes
- Social responsibility

◀ **FIGURE 15.7**
Measures of Overall Health of a Company

Source: Based on Peter Drucker, *Management: Tasks, Responsibilities, Practices* (New York: Harper and Row, 1974).

Profitability remains vitally important to the marketing department and the overall organization. Many IMC managers know that more than sales are at issue when assessing success. Sales must generate profits in order for the company to survive and thrive.

Manager performance and development is possibly an overlooked part of an IMC program. Effective marketing departments and advertising agencies must develop pipelines of new, talented creatives, media buyers, promotions managers, database Webmasters, and others in order to succeed in the long term. Also, new people must be trained and prepared for promotion for more important roles.

Employee performance and attitudes reflect not only morale within the marketing department, but also relations with other departments and groups. An effective IMC plan consists of building bridges with internal departments so that everyone is aware of the thrust and theme of the program. Satisfied and positive employees are more likely to help the firm promote its image.

Social responsibility can be linked to the long-term well-being of an organization. Brand equity and loyalty are hurt when the firm is known for illegal or unethical actions. Therefore, marketing leaders should encourage all of the members of an organization to act in ethical and socially responsible ways.

When these goals are being reached, the firm's IMC program is working well. Beyond these targets, IMC plans continually should emphasize the evolving nature of relationships with customers. Retail consumers and business-to-business buyers should be constantly contacted to find out how the company can best serve their needs.

Simply stated, every chapter in this book implies a series of key performance targets for IMC programs that should guide the actions of the marketing department and the advertising agency both in the short term and for the long haul. Firms that are able to maintain one clear voice in a cluttered marketplace stand the best chance of gaining customer interest and attention as well as developing long-term bonds with all key publics and stakeholders. An effective IMC program helps set the standards and measure performance and, in the end, becomes the model for marketing success for the entire organization.

8 How are evaluation programs adjusted to match international operations?

INTERNATIONAL IMPLICATIONS

Many of the techniques described in this chapter are available worldwide. IMC programs should be assessed in several ways, including: (1) domestic results, (2) results in other countries, and (3) as an overall organization.

Individual advertisements and promotional programs are examined within the countries in which they appear. Due to differing standards regarding advertising content, they must be evaluated in light of local cultures and purchasing habits.

Many times, advertising and promotional programs must be assessed across national boundaries. For example, a campaign launched in Europe leads to evaluations in individual countries such as France, Spain, and Italy, but also as a collective, such as the European Union. Measures of attitudes are difficult to collect. Sales are easier to assess due to the use of the Euro in all of these nations; however, inflation rates and other statistics are affected by local conditions.

It is advisable to contract with local advertising agencies to discover which techniques are most viable in other countries. In some nations using coupons may be viewed as a sign of poverty, and users are either secretive or embarrassed about redeeming them. In those situations it helps to study results in light of the cultural norms that are present.

Numerous multinational conglomerates assess advertising and promotional efforts through regional offices. Pacific Rim information will be combined with information from Europe, Africa, and other places. The goal is to make sure an overall image and theme is projected worldwide.

❝❝SUMMARY

Assessing an IMC program often involves examining the effects of individual advertisements. These efforts are conducted in three major ways: (1) message evaluations, (2) online evaluation metrics, and (3) evaluating respondent behaviors. A wide variety of techniques can be used. Most of the time, marketing managers and advertisement agencies use several different methods in order to get the best picture of an ad's potential for success. Advertisements are studied before they are developed, while they are being developed, and after they have been released or launched.

The guiding principles for any marketing tool include agreement on how test results will be used, preestablishing a cutoff score for a test's results, using multiple measures, basing studies on models of human behaviors, using multiple exposures, testing marketing instruments that are in the same stage of development, and preventing as many biases as possible while conducting the test. Many times, it is difficult for certain members of the marketing team to be objective, especially when they had the idea for the ad or campaign. In these instances, it is better to retain an outside research agency to study the project.

Message evaluations can be made at every stage of the development process. Methods that may be employed include advertising tracking research, copytesting, emotional reaction tests, and cognitive neuroscience.

Positioning advertising copytesting (PACT) is primarily used to evaluate television advertisements. Nine key principles are involved. The principles may be applied to any type of message evaluation system and all types of media.

Online evaluation metrics include the use of click-throughs, dwell rates, dwell time, and length of engagement. Interactive data are carefully evaluated in light of the company's IMC objectives. The newest form of evaluation is measuring and monitoring Web chat.

Behavioral evaluations consist of sales and response rates, toll-free number responses, response cards, Internet responses, and redemption rates. Test markets may be used to assess advertisements, consumer and trade promotions, pricing tactics, and acceptance of new products. Purchase simulation tests are cost-effective methods to analyze the impact of advertising and promotion on immediate consumer purchase responses.

IMC plans are general, overall plans for the entire company. Therefore, more general and long-term criteria should be included in any evaluation of an IMC program. When the IMC theme and voice are clear, the company is achieving its long-range objectives, the principles stated in this book are being applied efficiently and effectively, and the company is in the best position to succeed at all levels, including in all international operations.

KEY TERMS

metrics Measures that are designed to accurately portray the effectiveness of a marketing communications plan.

message evaluation techniques Methods used to examine the creative message and the physical design of an advertisement, coupon, or direct marketing piece.

online evaluation metrics Methods used to examine online advertising and marketing campaigns.

respondent behavior evaluations Methods used to examine visible customer actions, including making store visits, inquiries, or actual purchases.

storyboard A series of still photographs or sketches that outlines the structure of a television ad.

copytests Tests that are used to evaluate a marketing piece that is finished or is in its final stages prior to production.

portfolio test A test of an advertisement using a set of print ads, one of which is the ad being evaluated.

theater test A test of an advertisement using a set of television ads, including the one being evaluated.

warmth monitor A method to measure emotional responses to advertisements.

cognitive neuroscience A brain-image measurement process that tracks brain activity.

positioning advertising copytesting (PACT) Principles to use when assessing the effectiveness of various messages.

REVIEW QUESTIONS

1. What are the three categories of evaluation tools that can be used to evaluate IMC systems?
2. What common IMC objectives are matched with methods of evaluation?
3. What are message evaluations?
4. What is advertising tracking research? What does it help the marketing team assess?
5. Describe the use of portfolio tests and theater tests in copytesting programs.
6. What is a warmth monitor? What does it measure?

7. Describe the advantages and uses of cognitive neuroscience as a method for evaluating advertising and marketing programs.

8. What are the positioning advertising copytesting principles that are used to help advertisers prepare quality ads and campaigns?

9. Define the terms click-throughs, dwell rate, dwell time, and length of engagement. How are these measures used to evaluate marketing communications?

10. What are the primary forms of behavioral evaluations that can be used to test advertisements and other marketing pieces?

11. How are behavioral responses to marketing messages measured?

12. What items can be evaluated using test markets?

13. Describe a purchase simulation test.

14. Name and describe the criteria that can be used to assess the impact of the overall IMC program, as noted in this chapter.

15. What differences occur when international marketing programs are assessed?

CRITICAL THINKING EXERCISES

Discussion Questions

1. Create an advertising approach for one of the following products. Put the idea down in three or four sentences. Organize a small focus group of four other students in your class or individuals you know. Ask them to evaluate your advertising concept. What did you learn from the exercise?
   a. Retail pet store
   b. Baseball caps
   c. Computers
   d. Sweaters
   e. Watches

2. Pick out five print advertisements. Organize a small focus group of four to five other students in your class or individuals you know. Ask the group to discuss the ads. What do they like? What do they dislike? Write a summary of the evaluation of the ad and the process you used.

3. Form a group of five other students or individuals. Ask each person to write down two advertisements they enjoyed and their reasons. Ask individuals to write down two advertisements they dislike and their reasons. Finally, ask them to write down an advertisement they believe is offensive and their reasons. Ask each student to read his or her list comparing ads that were liked, disliked, or were considered to be offensive. What common elements did you find in each category? What were the differences?

4. Are sales figures important when evaluating integrated marketing communications? How should hard data such as redemption rates and store traffic be used in the evaluation of marketing communications? In terms of accountability, how important are behavioral measures of IMC effectiveness?

5. From the viewpoint of a marketing manager of a large sporting goods manufacturer, what types of measures of effectiveness would you want from the $5 million you pay to an advertising agency for an advertising campaign? Knowing that evaluation costs money, how much of the $5 million would you be willing to spend to measure effectiveness? What type of report would you prepare for your boss?

6. A clothing manufacturer spends $6 million on trade promotions and $3 million on consumer promotions. How would you measure the impact of these expenditures? If an agency was hired to manage these expenditures, what type of measures would you insist the company utilize?

7. Look through a magazine. Make a record of how many advertisements include methods for measuring responses. How many list a code number, a toll-free number, or a Web site? Just listing a toll-free number or a Web site does not ensure that the agency or firm will know where the customer obtained that information. How can the advertising agency or firm track the responses from a specific advertisement in the magazine you examined?

8. In some Asian countries, it is improper to talk about oneself. Therefore, people often are too embarrassed to answer questions about feelings and emotions. Those who do answer the questions would tend to provide superficial answers. Explain the advantages of a simulated purchasing test methodology in this situation. What other methods of evaluating feelings and emotions could an agency use in Asian countries?

INTEGRATED LEARNING EXERCISES

1. Pick three print or television advertisements that provide Web site URLs. Visit each site. Was the Web site a natural extension of the advertisement? What connection or similarities did you see between the Web site and the advertisement? Do you think your response was tracked? How can you tell?

2. Decision Analysts, Inc., is a leading provider of advertising and marketing research. The company's Web site is **www.decisionanalyst.com**. Access the site and investigate the various services the company offers. Examine the advertising research services that are available. Write a short report about how advertising research services provided by Decision Analysts could be used.

3. Reactions & Opinions, Inc., offers ad testing through the warmth meter technology discussed in this chapter. Access the Web site at **www.reactionsopinions.com**. Review how Reactions & Opinions conducts advertising research and write a report on when and how Reactions & Opinions could

be utilized for advertising research. What are the advantages and disadvantages of each research methodology offered?

4. Ipsos-ASI (**www.ipsos-asi.com**) is an advertising research firm with a high level of expertise in ad testing and measurements. Access the company's products and services. What services are offered? When would the various services be used? How would each be used?

5. AdKnowledge and comScore are two firms that excel at measuring Internet traffic and Internet advertising. Access the Web sites at **www.adknowledge.com** and **www.comscore.com**. What services does each company offer? Which companies do you like the best? Why? Describe a research project that you feel each company could do successfully to assist in advertising or Internet research.

6. Nielsen IAG measures the effectiveness of advertisements, marketing programs, and product placements. Access the Nielsen IAG Web site at **http://en-us.nielsen.com/tab/product_families/iag**. What type of services does the company offer? Pick one of the company's products and write a report on how it can be used by a company such as Reebok, John Deere, or Sony.

7. Millward Brown provides marketing and advertising evaluations. Access the company's Web site at **www.millwardbrown.com**. Describe the various services offered by the company. Suppose you want to evaluate an advertising campaign for Sunkist. Identify and discuss what Millward Brown tools you would use.

STUDENT PROJECT

Creative Corner

After leaders at PepsiCo and Starbucks became concerned about the diminishing supply of fresh, clean water, they teamed together to sell Ethos Water. The product's distribution has expanded, and it is now sold in major grocery stores, convenience stores, and drug stores. The goal of Ethos Water is to ensure that children throughout the world have clean water.

Access the Ethos Water Web site at **www.ethoswater.com**. After reviewing the site, design a print ad for a magazine aimed at college students in your area. When you have finished designing the ad, trade your ad with another student or ask him or her to show it to 10 students not enrolled in this class. Explain to the student how to conduct a copytest to gather attitudes and opinions about the ad. Before conducting the copytest, make a list of questions that you want to ask. Some suggestions are:

1. Have you ever heard of Ethos Water?
2. What do you think is the primary message of this advertisement?
3. Does the copy make sense? Is it understandable?
4. Does the visual attract your attention?
5. What types of feelings does the ad elicit?
6. How likely would you be to access the Ethos Water Web site for more information?
7. What is your overall evaluation of the advertisement?

It is important that someone else conduct the copytest for you to gain honest answers. Respondents are less likely to be honest, especially about any negative feedback, if you show them the advertisement and they know you designed it.

CASE 1

HANES: EVALUATION AND BRAND LOYALTY

Kelsey Van Sickle proudly accepted the promotion to brand manager for the Hanes line of men's undergarments. The line includes undershirts, briefs, boxers, and boxer briefs. The line has been widely distributed in a variety of stores, ranging from Kohl's and JCPenney to less expensive retailers.

The Hanes tagline "Wait 'til we get our Hanes on you" has served the company well. Brand awareness remains high. Kelsey was interested in enhancing or improving brand loyalty. She had all of the marketing tools at her disposal, including bonus packs, coupons, contests or sweepstakes, price-off deals, plus several incentives to be offered to retail stores, most notably cooperative advertising.

The advertising agency employed by Kelsey had recently encountered a public relations problem. Celebrity endorser Charlie Sheen had run into legal problems and was dropped. Sheen and basketball legend Michael Jordan appeared in a series of humor-based commercials for Hanes products.

The agency and Kelsey viewed the moment as an opportunity. Kelsey suggested that a new campaign should be developed, perhaps one more focused on product quality. She wondered whether greater long-term loyalty emerges from perceptions of quality as opposed to simply competing based on price or consumer promotions. She concluded that a well-designed consumer promotions program might enhance an advertising campaign.

The primary competitors for Hanes men's underwear may be found in three areas. First, higher-priced products designed to entice wealthy or fashion-conscious consumers are available in stores such as Saks Fifth Avenue. Second, comparable products, especially those produced by Fruit of the Loom, are on the market. Hanes competes for both consumer loyalty and shelf space with these items. Third, lower-end and generic undergarments are often sold side-by-side with Hanes and Fruit of the Loom.

Kelsey charged the advertising agency with engaging in some basic product and brand research. She wanted focus groups with members that purchase Hanes to tell her why they buy the items. She also wanted them to explain whether they were brand loyal or if buying Hanes was simply a habit that could be influenced by consumer promotions. Finally, she wanted to know what kinds of advertisements would cause them to take the time to watch the commercial and pay attention to its content.

Pricing was an additional concern. In 2008, a major recession had begun that reached many countries. Kelsey had heard that consumers had trended to more cost-conscious purchases, even for basic clothing necessities such as underwear. She wondered if an optimal price-quality perception could be established for Hanes.

Source: Thinkstock Royalty Free.

▲ Kelsey suggested a new campaign for the Hanes line of men's underwear she now managed.

1. What IMC objectives are important to Kelsey?

2. What types of message evaluation techniques should Hanes and the advertising agency use when developing the next set of commercials for television and print (magazines)?

3. Are there any online evaluation metrics that would be valuable to Kelsey's efforts?

4. What types of respondent behavior evaluations should Hanes and the advertising agency employ for the next set of commercials?

5. Which consumer promotions should Hanes use? How should they be evaluated?

6. What long-term IMC criteria should be used to assess the Hanes men's underwear brand?

CASE 2 CRUISING FOR INCREASED PROFITS

Adventure Cruises owns a fleet of ships that tour the Caribbean and the Bahamas and make trips to Hawaii. The company has been in operation for more than 20 years. Recently, there has been a drop in passengers on each voyage. Adventure's leadership believes increasing competition in the cruise ship industry, combined with additional new leisure-time activities, have led to the decline. Some worry that cruise ship tours are viewed as something "old people" do and that Disney has taken away the family cruise business.

To combat these problems, the marketing team at Adventure Cruises has decided on two tactics. First, the department will present a new ad campaign highlighting the advantages the company has compared to other lines. Second, a new type of passenger will be recruited, a "working business vacationer."

Adventure Cruise rebuilt the staterooms on 10 of its ships to accommodate business travelers. These individuals can be members of a company or guests of the company. The idea is to get the customer alone on a ship to conduct business for a series of days, all the while being able to enjoy the many features of cruise travel, including fine dining, gambling, shows, and stops at various ports. The advantage to the company is that it essentially has a "captive audience" when a customer is given a free cruise in exchange for doing business with the company footing the bill. Adventure Cruise intends to take out ads in business magazines and journals, selling these new packages to various business buyers. Adventure Cruise president Henry Crouch points out, "Lots of companies pay really big bucks to rent luxury boxes in football stadiums. They get the customer for what, 4 or 5 hours? We can offer them a chance to keep a customer for 4 or 5 *days.*"

Henry hired a large international advertising agency to prepare ads for both regular passengers and the new business-to-business market. Lauren Patterson was the account executive who signed the deal, by emphasizing that she would follow some basic principles . For cruise ship passengers, the ads would pass muster only if they met the following criteria:

1. *The eyes have it.* The ads must be clear and easy to follow.
2. *Never place copy above an illustration.* People see the picture first, so if the copy is higher it's ignored.
3. *Great visuals work.* The idea is to capture attention and interest.
4. *Make sure the headlines and visuals blend with the copy.* Don't confuse the reader.
5. *Don't use confusing visuals.* They distract the viewers.
6. *Don't use confusing headlines.* Readers will leave the message if they don't understand it.
7. *Testimonials increase believability and readership.* Provide them whenever possible.
8. *Size matters.* The ad must be big.
9. *Keep it simple.* Readers are not as interested in the product as you are, so make the ad easy to follow.
10. *Break the rules.* Be creative.

In the business-to-business marketplace, three problems routinely occur. Lauren is going to insist that the ads avoid these problems. She calls them the ABC sins in business-to-business marketing. The problems are:

a. Ads that are not visually appealing
b. Ads that are abstract rather than designed with a human appeal
c. Ads that fail to emphasize the benefit to the business buyer

Henry realizes that these two markets (regular passengers and business customers) are somewhat distinct. Still, he believes Adventure Cruises should speak with one voice. He believes his company has three major advantages: better food, unusual entertainment, and excellent service. He wants to be sure that Lauren incorporates these three elements into the ads that appear on television and in the trade journals that they select.

1. Design a print ad for Adventure Cruises' regular passengers.
2. Design a print ad for Adventure Cruises' business customers.
3. What type of testing should be done during the design phase of the advertisement?
4. What type of testing should be done after the ad is designed but prior to placing it in a magazine or other print media?
5. What type of testing should be done after the advertisement is launched? How can the effectiveness of the advertisement be measured?

Source: Thinkstock Royalty Free.

▲ Adventure Cruise decided to target a new type of passenger, the "working business vacationer."

ENDNOTES

Chapter 1

1. "1 on 1 with Twitter's Co-Founder," *CNNMoney.com* (**http://money.cnn.com/video/technology/2009/07/24/f_bst_twitter_biz_stone.fortune/**); "Rumor: Twitter's Worth $1B," *CNNMoney.com* (**http://money.cnn.com/video/technology/2009/09/25/f_tt_twitter_valuation.fortune/**).

2. Donald Baack, "Communication Processes," *Organizational Behavior* (Houston: Dame Publications, Inc., 1998), pp. 313–37.

3. Brian Morrissey, "Chick-fil-A's Strategy: Give Your Fans Something to Do," *Brandweek* 50, no. 35 (October 5, 2009), p. 40.

4. James G. Hutton, "Integrated Marketing Communications and the Evolution of Marketing Thought," *Journal of Business Research* 37 (November 1996), pp. 155–62.

5. Diane Brady, "Making Marketing Measure Up," *BusinessWeek* (December 13, 2004), pp. 112–13; "Top 10: Issues Facing Senior Marketers in 2007," *Advertising Age* 78, no. 17 (April 23, 2007), p. 23.

6. Andrew McMains, "Ad Spending Trends Reveal No Surprises," *Adweek* 48, no. 44 (December 3, 2007), p. 9.

7. Bob Liodice, "Essentials for Integrated Marketing," *Advertising Age* 79, no. 23 (June 9, 2008), p. 26.

8. Alison Circle, "Marketing Trends to Watch," *Library Journal* 134, no. 16 (October 1, 2009), pp. 26–29.

9. Lauren Keller Johnson, "Harnessing the Power of the Customer," *Harvard Management Update* 9 (March 2004), pp. 3–5; Patricia Seybold, *The Customer Revolution* (London: Random House Business Books, 2006).

10. Cate T. Corcoran, "Delivering the Goods: E-Tailing Sales to Rise But Gains Seen Slowing," *Women's Wear Daily* 197, no. 94 (May 5, 2009), p. 1; "Online Retail Spending, 2001–2007, and Projections, 2008," *The 2009 Statistical Abstract: Online Retail Sales* (**www.census.gov/compendia/statab/cats/wholesale_retail_trade/online_retail_sales**, accessed November 23, 2009).

11. "Wireless/Mobile Statistics" (**www.mobileisgood.com/statistics.php**, accessed November 13, 2009).

12. Matt Powell, "A Steady Stride," *SCB* 39, no. 11 (November 2006), p. 15.

13. M. N. Tripathi, "Customer Engagement—Key to Successful Brand Building," *The XIMB Journal of Management* 6, no. 1 (March 2009), pp. 131–40.

14. Jean-Noel Kapferer, "The Roots of Brand Loyalty Decline: An International Comparison," *Ivey Business Journal* 69, no. 4 (March–April 2005), pp. 1–6.

15. Debbie Howell, "Today's Consumers More Open to Try New Brands," *DSN Retailing Today* 43, no. 20 (October 25, 2004), pp. 29–32.

16. Jana Lay Hwa Bowden, "The Process of Customer Engagement: A Conceptual Framework," *Journal of Marketing Theory & Practice* 17, no. 1 (Winter 2009), pp. 63–74.

17. Arundhati Parmar, "10 Minutes with Rex Briggs," *Marketing News* 42, no. 6 (April 1, 2008), pp. 24–27.

18. Don E. Schultz and Philip J. Kitchen, "Integrated Marketing Communications in U.S. Advertising Agencies: An Exploratory Study," *Journal of Advertising Research* (September–October 1997), pp. 7–18.

19. Stephen J. Gould, Dawn B. Lerman, and Andreas F. Grein, "Agency Perceptions and Practices on Global IMC," *Journal of Advertising Research* (January–February 1999), pp. 7–26.

20. Ibid.

21. Parekh Rupal, "Febreze Sniffs Out New Target: Dorm Dwellers," *Advertising Age* (April, 2004), pp. 34–35.

Chapter 2

1. "Jury Awards Mattel $100 in Barbie-Bratz Lawsuit," *WCCO.* (**http://wcco.com/business/barbie.bratz.lawsuit.2.803672.html**, accessed August 10, 2010); Jeremy Deutchman, "After 50 Years, Barbie's Still a Living Doll," *USE News*, (**http://uscnews.usc.edu/business/after_50_years_barbies_still_a_living_doll.html** accessed August 10, 2010).

2. Arun Sudhaman, "Brand Quality Still Key to Corporate Reputation: Edelman," *Media Asia* (November 19, 2004), p. 8.

3. Kari Greenberg, "Mazda, Subaru Racing to Upgrade Dealerships," *Brandweek* 45, no. 39 (November 1, 2004), p. 10.

4. Joan Voight, "The Lady Means Business," *Adweek* 47, no. 15 (April 10, 2006), pp. 32–36.

5. Brad Dorfman, "Exclusive: Kraft's New Marching Orders: Make Today Delicious," *Reuters* (**http://uk.reuters.com/articlePrint?articleID=UKN15243520090217**), February 17, 2009.

6. Interview with Anne Gremillion, Gremillion & Pou Advertising Agency, Shreveport, Louisiana, December 10, 2009.

7. William J. McEwen, "How to Rejuvenate Your Brand, Changing a Brand Promise Involves a Lot More than Altering Your Advertising," *Gallup Management Journal Online* (September 11, 2008), pp. 1–4.

8. David Kiley, "Holiday Inn's $1 Billion Revamp," *BusinessWeek Online* (October 39, 2007), p. 19.

9. Matt Vella, "AT&T Rebrands. Again," *BusinessWeek Online* (September 12, 2007), p. 20.

10. Jennifer McFarland, "Branding from the Inside Out, and from the Outside In," *Harvard Management Update* 7, no. 2 (February 2002), pp. 3–4.

11. Paul McNamara, "The Name Game," *Network World* (April 20, 1998), pp. 77–78.

12. Max Du Bois, "Making Your Company One in a Million," *Brand Strategy,* no. 153 (November 2001), pp. 10–11.

13. Pamela W. Henderson and Joseph A. Cote, "Guidelines for Selecting or Modifying Logos," *Journal of Marketing* (April 1998), pp. 14–30.

14. Natalie Zmuda, "What Went into the Updated Pepsi Logo," *Advertising Age* (**http://adage.com/print?article_id=132016**), October 27, 2008.

15. Elaine Wong, "New Hormel Campaign Beefs Up Portfolio Strength," *Brandweek* (**www.brandweek.com/bw/content_display/news-and-features/direct/e3ia613cdbc5ebe**), February 8, 2010.

16. Natalie Zmuda, "What Went Into the Updated Pepsi Logo."

17. "Branding Isn't Just for Large Companies with Deep Pockets Anymore," *Smart Business* 4, no. 2 (May 2009), pp. 20–21.

18. Andrew Ehrenberg, Neil Barnard, and John Scriven, "Differentiation or Salience," *Journal of Advertising Research* (November–December 1997), pp. 7–14.

19. Stuart Elliott, "A Campaign Linking Clean Clothes with Stylish Living," *The New York Times* (**www.nytimes.com/2010/01/08/business/media/08adco.html**), January 8, 2010.

20. Debra Semans, "The Brand You Save," *Marketing Management* 13, no. 3 (May–June 2004), pp. 29–32.

21. Nanette Byrnes, Robert Berner, Wendy Zellner, and William C. Symonds, "Branding: Five New Lessons," *BusinessWeek* (February 14, 2005), pp. 26–28.

22. Ibid.

23. Andrew Hampp, "Mtn Dew Banks on Branded Entertainment," *Advertising Age* (**http://adage.com/print?article_id_137086**), June 4, 2009.

24. Stuart Elliott, "Making Social Connections and Selling Cookies" (**www.nytimes.com/2007/11/21/business/media/21adco.html**, accessed November 21, 2007).

25. Ibid.

26. Don E. Schultz, "Mastering Brand Metrics," *Marketing Management* 11, no. 3 (May–June 2002), pp. 8–9; Daniel Baack and Mark N. Hatala, "Predictors of Brand Rating and Brand Recall: An Empirical Investigation," *Regional Business Review* 17 (1998), pp. 17–34.

27. Fred Crawford, "Branding Isn't Like High School," *Retail Merchandiser* 47, no. 6 (July–August 2007), pp. S4–S9.

28. Debbie Howell, "Top Brands," *DSN Retailing Today* 33, no. 20 (October 24, 2005), pp. 38–42.

29. Kusum L. Ailawaldi, Scott A. Neslin, and Donald R. Lehman, "Revenue Premium as an Outcome Measure of Brand Equity," *Journal of Marketing* 67, no. 4 (October 2003), pp. 1–18.

30. John Kalkowski, "Private Labels Are Booming," *Packaging Digest* 46, no. 7 (July 2009), pp. 25–27.

31. Elaine Wong, "Nieslen: Private Label Deemed Equal to Name Brands," *Brandweek* (**www.brandweek.com/bw/content_display/news-and-features/packaged-goods/e3i3**), November 17, 2008.

32. Terri Goldstein, "Battling Brand Malpractice," *BrandWeek* (**www.brandweek.com/bw/content_display/news-and-features/direct/e3i422dde68f61e91f2f602f6a04ac4d207**), November 2, 2009; Ellen Byron, "At the Supermarket Checkout, Frugality Trumps Brand Loyalty," *The Wall Street Journal* (**http://online.wsj.com/article/SB122592835021203025.html**), November 6, 2008.

33. Dongdae Lee, "Image Congruence and Attitude Toward Private Brands," *Advances in Consumer Research* 31 (2004), pp. 435–41.

34. Rusty Williamson, "Penney's Launching New Line," *Women's Wear Daily (WWD)* 191, no. 83 (April 19, 2006), p. 2.

35. Kelly Nolan, "Apparel & Accessories: A Label for Every Style at JCP," *Retailing Today* 45, no. 14 (August 7, 2006), pp. 27, 36.

36. Cheryl Lu-Lien Tan, "Penney to Focus Advertising on Trendier Fashion Lines," *The Wall Street Journal* (**http://online.wsj.com/article/SJ12342216164826505405.html**), February 10, 2009.

37. John Kalkowski, "Private Labels Are Booming."

38. Vanessa L. Facenda, "A Swift Kick to the Privates," *Brandweek* 48, No. 31 (September 3, 2007), pp. 24–28.

39. Jack Neff, "Study: Cutting Spending Hurts Brand Long Term," *Advertising Age* (**http://adage.com/print?article_id=135790**), April 6, 2009.

40. Kris Perry, "Do You Help Your Customers Sell or Market?" *Paperboard Packaging* 89, no. 11 (November 2004), p. 8.

41. Vicki Jayne, "Packaging: The Wrap Up," *NZ Marketing Magazine* 28, no. 1 (February 2009), pp. 30–34.

42. Victoria Moore and Frances Stonor Saunders, "Message on a Bottle," *New Statesman* 130, no. 4538 (May 21, 2001), pp. 49–53.

43. "Packaging Affects Brand Loyalty," *Supermarket News* 53, no. 45 (November 7, 2005), p. 36.

44. Andrea Zoe Aster, "Good Drinks Come in Smart Packaging," *Marketing Magazine* 109, no. 32 (October 4–11, 2004), pp. 13–15.

45. Vicki Jayne, "Packaging: The Wrap Up."

46. Johnny K. Johansson and Ilkka A. Ronkainen, "Consider Implications of Local Brands in a Global Arena," *Marketing News* 38 (May 15, 2004), pp. 46–48.

47. Ibid.

48. Andrew McMains, "To Compete Locally, Global Brands Must Adapt," *Adweek.com* (**http://adweek.com/pt//cpt&title=To+compete+locally.html**), September 25, 2008.

49. Karlene Lukovitz, "Brands Lose Relevance in Food-Buying Decisions," *MediaPost Publications* (**www.mediapost.com/publications/?fa=Articles.san&s=93124&Nid=48584&p=925.html**), October 22, 2008.

50. Johnny K. Johansson and Ilkka A. Ronkainen, "Consider Implications of Local Brands in a Global Arena."

51. Material furnished by Gremillion & Pou Marketing, August 2010.

Chapter 3

1. "Chipotle Mexican Grill, Inc." (**www.fundinguniverse.com/company-histories/Chipotle-Mexican-Grill-Inc-Company-History.html**, accessed November 3, 2009); "Happy Pig, Happy Customer," ABC News "Nightline" (**http://abcnews.go.com/video/playerIndex?id=8018211**), July 6, 2009.

2. Jeffrey B. Schmidt and Richard A. Spreng, "A Proposed Model of External Consumer Information Search," *Journal of Academy of Marketing Science* 24, no. 3 (Summer 1996), pp. 246–56.

3. Merrie Brucks, "The Effect of Product Class Knowledge on Information Search Behavior," *Journal of Consumer Research* 12 (June 1985), pp. 1–15; Schmidt and Spreng, "A Proposed Model of External Consumer Information Search."

4. Laura M. Buchholz and Robert E. Smith, "The Role of Consumer Involvement in Determining Cognitive Responses to Broadcast Advertising," *Journal of Advertising* 20, no. 1 (1991), pp. 4–17; Schmidt and Spreng, "A Proposed Model of External Consumer Information Search"; Jeffrey J. Inman, Leigh McAllister, and Wayne D. Hoyer, "Promotion Signal: Proxy for a Price Cut," *Journal of Consumer Research* 17 (June 1990), pp. 74–81; Barry J. Babin, William R. Darden, and Mitch Griffin, "Work and/or Fun: Measuring Hedonic and Utilitarian Shopping Value," *Journal of Consumer Research* 20 (March 1994), pp. 644–56.

5. Schmidt and Spreng, "A Proposed Model of External Consumer Information Search."

6. M. Fishbein and Icek Ajzen, *Belief, Attitude, Intention, and Behavior: An Introduction to Theory and Research* (Reading, MA: Addison-Wesley, 1975).

7. Richard P. Bagozzi, Alice M. Tybout, C. Samuel Craig, and Brian Sternathal, "The Construct Validity of the Tripartite

Classification of Attitudes," *Journal of Marketing* 16, no. 1 (February 1979), pp. 88–95.

8. Stuart Elliott, "Levi's Courts the Young with a Hopeful Call," *The New York Times* (**www.nytimes.com/2009/06/30/business/media/30adco.html**), June 30, 2009.

9. Discussion of cognitive mapping based on Anne R. Kearny and Stephan Kaplan, "Toward a Methodology for the Measurement of Knowledge Structures of Ordinary People: The Conceptual Content Cognitive Map (3CM)," *Environment and Behavior* 29, no. 5 (September 1997), pp. 579–617; Stephan Kaplan and R. Kaplan, *Cognition and Environment, Functioning in an Uncertain World* (Ann Arbor, MI: Ulrich's, 1982, 1989).

10. Discussion of heuristics and multiattribute model based on William L. Wilkie and Edgar A. Pessemier, "Issues in Marketing's Use of Multiattribute Models," *Journal of Marketing Research* 10 (November 1983), pp. 428–41; Peter L. Wright, "Consumer Choice Strategies: Simplifying vs. Optimizing," *Journal of Marketing Research* 11 (February 1975), pp. 60–67; James B. Bettman, *An Information Processing Theory of Consumer Choice* (Reading, MA: Addison-Wesley, 1979).

11. Mark Sneider, "Create Emotional Ties with Brand for Sales," *Marketing News* 38 (May 15, 2004), pp. 44–45.

12. This section is based on "Are Latest 'Megatrends' a Road Map for New Products?" *Candy Industry* 170, no. 1 (January 2005), pp. 14–15; "The Changing Face of 2005," *International Food Ingredients* (February–March 2005), p. 20; "Global Consumer Trends," *Datamonitor* (**www.market-research-report.com/datamonitor/DMCM0683.htm**), July 21, 2004.

13. Peter Leimbach, "Role Reversal: Mr. Mom Goes Shopping," *Adweek.com* (**www.adweek.com/aw/content_display/news/agency/33i1a1890f91e4cda9a5b3c3348b4c85509**), July 1, 2009.

14. Elizabeth Fuhrman, "Consumer Trends Driving New Products," *Beverage Industry* 98, no. 4 (April 2007), pp. 4–8.

15. Mark Dolliver, "Alas, Free Time Comes at a Price," *Adweek* 45, no. 34 (September 13, 2004), p. 42; Mark Dolliver, "More Money or More Time?" *Adweek* 42, no. 11 (March 12, 2001), p. 44.

16. Discussion of second-chancers based on Richard Halverson, "The Customer Connection: Second-Chancers," *Discount Store News* 37, no. 20 (October 26, 1998), pp. 91–95.

17. "Boomers Bend the Trends," *Private Label Buyer* 21, no. 4 (April 2007), p. 14.

18. Dave Carpenter, "Diets Force Kraft to Change Marketing Approach," *Marketing News* 38 (September 15, 2004), p. 37.

19. Christine Blank, "Convenience, Health Top Consumer Trends," *Supermarket News* 55, no. 23 (June 4, 2007), p. 45.

20. Discussion based on Frederick E. Webster, Jr., and Yoram Wind, "A General Model for Understanding Organizational Buyer Behavior," *Marketing Management* 4, no. 4 (Winter–Spring 1996), pp. 52–57; Patricia M. Doney and Gary M. Armstrong, "Effects of Accountability on Symbolic Information Search and Information Analysis by Organizational Buyers," *Journal of the Academy of Marketing Science* 24, no. 1 (Winter 1996), pp. 57–66; Rob Smith, "For Best Results, Treat Business Decision Makers as Individuals," *Advertising Age's Business Marketing* 84, no. 3 (1998), p. 39.

21. Patricia M. Doney and Gary M. Armstrong, "Effects of Accountability on Symbolic Information Search and Information Analysis by Organizational Buyers," *Journal of the Academy of Marketing Science* 24, no. 1 (Winter 1996), pp. 57–66.

22. Herbert Simon, *The New Science of Management Decisions,* rev. ed. (Upper Saddle River, NJ: Prentice Hall, 1977).

23. Webster and Wind, "A General Model for Understanding Organizational Buyer Behavior"; Doney and Armstrong, "Effects of Accountability on Symbolic Information Search and Information Analysis by Organizational Buyers"; James A. Eckert and Thomas J. Goldsby, "Using the Elaboration Likelihood Model to Guide Customer Service-Based Segmentation," *International Journal of Physical Distribution & Logistics Management* 27, no. 9–10 (1997), pp. 600–15.

24. Patrick J. Robinson, Charles W. Faris, and Yoram Wind, "Industrial Buying and Creative Marketing," *Marketing Science Institute Series* (Boston: Allyn & Bacon, 1967).

25. Adapted from Webster and Wind, "A General Model for Understanding Organizational Buyer Behavior."

26. Eugene F. Brigham and James L. Pappas, *Managerial Economics,* 2d ed. (Hinsdale, IL: Dryden Press, 1976).

27. Charles A. Weber, John R. Current, and Desai Anand, "Vendor: A Structured Approach to Vendor Selection and Negotiation," *Journal of Business Logistics* 21, no. 1 (2000), pp. 134–69.

28. Discussion of dual channel marketing is based on Wim G. Biemans, "Marketing in the Twilight Zone," *Business Horizons* 41, no. 6 (November–December 1998), pp. 69–76.

29. Ibid.

30. Ibid.

31. Robert Duboff, "True Brand Strategies Do Much More Than Name," *Marketing News* 35, no. 11 (May 21, 2001), p. 16.

32. Interview with Brian and Sarah Warren, Emogen Marketing Group, February 15, 2010; Emogen Marketing Group (**www.emogenmarketing.com**, accessed May 22, 2010).

Chapter 4

1. **www.petsmart.com** (accessed November 26, 2007); Elizabeth Weise, "We Really Love—and Spend On—Our Pets," *USA Today* (December 11, 2006), p. 1-D.

2. Nancy Pekala, "Marketing to Today's Women: Focus on Life Stages, Not Ages," *Marketing Matters Newsletter*, American Marketing Association, November 10, 2009.

3. Ibid.

4. Kitty Bean Yancey, "More Women Head Out, Leave the Menfolk Behind," *USA Today* (**www.usatoday.com/travel/destinations/2007–10–25-gal-getaways_N.htm**), October 25, 2007.

5. Patricia Moore, "The Kids Are Alright," *AdMedia* 23, no. 6 (July 2008), pp. 30–33.

6. Chris Cormack, "Why Vega Got It So Wrong," *B&T Weekly* 56, no. 2574 (July 28, 2006), p. 14.

7. Gary Evans, "This Consumer Has Cash, But She's Tired," *Furniture Today* 31, no. 50 (August 27, 2007), pp. 1, 42.

8. Rebecca Piirto Heath, "Psychographics," *Marketing Tools* (November–December 1995), pp. 74–81.

9. SRI Consulting Business Intelligence (**www.sric-bi.com**, accessed January 3, 2008); Dana-Nicoleta Lascu and Kenneth E. Clow, *Essentials of Marketing* (Cincinnati, OH: Atomic Dog Publishing, 2007), p. 169.

10. Stacy Straczynski, "Probing the Minds of Teenage Consumers," *Adweek.com* (**www.adweek.com/aw/content_display/news/client/e3ie2038d49cf28a730c4ebeb20d2fd2604**), September 23, 2009.

11. David Feldman, "Segmentation Building Blocks," *Marketing Research* (Summer 2006), pp. 23–29.

12. PRIZM, "My Best Segments" (**www.claritas.com/ MyBestSegments/ Default.jsp**, accessed January 3, 2008).

13. Ronald L. Zallocco, "Benefit Segmentation of the Fitness Market," *Journal of Health Care Marketing* 12, no. 4 (December 1992), p. 80.

14. Susan Pechman, "Custom Clusters: Finding Your True Customer Segments," *Bank Marketing* 26, no. 7 (July 1994), pp. 33–35.

15. Gene Koprowski, "Bovine Inspiration," *Marketing Tools* (October 1996), pp. 10–11.

16. Pat Sloan, "Gillette Bets $80 Mil on Women," *Advertising Age* (May 4, 1998), p. 63.

17. "Intercontinental Hotels Group," *Business Travel News* 21, no. 6 (April 19, 2004), p. 67.

18. Margaret Henderson Blair, "An Empirical Investigation of Advertising Wearin and Wearout," *Journal of Advertising Research* 40, no. 6 (November–December 2000), pp. 95–100.

19. Ibid.

20. Lionell A. Mitchell, "An Examination of Methods of Setting Advertising Budgets: Practice and Literature," *European Journal of Marketing* 27, no. 5 (1993), pp. 5–22.

21. James E. Lynch and Graham J. Hooley, "Increased Sophistication in Advertising Budget Setting," *Journal of Advertising Research* 30, no. 1 (February–March 1990), pp. 67–76.

22. James O. Peckham, "Can We Relate Advertising Dollars to Market Share Objectives?" *How Much to Spend for Advertising,* M. A. McNiver (ed.) (New York: Association of National Advertisers, 1969), p. 30.

23. "Higher Gear," *Promo Industry Trends Report* (**www. promomagazine.com**, accessed January 2, 2008).

24. "2004 Advertising to Sales Ratios for 200 Largest Ad Spending Industries," *Adage* (**www.adage.com**, accessed February 26, 2005).

25. "U.S. Ad Expenditures," *2008 Marketing Fact Book, Marketing News* (July 15, 2008), p. 22.

26. "U.S. Alternative Media Spending," *2008 Marketing Fact Book, Marketing News* (July 15, 2008), pp. 18, 22.

27. Shannon Dortch, "Going to the Movies," *American Demographics* 18, no. 12 (December 1996), pp. 4–8.

Chapter 5

1. Interview with Stan Richards by Donald Baack and Kenneth E. Clow, January 20, 2010. Marketing materials provided by The Richards Group, including excerpts from "It's Been a Rocket Ride," an article reprinted from the *Dallas Business Journal.*

2. Rupal Parekh, "Thinking of Pulling a CareerBuilder? Pros and Cons of Bringing an Account In-House," *Advertising Age* (**http://adage.com/print?article_id=136701**), May 18, 2009.

3. Emma Hall, "A Pair of Advertising Pros Win Peperami's Crowdsourcing Contest," *Advertising Age* (**http://adage.com/ print?article_id=140712**), November 24, 2009.

4. Doritos Puts up $1 Million for Consumer-Created Doritos Commercial that Beats Seasoned Ad Pros During Super Bowl XLIII. **http://www.fritolay.com/about-us/press-release-20080924.html**, accessed August 16, 2010.

5. Rob Neill, "Doritos' House Rules Ad Is Tops with Users," *MSNBC.com* (**www.msnbc.com/id35300918/ns/ business-business_of_superbowl_xliv**), February 8, 2010.

6. G+G Advertising (**www.gng.net**, accessed January 16, 2010); "G&G Advertising," *Agency Compile* (**www.agencycompile.com/ factsheet/factsheet.aspx?agency_id=7823**, accessed January 16, 2010).

7. Beth Snyder and Laurel Wentz, "Whole Egg Theory Finally Fits the Bill for Y&R Clients," *Advertising Age* 70, no. 4 (July 25, 1999), pp. 12–13.

8. Heather Jacobs, "How to Make Sure Your Pitch Is Heard," *B&T Weekly* 57, no. 2597 (February 8, 2007), pp. 14–16.

9. Interview with Jane Hilk, Senior Vice-President of Marketing, Oscar Mayer, January 28, 2010.

10. Emily Bryson York, "Behind Kraft's Marketing Makeover: From New Ad Agencies to New Attitude," *Advertising Age* (**http://adage.com/article?article_id=141943**), February 8, 2010.

11. Jacobs, "How to Make Sure Your Pitch Is Heard."

12. Rupal Parekh, "Want More Out of Your Agencies? Write Better Briefs," *Advertising Age* (**http://adage.com/print?article_id= 138468**), August 17, 2009.

13. Laura Petrecca, "Agencies Urged to Show the Worth of Their Work," *Advertising Age* 68, no. 15 (April 14, 1997), pp. 3–4.

14. Interview with Stan Richards, The Richards Group, February 5, 2010.

15. Robert J. Lavidge and Gary A. Steiner, "A Model for Predictive Measurements of Advertising Effectiveness," *Journal of Marketing* 24 (October 1961), pp. 59–62.

16. Steve Miller, "VW is Going Outdoors, Literally," *Brandweek.com* (**http://brandweek.com/VW+IS+Going+Outdoor**), June 23, 2008.

17. Jack Neff, "The Newest Ad Agencies: Major Media Companies," *Advertising Age* (**http://adage.com/print?article_id=140712**), November 3, 2008.

18. Rupal Parekh, "Want More Out of Your Agencies? Write Better Briefs," *Advertising Age* (**http://adage.com/print?article_id= 138468**), August 17, 2009.

19. Henry A. Laskey and Richard J. Fox, "The Relationship Between Advertising Message Strategy and Television Commercial Effectiveness," *Journal of Advertising Research* 35, no. 2 (March–April 1995), pp. 31–39.

20. Herbert E. Krugman, "Memory Without Recall, Exposure Without Perception," *Journal of Advertising Research* 40, no. 6 (November– December 2000), pp. 49–55; David Kay, "Left Brain Versus Right Brain," *Marketing Magazine* 108, no. 36 (October 27, 2003), p. 37.

21. "Picking up the Pace," *Marketing News* 36, no. 7 (April 1, 2002), p. 3.

22. Laurel Wentz and Bradley Johnson, "Top 100 Global Advertisers Heap Their Spending Abroad," *Advertising Age* (**http://adage.com/ print?article_id=140723**), November 30, 2009.

23. Interview with Rick Thornhill, Jeremy Smallwood, Sean Girardin, and Victoria Emery, mcgarrybowen agency, March 25, 2010.

24. Interview with Jane Hilk, Vice-President of Marketing, Oscar Mayer, January 28, 2010.

Chapter 6

1. "About Us: Our Company," Hyundai USA (**www. hyundaiusa.com/about-hyundai/our-company/**, accessed March 29, 2010); George Perry, "Hyundai Founder, Ju-Yung Chung" (**www.thehyway. com/Hyundai_History.htm**, accessed March 29, 2010).

2. Mark Dolliver, "Assessing the Power of Ads," *Adweek.com* (**http://adweek.com/aw/content_display/news/agency/e3i34e2 ede5adb7e1e8aa21d1f4fa3b2d0b**), June 22, 2009.

3. Jerry Olson and Thomas J. Reynolds, "Understanding Consumers' Cognitive Structures: Implications for Advertising Strategy," *Advertising Consumer Psychology,* L. Percy and A. Woodside, eds. (Lexington, MA: Lexington Books, 1983), pp. 77–90; Thomas J. Reynolds and Alyce Craddock, "The Application of the MECCAS Model to Development and Assessment of Advertising Strategy," *Journal of Advertising Research* 28, no. 2 (1988), pp. 43–54.

4. Interview with Jane Hilk, Sr. Vice-President of Marketing, Oscar Mayer, January 28, 2010.

5. Laurie A. Babin and Alvin C. Burns, "Effects of Print Ad Pictures and Copy Containing Instructions to Imagine on Mental Imagery That Mediates Attitudes," *Journal of Advertising* 26, no. 3 (Fall 1997), pp. 33–44.

6. Marc Bourgery and George Guimaraes, "Global Ads: Say It with Pictures," *Journal of European Business* 4, no. 5 (May–June 1993), pp. 22–26.

7. Based on Rosemary M. Murtaugh, "Designing Effective Health Promotion Messages Using Components of Protection Motivation Theory," *Proceedings of the Atlantic Marketing Association* (1999), pp. 553–57; R. W. Rogers and S. Prentice-Dunn, "Protection Motivation Theory," *Handbook of Health Behavior Research I: Personal and Social Determinants,* D. Gochman, ed. (New York: Plenum Press, 1997), pp. 130–32.

8. Ibid.

9. Michael S. Latour and Robin L. Snipes, "Don't Be Afraid to Use Fear Appeals: An Experimental Study," *Journal of Advertising Research* 36, no. 2 (March–April 1996), pp. 59–68.

10. Martin Eisend, "A Meta-Analysis of Humor Effects in Advertising," *Advances in Consumer Research–North American Conference Proceedings* 34 (2007), pp. 320–23.

11. James J. Kellaris and Thomas W. Cline, "Humor and Ad Memorability," *Psychology & Marketing* 24, no. 6 (June 2007), pp. 497–509.

12. Theresa Howard, "Windex Birds Make Clean Sweep as Most-Liked Ads," *USA Today* (December 18, 2006), p. 7B (Money).

13. Jeremy Mullman, "How Bud Light Lost the Sense of Humor—and Subsequently, Sales," *Advertising Age* 80, no. 27 (August 10, 2009), pp. 1, 21.

14. Matthew Creamer, "Marketing's Era of Outrage," *Advertising Age* 78, no. 7 (February 12, 2007), pp. 1, 26.

15. Jimmy Yap, "McDonald's Finds Humor a Hit with Singapore Viewers," *Media Asia* (February 7, 2004), p. 22; Bill Britt, "Ford Tries Witty, Edgy Advertising to Promote the Kia," *Automotive News Europe* 9, no. 2 (January 26, 2004), p. 4.

16. "Sex Doesn't Sell," *The Economist* 373, no. 8399 (October 30, 2004), pp. 62–63.

17. Andrew Adam Newman, "Selling a Household Cleaning Product on Its...Sex Appeal?" *The New York Times* (**www.nytimes.com/ 2009/11/13/business/media/13adco.html**), November 13, 2009.

18. Sandra O'Loughlin, "Hanes Shows Some 'Love' in Battle for Intimates," *Brandweek* 48, no. 9 (February 26, 2007), p. 11.

19. Based on G. Smith and R. Engel, "Influence of a Female Model on Perceived Characteristics of an Automobile," *Proceedings of the 76th Annual Convention of the American Psychological Association* 15, no. 3 (1968), pp. 46–54; Leonard Reid and

Lawrence C. Soley, "Decorative Models and the Readership of Magazine Ads," *Journal of Advertising Research* 23 (April–May 1983), pp. 27 32; R. Chestnut, C. LaChance, and A. Lubitz, "The Decorative Female Model: Sexual Stimuli and the Recognition of Advertisements," *Journal of Advertising* 6 (Fall 1977), pp. 11–14.

20. Bob Garfield, "Dentyne Spot Makes It Seem That Naysayers Have a Point," *Advertising Age* 76, no. 5 (January 31, 2005), p. 41.

21. Jessica Severn, George E. Belch, and Michael A. Belch, "The Effects of Sexual and Non-Sexual Advertising Appeals and Information Level on Cognitive Processing and Communication Effectiveness," *Journal of Advertising* 19, no. 1 (1990), pp. 14–22.

22. Tom Reichart, "Sex in Advertising Research: A Review of Content, Effects, and Functions of Sexual Information in Consumer Advertising," *Annual Review of Sex Research* 13 (2002), pp. 242–74; D. C. Bello, R. E. Pitts, and M. J. Etzel, "The Communication Effects of Controversial Sexual Content in Television Programs and Commercials," *Journal of Advertising* 3, no. 12 (1983), pp. 32–42.

23. "Note to Chrysler: Gutter Humor Has No Place in Ads," *Automotive News* 78, no. 6064 (October 27, 2003), p. 12.

24. Tom Reichart, "Sex in Advertising Research: A Review of Content, Effects, and Functions of Sexual Information in Consumer Advertising," *Annual Review of Sex Research* 13 (2002), pp. 242–74; Andrew A. Mitchell, "The Effect of Verbal and Visual Components of Advertisements on Brand Attitude and Attitude Toward the Advertisement," *Journal of Consumer Research* 13 (June 1986), pp. 12–24.

25. Bruce Horovitz, "Risqué May Be Too Risky for Ads," *USA Today* (April 16, 2004), p. 1B.

26. Julie Naughton and Amy Wicks, "Eva's Seduction: Calvin Klein Stirs Controversy with Mendes Ads," *Women's Wear Daily* 196, no. 25 (August 4, 2008), p. 1.

27. Kate Lunau, "Study Finds Real Women Don't Sell," *Maclean's* 121, no. 33 (August 25, 2008), p. 34.

28. Howard Levine, Donna Sweeney, and Stephen H. Wagner, "Depicting Women as Sex Objects in Television Advertising," *Personality and Social Psychology Bulletin* 25, no. 8 (August 1999), pp. 1049–58.

29. Daniel A. Joelson, "Rebel Sell," *Latin Trade* 12, no. 8 (August 2004), p. 16.

30. Elizabeth Bryant, "P&G Pushes the Envelope in Egypt with TV Show on Feminine Hygiene," *Advertising Age International* (December 14, 1998), p. 2.

31. Gerard Stamp and Mark Stockdale, "Sex in Advertising," *Advertising Age's Creativity* 7, no. 6 (July–August 1999), pp. 35–36; Bob Garfield, "Pushing the Envelope: The Performing Penis," *Advertising Age International* (July 12, 1999), p. 4; Jean J. Boddewyn, "Sex and Decency Issues in Advertising: General and International Dimensions," *Business Horizons* 34, no. 5 (September–October 1991), pp. 13–20.

32. Boddewyn, "Sex and Decency Issues in Advertising: General and International Dimensions."

33. Steve Oakes, "Evaluating Empirical Research into Music in Advertising: A Congruity Perspective," *Journal of Advertising Research* 47, no. 1 (March 2007), pp. 38–50.

34. Felicity Shea, "Reaching Youth with Music," *B&T Weekly* 54, no. 2491 (October 1, 2004), pp. 16–17.

35. Brian Steinberg, "The Times Are a-Changin' for Musicians and Marketers," *Advertising Age* 78, no. 43 (October 29, 2005) p. 43.

36. Nicole Rivard, "Maximizing Music," *SHOOT* 48, no. 4 (February 23, 2007), pp. 17–21.

37. Douglas Quenqua, "What's That Catchy Tune? A Song for Car Insurance Makes the Charts," *The New York Times* (**www.nytimes. com/2007/12/31/business/ media/31 allstate.html**), December 31, 2007.

38. Stuart Elliott, "Godiva Rides in a New Direction," *The New York Times* (**www.nytimes.com/2009/11/16/business/media/ 16adnewsletter1.html**), November 16, 2009.

39. Joanne Lynch and Leslie de Chernatony, "The Power of Emotion: Brand Communication in Business-to-Business Markets," *Journal of Brand Management* 11, no. 5 (May 2004), pp. 403–420; Karalynn Ott, "B-to-B Marketers Display Their Creative Side," *Advertising Age's Business Marketing* 84, no. 1 (January 1999), pp. 3–4.

40. Stephanie Thompson, "Big Deal," *Mediaweek* 7, no. 44 (November 24, 1997), p. 36; Judann Pollack, "Big G Has Special Cheerios for Big '00,'" *Advertising Age* (June 14, 1999), pp. 1–2.

41. Gregg Cebrzynski, "Teachers Hot about Hot Teacher Dancing in 'Sexually Exploitive' Hardee's TV Spot," *Nation's Restaurant News* 41, no. 37 (September 17, 2007), p. 12.

Chapter 7

1. Rebecca Winters Keegan, "Top 10 TV ads" (**www.time.com/ specials/2007/top 10/article**, accessed January 9, 2008).

2. Henry A. Laskey, Ellen Day, and Melvin R. Crask, "Typology of Main Message Strategies for Television Commercials," *Journal of Advertising* 18, no. 1 (1989), pp. 36–41.

3. David Aaker and Donald Norris, "Characteristics of TV Commercials Perceived As Informative," *Journal of Advertising Research* 22, no. 2 (1982), pp. 61–70.

4. **www.campbellsoupcompany.com/atw_usa.asp** (accessed January 12, 2008).

5. Wolfgang Gruener, "Nintendo Wii Surrenders Market Share in Weak Game Console Market," *TG Daily* (**www.tgdaily.com/ trendwatch-features/43289**), July 17, 2009.

6. Tony Smith, "Intel Extends Market Share Gains," *Register Hardware* (**www.reghardware.co.uk/2007/04/20/intel_vs_amd_ q1_07/print.html**), April 20, 2007.

7. Shailendra Pratap Jain and Steven S. Posavac, "Valenced Comparisons," *Journal of Marketing Research* 41, no. 1 (February 2004), pp. 46–56.

8. Dhruv Grewal and Sukumar Kavanoor, "Comparative Versus Noncomparative Advertising: A Meta-Analysis," *Journal of Marketing* 61, no. 4 (October 1997), pp. 1–15; Shailendra Pratap Jain and Steven S. Posavac, "Valenced Comparisons," *Journal of Marketing Research* 41, no. 1 (February 2004), pp. 46–56.

9. Joseph R. Priester, John Godek, D. J. Nayakankuppum, and Kiwan Park, "Brand Congruity and Comparative Advertising: When and Why Comparative Advertisements Lead to Greater Elaboration," *Journal of Consumer Psychology* 14, no. 1/2 (2004), pp. 115–24; Grewal and Kavanoor, "Comparative Versus Noncomparative Advertising: A Meta-Analysis."

10. Joanne Lynch and Leslie de Chernatony, "The Power of Emotion: Brand Communication in Business-to-Business Markets," *Journal of Brand Management* 11, no. 5 (May 2004), pp. 403–420.

11. Jim Hanas, "Rotoscope Redux," *Creativity* 10, no. 1 (February 2002), pp. 40–41.

12. Interview with Stan Richards by Donald Baack and Kenneth E. Clow, January 20, 2010.

13. Matthew Warren, "Do Celebrity Endorsements Still Work?" *Campaign (UK)* 44 (November 2, 2007) p. 13.

14. Wayne Friedman, "Star Power: Celeb Endorsements Click with Younger Demos," *MediaPost News* (**www.mediapost.com/ publications/?fa=Articles.printFriendly&art_aid=117548**), November 17, 2009.

15. Jonathan Wexler, "Who Is the Athlete With the Most Endorsements?" *Playing Field Promotions* (**www. playingfieldpromotions.com/blog/438/who-is-the-athlete-with- the-most-endorsements**), June 9, 2009.

16. Interview with Stan Richards by Donald Baack and Kenneth E. Clow, January 20, 2010.

17. Claire Murphy, "Stars Brought Down to Earth in TV Ads Research," *Marketing* (January 22, 1998), p. 1.

18. Kamile Junokaite, Sonata Alijosiene, and Rasa Gudonaviciene, "The Solutions of Celebrity Endorsers Selection for Advertising Products," *Economics & Management* 12, no. 3 (2007), pp. 384–90.

19. Lacey Rose, "The 10 Most Trusted Celebrities," *Forbes.com* (**www.forbes.com/2010/01/25/most-trusted-celebrities-business- intertainment**), January 25, 2010.

20. Roobina Ohanian, "Construction and Validation of a Scale to Measure Celebrity Endorsers' Perceived Expertise," *Journal of Advertising* 19, no. 3 (1990), pp. 39–52.

21. Cathy Yingling, "Beware the Lure of Celebrity Endorsers," *Advertising Age* (**www.adage.com/print?article_ide=120560**), September 24, 2007.

22. Kenneth Hein, "Danica Patrick Talks GoDaddy, Pepsi," *Brandweek* (**www.brandweek.com/bw/content_display/news- and-features/direct/e3i7a35e791d5c**), November 30, 2009.

23. Carolyn Tripp, Thomas D. Jensen, and Les Carlson, "The Effects of Multiple Product Endorsements by Celebrities on Consumers' Attitudes and Intentions," *Journal of Consumer Research* 20 (March 1994), pp. 535–47.

24. Dipayan Biswas, Abhijit Biswas, and Neel Das, "The Differential Effects of Celebrity and Expert Endorsements on Consumer Risk Perceptions," *Journal of Advertising* 35, no. 2 (Summer 2006), pp. 17–31.

25. David J. Moore and John C. Mowen, "Multiple Sources in Advertising Appeals: When Product Endorsers Are Paid by the Advertising Sponsor," *Journal of Academy of Marketing Science* 22, no. 3 (Summer 1994), pp. 234–43.

26. Raymond R. Burke and Thomas K. Srull, "Competitive Interference and Consumer Memory for Advertising," *Journal of Consumer Research* 15 (June 1988), pp. 55–68.

27. Andrew Adam Newman, "Pitching a Product, Without Showing It," *The New York Times* (**www.nytimes.com/2010/01/05/ business/media/05adco.html**), January 5, 2010.

28. A. W. Melton, "The Situation with Respect to the Spacing of Repetitions and Memory," *Journal of Verbal Learning and Verbal Behavior* 9 (1970), pp. 596–606.

29. H. Rao Unnava and Deepak Sirdeshmukh, "Reducing Competitive Ad Interference," *Journal of Marketing Research* 31, no. 3 (August 1994), pp. 403–411.

30. Naveen Donthu, "A Cross-Country Investigation of Recall of and Attitudes Toward Comparative Advertising," *Journal of Advertising* 27, no. 2 (Summer 1998), pp. 111–21.

31. Grewal and Kavanoor, "Comparative Versus Noncomparative Advertising: A Meta-Analysis."

32. Michael L. Maynard, "Slice-of-Life: A Persuasive Mini Drama in Japanese Television Advertising," *Journal of Popular Culture* 31, no. 2 (Fall 1997), pp. 131–42.

33. Information and materials supplied by Emogen Marketing, Ruston, Louisiana, February 2010.

34. Grewal and Kavanoor, "Comparative Versus Noncomparative Advertising: A Meta-Analysis."

35. Stuart Elliott, "With Economy Volatile, Financial Firms Start to Stress Stability," *The New York Times* (**www.nytimes.com/ 2007/09/19/business/media/19adco.html**), September 19, 2007.

Chapter 8

1. Steve McClellan, "SB TV Advertisers See Online Gains," *Adweek Media* (**www.adweek.com/aw/content_display/ custom-reports/superbowl/e3ib96053a9e47796d76708c1d3b1 73fc76**), February 8, 2010; Jack Neff, "Future of Advertising? Print, TV, Online Ads," *Advertising Age* (**www.adage.com/ print?article_id=136993**), June 1, 2009; Aishwarya Bhatthttp, "GoDaddy.com–Lola SuperBowl Ad Controversy," Thaindian News (**www.thaindian.com/newsportal/tech-news/godaddy- com-lola-superbowl-ad-controversy_100316040.html**, accessed May 19, 2010), February 6, 2010; Peter Hartlaub, "The Sleaziest Super Bowl Commercials of all Time," MSNBC.com (**www. msnbc.msn.com/id/22871730/**, accessed May 18, 2010); GoDaddy.com (accessed May 18, 2010).

2. Mickey Marks, "Millennial Satiation," *Advertising Age* 14 (February 2000), p. S16; J. Thomas Russell and W. Ronald Lane, *Kleppner's Advertising Procedure*, 15th ed. (Upper Saddle River, NJ: Prentice Hall), 2002, pp. 174–75.

3. Larry Percy, John R. Rossiter, and Richard Elliott, "Media Strategy," *Strategic Advertising Management* (2001), pp. 151–63.

4. Kate Maddox, "Media Planners in High Demand," *BtoB* 89, no. 13 (November 8, 2004), p. 24.

5. Arthur A. Andersen, "Clout Only a Part of Media Buyer's Value," *Advertising Age* 70, no. 15 (April 5, 1999), p. 26.

6. Ibid.

7. Herbert E. Krugman, "Why Three Exposures May Be Enough," *Journal of Advertising Research* 12, no. 6 (1972), pp. 11–14.

8. Erwin Ephron and Colin McDonald, "Media Scheduling and Carry-over Effects: Is Adstock a Useful Planning Tool," *Journal of Advertising Research* 42, no. 4 (July–August 2002), pp. 66–70; Laurie Freeman, "Added Theories Drive Need for Client Solutions," *Advertising Age* 68, no. 31, p. 18.

9. Larry Percy, John R. Rossiter, and Richard Elliott, "Media Strategy," *Strategic Advertising Management* (2001), pp. 151–63.

10. Ibid.

11. Michael Schneider, "Nielsen: Traditional TV Still King," *Variety* (**www.variety.com/index.article=VR11180112369**), December 7, 2009.

12. Diane Holloway, "What's On? Ads, Ads, and Maybe a TV Show," *Austin American Statesman* (**www.austin360.com/tv/content/ movies/** television/2005/10/11tvcolumn.html, accessed January 17, 2008), October 11, 2005.

13. Jack Neff, "Future of Advertising? Print, TV, Online Ads," *Advertising Age* (**www.adage.com/print?article_id=136993**), June 1, 2009; Gregory Solman, "Forward Thought: Ads A-Ok on DVRs," *Hollywood Reporter* (**http://hollywoodreporter.com**), December 27, 2007.

14. "AAAA Survey Finds Eight Percent Hike in Cost to Produce 30-Second TV Commercials," *Film & Video Production & Postproduction Magazine (ICOM)* (**www.icommag.com/november- 2002/november-page-1b.html**, accessed January 14, 2005).

15. Adapted from Brian Steinberg, "Sunday Night Football Remains Costliest TV Show," *Advertising Age* (**http://adage.com/ article?article_id=139923**), October 26, 2009; "List of Top 20 Prime-time Programs in the Nielsen Ratings for Sept. 28–Oct. 4," *Entertainment Daily* (**http://blog.taragana.com/e/2009/10/06/ list-of-top-20-prime-time-programs-in-the-nielsen-ratings-for- sept28-oct4**), October 6, 2009.

16. Interview with Mary Price by Donald Baack and Kenneth E. Clow, January 20, 2010.

17. Interview with Stan Richards, The Richards Group, February 4, 2010; Rupal Parekh, "Behind the Scenes of Bridgestone's Super Bowl Spots," *Advertising Age*, February 8, 2010, pp. 4–5.

18. Doug McPherson, "Into Thin Air," *Response* 18, no. 5 (February 2010), pp. 40–45.

19. Interview with Mary Price by Donald Baack and Kenneth E. Clow, January 20, 2010.

20. Ibid.

21. Morianna Morello, "Why Print Media—and Why Now?" *Response* 17, no. 8 (May 2009), p. 77.

22. Jamie LaReau, "Magazines Are Pricey—But a Bargain, Publishers Say," *Automotive News* 79, no. 6139 (March 21, 2005), p. 46.

23. Nat Ives, "If You're Rich, You Still Have Time to Read," *Advertising Age* (**www.adage.com/print?article_id=130685**), September 2, 2008.

24. Bill Gloede, "Best Use of Newspapers," *Adweek* 48, no. 25 (June 18, 2007), pp. SR22–23.

25. "*Marketer Trees 2009*" (**http://adage.com/marketertres09**), December 28, 2009.

26. Lindsay Morris, "Studies Give 'Thumbs Up' to Mags for Ad Awareness," *Advertising Age* 70, no. 32 (August 2, 1999), pp. 16–17; Rachel X. Weissman, "Broadcasters Mine the Gold," *American Demographics* 21, no. 6 (June 1999), pp. 35–37.

27. Stacey Pratt, "Planning Casebook," *Mediaweek*, no. 1230 (October 20, 2009), p. 17.

28. "ABM Releases Harris Study Data: B2B Advertising Highly Effective," *Min's B2B* 9, no. 26 (June 26, 2006), p. 8.

29. Kate Maddox, "Top 100 B-to-B Advertisers Increased Spending 3% in '06," *BtoB* 92, no. 11 (September 10, 2007), pp. 25–30.

30. Carol Krol, "Office Depot Puts Focus on 'Business' in New Year," *BtoB* 90, no. 1 (January 17, 2005), p. 3.

31. Kate Maddox, "Top 100 B-to-B Advertisers Increased Spending 3% in '06."

32. Eric Pfanner, "TV Still Has a Hold on Teenagers," *The New York Times* (**www.nytimes.com/2009/12/14/business/media/14iht- cache14.html**), December 14, 2009.

33. Joe Mandese, "Power Shift," *Broadcasting & Cable* 135, no. 53 (December 12, 2005), p. 12.

34. Martin Croft, "Media Indies Take on Networks with Consortium," *Marketing Week* 29, no. 28 (July 13, 2006), p. 13.

35. Interview with Bill Breedlove by Donald Baack and Kenneth E. Clow, January 21, 2010.

36. Jack Neff, "Media Buying & Planning." *Advertising Age* 70, no. 32 (August 2, 1999), pp. 1–2.

37. Natalie Zmuda, "Coca-Cola Gets Hands-on with Its Own Digital Billboards," *Advertising Age* (**http://adage.com/mediaworks/article?article_id=142179**), February 18, 2010.

Chapter 9

1. Interview with Shama Kabini by Donald Baack and Kenneth E. Clow, January 19, 2010.

2. Brian Morrissey, "Marketers Get Real," *Adweek* (**www.adweek.com/aw/content_display/news/agency/e3i26911e62celee0f7ela76831**), November 2, 2009.

3. Brian Morrissey, "Real Time: The Web's New Prime Time," *Adweek* (**www.adweek.com/aw/content_display/news/digital/e3i15f4e2b3b4a487b3b5cd5347ebd07cbf**), May 25, 2009.

4. "The Decline of 'Old Media' and the Rise of Web 2.0," *Trends E-Magazine* 6, no. 11 (November 2009), pp. 33–36.

5. Cate T. Corcoran, "Delivering the Goods: E-tailing Sales to Rise But Gains Seen Slowing," *Women's Wear Daily* 197, no. 94 (May 5, 2009), p. 94.

6. Ibid.

7. Michael Stich, Jim Leonard, and Jennifer Rooney, "Ring Up E-Commerce Gains with True Multichannel Strategy," *Advertising Age* 79, no. 10 (March 10, 2008), p. 15.

8. "Consumers Embrace Internet as Regular Shopping Tool," *Australian Giftguide* (October–December 2009), p. 10.

9. David Sparrow, "Get 'em to Bite," *Catalog Age* 20, no. 4 (April 2003), pp. 35–36.

10. Amanda Gaines, "Leading the Charge," *Retail Merchandiser* 49, no. 6 (November–December 2009), pp. 16–19.

11. Gwen Moran, "Check Out Your Checkout," *Entrepreneur* 38, no. 1 (January 2010), p. 38.

12. Christine Dugas, "E-Retailers Increase Alternative Pay Options," *USA Today* (November 13, 2007).

13. Joab Jackson, "E-Consumers Get Smart," *CIO* 23, no. 7 (February 1, 2010), p. 18.

14. Mike Fletcher, "How to Create the Perfect E-Commerce Website," *Revolution* (March 2009), pp. 60–63.

15. Maya Dollarhide, "Bluefly Buzz Bags Shoppers," *Incentive* 180, no. 1 (June 2006), p. 10.

16. Lisa Cervini, "Free Shipping Offers Fueling Online Sales," *This Week in Consumer Electronics* 20, no. 24 (November 21, 2005), p. 16.

17. Nanette Byrnes, "More Clicks at the Bricks," *BusinessWeek,* no. 4063 (December 17, 2007), pp. 50–52.

18. Andrew Burgess, "At Your Convenience," *Marketing Week* 29, no. 38 (September 21, 2006), pp. 34–35.

19. Mark Del Franco, "Mailers Say, Webward Ho!" *Catalog Age* 19, no. 4 (March 15, 2002), pp. 1–3.

20. Paul A. Pavlou, Huigang Liang, and Yajiong Xue, "Understanding and Mitigating Uncertainty in Online Exchange Relationships: A Principal-Agent Perspective," *MIS Quarterly* 31, no. 1 (March 2007), pp. 105–36.

21. Dongmin Kim and Izak Benbasat, "Designs for Effective Implementation of Trust Assurances in Internet Stores," *Communications of the ACM* 53, no. 2 (February 2010), pp. 121–26.

22. "Data-Insecurity Fears Said to Hamper Online Shopping," *CardLine* 9, no. 13 (March 27, 2009), p. 34.

23. Suzanne Beame, "Consumer Confidence in Online Shopping Sites Is on the Rise," *New Media Age* (November 15, 2007), p. 15.

24. Nanette Byrnes, "More Clicks at the Bricks," *BusinessWeek,* no. 4063 (December 17, 2007), pp. 50–52.

25. Carol Patton, "Marketers Promote Online Traffic Through Traditional Media," *Advertising Age's Business Marketing* 84, no. 8 (August 1999), p. 40.

26. Shama Hyder Kabani, "Online Marketing Plan," The Marketing Zen Group (**www.marketingzen.com**), pp. 9–13.

27. Rory J. Thompson, "Can't Skip This: Consumers Acclimating to Internet Ads," *Brandweek* 48, no. 7 (December 31, 2007), p. 5; "Word of Mouse," *Economist* 385, no. 8554 (November 10, 2007), pp. 77–78.

28. Brian Morrissey, "Beefing Up Banner Ads," *Adweek* (**www.adweek.com/aw/content_display/news/digital/e3if04360897e1103df4b92464543af6649**), February 15, 2010.

29. Mike Shields, "Social Sites Not as Video Ad Friendly as Content, E-mail," *Mediaweek* (**www.mediaweek.com/mw/content_display/news/digital-downloads/metrics**), November 18, 2009.

30. "Problem Solved," *BtoB* 92, no. 15 (November 12, 2007), p. 21.

31. Ibid.

32. Jack Neff, "Why CPG Brands Better Buy Paid Search," *Advertising Age* (**http://adage.com/print?article_id=130353**), August 18, 2008.

33. Josh Quittner, Jessi Hempel, and Lindsay Blakely, "The Battle for Your Social Circle," *Fortune* 156, no. 10 (November 26, 2007), pp. 11–13.

34. Ibid.

35. Michael Fielding, "We Can All Get Along," *Marketing News*, May 15, 2007, p. 4.

36. Paula Andruss, "Personalized URLS," *Marketing News*, September 1, 2008, p. 10.

37. Rory J. Thompson, "Study: Chat Rooms Influence Holiday Purchases," *Marketing Power* (**www.marketingpower.com/content/OPTEDRELEASE12–06.pdf**), December 13, 2007.

38. Lorrie Grant, "Retailers Hope Shoppers Buy Blogs as the Place to Go," *USA Today,* August 25, 2005, Money Section, p. 5b.

39. Beth Snyder Bulik, "Does Your Company Need a Chief Blogger?" *Advertising Age* 79, no. 15 (April 14, 2008), p. 24.

40. Sarah Halzack, "Marketing Moves to the Blogosphere," *Washingtonpost.com* (**www.washingtonpost.com/wp-dyn/content/article/2008/08/24/AR20080824051517**), August 25, 2008.

41. Ibid.

42. Brian Morrissey, "Forrester: Social Web Now Mainstream," *Adweek.com* (**http://adweek.com/aw/content_display/news/digital/e3icc3b73373ecfd4eb35823e7a5e43da05**), October 24, 2008.

43. Lisa Lacy, "Nielsen: Social Ad Spending up Sharply," *ClickZ News* (**http://www.clickz.com/3635095**), September 25, 2009.

44. Brian Morrissey, "Brands Seek Fans on Facebook," *Adweek.com* (**http://adweek.com/aw/content_display/news/digital/e3id3d058ba458918f0fc8ec45**), October 12, 2009.

45. Mark Walsh, "Study: Social Media Pays," *Media Post News, Online Media Daily,* (**www.mediapost.com/publications/? fa=Articles_aid=110120**), July 20, 2009.

46. Mark Walsh, "Razorfish Study: Special Offers Drive Engagement in Social Media," *Media Post News, Online Media Daily* (**www.mediapost.com/publications/?fa=Articles_aid= 117008**), November 8, 2009.

47. Brian Morrissey, "Brands Seek Fans on Facebook."

48. Rachael King, "How Companies Use Twitter to Bolster Their Brands," *BusinessWeek* (**www.businessweek/com/ print/technology/content/sep2008/tc2008095_320491.htm**), September 6, 2008.

49. Claire Cain Miller, "Marketing Small Businesses with Twitter," *The New York Times* (**www.nytimes.com/2009/07/23/business/ smallbusiness/23twitter.html**), July 23, 2009.

50. Tim Bradshawn, "Twitter Do's and Don'ts for Brands," *FT.com* (**www.ft.com/cms/s/0/9f569d94-7546-11de-9ed-00144feabdc0. html**), July 20, 2009.

51. Jon Swartz, "More Marketers Use Social Networking to Reach Customers," *USA Today* (**www.usatoday.com/tech/news/2009- 08-27-social-networks_N.htm**), August 27, 2009.

52. Natalie Zmuda, "Behind Coca-Cola's Biggest Social-Media Push Yet," *Advertising Age* (**http://adage.com/print?article_id= 140591**), November 17, 2009.

53. Bruce Horovitz, "Doritos Ad Contest Raises the Stakes: Winners Could Earn $5M," *USA Today* (**www.usatoday.com/money/ advertising/2009-09-09-a-contest-doritos_N.htm**), September 9, 2009.

54. Eric Pfanner, "When Consumers Help, Ads Are Free," *The New York Times* (**www.nytimes.com/2009/06/22/business/media/ 22adco.html**), June 22, 2009.

55. Stuart Elliott, "Student's Ad Gets a Remake, and Makes the Big Time," *The New York Times* (**www.nytimes.com/2007/10/26/ business/media/26appleweb.html**), October 26, 2007.

56. Ibid.

57. Karen J. Bannan, "The Mandate to Integrate," *BtoB* 94, no. 12 (September 28, 2009), p. 23.

58. "Re-Marketing Helps Boost Online Shoppers' Baskets," *Data Strategy* 3, no. 7 (May 2007), p. 9.

59. Basil Katz, "Email Newsletters Aim for Inbox and Wallet," *Reuters* (**www.reuters.com/articlePrint?articleId=USTRE5894XI2009 0910**), September 10, 2009.

60. Andrew Adam Newman, "A Campaign for Clothes by a Guy Not Wearing Any," *The New York Times* (**www.nytimes.com/2009/10/ 29/business/media/29zappos.html**), October 29, 2009.

61. **www.elfyourself.com**, accessed August 30, 2010.

62. Lynda Radosevich, "Going Global Overnight," *InfoWorld* 21, no. 16 (April 19, 1999), pp. 1–3.

63. "The Worldly Web," *CFO* 19, no. 7 (June 2003), p. 30.

Chapter 10

1. WomenGamers.com (**www.womengamers.com/news/2010/03/11/ breaking-down-female-demographic**), May 3, 2010; Yukari Iwatani Kane, "Videogame Firms Make a Play for Women," *The Wall Street Journal* (**http://online.wsj.com/article/SB1000142405274870 4882404574463652777885432.html**), October 13, 2009; CNN.com (**www.cnn.com/2008/TECH/ptech/02/28/women.gamers.index. html**), May 3, 2010.

2. Joan Voight, "The New Brand Ambassadors," *Adweek.com* (**http://adweek.com/pt/cpt/The + New + Brand+Ambassadors**), December 31, 2007.

3. Laurie Burkitt, "Procter & Gamble Taps Co-Eds to Sell Products," *Forbes.com* (**www.forbes.com/2009/09/09/procter-gamble- repnation-cmo-network-readyu_print.html**), September 9, 2009.

4. Laurie Burkitt, "Marketers Break Into Homes By Sponsoring Parties," *Forbes.com* (**www.forbes.com/2009/08/19/purina- house-party-cmo-network-houseparty_print.html**), August 19, 2009.

5. Patricia Odell, "Pepsi Uses Influencers to Launch a New Product," *Promo* (**www.promomagazine.com/eventmarketing/ news/pepsi-uses-influencers-launch-0618**), June 18, 2009.

6. Angelo Fernando, "Transparency Under Attack," *Communication World* 24, no. 2 (March–April 2007), pp. 9–11.

7. Ibid.

8. Jim Matorin, "Infectious 'Buzz Marketing' Is a Smart Way to Build Customer Loyalty at Your Operation," *Nation's Restaurant News* 41, no. 18 (April 30, 2007), pp. 18–20.

9. Kate Niederhoffer, Rob Mooth, David Wiesenfeld, and Jonathon Gordon, "The Origin and Impact of CPG New-Product Buzz: Emerging Trends and Implications," *Journal of Advertising Research* 47, no. 4 (December 2007), pp. 420–26.

10. Ibid.

11. Chris Powell, "The Perils of Posing," *Profit* 26, no. 2 (May 2007), pp. 95–96.

12. Rusty Williamson, "Armani Exchange Pursues Lifestyle Marketing Gains," *Women's Wear Daily* 190, no. 57 (September 13, 2005).

13. Becky Wilkerson, "Bringing Brands to Life," *Marketing* (**www.marketingmagazine.co.uk**), February 18, 2009, pp. 35–38.

14. "Experiential Marketing Budget over $1M," *Brandweek* 50, no. 14 (April 6, 2009), p. 22.

15. Stuart Elliott, "King Cotton Goes on Tour," *The New York Times* (**www.nytimes.com/2009/08/24/business/media/24adnewsletter1. html**), August 24, 2009.

16. Derek Drake, "Prove the Promise of Your Brand," *Adweek* 50, no. 35 (October 5, 2009), pp. S11–S12.

17. Simon Hudson and David Hudson, "Branded Entertainment: A New Advertising Technique or Product Placement in Disguise?" *Journal of Marketing Management* 22, no. 5/6 (July 2006), pp. 489–504.

18. Linda Moss, "Nielsen: Product Placements Succeed in 'Emotionally Engaging' Shows," *Multichannel News* (**www. multichannel.com/index.asp**), December 10, 2007.

19. Stacy Straczynski, "Harley-Davidson Revs Product Placement," *Adweek* (**www.advweek.com/aw/content_display/news/agency/ e3i84436228620cd549875945**), November 12, 2009.

20. Simon Hudson and David Hudson, "Branded Entertainment: A New Advertising Technique or Product Placement in Disguise?" *Journal of Marketing Management* 22, no. 5/6 (July 2006), pp. 489–504.

21. Andrew Hampp, "How American Airlines Got a Free Ride in 'Up in the Air,'" *Advertising Age* (**http://adage.com/print? article_id=141059**), December 14, 2009.

22. Cecily Hall, "Subliminal Messages," *Women's Wear Daily* 195, no. 2 (January 3, 2008), p.12.

23. Simon Hudson and David Hudson, "Branded Entertainment: A New Advertising Technique or Product Placement in Disguise?" *Journal of Marketing Management* 22, no. 5/6 (July 2006), pp. 489–504.

24. Raj Persaud, "The Art of Product Placement," *Brand Strategy,* no. 216 (October 2007), pp. 30–31.

25. Burt Helm, "Marketing: Queen of the Product Pitch," *BusinessWeek* (April 30, 2007), pp. 40–41.

26. Rebecca Harris, "Brand Watchers," *Marketing Magazine* 111, no. 18 (May 15, 2006), p. 6.

27. "Mobile Ad Spending Trends Upward," *Adweek* (**www.adweek. com/aw/content_display/news/agency/e3if5f773e59310e059c43 c9851**), January 7, 2010.

28. "Nielsen Says Mobile Ads Growing, Consumers Respond," *The New York Times* (**www.nytimes.com/reuters/business/business-nielsen-mobileads.html**), March 4, 2008.

29. Lucia Moses, "SI Promoting Swimsuit Issue with Mobile Barcodes," *Mediaweek* (**www.mediaweek.com/mw/content_display/news/ magazines-newspapers/e3i0bdeb9f**), January 6, 2010.

30. Theresa Howard, "As More People Play, Advertisers Devise Game Plans," *USA Today* (July 11, 2006), p. Money, 3b.

31. Ibid.

32. Ibid.

33. Rita Chang, "Advergames a Smart Move, If Done Well," *Advertising Age* (**http://adage.com/print?article_id=131786**), October 16, 2008.

34. Mike Shields, "IGA: Most Gamers Cool with In-Game Ads," *Mediaweek.com* (**http://mediaweek.com/mw/content_display/ news/digital-downloads/gaming/e3i8d91a7147083886bfb91a8 ee5978c1a7**), June 17, 2008.

35. Susan Catto, "Are You Game?" *Marketing Magazine* (November 26, 2007, Supplement), pp. 18–19.

36. Ibid.

37. Katy Bachman, "HP Employs Cinema Experience to Push Printer," *Mediaweek* (**www.mediaweek.com/mw/content_display/news/ out-there/place-based/e3i4cb8ab6**), November 29, 2009.

38. Kenneth Hein, "Study: In-Store Marketing Beats Traditional Ads," *Sales & Marketing Management* 161, no. 6 (November 2009), p. 57.

39. Amy Johannes, "Snap Decisions," *Promo* 18, no. 11 (October 2005), p. 16.

40. Kenneth Hein, "Study: In-Store Marketing Beats Traditional Ads," *Sales & Marketing Management* 161, no. 6 (November 2009), p. 57.

41. Tim Dreyer, "In-Store Technology Trends," *Display & Design Ideas* 19, no. 9 (September 2007), p. 92.

42. Ibid.

43. Steve McClellan, "Wal-Mart Takes Its Ads to a New Level: The Aisle," *Adweek* 47, no. 38 (October 16, 2006), p. 9.

44. Laura Blum and Steve McClellan, "Selling Where People Buy: The Rise of In-Store TV," *Adweek* 47, no. 28 (July 17, 2006), p. 11.

45. Michael Bellas, "Shopper Marketing's Instant Impact," *Beverage World* 126, no. 11 (November 15, 2007), p. 18.

46. Ibid.

47. "POP Sharpness in Focus," *Brandweek* 44, no. 24 (June 6, 2003), pp. 31–36; David Tossman, "The Final Push—POP Boom," *New Zealand Marketing Magazine* 18, no. 8 (September 1999), pp. 45–51.

48. Betsy Spethmann, "Retail Details," *Promo SourceBook 2005* 17 (2005), pp. 27–28.

49. RoxAnna Sway, "Four Critical Seconds," *Display & Design Ideas* 17, no. 11 (November 2005), p. 3.

50. Catja Prykop and Mark Heitmann, "Designing Mobile Brand Communities: Concept and Empirical Illustration," *Journal of Organizational Computing & Electronic Commerce* 16, no. 3/4 (2006), pp. 301–23.

51. Sinclair Stewart, "More Marketers Using Word of Mouth to Whip Up Sales," *Seattle PI* **www.seattlepi.com/business/344656_ wordofmouth24.html**, December 23, 2007.

52. James T. Areddy, "Starbucks, PepsiCo Bring 'Subopera' to Shanghai," *The Wall Street Journal Online* (**http://online. wsj.com/public/article_print/SB119387410336878365.html**), November 1, 2007, p. B1.

53. Thomas Clouse, "Camp Jeep Comes to China," *Automotive News* 82, no. 6281 (November 12, 2007), p. 48.

54. Interview with Bill Breedlove, Fusionista, February 4, 2010; **www.fusionsita.com**.

55. Jeff Weiss, "Building Brands Without Ads," *Marketing Magazine* 109, no. 32 (October 4–11, 2004), p. 22.

56. "Red Bull's Good Buzz," *Newsweek* (May 14, 2001), p. 83.

57. Jeff Weiss, "Building Brands Without Ads," *Marketing Magazine* 109, no. 32 (October 4–11, 2004), p. 22.

Chapter 11

1. Betsy Spethmann, "Can We Talk?" *American Demographics* 21, no. 3 (1999), pp. 42–45; Levi Strauss (**www.levistrauss.com**, accessed June 6, 2005).

2. Brian Sullivan, "Winners Focus on Customers," *Computerworld* 35, no. 24 (June 11, 2001), pp. 50–51.

3. Stephanie Clifford, "Ads Follow Web Users, and Get More Personal," *The New York Times* (**www.nytimes.com/2009/ 07/31/business/media/31privacy.html**), July 31, 2009.

4. Leo Rabinovitch, "America's 'First' Department Stores Mines Customer Data," *Direct Marketing* 62, no. 8 (December 1999), pp. 42–45.

5. Jason Q. Zhang, Ashutosh Dixit, and Roberto Friedman, "Customer Loyalty and Lifetime Value: An Empirical Investigation of Consumer Packaged Goods," *Journal of Marketing Theory & Practice* 18, no. 2 (February 2010), pp. 127–139.

6. Elliot Zwiebach, "Wholesalers Segment Shoppers Using Lifestyle Clusters," *Supermarket News* 55, no. 7 (February 12, 2007), p. 23.

7. Howard J. Stock, "Connecting the Dots," *Bank Investment Consultant* 13, no. 3 (March 2005), pp. 28–31.

8. Jordan K. Speer, "Digging Deep: Extreme Data Mining," *Apparel Magazine* 45, no. 12 (August 2004), p. 1.

9. Arthur M. Hughes, "The Importance of Customer Communications," *Database Marketing Institute* (**www. dbmarketing.com/articles/ART233.htm**), August 23, 2007.

10. "High-Fliers Are Attractive Buyers," *Marketing News* 38, no. 1 (September 15, 2004), p. 2.

11. Joseph Gatti, "Poor E-Mail Practices Provoking Considerable Customer Defection," *Direct Marketing* (December 2003), pp. 1–2.

12. Joseph Gatti, "Most Consumers Have Reached Permission E-Mail Threshold," *Direct Marketing* (December 2003), pp. 1–2.

13. Ibid.

14. J. Walker Smith, "Permission Is Not Enough," *Marketing Management* 13, no. 3 (May–June 2004), p. 52.

15. Mark Dolliver, "Gauging Customer Loyalty," *Adweek* (**www. adweek.com/aw/content_display/news/agency/e3i4a73f5d745 1749a37c7fca20**), February 16, 2010.

16. Mike Beime, "Miller Launches Year-Long Loyalty Program," *Brandweek.com* (**www.brandweek.com/bw/news/recent_display. jsp?vnu_content_id=1003719329**), March 4, 2008.

17. Ran Kivetz and Itamar Simonson, "Earning the Right to Indulge: Effort As a Determinant of Customer Preferences Toward Frequency Program Rewards," *Journal of Marketing Research* 39, no. 2 (May 2002), pp. 155–70.

18. Mark A. Santillo, "Active Engagement," *Greater Games Industry Catalog* 12 (Spring 2010), p. 14.

19. Arthur M. Hughes, "The Importance of Customer Communications," *Database Marketing Institute* (**www. dbmarketing. com/articles/ART233.htm**), August 23, 2007.

20. "CRM Metrics," *Harvard Management Update* 5, no. 3 (March 2000), pp. 3–4.

21. Darrell K. Rigby, Frederick F. Reichheld, and Phil Schefter, "Avoid the Four Perils of CRM," *Harvard Business Review* 80, no. 2 (February 2002), pp. 101–108.

22. Richard H. Levey, "Prospects Look Good," *Direct* 16, no. 6 (December 1, 2004), pp. 1–5.

23. Julie Appleby, "As Drug Ads Surge, More Rx's Filled," *USA Today* (**www.usatoday.com/news/health/2008–02–29-drugs-main_N.htm**), February 29, 2008.

24. Paula Andruss, "Personalized URLs," *Marketing News*, September 1, 2008, p. 10.

25. Jeff Borden, "Eat My Dust," *Marketing News* 42, no. 2, February 1, 2008, pp. 20–22.

26. Cara Beardi, "E-Commerce Still Favors Traditional Techniques," *Advertising Age* 71, no. 43 (October 16, 2000), pp. 2–3.

27. Patrick Totty, "Direct Mail Gets a New Lease on Life," *Credit Union Magazine* 66, no. 4 (April 2000), pp. 36–37.

28. Carol Krol, "USPS Magazine Touts Direct Mail," *BtoB* 90, no. 3 (March 14, 2005), p. 20.

29. Based on Jay Kiltsch, "Making Your Message Hit Home: Some Basics to Consider When...," *Direct Marketing* 61, no. 2 (June 1998), pp. 32–34.

30. Daniel B. Honigman, "Sweet Science," *Marketing News* 41, no. 16 (October 2, 2007), pp. 16–17.

31. Camille Sweeney, "Avon's Little Sister Is Calling," *The New York Times* (**www.nytimes.com/2010/01/14/fashion/14SKIN.html**), January 14, 2010.

32. Ken Le Meunier-FitsHugh and Nigel F. Piercy, "Does Collaboration Between Sales and Marketing Affect Business Performance," *Journal of Personal Selling & Sales Management* 27, no. 3 (Summer 2007), pp. 207–220.

33. Patricia R. Lysak, "Changing Times Demand Front-End Model," *Marketing News* 28, no. 9 (April 25, 1994), p. 9.

Chapter 12

1. Personal interview of Reid Ryan and Jay Miller by Donald Baack, March 12, 2008 (**www.cchooks.com**, accessed June 20, 2008).

2. Mariola Palazon-Vidal and Elena Delgado-Ballester, "Sales Promotions Effect on Consumer-Based Brand Equity," *International Journal of Market Research* 47, no. 2 (2005), pp. 179–205.

3. Bruce Horovitz, "2 Million Enjoy Free Breakfast at Denny's," *USA Today* (**www.usatoday.com/money/industries/foo.2009/ 02/03-denny's_N.htm**), February 10, 2009.

4. Patricia Odell, "Now in Vogue," *PROMO* (**http://promomagazine. com/incentives/marketing_vogue/index.html**), December 1, 2009.

5. "Do Coupons Make Sense," *Incentive* 177, no. 5 (May 2003), p. 19.

6. Erik Sass, "Is Digital Coupons' Rise Print Insert's Demise?" *MediaPost News* (**www.mediapost.com/publications/?fa=Articles. showArticle&art_aid=122690**), February 18, 2010; Patricia Odell, "Now in Vogue."*PROMO* (**http://promomagazine.com/incentives/ marketing_vogue/index.html**), December 1, 2009.

7. Erik Sass, "Is Digital Coupons' Rise Print Insert's Demise?" *MediaPost News* (**www.mediapost.com/publications/?fa= Articles.showArticle&art_aid=122690**), February 18, 2010; Allen Adamson, "CMOs: Your Brand Is on Digital Time," *Forbes* (**www.forbes.com/2010/02/02/digital-branding-apple-ipad-cmo-network-allen-adamson**), February 2, 2010.

8. Elizabeth Gardener and Minakshi Trivedi, "A Communication Framework to Evaluate Sales Promotion Strategies," *Journal of Advertising Research* 38, no. 3 (May–June 1998), pp. 67–71.

9. "Hyundai Adds Luxury Glitz with iPad-based Owner's Manual," *PROMO* (**http://promomagazine.com/incentives/news/0407-hyundai-adds-ipad-manual/index.html**), April 7, 2010.

10. Don Jagoda, "The Seven Habits of Highly Successful Promotions," *Incentive* 173, no. 8 (August 1999), pp. 104–105.

11. "Prizewinning Growth," *PROMO* (**http://promomagazine. com/contests/marketing_prizewinning_growth/index.html**), July 1, 1998.

12. Patricia Odell, "Spending up by a Nose," *PROMO* (**http:// promomagazine.com/contests/marketing_spending_nose/ index.html**), December 1, 2009.

13. Joseph DeAvilla, "Who Could Eat All This?" *The Wall Street Journal* (**http://online.wsj.com/article/SB2000142405274870468860457 5125653339035336.html**), March 17, 2010.

14. Sarah Mahoney, "Sears Launches Yard Guru Campaign," *Marketing Daily* (**www.mediapost.com/publications/?fa= Articles.printFriendly&art_aid=125255**), March 31, 2010.

15. Kathleen Joyce, "Not Just a Novelty," *PROMO* 17, no. 12 (November 2004), pp. 52–56

16. Brian Morrissey, "Brand Sweepstakes Get Twitterized," *Adweek* (**www.adweek.com/aw/cn\content_display/news/digital/e3ied5 661580e6e68a1834a7e3**), November 22, 2009.

17. Sandra Block, "Rattled About Rebate Hassles? Regulators Starting to Step In," *USA Today* (March 22, 2005), p. 3b.

18. Kenneth Hein, "Study: Sampling Works," *Brandweek.com* (**www. brandweek.com/bw/content_display/news-and-features/shopper-marketing/e3i32e9c3e84ea86c79e3ae157688c1ad0a**), September 29, 2008.

19. Andrew Adam Newman, "Dr. Scholl's Widens Its Insole Campaign," *The New York Times* (**www.nytimes.com/2010/04/ 01/business/media/01adco.html**), March 31, 2010.

20. Pete Wetmore, "Inserts Branch Out Beyond Print Fliers," *Advertising Age* 75, no. 16 (April 19, 2004), p. N-6.

21. Betsy Spethman, "Introductory Offer," *PROMO* 16 (2004), p. 27; Jennifer Kulpa, "Bristol-Myers Squibb Breaks Ground with

Direct Response Product Sampling Website," *Drug Store News* 19, no. 7 (April 7, 1997), p. 19.

22. Elaine Wong, "Mars Petcare Goes on Tour," *Brandweek.com* (**www.brandweek.com/bw/content_display/news-and-features/direct/e3ife0fdee78e1e858d60f8b337c62fac1c**), August 21, 2009.

23. Beng Soo Ong and Foo Nin Ho, "Consumer Perceptions of Bonus Packs: An Exploratory Analysis," *Journal of Consumer Marketing* 14, no. 2–3 (1997), pp. 102–12.

24. David R. Bell, Ganesh Iyer, and V. Padmanaghan, "Price Competition Under Stockpiling and Flexible Consumption," *Journal of Marketing Research* 39, no. 3 (August 2002), pp. 292–304.

25. Showwei Chu, "Welcome to Canada, Please Buy Something," *Canadian Business* 71, no. 9 (May 29, 1998), pp. 72–73.

26. Walter Heller, "Promotion Pullback," *Progressive Grocer* 81, no. 4 (March 1, 2002), p. 19.

27. Miguel Gomez, Vithala Rao, and Edward McLaughlin, "Empirical Analysis of Budget and Allocation of Trade Promotions in the U.S. Supermarket Industry," *Journal of Marketing Research* 44, no. 3 (August 2007), pp. 410–24.

28. Ibid.

29. K. Sudhir and Vithala Rao, "Do Slotting Allowances Enhance Efficiency or Hinder Competition?" *Journal of Marketing Research* 43, no. 2 (May 2006), pp. 137–55.

30. Paula Bone, Karen France, and Richard Riley, "A Multifirm Analysis of Slotting Fees," *Journal of Public Policy & Marketing* 25, no. 2 (Fall 2006), pp. 224–37.

31. "Study: Trade Dollars Up," *Frozen Food Age* 50, no. 2 (September 2001), p. 14.

32. Walter Heller, "Promotion Pullback," *Progressive Grocer* 81, no. 4 (March 1, 2002), p. 19.

33. "Cruise Selling Season Kicks Off with Agent Promotions and Optimism," *Travel Agent* 319 (January 3, 2005), p. 9.

34. Roger A. Slavens, "Getting a Grip on Co-Op," *Modern Tire Dealer* 75, no. 3 (March 1994), pp. 34–37.

35. Jack Neff, "Wal-Mart Ups the Ante with Brand Co-op Ads—in More Ways than One," *Advertising Age* (**http://adage.com/article?article_id=140743**), November 30, 2009.

36. Jennifer Gilber, "The Show Must Go On," *Sales & Marketing Management* 155, no. 5 (May 2003), p. 14.

37. Walter Heller, "Promotion Pullback," *Progressive Grocer* 81, no. 4 (March 1, 2002), p. 19.

38. Brian Sullivan, "Make Sure Promotional Items Fit Brand Perfectly," *Marketing News* 35, no. 19 (September 10, 2001), p. 15.

39. Personal interview with Bill Breedlove by Kenneth E. Clow and Donald Baack, January, 2010.

40. Liz Parks, "Chains See Today's Wealthy Teens as Tomorrow's Loyal Customers," *Drug Store News* 21, no. 15 (September 27, 1999), p. 84.

41. Donald Baack, *International Business* (New York: Glencoe McGraw-Hill, 2008), pp. 28–49.

Chapter 13

1. Interview with Benny Black, February 18, 2010, by Donald Baack and Kenneth E. Clow.

2. Jenny Dawkins, "Corporate Responsibility: The Communication Challenge," *Journal of Communication Management* 9, no. 2 (November 2004), pp. 106–17.

3. "Random Sample," *Marketing News* 38 (August 15, 2004), p. 3.

4. Sheila Bonini, David Court, and Alberto Marchi, "Rebuilding Corporate Reputations," *McKinsey Quarterly*, no. 3 (June 2009), pp. 75–83.

5. Ronald J. Alsop, "Corporate Reputation: Anything But Superficial—The Deep But Fragile Nature of Corporate Reputation," *Journal of Business Strategy* 25, no. 6 (2004), pp. 21–30.

6. Michael Fielding, "Companies that Behave Responsibly Earn Good Rep, Consumers' Attention," *Marketing News* 41, no. 8 (May 1, 2007), pp. 17–18.

7. Suzanne Vranica, "NBC Universal Tees Up Cause-Related Shows," *The Wall Street Journal* (**http://online.wsj.com/article/SB10001424052748704112904574477872926288910.html**), October 19, 2009.

8. Larry Chiagouris and Ipshita Ray, "Saving the World with Cause-Related Marketing," *Marketing Management* 16, no. 4 (July–August 2007), pp. 48–51.

9. Karlene Lukovitz, "Triscuit Helps Grow Home Farming Movement," *Marketing Daily, MediaPost News* (**www.mediapost.com/publications/?fa=Articles.showArticle&art_aid=124077**), March 11, 2010.

10. Nan Xiaoli and Heo Kwangiun, "Consumer Responses to Corporate Social Responsibility (CSR) Initiatives," *Journal of Advertising* 36, no. 2 (Summer 2007), pp. 63–74.

11. Andrew Adam Newman, "Tough on Crude Oil, Soft on Ducklings," *The New York Times* (**www.nytimes.com/2009/09/25/business/media/25adco.html**), September 25, 2009.

12. Dawkins, "Corporate Responsibility: The Communication Challenge."

13. Jill Meredith Ginsberg and Paul N. Bloom, "Choosing the Right Green Marketing Strategy," *MIT Sloan Management Review* 46, no. 1 (Fall 2004), pp. 79–84.

14. Ibid.

15. Jill Meredith Ginsberg and Paul N. Bloom, "Choosing the Right Green Marketing Strategy, *MIT Sloan Management Review* 40, no. 1 (Fall 2004) pp. 79–84.

16. Examples based on Ginsberg and Bloom, "Choosing the Right Green Marketing Strategy."

17. Valerie Seckler, "Causes and Effect," *Women's Wear Daily* 194, no. 93 (October 31, 2007), p. 9.

18. Tanya Irwin, "Seventh Generation Debuts First National Campaign," *Marketing Daily, MediaPost News* (**www.mediapost.com/publications/?fa=Articles.printFriendly&art_aid=120626**), January 14, 2010.

19. Marvin E. Shaw and Philip R. Costanzo, *Theories of Social Psychology,* 2nd ed. (New York: McGraw-Hill, 1982), p. 334.

20. Rich Thomaselli, "New Orleans is a Super Bowl Winner," *Advertising Age* (**http://adage.com/superbowl10/article?article_id=141988**), February 8, 2010.

21. Sarah E. Needleman, "For Companies, A Tweet in Time Can Avert PR Mess," *The Wall Street Journal* (**http://online.wsj.com/article/SB1249258302403003.html**), August 3, 2009.

22. Michael Bush, "The Cult of Toyota," *Advertising Age* (**http://adage.com/print?article_id=142335**), March 1, 2010; Rich Thomaselli, "Toyota Sends in Jimi Lentz for Cross-Media Saatchi-Led PR Control," *Advertising Age* (**http://adage.**

com/print?article_id=141856), February 1, 2010; Laurie Burkitt, "From Trusted to Busted: Brands Have a Credibility Crisis," *Forbes* (www.forbes.com/1010/02/25/toyota-tiger-consumer-faith-cmo-network-trusted-to-be-busted), February 25, 2010.

23. Shaw and Costanzo, *Theories of Social Psychology,* 2nd ed., p. 334.

24. Ibid, p. 329.

25. Ibid, p. 333.

26. Nigel Pope, Kevin E. Voges, and Mark Brown, "Winning Ways," *Journal of Advertising* 38, no. 2 (Summer 2009), pp. 5–20.

27. "Events & Sponsorships," *2008 Marketing Fact Book, Marketing News* 42, no. 12 (July 15, 2008), p. 26.

28. Karl Greenberg, "Ford Intros Integrated Push for F-Series," *Marketing Daily, MediaPost News* (www.mediapost.com/publications/?fa=Articles.printFriendly&art_aid=125753), April 8, 2010.

29. Natalie Zmuda, "Speedo Makes a Splash with LZR Racer Suit," *Advertising Age* (http://adage.com/print?article_id=128002), June 25, 2008.

30. Gail Schiller, "Idol Sponsors Coke, Ford, AT&T Paying More," *Brandweek.com* (http://login.vnuemedia.com/bw/esearch/article_display.jsp?vnu_content_id=1003696656), January 15, 2008.

31. Pradnya Joshi, "Approval by a Blogger May Please a Sponsor," *The New York Times* (www.nytimes.com/2009/07/13/technology/internet/13blog.html), July 13, 2009.

32. Patricia Cobe, "Working the Neighborhood," *Restaurant Business* 108, no. 11 (November 2009), pp. 20–26.

33. David Tanklefsky, "Events-based Campaigns, Experiential Marketing Prove Successful Among Hispanic Consumers," B&C (www.broadcastingcable.com/article/print/355270-Hispanic_TV_Summit_Promotion), September 24, 2009.

34. Betsy Spethmann, "A Winning Season," *PROMO* 18, no. 1 (December 2004), pp. 32–41.

35. Kenneth Hein, "Study: Purchase Intent Grows with Each Event," *Brandweek* 49, no. 4 (January 28, 2008), p. 4.

36. Diane Anderson, "eBay's Campy Road Tour: One on One, No Mosquitoes," *Brandweek* 46, no. 10 (March 7, 2005), p. R6.

37. Jonathan Clegg, "NBA, Adidas Shoot for Europe," *The Wall Street Journal* (http://online.wsj.com/article/ SB10001424052 7487048961045751400325745513978.html), March 23, 2010.

Chapter 14

1. www.nutrition.about.com, www.conagrafoods.com, www.mcdonalds.com, www.foodproductdesign.com, www.fritolay.com, and www.nlm.nih.gov, all accessed March 13, 2008.

2. "Broadcasters Breach Kids Rules," *Marketing Magazine* 109, no. 35 (November 1, 2004), p. 4.

3. Bart Lazar, "This Column Is the Best One You'll Ever Read," *Marketing News* 38, no. 13 (August 15, 2004), p. 8.

4. Gary D. Hailey and Jeffrey D. Knowles, "Claiming Sufficient Substantiation Is No Easy Task," *Response* 13, no. 4 (January 2005), p. 50.

5. "KFC's Claims That Fried Chicken Is a Way to 'Eat Better' Don't Fly," *Federal Trade Commission* (www.ftc.gov/opa/2004/06/kfccorp.htm, accessed June 30, 2002).

6. "FTC Takes Aim at Another Credit Counseling Firm," *Mortgage Servicing News* 8, no. 7 (August 2004), p. 21.

7. "Body Wise International to Pay $3.5 Million to Settle Federal and State Deceptive Advertising Charges," Federal Trade Commission (www.ftc.gov, accessed September 20, 2005).

8. Debbi Mack, "FTC Use of Corrective Advertising Upheld," *Corporate Legal Times* 10, no. 108 (November 2000), p. 80.

9. Tim Arango, "Soon, Bloggers Must Give Full Disclosure," *The New York Times* (www.nytimes.com/2009/10/06/business/media/06adco.html), October 6, 2009; Douglas MacMillan, "Blogola: The FTC Takes on Paid Posts," *BusinessWeek* (www.businessweek.com/print/technology/content/may2009/tc20090518_532031.htm), May 19, 2009.

10. Loraine Debonis, "FTC Sends Issuers a Message: Adequately Disclose Card Fees," *Cards & Payments* 20, no. 5 (May 2007), pp. 16–17.

11. Ann Zimmerman, "Wal-Mart Rapped on Ad Claim," *The Wall Street Journal* (http://online.wsj.com/article/SB1245703077 26138427.html), June 23, 2009.

12. Seth Stevenson, "How New Is New? How Improved Is Improved?" *Slate* (www.slate.com/toolbar.aspx?action=print&id=2221968), July 13, 2009.

13. "Minute Maid Complains, but NARB Forces Change," *Advertising Age* 68, no. 15 (April 14, 1997), p. 51.

14. "NARB Sends Winn-Dixie Complaint to FTC," *Advertising Age* 67, no. 52 (December 23, 1996), p. 2.

15. Wayne Keeley, "Toys and the Truth," *Playthings* 106, no. 2 (February 2008), p. 8.

16. Mary Pipher, *The Shelter of Each Other* (New York: Ballentine Books, 1996).

17. Internet Marketing Register (www.marketing-register.com, accessed February 28, 2005).

18. Beth Snyder Bulik, "Consumers to Providers: Do You Know Who I Am?" *Advertising Age* 79, no. 10 (March 10, 2008), p. 8.

19. Simon Chadwick and Nicholas Burton, "Ambush!" *The Wall Street Journal* (http://online.wsj.com/article/SB1000142405 2970204731804574391102699362862.html), January 25, 2010.

20. Ibid; Aaron Baar, "Olympics Sponsors Benefit, As Do Competitors," *Marketing Daily* (www.mediapost.com/-publications/?fa=Articles.printFriendly&art_aid=122665), February 17, 2010.

21. Chadwick and Burton, "Ambush!"; Anne Kingston, "The Outlaws," *Maclean's* 123, no. 8 (March 8, 2010), pp. 48–49.

22. Jacob E. Osterhout, "Stealth Marketing: When You're Being Pitched and You Don't Even Know It," *NY Daily-News* (www.nydailynews.com/lifestyle/2010/04/19_stealth_marketing), April 19, 2010.

23. Ibid.

24. Weight Loss Institute (www.weight-loss-institute.com/products/solidax_adx.html, accessed March 23, 2008).

Chapter 15

1. http://www.sandsresearch.com/, accessed September 14, 2010.

2. Gordon A. Wyner, "Narrowing the Gap," *Marketing Research* 16, no. 1 (Spring 2004), pp. 6–7.

3. Interview with Elena Petukhova, The Richards Group, May 17, 2010, by Kenneth E. Clow.

4. "Nielsen IAG" (**http://en-us.nielsen.com/tab/product_families/ iag**, accessed May 19, 2010).

5. Lucia Moses, "Publishers Offer TV-Like Metrics, But Will Buyers Bite?" *Mediaweek*, (**www.mediaweek.com/mw/content_ display/news/magazines-newspapers/e3ieea0d35**), January 17, 2010.

6. Interview of David Snell by Kenneth E. Clow, May 17, 2010.

7. Interview with Elena Petukhova, The Richards Group, May 17, 2010, by Kenneth E. Clow.

8. Steven P. Brown and Douglas M. Stayman, "Antecedents and Consequences of Attitude Toward the Ad: A Meta-Analysis," *Journal of Consumer Research* 19 (June 1992), pp. 34–51.

9. Douglas M. Stayman and David A. Aaker, "Continuous Measurement of Self-Report or Emotional Response," *Psychology and Marketing* 10 (May–June 1993), pp. 199–214.

10. Freddie Campos, "UH Facility Test Ads for $500," *Pacific Business News* 35, no. 23 (August 18, 1997), pp. A1–A2.

11. Patricia Riedman, "DiscoverWhy Tests TV Commercials Online," *Advertising Age* 71, no. 13 (March 27, 2000), pp. 46–47.

12. Steve Jarvis, "Minnesota Campaign Grabs Smokers by Throat," *Marketing News* 36, no. 8 (April 15, 2002), pp. 5–6.

13. Bruce F. Hall, "On Measuring the Power of Communications," *Journal of Advertising Research* 44, no. 2 (June 2004), pp. 181–88.

14. Hall, "On Measuring the Power of Communications."

15. John Capone, "Microsoft and Initiative Strive for Better Advertising Through Neuroscience," *Online Media Daily* (**www.mediapost.com/publications/?fa=Articles.printFriendly&**

art_aid=118835), December 9, 2009; Steve McClellan, "Mind Over Matter: New Tools Put Brands in Touch with Feelings," *Adweek* (**http://www.adweek.com/aw/content_display/news/ media/e3i975331243e08d74c5b66f857ff12cfd5**), February 18, 2008.

16. Laurie Burkitt, "Battle for the Brain," *Forbes* 184, no. 9 (November 16, 2009), pp. 76–78.

17. Based on PACT document published in *Journal of Marketing* 11, no. 4 (1982), pp. 4–29.

18. **http://www.adknowledge.com/usa/index.php**, accessed September 14, 2010.

19. Emily Steel, "Marketers Find Web Chat Can be Inspiring," *The Wall Street Journal* (**http://online.wsj.com/article/SB10001 424052748703819904574551562382557556.html**), November 23, 2009.

20. Amanda Beeler, "POPAI Initiates Study Tracking Effectiveness of Displays," *Advertising Age* 71, no. 15 (April 10, 2000), p. 54.

21. Chris Dillabough, "Web Lets Canadian Tourism Test Media Effectiveness," *New Media Age* (October 31, 2002), p. 12.

22. Kate MacArthur, "McDonald's Tests Ads That Focus on Service," *Advertising Age* 74, no. 1 (January 6, 2003), p. 3.

23. Tim Triplett, "Researchers Probe Ad Effectiveness Globally," *Marketing News* 28, no. 18 (August 29, 1994), pp. 6–7.

24. Paul J. Cough, "Study: Marketers Struggle to Measure Effectiveness," *Shoot* 45, no. 29 (August 20, 2004), pp. 7–8.

25. Peter Drucker, *Management: Tasks, Responsibilities, Practices* (New York: Harper & Row, 1974).

Name/Organization Index

Subject Index

OTHER MARKETING TITLES OF INTEREST

PRINCIPLES OF MARKETING

Marketing: An Introduction, 10/E
Armstrong & Kotler
ISBN-10: 0136102433 ■ ISBN-13: 9780136102434

Marketing Plan Handbook and Marketing Plan Pro Package, 4/E
Wood
ISBN-10: 0138020876 ■ ISBN-13: 9780138020873

Principles of Marketing, 14/E
Kotler & Armstrong
ISBN-10: 0132167123 ■ ISBN-13: 9780132167123

Marketing: Real People, Real Choices, 7/E
Solomon, Marshall & Stuart
ISBN-10: 013217684X ■ ISBN-13: 9780132176842

Marketing: Defined, Explained, Applied, 2/E
Levens
ISBN-10: 0132177153 ■ ISBN-13: 9780132177153

Hasselback Marketing Faculty Guide, 13/E
Hasselback
ISBN-10: 0136010024 ■ ISBN-13: 9780136010029

Marketing Ethics: Cases and Readings, 1/E
Murphy & Laczniak
ISBN-10: 0131330888 ■ ISBN-13: 9780131330887

Marketing in Virtual Worlds, 1/E
Wood
ISBN-10: 0136117171 ■ ISBN-13: 9780136117179

CONSUMER BEHAVIOR

Consumer Behavior, 9/E
Solomon
ISBN-10: 0136110924 ■ ISBN-13: 9780136110927

Consumer Behavior, 10/E
Schiffman & Kanuk
ISBN-10: 0135053013 ■ ISBN-13: 9780135053010

Critical Thinking in Consumer Behavior: Cases and Experiential Exercises, 2/E
Graham
ISBN-10: 0136027164 ■ ISBN-13: 9780136027164

Consumer Behavior and Managerial Decision Making, 2/E
Kardes
ISBN-10: 0130916021 ■ ISBN-13: 9780130916020

MARKETING RESEARCH

Basic Marketing Research Using Microsoft Excel Data Analysis, 3/E
Burns & Bush
ISBN-10: 0135078229 ■ ISBN-13: 9780135078228

Basic Marketing Research: A Decision-Making Approach with Qualtrics Access Card, 3/E
Malhotra
ISBN-10: 013715593X ■ ISBN-13: 9780137155934

Marketing Research, 6/E
Burns & Bush
ISBN-10: 0136027040 ■ ISBN-13: 9780136027041

Multivariate Data Analysis, 7/E
Hair, Black, Babin & Anderson
ISBN-10: 0138132631 ■ ISBN-13: 9780138132637

INTERNATIONAL MARKETING

Global Marketing, 6/E
Keegan & Green
ISBN-10: 0137023863 ■ ISBN-13: 9780137023868

Global Marketing Management, 7/E
Keegan
ISBN-10: 0130332712 ■ ISBN-13: 9780130332714

International Marketing Research, 1/E
Kumar
ISBN-10: 0130453862 ■ ISBN-13: 9780130453860

MARKETING MANAGEMENT

Marketing Management, 14/E
Kotler & Keller
ISBN-10: 0132102927 ■ ISBN-13: 9780132102926

A Framework for Marketing Management, 5/E
Kotler & Keller
ISBN-10: 0132539306 ■ ISBN-13: 9780132539302

A Framework for Marketing Management Integrated with PharmaSim, 4/E
Kotler & Keller
ISBN-10: 0136083447 ■ ISBN-13: 9780136083443

Market-Based Management, 5/E
Best
ISBN-10: 0132336537 ■ ISBN-13: 9780132336536

Marketing Management, 4/E
Winer & Dhar
ISBN-10: 0136074898 ■ ISBN-13: 9780136074892

Strategic Marketing Problems: Cases and Comments, 12/E
Kerin & Peterson
ISBN-10: 0136107060 ■ ISBN-13: 9780136107064

Strategic Marketing, 1/E
Mooradian, Matzler & Ring
ISBN-10: 0136028047 ■ ISBN-13: 9780136028048

SELLING

Selling Today: Creating Customer Value, 12/E
Manning, Reece & Ahearne
ISBN-10: 0132109867 ■ ISBN-13: 9780132109864

SALES MANAGEMENT

Sales Management: Shaping Future Sales Leaders, 1/E
Tanner, Honeycutt & Erffmeyer
ISBN-10: 0132324121 ■ ISBN-13: 9780132324120